THE CHURCH ON TRIAL

GOD REVEALS HIDDEN EVILS IN THE CHURCH

Reverend Dr. Eugene Edwards

Scripture quotations are taken from the **King James Version (KJV)** of the Holy Bible, unless otherwise noted.

Publisher's Name: Reverend Dr. Eugene Edwards
ISBN: 978-1-968442-77-4

Front Cover Description

THE CHURCH ON TRIAL
God Rebukes the Hidden Evil in the Church

This cover declares a sobering truth: **the Church now stands before the righteous judgment of God.**

The balance scale is not a symbol of human courts or public opinion—it represents **God's divine standard.** On one side rests the image of the Church—its structures, traditions, titles, and reputation. On the other side lies the open Word of God—unchanging, holy, and uncompromising.

The question is not whether the Church still gathers.
The question is whether the Church still **aligns with God's truth.**

A beam of light cuts through the darkness, revealing what has long been hidden. This is not the light of exposure for shame, but the light of **loving correction.** God does not place His Church on trial to abandon her—but to **purify her.**

This cover is both a warning and an invitation:

- A warning that no sin, compromise, abuse, or deception can remain concealed.
- An invitation to repentance, restoration, and renewed reverence for God.

The scales remind us that **when tradition outweighs truth, the balance is broken.** When leadership replaces obedience, and silence replaces righteousness, heaven responds.

Yet mercy still speaks.

The Church is on trial—not for destruction, but for **refinement.**
The verdict has not yet been rendered.
The gavel has not fallen.

There is still time to choose holiness over hypocrisy, truth over comfort, and obedience over appearance.

Prophetic Meaning of the Balance Scale:

- **The Scale** – God's righteous judgment and divine accountability (Daniel 5:27, 1 Peter 4:17)
- **The Church Building** – Human systems, institutional power, reputation, and tradition
- **The Open Bible** – God's living Word, truth, justice, and moral authority
- **The Light** – Revelation, exposure, conviction, and the mercy of God, calling His people back This image declares:

The Church is not measured by attendance, influence, or wealth—but by obedience to God's Word.

Dedication / Acknowledgments

This book is dedicated first to Almighty God, the Righteous Judge, who exposes what is hidden and brings truth to light.

To my beloved children, **Kareem Edwards and Kelysha Christian**, may your lives always be guided by God's Word and His unfailing love. You are both my joy and my inspiration.

To a faithful pastor and dear friend, Reverend Larry Henderson of Total Deliverance Church of the Nazarene, Aroma Park, who continues to stand firmly on the principles of God's Word and carries a burning passion for soul-winning, as commanded in the Great Commission, your example of obedience and faithfulness encourages me daily.

And to Pastor Alfonso Leonard Spencer, a true and dedicated friend and brother and faithful remnant of the Body of Christ who refuses to bow to compromise, I pray these words strengthen your faith. To every believer who has been wounded by deception, betrayal, or corruption within the Church—may you find healing, hope, and courage to walk in the light of Christ.

Reverend Dr. Eugene C. Edwards

Dr. Edwards with his mother   Dr. Edwards with his grandchildren

Foreword:

The church, the body of Christ, is meant to be a beacon of light, a sanctuary of truth, and a community of love. Yet, history and Scripture alike reveal that even within sacred walls, human weakness, sin, and hidden corruption can take root. *The Church on Trial: God Reveals Hidden Evil* is a timely and necessary examination of the reality that no assembly of believers is immune from the pressures, temptations, and failures of this world.

This book does not seek to condemn but to illuminate, exposing hidden evils so that they may be confronted, repented of, and removed. It reminds the reader that God's discipline and correction are acts of love, intended to restore the church to her rightful calling as the spotless, radiant bride of Christ. Here, the author challenges complacency, false comfort, and the danger of covering sin with appearances, offering a prophetic voice that calls the church back to holiness, truth, and accountability.

Through Scripture, historical examples, and spiritual insight, the book unveils how pride, hypocrisy, compromise, and moral failure can undermine the witness of the church. At the same time, it provides a vision of hope: a restored church that walks in integrity, unity, and holiness, ready for Christ's return. Readers will encounter both sobering truths and life-giving guidance for repentance, revival, and renewal, demonstrating that God's desire is not punishment but redemption.

The message is urgent: God's people are being tested, and His bride is on trial. But the grace of God is sufficient to cleanse, restore, and glorify the church, making her fit for the eternal wedding feast of the Lamb. This foreword invites readers to approach this book with humility, openness, and a willingness to be transformed. It is a call not merely to observe but to respond— to engage in self-examination, to embrace holiness, and to participate in the work of God's refining Spirit.

As you read *The Church on Trial*, allow the words to challenge you, convict you, and inspire you. Recognize that God's revelation of hidden evil is not a condemnation of the faithful but a call to greater faithfulness. May this book stir your heart to pursue righteousness, seek unity, and prepare the church to shine brightly in a world desperately in need of the light of Christ.

Mr. Courtney Allen

Former Church Secretary of Clapham Junction Church of the Nazarene, London
Accountant in New York

The church today stands at a crossroads. On one side is the calling to be a holy, radiant bride prepared for Christ's return; on the other is the peril of compromise, hidden sin, and moral decay. As I have walked through ministry, counseling, and pastoral oversight, I have witnessed both the glory and the brokenness within the body of Christ. This book is born from a heart deeply concerned for the church, a desire to see God's people restored to purity, unity, and faithfulness.

The Church on Trial: God Reveals Hidden Evil is a prophetic voice for our times. It seeks to uncover what many prefer to hide: the subtle and sometimes overt ways in which sin, hypocrisy, and deception infiltrate the life of the church. From leadership failures to hidden personal sins, from doctrinal compromise to generational patterns of error, no area is beyond God's scrutiny. Yet this exposure is not intended to shame but to awaken, convict, and inspire transformation.

Throughout Scripture, God has called His people to holiness, warned of judgment, and offered redemption. The purpose of this book is to help believers recognize when the church has strayed from her calling and to encourage a response that aligns with God's will. Each chapter examines a facet of spiritual life, calling the reader to repentance, revival, and renewal. From returning to the altar to pursuing holiness, from restoring unity to preparing the bride for Christ's return, this book presents both a mirror and a roadmap for the church today.

The reader will encounter truths that may be difficult to hear. But the intent is not condemnation; it is restoration. God's goal is a church without spot or wrinkle, a glorious bride reflecting His character, His love, and His glory to the world. This book invites you to join in that refining work, to confront personal and corporate sin, and to embrace a higher calling.

It is my prayer that as you journey through these pages, you will be stirred to action, inspired to holiness, and equipped to contribute to a church that honors God fully. May this book awaken a deep desire for truth, spark a renewed commitment to righteousness, and prepare the church— each believer individually and the body collectively—for the return of our Lord Jesus Christ.

The church is on trial. The question is: will we respond in faith, humility, and obedience, or will we cling to compromise and comfort? May God's Spirit open your eyes, soften your heart, and empower you to be part of a glorious church ready for His return.

About the Author

Reverend Dr. Eugene Edwards is a pastor, author, teacher, counselor, and advocate for spiritual and mental wellness. With decades of ministry experience, he has served in leadership roles across local churches and community programs, guiding believers toward deeper intimacy with God and a faithful, righteous walk.

Dr. Edwards is passionate about helping the church return to her intended glory—holy, unified, and prepared for Christ's return. He combines biblical teaching with practical guidance, calling both individuals and congregations to repentance, renewal, and revival. His work emphasizes the importance of integrity, accountability, and spiritual discernment in every area of life.

He is the author of *Love from a Distance, God Uses the Foolish to Confuse the Wise, Youth on Purpose -Unashamed, Unshaken, and Ignited for Kingdom Impact, The Church on Trial: God Reveals Hidden Evil, The Church & Politics – God's Mandate in a Corrupted World, and, Fear doesn't Own us - but Faith, Power, Love and Sound Mind and Hidden Queens: The African Women Leaders History Tried to Hide.* Each book carries a consistent message of faith, repentance, and living wholly for God in a broken world.

As a father to *Kareem Edwards and Kelysha Christian,* and my spiritual daughter, *Dr. La'Kesha Francis.* Reverend Edwards is deeply committed to leaving a spiritual legacy—not only to his children, but also to his community and to every believer who chooses to be sold out for Jesus Christ. His passion is to see lives transformed by the Word of God, families restored, and generations walking in holiness.

As an author, Reverend Dr. Edwards has dedicated his writing to equipping believers to recognize and confront hidden sin, embrace holiness, and pursue God's purpose for their lives. He believes in a church that reflects the beauty and righteousness of Christ, standing as a light to a world in need.

Beyond ministry, Dr. Edwards is a devoted father and grandfather, committed to modeling faith, love, and service in both family and community life.He is pursuing courses to become an advocate for mental health awareness, integrating professional insight with spiritual guidance to encourage holistic well-being among believers.

Through his teaching, writing, and pastoral leadership, Reverend Dr. Eugene Edwards inspires individuals and congregations alike to pursue a life of holiness, truth, and unwavering devotion to Christ. He has become a voice of encouragement, conviction, and truth for those who refuse to compromise their faith. His life's work is a testimony that when the Church stands firm on the unshakable foundation of God's Word, it can withstand every trial and reveal Christ's glory to the world.

Memoir: Honoring My Spiritual Mentors

Throughout my life and ministry, God has placed mentors whose wisdom has shaped my path. Their guidance reminds me of the African queens I chronicle in this book, leaders whose courage, discernment, and faithfulness left lasting legacies. This memoir section honors those who poured into my life and inspires readers to seek mentors who uplift and guide them spiritually and intellectually.

My calling began at the tender age of 21, yet it was under the guidance, wisdom, and example of my spiritual mentors that I learned the depth of commitment, humility, and love required for a life dedicated to God's work.

The late **Reverend Dr. Rosa Lee** of Beacon-Light Church of the Nazarene in Antigua and Barbuda was my first spiritual mentor, guiding me as I stepped into ministry as co-pastor at our home church. From her, I learned the significance of vision rooted in prayer and discernment. She taught me that leadership in the church is not merely about titles or influence, but about nurturing souls, building relationships, and walking humbly with God. Her encouragement and counsel instilled in me the discipline to persevere, even when challenges seemed insurmountable. Reverend Dr. Rosa Lee demonstrated a rare combination of spiritual insight, compassionate leadership, and unwavering dedication to God's people, and it was under her guidance that my initial calling to serve took shape and flourished.

Equally influential in my life was the late **Reverend Joseph Bentham**, whom I served alongside as co-pastor at Clapham Junction Church of the Nazarene in London, United Kingdom.

Reverend Bentham was not only my mentor but also my spiritual role model. From him, I learned how faith translates into action and how true pastoral leadership is exercised with both conviction and grace. His guidance was marked by a deep understanding of God's Word, a passion for teaching, and a love for the global community. Under his mentorship, I developed a vision that extended beyond my immediate congregation, inspiring me to travel, minister, and serve in diverse communities across the world.

To the late Mother Beryl Hart (1925–2025)

It is with deep honor and gratitude that I reflect on the life and legacy of **Mother Beryl Hart**, who graced this earth for a remarkable 100 years. A pillar of faith at **Clapham Junction Church of the Nazarene in London,** Mother Hart was more than a member; she was a **spiritual mother, a guide, and a tireless warrior for God's truth**.

Serving alongside her as co-pastor, I experienced firsthand the profound influence she had on my ministry and my walk with God. Mother Hart's life was a living testament to honesty, integrity, spiritual discipline, and unwavering faith. She nurtured those around her with wisdom and love, providing both guidance and accountability in the ways of the Lord.

She loved her pastors with a deep, sacrificial devotion. Beyond ministering through prayer and the Word of God, she extended her home and her heart. Traveling some 56 miles to worship on Sundays and during the week, I was often invited to share Sunday dinner with her family, an act of warmth, hospitality, and genuine care that revealed her deep commitment to nurturing both the soul and the spirit of God's servants.

Mother Hart was a woman who understood her history, both spiritual and physical, and used it as a foundation to stand firm for righteousness and truth. She embodied **a life of worth, divinely centered on God**, and lived in a way that exemplified what it means to be both steadfast and compassionate in faith.

Her life was a model of spiritual strength, and her legacy extends far beyond the walls of the church. She taught by example, inspiring countless lives through her devotion, her prayers, and her unshakable faith.

Today, Mother Hart rests with her Master and Maker, receiving her eternal reward. Though she has departed from this earthly plane, her influence endures. She remains a source of inspiration, a reminder that a life fully surrendered to God is a life that impacts generations, nurtures leaders, and leaves an indelible mark on His Kingdom.

Rest in peace, Mother Beryl Hart. Your faith, your discipline, and your love for God and His servants continue to guide us. May your memory be cherished, and may your reward be great in the presence of the Lord.

The Trio, Reverend Dr. Rosa Lee, Reverend Joseph Bentham, and Mother Beryl Hart, shaped my understanding of ministry as a calling that demands sacrifice, perseverance, and a relentless pursuit of God's will. They taught me that leadership is never about personal gain but about serving others faithfully and obediently to the calling God places upon our lives. Their examples of wisdom, integrity, and dedication continue to guide me, even today, as I carry the mantle of ministry into my senior years.

As I reflect on my decades of service, I recognize that the foundation laid by these remarkable mentors is the reason I have been able to faithfully minister across continents, build bridges in communities, and serve God's people with love, compassion, and dedication. Their lives remind me that mentorship is a divine instrument through which God shapes the next generation of leaders, equipping them with courage, insight, and vision to fulfill their calling. To Reverend Dr. Rosa Lee, Reverend Joseph Bentham, and Mother Beryl Hart, I owe a debt of gratitude that words can scarcely express. Their influence is embedded in every sermon preached, every life touched, and every act of service I have performed in obedience to God.

I honor their memory not only in words but in the continued pursuit of excellence, integrity, and faithful service in ministry, upholding the values and lessons they imparted to me decades ago. May their legacy continue to inspire ministers and servants of God around the world, reminding us that a life dedicated to God's work is the most enduring tribute we can leave behind.

Table of Contents

Introduction: A Holy Fire in God's Nostrils

(The burden of the Lord, why exposure is coming, the prophetic urgency)

There are moments in history when God allows His patience to stretch beyond what seems possible. For generations, He extends mercy, hoping His people will turn back to Him. But there also comes a time when His holiness demands action. We are now standing at such a crossroads. The Spirit of the Lord is stirring, and the sins that have long been covered, hidden, or tolerated within the Church are rising like smoke into His nostrils. It is no longer a sweet fragrance of worship; it is a stench of rebellion, corruption, and compromise.

This book carries a burden, not of human imagination but of divine urgency. God is about to expose evil within His Church—not to destroy His people, but to purify them. What is concealed will be revealed, what is whispered in shadows will be proclaimed on rooftops, and what has been tolerated will be judged. The Lord is not mocked, and He will not allow His bride to be defiled forever.

The Church is called to be a light to the nations, a city set on a hill that cannot be hidden. Yet instead of shining brightly, too many have dimmed their witness through hypocrisy, greed, lust, abuse of power, and distorted teaching. Rather than leading people to Christ, these compromises have driven many away. But God, in His jealous love, refuses to allow His name to be continually blasphemed because of the failures of those who claim to represent Him.

Throughout Scripture, when the people of God turned from holiness to compromise, He raised voices—prophets, watchmen, and messengers—to call His people back. Often these voices were ignored, ridiculed, or silenced. Yet their message carried the weight of heaven: Repent, for the Lord is nearby. The same prophetic urgency burns today. The Spirit is speaking, warning, and shaking His Church before the world witnesses an exposure unlike any we have seen in our lifetime.

This exposure will not be selective. From the smallest congregation to the largest denomination, from local ministers to international leaders, nothing and no one is beyond the reach of God's refining fire. The Lord is not partial. He is not impressed by titles, followers, or wealth. He looks at the heart, and where corruption has taken root, He will uproot it.

Some will see this exposure as judgment, and indeed it is also mercy. Judgment begins in the house of God so that His people might repent and be restored before the greater judgment comes upon the nations. The Lord disciplines those He loves, and His cleansing is not for the destruction of His Church but for its renewal.

We must understand that exposure is not man's doing but God's. News outlets, social media scandals, and court trials may play their part, but behind it all is the hand of the Lord. He is pulling back the veil because He will not allow wolves to masquerade as shepherds any longer, nor will He let sin remain hidden under the guise of holiness.

The burden of this message weighs heavily: the Church has grieved the Holy Spirit. Too often, we have substituted programs for prayer, popularity for purity, and entertainment for true worship. We have excused leaders' sins in the name of "grace" while failing to uphold righteousness. We have tolerated Jezebel spirits in pulpits and praised ministries that serve mammon rather than God. The Lord declares, "Enough!"

This is not a word of condemnation but of awakening. Just as a surgeon cuts open the body to remove cancer, so too is the Lord preparing to cut open His Church to remove the rot. The pain of exposure will be real, but it will also bring healing and freedom. For whom the Son sets free is free indeed.

The Spirit is calling for watchmen who will not remain silent, for intercessors who will weep between the porch and the altar, for shepherds who will feed the flock instead of feeding on them. He is raising a remnant within the Church who will carry His burden, walk in holiness, and lead with integrity. Through them, His glory will again shine.

The urgency of this hour cannot be overstated. We are living in the last days. The signs are all around us: wars, rumors of wars, deception, apostasy, lawlessness, and the love of many growing cold. Yet before the Bridegroom returns, the bride must be purified. Exposure is God's final mercy call to His people before the trumpet sounds.

This book is written as both a warning and a call to repentance. It is a mirror for the Church to examine itself and a trumpet to announce the coming shaking. The evil within the Church will be exposed, not because God hates His people, but because He loves them too much to leave them in corruption. May every page stir conviction, ignite prayer, and prepare us for the holy fire that is about to sweep across the body of Christ.

Part I – The Roots of Hidden Evil

Chapter 1: A Church that Lost Its First Love

Revelation 2:4, leaving intimacy with Christ)

The words of Christ to the church in Ephesus echo into our generation with piercing relevance: *"Nevertheless I have somewhat against thee, because thou hast left thy first love"* (Revelation 2:4). This was not a pagan culture being addressed, nor a rebellious world, but the *church itself.* God's people had once burned with devotion, but now their fire had cooled, replaced by ritual, formality, and empty religion.

The Church today faces a crisis that many refuse to see. Revelation 2:4 warns us: *"Nevertheless I have somewhat against thee, because thou hast left thy first love."* A church that drifts from intimacy with Christ loses its power, its purity, and its prophetic voice. As A. W. Tozer emphasizes in *The Pursuit of God*, superficial faith cannot experience the fullness of God's presence; the heart must be fully surrendered to Him.

The tragedy of leaving first love is not in the loss of good works, for Christ commended them for labor, patience, and endurance. The tragedy is that the *heart had shifted*—what was once intimacy with Jesus had been replaced with mechanical duty. The lamp of affection had grown dim, and the fragrance of devotion was lost. When love for Christ wanes, ritual takes precedence over relationship. Leaders may focus on programs, appearances, or statistics while the soul of the congregation withers. Leonard Ravenhill reminds us in *Why Revival Tarries* that revival always begins with broken hearts turned back to God, not with clever strategies or worldly success.

In these last days, God's Spirit is exposing a church that has substituted programs for prayer, entertainment for encounter, and charisma for character. Crowds may gather, music may swell, and sermons may resound, but heaven searches for a heart fully yielded in love to Christ.

Without that love, we are nothing (1 Corinthians 13:1-3). The first love is not merely sentimental; it is a dynamic, living devotion that fuels holiness, boldness, and spiritual discernment. Without it, even the most structured ministries collapse under the weight of hidden sin and hypocrisy. Scripture repeatedly warns that God's presence departs from lukewarm hearts, leaving only outward religiosity.

A church that loses its first love loses its anchor. It drifts from the passion of the Bride toward the cold professionalism of an institution. Where there was once trembling before the Word, now there is casual indifference. Where there was once all-night prayer, now there are strategy meetings. Where there was once brokenness, now there is pride. We see this pattern repeated throughout history: churches rich in resources but empty in spirit, congregations boasting of numbers while moral decay spreads silently within. As Tozer notes, God's children must cultivate a "constant, consuming hunger" for His presence or risk losing the fire that once ignited their faith.

The Lord Jesus walks among His lampstands even now, eyes aflame with fire, discerning where love has grown cold. He is not deceived by numbers, offerings, or social media platforms. His gaze penetrates deeper than appearances, searching for the heart that says, *"I am my Beloved's, and my Beloved is mine"* (Song of Solomon 6:3). A church that loses its first love also becomes vulnerable to deception. Without an intimate connection to Christ, members cannot discern truth from false teaching. Ravenhill repeatedly highlights that compromise is never harmless; the moment a church tolerates even subtle sin, it opens the door to corruption and spiritual decline.

To lose first love is not simply to backslide into sin. It is to begin replacing the intimacy of walking with Jesus with the machinery of religion. It is to serve without adoration, to preach without tears, to worship without surrender, to give without sacrifice, and to lead without being led by the Spirit. True intimacy with God transforms character, reshapes priorities, and strengthens resilience against worldly pressures. Leaders who have left their first love often create systems that protect appearances while ignoring the spiritual rot beneath. This mirrors the warning in Matthew 23 about leaders covering their own sins while preaching righteousness to others.

This shift is subtle but deadly. Like Samson, the church can rise to shake itself as before yet not realize that the Spirit of the Lord has departed (Judges 16:20). Activity continues, but power is gone. Voices remain, but anointing is absent. Religion lives, but relationships die. Restoring the first love requires humility, confession, and a willingness to forsake comforts that distract from devotion. Tozer exhorts believers to seek God with intensity, saying that only through focused, personal pursuit of Christ can revival of the heart occur.

God is grieved when His people abandon intimacy with Him. His covenant desire was never for ritual alone, but for union. *"I will betroth you to Me forever; Yes, I will betroth you to Me in righteousness and justice, in lovingkindness and compassion"* (Hosea 2:19). When that covenant love is forsaken, judgment begins at the house of God (1 Peter 4:17). A lukewarm church cannot fulfill its mission in the world. Revelation warns that God will spit out a church that professes faith but lacks fervor. The remedy is a return to Christ, untainted by tradition, complacency, or worldly influence.

The Lord has been patient, calling His church back to the bridal chamber of prayer, fasting, and worship in Spirit and in truth. But when His voice is ignored, exposure comes. The Lord will uncover what is hidden because He cannot bless a bride who no longer loves her Bridegroom. This chapter challenges every reader to evaluate the depth of their own love for Christ. Are we pursuing Him passionately, or have we settled for spiritual mediocrity? Ravenhill reminds us that revival is never mass-produced; it is born in the hearts of those desperate for God.

In this hour, the prophetic cry is rising *Return to your first love.* This is not an optional invitation; it is a divine summons. Without revival of love, the church will soon be stripped of its lampstand—its influence, authority, and witness in the earth. The Church's first love is a lamp for the world. Without it, darkness spreads, deception flourishes, and the mission of Christ is hindered. But a church that passionately pursues intimacy with God will shine brightly, exposing evil and drawing souls to the Savior.

When a church loses its first love, it loses intimacy with Christ—the very source of its life. What remains may still look like a church on the outside, but the inner flame that once warmed the house of God flickers low. Without that nearness, even the best intentions slowly drift into routine, and the heart grows distant from the One who walks among the lampstands.

Revelation 2:4 is not a mild suggestion; it is a holy indictment: "You have abandoned the love you had at first." The Lord then commands, "Remember... repent...do the works you did at first," reminding us that love can be recovered through memory, repentance, and obedience.

Heaven's remedy is simple yet searching return to Him, not merely to activity about Him.

Love is the foundation of faith; remove it, and all Christian work collapses into empty ritual. Without love, generosity becomes self-promotion, preaching becomes performance, and service becomes drudgery. Paul's warning echoes: if we have not love, we are nothing—even when we do the right things for the wrong reasons.

Many congregations unknowingly trade living passion for safe tradition. The calendar stays full, the building stays busy, yet a quiet drought settles over the people. Tradition can honor God, but when it replaces hunger for God, it hardens into a shell that hides a starving heart.

When love fades, compromise finds a welcome door. Cold affections give room to cold decisions; purity gives way to pragmatism; courage yields to convenience. As Jesus foretold, in days of growing lawlessness, the love of many grows cold—and with that chill, sin feels less shocking.

Leaders face a subtle temptation to prize programs over presence. Metrics, momentum, and marketing can become the altar where prayer is sacrificed. Shepherds must remember: our people need wells, not wheels—places where living water flows, not just machinery that moves.

Worship drifts toward the mechanical when the heart no longer beholds the King. Songs are sung but not offered; prayers are spoken but not poured out. The absence of awe turns praise into poetry and intercession into announcements.

God does not seek religious busyness; He desires burning devotion. The great command remains to love the Lord with all our heart, soul, mind, and strength. Where that command is obeyed, zeal and holiness rise naturally, because love fuels both.

Daily communion with the Holy Spirit is how first love is sustained. Unhurried Scripture, honest prayer, and quiet listening tune the soul to Christ's voice. Intimacy is not an event; it is a way of walking—step by step, breath by breath, with the Helper.

Exposure of hidden evil often begins where love has died, because lovelessness makes space for darkness. When affection for Christ wanes, lesser loves creep in—control, image, gain—and what was sacred becomes strategic. The Lord's exposing light is mercy, calling the church back to the warmth of His heart.

Intimacy with Christ sharpens discernment and strengthens endurance. Those who linger with the Shepherd learn His tone and recognize the voice of strangers. In close fellowship, the church senses danger early and stands firm when storms arise.

Where love is absent, manipulation easily masquerades as leadership. Coercion replaces counsel, and fear replaces faith. True authority flows from proximity to Jesus; counterfeits grasp for control when communion is gone. Sheep can begin to follow programs blindly when their own walk with God grows thin. They trade listening for attendance, hunger for habit. Pastors must call people to personal encounter, not just corporate events—disciples, not merely participants.

When the church turns from passion for God, His holy fire begins to burn—not to destroy, but to purify. The flame exposes what coldness tried to hide and invites us to the altar again. Judgment starts with the house of God so that mercy can flow from it. Lukewarmness welcomes hypocrisy and compromise like two old friends. It says just enough to sound faithful and does just enough to look faithful. The Lord of Laodicea still knocks, offering gold refined by fire, white garments, and eye salve for those who open.

Leaders must prize prayer, Scripture, and shepherding above numbers and notoriety. Crowds are not the same as health, and impact is not the same as intimacy. The pastoral call is first to God, then to people—not to platforms. Love is the antidote to legalism, pride, and apathy. Love fulfills the law without becoming law-driven; it humbles the heart without self-contempt; it awakens sleepy souls without shaming them. Where love reigns, holiness is beautiful, not burdensome.

The Bridegroom calls His bride to return with all her heart. "Remember…repent… do the first works"—renew your altar, restore your prayer life, reopen your ear to His whisper. First love is not nostalgia; it is fresh surrender today. When God exposes sin, He is offering a door to repentance and renewal. Confession becomes the pathway to cleansing; humility becomes the seedbed of healing. The church's greatest scandals can become its greatest testimonies if we respond quickly and truthfully.

Daily self-examination keeps love tender. "Search me, O God," is the prayer that prevents drift and invites delight. We examine not despair but to remain aligned, repenting early, rejoicing often, and returning fast. Where love is lacking, truth is easily ignored, softened, or twisted. We begin to preach for applause instead of alignment and to edit the Word to fit the room. Only love for Jesus keeps the church loyal to Jesus' words when they cut against culture.

Revival is not the child of programs; it is the fruit of a Person. Jesus at the center—not an event at the center—draws hearts, heals wounds, and gathers the lost. "When I am lifted," He promised, "I will draw all people to Myself." Strategy is a good servant but a poor substitute for spiritual fervor. Plans can organize fruit, but they cannot produce it. The flame on the altar provides power; structure merely gives it channels.

Leaders must guard their hearts from distraction and pride, for these are subtle thieves of first love. Public success can hide private starvation. Wise shepherds keep short accounts with God and long hours at His feet. True leadership flows from love for Christ, not from status, skill, or wealth. The risen Lord still asks His shepherds a single qualifying question: "Do you love Me?" From that love comes the authority and tenderness to feed His sheep.

When a church begins to tolerate sin, it is no longer a light but a dim flicker that cannot pierce through darkness. The congregation may still gather, sing, and preach, but the power and presence of God slowly lift. What remains is a shell of religion without relationship. People become content with programs, numbers, and appearances, while the Spirit of God grieves in silence. This is why Jesus warned the Ephesian church to return to its first love before it was too late.

Hidden evil rarely shows itself in the beginning, disguising itself as small compromises, acceptable traditions, or harmless entertainment. But what begins as a crack in the wall eventually becomes a gaping breach through which the enemy storms in. A church without watchmen is like a city without walls—defenseless and vulnerable. Satan does not need to destroy the church in one blow; he only needs to plant seeds of distraction, division, and deception. Over time, these seeds grow into strongholds that suffocate the love of Christ.

The first love that Jesus spoke of is not a shallow feeling but a fiery devotion rooted in surrender. It is a love that prays earnestly, serves joyfully, and worships with reverence. It is a love that pursues Christ above convenience, popularity, or comfort. When this love grows cold, the church becomes mechanical, going through motions without meaning. Revival can only come when God's people repent, weep before the altar, and cry out for His presence to return.

The danger of losing the first love is that the church may not even realize it. Like Samson, they may shake themselves and expect power, not knowing the Spirit has departed. They may continue to hold services, conferences, and revival meetings, but without intimacy with Christ, these are empty echoes. The greatest tragedy is not an empty building but a full sanctuary absent God's glory. The lampstand may remain for a season, but if repentance does not come, Christ Himself warns that He will remove it.

Yet, even in His warning, Jesus extends mercy. He calls His church not simply to regret but to remember, repent, and return. Remember the days of burning passion, repent for drifting away, and return to the place of intimacy. This is the only cure for hidden evil—the rekindling of first love. For when the church truly loves Christ again, sin loses its grip, unity is restored, and the power of the Holy Spirit flows without hindrance. A revived church is a weapon in God's hand, and through it, the gates of hell cannot prevail.

(Matthew 23, leaders covering sin)

Hypocrisy in the church is like leaven, small at first but spreading quickly until it corrupts the whole loaf. What begins as a seemingly minor compromise, a subtle inconsistency between what is preached and what is practiced, soon becomes a cancer that touches everything. Just as leaven works silently and invisibly until the entire dough is affected, hypocrisy slowly eats away at the credibility of leaders and the trust of the congregation. Hypocrisy within the Church is like yeast in dough—it spreads silently, changing the whole nature of the body. Jesus sternly warned in Matthew 23 against leaders who appear righteous outwardly while hiding sin in their hearts. This leaven is subtle, often unnoticed by those who are comfortable with appearances.

Jesus confronted this very issue in Matthew 23, where He boldly called out the Pharisees and teachers of the law. He exposed them for placing heavy burdens on others while refusing to lift a finger themselves. Their outward appearance of holiness was impressive, yet behind the façade lay pride, corruption, and a heart far from God. His words remind us that God sees beyond religious performance and desires truth in the inward parts. C. S. Lewis, in *Mere Christianity*, warns that spiritual hypocrisy begins when we convince ourselves that small compromises are harmless. The danger is that unchecked hypocrisy grows until it dominates the entire congregation, obscuring the truth of God's Word.

The danger of hypocrisy is that it hides behind spiritual language and religious rituals. Leaders can appear righteous, preach eloquently, and even perform acts of service, while inwardly remaining untouched by the transforming power of the Holy Spirit. This duplicity not only deceives the people but also hardens the leader's own heart, making repentance increasingly difficult. Leonard Ravenhill reminds us that revival cannot coexist with hypocrisy. A Church seeking genuine transformation must first confront the hidden sins of its leaders, exposing them to the light of God's Word. Without this exposure, false teaching flourishes and spiritual decline accelerates.

In today's church, hypocrisy can take many forms: pastors preaching purity while living in immorality, leaders teaching generosity while secretly greedy, or congregations worshiping loudly on Sunday but walking in dishonesty throughout the week. These contradictions weaken the witness of the church and cause unbelievers to mock the name of Christ. Hypocrisy does not merely affect leaders; it contaminates the entire community. Members begin to emulate behaviors they see, prioritizing reputation over righteousness. Tozer notes in *The Pursuit of God* that the heart's devotion determines the Church's authenticity—without sincere love for Christ, the entire body suffers.

Jesus warned that such hypocrisy is not harmless; it is deadly. He compared the Pharisees to whitewashed tombs — beautiful on the outside but filled with dead men's bones inside. This imagery is haunting because it reveals that hypocrisy is nothing more than spiritual death dressed in religious clothing. When leaders live in hypocrisy, they do not merely stumble privately; they poison the souls entrusted to their care.

The leaven of hypocrisy can also infiltrate worship. Outward displays of reverence may mask internal rebellion or moral compromise. Worship becomes performance rather than communion with God. Lewis emphasizes that the integrity of faith is measured not by appearances but by obedience and the heart's alignment with God.

The Pharisees believed they were defenders of God's law, yet they opposed the very Messiah whom the law foretold. In the same way, modern leaders can convince themselves that their actions are justified, even when they contradict the Word of God. Pride makes confession difficult, and the fear of losing influence makes covering sin more appealing than repentance. God's Word calls for leaders to be blameless and above reproach (1 Timothy 3:2). Hypocrisy violates this standard, endangering the Church's witness. Ravenhill underscores that when leaders fail morally or spiritually, revival is hindered, and the loss remains unreached.

One of the clearest marks of hypocrisy is the obsession with appearances. Leaders may focus on titles, robes, stages, or recognition, while neglecting the weightier matters of justice, mercy, and faithfulness. When reputation becomes more important than righteousness, the church slips into a dangerous culture of performance rather than genuine transformation. The exposure of hypocrisy is not an attack; it is a call to repentance. Matthew 23's warnings are designed to wake the Church to self-examination. Tozer emphasizes that God honors confession and humility, purging the leaven from hearts willing to return to holiness.

Jesus never tolerated hypocrisy, and neither should the church today. He exposed it with sharp rebukes because He knew that unchecked hypocrisy destroys entire generations of believers. If leaders cover sin rather than confess it, they model deception rather than holiness, teaching the flock to imitate their corruption. The call of the gospel is not perfection but authenticity — walking in repentance and truth before God. A Church that confronts its hypocrisy can restore credibility, faithfulness, and spiritual power. Leaders must model transparency, confess wrongdoing, and pursue Christ fervently. Lewis highlights that even the smallest act of sincere faith can produce exponential spiritual impact when hypocrisy is eradicated.

Sadly, when hypocrisy flourishes, people begin to lose confidence in the church altogether. Scandals of sexual immorality, financial abuse, or abuse of authority become headlines that confirm the suspicion of unbelievers: "Christians are no different from the world." This is why the leaven of hypocrisy must be addressed swiftly, for it brings reproach upon the name of Christ. Hypocrisy is a spiritual cancer that spreads silently unless addressed. Scripture, Tozer, Ravenhill, and Lewis all underscore that true revival begins with honesty, repentance, and a heart wholly devoted to God. A Church willing to remove leaven will flourish, shining as a beacon of truth in a darkened world.

The cure for hypocrisy is humility and repentance. Leaders must be willing to step into the light, confess their sins, and allow God to cleanse them. Covering sin may preserve a reputation temporarily, but it destroys the soul eternally. Only by acknowledging weakness and surrendering to Christ can leaders be restored to integrity and the church regain its credibility before a watching world.

Hypocrisy spreads like leaven, quietly infiltrating hearts until the whole lump of dough is affected. Just as yeast works its way invisibly through flour, hypocrisy seeps into the life of a believer or a church, reshaping everything it touches. What begins as a small compromise—an overlooked sin, a tolerated lie, or a public image carefully crafted to hide private corruption—can quickly become a culture of deception. Jesus warned that the leaven of the Pharisees was hypocrisy (Luke 12:1), and when left unchecked, it could transform a place meant for holiness into a stage for self-promotion and control.

Leaders who wear masks of righteousness while hiding sin confuse the people they lead.

When spiritual leaders present themselves as holy but live contrary behind closed doors, they create a distorted picture of God. The people who follow them are left bewildered, unsure if faith is genuine or simply a performance. This disillusionment can lead to distrust, cynicism, and in some cases, walking away from God altogether. The tragedy is that Christ is not the one at fault—it is the hypocrisy of leaders who misrepresent Him.

Instead of pointing others to Christ, they draw attention to themselves. Jesus confronted the Pharisees for loving the praise of men more than the praise of God (John 12:43). When leaders seek recognition, titles, and honor more than humility and service, they shift the focus from God's glory to human pride. The pulpit becomes a platform for applause rather than a place of proclamation, and worship is no longer about God but about maintaining appearances.

The leaven of hypocrisy blinds leaders to their own need for repentance. Just as yeast puffs up dough, hypocrisy inflates the ego. Leaders caught in its grip can preach repentance to others but fail to examine their own hearts. They may excuse or minimize their sins, convincing themselves that their public ministry outweighs their private failures. This blindness is dangerous, for it hardens the conscience and makes true repentance less likely.

Jesus declared "Woe to you" to such leaders, exposing their double lives. In Matthew 23, Jesus pronounced a series of woes upon the scribes and Pharisees. His words were sharp, exposing the contrast between their polished exteriors and their corrupt hearts. He called them whitewashed tombs—beautiful on the outside but full of death within. This divine rebuke was not cruelty but mercy, for only truth can break through the walls of deception.

Hypocrisy not only damages leaders; it poisons entire congregations. The spiritual sickness of one leader can spread like an infection, shaping the culture of a church. If hypocrisy is tolerated at the top, soon it will be mirrored in the pews. Members begin to believe that appearances matter more than authenticity, and the cycle of pretense continues. This results in churches that look alive but are spiritually dead (Revelation 3:1).

The leaven of hypocrisy makes worship a performance rather than an offering. True worship flows from a heart surrendered to God. But when hypocrisy rules, songs are sung with lips while hearts remain distant. Prayers become rehearsed speeches, sermons become showpieces, and the Spirit's presence is grieved. What should be holy becomes hollow, and what should be sacred becomes shallow.

Hypocritical leaders demand burdens from others they themselves will not carry. Jesus condemned the Pharisees for loading people with heavy religious demands while refusing to lift a finger to help (Matthew 23:4). In the same way, modern leaders consumed with hypocrisy often enforce rules and traditions on their people, while excusing themselves from obedience.

This double standard crushes the flock and drives them into bondage rather than freedom.

Their desire for titles and recognition reveals where their hearts truly lie. Jesus said they loved to be called "Rabbi" and to sit in places of honor. Today, the same spirit can be seen when leaders crave positions, platforms, and prestige. They may use spiritual language, but their ambition exposes them. True shepherds seek the well-being of their flock; hypocrites seek to be elevated above it. The leaven of hypocrisy disguises itself as holiness but is rooted in pride. Pride is the soil where hypocrisy grows. It whispers that reputation matters more than repentance, that being seen as righteous is more important than being righteous. Outward acts of devotion become a mask covering inner decay. But God sees beyond the mask, and He weighs the motives of the heart.

Hypocrisy destroys the credibility of the gospel. When leaders fail to live what they preach, the message of Christ is weakened. The Word of God, which has the power to save, becomes suspect in the eyes of the hearer. People begin to associate religion with performance, morality with manipulation, and faith with fear. The gospel itself becomes overshadowed by human failure, and many hearts remain untouched.

Leaders who cover sin teach deception to the next generation. Children and youth learn more from actions than words. When leaders pretend to be righteous while hiding wrongdoing, they model dishonesty as a strategy for success. Young believers may grow up thinking that duplicity is acceptable, that faith is about appearances, and that God's law can be bent to suit convenience. This perpetuates cycles of spiritual compromise and moral blindness. The leaven of hypocrisy thrives in secret. Just as yeast works invisibly, hypocrisy often operates behind closed doors.

Public ministry can appear exemplary, but private life tells a different story. Leaders may justify their actions, rationalize compromises, and compartmentalize sin. Yet God sees all, and no secret remains hidden from His sight. Exposure may be painful, but it is the pathway to restoration.

Hypocrisy fosters fear instead of faith. When people realize that leaders are not what they claim to be, trust erodes. Congregations become afraid to question, afraid to speak truth, and afraid to confess their own sins. Fear replaces faith, and a culture of silence develops. The church becomes a place of appearance rather than transformation, where people hide their struggles instead of finding help.

Covering sin delays repentance and prolongs judgment. Jesus warned that those who hide sin bring disaster upon themselves and others. The longer sin remains hidden, the stronger its grip, and the harder it becomes to break. Repentance is not optional; it is lifesaving. Hypocrisy prolongs suffering because it pretends there is no need for God's corrective hand.

Leaders must remember that God is not deceived by outward appearances. The Lord sees the heart, the secret motives, and the hidden sins that no human eye can detect. Public acts of piety do not impress Him if the heart is far from righteous. To lead faithfully, leaders must live in transparency and accountability, knowing that God values sincerity above spectacle.

The leaven of hypocrisy isolates the leader from true fellowship. A leader who lives in pretense gradually distances himself from those who might speak truth. Friends, mentors, and spiritual companions are avoided or silenced. In isolation, pride grows unchecked, and the leader becomes more entrenched in deception. Community is essential for correction, accountability, and humility.

It corrupts decision-making and spiritual discernment. When hypocrisy reigns, decisions are based on personal gain, fear of exposure, or desire for admiration rather than God's guidance. Leaders may justify actions that violate Scripture or conscience. The moral compass becomes warped, and the congregation suffers as a result.

Hypocrisy breeds division within the church. Members sense inconsistency, favoritism, and hidden agendas. Rumors, suspicion, and resentment arise. Instead of fostering unity and love, leaders who live hypocritically create factions and strife. Jesus' prayer for unity (John 17) is undermined when deceit infiltrates the leadership.

Spiritual authority becomes a tool of control rather than a channel of blessing. Leadership intended to guide, nurture, and protect becomes an instrument to manipulate, dominate, or enrich oneself. Power is misused, and the flock suffers. The church may grow numerically, but its spiritual health declines. True authority always flows from humility, service, and obedience to Christ.

. Leaders who live double lives gradually lose their ability to discern right from wrong. What was once clear in Scripture and conscience becomes blurred.

Rationalization replaces conviction, and moral compromise becomes normalized. Personal integrity, the foundation for authentic ministry, is eroded brick by brick. It diminishes the witness of the church in the community. Outsiders notice when leaders fail to practice what they preach. Neighbors, coworkers, and friends may conclude that Christianity is a façade. When hypocrisy becomes visible, the power of the gospel to transform lives is questioned. The church risks becoming irrelevant because its example no longer aligns with its message.

Hypocrisy feeds self-righteousness among leaders. Leaders may believe that their public works compensate for private failings. They may judge others harshly while excusing themselves. This self-righteousness blinds them to their own need for grace and mercy, and it prevents authentic confession and humility.

The congregation begins to imitate the hidden sins of leadership. When leaders model duplicity, members unconsciously learn to mimic it. People may speak Christian language while engaging in worldly behaviors. Integrity is replaced by imitation of convenience and compromise. The spiritual culture becomes corrupt from the top down.

Hypocrisy breeds complacency toward sin. When leaders cover sin, the church becomes desensitized. Acts once recognized as sinful are minimized or justified. Congregants accept behaviors that violate God's Word, believing that if leadership condones it, it must be acceptable.

God's judgment is certain against hypocrisy. Jesus' rebukes against the Pharisees were not hyperbole—they illustrate God's intolerance for deceit in leadership.

Hypocrisy provokes His wrath because it misrepresents His character and misleads His people. Ignoring this warning invites correction, exposure, and ultimately, loss of spiritual authority.

The antidote to hypocrisy is radical transparency. Confession, accountability, and authenticity restore trust. Leaders must be willing to be known fully by God and others. Transparency invites God's power to heal, convict, and purify, reversing the spread of leaven.

Teaching should reflect practice. Preaching about generosity must be accompanied by generous living. Preaching about purity must be accompanied by holiness in action. The Word comes alive when the messenger embodies the truth he proclaims. Accountability prevents hypocrisy from taking root. Spiritual mentors, peer leaders, and oversight boards can provide checks on behavior. When leaders have wise counsel, correction becomes possible, pride is restrained, and spiritual integrity is protected.

Humiliy is the foundation of authentic leadership. Leaders who submit to God first, and then to godly counsel, are protected from the creeping leaven of hypocrisy. Humility keeps ambition in check and ensures that ministry remains centered on Christ rather than personal glory. Hypocrisy often masquerades as zeal. Outward fervor can hide inner coldness. Leaders may appear passionate in public while privately indifferent to God's work or truth. External activity is no substitute for heart devotion, and the Lord searches for the soul to reveal hidden motives.

It blinds the church to its true condition. Congregants may believe they are healthy because everything appears active and full. Programs, attendance, and giving may look good externally, masking spiritual decay inside. The Lord warns that without holiness; the outward image is meaningless. Leaders who refuse correction deepen the spiritual rot.

Those who reject rebuke or resist accountability accelerate corruption. Without guidance, deception hardens into habit, pride takes root, and hypocrisy becomes entrenched. Spiritual rot spreads until revival seems impossible.

Hypocrisy provokes scandal and shame. Exposure is inevitable. Secret sins come to light, reputations crumble, and trust evaporates. Scandals become headlines that not only harm the leader but also wound innocent members and tarnish Christ's name. True leadership restores rather than exploits. Contrary to hypocrisy, godly leaders guide with honesty, integrity, and compassion. They shepherd the flock to God, not to personal gain. Restoration of trust and intimacy with God becomes the hallmark of their ministry.

Spiritual discernment protects the flock. Leaders who walk transparently and seek God's wisdom can spot deception before it spreads. Discernment allows correction and protection for the congregation, guarding against the destructive leaven of hypocrisy.

Prayers are fortified against hypocrisy. Constant communication with God keeps the heart aligned with truth. Prayer exposes hidden motives, strengthens humility, and opens the leader to divine correction before human failure sets in. Teaching by example strengthens the church.

Leaders who live what they teach create credibility and model holiness. Their life becomes a sermon that resonates more powerfully than words alone. Integrity becomes contagious, cultivating authentic faith in the congregation.

Repentance breaks the power of hypocrisy. Confession of hidden sin dismantles the leaven. God's grace cleanses, renews, and restores leaders and congregations. Repentance is not weakness—it is strength and a declaration that God's truth reigns over human pride. Only Christ- centered leadership sustains a healthy church. Leadership rooted in love for Christ, dependence on the Holy Spirit, and accountability to God produces a congregation resilient against deception. When leaders walk in honesty, humility, and faithfulness, the church thrives, and the lean of hypocrisy is overcome.

Chapter 3: Wolves in Shepherd's Clothing

(Ezekiel 34, John 10)

Jesus warned the Church of false leaders: *"Beware of false prophets, which come to you in sheep's clothing, but inwardly they are ravening wolves"* (Matthew 7:15). Wolves disguise

themselves as shepherds, offering guidance and protection while seeking to devour the flock. Their danger is subtle but devastating.

Wolves disguised as shepherds are one of the greatest threats to God's flock. These individuals appear to care for the sheep, yet their motives are self-serving. They promise guidance, protection, and spiritual nourishment, but in reality, they lead the congregation into danger, confusion, and spiritual harm. Deception is subtle at first; their actions mimic genuine care, making it difficult for people to discern their true intentions.

C. S. Lewis, in *Mere Christianity*, describes the danger of deceitful appearances. The heart of a leader determines the true nature of their ministry, and when self-interest drives leadership, the people suffer. Appearances of godliness cannot substitute for genuine obedience to God.

God's Word warns repeatedly against such leaders. In Ezekiel 34, the Lord condemned shepherds who fed themselves rather than the flock. They exploited the people for personal gain, neglected the weak, and scattered the sheep in every direction. These scriptures reveal God's intense displeasure with leaders who abuse their spiritual authority. They are not merely misguided—they are actively opposing God's design for His church.

False shepherds are skilled at manipulation. They use charisma, eloquence, and spiritual jargon to gain trust while covering their greed, pride, or immorality. Scripture repeatedly contrasts their outward show of righteousness with inward corruption, demonstrating that God sees the heart.

A true shepherd sacrifices for the flock; a wolf exploits it. The shepherd gives of himself—time, energy, and even safety—to ensure the sheep are nourished, protected, and guided. In contrast, a wolf in shepherd clothing seeks advantage: power, influence, wealth, or prestige. The difference is clear to God, though it may be hidden from human eyes. The flock suffers most when wolves take the form of leaders.

Leonard Ravenhill warns that the Church often tolerates wolves because it fears confrontation or loss of influence. When leaders are protected instead of being held accountable, sin spreads through the congregation unchecked. Wolves in leadership often prioritize appearance over authenticity. They maintain an image of piety, perform grandiose acts of ministry, and attract attention, while ignoring the real spiritual needs of their people. Charisma, eloquence, and spectacle are tools to manipulate rather than to serve. Congregants may admire their style, but their souls are neglected, and their faith is compromised.

The wolves' strategies are not limited to deception in speech. They often manipulate finances, positions, and emotional bonds. Tozer, in *The Pursuit of God*, emphasizes that a pure heart aligned with God is essential to discern and resist such subtle entrapments. Such leaders often exploit vulnerability. People who are grieving, lost, or searching for guidance are easy targets for wolves. The shepherd's role is to lift, protect, and restore, but the wolf feeds on pain and confusion, twisting it to serve personal agendas. These leaders may promise miracles, blessings, or advancement while subtly draining trust, faith, and resources.

History provides examples of wolf-like leadership. In biblical times, Eli's sons corrupted the sanctuary through greed and immorality, and the nation suffered consequences (1 Samuel 2:12- 17). These examples highlight the devastating effect of unchecked sin in leadership. Wolves sow division to maintain control. True shepherds unite and protect their flock. Wolves, however, create factions, jealousy, and suspicion to consolidate power. By keeping people distracted and at odds with each other, they prevent unity, making it easier to dominate and manipulate. Discord becomes the tool of exploitation.

Modern-day wolves are often hidden behind church programs, media presence, and impressive ministries. While they draw followers, their influence undermines biblical truth. Lewis underscores that evil often wears a mask, and spiritual discernment is crucial to detect it.

Deception is their primary weapon. Wolves masquerade as spiritual guides, often quoting Scripture selectively, twisting truth to justify their desires. Their words are persuasive, their counsel appears wise, yet every decision serves personal gain rather than God's glory. The sheep may follow faithfully, believing the leader is righteous, unaware of the spiritual danger they are in.

Accountability and transparency are God's remedy. Leaders must submit to oversight, Scripture, and prayerful counsel. Ravenhill repeatedly stresses that revival cannot flourish in environments where wolves are allowed to operate without correction. Recognition of wolves requires discernment and courage. The flock must learn to test the words and actions of leaders against God's Word. Spiritual discernment is essential, for wolves are skilled at hiding their true intentions. Courage is necessary because confronting or distancing from a disguised wolf may provoke conflict, criticism, or persecution. Yet obedience to God demands vigilance.

The responsibility also falls on the congregation to be vigilant. Believers must test every teaching against Scripture (1 John 4:1-3) and pray for discernment. Tozer reminds us that the pursuit of God equips His people to recognize deceit and remain faithful despite deception around them. Wolves thrive where accountability is absent. A leader left unchecked will increasingly exploit authority. Without peer review, counsel, or spiritual oversight, the wolf can act freely, unchecked by conscience or consequence. This highlights the importance of systems of accountability within the church that protect the flock and hold leaders to God's standard.

In conclusion, wolves in shepherd clothing are a pervasive threat. Scriptural warnings, combined with insights from Lewis, Tozer, and Ravenhill, make it clear that only a heart committed to Christ and grounded in His Word can withstand their influence. The Church must remain vigilant, discerning, and prayerful to preserve its purity and mission. The flock suffers most when wolves are blind to their own corruption. Many wolves do not see themselves as dangerous. Pride, ambition, or greed blinds them to the destruction they leave behind. The people they are meant to serve become collateral damage in their pursuit of status or material gain. Only God's intervention can expose the wolf, redirect the leader, and restore the flock to safety.

Wolves in spiritual leadership often disguise greed as vision. They may speak eloquently about growth, expansion, or revival, but underneath is a hunger for wealth, influence, or prestige. They entice followers with promises of blessings, advancement, or miracles, while quietly directing offerings, resources, and loyalty toward themselves. Their vision is self-serving, and the flock pays the cost.

They manipulate trust for control. A wolf builds confidence by providing counsel or encouragement, then uses that trust to pressure obedience or submission. Their flattery and charm mask their exploitative motives, leaving the flock dependent yet deceived. Trust becomes a tool to enforce authority rather than to guide or protect.

Wolves exploit the weak and the vulnerable. Those struggling with grief, loss, or trauma are often singled out for manipulation. Rather than offering healing or protection, wolves prey on emotional and spiritual vulnerability, twisting it to maintain influence. Their predatory behavior leaves long-lasting scars on the hearts of the faithful.

They use fear to dominate. Fear is an effective instrument for controlling congregations. Wolves warn of consequences for dissent, label questioning as rebellion, or portray themselves as God's chosen while intimidating the flock. By invoking fear, they silence criticism and prevent accountability, perpetuating their own authority.

Wolves cloak themselves in outward spirituality. Charisma, eloquence, and ritual become disguises for moral decay. Their lives appear upright, their ministries impressive, yet the inner reality is corruption. They mimic the behaviors of true shepherds to conceal selfish ambition and hidden sin. The damage is both immediate and generational. Beyond affecting current members, wolves leave a spiritual legacy of confusion, doubt, and mistrust. Children and youth growing up under such leadership may inherit skepticism toward authority, bitterness toward God, or a distorted understanding of faith. The harm extends far beyond their tenure.

Wolves divert attention from God to themselves. Sermons, programs, and initiatives often reflect the leader's personality, agenda, or ambition rather than God's call. The flock may praise the leader instead of God, and devotion becomes misdirected. A healthy church focuses on Christ; a compromised church elevates human authority.

They resist accountability at all costs. The wolf avoids spiritual oversight, council boards, or peer review. Confrontation is met with defensiveness, manipulation, or dismissal. Without accountability, they operate without restraint, unchecked by conscience or community standards. Wolves suppress truth and confrontations. Honest questioning is often labeled as rebellion.

Concerns about integrity, doctrine, or ethical behavior are dismissed or punished. This creates an environment where deception flourishes and the flock become complicit in silence.

Wolves foster dependency instead of discipleship. Rather than equipping the congregation to grow spiritually, wolves create reliance on themselves. Teaching, counseling, and decision- making are centralized in the leader, making the people dependent rather than empowered. The flock is left spiritually immature, unable to discern truth or resist deception.

They often justify their actions through selective Scripture. Wolves twist the Word of God to validate ambition, greed, or moral compromise. Passages emphasizing submission, honor, or obedience are used to manipulate, while warnings about greed, pride, and sin are ignored or reinterpreted. Scripture becomes a tool for deception rather than a guide to holiness.

Hypocrisy and wolfish behavior often coexist. Many wolves are also hypocrites, maintaining an appearance of righteousness while living contrary to God's Word. This combination is lethal for a congregation, as trust is destroyed, spiritual guidance is false, and sin is normalized within the church. Wolves manipulate generosity for personal gain. Offerings, donations, and tithes are misused to elevate the leader's status. Instead of funding the mission of God, resources are diverted to maintain lifestyle, influence, or programs that serve the leader. This exploitation can devastate both the spiritual and financial health of the congregation.

Wolves exploit loyalty to silence criticism. Followers who challenge or question the leader are often ashamed, marginalized, or accused of rebellion. Loyalty becomes a weapon, forcing conformity and suppressing truth. The church becomes a place where people fear speaking the Word of God boldly. They often present themselves as indispensable. Wolves cultivate the idea that without them, the church cannot survive or thrive. This false narrative secures obedience and deters scrutiny, while the leader gains disproportionate control over the congregation's life and resources.

The sheep suffer quietly under wolfish leadership. Congregants may endure manipulation, fear, and spiritual stagnation in silence. Their trust is betrayed, and they feel powerless to act. Spiritual vitality diminishes, and true ministry becomes stagnant or corrupted. Wolves exploit the authority given by God. Spiritual authority is a sacred trust meant to shepherd, protect, and guide. Wolves abuse this gift for personal ambition, turning a divine responsibility into a tool of exploitation. Their actions invite God's judgment, but the consequences often manifest first in the suffering of the flock.

They prioritize short-term gain over eternal impact. Ambition drives them to seek immediate recognition, wealth, or influence. They measure success in numbers, popularity, or financial prosperity rather than in transformed hearts and lives. This pursuit undermines the eternal mission of the church. Wolves often isolate the flock from outside counsel. By discouraging contact with mentors, other leaders, or spiritual authorities, wolves maintain control. They present themselves as the sole source of guidance, suppressing wisdom that might reveal deception. Isolation becomes a tool of oppression.

Fear and flattery are tools of control. Wolves use fear to intimidate and flattery to manipulate. The congregation is constantly reminded of the leader's "importance" while being subtly coerced into compliance. Spiritual discernment is dull, and critical thinking is stifled. They exploit grief and vulnerability. People experiencing loss, trauma, or life transitions are often preyed upon.

Wolves promise healing or comfort but use the situation to secure influence, loyalty, or financial gain. Healing becomes transactional rather than transformative.

Wolves distort the image of Christ. By blending charisma, ritual, and authority with corruption, wolves present a false version of Jesus. The people's understanding of God's character is skewed, leading to disillusionment, anger, or even abandonment of faith.

They prioritize power over prayer. Wolves invest in networking, influence, and visibility rather than intimate communion with God. Their spiritual life is secondary to personal ambition, leaving the flock spiritually malnourished. Wolves mislead with selective miracles or signs.

When they perform wonders or impressive acts, it often serves personal gain or validation, not the glory of God. People may be impressed, but hearts remain unchanged, and deception is reinforced.

They often disregard God's correction. Confrontation by peers or accountability structures is resisted, rationalized, or rejected. Wolves refuse to submit, believing they are beyond correction or reproach. Wolves silence those who see clearly. Those with discernment or boldness to expose wrongdoing are marginalized, accused of rebellion, or dismissed. This creates a culture where deception thrives, and truth is suppressed.

They exploit spiritual gifts for influence. Gifts of prophecy, teaching, or leadership are manipulated to enhance status rather than to serve God. Followers are impressed by the display but spiritually misled. Wolves encourage dependency over maturity. Instead of equipping the congregation to discern truth and live faithfully, they cultivate reliance on themselves, creating spiritual immaturity and vulnerability.

Their ambition blinds them to eternal consequences. Focused on temporal gain, wolves ignore warnings from God's Word. They fail to see that their corruption will result in judgment, loss of influence, and spiritual ruin. The sheep can be protected through discernment. Congregants must learn to test teachings, pray for wisdom, and evaluate leadership by Scripture. Awareness is essential to avoid being deceived by charismatic but corrupt leaders.

Wolves may appear righteous but lack heart transformation. External obedience or impressive works cannot substitute for inner devotion. The heart remains unchanged, leaving leaders susceptible to sin and the flock exposed to harm. Their spiritual agenda serves self, not God. Every program, initiative, or sermon is calculated to elevate personal influence rather than advance God's kingdom. This subverts true ministry and betrays divine trust.

Wolves thrive where accountability is absent. Structures of oversight, mentorship, and peer correction restrain exploitation. Without them, wolves act freely, and the flock remains vulnerable. Exposure is inevitable. God promises to reveal hidden corruption. Wolves may deceive for a season, but truth eventually comes to light, often with painful consequences for both leader and congregation.

The flock must be taught vigilance. Education in discernment, knowledge of Scripture, and prayer equips the church to recognize wolves and resist manipulation.

Ignorance leaves believers vulnerable. God raises faithful leaders to confront deception. True shepherds, committed to Christ and integrity, serve as guides and protectors. They call out wolves and restore the flock with wisdom and courage. Wolves hinder revival and spiritual growth. Spiritual stagnation results when deceit replaces authenticity. Hearts are hardened, prayer is muted, and true transformation is blocked.

Prayer and the Holy Spirit reveal hidden motives. Only through the Spirit's guidance can the church discern wolves. Vigilant prayer illuminates hidden agendas and equips the congregation for faithful response. God promises justice for His sheep. Ezekiel 34 assures that God Himself will seek, rescue, and judge the leaders who exploit His flock. The Lord is faithful to protect His people and restore what has been lost. Christ alone is the true shepherd. All other leadership is temporary; only Jesus leads with perfect love, wisdom, and sacrifice. Following Him protects the flock from wolves and restores spiritual safety, life, and hope.

Chapter 4: When Love Is Thrown to the Wolves:

Michal, David, and the Judgment Against Power That Betrays the Faithful The Ripple Effects of Silent Suffering in Palaces and Pulpits

Across nations and generations, empires rise cloaked in piety and thrones draped in holy garments, yet beneath sanctified robes lie hearts desperate to control, shape, and silence those who love sincerely. From ancient palace courts to today's religious institutions and political halls, there exists a spirit older than crowns and deeper than politics spirit that fears true loyalty, fears authentic love, fears the quiet strength of a woman whose devotion cannot be bought, manipulated, or erased. Michal stands as a timeless symbol of every woman who loved righteousness amid corrupted power, and her story echoes across every system, whether monarchy, mosque, cathedral, synagogue, temple, or church, where men wield God's name as a weapon against devotion they do not understand.

For in every age, there has been the palace daughter traded for alliance, the bride chosen not for affection but for strategy, the woman whose body and future served as bargaining chips between thrones and honor-bound families. Whether in ancient Israel's royal courts, arranged marriages in noble houses, political unions in dynastic empires, or holy-sealed marriages negotiated by elders and imams, the pattern remains—women offered at the altar of legacy, loyalty, and religious respectability, while their hearts cried silently beneath the sound of ceremonial blessings.

And in this modern hour, too many women look at the news, the church pew, the marriage bed, the cultural expectation, and whisper, "My trauma is biblical. My suffering is ancient. What they call obedience looks like bondage draped in scripture. They read about royal marriages that imprison women in golden cages, religious unions that stifle dreams in the name of honor, and political families where women are protected publicly and imprisoned privately. And as they whisper, heaven replies: *Daughter, you are not alone. Michal walked this path. Her tear-stained footprints still lie on the palace floor where honor and heartbreak collided.*

Michal's life teaches that a woman may love with purity while surrounded by men who love power. She adored David not because a crown commanded her loyalty, but because destiny stirred within her spirit. Yet she was handed over not as a bride chosen by heaven for joy, but as a pawn chosen by a king for control. There are women today who know this altar too well— where vows are sacred only to them, while families, leaders, and systems manipulate marriage as politics, tradition, or religious performance. They live in houses where honor is proclaimed but heartache is practiced; where wedding garments are holy, but motives behind them are unclean.

Some women walk down aisles with trembling hope while unseen forces family pressure, political agenda, cultural tradition, and religious decree, walk beside them, binding their wrists with expectations disguised as righteousness. And like Michal, they love sincerely, defend fiercely, sacrifice deeply… yet are repaid with betrayal, abandonment, and silence. Their devotion becomes erased, their loyalty forgotten once usefulness ends. Heaven records what earth hides, and the throne of God remembers every tear.

For abuse in holy garments is the most dangerous abuse of all. When love is twisted into obedience, when submission becomes servitude, when spiritual language is used to silence emotional pain, when scripture becomes a chain rather than comfort, then the wolf no longer prowls outside the folder stands in the pulpit, sits in the palace, shares the bed, leads the prayer. Michal's story is not ancient gossip; it is the prophetic script of women trapped beneath holy expectations while God whispers liberation through the cracks in their restraint.

This chapter cries not against faith but against those who weaponize it; not against covenant, but against those who counterfeit covenant to cloak control. In every faith tradition across time, God raised women who suffered beneath misused authority, women who prayed in silence while priests feasted, queens who bowed outwardly while their spirits groaned, daughters traded to secure kingdoms while God wrote deliverance through their tears. And to them heaven says: *Your suffering is not weakness; it is testimony. Your silence was not defeat; it was evidence presented in the courtrooms of eternity.*

Saul's spirit survives wherever power fears humility, wherever leadership distrusts love it cannot command, wherever men crowned by systems fear men chosen by God. Michal lived in the palace of a king who used her love as currency first to ensnare David, then to punish him, then to punish her. She stands today in every woman placed in marriages arranged for legacy, for wealth, for image, for family honor, for religious control, for cultural propriety. She stands beside daughters whose choice was overshadowed by duty and whose hearts were sacrificed upon the altar of alliances and tradition.

Yet her story does not end in palace halls; it extends into sanctuary pews where brides shed silent tears dressed in holy garments, believing obedience will become blessing, yet discovering that obedience to corrupted voices is not faithfulness to God. It echoes in mosque courtyards where honor protects men while shame binds women; in temples where sacrifice means silence; in Christian altars where priests and pastors urge forgiveness for a husband's tyranny but never accountability for his sin. And the Lord says: *I see. I judge. I defend.*

The ripple effects of Michal's story move like shockwaves across time. When love is betrayed, destiny is delayed. When loyalty is abused, nations shake. When women are silenced, generations bleed. When leaders misuse authority, God overturns thrones. There is nothing new under the sun—only hearts repeating ancient patterns, only voices echoing ancient cries, only systems trying once again to bury women God called to rise, to speak, to discern, to intercede, to see beyond the palace veil.

There are women today who sit in church pews with wedding rings that feel like shackles, praying their suffering does not dishonor God, unaware that heaven never authorized their captivity. They look at Michal and whisper, "She loved. She lost. She was forgotten." And heaven whispers back, "She was not forgotten by Me." For though man may erase a woman's name when she no longer serves his legacy, God inscribes her name when she suffers for righteousness, not the righteousness men demand, but the righteousness of a heart that loves truth even when truth costs everything.

And so we speak not against marriage, but against its perversion; not against faith, but against those who twist it; not against male leadership, but against male domination disguised as divine authority. For God never ordained a throne where women kneel, but men never bow. A kingdom that silences women is a kingdom already under judgment. A church that fears women's voices fears the Holy Spirit who fills them. A political system that uses women as bargaining tools has already provoked the God who defends the defenseless.

Michal is not merely a footnote in Scripture; she is a mirror held up to generations of women whose love stood tall but whose voices were pushed low. She is the reflection of every Christian wife who hides bruises under makeup and Bible verses under tears; every Muslim woman forced to bear family shame alone; every Hindu bride burdened with honor she did not choose; every Jewish wife whose security became her silent prison; every secular woman traded by politics and wealth; every royal bride whose crown is a cage. Her story stretches across belief systems because oppression is not religion—oppression is sin, and sin wears many robes.

When Saul gave Michal to David, he did not celebrate love. Love is never born where power plots. Marriage is sacred only when hearts unite under God, not when families unite under fear. Some women today were not married; they were assigned. Their vows were not holy; they were coerced. Their covenant was not mutual; it was dictated. And God, the righteous Judge, says: *"I saw who spoke for you. I saw who never asked you. I saw who decided your destiny without seeking mine."*

But hear this truth: arranged marriages throughout history were not always abusive; some were blessed by God, secured family honor, and protected communities. The sin is not arrangement, it is *coercion without consent, tradition without compassion, authority without humility*. Marriage becomes wicked not by culture, but by control. It becomes a cage not by custom, but by the crushing of the woman's spirit while pretending it honors God. God is not against tradition. God is against tyranny.

Likewise, within Islam, Judaism, Christianity, Hinduism, and tribal traditions around the world, there are marriages made with prayer, mutual honor, and community blessing. But there are also marriages where fathers negotiated futures without hearing a daughter's tears, where imams, rabbis, pastors, or elders forgot that daughters belong not to men but to God.

And to those daughters, heaven declares: *"Your worth was never in the contract. Your dignity was never in the dowry. Your calling was never in the marriage bed. You were Mine before you were theirs."*

Michal loved David, but her father used her. And in that tension, her heart lived between divine purpose and human manipulation. So do many women today, caught between God's calling and man's control, between heaven's voice and culture's demand, between love's promise and leadership's betrayal. These women wake up every day torn between loyalty to family and loyalty to the truth burning quietly inside their souls.

When power uses love, it corrupts the covenant. When leaders weaponize scripture to silence questions, they reveal fear, not faith. When pastors preach submission but ignore suffering, the pulpit becomes an accomplice to abuse. When political leaders parade their wives while privately humiliating them, they forget that every crown will fall, every microphone will fade, and every hidden humiliation will be replayed in heaven's courtroom.

The modern woman who suffers silently is not weak; she is weary. She does not lack faith; she has been drained of hope by those who should have protected it. The abused wife is not unspiritual; she is often more spiritual than those who judge her, for she wrestles with God in nights of tears like Hannah, walks faithfully despite pain like Leah, hides trauma like Tamar, navigates danger like Esther, and clings to covenant like Abigail. Scripture does not silence these women; Scripture honors them. It is men who silenced them. But God is restoring their voices.

Esther was chosen for a palace not because she desired it, but because God called her into a system to break its decree. Leah bore rejection but birthed destiny. Hannah wrestled until heaven opened. Tamar exposed unrighteousness with boldness. Abigail confronted a king with wisdom. Bathsheba, once exploited, became the mother of greatness. And Michal, though dismissed by men, remains a beacon for every woman whose loyalty was exploited and whose tears will be redeemed.

Power fears a woman's discernment. Kings lose sleep when a wife prays with purpose. Religious strongholds tremble when women study scripture for themselves. Political kingdoms shudder when women awaken their identity. Because when God restores a woman's voice, no throne can silence her. When a woman understands her worth, no culture can contain her. When a wife becomes a warrior, hell trembles. When a mother intercedes, nations shift. And when a daughter rises in truth, every generational chain begins to break.

To every woman who ever whispered, "God, do You see me?" heaven replies, *"I saw Michal. I see you."*

To every woman who prayed, "Why must I carry this quietly?" heaven answers, *"There will be justice for the quiet ones."*

To every woman who wonders why God allowed suffering, the Spirit says, *"Your tears planted future freedom. Your pain is prophecy. Your silence is evidence. Your endurance is testimony."*

But this chapter is not only comfort—it is a courtroom summons. For judgment comes not only to comfort the violated, but to confront the violators. Leaders who used sermons to suppress truth will tremble. Fathers who used culture to cage daughters will answer. Husbands who hid cruelty behind scripture will be exposed. Religious councils that favored male protection over female dignity will fall like Saul. No robe, no collar, no crown, no title will shield a man from justice when that justice is God's.

For Scripture declares: *"Woe to shepherds who scatter My sheep."* Woe to fathers who trade daughters like contracts. Woe to husbands who treat wives like servants. Woe to leaders who crown themselves kings in homes and pulpits. Woe to those who call control "covering" and domination "headship." Woe to every system that honored male desire and crucified female devotion. Heaven is convening. Thrones are trembling. Justice is marching.

Yet God does not destroy to humiliate—He dismantles to rebuild. He is exposed to heal. He seeks to liberate. For the Lord desires not the fall of men but the rising of families; not the shaming of husbands but the restoration of souls; not the war of genders but the return of holy partnership where man and woman walk side by side, each reflecting glory, each honoring the other, each fully seen, fully valued, fully free.

Modern Systems Called to Account

In political dynasties where marriages protect power instead of hearts, God is shaking foundations. Across kingdoms, empires, and modern institutions, the echo of Michal's betrayal reverberates. Systems built for protection and honor too often become engines of oppression. Royal marriages that trade for alliance, political unions that trade hearts for power, religious marriages that trade joy for duty all bear the same mark: power seeking control at the expense of the innocent. Leaders, elders, and institutions may call these acts tradition, strategy, or divine order, but God calls them corruption, and the Holy Spirit bears witness against every abuse hidden in plain sight. The Almighty sees behind gilded doors, into ceremonial halls, across silken veils, and into the silent hearts of daughters, wives, and mothers who are made invisible while the system celebrates appearances.

These systes survive through secrecy, through expectation, through the cultural logic that obedience is holiness and questioning is rebellion. Yet every hidden coercion, every silenced voice, every woman traded for advantage becomes an indictment against the institution itself. The Bible reminds us that the Lord is not mocked; the manipulation of love is not unnoticed; every coercive act is written in the ledger of eternity. Modern kingdoms—be they political, religious, or cultural—cannot escape the judgment of a God who lifts veils, exposes motives, and vindicates the oppressed.

Today, royal palaces, political offices, and religious hierarchies are filled with Michals whose voices are ignored, whose tears are unseen, whose devotion is twisted into leverage for control. God declares that no throne, no office, no pulpit, and no robe of tradition will hide the truth from Him. Leaders who think to silence women in the name of God or culture will discover that every hidden cry is cataloged in heaven. The injustice of yesterday is the prophetic declaration of tomorrow.

Societies cannot remain indifferent to these abuses. When institutions conceal corruption and dishonor the hearts of women, families fracture, communities falter, and nations bleed. It is the ripple effect of one corrupted system upon countless lives. The palace is not isolated; the pulpit is not hidden. The impact spreads like invisible roots beneath the soil, poisoning communities while leadership remains blind. God sees the pattern, and His justice is relentless.

Yet the exposure of these systems is not only condemnation but is an invitation. God calls for restoration, for accountability, for repentance, and for transformation. When a system betrays its people, heaven moves to correct it. He calls leaders humility, institutions to transparency, and communities to protection over control. The weight of systemic betrayal will not stand against the Spirit of justice; the truth of God will rise, and every hidden abuse will be accounted for, not by man, but by the Almighty Judge.

In religious councils where tradition weighs more than tears, God is flipping tables. In royal houses where brides bear crowns but not joy, God is opening palace windows to reveal hidden misery. In cultures where daughters are bargaining chips, God is raising prophetic daughters who refuse silence. In churches where purity culture protects men and polices women, God is lifting veils and writing truth on tablets of fire.

Healing and Deliverance for the Reader

To the woman trapped in duty, God releases you into dignity. To the woman silenced by religion, God anoints your mouth with fire. To the woman used for legacy, God restores your identity. To the wife told to "pray harder" instead of being protected, God says, *"Daughter, safety is not rebellion."* To the mother judged for leaving abuse, heaven says, *"You saved a generation."*

Michal was silenced by power, yet God's memory of her heart never faltered. She loved David with a purity that threatened Saul's pride. In every age, there are women who, like Michal, are dismissed, called bitter or rebellious, and whose loyalty is treated as insignificant. But heaven sees every tear, every quiet prayer, every act of devotion performed in secret. The Lord does not forget the silenced, the shamed, or the overlooked; He counts their love as testimony, their suffering as prophetic evidence, and their patience as a weapon against corruption.

Her barrenness, her isolation, her dismissal from the narrative of kings and princes was not a mark of divine neglect but of earthly injustice. Modern parallels abound women who are faithful in their homes, offices, churches, and nations, yet are marginalized for speaking truth, for resisting exploitation, for loving when love is endangered. God whispers, "You are not forgotten. Your loyalty is not lost. Your devotion is a seed that will bloom in My timing."

Back to Michal — the Forgotten Voice

Some theologians dismiss Michal, but heaven remembers her. Some call her bitter, but God calls her wounded. Some blame her silence, but God blames the system that silenced her. Some say she opposed worship, but truth says she confronted pride disguised as praise. Her barrenness hurt not because of judgment alone, but because she carried trauma unhealed, unseen, unspoken.

Michal's silence was forced by manipulation, her voice suppressed by the structures around her. Today, women across cultures experience the same tension: the clash between personal calling and systemic obedience. In some traditions, silence is praised as a virtue; in others, it is enforced as control. Yet in both, God's eyes are upon the faithful, and His heart beats for those who love sincerely while surrounded by tyranny.

Her story invites reflection: What happens when loyalty is exploited? What becomes of love when power corrupts its environment? Michal's heart was true, yet she endured neglect, manipulation, and abandonment. The modern woman learns from her story: faithfulness may not bring immediate recognition, but it secures eternal vindication. Every silent Michal of today carries the potential to awaken nations through God-ordained resilience.

Thus, Michal's legacy is prophetic: silence does not erase her worth. Suffering does not diminish her testimony. Betrayal does not cancel her destiny. God sees, remembers, and orchestrates justice that transcends human neglect. Every modern Michal reading these words is called to stand, to discern, to believe, and to anticipate a restoration that defies the injustices imposed by power.

Prophetic Declaration to Women Rising

No more holy cages. No more spiritual gaslighting. No more prophetic intimidation. No more pulpits policing women's obedience while excusing men's sin. No more hiding your calling to protect someone's ego.

Rise, daughters of valor. Heaven calls you from the shadows of neglect and oppression. Rise from cultural chains, from the weight of expectation, from the betrayal of those who should have protected you. Like Michal, your love is powerful, your devotion holy, your voice prophetic. Let no system, no tradition, no authority convince you that your loyalty is a liability.

Rise, not with rebellion, but with righteousness. Not with anger, but with authority granted by God. Your prayers are not wasted, your tears are not ignored, your obedience is not unnoticed. Every act of faithfulness becomes a seed for generations, a testimony for communities, and a challenge to systems built on fear, control, and manipulation.

Rise, daughters of discernment. Speak with courage, act with integrity, and stand firm against coercion disguised as piety. The palace, the pulpit, the marriage, the office—these cannot contain the Spirit of God when it moves through a heart awakened to truth.

Rise, daughters who have endured betrayal. Your pain has purpose. Your silence was temporary. Your witness is eternal. The Lord of justice is gathering your story, weaving your sorrow into strategy, and preparing your testimony to shake every throne built upon fear and control.

Rise, daughters called to lead, intercede, and transform. God's Spirit within you is stronger than every tradition that seeks to suppress, every culture that marginalizes, every leader who betrays. Your rise will not only honor your life, it will awaken nations and vindicate the legacy of every Michal who ever suffered silently.

Prophetic Warnings to Leaders

Pastor, if you silence abused women, your ministry will be weighed. Husband, if you demand obedience without humility, your prayers will be hindered. Father, if you value honor over her heart, heaven is watching. Imam, Rabbi, Priest, Elder — if you shield abusers, your throne is temporary. Religious gatekeepers — if you fear female power, you have already lost spiritual power.

Leaders, hear this warning: every act of manipulation, every silencing of women, every misuse of authority is seen and recorded by the Almighty. Thrones built on fear crumble; crowns placed by coercion are temporary. Your power is not above God's justice.

Pastors, if you conceal abuse in your congregation, if you silence the oppressed under holy language, heaven will expose you. Every sermon that defends control over care will be weighed. Every tradition used to justify oppression will be overturned.

Husbands, if you demand obedience through fear, if you protect your image over your wife's heart, every hidden act of cruelty will stand before the Judge of all the earth. Titles, influence, and wealth will shield you from the weight of righteousness.

Political rulers, elders, fathers—if you value legacy over humanity, strategy over love, power over protection, your dominion will be shaken. Every dynasty built on fear and oppression will face God's correction.

Religious authorities, if you fear the prophetic voice of women, if you refuse accountability, if you elevate pride above humility, the Lord declares: your thrones are temporary, your influence is measured, and your betrayal of trust will be exposed in due time.

Transformation and Restoration

God is raising women who will speak like Deborah, negotiate like Abigail, intercede like Hannah, resist manipulation like Esther, expose injustice like Tamar, and worship in truth like Mary. Men of humility will rise beside them, not threatened, but strengthened. Marriage will not die; it will be purified. Leadership will not fade; it will be refined. The church will not collapse; it will be cleansed.

God's judgment is always paired with restoration. Daughters abused will be healed; wives silenced will sing; communities harmed will awaken. What was stolen by power will be returned with abundance.

Leaders who repent will find wisdom; institutions that confess will find favor; marriages rebuilt in truth will flourish. The palace, the pulpit, the office, the home—anywhere oppression existed—God's Spirit can bring revival.

Women who were forced into silence will discover their voice. Their prayers, once unheard, will move mountains. Their obedience, once exploited, will inspire nations. Their loyalty, once dismissed, will define legacies.

Communities that once normalized abuse will be purified. Children will witness respect instead of coercion, love instead of manipulation, and courage instead of fear. The ripple effect will heal generational wounds and redirect destiny.

Restoration is not passive. It requires the rising of the faithful, the correction of the corrupt, and the intercession of those who know truth. God's hand guides the process, but human obedience activates the movement of His justice.

Ripple Effects Across Society

When women are silenced, children suffer. When mothers are oppressed, nations weaken. When brides become bargaining chips, societies fracture. When wives cry unnoticed, heaven's alarms ring. When daughters rise in identity, whole generations shift.

When a woman is silenced, her silence does not die with her—it flows outward like water pressed through a sieve, touching every life around her. Children learn that their voices can be ignored. Husbands learn that authority is more important than love. Communities learn to normalize fear as a virtue. When loyalty is exploited, obedience becomes a chain rather than a blessing, and every heart in proximity to her suffers the subtle erosion of trust, hope, and courage. What appears as private suffering becomes a societal wound, invisible to the casual observer but palpably present in the weakened moral and spiritual fabric of a generation.

When mothers and daughters are traded or marginalized for power, the cost is not only personal but also cultural. The home, intended to be a sanctuary of nurture, becomes a training ground for submission under duress. Sons grow up misunderstanding honor; daughters grow up undervaluing self-worth. Communities are built upon compromised principles, believing that obedience to authority supersedes justice and that fear of reprisal outweighs compassion. The ripple effect of one coerced heart is the erosion of ethical stability, spiritual integrity, and emotional resilience across entire cities.

When a leader, religious, political, or familial, exploits love for control, society internalizes the lie that power is sacred and manipulation is holy. The pulpit that silences women teaches children to fear the God who empowers them. The political office that protects patriarchy teaches citizens to respect the oppressor more than the oppressed. The ripple is systemic: laws and norms bend to justify exploitation, honor is weaponized, and culture itself becomes an accomplice to sin. The echoes of a single act of injustice resound across neighborhoods, workplaces, schools, and families, creating a hidden yet pervasive network of spiritual decay.

Conversely, when women are empowered, when their voices are honored, when their loyalty is treated with reverence rather than exploitation, the ripple is a tide of revival. Families heal; communities flourish; nations are recalibrated toward justice. When daughters of valor rise and declare truth, their courage inspires sons to protect rather than dominate. Their integrity teaches neighbors to act with compassion rather than convenience. Their devotion inspires leaders to pursue righteousness rather than reputation. Heaven uses these restored voices as levers, shifting the spiritual and moral trajectory of society itself.

The ripple effect is therefore dual: corruption spreads like an unseen poison, while redemption flows like living water. When love is weaponized, societies fracture and bleed quietly. When justice is restored, societies awaken and flourish visibly. Michal's story teaches that even a single silenced heart, when divinely remembered, can become the spark for collective revival. Every woman who endured exploitation, betrayal, or coercion carries within her the seed of societal transformation. God's Spirit is waiting for the moment when these seeds germinate, when hidden loyalty blossoms into public righteousness, and when the ripple effect of restored women reforms families, communities, and nations with enduring power.

The Turning

There is a shaking, and hidden stories are surfacing. There is a stirring, daughters are remembering who they are. There is a rumbling religious pride that is cracking. There is a wind, the breath of God, awakening forgotten voices. There is fire burning every false doctrine that justifies control.

There comes a moment in history when the quiet endurance of the faithful cannot remain hidden. The turning begins not with thunder, but with whispers—whispers of truth breaking through corridors of fear, whispers of courage piercing the walls of oppression. It is the subtle shift of hearts that have been silenced, the sudden awakening of voices long muted by tradition and coercion. Like a river redirected after years of damming, the Spirit begins to flow, reshaping landscapes, overturning entrenched power, and releasing the captive into freedom. What seemed dormant is alive; what seemed powerless is potent; what seemed hidden is now visible in the eyes of God and in the world that watches.

The turning is marked by awareness that suffering was never ignored by heaven, that oppression never went unnoticed, and that the systems built on manipulation are temporary, fragile, and accountable. Women who once bowed under weighty expectations rise with discernment, seeing clearly the mechanisms that sought to bind them. Communities that normalized silence are startled by the awakening of voices that carry authority, wisdom, and courage. Leaders who thought their control was eternal begin to tremble, for the Spirit is shifting allegiances, rewriting narratives, and unveiling truths that no human hand can suppress.

The turning is also a divine disruption. It challenges not only structures but mindsets, cultural assumptions, and spiritual complacency. Every family where obedience was demanded over understanding is confronted with the reality that love cannot be weaponized without consequences. Every religious institution that prioritizes hierarchy over heart faces scrutiny from heaven. Every political entity that sacrifices the innocent for expediency encounters divine evaluation. The turning exposes the hidden currents, illuminates the concealed patterns, and calls all hearts to witness the unraveling of corruption.

Yet the turning is not destruction alone; it is liberation. Those who were silenced discover agency in God's timing. Those who endured betrayal perceive the purpose behind their suffering. Nations, communities, and families begin to feel the momentum of restoration. The turning brings clarity: the faithful are not collateral; the loyal are not expendable; the silenced are not irrelevant. God redeems the pain of those who bore it quietly, and their rise transforms the spiritual climate around them, setting a precedent that cannot be erased.

The turning is prophetic, societal, and personal all at once. It signals a divine reordering of relationships, responsibilities, and power dynamics. Women rise as bearers of wisdom and justice; men who walk in humility rise as allies, not oppressors; communities rise to align with heaven rather than fear. Every tear that fell under abuse becomes a seed of awakening; every act of loyalty mistreated becomes a catalyst for revival. The Spirit orchestrates the turning, and when it sweeps through hearts, homes, and nations, no system built on fear or injustice can resist the current of God's restorative hand.

For Every Woman Reading

Your tears were prayers. Your survival was prophecy. Your endurance was warfare. Your silence was not weakness; it was evidence that God will now use. Your freedom is heaven's agenda.

Sound the alarm, daughters of the Highest. The Lord is raising His voice over nations, over kingdoms, over religious systems, and over every institution that has silenced, manipulated, or exploited you. From palace corridors to pulpit steps, from political chambers to religious temples, from cultural hierarchies to societal expectations, the pattern is the same: women's voices are often ignored, their loyalty exploited, their devotion twisted for control. You may have believed that your suffering is isolated, that the injustice is unique to your environment, or that your obedience is taken for granted. Hear this: God sees it all. God rebukes every hidden evil, every systemic manipulation, every heart hardened by pride or fear, and He remembers every tear shed in silence.

Across religious systems, Hinduism, Islam, Buddhism, and beyond, the subtle and overt mechanisms of control have often diminished the value of women's voices. Arranged marriages, prescribed obedience, gender hierarchies, and cultural rituals have been wielded as tools of authority rather than platforms of love. The faithful, the devoted, and the righteous are often forced into compliance, taught to fear speaking truth, and trained to sacrifice joy and personal destiny for the sake of tradition. The alarm God sounds is not a critique of faith itself, but a piercing revelation against the corruption of love and loyalty that turns sacred practice into oppression.

Political systems amplify these challenges. Women in leadership, advocacy, or influence are confronted with power that fears their insight, suppresses their agency, and manipulates their loyalty for advantage. From parliaments to courts, from grassroots governance to international diplomacy, the echoes of Michal's silencing are heard today. Obedience is mistaken for submission, devotion is mistaken for weakness, and courage is treated as defiance. The Lord is declaring you are not to be intimidated, your voice is not to be erased, and every act of silencing will face prophetic accountability.

The Lord calls you to see clearly, daughters, to understand why struggle has been part of your journey. Spiritual abuse, political manipulation, religious coercion, and cultural expectations are tools of the same adversary who seeks to diminish God's image in you. Yet in the midst of struggle lies revelation: God is forming within you discernment, resilience, and prophetic authority. The oppression you experience today is the training ground for the voice you will release tomorrow. Every challenge you endure is cataloged in heaven and prepared to be transformed into testimony, influence, and legacy.

Hear this prophetic alarm: God is raising women across nations, across religions, across cultures, and across political and religious boundaries. You are not isolated, your voice is not forgotten, and your suffering is not wasted. The chains placed upon you—whether by tradition, authority, or fear temporarily and the divine plan will elevate your insight, vindicate your loyalty, and amplify your voice. Women of all backgrounds, faiths, and experiences are being called to rise in understanding, to walk in courage, and to become instruments of justice and restoration in a world that has long sought to diminish their influence. The alarm is sounding—awake, discern, rise, and proclaim, for the Lord's justice will not be delayed.

For Men Reading With Humility

You are not accused, you are invited. You were born to protect freedom, not possess it. You are called to love, not rule. Your strength was created to shield, not silence. Honor your wife, and God honors you.

The Final Wave of Prophecy

God is rewriting family bloodlines through healing. God is restoring daughters who were traded, abandoned, controlled, or ignored. Heaven is recording every injustice done in His name. The tears of women are becoming the seeds of reformation. A global awakening of female purpose has begun not against men, but beside righteous men.

Hear the voice of the Lord thunder over the corridors of false religion, the chambers of deceitful politics, and the hidden chambers of hearts betrayed. The final wave of prophecy rises not gently, but as a tidal force, sweeping away pretense, exposing hidden corruption, and shaking the foundations of institutions built upon fear and manipulation. Those who have weaponized love to control, silence, or exploit women will be confronted by a God whose vision pierces every veil, whose justice touches every hidden heart, and whose Spirit awakens every silenced soul.

Michal's pain is not a relic of history; it is a mirror for today. Her love, tender and devoted, was twisted by the ambitions of her father, the fear of a king, and the manipulation of power. Across centuries, women endure the same anguish: devotion unappreciated, loyalty exploited, affection silenced. The Lord declares that every tear shed by a faithful heart in the face of power is stored in heaven, each one carrying prophetic weight, each one a testimony of love unjustly treated, yet eternally honored.

Churches, modern religious sects, and cultural movements are called to account. God sees the misused pulpits, the hidden hierarchies, the silenced voices, and the systemic betrayal of love. Leaders who manipulate devotion, who weaponize loyalty, who silence the faithful, and who elevate ritual above righteousness are warned: the final wave of prophecy rises against you. It does not merely expose transformation. It convicts hearts, awakens the oppressed, and calls institutions to repent before heaven's scrutiny becomes public reckoning.

Women of faith, listen with your hearts open: your struggle is not without meaning. The pain of rejection, the burden of silence, and the betrayal of loyalty are not indications of divine neglect. They are preparing. They are the soil in which God will plant your restoration, your voice, your influence, and your prophetic authority. Like Michal, your heart has loved from purity; like Michal, your loyalty has been tested; like Michal, your witness will rise as proof that God redeems every betrayal, every humiliation, and every silent prayer.

The wave crashes against every stronghold of corruption, revealing the truth behind veiled practices, hidden sins, and cultural distortions. It exposes arranged marriages that sacrifice hearts, religious hierarchies that silence devotion, political systems that exploit loyalty, and traditions that honor appearance over righteousness. Nothing remains concealed from the Spirit of God. Nothing escapes the prophetic declaration: every act of injustice, every hidden abuse, every heart silenced will be vindicated in God's timing.

This is a moment of awakening, daughters of courage. The Spirit calls you to see, to hear, and to understand the depth of systemic betrayal, to recognize the continuity of Michal's pain across centuries, and to know that your devotion, even when overlooked, carries eternal significance.

The final wave is not merely a warning; it is empowerment, an invitation to rise, to speak, to act, and to become co-laborers with heaven in exposing hidden evil and restoring honor.

Church leaders, religious authorities, political rulers, and cultural influencers share the clarion call: the time of concealment is over. The Spirit is moving in unprecedented ways to unmask those who exploit love, to expose every hidden injustice, and to vindicate those who have endured patiently. Every system that has manipulated devotion, controlled loyalty, or silenced the faithful is being called to repentance, and every institution that resists will face divine correction.

Women across every land, culture, and tradition—receive this final wave of prophecy as your personal mantle. Let the story of Michal awaken understanding:

your love is sacred, your loyalty is divine, your silence is not in vain. God is raising your voice, magnifying your witness, and preparing your testimony to be a catalyst for justice, restoration, and societal transformation.

What the world has diminished, God will exalt. What the world has ignored, God will illuminate. What the world has silenced, God will amplify.

The final wave does not only bring reckoning, it brings revelation. You are called to discern, to recognize every attempt to manipulate your heart, to resist every strategy that seeks to silence your devotion, and to embrace the God-given power of your voice. Every moment of suffering is a prophetic pointer to your destiny. Every act of loyalty exploited is evidence that you were chosen to stand, to witness, and to transform the systems that would have oppressed you.

Let's hear: the final wave of prophecy rises with clarity and authority. God rebukes the hidden evil in every church, every religious sect, every political palace, and every institution that marginalizes women. Michal's pain is no longer private; it is public in heaven's remembrance. Her loyalty is no longer dismissed; it is honored as a testimony. Her silence is no longer permanent; it is transformed into a prophetic cry that echoes across nations, awakening women, convicting leaders, and revealing that God's justice always prevails.

Closing Judgment and Glory

Wolves in shepherd clothing will be exposed. Saul's systems will fall before David's rise. Daughters once silent will prophesy with fire. Nations will feel the shift when women stand in truth. And God, the Defender of the forgotten Michals, will vindicate every silenced heart and rewrite the legacy of every woman whose love was thrown to the wolves.

Hear the voice of the Lord thunder across the ages: leaders who exalt themselves above God, who glorify their own names, who oppress the faithful, and who punish the innocent will not escape divine reckoning. Just as Pharaoh hardened his heart against Moses and Saul against David, so too today, men in positions of power harden their hearts, believing authority gives them the right to oppress women, families, and communities. The Lord warns: every crown worn in arrogance, every office occupied through fear, every throne built on manipulation will be stripped away by the righteous hand of justice.

God's judgment is precise and unrelenting. The daughter punished for loyalty—the Michal silenced and dismissed—represents every woman today whose voice is crushed by prideful leaders, every daughter, wife, and mother who suffered for doing right. Those who attempt to silence the righteous, whether through culture, race, religion, or political maneuvering, are warned: heaven sees every violation, every act of suppression, every heart coerced into submission. God declares, "I remember. I will judge. I vindicate."

The same power that hardened Pharaoh to the plagues, that hardened Saul to his pride and jealousy, is God's power to overturn injustice today. Nations, churches, institutions, and families that have marginalized women, exploited loyalty, and elevated pride over righteousness will face the glory of His corrective hand. No influence, no wealth, no tradition, no precedent can shield the oppressor from accountability. The Lord's eyes are upon every heart, and His Spirit moves to expose the hidden evil that has long gone unchallenged.

Hear the warning, rulers of men: oppression cannot endure. Authority misused against the innocent, power wielded to silence truth, pride elevated above justice—these provoke the wrath of God. Like Saul and Pharaoh, you may believe that your control is absolute, that your intimidation is permanent, that your punishment of the faithful is righteous. But the Almighty declares: every act of betrayal will return upon your head, every silenced voice will rise, and every injustice will be weighed against your throne.

God's glory is revealed in the vindication of the faithful. Women who endured, who persevered, who loved sincerely when love was exploited, are lifted into honor and recognition. Their loyalty, once ignored, becomes testimony. Their silence, once imposed, becomes a proclamation. Their suffering, once dismissed, becomes prophetic. Heaven's justice restores, elevates, and glorifies those who were faithful while exposing the corrupt hearts that tried to crush them.

The judgment of God is not mere retribution; it is a clarion call for repentance. Leaders who have hardened their hearts have a final opportunity to turn, to acknowledge the God above authority, to honor the loyalty they have exploited, and to cease punishing the innocent. The Lord calls: "Repent while there is time. Humble yourselves. Restore what you have stolen through pride and manipulation. Walk in My justice, not in your vanity."

For the faithful, the promise is unshakable: no throne, no office, no position, no worldly power can overshadow God's plan for restoration. Women silenced, marginalized, and exploited will rise, carrying the Spirit's authority. Communities bruised by leadership corruption will witness renewal. Societies blinded by injustice will be illuminated. The ripple effect of vindicated loyalty spreads beyond the individual, transforming families, institutions, and nations.

Let the warning resound: the God who delivered David, who raised Esther, who empowered Deborah, and who preserved Michal's heart still reigns. He sees the manipulation, oppression, the silencing, and the betrayal of today. Those who push women into submission, who suppress their voice through race, religion, or authority, are confronted with the same divine justice that struck Pharaoh's pride, that removed Saul from his throne, and that corrected the hearts of every leader who forgot God's supremacy.

Glory accompanies judgment. The power of God is displayed not only in correction but in restoration. Women silenced will be seen; loyalty exploited will be honored; hearts broken in injustice will be healed. Leaders who repent will witness the Spirit's transformative work.

Societies will glimpse heaven's standard for righteousness, mercy, and justice. Michal's pain, once hidden, now becomes the light of understanding for all women who have loved from the heart and been punished for it.

So, hear the final decree: the Lord Almighty warns, exposes, and vindicates. Power abused will be humbled. Love betrayed will be restored. Silence imposed will be shattered by truth. Glory and justice are His, and every heart that has endured faithfully will experience His vindication. Let this chapter, this wave of prophecy, this sound warning, echo across every palace, every pulpit, every political office, and every hidden chamber where hearts have been oppressed. God reigns. God judges. God restores. And His glory will not be thwarted.

Chapter 5: Merchandising the Gospel

(2 Peter 2:3 – greed, prosperity schemes, "selling" the anointing)

The gospel is not a commodity to be bought or sold. Christ's message of salvation, grace, and eternal life cannot be measured in dollars, programs, or status. When leaders attempt to monetize spiritual gifts, anointing, or ministry, they distort God's purpose. Faith becomes transactional rather than transformative, and the flock is led to value material gain over spiritual growth. The commercialization of the Gospel is a plague on the modern Church. 2 Peter 2:3 warns of false teachers who exploit believers with fabricated words. When ministry becomes a business, the sacred is diminished, and the sheep are preyed upon.

The selling of anointing is a perversion of God's power. The Holy Spirit equips believers for service, not for profit. Leaders who suggest that financial contributions can purchase miracles, blessings, or divine favor undermine the integrity of God's work. The anointing is a gift, freely given, and cannot be transferred through cash, promises, or manipulation. John MacArthur, in *The Gospel According to Jesus*, emphasizes that the true Gospel cannot be bought or sold. Any attempt to commodify spiritual gifts or manipulate offerings for personal gain distorts the mission of Christ and harms the integrity of the Church.

Prosperity schemes exploit the vulnerable. Many believers contribute faithfully, trusting that God will act through their giving. Wolves exploit this trust, offering material or spiritual rewards in exchange for money. The result is not spiritual blessing but financial and emotional harm, leaving the congregation disillusioned and spiritually drained. Prosperity schemes and "anointing for sale" ministries are examples of merchandise within the Church. These distort biblical teaching and exploit the faithful, turning faith into a transaction rather than a relationship with God.

Greed undermines spiritual integrity. When leaders prioritize wealth over obedience, they betray the very principles they preach. God's Word repeatedly warns that love of money is a root of all kinds of evil (1 Timothy 6:10). Prosperity-focused ministries risk replacing Christ-centered devotion with material obsession. Merchandising the gospel creates inequality in the church.

Only those who can give are promised blessing, advancement, or recognition. The poor and struggling members are marginalized, their faith questioned, and their participation undervalued. This breeds resentment, division, and spiritual disillusionment. Leonard Ravenhill reminds us that revival and spiritual vitality are never for sale. Genuine ministry flows from obedience, humility, and a heart wholly surrendered to God. When leaders pursue wealth over righteousness, the Gospel message becomes polluted.

Leaders who commodify faith misrepresent God's character. The Lord is generous, loving, and just. Reducing His grace and power to a financial transaction distorts His nature. Congregants may begin to see God as a vending machine, waiting for payment to respond, rather than a loving Father inviting relationship and obedience. Manipulation replaces discipleship. The focus shifts from teaching, mentoring, and equipping believers to controlling giving and attendance.

Followers are motivated by fear of missing out on blessings or favor, rather than by love, faith, and devotion. This undermines authentic spiritual growth. The Scripture repeatedly condemns greed within spiritual leadership. 1 Timothy 6:5-10 highlights the dangers of loving money, equating it with spiritual ruin. A Church that commodifies faith loses its witness and betrays the trust of its people.

Merchandising fosters spiritual immaturity. Believers learn to expect miracles, material gain, or recognition without surrendering to God's will. Prayer becomes transactional, worship becomes performance, and faith becomes conditional. Spiritual maturity, rooted in humility, obedience, and perseverance, is neglected. Financial exploitation damages trust. When leaders use Scripture to pressure contributions or suggest that giving guarantees divine favor, trust erodes. Members become skeptical, cynical, and hesitant to engage in genuine acts of service or generosity. The entire church culture suffers as a result. A. W. Tozer stresses that God is glorified through holiness, not financial schemes. Ministries that chase profits rather than God's call operate in a vacuum of spiritual power, leaving the flock spiritually malnourished

God's judgment is certain against those who sell His gifts. 2 Peter 2:3 warns that those who exploit the faithful for personal gain face condemnation. The Lord detests the commercialization of His work, and exposure of such practices is inevitable. Those who trust in God rather than money are the ones truly blessed. Leaders who monetize faith erode the spiritual foundation of their congregation.

By focusing on wealth, status, or influence, they shift attention away from Christ and His teachings. The church becomes an enterprise rather than a sanctuary, and members learn to value material gain above obedience and devotion to God. Selling blessings encourages entitlement rather than gratitude. Commercialized faith also fosters deception.

Followers may be convinced that financial contributions guarantee blessings or spiritual favor. Lewis, in *Mere Christianity*, warns against substituting ritualistic or transactional acts for genuine repentance and obedience.

When members are taught to expect rewards for giving, they begin to measure their faith by what they receive. True worship, humility, and service are replaced by calculation and expectation, distorting the purpose of Christian life. Prosperity teachings often misinterpret Scripture.

Passages about God's provision are twisted to suggest that giving money can manipulate divine outcomes. The Word is misapplied, and members are misled about God's will and timing, fostering confusion and spiritual disillusionment. The gospel is a message of transformation, not transaction. True faith changes hearts, relationships, and communities. It is not dependent on payments or material exchange. Leaders who convert spiritual truths into business transactions compromise the life-changing power of the gospel. The damage extends beyond finances. Souls are hardened, spiritual discernment dulled, and the Church becomes a marketplace rather than a sanctuary. Ravenhill emphasizes that such practices quench the Spirit and resist revival.

Merchandising fosters comparison and competition among believers. When blessings are tied to giving, congregants may compete for recognition, titles, or special treatment. Spiritual pride replaces humility, and envy replaces love. The church becomes a stage for status rather than a sanctuary for souls. Correcting this requires courage and transparency. Leaders must renounce greed, prioritize biblical teaching, and model stewardship without manipulation. Scriptural principles must always guide ministry, not trends or personal gain.

It creates spiritual insecurity. Believers may doubt God's favor if they cannot give as instructed or if promised blessings fail to materialize. Fear, anxiety, and guilt replace confidence in God's grace, leaving hearts burdened and confused. Manipulative teaching often masks personal ambition. Leaders may justify wealth accumulation, luxurious lifestyles, or influence as God's reward, while their motives are self-serving. Congregants are led to believe that such outcomes are divine endorsement rather than human desire. In conclusion, merchandising the Gospel is a subtle yet destructive force. With the guidance of Scripture and insights from MacArthur, Tozer, Lewis, and Ravenhill, the Church can reclaim the sacredness of the Gospel, restore integrity, and refocus on its divine mission to reach souls with truth and love.

Congregations can be financially and emotionally drained. Over time, members give beyond their means or sacrifice essential needs to follow promises of blessing. This exploitation results in stress, resentment, and spiritual exhaustion, weakening the church's witness and vitality.

Leaders who sell the anointing diminish God's credibility. When promised miracles or favors do not occur as claimed, believers may blame God rather than the deceitful messenger. This undermines faith and can lead to cynicism, doubt, and spiritual withdrawal.

True anointing cannot be purchased or traded. The Holy Spirit's gifts are sovereignly distributed according to God's wisdom and purpose. Any attempt to commodify them is futile and dangerous. Authentic ministry flows from obedience, humility, and dependence on God—not from monetary transactions. Merchandising encourages spiritual shortcuts. Believers may think that giving money guarantees spiritual success, bypassing prayer, repentance, and personal growth. This fosters a shallow, transactional faith rather than one rooted in obedience and transformation.

It promotes deception and dishonesty. Leaders may exaggerate miracles, manipulate statistics, or fabricate testimonies to encourage giving. This deceit becomes normalized, eroding ethical standards and diminishing the church's credibility. The practice fosters a culture of entitlement. Congregants may expect blessings, positions, or recognition as rewards for financial contributions. Faith becomes conditional, measured by what is received rather than by commitment to Christ and His will. Spiritual leadership should model stewardship, not exploitation. Leaders are entrusted with guiding resources responsibly, teaching generosity, and serving the flock. Those who monetize faith distort this trust, turning sacred responsibility into personal profit.

The pursuit of wealth can blind leaders to sin. When ambition drives ministry, ethical boundaries are easily crossed. Manipulation, deceit, and greed replace compassion and integrity, and leaders fail to recognize their own spiritual decay. Congregants are often unaware of subtle exploitation. Promises of favor, miracle, or blessing may seem benign at first. Over time, the pattern of manipulation emerges, leaving believers financially, emotionally, and spiritually compromised.

Prosperity schemes exploit hope and desperation. People facing financial hardship, illness, or life challenges may be targeted with promises of divine intervention tied to giving. Instead of comfort and guidance, they encounter exploitation masked as spiritual opportunity.

Merchandising the gospel diminishes spiritual discernment. Constant focus on giving to receive blessings distracts believers from studying Scripture, seeking God personally, and discerning His will. The flock becomes conditioned to transactional thinking rather than obedience and faith.

Leaders often justify exploitation as a test of faith. Members are encouraged to give beyond their means to demonstrate devotion. While obedience is biblical, coercion through financial pressure or promises of reward corrupts genuine faith. Practice discourages genuine generosity.

Giving should flow from love, gratitude, and service, not obligation or expectation of reward. When financial contributions are manipulated, the natural outpour of generosity is stifled.

Merchandising the gospel fosters disillusionment. When promises fail or the church becomes focused on wealth, believers feel betrayed. Faith that once burned brightly can dim, leaving cynicism and spiritual fatigue. Greed in leadership leads to division. Conflict over resources, recognition, and power creates factions within the church. Members are pitted against one another, competing for favor or approval rather than united in mission and worship.

Wolves use charismatic displays to sell the gospel. They may perform miracles, speak eloquently, or demonstrate power, all to attract attention and contributions. Spectacle substitutes for substance, and awe replaces genuine transformation. The anointing is a divine gift, not a commodity. True spiritual empowerment comes from submission, prayer, and obedience, not from human transaction. Misrepresenting the Spirit as purchasable undermines God's authority and integrity.

Prosperity schemes corrupt spiritual priorities. Followers focus on financial gain, personal blessing, and status instead of prayer, service, and obedience. The mission of Christ is displaced by material ambition. Leaders often manipulate guilt to increase giving. Believers are ashamed of insufficient contributions, taught that lack of faith or obedience is demonstrated by financial withholding. Spiritual growth is twisted into financial compliance. Merchandising creates spiritual confusion. Promises of blessings, miracles, or advancement based on giving distort the understanding of God's will. Congregants struggle to discern genuine divine guidance and human exploitation. Exploitation often goes unnoticed until harm is done.

Small steps of manipulation accumulate over time. By the time deception is recognized, trust has been broken, and damage to faith and finances is significant.

God's justice confronts those who exploit His people. 2 Peter 2:3 warns that greedy leaders face judgment. Deception, exploitation, and misuse of spiritual authority will not go unpunished. God honors those who act in faithfulness and integrity. The antidote is transparency and accountability. Churches must establish systems for oversight, reporting, and ethical stewardship. Leaders accountable to peers and God are less likely to exploit the flock for personal gain.

Teaching on giving must be grounded in Scripture. Generosity is a response to God's love, not a means to manipulate blessings. Biblical teaching ensures members understand the purpose of giving, rooted in service rather than reward. Discipleship should focus on heart transformation. Faithfulness is measured by love, obedience, and character, not by financial contributions.

Leaders must prioritize spiritual growth over monetary gain. Authentic leaders serve, not sell. Christ exemplified servant leadership, giving Himself for the flock without seeking profit. Leaders must follow His model to guide the church faithfully.

Prosperity schemes erode trust in the church. When members experience exploitation, skepticism toward the ministry increases. Trust must be rebuilt through transparency, accountability, and Christ-centered teaching. The flock learns to discern truth from manipulation.

Awareness, prayer, and Scriptural knowledge equip believers to recognize transactional teachings and resist exploitation.

God calls His leaders to humility and stewardship. Ministry is a calling to serve, teach, and shepherd—not to enrich oneself. Humility safeguards integrity and honors God. Financial exploitation provokes God's wrath. Leaders who prioritize gain over obedience face correction. The Lord defends the vulnerable and restores justice to His people.

Prosperity-driven leadership blinds members to God's work. Focusing on material rewards distracts from spiritual growth, obedience, and service. The true mission of the church is obscured. Redemption is possible through confession and accountability. Leaders who recognize exploitation, repent, and submit to oversight can restore trust and rebuild faithful ministry.

True ministry reflects Christ's love, not commerce. Service, sacrifice, and shepherding reflect God's heart. Authentic leadership nurtures the flock, honors God, and resists the leaven of greed. The gospel is not a commodity to be bought or sold. Christ's message of salvation, grace, and eternal life cannot be measured in dollars, programs, or status. When leaders attempt to monetize spiritual gifts, anointing, or ministry, they distort God's purpose. Faith becomes transactional rather than transformative, and the flock is led to value material gain over spiritual growth.

The selling of anointing is a perversion of God's power. The Holy Spirit equips believers for service, not for profit. Leaders who suggest that financial contributions can purchase miracles, blessings, or divine favor undermine the integrity of God's work. The anointing is a gift, freely given, and cannot be transferred through cash, promises, or manipulation.

Prosperity schemes exploit the vulnerable. Many believers contribute faithfully, trusting that God will act through their giving. Wolves exploit this trust, offering material or spiritual rewards in exchange for money. The result is not spiritual blessing but financial and emotional harm, leaving the congregation disillusioned and spiritually drained.

Greed undermines spiritual integrity. When leaders prioritize wealth over obedience, they betray the very principles they preach. God's Word repeatedly warns that love of money is a root of all kinds of evil (1 Timothy 6:10). Prosperity-focused ministries risk replacing Christ-centered devotion with material obsession.

Merchandising the gospel creates inequality in the church. Only those who can give are promised blessings, advancement, or recognition. The poor and struggling members are marginalized, their faith questioned, and their participation undervalued. This breeds resentment, division, and spiritual disillusionment.

Leaders who commodify faith misrepresent God's character. The Lord is generous, loving, and just. Reducing His grace and power to a financial transaction distorts His nature. Congregants may begin to see God as a vending machine, waiting for payment to respond, rather than a loving Father inviting relationship and obedience.

Manipulation replaces discipleship. The focus shifts from teaching, mentoring, and equipping believers to controlling giving and attendance. Followers are motivated by fear of missing out on blessings or favor, rather than by love, faith, and devotion. This undermines authentic spiritual growth. Merchandising fosters spiritual immaturity. Believers learn to expect miracles, material gain, or recognition without surrendering to God's will. Prayer becomes transactional, worship becomes performance, and faith becomes conditional. Spiritual maturity, rooted in humility, obedience, and perseverance, is neglected.

Financial exploitation damages trust. When leaders use Scripture to pressure contributions or suggest that giving guarantees divine favor, trust erodes. Members become skeptical, cynical, and hesitant to engage in genuine acts of service or generosity. The entire church culture suffers as a result. God's judgment is certain against those who sell His gifts. 2 Peter 2:3 warns that those who exploit the faithful for personal gain face condemnation. The Lord detests the commercialization of His work, and exposure to such practices is inevitable. Those who trust in God rather than money are the ones truly blessed.

Leaders who monetize faith erode the spiritual foundation of their congregation. By focusing on wealth, status, or influence, they shift attention away from Christ and His teachings. The church becomes an enterprise rather than a sanctuary, and members learn to value material gain above obedience and devotion to God. Selling blessings encourages entitlement rather than gratitude. When members are taught to expect rewards for giving, they begin to measure their faith by what they receive. True worship, humility, and service are replaced by calculation and expectation, distorting the purpose of Christian life.

Prosperity teachings often misinterpret Scripture. Passages about God's provision are twisted to suggest that giving money can manipulate divine outcomes. The Word is misapplied, and members are misled about God's will and timing, fostering confusion and spiritual disillusionment. The gospel is a message of transformation, not transaction. True faith changes hearts, relationships, and communities. It is not dependent on payments or material exchange.

Leaders who convert spiritual truths into business transactions compromise the life-changing power of the gospel.

Merchandising fosters comparison and competition among believers. When blessings are tied to giving, congregants may compete for recognition, titles, or special treatment. Spiritual pride replaces humility, and envy replaces love. The church becomes a stage for status rather than a sanctuary for souls. It creates spiritual insecurity. Believers may doubt God's favor if they cannot give as instructed or if promised blessings fail to materialize. Fear, anxiety, and guilt replace confidence in God's grace, leaving hearts burdened and confused.

Manipulative teaching often masks personal ambition. Leaders may justify wealth accumulation, luxurious lifestyles, or influence as God's reward, while their motives are self-serving.

Congregants are led to believe that such outcomes are divine endorsement rather than human desire. Congregations can be financially and emotionally drained. Over time, members give beyond their means or sacrifice essential needs to follow promises of blessing. This exploitation results in stress, resentment, and spiritual exhaustion, weakening the church's witness and vitality.

Leaders who sell the anointing diminish God's credibility. When promised miracles or favors do not occur as claimed, believers may blame God rather than the deceitful messenger. This undermines faith and can lead to cynicism, doubt, and spiritual withdrawal. True anointing cannot be purchased or traded. The Holy Spirit's gifts are sovereignly distributed according to God's wisdom and purpose. Any attempt to commodify them is futile and dangerous. Authentic ministry flows from obedience, humility, and dependence on God—not from monetary transactions.

Merchandising encourages spiritual shortcuts. Believers may think that giving money guarantees spiritual success, bypassing prayer, repentance, and personal growth. This fosters a shallow, transactional faith rather than one rooted in obedience and transformation. It promotes deception and dishonesty. Leaders may exaggerate miracles, manipulate statistics, or fabricate testimonies to encourage giving. This deceit becomes normalized, eroding ethical standards and diminishing the church's credibility.

Practice fosters a culture of entitlement. Congregants may expect blessings, positions, or recognition as rewards for financial contributions. Faith becomes conditional, measured by what is received rather than by commitment to Christ and His will. Spiritual leadership should model stewardship, not exploitation. Leaders are entrusted with guiding resources responsibly, teaching generosity, and serving the flock. Those who monetize faith distort this trust, turning sacred responsibility into personal profit.

The pursuit of wealth can blind leaders to sin. When ambition drives ministry, ethical boundaries are easily crossed. Manipulation, deceit, and greed replace compassion and integrity, and leaders fail to recognize their own spiritual decay. Congregants are often unaware of subtle exploitation. Promises of favor, miracle, or blessing may seem benign at first. Over time, the pattern of manipulation emerges, leaving believers financially, emotionally, and spiritually compromised.

Prosperity schemes exploit hope and desperation. People facing financial hardship, illness, or life challenges may be targeted with promises of divine intervention tied to giving. Instead of comfort and guidance, they encounter exploitation masked as spiritual opportunity.

Merchandising the gospel diminishes spiritual discernment. Constant focus on giving to receive blessings distracts believers from studying Scripture, seeking God personally, and discerning His will. The flock becomes conditioned to transactional thinking rather than obedience and faith.

Leaders often justify exploitation as a test of faith. Members are encouraged to give beyond their means to demonstrate devotion. While obedience is biblical, coercion through financial pressure or promises of reward corrupts genuine faith. Practice discourages genuine generosity.

Giving should flow from love, gratitude, and service, not obligation or expectation of reward. When financial contributions are manipulated, the natural outpour of generosity is stifled.

Merchandising the gospel fosters disillusionment. When promises fail or the church becomes focused on wealth, believers feel betrayed. Faith that once burned brightly can dim, leaving cynicism and spiritual fatigue. Greed in leadership leads to division. Conflict over resources, recognition, and power creates factions within the church. Members are pitted against one another, competing for favor or approval rather than united in mission and worship.

Wolves use charismatic displays to sell the gospel. They may perform miracles, speak eloquently, or demonstrate power, all to attract attention and contributions. Spectacle substitutes for substance, and awe replaces genuine transformation. The anointing is a divine gift, not a commodity. True spiritual empowerment comes from submission, prayer, and obedience, not from human transaction. Misrepresenting the Spirit as purchasable undermines God's authority and integrity.

Prosperity schemes corrupt spiritual priorities. Followers focus on financial gain, personal blessing, and status instead of prayer, service, and obedience. The mission of Christ is displaced by material ambition. Leaders often manipulate guilt to increase giving. Believers are shamed for insufficient contributions, taught that lack of faith or obedience is demonstrated by financial withholding. Spiritual growth is twisted into financial compliance.

Merchandising creates spiritual confusion. Promises of blessings, miracles, or advancement based on giving distort the understanding of God's will. Congregants struggle to discern genuine divine guidance and human exploitation. Exploitation often goes unnoticed until harm is done. Small steps of manipulation accumulate over time. By the time deception is recognized, trust has been broken, and damage to faith and finances is significant.

God's justice confronts those who exploit His people. 2 Peter 2:3 warns that greedy leaders face judgment. Deception, exploitation, and misuse of spiritual authority will not go unpunished. God honors those who act in faithfulness and integrity. The antidote is transparency and accountability. Churches must establish systems for oversight, reporting, and ethical stewardship. Leaders accountable to peers and God are less likely to exploit the flock for personal gain.

Teaching on giving must be grounded in Scripture. Generosity is a response to God's love, not a means to manipulate blessings. Biblical teaching ensures members understand the purpose of giving, rooted in service rather than reward. Discipleship should focus on heart transformation. Faithfulness is measured by love, obedience, and character, not by financial contributions.

Leaders must prioritize spiritual growth over monetary gain.

Authentic leaders serve, not sell. Christ exemplified servant leadership, giving Himself for the flock without seeking profit. Leaders must follow His model to guide the church faithfully.

Prosperity schemes erode trust in the church. When members experience exploitation, skepticism toward the ministry increases. Trust must be rebuilt through transparency, accountability, and Christ-centered teaching.

The flock learns to discern truth from manipulation. Awareness, prayer, and Scriptural knowledge equip believers to recognize transactional teachings and resist exploitation. God calls

His leaders to humility and stewardship. Ministry is a calling to serve, teach, and shepherd—not to enrich oneself. Humility safeguards integrity and honors God.

Financial exploitation provokes God's wrath. Leaders who prioritize gain over obedience face correction. The Lord defends the vulnerable and restores justice to His people. Prosperity-driven leadership blinds members to God's work. Focus on material reward distracts from spiritual growth, obedience, and service. The true mission of the church is obscured.

Redemption is possible through confession and accountability. Leaders who recognize exploitation, repent, and submit to oversight can restore trust and rebuild faithful ministry. True ministry reflects Christ's love, not commerce. Service, sacrifice, and shepherding reflect God's heart. Authentic leadership nurtures the flock, honors God, and resists the leaven of greed.

The Apostle Peter warned long ago, "Through covetousness shall they with feigned words make merchandise of you" (2 Peter 2:3). His words echo like thunder across the centuries, a prophetic alarm against a sin that would creep into the Church—the selling of what was meant to be freely given. The Gospel of Jesus Christ was never intended to be a product for sale. It is the message of God's redeeming love, the blood of His Son, offered without cost to all who believe. Yet in many pulpits today, it is packaged, marketed, and sold as though salvation were a commodity.

This merchandising spirit disguises itself as ministry, but its fruit reveals greed, manipulation, and exploitation of the flock. It turns sacred offerings into price tags, and the holy altar into a market stall. The prophets of old railed against priests who sold sacrifices for gain, and Jesus Himself overturned the tables of the money changers in the Temple. What he confronted in Jerusalem has resurfaced in modern pulpits.

The danger of this spirit is not just financial—it corrupts hearts, distorts doctrine, and perverts the nature of God's love. True ministry points people to Christ. False ministry points people to cash registers. When a minister spends more time crafting sales pitches than preaching repentance, something has shifted. The shepherd has become a salesman, and the sheep have become customers. Prosperity schemes often cloak themselves in half truths. Yes, God blesses His people. Yes, sowing and reaping are biblical. But when the promise of wealth becomes the central message, Christ is pushed aside.

This is why Paul declared, "We are not as many, which corrupt the word of God" (2 Corinthians 2:17). The word *corrupt* here literally means to "peddle for profit." Today, many pulpits echo with promises of a hundredfold return if only you "sow a seed" into the preacher's ministry. This is not faith—it is spiritual gambling. The merchandising of the Gospel thrives on manipulation. Emotional music, persuasive stories, and urgent appeals are used to loosen wallets, not break chains of sin. Instead of pointing people to the free grace of Christ, it burdens them with financial pressure disguised as "faith steps."

How far we have drifted from the words of Isaiah: "Ho, everyone that thirsteth, come ye to the waters, and he that hath no money; come ye, buy, and eat" (Isaiah 55:1). The Gospel was never for sale. In Acts 8, Simon the sorcerer offered the apostles money to purchase the power of laying hands on people to receive the Holy Spirit. Peter rebuked him sharply: "Thy money perish

with thee!" That same spirit of Simon is alive today, buying and selling the anointing as if it were a franchise.

The merchandising spirit thrives in a church culture obsessed with celebrity preachers, branded conferences, and VIP tickets to "anointed" events. Jesus sent His disciples out saying, "Freely ye have received, freely give" (Matthew 10:8). Any preacher who cannot minister unless there is a financial incentive has missed the heart of Christ. The danger of merchandising the Gospel is not just external—it reshapes the church into a business instead of a body. Instead of discipleship, we get consumers. Instead of altars, we get stages. Instead of shepherds, we get CEOs. The merchandising spirit turns church members into "donors," revival into "products," and miracles into "packages."

This is why judgment is coming. God will not allow His holy name to be dragged through the mud of greed. Jesus warned of hirelings—those who care not for the sheep but only for what they can gain. When trouble comes, they flee. A true shepherd lays down his life for the sheep. A hireling calculates what he can gain. The Church today must examine itself. Are we building altars or businesses? Are we serving Christ or our bank accounts?

It is not wrong for ministers to be supported. Scripture teaches that those who preach the Gospel should live on the Gospel (1 Corinthians 9:14). But when money becomes the message, it becomes idolatry. The merchandising spirit corrupts motives. What begins as a genuine need for ministry support often drifts into greed and exploitation. We must ask: Do our conferences exalt Christ, or do they exalt brands?

Do our tithes and offerings reflect worship, or do they reflect manipulation? Do our leaders carry crosses, or do they carry price tags? The merchandising of the Gospel turns the Church into a den of thieves. This is why Jesus drove them out of the Temple with a whip of cords. His zeal for His Father's house burned hot against corruption. The same zeal burns in His heart today, and judgment will begin in the house of God.

Many believers have grown disillusioned, not with Christ, but with leaders who have sold Him out for profit. The merchandising spirit drives people away from the true Gospel, leaving them empty, wounded, and cynical. But God is raising a remnant who will preach the unpolluted Word without price or profit motive. These men and women will not be for sale. They will not bow to Mammon. They will stand in pulpits with fire in their bones, declaring the truth even if it costs them everything.

God is restoring the purity of His Gospel. He cleans His Church from the spirit of Simon, the money changers, and the hirelings. Those who have turned His house into a marketplace will be exposed. Those who have used the poor to line their pockets will be judged. Those who merchandise the anointing will discover that God's fire cannot be bought or sold.

The Holy Spirit is not for sale. The blood of Jesus cannot be marketed. Salvation cannot be franchised. Deliverance cannot be auctioned. The Cross stands as a rebuke to every scheme that seeks to profit from Christ's sacrifice. At Calvary, Jesus did not collect an offering—He poured out His life. The apostles did not sell tickets to Pentecost—they prayed until the fire fell.

Revival cannot be purchased with dollars. It comes through brokenness, repentance, and prayer. A merchandising church is powerless. Church giving is powerful. The Lord is calling His people back to purity: "Buy of me gold tried in the fire" (Revelation 3:18). That gold cannot be bought with money—it is received through surrender. The merchandising of the Gospel is coming to an end. God will expose, judge, and remove it, for the Bride must be purified before the Bridegroom returns.

(Revelation 2:20 – manipulation, control, seduction)

Revelation 2:20 warns of the Spirit of Jezebel, a spirit of manipulation, control, and seduction infiltrating the Church. This spirit promotes power over humility, ambition over obedience, and deception over truth. The Spirit of Jezebel is a subtle yet destructive force in the church.

It operates under the guise of authority, influence, or spiritual insight, yet its purpose is to manipulate, control, and seduce. Unlike overt sin, this spirit often appears attractive and compelling, drawing leaders and congregants into compromise. Its presence destabilizes churches, relationships, and individual faith.

This spirit thrives on pride and ambition. Those who harbor selfish desires, crave influence, or seek recognition become susceptible. Jezebel's spirit preys on human weakness, promising power and status while masking the eventual consequences of manipulation and rebellion against God. C. S. Lewis, in *Mere Christianity*, observes that pride and ambition often masquerade as virtue. When leaders or members operate under a controlling spirit, they distort God's call and stifle genuine spiritual growth.

Manipulation is a hallmark of Jezebel's influence. Individuals influenced by this spirit skillfully twist Scripture, exploit emotions, and maneuver situations to achieve control. They prioritize personal agendas over God's purposes, often creating environments where obedience to them supersedes obedience to Christ. The Jezebel spirit thrives where accountability is absent. Leaders and members may manipulate others for personal gain or status, often cloaked in religious language. Scripture reveals that unchecked control and seduction are offensive to God, burning in His nostrils like unrepentant sin.

Seduction extends beyond sexuality. While Jezebel's story in Scripture includes sexual immorality, the modern manifestation also seduces through flattery, charm, and promises of success. It lures hearts away from God by appealing to vanity, ambition, and desire for recognition. Leonard Ravenhill, in *Why Revival Tarries*, emphasizes that revival cannot occur where manipulation and control dominate.

The Jezebel spirit quenches the Spirit of God, suppresses truth, and creates fear and deception within the Church.

This spirit seeks to dominate leaders and the flock. Jezebel's influence is not passive; it actively attempts to control decision-making, influence ministry direction, and suppress dissent. Its goal is power over others, often cloaked in spiritual rhetoric, making it difficult to discern. This spirit is not limited to women; it manifests wherever ambition, pride, and manipulation exist. Leaders influenced by it may resist correction, silence dissent, and foster an environment where compromise thrives.

False prophecy and manipulation often accompany Jezebel's spirit. Words of encouragement, guidance, or insight are twisted to serve control rather than truth. Leaders may be convinced that they are following God's will while actually being guided by deception. This leads to compromised leadership and damaged congregations. Tozer, in *The Pursuit of God*, highlights that God desires wholehearted devotion. The Jezebel spirit diverts attention from Christ, replacing worship with control, intimidation, and human agendas.

Churches under Jezebel's influence experience division. Conflict, rivalry, and mistrust grow as this spirit exploits relationships. Leaders may be pitted against one another, and congregants may be manipulated into loyalty or fear, fragmenting the unity of the body of Christ. The consequences of ignoring this spirit are severe. Churches influenced by Jezebel often experience division, doctrinal error, and spiritual stagnation. Scripture shows that Ahab's allowance of Jezebel's manipulation led Israel into idolatry and destruction (1 Kings 21).

Accountability is resisted under Jezebel's influence. Those operating under this spirit often reject oversight, critique, or correction. Attempts at accountability are met with hostility, deflection, or subtle manipulation, creating an environment where deception thrives unchecked. Discernment is essential. Congregations must recognize the signs of manipulation, control, and spiritual seduction. Lewis reminds us that false appearances often cloak dangerous motives, making vigilance and obedience to God's Word vital.

Spiritual seduction replaces true discipleship.

Followers may be enticed to pursue recognition, favor, or personal advantage rather than cultivating intimacy with God. The focus shifts from obedience, humility, and service to manipulation, influence, and self-interest. Accountability structures and transparent leadership are God's remedies. Leaders must submit to Scripture, counsel, and prayer, ensuring that no spirit of control or manipulation can take root. Ravenhill stresses that revival depends on leaders who submit fully to God rather than human ambition.

The goal of this spirit is destruction. Jezebel's influence undermines faith, corrupts leadership, and weakens the church's mission. By enticing hearts away from God's truth, it sets the stage for spiritual decay, scandal, and the erosion of godly authority. In conclusion, the Spirit of Jezebel is a pervasive, destructive influence that infiltrates the Church whenever pride, ambition, or manipulation is tolerated. Scripture, combined with insights from Lewis, Tozer, and Ravenhill, equips the Church to identify, confront, and expel this spirit, restoring purity, freedom, and true devotion to Christ.

Jezebel's spirit fosters deception through appearances. Those influenced often appear godly, wise, and authoritative. They use charisma and perceived spiritual maturity to cloak manipulation, making it difficult for the flock to recognize the underlying corruption. It thrives on controlling information. Decisions, guidance, and counsel are centralized, leaving others dependent. Transparency is minimized, and truth is obscured to maintain influence and control.

Fear is used as a tool of submission. Followers are warned of spiritual consequences, exclusion, or divine disfavor if they question authority. Fear suppresses critical thought and ensures compliance without genuine conviction. The spirit manipulates relationships for loyalty.

Leaders and key influencers are drawn into alliances through flattery, promises, or coercion. Personal relationships are leveraged to enforce obedience, create dependency, and isolate dissenters.

Jezebel's influence targets spiritual vulnerability. Individuals with a deep desire for affirmation, recognition, or acceptance are most susceptible. Their longing is exploited to maintain control and propagate deception. It distorts biblical truth. Scripture is selectively interpreted to justify actions, decisions, or ambitions. Verses about submission, honor, or faithfulness are twisted to enforce obedience to the manipulator rather than obedience to Christ.

Gossip and rumors are weaponized. Jezebel's spirit thrives on division, often using misinformation to undermine trust, create suspicion, and isolate targets. Relationships are strained, and community unity is weakened. It undermines a spiritual authority legitimately established. True leaders are challenged or discredited through manipulation, deception, or covert attacks. Jezebel's spirit seeks to elevate itself above God's appointed authority.

Seduction often comes disguised as encouragement. Compliments, praise, and promises of favor are used to lure individuals into complicity or submission. What seems like mentorship or guidance is often a strategic ploy for control. Jezebel's influence encourages compromise.

Followers may be subtly persuaded to participate in unethical decisions, tolerate sin, or endorse manipulation. Over time, moral boundaries erode, normalizing deception and corruption.

Churches under this spirit often prioritize image over truth. Reputation, influence, and outward success are elevated above obedience, holiness, and discipleship. Appearance becomes a tool to attract followers while masking corruption. The spirit cultivates pride and self-exaltation.

Leaders influenced by Jezebel may present themselves as indispensable or uniquely gifted, cultivating adoration and dependence. This pride fuels further manipulation and suppresses accountability.

Vulnerable members are often isolated. By controlling information, influence, and relationships, the spirit ensures that dissenting voices are marginalized. The flock is divided, and the ability to challenge deception is diminished. Jezebel's spirit opposes prophetic voices.

God's messengers, who speak truth or call for repentance, are resisted, ignored, or persecuted. The spirit seeks to maintain deception and prevent correction from

God's word.

It often operates in subtle, incremental ways. Change occurs slowly, making manipulation hard to detect. Members may not realize the influence until spiritual harm or corruption is deeply rooted. The spirit fosters dependency on human leaders. Followers are encouraged to seek approval, guidance, or validation from leaders rather than God. Spiritual maturity is stunted as reliance on divine guidance is replaced by obedience to human influence.

Jezebel encourages control through seduction and intimidation. Compliance is enforced through a mixture of allure, reward, and threat. Emotional, spiritual, or social pressure ensures obedience and reinforces the manipulator's position. It targets both leaders and followers. The spirit does not discriminate. Ambitious leaders are seduced into control, while the flock is manipulated into submission. This dual reach amplifies its destructive power.

Spiritual discernment is clouded. Members may struggle to distinguish God's guidance from deception. False authority appears legitimate, and hearts are drawn away from truth and obedience. Jezebel fosters compromise in leadership decisions. Decisions that should align with Scripture are influenced by ambition, manipulation, or personal gain. Spiritual objectives are subordinated to human agendas. Accountability structures are undermined. Oversight boards, elder councils, or peer accountability may be bypassed, manipulated, or neutralized to prevent exposure. The spirit protects itself through control and deception.

Leaders influenced by Jezebel often manipulate offerings and resources. Financial and human resources may be exploited to reinforce control, reward loyalty, or further personal ambitions, masking spiritual objectives with spiritual language. Relationships become transactional.

Loyalty, obedience, and favor are exchanged for reward or protection. An authentic community is replaced with dependence, fear, and strategic alliances.

Spiritual maturity is suppressed. Discipleship, prayer, and independent discernment are discouraged. Followers are taught to rely on human guidance rather than cultivating a personal relationship with Christ. Jezebel's spirit manipulates gender and authority dynamics.

Traditional roles, influence, and expectations may be exploited to advance control. Manipulation often capitalizes on cultural or structural dynamics to consolidate power.

It exploits ambition under the guise of spiritual opportunity. Followers may be drawn into leadership or ministry opportunities framed as God's calling when, in reality, it is a mechanism to extend control. Lies are reinforced with partial truths.

Selective Scripture, anecdotal experiences, or apparent spiritual insight are used to validate deception. Partial truths make discernment difficult and entice followers to accept manipulation.

Jezebel sows seeds of fear and doubt. Fear of exclusion, divine disfavor, or failure is used to ensure submission. Doubt of personal judgment or spiritual insight keeps followers dependent and compliant. It fosters pride masked as spiritual authority.

Leaders influenced by this spirit often project superiority, spiritual insight, or divine favor to command loyalty. Pride becomes the engine of manipulation, disguised as godliness.

Subtle coercion replaces open confrontation. Manipulation is often gentle, persuasive, and layered. Confrontation is avoided to maintain the illusion of spiritual integrity. The spirit destabilizes the church's mission. Focus shifts from outreach, discipleship, and Christ-centered ministry to human agendas, manipulation, and control, undermining true purpose. It exploits spiritual gifts for influence. Gifts of teaching, prophecy, or discernment may be used to manipulate or control rather than to serve. Followers are impressed but misled. Jezebel thrives where humility is lacking. Ambitious, prideful, or insecure leaders are particularly vulnerable. Their desire for influence, recognition, or approval opens the door to manipulation.

It resists exposure. Efforts to confront or reveal manipulation are often met with denial, rationalization, or counteraccusations. This prolongs deception and increases harm. Spiritual vigilance is essential. Prayer, discernment, and accountability are the only defenses against this spirit. Awareness and reliance on Scripture equip believers to recognize and resist manipulation.

God calls His people to stand firm. Confronting Jezebel's influence requires courage, faith, and submission to divine guidance. The flock is protected through obedience to God, not fear of human authority. Healing begins with exposure and repentance. Acknowledging manipulation, seeking truth, and returning to God-centered leadership restores spiritual health and unity.

True ministry reflects Christ's character. Service, humility, and integrity counteract the influence of manipulation. Leaders who prioritize God over personal gain safeguard the church. God promises justice for His people. Revelation 2:20 assures that those who deceive, manipulate, or lead the flock astray will face divine judgment. Protection and restoration are promised to the faithful. The ultimate authority remains Christ alone. No human leader, influence, or manipulation can override God's sovereignty. Following Christ ensures safety, truth, and spiritual growth for the flock.

Part II – The Smoke that Reaches Heaven

Chapter 7: Sin That Burns in God's Nostrils

(Isaiah 65:5–7)

Some sins are more than mere offenses; they are a direct affront to God's holiness. Isaiah describes behaviors and attitudes that inflame the Lord's righteous anger, emphasizing that sin is not merely private or personal but has cosmic and spiritual consequences. God sees beyond appearances. While humans may overlook hypocrisy, deceit, or secret sins, God perceives every action, intention, and thought. Nothing hidden escapes His notice. Isaiah 65:5-7 describes sin that provokes God's wrath, highlighting practices that grieve His Spirit. Sin in the Church is especially offensive when it is hidden, tolerated, or embraced by leaders and congregations alike.

Profane acts in sacred spaces intensify the offense. When sin is practiced within places of worship or under the guise of religiosity, it is especially grievous, provoking divine indignation. Selfish indulgence fuels sin that burns in God's nostrils. Seeking personal gain, pleasure, or status at the expense of God's will demonstrates rebellion, greed, and a lack of reverence for His authority. C. S. Lewis, in *Mere Christianity*, warns that sin is not just the breaking of rules but a turning away from God's order and goodness. When spiritual leaders or members ignore sin, the Church becomes a vessel of offense rather than a refuge of holiness.

Manipulation and deceit compound the offense. Those who exploit others for personal benefit, while masking their actions with a veneer of righteousness, deepen the spiritual breach. God's patience is tested by repeated disobedience. Persistent sin, unrepentant and unapologetic, reflects hearts hardened against correction, inviting judgment and exposing the spiritual danger of complacency. The Smoke of sin rises to heaven, demanding God's attention. A. W. Tozer, in *The Pursuit of God*, emphasizes that unrepentant sin diminishes the Church's intimacy with God, dulling its spiritual discernment and influence in the world.

Pride amplifies sinful behavior. Arrogance, self-exaltation, and the pursuit of glory over God magnify offense, creating a culture where sin flourishes unchecked. Social injustice intensifies God's anger. Ignoring the needs of the vulnerable, exploiting the poor, and oppressing the marginalized are sins that deeply grieve the heart of God. Sin is not only personal but corporate. When leaders fail to confront corruption, hypocrisy, and injustice within the Church, the collective offenses intensify. Leonard Ravenhill notes that revival cannot flourish where sin is excused or ignored.

Secret sins are no less offensive than public ones. Hidden deceit, covetousness, and idolatry, even when unnoticed by people, provoke God's righteous judgment and disrupt spiritual integrity. God's fire is a refining fire. Though His anger burns against sin, His ultimate purpose is restoration and purification, calling people to repentance, humility, and alignment with His will. Hidden sin manifests in pride, greed, immorality, and the abuse of spiritual authority.

Scripture repeatedly condemns such behavior, as it undermines the holiness God requires and damages the witness of the Church to the outside world.

False worship intensifies God's displeasure. Offering praise with insincere hearts, performing rituals without obedience, or honoring God in words but rejecting Him in actions provokes His righteous anger. Corruption in leadership is especially grievous. Religious leaders who exploit their positions for personal gain, manipulate followers, or condone sinful practices amplify the offense against God. The Scriptures describe God's indignation at sin that masquerades as righteousness. Isaiah's warnings are timeless: the Lord's displeasure is not for show but a holy reaction to persistent rebellion. Lewis explains that tolerating sin within the Church dulls the moral and spiritual compass of believers.

Unrepentant sin contaminates communities. When sin is normalized or tolerated, it spreads like smoke, affecting not only the sinner but those around them, creating spiritual decay within the congregation. Hypocrisy magnifies the offense. Pretending righteousness while secretly indulging in sin undermines God's authority and misleads the faithful, drawing condemnation. Tozer highlights the importance of confession and repentance. A Church willing to confront sin and pursue holiness can restore intimacy with God and revive its spiritual vitality. The smoke dissipates only when hearts are purified and aligned with God's will.

God's awareness of every action ensures accountability. No act, however concealed, escapes His sight. Every thought, decision, and deed carries weight in His judgment. Sins of oppression particularly burn in His nostrils. Exploiting the weak, ignoring justice, or perverting fairness reflects rebellion and injustice, causing grief to the Almighty. Corporate accountability is vital. Leaders and members must submit to Scripture, prayer, and godly counsel. Hidden sin thrives where accountability is absent.

Lewis reminds us that spiritual vigilance and moral courage are essential to preserving the Church from decay. Idolatry is a recurring theme of provocation. Worshipping created things, elevating human leaders above God, or valuing possessions more than obedience invites divine wrath. , sin that burns in God's nostrils is not just a personal matter but a corporate concern.

Scripture, Lewis, Tozer, and Ravenhill all emphasize that confronting sin openly, pursuing holiness, and maintaining accountability are essential for the Church to fulfill its mission and avoid God's judgment.

Selfish ambition leads to spiritual destruction. Pursuing power, status, or wealth at the expense of moral integrity separates individuals from God and corrupts spiritual communities. Secretive alliances with sin strengthen its hold. Collaborating with others to conceal wrongdoing, justify behavior, or manipulate outcomes compounds guilt and magnifies offense. A. W. Tozer emphasizes that the pulpit must ignite hearts, not simply entertain. Messages must confront sin, challenge pride, and call for repentance. Silence softens the edge of God's Word, leaving congregants unprepared for spiritual warfare.

God's anger is a call to repentance. The burning indignation is not solely punitive; it is intended to awaken hearts to righteousness and restore alignment with His holy standards. Sin blinds the soul to truth. Continuous indulgence in wrongdoing clouds judgment, weakens spiritual discernment, and desensitizes the conscience, making correction more difficult.

The complacency of the heart invites divine wrath. Ignoring sin, excusing wrongdoing, or refusing accountability demonstrates spiritual apathy and intensifies the gravity of offense. Words carry weight in the eyes of God. Gossip, slander, lies, and harmful speech are not trivial; they contribute to sin that burns and affect both individuals and communities. Injustice in courts and governance grieves God. Leaders who fail to uphold justice, favor the powerful, or oppress the vulnerable provoke His anger and disrupt societal order.

Ignoring the poor and needy compounds sin. Neglecting those in distress, failing to feed the hungry, or protect the oppressed is a direct violation of God's commands and provokes His righteous indignation. Secret covetousness corrodes the soul. Desiring what belongs to others, fostering envy, or plotting to acquire wealth at another's expense accumulates sin that is visible to God.

Spiritual adultery reflects deep rebellion. Idolatry, divided loyalties, or prioritizing worldly desires over God represent unfaithfulness that burns in His nostrils. God detests hypocrisy in judgment. Condemning others while excusing oneself, or applying standards unevenly, is a grievous sin that undermines divine justice. Neglecting worship from the heart provokes Him. Mechanical rituals without devotion, prayer without sincerity, or offerings without obedience fail to honor God and invite His wrath. Rebellion against divine instruction intensifies the offense. Refusing to follow God's commands, teaching false doctrines, or leading others astray reflects active defiance of His authority.

Hidden sins influence entire generations. Unaddressed wrongdoing, especially in leaders, establishes patterns that affect families, congregations, and communities for years. God's justice demands correction. The burning of His nostrils is both a warning and a consequence, signaling that unrepentant sin cannot stand unchallenged.

Secret indulgences of the flesh offend Him. Lust, greed, gluttony, and uncontrolled appetites, when hidden behind piety, intensify divine displeasure. Disregard for mercy and compassion is grievous. Failing to love, forgive, and act justly toward others violates God's commands and provokes righteous anger. Sin in the sanctuary is magnified. When wrongdoing occurs within holy spaces or religious institutions, the offense is greater because it defiles what is meant to be consecrated. Arrogance compounds guilt. Pride, self-righteousness, and disdain for correction deepen the offense, making repentance more difficult and the sin more severe.

Manipulating truth is an abomination. Twisting God's Word to justify wrongdoing, deceive, or mislead others provokes His holy anger. God's fire purifies as well as punishes.

While His wrath burns against sin, it also seeks to refine, cleanse, and restore hearts to holiness and obedience. Neglecting justice and righteousness invites calamity.

Communities that tolerate corruption, oppression, or exploitation become vulnerable to judgment and societal decay.

Hidden sins poison spiritual leadership. Leaders who conceal transgressions undermine trust, accountability, and the moral foundation of their ministries. Unrepentant sins accumulate weight. Like smoke that fills a room, repeated offenses create an atmosphere of spiritual suffocation, affecting all who dwell within the community. God's awareness ensures eventual accountability.

No sin, whether hidden or public, escapes His notice; judgment or correction is inevitable if hearts remain unrepentant.

Sin clouds discernment. Individuals entangled in wrongdoing struggle to see the truth, make righteous decisions, or guide others in Godly paths. Hypocrisy undermines faith communities. Members become disillusioned when leaders preach righteousness but practice deceit, fostering cynicism and spiritual decay. Greed and selfish ambition are particularly offensive.

Pursuing wealth, influence, or recognition at the expense of obedience and justice provokes God's anger and corrupts spiritual environments. Secret alliances with evil amplify sin's effects. Collaborating to conceal wrongdoing, exploit others, or pervert justice compounds guilt and spreads corruption. Disobedience without repentance invites judgment. Ignoring correction, hardening hearts, and persisting in sin set the stage for divine intervention. God desires hearts aligned with His will. The purpose of His indignation is not mere punishment but to call His people to genuine holiness, obedience, and love.

True repentance restores spiritual health. Confession, humility, and turning from sin extinguish the fire that provokes God, bringing peace to individuals and communities. Sin that burns in God's nostrils is ultimately overcome through obedience. Living according to His Word, pursuing justice, and walking humbly with Him aligns hearts with His standards, ensuring His favor and protection. Spiritual leaders are called to model holiness. When they participate in sin or conceal it, the smoke reaches heaven, affecting not only themselves but the entire congregation. Ravenhill asserts that leadership without holiness is leadership without spiritual authority.

False Prophets and the Masked Ministers

Exposing those who preach lies and manipulate the flock

God's judgment begins in His house. False prophets, masquerading as shepherds, are among the first to be revealed. Their words may sound anointed, their presence compelling, but their hearts are far from God. Matthew 7:15 warns, *"Beware of false prophets, which come to you in sheep's clothing, but inwardly they are ravening wolves."* The Church is under siege not from outside enemies, but from within. A masked minister may preach holiness on Sundays, yet live in secret sin during the week. He may call himself a man of God, yet his heart beats for wealth, fame, or control.

The faces of exposure are many: the preacher who manipulates emotions for money, the teacher who twists Scripture for personal gain, the worship leader who seeks applause rather than God's presence. These wolves operate subtly. Their sins are often hidden behind layers of ministry success, glowing testimonies, or spiritual jargon. The Lord has given His Spirit as a discerner.

He exposes darkness when hearts are ready to see, and when the time for correction has arrived. When God lifts the veil, the truth becomes undeniable. Masks fall. Charisma cannot hide corruption. Titles cannot conceal rebellion.

The Church today is beginning to see the faces of those who have misled, manipulated, and misrepresented the Word of God. Exposure brings accountability, healing, and cleansing.

Ezekiel 34:2–4 condemns shepherds who feed themselves and not the flock. God calls them to account. The time is coming when every leader who has exploited the sheep will stand before the Lord. Exposure is not only a warning but a mercy. By revealing false teachers and corrupt leaders, God preserves the faithful, redirects wandering hearts, and restores integrity to His Church. False prophets often cloak their motives in scripture, twisting verses to suit personal agendas. Many unsuspecting believers follow, thinking the words are inspired when they are manipulated.

Their teachings may be partial truths, mixed with deception. This creates confusion, leading sincere Christians into compromise and disillusionment. The Lord warns that many will be deceived in the last days (Matthew 24:24). We see this happening in plain sight through the growing influence of motivational preaching over biblical truth. One of the most dangerous faces of exposure is the masked minister who thrives on fear. Fear of missing blessings, fear of God's judgment, and fear of personal loss are tools they exploit.

Many ministries today operate with emotional manipulation, promising miracles, healing, or prosperity contingent on financial offerings. This is not true faith; it is transactional religion. God's blessing cannot be bought, sold, or manipulated by human hands. Exposure reveals hypocrisy. Leaders who demand submission but refuse accountability are no longer hidden. The light of God exposes darkness that has long operated in secrecy. Prophets who cry truth often face opposition. Jezebel-like spirits and masked ministers attempt to silence them through intimidation, slander, or social ostracization.

The sheep are not left powerless. God provides discernment through His Spirit, guiding hearts to recognize false teaching and resist deception. Modern churches face subtle forms of false prophecy: teachings that make believers dependent on men rather than God, encouraging loyalty to personalities instead of Christ. Exposure is merciful. It uncovers hidden agendas, false promises, and manipulation. Without exposure, believers may continue blindly, unknowingly following wolves instead of the Good Shepherd.

The Apostle John exhorted believers to test the spirits (1 John 4:1). This is vital today as many voices masquerade as anointed but are ultimately self-serving. Another face of exposure is prosperity preaching that emphasizes wealth as the proof of divine favor. While God does bless, this distorted message prioritizes riches over righteousness. Leaders exploiting these teachings often live lavish lifestyles while the flock gives sacrificially, believing that their offering guarantees God's blessing.

God sees this as theft from His people. He will expose the fraud and restore integrity to His Church. Exposure also addresses sexual immorality hidden under the guise of spiritual authority. Leaders who seduce, manipulate, or abuse trust are revealed through God's justice. Silence and tolerance enable corruption. Exposure begins when the church refuses to ignore the evidence of sin and deceit.

This exposure is not intended to shame believers but to call the Church to repentance, restoration, and vigilance. The mask of spiritual authority is often convincing. Many can quote Scripture, lead worship, and preach compelling messages, but their lives contradict the Word they proclaim. The Spirit of God brings truth to light. What was once hidden in darkness becomes visible. Those who have led others astray cannot escape God's judgment. Exposure also brings clarity for the faithful. Believers can distinguish between those who lead with integrity and those who manipulate for self-interest.

The Lord is raising a remnant of shepherds and teachers who will stand uncompromisingly in truth, even when popular opinion resists. These faithful leaders are willing to risk rejection, criticism, and persecution to protect the flock. Exposure encourages accountability. Ministries that are transparent, honest, and Christ-centered will be strengthened as false leaders are removed. Revelation of hidden evil purifies the Church, preventing deeper spiritual decay. The faces of exposure are not always dramatic. Sometimes they are quiet, whispered deception, a subtle manipulation, or a hidden agenda.

God exposes even the small things because they have eternal consequences. The Church must embrace accountability, ensuring leaders are answerable to God and community, preventing the rise of wolves in sheep's clothing. Exposure reminds us that the gospel is not a platform for personal gain. True ministry sacrifices for the sake of others and glorifies Christ alone. Every deception brought to light allows the faithful to worship without distraction and to follow Christ without compromise.

Exposure also inspires vigilance. Believers learn to weigh words against Scripture, discern motives, and follow the Spirit's guidance. False prophets, masked ministers, and manipulative leaders will ultimately face God's judgment. Their influence may persist for a time, but truth will always triumph. God's Word is sharper than a two-edged sword, piercing every hidden heart (Hebrews 4:12). The Church on trial will see the removal of corrupted leadership, allowing the righteous to rise and serve with integrity.

Exposure reveals hypocrisy and calls the Church back to holiness, devotion, and fear of the Lord. God is patient, providing time for repentance and correction, but His justice is certain. The unveiling of masked ministers is part of a divine cleansing that restores honor to His Name.

Believers are called to pray for discernment, courage, and protection from deception. Exposure is a gift from God—it saves the Church from deeper compromise and preserves the purity of the gospel. In this hour, God is revealing hidden faces so that His people may be purified, empowered, and ready for the Bridegroom. The Church on trial is not abandoned; it is being refined.

The pulpit was once the most powerful place in society. From it, truth thundered, sin was confronted, and righteousness was upheld. Yet today, in many churches, silence reigns where boldness once stood. It was never meant to be silent. It was created to be a voice crying out in the wilderness, declaring the Word of the Lord with power and clarity. Yet in our day, too many pulpits echo with empty words or remain disturbingly quiet where truth should thunder. Fear has silenced too many pulpits. Preachers are hesitant to speak the full truth of God's Word, worried about offending congregants or losing influence. Yet Scripture commands boldness: *"Preach the word; be ready in season and out of season"* (2 Timothy 4:2).

This silence is not born of reverence, but of fear. Many preachers fear losing members, offerings, or their reputation more than they fear losing the presence of God. When a preacher chooses silence over truth, it is not merely a personal decision—it is a betrayal of the call of God. The pulpit is not a performance stage, but a sacred platform for proclamation. Silence in such a place is deadly. C. S. Lewis, in *Mere Christianity*, underscores that moral courage is essential in the Christian life. The pulpit must be a place of clarity, not compromise. Silence in the face of injustice or sin is a betrayal of Christ's call.

The prophet Ezekiel warned that the watchman who fails to sound the alarm when danger approaches will be held accountable for the blood of the people (Ezekiel 33:6). Today's pulpits too often resemble watchtowers where the trumpet has been laid aside. God appointed His messengers as watchmen (Ezekiel 33:7). A watchman who sees danger and refuses to sound the trumpet is guilty of the blood of the people. In the same way, a preacher who refuses to warn of sin, judgment, and hell has blood on his hands.

Where warnings of sin and hell once resounded, there is now an echo of motivational speeches, self-help strategies, and watered-down messages designed to entertain rather than convict. The modern church has often replaced the cry of "Repent, for the kingdom of heaven is at hand" (Matthew 3:2) with soft affirmations of self-esteem, prosperity, and comfort. Yet comfort without conviction is deception, and prosperity without holiness is a trap. The consequences of a silent pulpit are severe. Congregants may be misled, remain ignorant of God's standards, or fall prey to false teaching. A. W. Tozer, in *The Pursuit of God*, warns that a pulpit devoid of conviction and truth becomes a vehicle for mediocrity and spiritual decline.

The silence of the pulpit is not merely the absence of words—it is the absence of truth. And when truth is absent, deception multiplies. Many sermons are long, but few are weighty. They fill time but fail to pierce hearts. A message that avoids sin, repentance, and holiness may soothe the crowd, but it grieves the Spirit of God. The silence often stems from fear: fear of losing membership, financial support, or personal reputation. Leonard Ravenhill reminds us that true revival requires preachers willing to confront sin boldly, regardless of public opinion.

Jesus said, "You shall know the truth, and the truth shall make you free" (John 8:32). But if truth is never proclaimed, how can the people be set free? Many pastors avoid preaching on sin because they fear offending the congregation. Yet sin left unchecked is far more offensive to God than any sermon could be to man. Paul warned Timothy that a time would come when people would not endure sound teaching but would gather teachers to suit their own desires (2 Timothy 4:3). That time is now, and pulpits have grown silent to cater to itching ears. Leonard Ravenhill's writing reminds us that revival movements throughout history were preceded by preachers who spoke boldly against societal and spiritual compromise. The Church thrives when leaders prioritize truth over popularity.

The danger of silence is that it gives sin permission to grow. When the pulpit does not confront sin, the congregation learns to tolerate it. And what the pulpit tolerates, the pew embraces. Paul further charged Timothy to "preach the word; be ready in season and out of season; reprove, rebuke, and exhort, with complete patience and teaching" (2 Timothy 4:2). This mandate has not expired. The silence of the pulpit allows sin to flourish unchecked within the pews.

Congregations become comfortable in their compromises because the Word of God is not cutting deep into their hearts.

Silence breeds lukewarmness, and lukewarmness makes the Church nauseating to Christ (Revelation 3:16). It also compromises, and compromise weakens the Church's witness. A church that refuses to speak against unrighteousness becomes indistinguishable from the world. Jesus warned that salt that loses its savor is good for nothing (Matthew 5:13). Silence also allows societal pressures to infiltrate the Church. When preachers avoid preaching on topics such as moral compromise, social injustice, or spiritual warfare, the flock becomes unequipped for the realities of life. Lewis stresses that truth cannot be separated from love; speaking God's Word is a form of divine care.

The prophets of old did not whisper when Israel strayed—they cried out. Isaiah declared, "Cry aloud, spare not, lift your voice like a trumpet, and show my people their transgression" (Isaiah 58:1). Today, too many ministers cry softly so as not to disturb the slumber of a sinful culture. The silence of the pulpit has opened the door for cultural compromise. When the Church no longer confronts sin, it begins to conform to the world. Accountability and courage are essential. Preachers must be grounded in Scripture, prayer, and personal holiness. Congregations should support courageous truth-tellers and resist the temptation to silence challenging messages.

Instead of shaping society, the Church has allowed society to reshape it. The pulpit's silence has led to the congregation's confusion. Where are the voices that will rise and declare, "Thus saith the Lord"? John the Baptist confronted Herod's sin, even though it cost him his life. Nathan confronted David's adultery, though David was king. Elijah confronted Ahab, though Ahab had power. True prophets did not keep silent in the face of sin. But today, silence confronts no one.

The enemy rejoices when pulpits fall silent. For he knows that "faith comes by hearing, and hearing by the word of God" (Romans 10:17). If no Word is preached, no faith will rise. Silence is not neutral; it is deadly. A watchman who does not warn is complicit in the destruction of the people. Congregations starve spiritually when pulpits grow silent. They receive stale bread, milk that is spoiled, and water that is polluted. For silence does not stop the advance of sin—it strengthens it. Darkness thrives where light refuses to shine. In conclusion, the silence of the pulpit hinders God's work and endangers the flock. Scriptural mandates, combined with insights from Lewis, Tozer, and Ravenhill, affirm that bold, uncompromising preaching is necessary to expose sin, promote holiness, and prepare the Church for God's return.

The Church is weakened when pulpits are silent, but society is also endangered. If the Church does not declare God's truth, then lies become law, and deception rules the day. A silent pulpit is not only a betrayal of the Church but also a curse upon the nation. Jesus described Himself as the Bread of Life (John 6:35). Yet many churches offer their people crumbs of entertainment instead of the feast of truth. The silence of the pulpit leaves a generation biblically illiterate, unable to discern truth from error, good from evil. This generation knows more about celebrities than about the apostles, more about sports than about Scripture, and more about politics than about prophecy.

And why? Because pulpits have failed to prioritize the eternal Word over the temporary noise of culture. The silence of the pulpit has consequences that echo into eternity. Souls that were never warned of hell will spend eternity there. God declared through the prophet Hosea, "My people are destroyed for lack of knowledge" (Hosea 4:6). When pulpits are silent, knowledge is withheld, and destruction follows. Silence in the pulpit has led to confusion in the pews.

Believers who are not fed truth grow spiritually malnourished. They cannot discern right from wrong, nor can they stand firm when temptation comes. A weak word produces a weak Church.

When the pulpit avoids addressing sin, families suffer. Marriages crumble because no one preaches faithfulness. Children are lost to worldly ideologies because no one proclaims holiness. Generations are destroyed because pulpits remain silent. The pulpit is meant to be a place of courage, not compromise. A preacher is called to speak for God, not to please men. Paul said, "For am I now seeking the approval of man, or of God? … If I were still trying to please man, I would not be a servant of Christ" (Galatians 1:10). Silence is often a form of seeking man's approval. To remain quiet about sin is to silently approve of it.

The silence of the pulpit is often cloaked in excuses. Some claim they do not want to "judge." Others say they want to focus only on "love." But true love warns. True love confronts sin before sin destroys. The pulpit's silence has emboldened sin in the pews. Divorce, fornication, greed, and worldliness go unchallenged. What the pulpit ignores, the congregation embraces. The silence of the pulpit has also crippled the Church's prophetic voice in the world. Instead of being salty, the light, the Church has become bland and dim. Scripture illustrates the danger of unspoken truth. Ezekiel 33 records the watchman's responsibility to warn the people. Failure to proclaim God's message brings judgment upon both the messenger and the congregation.

Jesus Himself preached on sin, hell, and judgment more than any other subject. To avoid such topics is to avoid the ministry of Christ. A Christless pulpit is not a Christian pulpit—it is an empty shell. Jesus warned that salt that loses its savor is good for nothing but to be trampled underfoot (Matthew 5:13). When pulpits go silent, the Church loses its savor. It becomes a powerless institution rather than a Spirit-filled movement. The early Church turned the world upside down because it refused to be silent. They preached Christ crucified, risen, and coming again.

Today, many churches cannot turn their own communities' right side up because the pulpit has grown mute. Pastors who choose silence often do so out of fear. Fear of losing members. Fear of offending wealthy tithers. Fear of being labeled intolerant. Yet the Bible declares, "The fear of man brings a snare" (Proverbs 29:25). Silence born of fear is disobedience to God.

A pulpit that refuses to preach truth is like a doctor refusing to diagnose a disease. He may comfort the patient, but his silence ensures their death. In the same way, preachers who remain silent about sin ensure the spiritual death of their people. God never called His messengers to be popular. He called them to be faithful. Jeremiah was thrown into a pit. John the Baptist lost his head. Jesus was nailed to a cross. None of them was silent, and none of them was applauded by the world. Yet the silence of the modern pulpit suggests that applause is more desirable than anointing.

The silence of the pulpit has also opened the door for false teachers. Where truth is absent, deception rushes in. Wolves thrive in an atmosphere where shepherds are silent. The silence of the pulpit also emboldens false teachers. When truth is withheld, lies rush in to fill the vacuum. Wolves thrive when shepherds are silent. The Church needs preachers who will roar like lions, not whisper like mice. The silence of the pulpit is a betrayal of calling, a denial of truth, and a surrender to darkness.

Jesus warned that many false prophets would rise in the last days and deceive many (Matthew 24:11). They promise blessings without repentance, crowns without crosses, and heaven without holiness. And their influence grows because pulpits stay silent. A silent pulpit cannot produce a holy people. Holiness comes through the washing of the Word (Ephesians 5:26). If the Word is not boldly preached, the Church remains defiled.

The hour is late, and the need is urgent. This is not a time for silence, but for bold proclamation. The world is not ashamed to flaunt its sin; why should the Church be ashamed to proclaim the Savior? The pulpit must rise again as the platform of prophetic truth. It must resound with the Word of God, not the opinions of man. Silence also robs the Church of its prophetic voice in the world. Instead of confronting wickedness in high places, the Church bows in compromise.

Instead of standing as a city on a hill, it blends into the darkness.

Revival will not come through silent pulpits, but through pulpits set ablaze with the fire of the Holy Spirit. Silence will not awaken the Church; only a sound from heaven can. That sound must begin in the pulpit—with men and women who refuse to be silent, no matter the cost. The world is not ashamed to flaunt its sin. Why then is the Church ashamed to proclaim its Savior? This is the tragedy of a silent pulpit: it fears offending men while failing to fear offending God.

Revival will never come through silent pulpits. It will only come through pulpits set aflame with the fire of God's Word. Silence quenches the Spirit; bold preaching invites His power. The silence of the pulpit is the death of the Church. The boldness of the pulpit is its revival. May God raise voices in this generation who will break the silence, declare His truth, and prepare His people for the coming King.

Yet, silence can also become a stumbling block. When pastors and leaders avoid speaking on matters of sin, justice, or holiness, the flock may wander without guidance. This silence often communicates, even without words, that the church should conform to cultural trends rather than to God's Word. Jesus warned that those entrusted with leadership must shepherd the flock faithfully. A shepherd who refuses to warn of wolves endangers the sheep. Similarly, a pulpit that avoids the truth endangers souls by failing to prepare them for temptation, suffering, or judgment.

Silence can be motivated by fear of offending. Many leaders dread losing members, offerings, or popularity. But when financial stability or personal reputation outweighs the call to preach truth, the pulpit becomes compromised. In these cases, silence is not humility; it is disobedience.

Silence can also come from weariness. Pastors who face criticism, rejection, or burnout may retreat from bold preaching. They may choose quiet resignation rather than courageous confrontation. While their pain is real, their silence still leaves God's people vulnerable.

In other instances, silence is strategic. Some leaders wait for God's timing, choosing restraint until the Spirit directs them to speak. Jesus Himself remained silent before Herod, knowing that words would not be received. In such moments, silence is wisdom, not weakness. Discernment is therefore essential. Not every silence is sinful, but every silence carries consequences. The silence of a preacher can either be an act of obedience to God's Spirit or an abdication of responsibility.

The congregation also bears responsibility. If believers demand only comforting messages, they pressure leaders to remain silent on difficult truths. When churches crave entertainment over edification, the pulpit becomes muted by popular demand. The Bible describes seasons when prophets were scarce and visions were rare. These were times of judgment, where silence signified God's withdrawal. Such silence was devastating, for without God's Word, the people perished in ignorance and idolatry.

Today, the silence of the pulpit may be one of the greatest crises in the modern church. With so many competing voices in media, politics, and culture, the absence of a clear prophetic word leaves the flock vulnerable to deception. Yet, even in silence, God always preserves a remnant. He raises voices in unexpected places—sometimes outside the pulpit—to cry aloud and spare not. When official platforms go quiet, the Spirit empowers ordinary believers to speak truth with boldness.

The silence of the pulpit should stir believers to pray. Instead of criticizing leaders, the church must intercede for them to find renewed courage and clarity. Prayer breaks spiritual chains and empowers pastors to speak boldly once more. Ultimately, silence in the pulpit must be tested against Scripture. If it aligns with God's will, it is holy restraint. If it contradicts His commission to "preach the Word in season and out of season," it is a compromise. Only the Spirit can reveal which is which.

(Amos 5:24 – Social Justice in God's Eyes)

God's heart is deeply moved by injustice against the vulnerable. The prophet Amos reminds us that God desires justice, mercy, and righteousness above rituals, highlighting His concern for those marginalized in society. Neglecting the poor is a spiritual offense.

When leaders, communities, or individuals ignore the needs of the marginalized, they are participating in sin that grieves God's heart. God's Word is clear: He cares deeply for the poor, the oppressed, and the marginalized. *"But let justice roll down like waters, and righteousness like an ever-flowing stream"* (Amos 5:24). Neglecting the poor is a sin that grieves God's heart and burns in His nostrils.

Wealth without compassion is meaningless. Prosperity, when hoarded or used selfishly, does not honor God. True riches are measured by generosity and care for those in need. Social neglect perpetuates cycles of poverty. Ignoring systemic issues and failing to support the disadvantaged allows injustice to continue, harming generations and destabilizing communities.

Spiritual leaders are accountable for the oppressed. Pastors and ministry leaders who focus solely on internal affairs, entertainment, or personal gain fail to reflect God's justice and compassion.

God calls His people to advocacy.

True faith manifests in action: defending the marginalized, speaking for those who cannot, and implementing structures that promote equity and fairness. C. S. Lewis, in *Mere Christianity*, teaches that love of neighbor is inseparable from love of God. A Church that ignores the needy violates the very essence of Christ's command to serve others selflessly.

Indifference to suffering is a mark of spiritual decay. A community that tolerates injustice or turns a blind eye to the poor reveals hearts hardened to God's commands and compassionate character. Justice is inseparable from worship. Rituals and religious ceremonies are meaningless if the community ignores the cries of the oppressed and fails to act righteously. God values mercy over sacrifice. He desires that His people act justly, love mercy, and walk humbly, prioritizing care for the vulnerable above empty religious acts. Neglecting the poor creates spiritual and social consequences. When churches prioritize comfort, status, or financial gain over justice and mercy, God's presence is hindered, and the communities they serve suffer. Leonard Ravenhill warns that revival cannot flourish where indifference to the needy persists.

Neglecting the poor invites divine judgment. Societies and leaders who disregard social justice provoke God's wrath, and history consistently demonstrates the consequences of systemic neglect. Silence in the face of suffering is complicity. Failing to speak or act on behalf of the oppressed communicates acceptance of injustice, which grieves God and undermines moral integrity. God's people are called to be a voice for the voiceless. Advocacy is not optional; it is a spiritual mandate to confront systemic oppression and defend those without power or privilege. A. W. Tozer, in *The Pursuit of God*, emphasizes that worship and service are inseparable. True worship manifests in tangible acts of compassion, especially toward those society overlooks. Failing to minister to the poor indicates spiritual apathy.

Poverty is not only an economic issue; it is also relational and spiritual. Those neglected often lack access to education, healthcare, justice, and spiritual guidance, compounding the harm they experience. Neglect of marginalization damages society. When communities ignore the needs of the poor, social cohesion, trust, and stability are eroded, leading to unrest and further inequity. Leaders must model justice and mercy. Spiritual and civic leaders who actively support equitable policies, charitable programs, and ethical conduct demonstrate God's heart in tangible ways. Scripture repeatedly connects justice and righteousness with the treatment of the vulnerable. Isaiah 1:17 calls believers to "learn to do good; seek justice, correct oppression; bring justice to the fatherless, plead the widow's cause." Ignoring these responsibilities invites God's judgment.

God measures the righteousness of a community by how it treats the vulnerable. Nations, churches, and individuals are evaluated not only by personal piety but by their commitment to social justice. Self-interest corrupts spiritual leadership. When leaders prioritize personal gain, comfort, or status over the needs of the poor, they act in direct opposition to God's commands. Jesus' ministry exemplified concern for the marginalized. He fed the hungry, healed the sick, and advocated for the oppressed. The Church today must emulate His example, aligning its actions with His compassion and justice.

Neglect fosters despair and hopelessness. Ignored individuals may feel abandoned, rejected, or forgotten, which can lead to spiritual, emotional, and psychological decline. Compassion must be translated into action. Prayers alone, without practical engagement, do not fulfill God's mandate to care for the marginalized; deeds validate faith. Ignoring social injustice perpetuates sin. Communities that fail to address inequality, exploitation, and oppression allow evil to fester, creating fertile ground for further corruption. The consequences of neglect are not merely spiritual; communities suffer economically, socially, and morally. Churches that ignore systemic poverty or fail to support struggling families contribute indirectly to cycles of oppression. Lewis reminds us that Christian love requires action, not passive sentiment.

God's perspective is eternal. Human systems may tolerate neglect or injustice temporarily, but God sees the cumulative effects of indifference and holds people accountable. True worship includes justice. Celebrations, songs, and rituals are hollow if accompanied by apathy toward the suffering and marginalized members of society. Social responsibility is an expression of faith. Caring for the poor is not a suggestion but a reflection of God's love in practice, aligning actions with spiritual convictions. Tozer emphasizes that God's Kingdom advances when believers actively engage in justice. Ministries should prioritize social programs, advocacy, and outreach as expressions of Christlike love. Neglecting the poor undermines the Church's mission and testimony.

Neglect of children and youth is particularly grievous. Failing to provide guidance, protection, and opportunity to young people damages not only their future but the moral and spiritual fabric of society. Justice delayed is justice denied. Hesitation to act on behalf of the oppressed compounds suffering and demonstrates a lack of commitment to God's standards. Leonard Ravenhill asserts that revival is inseparable from social responsibility. Leaders who teach holiness but ignore the plight of the oppressed cultivate hollow faith that God cannot honor. True obedience requires both spiritual and social engagement.

Spiritual apathy affects credibility. Churches and leaders who ignore social issues risk being perceived as irrelevant or hypocritical, weakening their witness. Scripture repeatedly emphasizes the rights of the poor. From Proverbs to Isaiah to Amos, God underscores His concern for justice, fairness, and care for those most vulnerable. God's anger is provoked by societal neglect. When systemic injustice persists, it burns in His nostrils, signaling a call for repentance and immediate corrective action. In conclusion, neglecting the poor is a sin that provokes God's wrath and hinders the Church's witness. Scripture, Lewis, Tozer, and Ravenhill collectively remind us that genuine faith must express itself in justice, mercy, and compassion, ensuring that the Church becomes a beacon of hope for all, especially the most vulnerable.

Leaders must balance charity and empowerment. Supporting the poor requires both immediate relief and long-term strategies to equip them with skills, education, and resources. Neglect fosters spiritual blindness. Communities that turn away from the poor often lose discernment, becoming blind to sin, injustice, and the moral consequences of their actions. God's covenant includes justice. Faithfulness to Him is inseparable from upholding fairness, righteousness, and protection for the weak. Disregard for the marginalized erodes compassion. Habitual neglect hardens hearts, diminishes empathy, and distances communities from the character of Christ.

Public policies reflect moral priorities. Governments, organizations, and faith communities that neglect social justice reveal their values, which can either honor or grieve God. The church is called to be a refuge. Congregations must actively provide support, safety, and hope for the marginalized, modeling God's love and justice. Ignoring poverty undermines stewardship. Resources, time, and influence entrusted to communities and leaders must be used to uplift the needy, demonstrating faithfulness to God's mandate.

Social justice is inseparable from spiritual health. Congregations that neglect equity, fairness, and compassion risk moral and spiritual decay, eroding the foundation of faith. The cries of the oppressed reach heaven. God hears the lamentations of the poor and oppressed, and their suffering becomes a testimony of societal neglect. Faith without action is incomplete. Genuine belief manifests in deeds; neglecting social responsibility invalidates the authenticity of one's faith. Leaders must address both individual and systemic needs. True justice requires confronting personal failings and advocating for structural changes that benefit the marginalized.

Ignoring the poor invites divine correction. History demonstrates that persistent neglect provokes God's judgment, signaling the seriousness of this sin. Community engagement is essential. Churches, organizations, and leaders must collaborate with local resources to create holistic solutions for poverty and injustice. Education empowers the marginalized. Investing in learning and vocational skills equips vulnerable individuals to break cycles of oppression and dependence.

Advocacy is a spiritual mandate. Speaking truth to power, challenging unjust systems, and championing equity fulfill God's call to His people. Neglect corrodes moral conscience. Turning a blind eye to suffering dulls sensitivity to wrongdoing, leading to spiritual indifference and apathy. Generosity reflects God's character. Providing for the needy demonstrates alignment with His love, mercy, and compassion, fulfilling His commands. Prayer and action must work together. Intercession for the poor is strengthened when accompanied by tangible support and advocacy.

Social justice fosters community cohesion. Addressing inequality and supporting the vulnerable builds trust, reduces conflict, and creates stronger, healthier communities. Spiritual leadership requires moral courage. Confronting poverty, injustice, and systemic oppression challenges comfort zones but honors God and safeguards communities. God's timing is perfect.

He observes the neglect, hears the cries of the oppressed, and works to bring accountability and restoration at the appointed time. True faith honors the poor. Walking in obedience, actively supporting the marginalized, and promoting justice ensures alignment with God's heart and demonstrates genuine holiness.

(Isaiah 14 – Leaders Seeking Glory Instead of God)

Pride has become a hidden epidemic in many sanctuaries today. Leaders seeking recognition, honor, or influence often prioritize personal acclaim over God's glory, distorting the purpose of ministry. Isaiah 14 exposes the dangers of pride, revealing how self-exaltation provokes God's anger. Pride in the sanctuary manifests when leaders or congregants seek glory, recognition, or influence above God's will. The desire for human praise undermines spiritual integrity. When leaders crave approval from people more than obedience to God, decisions are influenced by popularity rather than righteousness.

Ambition can blind leaders to God's calling. Those consumed with advancement or status may overlook humility, service, and the responsibilities entrusted to them by God. C. S. Lewis, in *Mere Christianity*, warns that pride is the "anti-God" sin, the root of rebellion. Within the Church, pride misguides hearts, distorts teaching, and elevates human ambition over divine purpose. Pride leads to self-exaltation. Leaders may manipulate, dominate, or control congregants to elevate their own status, creating an environment that honors the individual over the Creator.

God opposes the proud. Isaiah 14 reveals that arrogance and self-glorification provoke divine judgment, reminding leaders that their authority is accountable to God. Spiritual pride distorts teaching. When ministers emphasize personal success, achievements, or charisma, they risk shifting focus from God's Word to themselves. A. W. Tozer emphasizes that God resists the proud and gives grace to the humble (*James 4:6*). Sanctuaries tainted with pride lose spiritual vitality and hinder the movement of the Holy Spirit.

Humility is essential for effective leadership. True leaders model servanthood, acknowledging God as the source of all wisdom, strength, and influence. Pride also breeds division. Leaders competing for status, recognition, or influence are fracturing congregations. Leonard Ravenhill highlights that revival cannot thrive where egos dominate ministry, and spiritual authority is misused for personal gain. Congregations suffer under prideful leadership. When leaders seek their own glory, members may be misled, manipulated, or spiritually stunted, unable to grow in true faith.

Pride erodes accountability. Leaders who prioritize self over God often resist correction, peer oversight, or spiritual guidance, fostering corruption within the church. The consequences of pride extend beyond leadership. Congregants often emulate prideful behaviors, valuing appearance, position, or performance over devotion and obedience. Scripture reminds us, *"Humble yourselves before the Lord, and he will lift you"* (James 4:10). God's glory must be the goal. Leadership is a stewardship of influence and responsibility, not a platform for self- promotion, recognition, or personal gain.

Pride blinds leaders to their own weaknesses. Arrogance prevents self-reflection, making it difficult to recognize errors, repent, or grow in godly character. Spiritual authority is a divine trust, not a personal entitlement. Leaders are stewards of God's people, called to guide and serve, not to dominate or aggrandize themselves. Lewis explains that spiritual pride blinds believers to their own shortcomings. In sanctuaries where humility is absent, sin goes unchecked, and God's justice and mercy are ignored. Tozer further asserts that true worship and ministry flourish only in humility. Leaders must cultivate hearts surrendered to God, not inflated by applause, status, or worldly accolades. Seeking applause distorts ministry priorities. Efforts shift from shepherding souls to creating spectacle, entertainment, or programs that elevate the leader rather than glorify God.

Pride fosters division in congregations. Leaders who exalt themselves can create favoritism, cliques, or competition, fracturing unity and undermining community. Ravenhill's analysis of revival movements shows a pattern: the presence of humility in leadership consistently precedes outpourings of God's Spirit. Conversely, pride delays or prevents spiritual awakening. God resists the proud but gives grace to the humble. Leadership rooted in humility invites divine favor, discernment, and empowerment to fulfill God's purpose faithfully.

Vanity leads to spiritual blind spots. Prideful leaders may ignore injustice, sin, or doctrinal error to maintain image or popularity. Humility attracts God's guidance. Leaders who submit to God and prioritize His glory receive wisdom, clarity, and discernment for difficult decisions. A proud sanctuary also discourages accountability. Leaders or members resistant to correction perpetuate false teaching, compromise, and mismanagement. Scripture consistently calls the Church to communal humility and submission to God's Word.

Pride corrupts motivation. Self-centered ambition replaces love for God and people, making ministry a platform for ego rather than service. Congregants recognize insincerity. People can sense when leaders act for recognition or applause, which erodes trust and respect. Pride in the sanctuary provokes God's anger and disrupts spiritual growth. By integrating Scripture, Lewis, Tozer, and Ravenhill's insights, the Church is reminded that humility, obedience, and God- centered leadership are indispensable for revival, spiritual health, and true worship.

Leaders must guard against subtle forms of pride. Even small acts of self-promotion, favoritism, or personal glorification can accumulate, creating a culture of arrogance. The heart of leadership is servanthood. Jesus exemplified humility, washing the feet of His disciples and prioritizing God's mission over personal honor.

Pride invites judgment. Isaiah 14 demonstrates that those who exalt themselves will ultimately face correction, humiliation, and accountability before God. Spiritual pride distorts vision.

Leaders may pursue programs, growth, or influence self-interest, losing sight of the Kingdom's priorities. Humility fosters collaboration. Leaders who acknowledge God's guidance and empower others cultivate healthy, productive, and unified communities.

Pride is often masked by good intentions. Leaders may rationalize self-promotion or authority as necessary for ministry, yet God examines motives beyond appearances. Accountability structures curb arrogance. Oversight, mentorship, and peer evaluation protect leaders from the temptation to seek personal glory.

Pride disrupts teaching. Messages may become self-referential, highlighting the leader rather than focusing on God's Word and transformative truth. Servant leadership strengthens the church. Communities flourish when leaders serve, guide, and uplift others, prioritizing God's will over personal ambition. Pride leads to spiritual isolation. Leaders consumed by self- importance distance themselves from God, peers, and the people they are called to serve.

Humility invites correction. Leaders willing to receive guidance, rebuke, and counsel remain aligned with God's purpose, fostering personal and communal growth. Pride blinds leaders to sin in the church. Self-focus diminishes sensitivity to corruption, injustice, or neglect within the community. God exalts the humble and humbles the proud. Spiritual elevation comes not from human applause but from obedience, integrity, and alignment with divine will.

Leaders must resist comparison. Seeking status relative to others fosters pride, envy, and competition, which corrupts ministry. True leadership seeks God's approval, not man's. Recognition and honor are byproducts of obedience, not goals in themselves. Pride hinders mentoring. Arrogance can prevent leaders from teaching, empowering, or investing in the next generation of faithful servants.

Humility encourages unity. Leaders who model Christlike behavior foster trust, collaboration, and a sense of shared purpose. Pride distorts worship. Focus shifts from glorifying God to highlighting human achievement, undermining spiritual authenticity. God detests self-exaltation. Isaiah 14 illustrates that arrogance challenges divine authority, provoking righteous judgment.

Leaders must cultivate self-awareness. Regular reflection, prayer, and accountability prevent pride from taking root in their hearts. Humble leaders prioritize God's vision over personal ambition. Their actions reflect obedience, service, and fidelity to divine instruction rather than personal gain. Pride undermines credibility. Congregants and communities quickly detect leaders who elevate themselves, diminishing trust and influence.

Accountability enhances humility. Structures of supervision, peer counsel, and transparency protect leaders from succumbing to arrogance. Spiritual arrogance impacts decisions.

Prideful leaders may make choices for personal benefit rather than the welfare of the community or God's Kingdom. Humility fosters longevity in ministry. Leaders who prioritize God and serve others sustain effective, influential, and spiritually fruitful ministries.

Pride creates barriers to collaboration. Ego-driven leaders resist partnership, peer input, and team engagement, isolating themselves and weakening their impact. God rewards faithfulness, not fame. Divine recognition is based on obedience, service, and integrity, not popularity or applause. Leaders must recognize their dependence on God. All influence, wisdom, and authority are gifts from the Creator, not personal achievements to be glorified.

Pride distorts vision for the flock. Goals become centered on personal gain rather than spiritual growth, discipleship, and communal flourishing. Humility protects against corruption.

Leaders who submit to God's authority remain grounded, accountable, and guided by His principles. True leadership honors God above self. Prioritizing divine purpose, servant-hearted service, and integrity ensures the sanctuary reflects God's glory, not human ambition.

Chapter 11: False Unity and Compromise

Exposing false teachings and restoring biblical truth in the Church 2 Corinthians 6:14 – Alliances with Darkness

1. Compromise often masquerades as unity.
Leaders may seek agreement or harmony at the expense of God's truth, creating a veneer of peace while ignoring spiritual corruption. False unity diminishes accountability.

When principles are sacrificed for the sake of relationships or appearances, ethical standards erode, and sin goes unchallenged. 2 Corinthians 6:14 warns against being unequally yoked with unbelievers. False unity and compromise within the Church arise when leaders or congregants prioritize harmony over truth, accommodating sin, or worldliness for the sake of peace.

Compromising God's Word has serious consequences.
Short-term benefits or fleeting peace can cause widespread deception, spiritual confusion, and moral decline within the church. C. S. Lewis, in Mere Christianity, highlights that moral compromise is never harmless; it dulls conscience and draws believers away from God's standards. Unity without holiness is just an appearance that distorts God's Church. Alliances with darkness create moral risks. Partnerships with individuals or groups who are unrepentant or spiritually compromised can damage values, mission, and testimony.

God calls for separation from evil. 2 Corinthians 6:14 warns against being yoked with unbelievers in matters that violate God's commands, emphasizing the need for holiness and discernment. False unity undermines spiritual authority. Leaders who tolerate sin or align with morally compromised entities lose credibility and weaken the church's witness. A. W. Tozer, in *The Pursuit of God*, asserts that God demands purity in His people. Churches that compromise with secular values, tolerate sin, or avoid confrontation in the name of unity risk forfeiting God's blessing.

Compromise often begins subtly. Small concessions, seemingly insignificant agreements, or unchallenged behaviors gradually shift the moral compass of leaders and congregations. False unity manifests when leaders prioritize public image over obedience to Scripture. Leonard Ravenhill emphasizes that revival often necessitates confrontation, correction, and a willingness to resist cultural pressures. Compromise undermines spiritual integrity. God values integrity over popularity. Seeking approval or acceptance at the cost of truth is a dangerous path that invites judgment and spiritual decline.

True unity is rooted in God's standards. Harmonious relationships should reflect obedience, righteousness, and shared commitment to God's Word, not human convenience or ambition. Compromise is a slippery slope. Once moral boundaries are crossed, the erosion of truth accelerates, leading to widespread corruption and loss of spiritual discernment. Scripture consistently calls God's people to holiness, even if it leads to discomfort or conflict. Jesus' ministry demonstrated that obedience to God sometimes leads to opposition, but it honors Him and protects the spiritual health of the community.

Compromise erodes spiritual discernment. Leaders who consistently seek agreement at the expense of truth gradually lose the ability to distinguish God's will from human preference. Appeasing others can become idolatry. Prioritizing human approval over divine instruction subtly shifts allegiance from God to people, undermining spiritual authority. Lewis observes that a Church that compromises truth for peace fosters moral ambiguity. Congregants become confused about right and wrong, weakening spiritual discernment and paving the way for hidden evil.

False unity can silence correction. When leaders avoid conflict to maintain harmony, sin and error go unchecked, harming the church and its members. God's Word is the ultimate standard. Any alliance or agreement that contradicts Scripture cannot be considered true unity but rather a compromise of faith. Compromise invites deception. Those who normalize morally questionable practices make it easier for evil to infiltrate and remain undetected in the church. Tozer emphasizes that true unity is only possible in Christ-centered obedience. A congregation committed to holiness can experience harmony without abandoning God's standards. False peace that sacrifices truth is destructive.

Spiritual leaders must maintain moral boundaries. Clear lines of integrity protect the congregation and ensure alignment with God's purposes rather than human agendas. Compromise can fracture communities. Superficial unity often leads to confusion, resentment, and division when the underlying moral inconsistencies surface. Ravenhill underscores that historical revivals were preceded by churches willing to confront sin, reject compromise, and uphold God's Word boldly. Leaders who cling to comfort or popularity stifle revival and invite judgment.

God detests alliances that corrupt His people. Partnerships with individuals, organizations, or ideologies that contradict His truth provoke His displeasure and bring accountability. False unity and compromise threaten the Church from within. Scripture, combined with insights from Lewis, Tozer, and Ravenhill, reminds believers that genuine unity is founded on holiness, truth, and unwavering devotion to God, rather than mere agreement or convenience. True unity builds; compromise destroys. Unity aligned with God's Word strengthens faith communities, while compromise weakens trust, values, and spiritual health.

False unity undermines discipleship. Congregants may adopt inconsistent beliefs or behaviors when leaders prioritize compromise over instruction in righteousness. Leaders are accountable for every alliance. God holds shepherds responsible for the associations they form and the influence these partnerships have on the flock. Compromise is often rationalized. Leaders may justify morally ambiguous agreements as necessary for growth, funding, or influence, ignoring the spiritual cost.

God calls for courage, not convenience. Obedience to His Word requires standing firm, even when separation from compromise is uncomfortable or unpopular. Alliances with darkness distort the mission. Efforts meant to spread truth or serve communities may become compromised, diluting the message of the Gospel. Compromise erodes spiritual authority.

Congregants notice inconsistency, reducing respect for leadership and weakening the church's witness in the broader community. God honors integrity over compromise. Leaders who maintain moral and spiritual boundaries demonstrate faithfulness and attract divine guidance and blessing.

False unity breeds complacency. Acceptance of error or sin to maintain peace fosters stagnation and spiritual lethargy. Compromise misleads future generations. Young believers may be taught that bending the truth is acceptable, perpetuating cycles of spiritual weakness and deception.

Leaders must resist peer pressure. Influence from colleagues or influential partners can pressure leaders to compromise, making discernment essential.

Scripture warns against being unequally yoked. God's design for relationships, partnerships, and alliances is rooted in obedience and shared commitment to holiness. False unity creates false security. Appearances of peace can mask underlying sin, leaving communities vulnerable to moral and spiritual collapse. Compromise diminishes accountability. When wrongdoing is tolerated to maintain unity, personal and collective responsibility erodes, creating a permissive environment.

God calls leaders to radical fidelity. Standing firm in truth, even when it is unpopular or difficult, honors Him and safeguards the flock. False unity hinders spiritual growth. Communities that compromise on principle stagnate, as members are not challenged to pursue holiness and righteousness. True unity requires sacrifice. Leaders and congregations must sometimes separate from comfortable arrangements to remain aligned with God's standards.

Compromise distorts moral clarity. Allowing morally ambiguous practices blurs distinctions between right and wrong, weakening spiritual discernment. Leaders must model courage and integrity. Upholding God's truth sets an example for others, encouraging obedience and principled living within the church. Compromise can be subtle and incremental. Small concessions, left unchecked, accumulate, leading to widespread deviation from God's Word.

God's blessing accompanies obedience. Choosing truth over convenience invites divine favor, protection, and spiritual fruitfulness. False unity undermines evangelism. When compromise distorts the Gospel message, outreach efforts lose credibility, and the truth is obscured. Spiritual vigilance is essential. Leaders must continually evaluate alliances and decisions to ensure alignment with God's Word.

Compromise diminishes moral influence. Communities that tolerate error lose the power to shape ethical, just, and godly behavior in society. God calls for separation, not isolation. Rejecting compromise does not mean withdrawing from the world but engaging with integrity and discernment. True unity is built on shared commitment to God. Partnerships and relationships grounded in Scripture foster lasting strength, faithfulness, and witness.

Compromise masks weakness. Leaders who bend the truth to maintain appearances reveal insecurity and lack of reliance on God. God demands discernment in every alliance. Evaluating relationships through the lens of Scripture ensures alignment with His standards and purposes. False unity leads to illusion. When compromise surfaces, members may feel betrayed, confused, or spiritually abandoned. Leaders must be proactive in setting boundaries. Clear ethical, moral, and spiritual standards prevent compromise and protect the church from deception.

God honors leaders who uphold truth despite opposition. Courage, integrity, and fidelity to His Word bring His favor and strengthen communities spiritually. True unity glorifies God, not man. Alliances rooted in obedience, holiness, and principle ensure the church remains a beacon of truth, light, and righteousness.

Confronting Deception and Heresy

Deception and heresy undermine the Church by diverting believers from God's truth. Revealing hidden evils clarifies doctrines that distort the Gospel. Church leaders must teach discernment to help believers identify false teachings. Heresy often begins subtly, disguised as wisdom, innovation, or spiritual insight. By exposing these deceptions, we can see how they infiltrate ministries through pride, manipulation, or compromise. Believers need to ground themselves in Scripture to resist such errors. Leaders have a crucial role in correcting false doctrines using truth and authority.

Exposure highlights the consequences of allowing heresy to spread unchecked. Deception can corrupt faith, obedience, and the Church's witness in society. Leaders must model humility, knowledge, and courage when confronting errors. Exposure teaches that silence or passivity enables deception to thrive. Believers must test all teachings, practices, and spiritual claims against God's Word. Leaders must equip the Church to discern truth from error in every context.

Exposure reveals hidden agendas, manipulative tactics, and spiritual distractions. False teachings often exploit fear, greed, or desire for power. Leaders must provide clear, consistent, and biblically grounded teaching. Exposure ensures the Church confronts error without compromising love or truth. Deception can masquerade as revelation, personal experience, or modern insight.

Leaders must cultivate spiritual maturity and discernment among members. Exposure teaches believers to rely on God's Word, not human authority, for guidance. False teachings often appeal to convenience, emotion, or self-interest. Leaders must confront heresy boldly, providing evidence and Scripture to correct errors. Exposure helps the Church recognize patterns of deception in culture, media, and ministry. Believers must embrace accountability, mentorship, and study to remain grounded.

Leaders must act decisively to remove false teaching without fear or compromise. Exposure protects the Church from spiritual confusion, division, and compromise. Deception seeks to distort truth, divide congregations, and weaken spiritual authority. Leaders must provide pastoral care while addressing doctrinal errors. Exposure strengthens confidence in God's Word and His guiding Spirit. Believers must cultivate discernment, prayer, and vigilance in all spiritual matters.

Leaders must identify heretical influences and teach corrective measures. Exposure ensures that the Church is aligned with Scripture, holiness, and truth. Deception thrives where ignorance, apathy, or pride exist. Leaders must nurture humility, obedience, and submission to God's authority. Exposure clarifies the dangers of popular culture, trends, or untested spiritual claims. Believers must actively reject teachings that contradict God's Word. Leaders must communicate the consequences of error while providing paths to correction. Exposure strengthens the Church's ability to discern God's voice from false voices. Deception often exploits emotional, social, or financial vulnerabilities. Leaders must teach vigilance, spiritual awareness, and obedience to God's commands.

Exposure fosters courage, conviction, and boldness in proclaiming truth. Believers must remain steadfast, prayerful, and rooted in Scripture. Leaders must maintain accountability, teaching, and discernment to protect the Church. Exposure equips the Church to confront deception with wisdom, courage, and love. Ultimately, confronting deception and heresy restores biblical truth, strengthens faith, and protects the Church from spiritual ruin, enabling it to fulfill God's mission faithfully.

Part III – God's Shaking and Exposure
Chapter 12: Judgment Begins in the House of God

1 Peter 4:17 – God's Standard of Accountability for His People

God's judgment is impartial and begins with His own house. Spiritual accountability starts within the church because leaders and believers are entrusted with the truth of His Word. The Church cannot escape scrutiny. God examines the lives of those who claim to serve Him, measuring obedience, integrity, and faithfulness against His standards. 1 Peter 4:17 reminds believers that judgment begins at the household of God. When sin is tolerated, hypocrisy ignored, or compromise accepted within the Church, God's correction is inevitable.

Judgment is a refining process. Rather than mere condemnation, divine correction purges hypocrisy, sin, and neglect, revealing true character and intent. Leaders bear greater responsibility. C. S. Lewis, in *Mere Christianity*, emphasizes that God's discipline is a form of love aimed at restoration. Judgment is not solely punitive but seeks to bring believers back into holiness and intimacy with Him. Those who shepherd God's people will be held to higher standards, as their influence directly impacts the spiritual well-being of the congregation.

God sees what is hidden. Private sins, concealed motives, and secret compromises cannot escape His notice; He brings everything to light for correction and accountability. The faithful are encouraged to live in holiness. Knowing that God begins judgment with His own people motivates believers to pursue righteousness and genuine devotion. A. W. Tozer, in *The Pursuit of God*, notes that the Church cannot escape scrutiny. Hidden sin, unrepentant compromise, or spiritual neglect draws God's attention and necessitates correction

Ignorance does not excuse sin. Pretending not to see wrongdoing or claiming unawareness of God's standards does not remove accountability for actions or leadership failures. Judgment protects the integrity of the Church. By confronting sin internally, God ensures that His Word is not misrepresented and His name is not profaned through hypocrisy or neglect. The exposure of sin serves as a warning. God uses the consequences of unrighteousness within His house to instruct, redirect, and awaken both leaders and congregants.

Judgment begins with repentance. The church is called to humility, confession, and restoration, allowing God's corrective hand to guide them back to righteousness. God's judgment exposes both leaders and members. No one within His church is exempt from scrutiny; all are accountable for how they live, teach, and represent His Word. Historical examples illustrate this principle. Eli's sons, Ananias and Sapphira, and Judas serve as warnings of how God's judgment touches leaders who fail to uphold integrity and righteousness.

Trials are often tools of refinement. Difficulties, exposures, and challenges are not always punishment; they can serve to correct and purify those in God's house. Concealed sin is dangerous. Secret transgressions in leadership or membership erode spiritual authority and weaken the church's witness externally. Leonard Ravenhill emphasizes that revival is preceded by God shaking His Church, exposing hidden sin, and calling leaders to accountability. The shaking is a purification process meant to prepare the Church for His glory.

Judgment prompts self-examination. God's corrective hand encourages believers to assess motives, actions, and attitudes to ensure alignment with His Word. Leaders are under intensified scrutiny. Just as Eli's sons faced consequences for their corruption, modern church leaders are accountable for protecting holiness and guiding rightly. Judgment is not limited to leaders; congregants are equally accountable. Complicity, indifference, and silent approval of sin all contribute to God's displeasure and corrective action.

Integrity cannot be faked. Public appearances, eloquence, or influence cannot conceal disobedience; God sees the heart and intentions. Exposure leads to awakening. When sin is brought to light, individuals are prompted to repent, adjust, and recommit to God's standards. Lewis reminds us that God's holiness cannot tolerate compromise. Even subtle disobedience, when multiplied across the Church, produces spiritual decay that invites divine correction.

Judgment encourages transparency. God desires openness and honesty, discouraging hidden agendas, manipulation, or spiritual hypocrisy. The church must prioritize holiness. Spiritual growth and community strength depend on obedience, integrity, and sincere devotion to God. Tozer warns that a Church comfortable with mediocrity or false security will face exposure. God uses trials, scrutiny, and shaking to awaken His people to repentance and restoration. Consequences are immediate and eternal. Neglect or disobedience may carry earthly ramifications, but spiritual misalignment has eternal significance.

God uses examples from Scripture to teach. Historical accounts such as Ananias and Sapphira illustrate the severity of sin and the importance of accountability within God's house. Disobedience leads to loss of influence. Scripture calls for self-examination. Leaders and members alike must evaluate their hearts, motives, and actions, ensuring that they align with God's Word and not human approval or comfort. Leaders who compromise moral or spiritual principles diminish their credibility and the church's impact.

Judgment reveals true faith. Those who remain steadfast under scrutiny demonstrate genuine devotion and reliance on God. Exposure refines leadership. Difficult revelations identify weaknesses and provide opportunities for leaders to repent, learn, and mature spiritually. Concealed wrongs endanger the flock.
→ Hidden sin in leadership sets a precedent for members, potentially normalizing disobedience and moral compromise. Judgment in the house of God is a manifestation of divine love and a call to holiness. Scripture, Lewis, Tozer, and Ravenhill collectively affirm that God's shaking exposes hidden evil, purifies His Church, and prepares it for revival and spiritual strength.

God's hand of discipline is a demonstration of love. His corrective measures are intended to protect, guide, and restore, not merely punish. Accountability prevents systemic corruption. When leaders are held responsible, the entire church maintains moral and spiritual integrity. Public exposure can strengthen the community. Transparent correction fosters trust, encourages ethical conduct, and reinforces commitment to God's Word. Judgment fosters humility. Realizing God's omniscience encourages leaders and members to remain humble and dependent on His guidance.

Leaders must model repentance. Public acknowledgment of error reinforces spiritual authenticity and encourages congregants to pursue holiness. Judgment protects the reputation of God's name. The church, as God's representative, must reflect His holiness and truth to the world. Sin tolerated in the house invites further judgment. Ignoring wrongdoing allows corruption to multiply, creating consequences beyond the initial offense. Exposure encourages vigilance.

Believers learn to remain alert, discerning, and aligned with Scripture in all actions and decisions.

God's judgment is purposeful. It aims to restore righteousness, correct errors, and cultivate spiritual maturity. Leaders must examine their hearts continually. Daily reflection and accountability guard against pride, hypocrisy, and compromise. God calls the church to purity. Spiritual health depends on unwavering commitment to His Word and moral standards. The consequences of sin are sobering. Historical examples remind the church that disobedience has both immediate and eternal repercussions.

Judgment instills fear of God, not man. Reverence for God's authority fosters obedience, humility, and accountability. Exposure strengthens leadership succession. Corrective measures create opportunities to mentor, train, and develop spiritually mature leaders. God's Word is the ultimate standard of judgment. Personal opinion, tradition, or popularity cannot override His commands or principles. Accountability must be proactive. Waiting until sin becomes public can be destructive; early correction preserves integrity and credibility.

Judgment reveals motives. God distinguishes between those acting for self-interest and those truly serving His purposes. Leaders must cultivate transparency in all dealings. Open communication, honest decision-making, and integrity prevent the concealment of sin. Exposure should lead to restoration. God desires repentance, correction, and spiritual renewal, not merely punishment. Judgment fosters spiritual growth. Facing correction and alignment with God's standards develops character, maturity, and resilience.

Leaders must embrace correction gracefully. Resistance to accountability invites further consequences and diminishes divine favor. God honors those who learn from exposure. Repentance and renewed commitment demonstrate faithfulness and obedience. The congregation benefits from righteous leadership. Transparent, accountable, and obedient leaders cultivate trust, faith, and spiritual vitality among members.

Judgment ensures the church reflects God's holiness. Maintaining purity in His house preserves the church as a beacon of truth in a world of compromise. The call is clear: holiness begins within. God's shaking and exposure in His house are not arbitrary; they are essential for the church to fulfill its divine purpose faithfully.

It is imperative to confront and overcome spiritual oppression, corruption, and satanic influence within the Church. Darkness actively establishes strongholds in the hearts, minds, and institutions of the Church, and we must take action. By exposing hidden evils, we can identify and dismantle these spiritual strongholds and their harmful effects. These strongholds manifest as deception, pride, manipulation, fear, and rebellion, and it is our duty to confront them head- *on.* God calls His people to dismantle every barrier to His truth and holiness. Leaders must recognize that strongholds thrive where sin, compromise, and ignorance exist. Exposure provides clarity on the tactics of the enemy and the areas needing intervention.

Breaking strongholds requires prayer, fasting, and the authority of God's Word. Leaders must equip the Church to confront spiritual oppression with faith and discernment. Exposure ensures that hidden sin, corruption, or compromise is not ignored. Spiritual warfare is necessary to reclaim territory for God and restore His glory. Leaders must model courage, integrity, and faith when confronting spiritual strongholds.

Exposure clarifies the sources of deception, control, and oppression within the Church. Believers must recognize the spiritual battles that underlie visible challenges. Leaders must guide the Church in both corporate and personal spiritual warfare. Exposure strengthens the Church's resolve to stand firm against satanic influence. Breaking strongholds requires unity, prayer, and obedience to God's commands.

Leaders must identify root causes, not just symptoms, when addressing darkness. Exposure reveals patterns of deception, manipulation, and unrepentant sin. Believers must exercise authority in Christ, declaring freedom over lives, ministries, and nations. Leaders must teach spiritual discernment, accountability, and righteous boldness. Exposure helps the Church avoid repeating cycles of deception and compromise. Breaking strongholds restores freedom, holiness, and spiritual authority.

Leaders must cultivate environments that foster spiritual maturity, vigilance, and integrity. Exposure highlights the areas where repentance and renewal are essential. Believers must confront fear, doubt, and spiritual oppression with faith and prayer. Leaders must ensure that deliverance is grounded in Scripture, not emotion or gimmicks. Exposure protects the Church from allowing darkness to go unchallenged. Breaking strongholds requires sustained commitment, perseverance, and spiritual discipline. Leaders must empower members to actively participate in spiritual warfare.

Exposure strengthens awareness of subtle manipulation, deception, and worldly influence. Believers are equipped to resist temptation, deception, and oppression. Leaders must provide guidance, mentoring, and support for spiritual battle. Exposure clarifies where leadership, teaching, or accountability has failed. Breaking strongholds restores faith, courage, and spiritual vitality. Leaders must demonstrate authority in Christ while maintaining humility and love.

Exposure teaches that ignorance or passivity enables the enemy to entrench strongholds. Believers must cultivate prayer, fasting, worship, and obedience to maintain freedom. Leaders must model consistency, integrity, and reliance on God's Spirit. Exposure motivates the Church to confront darkness boldly, not fearfully. Breaking strongholds strengthens unity, faith, and spiritual resilience. Leaders must encourage the Church to live in continual submission to God's authority.

Exposure ensures that evil is confronted, purified, and removed with wisdom. Believers gain spiritual confidence, boldness, and authority through persistent confrontation. Leaders must teach the principles of spiritual warfare, discernment, and victory in Christ. Ultimately, breaking the strongholds of darkness restores the Church to its divine calling, empowering it to serve, proclaim, and impact the world with God's truth and glory.

Eli's Sons, Ananias & Sapphira, Judas – God's Correction of Corrupt Leadership

God shakes leaders to reveal hidden corruption. Those entrusted with spiritual authority may develop pride, greed, or moral compromise, which God exposes through divine correction. Eli's sons serve as a warning. Their misuse of priestly duties, indulgence in sin, and disregard for God's instructions demonstrate the consequences of neglecting sacred responsibility. God's Word reveals that leaders are not exempt from scrutiny. *"For the time has come for judgment to begin at the house of God; and if it begins with us, what will be the outcome for those who do not obey the gospel of God?"* (1 Peter 4:17). Leaders must recognize the weight of responsibility and accountability before God.

Leadership accountability begins with personal integrity. God expects those in authority to model righteousness, discipline, and devotion, not exploit their position for self-gain. Ananias and Sapphira illustrate deceit in leadership. Their attempt to manipulate appearances for personal recognition resulted in immediate divine judgment, highlighting the seriousness of hypocrisy. C. S. Lewis, in *Mere Christianity*, highlights that leadership carries spiritual consequences. Those entrusted with guiding others are held to higher standards, and their failures have repercussions that ripple through the congregation.

Judas represents betrayal from within. Even those closest to Jesus were not immune to corruption; secret motives and covetousness led to catastrophic consequences. The shaking of leaders preserves the flock. By correcting or removing corrupt leadership, God protects the congregation from spiritual harm and moral compromise. The Bible provides sobering examples. Eli's sons abused their position and faced God's judgment (1 Samuel 2:12–17). Ananias and Sapphira attempted to deceive the Church and were struck dead (Acts 5:1-11). Judas betrayed Christ, succumbing to greed and deceit (Matthew 26:14-16).

God's correction is often public to instruct others. Exposures of sin in leadership serve as warnings, teaching accountability, vigilance, and obedience throughout the church. Leaders are entrusted with God's reputation. Their actions reflect God's holiness, and failure to uphold standards diminishes the church's witness and integrity. A. W. Tozer, in *The Pursuit of God*, reminds us that spiritual authority without humility and obedience leads to corruption and disgrace. Leaders must serve with integrity, placing God's will above personal ambition or gain.

Divine shaking encourages humility. Recognizing God's sovereignty and corrective power prevents arrogance, fosters repentance, and nurtures servant-hearted leadership. The fear of God is a deterrent against corruption. Awareness that God observes motives, decisions, and actions motivates leaders to remain faithful, upright, and accountable. The shaking of leaders often exposes hidden sin, character flaws, or spiritual weaknesses that would otherwise remain concealed. Leonard Ravenhill emphasizes that God uses trials, correction, and sometimes public exposure to purify leadership and restore integrity.

Leaders are accountable for spiritual guidance. God entrusts authority to shepherd His people, and failure to lead rightly invites His corrective action. The pattern of compromise begins subtly. Small acts of greed, favoritism, or indulgence, when unchecked, accumulate and corrupt leadership from within. God's shaking exposes hidden motives. Intentions that are selfish, manipulative, or deceitful cannot remain concealed before His omniscient gaze.

Leadership is not merely about position or visibility; it is stewardship of God's people. Failures at the top can mislead congregants, propagate false teaching, and hinder revival. Lewis notes that leaders must remain vigilant, disciplined, and grounded in God's Word. Eli's sons ignored the correction. Despite warnings, they continued in wrongdoing, demonstrating how refusal to repent magnifies judgment.

Ananias and Sapphira sought recognition over obedience. Their desire for status led them to deceive both Peter and the Holy Spirit, a deadly combination in God's eyes. Judas allowed personal ambition to override loyalty. Tozer underscores the necessity of self-examination. Leaders must confront their own pride, selfishness, and hidden compromises before God exposes them externally. Spiritual health begins with inward reflection and repentance. Covetousness, greed, and disloyalty created a breach between him and Christ, culminating in betrayal.

God shakes leadership to protect His people. Exposing corrupt leaders prevents further spiritual damage and safeguards the integrity of the church community. Shaking fosters repentance and renewal. Ravenhill illustrates that historical revivals were often preceded by God shaking leadership. He contends that such shaking is merciful, providing leaders with the opportunity to realign with God before consequences escalate. Confrontation with sin provides an opportunity to realign with God's standards, restoring leaders to righteousness if they respond rightly.

Spiritual vigilance is necessary for every leader. Awareness of temptation, pride, and subtle compromise helps maintain obedience and accountability. God's corrective measures are a form of divine love. The congregation also plays a role. Churches should cultivate accountability structures, encourage transparency, and support leaders who demonstrate humility and obedience. Ignoring warning signs can exacerbate failures and allow sin to fester. Shaking may be painful, but it protects leaders and the congregation from destruction, revealing His care and sovereignty.

Leaders must prioritize God's commands over personal gain. Authority is a stewardship, not a tool for self-promotion or advantage. The consequences of hidden sin are severe. The shaking of leaders is both a warning and an opportunity. Scripture, Lewis, Tozer, and Ravenhill collectively affirm that God exposes and purifies leadership to safeguard the Church, ensure faithful guidance, and prepare His people for revival and spiritual maturity. When leadership fails in integrity, the effects ripple through the congregation, breeding confusion, deception, and mistrust. Public exposure teaches humility to others. Congregants witness the seriousness of sin and the necessity of righteous living, reinforcing accountability in the entire church.

Leaders must embrace transparency. Open acknowledgment of weaknesses and accountability to peers or spiritual mentors prevents hidden corruption. Shaking refines character. God allows trials to strip away pride, expose weaknesses, and cultivate resilience and spiritual maturity. God honors repentance in leadership. Leaders who acknowledge wrongdoing, seek forgiveness, and make amends demonstrate faithfulness and earn His favor. Leadership carries spiritual risk.

Authority without accountability can amplify sin, correcting both necessary and urgent. The church's witness depends on faithful leaders. Integrity in leadership directly influences the congregation's trust, morale, and ability to minister effectively.

Shaking is a preventive measure. God often acts before corruption spreads widely, preventing extensive damage and spiritual collapse. Leadership requires constant self-examination. Daily reflection on motives, actions, and influence helps maintain obedience, humility, and accountability. God's eyes are always on leaders. Spiritual authority brings visibility before God, requiring diligence in integrity and discernment.

Shaking leaders serves as an instruction for others. Biblical examples demonstrate the consequences of sin in leadership, guiding future leaders toward obedience. Compromise in leadership erodes spiritual culture. Once corruption takes root, it becomes normalized, affecting the entire church's values and practices. Leaders must rely on God's guidance continually. Prayer, study of Scripture, and sensitivity to the Holy Spirit guard against pride and error.

The Holy Spirit convicts and corrects. God uses inner conviction to alert leaders to wrongdoing before consequences escalate. Leaders who resist correction invite judgment. Ignoring God's warnings magnifies the shaking and increases personal and communal consequences. Accountability structures protect leaders and congregations. Mentorship, oversight, and peer review help maintain ethical and spiritual standards.

Transparency fosters trust. Honest communication about challenges and failures encourages authenticity and spiritual growth in the church. Shaking demonstrates God's holiness. His corrective actions remind leaders that He is just, righteous, and intolerant of sin in His house. Leadership is both a privilege and a responsibility. Authority entrusted by God requires stewardship, vigilance, and unwavering commitment to His commands.

Failure in leadership has a communal impact. Sin at the top ripples downward, affecting members' faith, confidence, and spiritual health. God's shaking separates wheat from chaff. Testing, exposure, and correction reveal those who are faithful and those who are compromised. Shaking cultivates humility and reliance on God. Leaders learn to submit to divine authority, trusting His wisdom above personal ambition.

God's discipline protects His reputation. By correcting leaders, He ensures that His name is honored, and His church remains a light in the world. Leaders must remain teachable. Openness to instruction, correction, and guidance prevents long-term compromise and spiritual decline. God exposes hidden sins to preserve the flock. The well-being of the congregation is central to His corrective action, safeguarding spiritual health and integrity.

Shaking encourages leaders to prioritize holiness. Continuous alignment with God's standards ensures moral clarity and faithful leadership. Leaders must not fear accountability. Accepting correction reflects humility, strengthens credibility, and demonstrates spiritual maturity. God's correction produces lasting impact. Leaders who respond rightly influence their congregations positively, fostering obedience, faithfulness, and growth. The shaking of leaders reveals God's ultimate authority. His power to expose, correct, and restore ensures that His will prevails and that His church remains true to His Word.

Chapter 14: Hidden Sin Brought to Light

Ephesians 5:11–14 – Exposing Darkness and Walking in the Light

God calls His church to expose hidden sin. Darkness cannot be allowed to fester in His house; uncovering secret transgressions is necessary for spiritual health. Sin that hides in plain sight threatens the community. Unchecked wrongdoing corrodes trust, spiritual authority, and the moral fabric of the church. Light is the standard for righteousness. God commands His people to live transparently, rejecting secretive, deceptive, or hypocritical behavior. Ephesians 5:11-14 calls believers to expose the unfruitful works of darkness. Hidden sin in the Church often lurks behind a mask of righteousness, but God's truth will inevitably bring it to light.

Hidden sin impacts the spiritual atmosphere. Concealed wrongdoing contaminates worship, teaching, and fellowship, subtly affecting all who participate. Confrontation is an act of love. Addressing sin, though uncomfortable, protects individuals and the congregation from further harm. Leaders must model exposure of sin. C. S. Lewis, in *Mere Christianity*, emphasizes that truth cannot remain hidden indefinitely. Deception, hypocrisy, and sin will eventually surface, requiring correction and accountability.

By confessing mistakes and maintaining transparency, they encourage members to live in truth and integrity. Silence allows darkness to multiply. Ignoring sin gives it strength, spreading corruption and diminishing accountability across the church. A. W. Tozer, in *The Pursuit of God*, warns that the Church is often lulled into complacency, failing to confront sin until it becomes destructive. The light of God exposes what was hidden, urging repentance.

God uses exposure to restore. Bringing hidden sins to light opens the door for repentance, healing, and renewed spiritual vitality. Members are called to walk in the light. Obedience, accountability, and openness reflect God's standard and nurture a culture of holiness. Leonard Ravenhill stresses that revival cannot occur where hidden sin is tolerated. God's shaking and exposure bring opportunity for purification, spiritual awakening, and renewed holiness within His people. Exposure strengthens spiritual resilience. Facing and correcting hidden sins fortifies the church, producing maturity, wisdom, and steadfastness in faith. Darkness thrives where accountability is absent.

When the church ignores wrongdoing, it allows sin to multiply, creating spiritual decay and moral compromise. Hidden sin manifests in multiple ways: gossip, pride, financial deceit, sexual immorality, and compromise with the world. Leaders and congregants alike are accountable to God for allowing such sin to continue unchecked. God commands exposure for the sake of truth. Uncovering sin is not meant to shame but to realign hearts with His righteousness and restore integrity. Members must be vigilant observers. Lewis explains that spiritual blindness often accompanies hidden sin. Believers may justify or rationalize wrongdoing, failing to see the spiritual danger or the offense caused to God's holiness.

Awareness of spiritual health within the congregation helps identify subtle sins and intervene with love and guidance. Sin affects more than the individual. Hidden wrongdoing in one person can influence decisions, culture, and the spiritual direction of the entire church. Leaders bear the weight of correction. Those in positions of authority must confront hidden sin, guiding others toward confession, repentance, and accountability. Tozer emphasizes that the fear of man can silence the Church. Leaders often avoid addressing sin for fear of conflict, disapproval, or reputational damage, inadvertently fostering an environment where sin flourishes.

God's light exposes even the darkest corners. Nothing can remain hidden from His sight; secrets will eventually be revealed for correction and justice. Fear of exposure should not prevent obedience. While confrontation may be uncomfortable, it is necessary for maintaining holiness and protecting the community. Scripture calls the Church to accountability, transparency, and discipline. When sin is hidden, it erodes trust, damages testimony, and hinders the work of God. Restoration follows exposure. Confession, repentance, and accountability lead to healing, renewal, and a stronger spiritual foundation. Walking in the light requires humility. Admitting wrongs, seeking forgiveness, and accepting correction demonstrate maturity and dependence on God.

Hidden sin undermines spiritual authority. Leaders who conceal wrongdoing lose credibility, erode trust, and compromise the influence of the church. Exposure is a preventative measure. Addressing sin early prevents further escalation and helps maintain moral and spiritual health within the congregation. God's corrective action is loving. Though it may be painful, exposure protects the church and provides an opportunity for alignment with His Word. Ravenhill observes that historical revivals were preceded by moments when God exposed the sin of His people. This exposure acted as a catalyst for confession, repentance, and spiritual renewal.

Members learn accountability through observation. Seeing sin addressed transparently teaches the congregation to value honesty, responsibility, and repentance. Hidden sin creates spiritual confusion. When wrong behavior is tolerated, the church risks normalizing compromise and weakening its witness. God calls for a culture of transparency. Openness about struggles and failures fosters spiritual growth, trust, and integrity across leadership and membership. Exposure strengthens communal bonds. When sin is confronted and resolved, the church experiences restoration, unity, and renewed purpose. Leaders must lead by example. Their willingness to confess mistakes and walk in the light inspires members to do the same.

Concealed sins disrupt spiritual vitality. Unaddressed wrongdoing hinders worship, ministry effectiveness, and discipleship within the church. God uses exposure for spiritual refinement. Corrective measures illuminate character flaws, enabling growth, maturity, and obedience. Accountability is a spiritual safeguard. Systems for oversight, mentorship, and peer review help prevent sin from spreading unnoticed. The fear of God motivates transparency. Hidden sin will not remain concealed. Scripture, Lewis, Tozer, and Ravenhill collectively remind the Church that God's light brings exposure, accountability, and the opportunity for purification and revival. Reverence for His omniscience encourages leaders and members to live openly, honestly, and righteously.

Exposure fosters humility and teachability. Confronting sin nurtures a heart willing to learn, repent, and grow spiritually. Hidden sin can undermine outreach. A compromised church loses credibility, reducing its effectiveness in ministering to the community. God's Word reveals wrongdoing. Scripture offers the moral compass and standards for recognizing, confronting, and addressing sin. Exposure promotes vigilance in leadership. Awareness and oversight help leaders prevent small compromises from turning into systemic corruption.

Correcting sin requires courage. Addressing wrongdoing, especially among peers or superiors, demands boldness rooted in love and righteousness. Accountability nurtures spiritual growth. Regular correction strengthens character, obedience, and reliance on God's guidance. Exposure affirms God's justice. By bringing hidden sin to light, He ensures fairness, equity, and the preservation of truth within the church. Leaders must confront sin with wisdom. Approach, timing, and method matter, as correction should restore rather than alienate.

Public consequences may follow concealed sin. God sometimes allows exposure to teach lessons and prevent widespread harm. Walking in the light produces clarity. Transparency dispels confusion, strengthens faith, and fosters a culture of trust. God's exposure protects His reputation. The church reflects His holiness; addressing hidden sin safeguards His name and authority. Sin tolerated in leadership sets dangerous precedents. Members learn by example; failure to confront wrong behavior normalizes compromise.

Exposure can lead to repentance and renewal. Once sin is addressed, the path is open for confession, transformation, and spiritual strengthening. Accountability structures are essential. Mentorship, peer support, and oversight help leaders maintain transparency and uphold God's standards. Confrontation must be rooted in love. Correcting sin without compassion can harm relationships; love ensures restoration is the goal. Exposure cultivates integrity. Living openly in alignment with God's Word fosters a culture of honesty, responsibility, and trustworthiness.

The congregation benefits from transparency. Witnessing proper correction and repentance encourages members to pursue holiness themselves. God's light brings hope. Even in exposing wrongdoing, He offers restoration, renewal, and the opportunity to walk in obedience. Hidden sin brought to light leads to spiritual revival. By addressing concealed wrongdoing, the church becomes stronger, purer, and more effective in fulfilling God's mission.

Revelation 3:15–16 – God's Warning Against Spiritual Apathy

God's Word warns against lukewarmness. God desires wholehearted devotion. Spiritual complacency, neither hot nor cold, displeases Him and hinders the church's mission. A lukewarm church lacks passion for God. Worship, prayer, and obedience become mechanical, devoid of zeal, love, and wholehearted devotion. Revelation 3:15–16 exposes the danger of lukewarm faith. God warns the Church that complacency, half-hearted devotion, and indifference are offensive to Him, and He will not tolerate spiritual mediocrity.

Spiritual indifference leads to vulnerability. Without fervent faith, the church is susceptible to deception, compromise, and internal decay. Lukewarmness obscures God's power. Half-hearted commitment diminishes the effectiveness of ministry and reduces spiritual impact. Passion, obedience, and love for Him should define the life of the church and its members. C. S. Lewis, in *Mere Christianity*, explains that half-hearted obedience is a form of self-deception. Believers may claim faith, but without zeal and sincerity, their devotion lacks the transformative power of God.

Complacency is contagious. When leaders or influential members are lukewarm, it spreads throughout the congregation, weakening faith and commitment. Lukewarmness diminishes testimony. The world sees a church without zeal, causing unbelievers to doubt God's authenticity and power. Spiritual heat fuels transformation. God uses passionate worship, faithful service, and obedient living to impact lives and communities.

A lukewarm church invites divine rebuke. God's warning is clear: apathy will not be tolerated, and corrective action is inevitable. Repentance restores fervor. Turning from spiritual indifference to wholehearted commitment renews vitality, purpose, and alignment with God's will. A. W. Tozer, in *The Pursuit of God*, emphasizes that lukewarmness in the Church leads to spiritual stagnation. Worship becomes routine, prayer loses intensity, and the mission of God is neglected.

Lukewarmness is rooted in self-satisfaction. Believers may feel comfortable with minimal obedience, prioritizing convenience over spiritual growth. Complacency masks spiritual danger. A church that appears active externally may be cold in faith internally, deceiving both members and leaders. Passionless worship displeases God. Rituals without devotion or love do not honor Him; He seeks hearts fully surrendered. Spiritual mediocrity breeds compromise. Indifference opens doors to false teaching, moral laxity, and corrupted values. Leaders must model fervent devotion. Their zeal, prayer life, and obedience set the tone for the congregation's spiritual health.

Lukewarmness diminishes influence. A church without zeal loses credibility in its community, failing to inspire faith or enact change. God calls for renewed passion. He desires revival within hearts and congregations, igniting love, obedience, and commitment. A lukewarm church ignores the needs of others. When focus is inward or self-serving, it neglects ministry, outreach, and marginalization.

God disciplines spiritual apathy. His corrective measures may include reduced influence, exposure of sin, or withdrawal of blessings. Repentance rekindles spiritual fire. Turning from indifference and embracing wholehearted devotion restores vitality and favor. Members must examine their hearts. Self-reflection uncovers areas of half-hearted faith and prompts renewed commitment. Spiritual zeal strengthens community. Passionate believers inspire collective growth, accountability, and effectiveness in ministry.

Lukewarmness can blind leaders. Comfort and routine dull discernment, allowing sin or compromise to go unnoticed. God desires wholehearted obedience. Commitment, sacrifice, and consistent faithfulness please Him and empower His work. A church must prioritize intimacy with God. Personal and corporate devotion fuels zeal, mission, and spiritual authority.

Lukewarm hearts hinder revival. Without fervor, the movement of the Holy Spirit is limited, and opportunities for transformation are missed. God exposes spiritual apathy through challenges.

Trials, confrontations, or prophetic warnings often reveal lukewarm attitudes that require correction. Leadership accountability combats mediocrity. Oversight, mentorship, and guidance ensure that leaders maintain zeal and integrity. Zeal inspires obedience in others. Passionate faith encourages members to pursue God diligently, creating a ripple effect of spiritual growth.

Lukewarmness undermines mission. Ministries stagnate when passion wanes, preventing outreach, discipleship, and effective service. God rewards wholehearted commitment. Fervent obedience attracts His favor, blessings, and empowerment for ministry. Spiritual laziness leads to vulnerability. A complacent church is easily influenced by false teachings, world values, or internal corruption. Leonard Ravenhill warns that revival is impossible where the Church tolerates indifference. Spiritual lethargy breeds compromise, moral weakness, and susceptibility to deception

Leaders must fan the flame of faith. Regular preaching, prayer, and encouragement keep the congregation spiritually alive and motivated. Lukewarmness hinders personal growth.

Individuals who settle for mediocrity fail to develop in character, understanding, and Christlike maturity. God's Word calls for full devotion. Scripture consistently demands obedience, diligence, and wholehearted love for Him. Lukewarmness often manifests in complacency toward sin, neglect of discipleship, and prioritizing comfort over obedience. God desires wholehearted devotion, not superficial participation.

Zeal combats spiritual stagnation. Passion drives engagement, service, and deepens intimacy with God. Lukewarmness fosters complacency in giving. Generosity, service, and sacrificial living decline when faith becomes indifferent. God honors renewed passion. Lewis points out that self-satisfaction blinds believers to their spiritual condition. The Church may appear vibrant externally but be spiritually dead internally. Repentance and wholehearted commitment establish divine favor and empower ministry impact.

Spiritual passion is contagious. Driven leaders and members ignite enthusiasm, inspiring others to pursue God earnestly. Lukewarmness weakens spiritual authority. Tozer stresses that God's people must pursue a passion for holiness and revival. Lukewarm attitudes hinder the movement of the Holy Spirit and the Church's ability to impact the world.

Without zeal, the church cannot effectively lead, disciple, or influence the community. God's rebuke serves as a call to revival. Warnings against lukewarmness are chances to repent, rekindle faith, and restore purpose. Passionate worship attracts the Holy Spirit. Wholehearted devotion invites God's presence, power, and transformation into the church. Leaders must resist comfort- driven ministry.

Ravenhill illustrates that historical awakenings occurred when the Church confronted its lukewarmness, confessed spiritual apathy, and recommitted to God's standards.

Routine, ease, and self-interest threaten zeal and weaken mission effectiveness. Lukewarm hearts lead to spiritual confusion. Mixed motives, apathy, and indifference cause instability in doctrine, teaching, and fellowship. God calls for a clear, decisive stance. Scripture calls for zeal, love, and obedience. A lukewarm Church is a Church in danger of judgment, yet God's corrective action is an invitation to return to fervent faith.

Faith must be fully surrendered, active, and uncompromising to honor Him and advance His kingdom. Spiritual apathy hinders discipleship. Indifference in leaders or members prevents the cultivation of mature, obedient followers of Christ. Repentance restores impact. The lukewarm Church will not escape God's scrutiny. Revelation 3:15-16, supported by Lewis, Tozer, and Ravenhill, affirms that wholehearted devotion, zeal for God, and obedience are essential to remain in His favor and participate in His redemptive work. Turning from indifference reinvigorates personal and corporate influence, ministry, and witness.

Zeal protects the church from compromise. Passionate faith resists cultural pressures, false teaching, and moral drift. Wholehearted devotion strengthens legacy. A fervent church leaves a lasting spiritual imprint, impacting generations and communities. God's warning is clear: choose heat over lukewarmness. Commitment, zeal, and obedience ensure the church thrives, honors God, and fulfills its divine calling.

"The Deception of White Christian Nationalism" illustrates how distorted faith can mislead and divide the Church, highlighting the trials believers encounter today. This chapter encourages readers to develop discernment, courage, and unwavering faith, trusting God to lead His Church through all challenges.

In every generation, a deception arises that cloaks itself in the language of faith but serves the purposes of power. In our time, one of the most dangerous of these deceptions is **White Christian Nationalism**. This movement confuses loyalty to Christ with loyalty to a nation, and spiritual identity with racial superiority. It presents itself as a revival of Christian values, but beneath its surface lies the old spirit of pride, domination, and exclusion that Christ came to destroy. This false gospel seeks to merge the cross with the flag, and the Kingdom of God with the kingdoms of men.

White Christian Nationalism can be defined as the belief that a nation—particularly America— was founded as a "Christian nation" meant to be ruled by a specific form of Christianity dominated by white culture and leadership. It preaches that only when "Christian laws" and "Christian leaders" govern the state can the nation be saved. But this ideology does not reflect the Gospel of Jesus Christ; instead, it reimagines Christ as a political mascot for earthly agendas. It corrupts the mission of the Church, turning worship into warfare and evangelism into exclusion.

This movement is not new. Its roots stretch back through centuries of colonial conquest, slavery, segregation, and political dominance under the banner of Christendom. From the European crusades to the American slave plantations, religion has too often been used as a tool to justify power. The Bible was misquoted to bless the slave ships, to defend apartheid, and to silence voices calling for freedom. White Christian Nationalism is the modern heir of these same distortions—a spiritual counterfeit born from pride, not repentance.

Many of its followers believe they are defending Christianity, but in truth they are defending cultural dominance. They equate God's blessing with political control and mistake privilege for divine favor. Yet Jesus said, *"My kingdom is not of this world"* (John 18:36). He refused every temptation to seize earthly power, for His

134

mission was not to build a nation, but to redeem humanity. Any movement that seeks to enthrone one race or nation as the guardian of God's truth has already departed from the Gospel of grace.

At its heart, White Christian Nationalism is not about Christ—it is about control. It uses religious symbols to mask political ambition. It baptizes nationalism with the language of Scripture, claiming divine endorsement for human agendas. But God does not share His glory with earthly empires. The prophets of old warned against nations that exalted themselves above others, saying, *"The Lord is a great King over all the earth"* (Psalm 47:2). To confuse God's eternal Kingdom with any temporary government is to commit spiritual idolatry.

Historically, this ideology found fertile ground in America's story. The early colonists declared the land a "New Israel," sent by God to conquer a wilderness and establish a city on a hill. That vision was noble in part, but quickly tainted by greed, slavery, and genocide. They claimed divine favor while enslaving Africans and erasing Indigenous peoples. Thus, the foundation of "Christian America" was mixed with injustice from the beginning. White Christian Nationalism today simply rebrands that old illusion, pretending that God endorses the political power of one race above all others.

The same spirit that once justified slavery now justifies exclusion and fear. The same twisted theology that segregated churches in the 20th century now fuels the rejection of immigrants, Muslims, and people of color in the 21st century. When people claim they are "taking back" their country for God, what they often mean is taking it back for themselves—restoring their privilege, not Christ's presence. But the Church of Jesus Christ does not belong to one culture, language, or color. It is a Kingdom of every tribe, nation, and tongue.

Scripture is clear: God does not favor one people group over another. Acts 10:34 declares, *"God shows no partiality, but in every nation anyone who fears Him and does what is right is acceptable to Him."* When a movement teaches that one nation is God's favorite, or one race is His chosen instrument for leadership, it directly contradicts the Gospel. White Christian Nationalism is therefore not a revival—it is rebellion against the cross that made all humanity one.

This deception thrives on fear—the fear of losing power, status, or identity. Many white Christians have been told that demographic change and diversity threaten their way of life. Instead of seeing God's hand in the expansion of His Kingdom among every people, they see enemies. The devil capitalizes on this fear to turn brothers into rivals and neighbors into threats. But fear and faith cannot coexist. Jesus called His followers to love, not to dominate. He said, *"Love your enemies and pray for those who persecute you"* (Matthew 5:44).

White Christian Nationalism disguises itself as patriotism, but patriotism becomes idolatry when it replaces devotion to God. The prophets of Israel repeatedly warned against trusting in national identity for salvation. Jeremiah cried, *"Do not trust in these deceptive words: 'This is the temple of the Lord'"* (Jeremiah 7:4), reminding Israel that no nation, not even one chosen by God, is immune to judgment. Likewise, no modern nation can claim divine immunity while practicing injustice.

The deception is subtle. It often begins with slogans like "God and country," or "America first," which sound harmless but hide deeper allegiances. It appeals to Christians who feel disoriented by cultural change, offering a sense of belonging and moral certainty. Yet beneath the surface, it preaches a distorted gospel where salvation depends on preserving power, not pursuing holiness. It replaces the Great Commission with a call for cultural conquest, urging believers to "take back" the seven mountains of influence instead of taking up the cross.

This ideology thrives in churches that mistake political enthusiasm for spiritual revival. When congregations cheer for political candidates more than they weep for the lost, something sacred has been exchanged. The altar becomes a stage for nationalism, and the sanctuary a rally for worldly power. Jesus warned of such confusion when He said, *"You cannot serve God and money"* (Matthew 6:24). Likewise, you cannot serve God and empire. The Church must choose whom it will worship—Christ the King, or Caesar in disguise.

At its worst, White Christian Nationalism becomes a form of heresy—a false gospel that claims God needs earthly government to accomplish His will. But the true Church knows that the Kingdom of God grows not by legislation but by transformation of hearts. It does not depend on ballots but on the blood of Jesus. When the Church forgets this, it becomes an agent of oppression rather than liberation. As Paul wrote, *"The weapons of our warfare are not carnal, but mighty through God to the pulling down of strongholds"* (2 Corinthians 10:4).

This false movement not only distorts theology but endangers democracy. When any group claims divine authority to rule, it undermines the principle of equality before God and law. It seeks to silence dissent and punish difference. In the name of defending Christianity, it destroys the very freedoms that allow faith to flourish. Yet true Christianity does not fear freedom—it thrives in it, because the truth of Christ stands on its own without coercion.

The rise of White Christian Nationalism is therefore both a political and spiritual crisis. It exposes how far the Church has drifted from the humility of Christ. God is not raising this movement—He is exposing it. Just as He revealed the idols of Baal in Elijah's day, He is uncovering the idols of nationalism in ours. The Church must decide whether to defend false power or to return to true repentance. For Scripture declares, *"Judgment begins with the house of God"* (1 Peter 4:17).

A Counterfeit Gospel Arises

In every generation, the enemy of truth disguises himself as an angel of light. Today, one of his most cunning disguises is the rise of *White Christian Nationalism*—a movement that wraps itself in the language of faith while promoting a gospel of exclusion, racial pride, and political domination. Many believers are deceived because it speaks the familiar language of Christianity but lacks the heart of Christ. The Church must discern this spirit, for it is not of God; it is a distortion that threatens both democracy and the mission of the Body of Christ in the world.

The Subtle Corruption of Faith

White Christian Nationalism presents itself as patriotism guided by faith, but beneath the surface lies an idol of racial supremacy and power. It substitutes the cross of Christ with the flag of a single nation and elevates cultural identity above spiritual rebirth. Instead of exalting Christ's kingdom, it exalts human institutions, seeking to merge the will of God with the ambitions of men. This is precisely the kind of corruption Jesus condemned when He said, "My Kingdom is not of this world" (John 18:36).

A Distorted Identity

This movement teaches that to be a "true Christian" is to belong to a specific political or ethnic group, which contradicts the very foundation of the Gospel.

Scripture declares that in Christ there is neither Jew nor Greek, bond nor free, male nor female, for all are one in Him (Galatians 3:28). White Christian Nationalism divides where Christ unites. It creates an earthly hierarchy of power that has no place in the Kingdom of God.

The Historical Roots

The roots of this deception reach deep into the soil of America's history—into eras of slavery, segregation, and colonial expansion. Many churches during those times used Scripture to justify racial oppression and to sanctify systems of inequality. These same justifications have been repackaged under modern slogans of "heritage" and "Christian identity," but the spirit behind them remains the same. It is the spirit of pride, domination, and idolatry.

The Weaponization of Religion

Throughout history, religion has often been used as a tool of control. In White Christian Nationalism, Scripture is selectively quoted to legitimize nationalism and racial hierarchy. God's Word, which was meant to liberate, is instead twisted to enslave minds and hearts. This is reminiscent of Satan's temptation of Jesus in the wilderness—using pieces of God's Word to promote his own agenda (Matthew 4:6). In the same way, Christian Nationalism manipulates the Word of God to promote earthly power.

The Illusion of Righteousness

One of the most dangerous aspects of this movement is its *appearance* of holiness. Its followers pray, worship, and quote Scripture, yet their hearts are far from the message of Christ. Jesus warned of this hypocrisy when He said, "This people honors Me with their lips, but their heart is far from Me" (Matthew 15:8). Outward religiosity does not guarantee inward righteousness. The measure of faith is not how loudly we proclaim God's name but how deeply we love His creation.

Nationalism vs. God's Kingdom

The ideology of nationalism teaches that one nation or people group is chosen above others, but God's plan has always been global and inclusive. The Great Commission commands us to make disciples of *all nations* (Matthew 28:19). Any movement that elevates one nation, race, or culture as more divine than another opposes God's redemptive plan. God's Kingdom transcends all borders; it is not confined by race, geography, or politics.

The Political Seduction

White Christian Nationalism thrives on fear and division. It convinces believers that their faith is under attack unless their political party controls the nation. This manipulates sincere Christians into viewing political battles as spiritual warfare, when in truth, the real war is not between left and right, but between truth and deception. The Apostle Paul reminds us that "we wrestle not against flesh and blood" (Ephesians 6:12), but against spiritual wickedness that can even wear a religious mask.

The False Promise of Power

At the heart of this deception lies a craving for power—the same temptation that caused Lucifer to fall. The devil said to Jesus, "All these kingdoms I will give you if you will bow down and worship me" (Matthew 4:9). The pursuit of earthly dominance masquerading as divine purpose is the ancient lie repeated. God's true power is not in control of governments but in the transformation of hearts.

The Role of Fear

Fear is the currency of Christian Nationalism. It preaches that outsiders, immigrants, and minorities threaten the "Christian way of life." But God has not given us a spirit of fear, but of power, love, and a sound mind (2 Timothy 1:7). When fear replaces faith, love is cast out. And where love is absent, Christ is absent. Any gospel built on fear of others cannot be the Gospel of Jesus Christ.

The Racial Stronghold

Racism is not merely a social issue; it is a spiritual stronghold. It thrives in hearts that have not fully submitted to Christ's lordship. White Christian Nationalism baptizes racism in religious language, calling it "heritage," "tradition," or "biblical order." But God makes no distinction among His children. From the first covenant with Abraham to the revelation of John, God's plan has always been to bless *all families of the earth.*

The Danger to Democracy

Democracy, when functioning rightly, reflects God's justice and equality—it gives every person dignity and voice. White Christian Nationalism seeks to dismantle that system by fusing faith with authoritarianism. It portrays opposition as ungodly and demands loyalty to political leaders rather than to Christ. This is dangerous because it replaces moral authority with human authority, paving the way for tyranny in both church and state.

A Counterfeit Revival

Some view the rise of Christian Nationalism as a spiritual awakening, but it is actually a counterfeit revival. True revival produces humility, repentance, and love; counterfeit revival breeds pride, anger, and exclusion. The book of James warns that the wisdom from above is "pure, peaceable, gentle," while the wisdom from below is "earthly, unspiritual, and demonic" (James 3:15-17). Any movement that exalts one race or nation over another cannot be born of the Holy Spirit.

False Prophets and Political Idols

Jesus warned that in the last days, false prophets would arise and deceive many (Matthew 24:11). Today, some preachers bless political agendas instead of preaching repentance and righteousness. They exchange the anointing of the Holy Spirit for influence and applause. This is not ministry, it is manipulation. God is calling His true servants to stand apart, to proclaim His Kingdom above every earthly allegiance.

The Deception of "Chosen Nation" Theology

White Christian Nationalism often claims that America holds a unique covenant with God, as if it were the new Israel. This belief twists biblical covenants and confuses patriotism with divine election. While we can thank God for national blessings, no modern nation replaces the Church as God's chosen people. The Church—composed of believers from every tribe and tongue—is the true nation of God's heart.

When Church Becomes Empire

History shows that when the Church aligns itself too closely with political power, it loses its prophetic voice. The early Church grew strongest under persecution, not privilege. Yet, White Christian Nationalism seeks to restore a form of Christendom where faith and government are inseparable. God never called His Church to rule nations through legislation but to transform them through love and truth.

The Misuse of Scripture

Passages about obedience to authority (like Romans 13) are often quoted to demand unquestioning loyalty to political leaders. But Scripture must be read in context—Paul wrote those words while living under pagan Rome, not a theocracy. His point was to encourage peace, not to justify oppression. When the Word of God is twisted to sanctify injustice, it becomes a weapon in the enemy's hand.

The Spirit of Division

Christian Nationalism thrives by creating "us versus them" mentalities. It divides believers into camps—liberal vs. conservative, black vs. white, citizen vs. immigrant. But Jesus prayed that His followers "may be one, even as We are one" (John 17:21). Division weakens the Church's witness. Satan knows that a divided Church cannot stand, so he sows seeds of nationalism to fracture the body of Christ.

The Seduction of Cultural Christianity

In many circles, being Christian is no longer defined by following Christ but by belonging to a cultural group. This shallow form of religion celebrates outward identity rather than inward transformation. White Christian Nationalism thrives in such soil—it promises belonging without repentance, pride without humility, and culture without cross-bearing. Yet Jesus calls His followers to deny themselves and carry their cross daily.

God's Rebuke of Hidden Evil

In Revelation 2 and 3, Christ rebuked churches that tolerated corruption within their midst. He warned that He would come quickly and remove their lampstand if they did not repent. The same warning applies to the modern Church. God sees the hidden evil masquerading as righteousness. He will not share His glory with any idol of race, nation, or political power. His judgment begins in His house.

Who Are They?

White Christian Nationalists are not merely political actors; they are a spiritual movement that merges faith with ideology. They claim to uphold biblical truth, but their focus is on preserving racial and cultural dominance. Many are well-meaning but deceived, believing that supporting certain leaders or policies is synonymous with obedience to God. Yet obedience to Christ requires humility, justice, and love, not the elevation of one group above others.

Their Ultimate Goal

The ultimate goal of White Christian Nationalism is to establish a theocratic society that reflects their interpretation of God's will, limited by race, nationality, and culture. They aim to consolidate power in political, social, and religious institutions, seeking control over law, education, and public life. What they fail to realize is that God's Kingdom cannot be enforced by legislation or intimidation; it grows through hearts transformed by the Spirit.

The Misuse of God's Name

This movement frequently invokes the name of Jesus to justify exclusion and oppression. They claim divine sanction for policies that marginalize minorities, immigrants, and dissenters. But Scripture warns that God cannot be mocked (Galatians 6:7), and any attempt to co-opt His name for personal agendas is ultimately rebellion. God blesses righteousness, not the preservation of power at the expense of His creation.

Weaponizing Fear and Threat

Fear is a primary tool of Christian Nationalists. They portray the world as under siege by forces opposed to God, often exaggerating threats to stir loyalty and obedience. By creating panic, they manipulate believers into supporting their agenda. But Jesus said, "Peace I leave with you; My peace I give to you" (John 14:27). Faith in God dispels fear, yet fear-based politics leads believers away from true spiritual freedom.

Disguised Racism

Although presented as religious conviction, White Christian Nationalism often carries an undercurrent of racial supremacy. It teaches that white Christians are the true inheritors of God's blessing, while others are outsiders or threats. The Bible contradicts this notion repeatedly: God created every nation and tribe, and all are equal in His sight (Acts 10:34-35). Any theology that elevates one race is contrary to the heart of God.

Political Ambition Masquerading as Faith

Many adherents place political loyalty above spiritual obedience. They champion certain leaders as God's chosen while overlooking moral failures and corruption. Yet Scripture reminds us that earthly kings are mortal, fallible, and accountable to God (Proverbs 21:1). Faithfulness to God must never be subordinated to allegiance to political figures, no matter how appealing their platform.

Misreading Prophecy

White Christian Nationalists often claim biblical prophecy to legitimize political power. They interpret visions, promises, and apocalyptic texts as direct mandates for national dominance. Yet God's prophecy always centers on repentance, redemption, and justice—not political conquest. Prophecy is fulfilled in hearts and communities, not through legislation or racial hierarchy. Misusing prophecy for personal gain is a distortion of God's Word.

The Global Threat

While this movement is most visible in the United States, its influence is spreading worldwide. Christian Nationalist ideologies appear in parts of Europe, Africa, and Latin America, often intertwined with populist politics and authoritarianism. Wherever it arises, it undermines the Church's witness, fuels division, and hinders the expansion of Christ's Kingdom. The global Church must recognize this threat and respond with discernment and love.

The Attack on Democracy

White Christian Nationalism seeks to dismantle democratic principles in favor of a system controlled by a select group of believers. This endangers freedom of religion, equality under the law, and civil liberties. Such movements blur the line between Church and state, risking the very liberties that allow the Gospel to flourish. True Christians must defend justice and equality as part of their obedience to God's moral law.

The Church's Complicity

Sadly, some churches unknowingly support this movement by prioritizing political agendas over the Gospel. When pastors and congregations focus on partisan loyalty rather than spiritual formation, they become instruments of deception. God's Word calls His Church to speak truth, protect the oppressed, and promote righteousness (Isaiah 1:17). Complicity in nationalism is complicity in injustice.

The Danger of False Security

White Christian Nationalism promises safety, blessing, and divine favor to those who conform. Yet these promises are false. True security is found only in Christ (Psalm 46:1). Believers who place their hope in politics, power, or privilege will face disappointment and divine rebuke.

God's blessing follows obedience to His Word, not alignment with human ideology.

Idolatry of Race and Nation

Idolatry is not limited to carved images; it can take the form of ideas, nations, or cultural identity. White Christian Nationalists worship a distorted image of God—a God who supposedly favors one race and one country. This is idolatry, plain and simple. God commands, "You shall have no other gods before Me" (Exodus 20:3). Elevating a nation or race above God is rebellion.

Misguided Enforcement of Morality

Christian Nationalists claim moral authority over laws and culture, but morality imposed by fear is not true righteousness. God desires hearts that love Him freely, not subjects who obey out of coercion. The Old Testament repeatedly demonstrates that external enforcement without inner transformation is empty ritual. True revival begins with repentance, not legislation.

The Consequences of Deception

The deception of White Christian Nationalism has real consequences for believers and society. It breeds division, hatred, and spiritual pride. It can lead churches to become echo chambers of fear and exclusion rather than communities of grace. The prophetic voice of the Church must confront this deception, warning that God will hold all accountable who distort His Word for human agendas (Isaiah 5:20–23).

Confusing Patriotism with Piety

Patriotism is honorable, but it becomes idolatrous when mistaken for piety. Love for one's country must never supersede love for God and neighbor. Jesus taught that the greatest commandments are love for God and love for others (Matthew 22:37-39). Any ideology that promotes exclusion, supremacy, or violence in the name of God contradicts His commandments.

The Danger of Seducing the Young

Christian Nationalist movements often target youth, teaching them that political allegiance equals spiritual maturity. This is a subtle form of indoctrination that distorts faith and harms future generations. God calls young believers to pursue wisdom, justice, and mercy (Micah 6:8), not to embrace ideologies that oppress others. The Church must protect its children from this spiritual seduction.

A Kingdom Perspective

Christ's Kingdom is not built on power, fear, or exclusion. It is built on love, humility, and sacrifice. White Christian Nationalism seeks to invert this order, promising earthly authority instead of eternal reward. Jesus said, "Whoever wants to become great among you must be your *servant*" (Matthew 20:26). True greatness in God's eyes is service, not dominance.

The Call to Discernment

Believers must learn to discern spirits. White Christian Nationalism is a spirit of pride, fear, and division masquerading as righteousness. Discernment requires studying God's Word, praying for wisdom, and seeking counsel from mature, Spirit-filled leaders. Without discernment, Christians can unknowingly participate in movements contrary to God's will.

The Weaponization of Worship

In some contexts, worship is co-opted to promote political ideology. Hymns, prayers, and sermons are turned into tools of nationalism rather than instruments of praise. God sees worship not as a means to influence political power but as a heartfelt response to His glory. Any distortion of worship for human agendas is offensive to God and undermines the Church's mission.

The Urgency of Awareness

Time is short, and the Church must wake from spiritual slumber. White Christian Nationalism is spreading rapidly, and ignorance of its tactics leaves believers vulnerable. The Church must educate, warn, and equip the faithful to recognize deception. God's people are called to be the salt and light in a world where faith is too often misused for control and fear.

God's Warning Through Scripture

The Bible is filled with warnings against idolatry, pride, and the misuse of power. God repeatedly condemned nations and leaders who exalted themselves while oppressing others (Isaiah 10:1–2). White Christian Nationalism embodies these very sins today. By cloaking prejudice and power in religious language, it ignores the commands of justice, mercy, and humility. God calls His Church to recognize this evil, resist it, and return to His ways.

Lessons from Israel

Israel repeatedly experienced the consequences of failing to follow God rather than human kings or idols. When the people trusted in their monarchy or military might, judgment came swiftly (1 Samuel 8:7). Similarly, Christians who place faith in earthly power rather than God's Kingdom risk spiritual ruin. The history of God's chosen people provides a sobering lesson: allegiance to God alone secures life, blessing, and true security.

The Danger of Hidden Evil

White Christian Nationalism often hides behind good intentions, making it even more dangerous. It appeals to righteousness while spreading division, pride, and fear. God rebukes hidden evil in the Church (Revelation 2:23). Believers must be vigilant, recognizing that not all that glitters is godly. True faith is tested by love, humility, and obedience, not by slogans or cultural dominance.

The Misguided Quest for Dominion

This movement seeks dominion in ways that contradict God's Kingdom. Instead of bringing people to Christ, it seeks to dominate hearts, minds, and institutions. True dominion in God's Kingdom comes through spiritual authority, love, and service, not coercion or intimidation. White Christian Nationalism misrepresents God's purpose, offering control rather than redemption.

The False Comfort of Conformity

Adherents often find comfort in conformity and belonging to a group that claims divine favor. But this comfort is illusory. God does not bless conformity to human systems that oppress or divide. True comfort comes from obedience, prayer, and reliance on the Spirit (Psalm 34:18). Followers must discern between societal approval and God's approval.

Global Implications

The influence of White Christian Nationalism is not confined to one nation. It undermines the Church worldwide, emboldens authoritarian leaders, and inspires similar movements abroad. Wherever this ideology spreads, it threatens the Church's unity, damages interfaith relations, and distorts the message of Christ. The Church must remain vigilant, global in perspective, and committed to truth.

The Deception of Power as Blessing

Many followers equate political or racial power with divine blessing. Yet God's favor is never contingent on dominance. Jesus said, *"Blessed are the meek, for they shall inherit the earth"* (Matthew 5:5). The pursuit of earthly authority as a measure of God's favor is a dangerous illusion. True inheritance comes through humility, obedience, and righteousness.

Role of the Church

The Church has a responsibility to expose deception and teach truth. It must distinguish between nationalism disguised as Christianity and the genuine Gospel of Christ. This requires courage, discernment, and a willingness to confront uncomfortable realities. Believers are called to love the oppressed, speak against injustice, and uphold the dignity of all people (Micah 6:8).

Restoration Through Repentance

God offers restoration to any believer or community willing to repent. Even those who have been deceived by White Christian Nationalism can be restored through humility and obedience. True repentance involves turning away from pride, fear, and division, and turning toward Christ in love and service. God's mercy is vast, but it requires honesty, confession, and action.

The Necessity of Education

Ignorance allows deception to thrive. Many Christians unknowingly support nationalist ideologies because they have not studied Scripture, history, or current events in context. Education equips the Church to discern truth from falsehood. Believers must understand the signs of deception and the principles of God's Kingdom to stand firm in faith.

The Threat to Unity

White Christian Nationalism fractures the Church, creating factions and silos. It pits believers against one another over politics, race, and culture rather than uniting them under Christ. The Apostle Paul exhorted the Church to maintain unity through the Spirit (Ephesians 4:3). Division weakens the witness of the Church and allows the enemy to flourish.

The Misuse of Worship and Prayer

In some circles, worship and prayer are weaponized to serve nationalist agendas. Songs, liturgies, and sermons become tools to reinforce fear, pride, and exclusion. God desires worship that glorifies Him, not human ambition. Worship must remain pure, focused on God's glory, and free from political manipulation.

The Illusion of Spiritual Authority

Leaders within White Christian Nationalism often claim spiritual authority to legitimize political agendas. Yet true authority comes from God and is exercised in humility, service, and obedience (Matthew 20:25-28). Authority that enforces domination rather than discipleship is counterfeit and subject to divine judgment.

The Biblical Response to Injustice

Scripture calls the Church to resist oppression, defend the vulnerable, and uphold justice (Isaiah 1:17). Silence in the face of injustice is complicity. Believers must act boldly to expose deception, challenge false teachings, and demonstrate God's love through concrete action. Faith without works is dead (James 2:17).

Recognizing the Signs

Christian Nationalism often presents as concern for morality, family, or faith, making it difficult to recognize. Believers must discern the underlying motives: pride, fear, domination, and exclusion. When rhetoric elevates one group while marginalizing others, the Church must speak truth and call for repentance.

A Call to Spiritual Vigilance

Believers are warned to remain vigilant against deception. The enemy often hides in plain sight, cloaked in religious language. Prayer, study of God's Word, and reliance on the Holy Spirit are essential to recognizing false teachings and resisting manipulation. Spiritual vigilance preserves both personal faith and the integrity of the Church.

The Power of Truth

Truth is the weapon of the Kingdom. When believers proclaim God's justice, mercy, and love, the lies of nationalism are exposed. Scripture is clear: God is not partial and shows no favoritism (Acts 10:34). By proclaiming the truth, the Church dismantles deception and restores hope to the oppressed.

Hope for the Church

Despite the rise of White Christian Nationalism, hope remains. God is still sovereign, and His Kingdom cannot be thwarted by human pride or political ambition. Believers who remain faithful, humble, and obedient can participate in the transformation of society according to His will. Christ's light will always shine in the darkness.

The Call to Repentance

The Church must turn from compromise and align fully with God's Kingdom. Repentance involves renouncing pride, fear, and division, confessing complicity, and committing to love and justice. God promises forgiveness and restoration to those who seek Him sincerely (1 John 1:9). The faithful are called to lead by example, demonstrating God's righteousness in all spheres of life.

Closing Prayer and Prophetic Declaration

Heavenly Father, we repent for the ways Your name has been misused to justify pride, exclusion, and oppression. Forgive us, Lord, for the times we have trusted human power above Your Kingdom. Raise a Church that stands in truth, loves all people, and shines Your light into every nation. Guide us, Holy Spirit, to discern deception, embrace justice, and lead with humility. Let Your Kingdom come, Your will be done, on earth as it is in Heaven. In Jesus' name, Amen.

Chapter 17: The Spirit of Division Masquerading as Prophecy

Acts 16:16–18 – Exposing False Prophecy in the Church

God warns against counterfeit prophecy. False spiritual authority can mislead the church, corrupting faith and distorting God's Word. The spirit of divination often hides behind prophetic language. It may appear holy or inspired, but its purpose is deception, manipulation, and control. In Acts 16, the slave girl demonstrates this danger. Though seemingly prophetic, her pronouncements were driven by a demonic spirit, not God's guidance. Acts 16:16-18 warns of spirits that masquerade as prophetic voices. False prophecy infiltrates the Church, misleading congregants, promoting manipulation, and obscuring the truth of God's Word.

Leaders must discern the truth from false prophecy. Biblical knowledge, spiritual sensitivity, and accountability are essential tools in identifying deception. False prophecy disrupts church unity. Misleading messages create confusion, division, and mistrust among members. Counterfeit prophets often pursue gain or influence. Their motives are self-serving, seeking recognition, control, or material benefit rather than God's glory. Many misunderstood Lucifer's role before his fall. Contrary to popular belief, he was not in charge of worship but served as a chief prosecutor in God's heavenly court, bringing sin to light (Ezekiel 28:12–15).

God exposes deception to protect His people. The removal of the demonic influence in Acts 16 illustrates His commitment to safeguarding believers. Spiritual maturity aids discernment. Leaders and members who cultivate prayer, Scripture study, and the Holy Spirit's guidance are less likely to be deceived. God uses exposure as a teaching moment. His name, Lucifer, derives from Latin: *lux* (light) and *ferre* (to bring), meaning "light bringer." His role involved clarity and accountability, not worship leadership, highlighting his legal responsibilities before rebellion.

When false prophecy is revealed, it educates the church on vigilance, discernment, and reliance on God's Word. C. S. Lewis, in *Mere Christianity*, emphasizes discernment in spiritual matters. Misunderstanding God's order can lead believers to attribute divine authority incorrectly, opening the door for deception. True prophecy aligns with God's character. Messages that glorify God, edify the church, and uphold Scripture reflect authentic divine inspiration.

False prophecy often appeals to emotion rather than truth. Manipulating fear, hope, or desire can make the deception seem credible, drawing people away from God's guidance. Leaders must test their spirits. A. W. Tozer, in *The Pursuit of God*, stresses the necessity of grounding prophecy in Scripture. False prophets manipulate truth, mislead the faithful, and cultivate confusion under the guise of revelation. Discernment involves prayer, Scripture alignment, and consultation with wise, accountable believers.

The church is vulnerable to spiritual impostors. Members seeking direction, miracles, or affirmation may easily be misled if discernment is absent. Counterfeit prophecy can lead to bondage. Demonic influence behind false messages often manipulates, pressures, or controls individuals spiritually and emotionally. Exposure restores God's authority. Leonard Ravenhill highlights that spiritual deception often appears attractive. Leaders or self-proclaimed prophets may display charisma or insight, but their message deviates from God's Word, revealing a spirit of divination. Revealing false prophecy reinstates His power and truth, correcting the direction of the congregation.

False prophets may claim divine endorsement. They often present themselves as vessels of God's will, making it essential to verify claims with Scripture. God provides warnings through His Word. The Bible equips believers to identify deception, uphold truth, and reject misleading voices. Discernment requires spiritual vigilance. Constant prayer, meditation, and reliance on the Holy Spirit prevent believers from accepting counterfeit messages. Lucifer's post-fall activity, now as Satan, demonstrates a continuous role of accusation and deception. He tempts, prosecutes, and accuses, seeking to derail God's people from obedience and truth.

God uses confrontation to expose deception. In Acts 16, the apostles' authority silenced the demonic influence, demonstrating God's intervention. Members must remain humble and teachable. Pride and spiritual arrogance can blind the church to deception, making humility a safeguard. Scripture consistently differentiates between God's true prophets and those influenced by Satan. False prophecy tempts believers to rely on visions, manipulations, or human wisdom rather than Scripture and the Holy Spirit.

Authentic prophecy builds the church. True messages from God edify, correct, and guide believers toward obedience and spiritual growth. Counterfeit prophecy sows confusion. Mixed messages divide congregations, erode trust, and compromise unity in Christ. Leadership accountability prevents exploitation. Oversight, mentoring, and peer evaluation help detect and eliminate false prophetic influence.

God honors those who confront deception. Courageous leaders who expose counterfeit prophecy protect the congregation and uphold His glory. False prophecy often distracts from God's mission. The focus shifts from obedience, evangelism, and discipleship to sensationalism and personal gain. Exposure encourages spiritual growth. The spirit of divination masquerading as prophecy is a persistent threat. Scripture, supported by Lewis, Tozer, and Ravenhill, underscores the importance of vigilance, discernment, and adherence to God's Word to expose and reject false prophecy.

Confronting deception educates believers, strengthens discernment, and fosters maturity in faith. Prayer is essential in discerning prophecy. Constant communion with God reveals truth, guards against manipulation, and empowers accurate interpretation. God's Word is the ultimate standard. Any prophetic message inconsistent with Scripture must be rejected, regardless of charisma or persuasion.

False prophets manipulate scripture. Twisting passages for personal advantage or deception undermines the integrity of God's Word. Exposure restores confidence in God. Revealing false prophecy reassures the congregation of His guidance, protection, and omnipotence. Spiritual maturity safeguards against deception. Knowledge of Scripture, prayer, and reliance on the Holy Spirit equip leaders to discern truth from falsehood.

God empowers leaders to act. Confronting spiritual deception requires courage, authority, and dependence on His wisdom. False prophecy thrives in secrecy. Hidden agendas, private manipulation, and unchecked authority allow deception to persist undetected. Exposure cultivates vigilance. Awareness of past deception trains the church to detect future counterfeit messages. Discernment protects the flock. Leaders who actively evaluate prophetic claims safeguard believers from spiritual and emotional Lewis observes that spiritual deception thrives where discernment is absent. The Church must cultivate wisdom, study Scripture diligently, and test all prophetic words against the Word of God.

God's intervention demonstrates His sovereignty. The removal of demonic influence in Acts 16 illustrates that He controls all spiritual matters. Counterfeit prophecy undermines credibility. When exposed, false prophets diminish trust, emphasizing the need for careful evaluation and accountability.

God's truth cannot be obscured. Divine guidance, when sought earnestly, pierces through deception and restores clarity. Spiritual deception often promises quick results. Miracles, wealth, or fame may be offered as enticements, contrasting God's call for faithful obedience. Exposure reinforces God's standards. Revealing false prophecy underscores the necessity of Scripture, integrity, and divine alignment. Leaders must maintain humility. Even spiritual authority requires dependence on God, prayerful discernment, and accountability.

. Members must practice critical thinking. Evaluating prophetic messages against God's Word prevents manipulation and strengthens spiritual maturity. Exposure restores order in the church. By confronting deception, God ensures that His authority, mission, and truth prevail. False prophecy tests the faith of believers. Challenges reveal loyalty, discernment, and the commitment to follow God above all.

God equips leaders to discern accurately. The Holy Spirit provides wisdom, insight, and courage to identify counterfeit messages and act decisively. Exposure strengthens the spiritual foundation. Correcting deception builds trust, promotes accountability, and reinforces a culture of truth.

Leadership must be rooted in Scripture. Knowledge of God's Word protects against manipulation, misinterpretation, and spiritual compromise. False prophecy tempts the inexperienced. Novice believers may accept it without question, highlighting the importance of mentorship and teaching.

Exposure encourages a culture of discernment. Congregations learn to evaluate, question, and rely on God's Word rather than human charisma. God's light triumphs over deception. Ultimately, all counterfeit prophecy is revealed and nullified by His truth, authority, and sovereign power.

Racism is not just a social or cultural problem—it is a **sin problem.** It denies the truth that every human is made in the image of God. It distorts the gospel by elevating one group over another. And it resists the work of the Holy Spirit, who unites people from every nation into one body. The church cannot remain silent about this sin if it hopes to walk in holiness.

When racism is left unchallenged, it becomes like leaven, spreading quietly through the congregation. It corrupts worship, poisons fellowship, and undermines the credibility of the church's witness to the world. Just as Paul warned about hypocrisy and immorality in the early church, so too must we confront racial prejudice wherever it takes root.

One of Satan's greatest strategies has been to pit God's people against each other based on skin color, culture, or nationality. He knows that a divided church is a powerless church. By sowing seeds of suspicion and superiority, he has weakened the church's ability to stand united in truth.

Throughout history, counterfeit prophecy has often carried the undertones of racism. Religious leaders declared doctrines that God never ordained, claiming that certain races were cursed, inferior, or outside God's plan. These were lies of the enemy, meant to keep people in bondage and blind the church to God's inclusive kingdom.

Yet Scripture consistently reveals God's love for all nations. The book of Revelation paints a vision of the redeemed as "a great multitude which no one could number, of all nations, tribes, peoples, and tongues, standing before the throne and before the Lamb" (Revelation 7:9). Heaven itself will be filled with diversity—proof that God values every ethnicity equally.

The suppression of Black contributions to the Bible has left generations feeling excluded from God's story. When young people of color are told, directly or indirectly, that the Bible is not for them, it creates spiritual alienation. But when they learn of Zephaniah, Ebed-Melech, the Queen of Sheba, and the Ethiopian eunuch in Acts 8, their eyes open to the reality that they, too, have always been part of God's redemptive plan.

Consider the Ethiopian eunuch in Acts 8. He was a high-ranking official in the court of Candace, queen of Ethiopia, and he was seeking God when Philip explained the gospel to him. This man of African descent became one of the first Gentile converts in the early church, carrying the gospel back to his homeland. This is evidence of God's strategy to spread His Word across continents through diverse vessels.

Why have we not heard more sermons about these figures? Why has the ethnicity of these faithful servants been brushed aside or hidden? It is because the enemy wants to keep God's people in ignorance. Ignorance breeds division, and division prevents revival.

The truth is that the gospel does not belong to the West or the East, to the North or the South. It belongs to the Lord, who gave His Son for the whole world. When we allow cultural pride or racial prejudice to claim ownership of the gospel, we fall into idolatry, worshipping our own identity rather than the God who made us one.

The church must repent of its complicity in racism. Repentance means more than feeling sorry— it means confessing the sin, turning away from it, and actively pursuing reconciliation and justice. Only then can the church walk in true holiness and be a credible witness of God's kingdom.

Some argue that speaking about race divides the church. But silence in the face of sin has never produced unity. It is only by naming and exposing hidden evil that healing can begin. Just as hidden immorality or greed must be confronted, so too must racism be brought into the light.

The prophets of old did not shy away from naming the sins of their generation. They spoke against oppression, injustice, and pride. Today, if the church refuses to speak against racism, it forfeits its prophetic voice and becomes complicit in the very evil God abhors.

God has always had a remnant who refused to bow to cultural idols. In every generation, some men and women stand up for truth, even when it is unpopular. Just as Ebed-Melech stood for Jeremiah, so too must believers today stand against racism in defense of God's truth and His people.

When we look at Jesus' ministry, we see that He consistently crossed cultural and racial boundaries. He spoke with the Samaritan woman at the well, healed the servant of a Roman centurion, and praised the faith of a Syrophoenician woman. Each of these actions was radical for His time, breaking through barriers of race and class.

Jesus demonstrated that the kingdom of God is not bound by human divisions. His parable of the Good Samaritan explicitly rebuked ethnic prejudice, teaching that love transcends boundaries of nationality and race. In Christ's kingdom, neighborliness is defined not by similarity but by compassion.

The early church also embraced this reality. On the Day of Pentecost, the Holy Spirit fell on people from many nations, and they heard the gospel in their own languages. The Spirit intentionally broke down cultural walls, showing that the gospel was for all people everywhere.

Paul's missionary journeys further emphasized this truth. He traveled across Asia Minor, Greece, and Rome, reaching Jews and Gentiles alike. His letters consistently call for unity among diverse believers, urging them to set aside divisions and be one in Christ.

Despite this biblical foundation, the church has often fallen into the same trap as the world— judging people by outward appearance. James warned against showing favoritism to the rich over the poor, but the same principle applies to race. To show partiality is to sin against the law of love.

Racism not only hurts individuals but also quenches the Spirit within the church. When believers reject one another based on skin color or culture, they grieve the Holy Spirit, who longs to bring them together in unity. Division is the enemy's tool; unity is God's weapon.

The church cannot fulfill its mission until it embraces the full diversity of God's kingdom. How can we reach all nations if we refuse to honor the voices and contributions of those nations? How can we preach unity in Christ if we harbor prejudice in our hearts?

The exposure of racism within the church is not meant to shame but to cleanse. Just as God exposes hidden immorality or false prophecy, He is now exposing the sin of racism so that His bride may be purified. Judgment begins in the house of God, and this is one of the sins He is bringing into the light.

This exposure is a sign of God's mercy. If He did not care, He would allow the church to continue in deception. But because He desires a spotless bride, He is revealing what has been hidden so that His people may repent and be restored.

The enemy has long used racism as a weapon to discredit the church in the eyes of the world. Outsiders see the hypocrisy of a church that preaches love but practices division. Only repentance and reconciliation can restore credibility to our witness.

The time has come for the church to celebrate the contributions of all God's people. Black inventors, leaders, prophets, and saints have shaped not only history but also the story of redemption. Their voices must no longer be silenced or minimized.

When the church embraces the truth of Scripture's diversity, it reflects the beauty of God's design. Unity does not mean uniformity; it means harmony among differences, like the notes of a symphony blending into one song of praise.

The vision of a glorious church without spot or wrinkle includes a church free from racism. Just as Christ cleanses His bride from immorality and idolatry, so too must He cleanse her from prejudice and division. Only then will she shine as a light to the nations.

The revelation of Black and African contributions in Scripture is not just about history—it is about destiny. It reminds us that God has always included all peoples in His plan, and He continues to call a diverse people to proclaim His name in this generation.

The church must teach these truths boldly. Pastors and leaders must not shy away from preaching about racism, biblical diversity, and unity in Christ. To remain silent is to allow the deception to continue unchallenged.

Let us, then, be a people who walk in transparency, who acknowledge the sins of the past, who repent of hidden prejudice, and who embrace the fullness of God's vision for His church. Only then will we be prepared for the revival and final exposure God is bringing.

In Christ, there is no Black church, White church, Asian church, or Hispanic church—there is only His church. A holy, unified, multi-ethnic bride, washed in His blood, standing together as one. This is the church that will overcome deception, silence the accuser, and be ready for the return of her King.

Political violence is not a new phenomenon. Throughout history, we have seen rulers, governments, and movements use power to dominate, oppress, and silence the voices of justice. The Bible reminds us that "there is nothing new under the sun" (Ecclesiastes 1:9). From the violence of Pharaoh against Israel in Egypt to the persecution of the early church under Roman rule, Scripture records how power in the wrong hands can become a tool of destruction. Political violence is the misuse of authority to enforce fear, strip dignity, and uphold unjust systems. It thrives wherever human ambition replaces God's righteousness.

At its root, political violence is not just a social or governmental problem; it is a spiritual problem. James 4:1 asks, *"What causes fights and quarrels among you? Don't they come from your desires that battle within you?"* Violence begins in the heart when envy, greed, and pride take hold. When leaders or nations give in to these corrupt desires, the result is widespread destruction. Political violence is therefore not only the clash of armies or protestors but also the policies, laws, and manipulations that crush the vulnerable and exalt the oppressor.

The rise of Christian nationalism in our day is a disturbing example of how political violence and counterfeit religion walk hand in hand. Christian nationalism cloaks political agendas in religious language, making it appear as though God Himself endorses hatred, exclusion, and domination. But Jesus taught that His Kingdom is *not of this world* (John 18:36). Whenever religion is used to justify violence, racism, or the subjugation of others, it ceases to be true Christianity and becomes idolatry—a false gospel that God Himself rejects.

James strongly warns against performative religion, saying, *"Do not merely listen to the word, and so deceive yourselves. Do what it says"* (James 1:22). Many who wave the banner of "Christian nation" or "family values" live lives that betray the gospel. They profess faith with their lips while their actions spread hatred and division. Jesus called such people hypocrites, comparing them to whitewashed tombs: beautiful on the outside but full of death inside (Matthew 23:27). Political violence thrives when religion becomes a performance rather than a practice of justice, mercy, and humility before God (Micah 6:8).

History shows us that counterfeit religion often aligns with oppressive politics. In Nazi Germany, many churches compromised and supported Hitler's regime, remaining silent as Jewish families were slaughtered. In the United States, many white churches supported slavery and segregation, twisting Scripture to justify their sins. Today, the same counterfeit spirit rises in the form of Christian nationalism and white supremacy. It disguises itself as patriotism and holiness, but its fruits are hatred, exclusion, and violence.

God's anger is revealed against the church when it supports evil against His people. Jesus declared that whatever is done to "the least of these" is done to Him (Matthew 25:40). To endorse racism, violence, or injustice is to reject Christ Himself. The prophets of old did not hesitate to rebuke nations and religious leaders who sided with the oppressor. Isaiah cried out, *"Woe to those who make unjust laws, to those who issue oppressive decrees"* (Isaiah 10:1). God still rebukes His church today when it becomes a tool for political corruption rather than a voice of righteousness.

When we lack critical thinking, we open the door to deception. Hosea 4:6 says, *"My people are destroyed from lack of knowledge."* The church is called to discern spirits and test every teaching against the Word of God (1 John 4:1). Yet when believers uncritically accept propaganda, conspiracy theories, or nationalist rhetoric, they abandon the wisdom of Christ for the foolishness of men. This intellectual laziness is dangerous, for it allows political violence to masquerade as righteousness.

The biblical truth is that every person bears the image of God (Genesis 1:27). Racism, nationalism, and political dominance deny this truth by elevating one group above another. Paul reminds us that in Christ there is neither Jew nor Greek, slave nor free, male nor female, for all are one in Him (Galatians 3:28). Any ideology that creates hierarchy among races or cultures is anti-Christ in spirit. A nation cannot call itself Christian while denying the equal worth of all people.

Christian nationalism often equates the identity of a nation with a specific race, culture, or political party. But the Kingdom of God is not bound by national borders or political affiliations. Revelation 7:9 describes the redeemed as *"a great multitude... from every nation, tribe, people and language, standing before the throne and before the Lamb."* The church must resist the temptation to fuse faith with nationalism, for doing so corrupts the gospel and reduces the cross to a political weapon.

The fundamental root of much political violence is white supremacy. White supremacy is not merely prejudice; it is a false religion that elevates whiteness as divine and superior. It creates systems designed to oppress people of color, silence dissent, and maintain power at all costs. Jesus declared, *"You cannot serve both God and money"* (Matthew 6:24). Likewise, you cannot serve both Christ and white supremacy. They are incompatible, for one produces humility and love, while the other breeds violence and pride.

The Scriptures remind us of rulers who used violence to secure their power. Pharaoh enslaved Israel, Herod slaughtered infants to protect his throne, and Nebuchadnezzar built a golden statue demanding worship. Each time, God raised prophets, leaders, or deliverers to expose the evil and remind His people that power belongs to Him alone. Political violence, no matter how entrenched, cannot stand against the justice of God.

One striking example is the story of Daniel and the lions' den. Political violence was used to trap Daniel, a faithful servant of God, because he refused to bow to the king's decree (Daniel 6). Yet God shut the mouths of the lions and vindicated His servant. This story reveals that political violence, though powerful for a moment, cannot silence those who stand in truth. The same God who delivered Daniel still defends His people today.

Jesus Himself was a victim of political violence. The religious elite conspired with Roman authorities to crucify Him, using both false religion and state power to execute the Son of God. Yet what seemed like defeat became victory, for through the cross, Christ triumphed over every principality and power (Colossians 2:15). The crucifixion reveals how counterfeit religion and political violence unite to oppose God's kingdom—but it also shows that their power is temporary.

The early church lived under constant political violence. Believers were arrested, beaten, and martyred for refusing to deny Christ. Yet their testimony shook the world. Acts 17:6 describes how the apostles were accused of *"turning the world upside down."* Despite violence, the church grew because it did not bow to political corruption. Instead, it stood firm on the truth of the gospel. The modern church must reclaim this boldness.

Today's rise of performative religion and counterfeit Christianity is a warning sign. Jesus prophesied in Matthew 24:10-12 that in the last days, *"many will turn away from the faith... and because of the increase of wickedness, the love of most will grow cold."* Political violence and nationalism are part of this falling away. The church must guard against deception and hold fast to the truth, lest it becomes complicit in the very evil God condemns.

Political violence does not only happen in far-off nations—it is present in our streets, our policies, and even our pulpits. When churches endorse leaders who promote division, when sermons excuse racism, and when believers remain silent in the face of injustice, the church itself becomes a breeding ground for violence. This is why judgment begins in the house of God (1 Peter 4:17). The Lord will not allow His bride to continue in hypocrisy without rebuke.

The witness of the church is at stake. Jesus said the world would know His disciples by their love (John 13:35). When the church instead becomes known for hatred, violence, and political idolatry, it forfeits its testimony. A compromised church cannot heal a broken world. Only when the church returns to the simplicity of Christ—loving God and neighbor can it reclaim its power to bring transformation.

We must also recognize that silence in the face of political violence is itself a form of complicity. Dietrich Bonhoeffer, who resisted Hitler, famously said, "Silence in the face of evil is itself evil." The prophets cried aloud against oppression, and Jesus overturned the tables of corrupt power. Likewise, the church today must not remain silent but boldly confront the evils of racism, nationalism, and political corruption.

God's call is for the church to be a prophetic voice, not a political pawn. We are called to be the light of the world and the salt of the earth (Matthew 5:13-14). Light exposes hidden evil, and salt preserves righteousness in a decaying culture. If we lose our saltiness—our distinctiveness as God's people—we become useless. To confront political violence, the church must recover its prophetic calling, declaring truth even when it is costly.

In the end, political violence, white supremacy, and counterfeit religion will not prevail. Revelation 11:15 declares, *"The kingdom of the world has become the kingdom of our Lord and of his Messiah, and he will reign for ever and ever."* God will dismantle every corrupt system and establish His justice. Until then, the church must stand boldly, rebuking hidden evil, defending the oppressed, and embodying the love of Christ. This is not optional—it is the very essence of our faith.

Biblical Warnings & Prophetic Voices

Throughout Scripture, God raises prophets to warn His people when they stray into injustice, idolatry, or corruption. From Moses confronting Pharaoh to Isaiah rebuking Judah, prophetic voices expose sin and call for repentance. Today, the church must listen carefully to these warnings. Political violence, Christian nationalism, and counterfeit faith are the modern Pharaohs that need confrontation.

Prophets are often rejected, mocked, or persecuted. Jeremiah was thrown into a cistern for speaking God's truth (Jeremiah 38:6). Likewise, contemporary prophetic voices are marginalized when they challenge Christian nationalism or political collusion. The church on trial must remember that rejecting the prophet invites judgment on itself.

God's warnings are not abstract; they are urgent. Hosea 4:6 declares, *"My people are destroyed for lack of knowledge."* Ignorance, indifference, and blind allegiance to counterfeit systems make believers vulnerable to deception and political manipulation. Understanding God's Word is the foundation for resisting false ideologies.

Isaiah 5:20–21 warns against calling evil good and good evil. Christian nationalism and political violence are prime examples of this distortion. Leaders and believers who defend oppression while claiming righteousness are guilty of this sin. Scripture calls the church to discernment, not blind loyalty to political power.

Prophetic voices also expose the consequences of sin. Amos warned Israel that injustice toward the poor would lead to exile (Amos 5:11–12). Modern Christian nationalism, white supremacy, and counterfeit churches may seem powerful, but God's justice is inevitable. No ideology or political alliance can escape His judgment.

The danger of ignoring prophetic warnings is spiritual numbness. Habakkuk 1:5 reminds us,

"Look among the nations and watch—be utterly amazed! For I am going to do something in your days that you would not believe, even if you were told." God works through history, often using unexpected means, to bring His people back to righteousness.

The Bible also teaches that leaders who ignore God's commands bring calamity to the nation. King Saul lost favor with God because he prioritized political ambition over obedience (1 Samuel 15:23). Similarly, churches that align with political violence or Christian nationalism for influence betray the Lord and invite destruction.

Prophetic voices call for justice, mercy, and humility. Micah 6:8 instructs, *"He has shown you, O mortal, what is good. And what does the LORD require of you? To act justly and to love mercy and to walk humbly with your God."* Counterfeit churches invert this call, promoting pride, fear, and exclusion instead of love and justice.

The prophets remind us that God sees all hidden evil. Nothing is concealed from His eyes (Hebrews 4:13). When churches support oppression, political violence, or supremacy, they cannot hide behind slogans or performative rituals. God will bring accountability to those who use His name to bless evil.

Prophetic voices also encourage courage in the faithful. Just as Elijah confronted Ahab and the prophets of Baal (1 Kings 18), the church today must stand boldly against Christian nationalism, racism, and counterfeit faith. Courageous voices awaken the conscience of the people and reveal God's truth in a world of deception.

The prophetic tradition also shows the power of a faithful remnant. Daniel, Shadrach, Meshach, and Abednego remained obedient in hostile political environments. Their unwavering commitment to God preserved them and testified to His sovereignty. The church today must nurture a similar remnant of faithful believers.

Ultimately, biblical warnings teach that God's justice will prevail. Political violence, Christian nationalism, and counterfeit churches may appear dominant, but they are temporary. Revelation 19:11-16 portrays Christ returning as King of Kings, exposing and judging all evil, and establishing His eternal Kingdom of justice and peace.

Living the True Gospel in a Divided World

Living the true Gospel begins with recognizing that Christ's Kingdom is not of this world. Jesus said, *"My Kingdom is not of this world"* (John 18:36). Therefore, believers must resist the temptation to conflate political power, nationalism, or cultural dominance with God's authority. Faithful discipleship requires loyalty to God above all earthly allegiances.

The first step in living faithfully is discernment. Believers must test every teaching, every leader, and every ideology against the Word of God (1 John 4:1). Critical thinking is not optional; it is a spiritual discipline. Without it, the church becomes vulnerable to deception, false prophets, and counterfeit religion.

Love must guide every action. In a world divided by race, politics, and ideology, the Gospel calls believers to love their neighbors as themselves (Mark 12:31). Political loyalty cannot replace love. Racism, white supremacy, or favoritism violates the command to love all people equally.

Faithful living also means confronting injustice. Christians are called to speak truth boldly, even when it is unpopular. Proverbs 31:8-9 exhorts, *"Speak up for those who cannot speak for themselves, for the rights of all who are destitute."* Silence in the face of oppression allows evil to flourish.

The true Gospel rejects fear and intimidation. Followers of Christ are not to be swayed by threats, propaganda, or political coercion. 2 Timothy 1:7 reminds us, *"For God has not given us a spirit of fear, but of power and of love and of a sound mind."* Courageous faith confronts counterfeit religion and political manipulation.

Prayer is a central weapon against counterfeit faith and political violence. Believers must pray for wisdom, discernment, and God's justice to prevail. Daniel prayed for his nation and his people even under hostile regimes, and God answered, demonstrating that prayer aligns the heart with His purposes (Daniel 9:3–19).

Community is essential. Believers must surround themselves with others who uphold truth and justice. Fellowship strengthens resistance to deception and reinforces the Kingdom's values. Hebrews 10:24-25 instructs, *"Let us consider how we may spur one another on toward love and good deeds, not giving up meeting together."*

Equipping the next generation is also vital. Teaching children and young believers about true discipleship, racial equality, and biblical justice prepares them to resist Christian nationalism and counterfeit churches. Deuteronomy 6:6-7 reminds parents to impress God's commandments on their children diligently.

Faithful living includes engaging culture without being conformed to it. Romans 12:2 teaches, *"Do not conform to the pattern of this world, but be transformed by the renewing of your mind.*" Christians can participate in society while upholding justice, mercy, and truth without succumbing to political or cultural idolatry.

Standing for truth often comes at a cost. The early church endured persecution for refusing to compromise the Gospel (Acts 5:29). Today, believers may face criticism, exclusion, or even threats when opposing Christian nationalism and counterfeit churches. Yet obedience to God must outweigh fear of human judgment.

Forgiveness and reconciliation are also marks of the true Gospel. In a world torn by division, the church demonstrates the Kingdom by restoring relationships and breaking cycles of hatred (Matthew 5:23-24). True discipleship does not retaliate or seek revenge; it seeks restoration under God's guidance.

Finally, living the true Gospel requires hope. No matter how pervasive political violence or counterfeit churches may seem, God's Kingdom will triumph. Revelation 21:4 promises, *"He will wipe every tear from their eyes. There will be no more death or mourning or crying or pain, for the old order of things has passed away."* Believers are called to live faithfully now, anticipating the full restoration of God's Kingdom.

The Nature of False Prophecy

The Spirit of division arrives veiled in righteousness, wearing the mask of holy intent, whispering promises of insight while planting seeds of mistrust. It exploits the human desire for direction, using the language of God to conceal the intent of self-exaltation, knowing that untested hearts will accept authority without discernment.

True prophecy aligns with God's Word and builds unity, yet the counterfeit fragments families, churches, and communities, leaving wounded hearts in its wake. The subtlety of its intrusion is its most dangerous weapon; it convinces the faithful that division itself is sanctified. This spirit thrives on pride, ego, and ambition. It presents obedience to the messenger as equivalent to obedience to God, and it transforms accountability into judgment, making the sheep dependent on human will rather than divine guidance.

Division masquerading as prophecy often appeals to fear. It warns of consequences, misrepresents God's heart, and exploits uncertainty, using visions, dreams, or selective Scripture to manipulate the conscience of the obedient and the vulnerable. The false prophetic voice can sound urgent, compelling, and convincing. Yet it leaves trails of confusion, pitting friends against friends, leader against leader, and churches against churches. The Spirit of God, patient and discerning, is often drowned out by human interpretation and ambition.

In the hidden corridors of influence, this spirit weaves its webs, promising revelation while spreading discord. The unwise follow, believing that those who speak loudly and with apparent authority carry the mantle of God, not realizing that the Spirit of God never demands fear or blind allegiance. God warns that every prophetic word must be tested. Discernment is not optional; it is a divine mandate. A heart aligned with truth recognizes unity as the fruit of God, while division, pride, and fear mark the counterfeit.

The Spirit of division uses subtle intimidation, portraying disagreement as rebellion and correction as betrayal. It seeks to silence honest voices, marginalize humility, and glorify the messenger above the mission of God. Every community that has yielded to untested prophetic words suffers in silence. Families fracture; leaders fall into envy, ministries splinter, and loyalty is weaponized. What masquerades as guidance leaves in its path a harvest of pain, mistrust, and broken relationships.

Counterfeit prophecy is often patient, waiting for the opportune moment to fracture the body of Christ. One word of accusation here, one misapplied vision there, until the seeds of division sprout unseen and unopposed. Pride is the lifeblood of this spirit. It thrives on the elevation of the self over the Spirit of God, on the desire to be seen as chosen, exceptional, or indispensable. The false prophet craves influence more than the holiness of God.

The Spirit of God fosters unity, love, and accountability. The counterfeit seeks isolation, manipulation, and fear. Those who are rooted in His Word recognize the difference, yet many fall victim to subtle distortions disguised as revelation. In churches, ministries, and communities, this spirit thrives where humility is absent and accountability is ignored. It exploits gaps in leadership, spiritual immaturity, and unhealed wounds, transforming vulnerability into a tool for control.

The voice of division masquerading as prophecy is loud, confident, and persuasive. It promises insight, positions itself as visionary, and calls obedience to itself rather than to God. Its goal is domination, not guidance, manipulation, not edification.

God calls the faithful to vigilance, humility, and discernment. Prophecy must align with Scripture, build community, and magnify God rather than men. Any word that divides, manipulates, or exalts the messenger above the mission of God must be rejected, prayed through, and confronted with courage.

Recognizing the Spirit of Division

Signs of the counterfeit prophetic spirit appear in patterns, not isolated moments. Repeated accusations, manipulation through fear, and pressure to conform are hallmarks. The discerning heart watches for these indicators as markers of deception. When a prophetic message demands allegiance to the speaker rather than obedience to God, it has crossed into counterfeit territory. True prophecy honors God uplifts the body, and leaves the faithful free to serve without coercion.

Division masquerading as prophecy often exploits existing conflict, inflating minor disagreements into spiritual battles. It thrives in unresolved wounds, unhealed trauma, and unchecked ambition. A community under the influence of this spirit experiences chronic instability. Leadership turnover, shifting alliances, and fractured relationships are the visible fruits, while invisible wounds fester in silence. The false prophet often portrays themselves as the gatekeeper of truth. Questioning or dissent is labeled rebellion, loyalty to God is reframed as disobedience, and obedience to God is replaced with obedience to a human standard.

The Spirit of God never isolates; it always seeks the flourishing of the body. Where manipulation and secrecy prevail, the counterfeit spirit is at work, and discernment becomes vital. Words that alienate, accuse unjustly, or create factions within families, congregations, or ministries are signs. A true prophetic message will build, heal, and guide, not divide or destroy.

The counterfeit spirit often masquerades as zeal. It measures loyalty, monitors compliance, and enforces a standard that exalts the messenger while diminishing God's authority. Leaders are warned: do not confuse personal ambition or passion with the voice of God. True prophecy aligns with humility, Scripture, and the Spirit's fruit: unity, peace, and love.

False prophetic words often employ selective Scripture, manipulating context to serve human agendas. Knowledge without discernment becomes a weapon in the hands of pride. The Spirit of division thrives on emotional manipulation. Guilt, shame, and fear are its tools; obedience, humility, and love are its obstacles. Even the most faithful can be misled if the spirit's voice is untested. Prayer, Scripture, and accountability act as safeguards to discern truth from deception.

Division masquerading as prophecy seeks to control conversation, limit access, and silence those who question. Its tactics are subtle, often cloaked in concern, yet destructive in outcome. God's people must be anchored in His Word. Only alignment with truth, love, and humility can withstand the seduction of counterfeit revelation. A discerning community protects itself through transparency, accountability, and spiritual maturity, refusing to allow a single voice to dominate under the guise of divine authority.

Biblical Examples and Modern Parallels

Saul's jealousy of David is an archetype of the Spirit of division. His prophetic counselors became instruments of fear, control, and manipulation, enforcing his pride while punishing the righteous. Korah's rebellion in Numbers shows how misused authority and counterfeit spiritual motives can fracture entire communities. God exposed the deception, but the damage left a scar in Israel for generations. Modern parallels abound. Ministries fracture under self-appointed prophets, families are torn apart by leaders claiming divine authority, and churches are destabilized by untested visions and selective interpretations.

False prophecy can masquerade as encouragement, but its fruit is unrest. Decisions that should unify instead of divide. Obedience that should serve God instead serves the ego. Loyalty that should glorify the Lord instead glorifies man. The counterfeit spirit seeks admiration and fear, positioning itself as the mediator of God's will. It measures faithfulness by conformity, not devotion to truth.

In today's religious climate, social media amplifies the counterfeit voice. One unchecked prophetic statement can spread division globally, magnifying confusion and fracture in congregations, networks, and denominations. Women, youth, and vulnerable members are often targeted. Their doubts are weaponized, their obedience tested, and their loyalty exploited.

The Spirit of God calls for restoration of hearts, healing of divisions, and accountability among leaders, so that God's purposes prevail over human ambition.

The Spirit of division masquerading as prophecy is patient. It waits for insecurity, ambition, or unhealed pain to create an opening. Once lodged, it manipulates perception, reshaping reality around prideful narratives.

Communities are cautioned: discernment is a spiritual discipline. Test every word, every dream, every vision, and every declaration against Scripture and the fruit it produces. Leaders must cultivate humility. The prophetic gift is not for personal elevation but for edification, encouragement, and guidance aligned with God's Word.

Division arises where accountability is absent. Where no one tests prophetic utterances, the counterfeit flourishes, spreading confusion and fear. Historically, religious movements fell because false prophecy silenced the wise and elevated prideful ambition. Today, the pattern repeats unless vigilance prevails. False prophets masquerading as messengers of God often exploit respect, fear, and devotion, creating a climate where questioning becomes spiritual rebellion.

Even well-meaning leaders can be deceived if they fail to align every word with God's heart and Scripture. Pride is the doorway; discernment is the guard. Churches fractured, ministries destabilized, and families divided are testimonies to the destructive power of the counterfeit prophetic spirit. God's warning is clear: those who elevate themselves above truth will be exposed. Those who manipulate love and loyalty will face accountability.

Faithful voices must be bold in discernment, courageous in correction, and unwavering in obedience to God, even when confrontation is uncomfortable. The Spirit of division uses isolation to multiply impact. When individuals are separated from the community, their discernment weakens and their exposure to deception increases. True prophecy seeks collaboration. It invites counsel, humility, and alignment with God's Word. Counterfeit prophecy isolates and controls.

Spiritual maturity is the key to resistance. Those grounded in Scripture, prayer, and community are less likely to be deceived. God honors transparency. Prophetic voices should operate in the light, open to correction, willing to submit to accountability, and sensitive to the unity of the body. False prophecy manipulates emotions, pressures loyalty, and fosters fear. It masquerades as zeal for God, but its fruit is envy, division, and unrest.

Vigilance requires both courage and humility. Rejecting counterfeit prophecy may provoke opposition, but God will uphold those who honor truth over manipulation. The final test of prophetic authenticity is fruit: unity, encouragement, and alignment with God's Word. Anything contrary signals the Spirit of division at work.

Prophetic Warnings to Leaders

Leaders who claim God's authority yet operate from pride, jealousy, or ambition are warned: the eyes of heaven pierce every veil. No manipulation, no selective revelation, no carefully orchestrated fear can escape divine scrutiny. Every whispered command that silences the faithful is recorded, every exalted word above God's Word is marked. You who sit in pulpit, council, or throne, hear this: your authority is temporary, your gifts borrowed, your legacy measured by obedience, humility, and love, not by the fear you inspire or the loyalty you extract. Heaven observes all; the Spirit of God does not slumber.

False prophecy masquerading as divine instruction is a snare to the proud, a test to the meek, and a trial for the community. When the faithful confront it with Scripture and discernment, the deception is revealed. Do not mistake silence for consent; do not confuse submission to manipulation with true obedience. Leaders who exalt themselves above God's Word and manipulate loyalty under the guise of prophecy will face the echo of their own pride. What was meant to serve God becomes a weapon against His people, and judgment comes with weight and certainty.

Beware the temptation to silence dissent, to control the narrative, to demand allegiance over alignment. God is not served through fear; His Spirit does not dwell in manipulation. Leadership without love is an empty vessel, and every heart that bleeds under false prophecy is a witness to your accountability. Prophetic authority is a calling to serve, not dominate; to edify, not enslave; to unify, not divide. Those who pervert it for self-interest will see their house built on sand, and the storms of truth will expose the empty throne.

Leaders, take heed: the Spirit of God favors discernment, humility, and accountability. Your power is a tool, not a crown. Every misused word, every hidden manipulation, every silenced voice cries out for vindication. God will respond. The Spirit of division seeks to fracture the obedient and elevate the manipulator. Yet heaven's scales never tip toward injustice. Every act of coercion, every distorted prophetic word, every act of silence is noted, and every faithful heart is remembered.

Leaders are accountable to more than human eyes. The same God who disciplines Saul, exposes Korah, and vindicates Michal watches over all who wield spiritual authority. The veil of secrecy will be torn aside; the truth will rise like a wave over pride. The warning is clear: humility, obedience to Scripture, and love for the flock are the antidotes to division masquerading as prophecy. Reject pride, reject manipulation, reject fear-based control, and honor the Spirit whose fruit is peace, unity, and righteousness.

Ripple Effects Across Society

When prophetic words are distorted into instruments of control, the ripple spreads beyond the walls of the church or ministry. Families fracture, friendships collapse, and communities are burdened with distrust, suspicion, and fear. The consequences of spiritual deception are never contained; they echo across generations. Young women silenced in congregations grow into adults questioning their faith. Children raised under fear and manipulation learn submission to power over submission to God. Society bears the cost of what was intended as spiritual guidance.

The Spirit of division masquerading as prophecy seeps into politics, workplaces, and social networks. Authority becomes toxic; loyalty is weaponized; love is measured by obedience to flawed men rather than faithfulness to God. Trust erodes in every institution where manipulation masquerades as revelation. Communities once vibrant with hope now harbor doubt, resentment, and division. What was meant to unify has fractured society, leaving wounds that fester unseen but felt by all.

The ripple extends to policy, governance, and leadership beyond the church. Leaders who mimic prideful prophets in behavior and ambition distort justice, marginalize voices, and institutionalize oppression. The people bear the consequences. Spiritual division that begins in the sanctuary echoes in the marketplace, the courts, and the halls of power. Communities experience broken families, unhealed trauma, and generations burdened by fear rather than liberated by truth.

Women who are silenced become invisible in the public square, their insights overlooked, their voices suppressed. Societies lose wisdom, compassion, and

172

moral clarity when God's daughters are pushed to the margins.

The ripple effect also reaches the faithful who remain vigilant. They carry the burden of discernment, teaching, and restoration, often at great personal cost. Yet these faithful hearts are the seeds of restoration and the bearers of God's justice. Communities that reject discernment, accountability, and humility in leadership are doomed to repeat cycles of division, manipulation, and silencing. Healing is delayed, and the consequences of prideful leadership multiply.

God's perspective sees every ripple. Every tear, every silenced word, every heart broken under false prophecy is remembered. Justice is coming, and the restoration of integrity and truth will roll like a wave across families, congregations, and nations.

Restoration and God's Glory

God promises vindication for the faithful. Every distorted word, every act of manipulation, every silent voice will be answered with restoration, honor, and divine clarity. The Spirit of God will heal wounds, restore relationships, and expose deception in its entirety. Faithful voices, once silenced, will rise with clarity and authority, no longer bound by fear or oppression. Their words, hearts, and actions will glorify God rather than man, and their witness will bring revival to broken communities.

Leaders who repent, humble themselves, and align with God's Word will experience a transformation that restores credibility, trust, and fruitfulness. God's mercy awaits those who turn from pride to obedience. Communities and congregations will witness the power of God as division is dismantled, unity restored, and truth reigns supreme. The faithful are lifted; the manipulative is exposed. God's justice is unwavering.

Generational consequences are reversed when the Spirit of God restores honor, heals hearts, and equips the silenced to speak boldly. The ripple of restoration spreads farther than the ripple of division ever did. God's glory manifests when His people choose discernment, humility, and truth over manipulation, fear, and pride. Division may linger, but His Spirit will prevail, uniting hearts and communities in righteous authority.

The final wave of prophecy declares that no power, no human ambition, no counterfeit voice can overturn God's plan. His Word, His Spirit, and His judgment endure forever. Every prophetic word that sought to divide, manipulate, or control will be exposed. Every faithful heart that endured in humility will be honored. God's justice is certain, His timing perfect, and His glory unshakable.

The faithful are called to stand, speak, and witness. They must uphold truth, guard unity, and reject manipulation. Their obedience becomes a testimony to God's power to restore, vindicate, and heal. Let every reader understand: the Spirit of division masquerading as prophecy will be defeated. God's justice will prevail. Love, truth, humility, and discernment will rise. And His glory will shine over every heart that seeks Him faithfully, revealing light where darkness once masqueraded.

The Ultimate Danger and Divine Judgment

The Spirit of division masquerading as prophecy, once allowed to operate unchecked, carries a weight of danger that spans generations. It begins quietly, a whisper of misdirection in the ears of the faithful, and grows into a roaring storm, fracturing families, congregations, and societies.

God's eyes are not deceived; every heart, every hidden ambition, every corrupted declaration is known. *"The Lord looks down from heaven on the children of men, to see if there are any who understand, who seek God"* (Psalm 14:2). The silence of those misled is not unnoticed, and the sorrow of the oppressed reaches the throne of heaven.

Leaders who elevate themselves above God's Word, who manipulate love, loyalty, and obedience as Saul did, are treading a path of destruction. The same God who exposed Saul's envy, punished his oppression, and silenced the innocent Michal will execute justice for every modern ruler—religious, political, or sectarian—who weaponizes faith for personal gain. *"Woe unto the shepherds that destroy and scatter the sheep of my pasture! saith the Lord"* (Jeremiah 23:1).

The danger is ultimate because God's judgment is both personal and communal. When the Spirit of division fractures the congregation, those deceived carry unseen scars. Children of the church, women silenced in the corners, youth manipulated by fear, and faithful servants bound by loyalty suffer quietly—but God sees every tear. *"The Lord trieth the righteous: but the wicked and him that loveth violence his soul hateth"* (Psalm 7:10). Every act of deception will be answered; every hidden wound vindicated.

God warns that false prophets, those who mislead the flock under the guise of revelation, will face swift and certain destruction if unrepentant. The proud are held accountable, the manipulative exposed, and the innocent restored. *"But there were also false prophets among the people, even as there shall be false teachers among you... and bring upon themselves swift destruction"* (2 Peter 2:1). The lessons of Michal's silence echo across time: every daughter, every faithful woman, every misled believer will be accounted for in God's eyes.

The ripple of deception is not contained within church walls. It spills into society, politics, and families. Leaders who silence truth, marginalize women, or manipulate justice under the guise of prophecy create structures of oppression that mirror Pharaoh, Saul, and the prideful kings of old. *"Woe unto them that call evil good, and good evil; that put darkness for light, and light for darkness"* (Isaiah 5:20). The judgment is both immediate and prophetic, exposing hidden evil before heaven and men.

God's punishment is thorough. Those who persist in deception, refuse correction, and harden their hearts will face consequences in both time and eternity. *"But the fearful, and unbelieving, and the abominable... shall have their part in the lake which burneth with fire and brimstone"* (Revelation 21:8). Every calculated word that divided the faithful, every act of control, and every silenced voice will be brought to light.

Yet God's judgment is not only punitive—it is restorative. The silenced Michals, the oppressed faithful, and the manipulated congregations will be vindicated. *"The Lord is a God of knowledge, and by him actions are weighed"* (Psalm 7:9). Honor will be restored to the meek, courage elevated in the humble, and truth restored in places where deception once reigned.

The faithful are called vigilance. Test every prophetic word, examine every vision, and measure every declaration against Scripture. *"Beloved, believe not every spirit, but try the spirits whether they are of God"* (1 John 4:1). Your discernment is a shield against the Spirit of division, and your obedience a witness to the glory of God.

The warning to leaders is loud and clear: God despises manipulation, division, and the misuse of authority. *"Woe unto them that are wise in their own eyes, and prudent in their own sight"* (Isaiah 5:21). Just as Saul punished Michal for loving David, so will God bring retribution to those who punish the faithful for doing right. Every attempt to silence, control, or dominate will be overturned in His time.

God's glory will be revealed over every heart that suffered under deception, every woman misled, every congregation divided. The Spirit of division will be exposed, the proud humbled, and the faithful vindicated. *"For the day of the Lord cometh as a thief in the night; ... the earth also and the works that are therein shall be burned up"* (2 Peter 3:10). Let every heart tremble, every leader repent, and every believer rise in discernment, for the Lord's justice and glory will prevail over every hidden evil.

Chapter 18: Exposing the Sin of Racism and the Forgotten Voices in Scripture

One of the most dangerous deceptions that has plagued the church is the idea that the Bible belongs to one race, one culture, or one ethnic group. This lie has been used to justify slavery, segregation, nationalism, and discrimination within the very house of God. Yet when we return to Scripture itself, we discover a different truth: the Word of God was never written for Black or White people—it was written for humanity, for all nations, tribes, and tongues.

At the very beginning of creation, God designed humanity in His image, male and female, without distinction of race or superiority. Genesis does not describe Adam and Eve as belonging to a category of White or Black, but as the parents of all mankind. Race, as we know it today, is a social construct that emerged after sin entered the world and fractured human unity. The divisions we wrestle with are not God's design but man's distortion.

When sin entered the Garden of Eden, Adam and Eve were expelled from their perfect dwelling. It was not their skin color that separated them from God's presence, but their disobedience. From the beginning, God made clear that His concern was not external appearance, but the condition of the heart. Humanity's obsession with race is evidence of our fallen nature, not our divine origin.

As we trace through the Old Testament, we see the interconnectedness of nations and ethnicities within God's unfolding plan. For example, the Kenites—descendants of Moses' Midianite father-in-law—were welcomed into Israel's covenant community and lived among the children of Judah (Judges 1:16). This demonstrates that God's covenant family was never bound by ethnicity alone but by obedience and faith in Him.

The Midianites themselves were descendants of Abraham through Keturah, and though they often opposed Israel, individuals among them—like Hobab, who guided Israel in the wilderness—became instruments of God's purpose. Their story reminds us that God works through all peoples, not just through a single bloodline or culture.

The word *Kenite* is often overlooked in Scripture, yet its meaning reveals a connection to the Canaanite tribes and the Midianites. These were people descended from Ham, the son of Noah, who was a man of color. The presence of Ham's descendants throughout biblical history proves that people of African lineage were woven into God's redemptive plan from the earliest days.

One striking example is the prophet Zephaniah. Many believers read his book without realizing that Zephaniah was a man of African descent. Zephaniah 1:1 introduces him as "the son of Cushi," which directly connects him to Cush, the ancient region of Ethiopia. According to Strong's Concordance, Cush is synonymous with Ethiopia, and Ethiopians are people of dark skin. Zephaniah, then, was a Black man chosen by God to record His Word.

This truth has been hidden from many pulpits, ignored by scholars, and dismissed by those who would rather preserve a Eurocentric narrative of Scripture. Yet it cannot be denied: one of the 39 Old Testament books was written by a man of African descent. This shatters the myth that Black people contributed nothing of significance to God's revelation.

Zephaniah's presence in the biblical canon proves that God transcends race in His selection of vessels. He is no respecter of persons, and He does not choose prophets based on the shade of their skin but on the posture of their heart. By silencing the truth of Zephaniah's ethnicity, the church has robbed generations of believers of the richness of God's diverse kingdom.

The erasure of Black and non-European contributions in Scripture is not accidental—it is part of Satan's strategy of deception. Just as counterfeit prophecy twists God's Word for selfish gain, so too has racism twisted biblical truth to uphold systems of oppression. When the church refuses to acknowledge the fullness of biblical diversity, it participates in a lie.

Another overlooked figure is Ebed-Melech, the Ethiopian eunuch who rescued the prophet Jeremiah from the dungeon (Jeremiah 38:7–13). Ebed-Melech was a man of African descent, marginalized both by race and by his status as a eunuch, yet God used him mightily to preserve the life of His prophet. His courage and compassion shine as a testimony of God's willingness to elevate the humble and use the rejected.

Ebed-Melech's intervention also carries prophetic weight. While Israelite leaders were silent or complicit in Jeremiah's suffering, it was a foreigner—a Cushite—

who acted with justice. This foreshadows the inclusion of the nations in God's plan of salvation and exposes the hypocrisy of God's people when they fail to live by His standard.

God later vindicated Ebed-Melech, promising him protection during the Babylonian invasion because he trusted in the Lord (Jeremiah 39:15–18). This divine commendation affirms that God does not measure worth by nationality or race but by faithfulness. A Cushite eunuch received the promise of life because he feared God when others did not.

When we piece together these biblical accounts, a clear pattern emerges: the narrative of Scripture includes Africans, Middle Easterners, and people of varied ethnic backgrounds as central actors in God's drama of redemption. To deny this truth is to deny the authority of Scripture itself.

Unfortunately, throughout history, the church has been guilty of downplaying or erasing these truths. During the era of transatlantic slavery, Scripture was weaponized to justify racial hierarchy. Passages were selectively taught or distorted to suggest that people of African descent were cursed, inferior, or destined for servitude. This was not biblical truth—it was satanic deception masquerading as doctrine.

The so-called "curse of Ham" is a prime example. Misinterpreted and misapplied, it was used to validate centuries of racism, even though the Bible never declares that Ham's descendants were cursed with black skin or destined for slavery. Such teachings were counterfeit prophecy—lies disguised as divine authority.

In America and other nations shaped by colonialism, this distortion became deeply ingrained. People were no longer seen as simply Americans, Britons, or believers in Christ—they were divided by racial categories: African Americans, Asian Americans, Hispanic Americans, and so on. While cultural identity has value, the overemphasis on division undermines the unity of God's kingdom.

Just as the Kenites and Midianites lived among the Israelites and became part of their story, so too do diverse peoples today form one family under God. The church must recognize that whether one is African American, Asian American, Hispanic, or White American, in Christ, all are simply children of God. National or racial labels cannot define what only the Spirit of adoption establishes.

Paul's declaration in Galatians 3:28 resounds as a rebuke to racism: "There is neither Jew nor Greek, there is neither slave nor free, there is neither male nor female; for you are all one in Christ Jesus." This was not a call to erase cultural identity but to elevate unity in Christ above all other distinctions.

Tragically, the church has often failed to live out this truth. Many pulpits have ignored the sin of racism, treating it as a political issue rather than a spiritual one. Silence in the face of racial injustice is itself a form of complicity, echoing the silence of the pulpit in other areas of sin.

The Destructive Power of Rhetoric and Racism

Throughout history, words have carried the power to heal or to wound, to unify or to divide. What may appear to some as a passing comment, a fiery debate, or a clever piece of rhetoric can, in reality, plant seeds of hatred in the minds of many. When leaders, teachers, or influencers use their platform to degrade another race, ethnicity, or people group, the damage runs deeper than headlines or sound bites—it reaches the very soul of communities. Scripture reminds us that "death and life are in the power of the tongue" (Proverbs 18:21). Careless, divisive speech can destroy lives, reputations, and futures.

One modern incident serves as a painful reminder of this truth. A prominent figure, admired by many, used his influence to stir up rhetoric against a community based on race and ethnicity. He may not have lifted a weapon, but his words acted like daggers, cutting deep into the dignity and worth of people created in the image of God. The tragic outcome of such rhetoric reveals that racism is not always expressed in violent acts first—it often begins in careless, hateful words that pave the way for violence, exclusion, and despair.

Jesus' teaching in Matthew 5:21–22 warns us that murder begins in the heart. Anger, hatred, and resentment, when fueled by fiery rhetoric, can lead to outcomes as destructive as physical violence. A word spoken in malice can strip someone of hope, break down their humanity, and in some cases even push individuals toward self-destruction. This is why God takes both words and intentions seriously. He is not pleased when leaders—whether in politics, media, or even the church—use their voices to divide rather than unite.

The incident also exposes how racism disguises itself in cultural commentary or political rhetoric. What many dismiss as "just words" is actually a form of poison. When those words echo in the hearts of listeners, they stir up animosity and normalize prejudice. Over time, this climate of hostility can destroy lives as surely as any weapon. The Bible tells us plainly: "But I say unto you, that for every idle word man shall speak, they shall give account thereof in the day of judgment" (Matthew 12:36). Racist rhetoric will not escape God's judgment.

God created humanity as one family, tracing back to Adam and Eve, and later reminding us through Paul that in Christ "there is neither Jew nor Greek, bond nor free" (Galatians 3:28). Yet when society entertains rhetoric that divides us by skin color, heritage, or ethnicity, we rebel against God's vision for His people. The incident we are reflecting on shows how quickly racism, fueled by words, can unravel the dignity of an individual and the unity of a community. God is not pleased when His creation is treated with contempt.

We must also recognize the ripple effects of such rhetoric. Words of racism not only destroy one life but also perpetuate cycles of fear, mistrust, and generational trauma. Children grow up hearing these divisive messages and begin to internalize them, either as feelings of superiority or as wounds of inferiority. In either case, the image of God in each person is distorted, and the heart of the gospel—which is reconciliation through Christ—is rejected. This is why the church must speak out against rhetoric that demeans and destroys.

The tragedy of the incident demonstrates how far-reaching the consequences can be when society tolerates racism disguised as free speech. Though nations may permit it, heaven does not endorse it. God holds His people to a higher standard. When rhetoric takes root in hatred, the outcome can be as devastating as the story of Cain and Abel, where jealousy and anger led to murder. The connection between words, hatred, and destruction is undeniable. Our silence in the face of such rhetoric makes us complicit.

This Chapter calls us to see beyond race, ethnicity, and division—to the God who sees all His children as one. The incident we have considered reminds us that racism begins not only in actions but in the heart and on the tongue. God is not pleased with rhetoric that destroys lives because it opposes His very nature of love, justice, and reconciliation. As believers, we are called to resist such language, to speak truth in love, and to live out the gospel that unites rather than divides. In doing so, we embody the heart of Christ, who came not to destroy lives but to save them.

Speaking Truth in an Age of Silencing

In every generation, God raises voices to cry out against injustice and deception. Yet today we live in a climate where political leaders and their administrations seek to silence dissent, and even the news media often becomes cautious, fearful, or compromised in reporting the truth. When truth is filtered, altered, or ignored for the sake of political convenience, the result is the erosion of democracy and the loss of the people's voice. Scripture reminds us: "Woe to those who call evil good, and good evil; who put darkness for light and light for darkness" (Isaiah 5:20).

When leaders spread lies, and media platforms amplify those lies without scrutiny, a nation becomes enslaved to deception. Jesus declared, "You shall know the truth, and the truth shall make you free" (John 8:32). Lies enslave; truth liberates. A democracy cannot survive when its people are denied truth, and the church cannot remain healthy if it imitates this pattern of silence and compromise.

Far too often, the church has followed the culture in its silence. Instead of being prophetic voices that hold leaders accountable, many pastors and Christian leaders have chosen comfort, financial security, or political favor over speaking out. This silence grieves God. Ezekiel 33:6 warns: "But if the watchman sees the sword coming and does not blow the trumpet to warn the people... I will hold the watchman accountable for their blood." Silence in the face of deception is complicity.

Throughout Scripture, God used courageous men and women who refused to stay quiet. Esther, though fearful, stood before the king to expose the plot against her people (Esther 4:14).

Jeremiah, though imprisoned, declared truth to kings who wanted him silenced (Jeremiah 38:6– 9). Zephaniah, a Cushite prophet, spoke to a nation facing judgment. Their courage reminds us that God expects His people to speak truth even when it costs them their position, comfort, or life.

When the meia fails to fact-check leaders' lies and instead spreads half-truths or one-sided reports, it becomes an instrument of manipulation. The prophet Micah warned against leaders and prophets who cry "Peace" when there is no peace (Micah 3:5). Their words comfort the powerful while oppressing the vulnerable. Today's media, when it abandons truth, repeats this same sin.

But the greater indictment rests upon the church. Too many pulpits have exchanged the courage to preach against sin for the comfort of political connections or financial donations. Some leaders, instead of condemning injustice, have taken money to remain silent, allowing corruption to flourish unchallenged. Jesus called such leaders "hirelings" who abandon the sheep when the wolf comes (John 10:12-13).

God is not pleased when the church loses its prophetic voice. Silence in the face of lies is not neutral; it is betrayal. Proverbs 29:18 declares: "Where there is no vision, the people perish." When pastors and spiritual leaders refuse to cast God's vision of justice and holiness, the people wander in confusion, enslaved by political rhetoric instead of anchored in divine truth.

In God's eyes, there are no conservative Christians, liberal Christians, right-wing or left-wing believers. There is only one body, unified under Christ. Paul reminds us: "For we were all baptized by one Spirit to form one body—whether Jews or Gentiles, slave or free" (1 Corinthians 12:13). Dividing Christ's body along political lines is a man-made deception that weakens the witness of the gospel.

When church leaders align themselves with political factions, they risk exchanging the kingdom of God for the kingdoms of men. Jesus warned Pilate, "My kingdom is not of this world" (John 18:36). Yet many churches have made politics their pulpit, echoing party lines instead of proclaiming the gospel. God will hold accountable every leader who misuses His pulpit to advance earthly agendas over heavenly truth.

Silence is not an option. Amos was clear: "Let justice roll down like waters, and righteousness like an ever-flowing stream" (Amos 5:24). Justice and truth are not political issues—they are kingdom issues. When the church refuses to speak against lies, corruption, and exploitation, it has abandoned its calling to be salt and light (Matthew 5:13-16).

Consider Nathan, the prophet who stood before King David and declared, "You are the man!" (2 Samuel 12:7). He risked his life to confront a king with his sin. Or John the Baptist, who boldly rebuked Herod for his immoral actions (Mark

6:18). Both men remind us that God calls His messengers to confront leaders with truth, not flatter them with silence.

When leaders lie, nations stumble. Hosea 4:6 warns, "My people are destroyed for lack of knowledge." If truth is withheld, manipulated, or silenced, the people suffer. Families become divided, communities crumble, and the vulnerable are crushed under the weight of deception. God will not overlook leaders who misuse their influence to promote falsehood.

Likewise, He will not excuse churches that turn a blind eye. Malachi 2:7 declares, "For the lips of a priest ought to preserve knowledge, because he is the messenger of the Lord Almighty." Pastors and leaders are called to guard and proclaim truth. When they exchange this duty for silence, wealth, or influence, they betray both God and His people.

The pattern is clear: when political leaders silence truth, when media echoes their lies, and when the church stays quiet, nations descend into darkness. But God will always raise up a remnant—a people who refuse to bow to falsehood. Just as Daniel stood firm in Babylon and Shadrach, Meshach, and Abednego refused to bow to Nebuchadnezzar's image, so must believers today resist the idols of political power and compromised truth.

The church must recover its prophetic boldness. It must be willing to say what others will not, to confront lies with Scripture, and to expose injustice even when unpopular. Jesus Himself warned: "If these should hold their peace, the stones would immediately cry out" (Luke 19:40). God will not allow silence to cover sin forever.

At the heart of this battle lies the question: Who will the church fear—God or man? Proverbs 29:25 warns, "The fear of man brings a snare: but whoso puts his trust in the Lord shall be safe." Too many leaders fear losing members, money, or influence, when they should fear the judgment of God for failing to shepherd His flock faithfully.

God's way of revealing evil is thorough. He exposes corruption not only in politics but also in the pulpit. Leaders who take money to remain silent, who promote lies to gain influence, or who misuse the gospel for personal gain will be exposed. Luke 12:2–3 promises: "For there is nothing covered that shall not be revealed;

neither hid, that shall not be known."

History proves that silence never protects. Had Esther remained silent, her people would have been destroyed. Had Jeremiah withheld his words, Judah would have been left unprepared for exile. Had Zephaniah hidden his message, the people would have remained in their sin. Silence may preserve temporary safety, but it forfeits eternal accountability.

This is why God is calling His church today to reject political labels, to rise above media manipulation, and to return to the simplicity of His Word. Believers are to be known not for their party but for their proclamation of Christ, not for their silence but for their courage, not for compromise but for truth. "For we cannot do anything against the truth, but only for the truth" (2 Corinthians 13:8).

The message again is clear: God is not mocked, and He will not be pleased with a silent church. He calls His people to speak truth boldly, to resist lies, and to stand united in Christ beyond all political divisions. Whether political leaders, organizational heads, popes, kings, or queens— God will expose every hidden evil. And He will hold accountable not only those who lied, but also those who remained silent when they should have spoken.

When Silence Becomes Sin

In every generation, political leaders and administrations have attempted to silence the voice of truth. When leaders manipulate narratives and suppress facts, the media often becomes a tool rather than a watchdog. Instead of serving the people with honesty, news outlets can be tempted to present a one-sided story, either out of fear, financial pressure, or political influence. When this happens, the democratic right of the people to know the truth is compromised, and a nation begins to stumble.

Truth is not optional in God's eyes. Scripture declares, *"You shall know the truth, and the truth shall make you free"* (John 8:32). When lies dominate the airwaves and leaders speak unchallenged, the people remain in bondage. A society built on deception cannot stand for long. Jesus warned that a house divided against itself cannot stand (Mark 3:25), and when facts are distorted, the very foundation of justice and unity is shaken.

185

The church, sadly, has not always stood as the voice of truth. Too often, religious leaders have remained silent when faced with corruption, racism, and oppression. Some have accepted financial incentives, political favor, or social standing in exchange for their silence. Yet the Word of God makes it clear: *"For we cannot but speak the things which we have seen and heard"* (Acts 4:20). When church leaders refuse to speak, they betray their calling as watchmen on the wall (Ezekiel 33:7–9).

God is not pleased with a silent church. He will hold leaders accountable for their refusal to stand for justice. Silence in the face of lies is complicity. Silence in the face of injustice is approval.

Just as the prophet Isaiah declared, *"Woe to those who call evil good and good evil"* (Isaiah 5:20), so too must the church remember that neutrality in times of moral crisis is not an option.

In God's kingdom, there are no conservative Christians, no liberal Christians, no right-wing or left-wing Christians. There is only the body of Christ. Paul reminds us in Galatians 3:28 that *"there is neither Jew nor Greek, slave nor free, male nor female, for you are all one in Christ Jesus."* To divide the body along political lines is to weaken its witness. Christ came to establish unity in truth, not factions built on worldly ideologies.

History and Scripture are filled with examples of those who refused to stay silent when silence would have been easier. Esther, a young queen in Persia, risked her life to confront the king and save her people. She was reminded by Mordecai that silence was not an option: *"For if you remain silent at this time, relief and deliverance for the Jews will arise from another place… And who knows but that you have come to your royal position for such a time as this?"* (Esther 4:14). Esther understood that silence would cost lives.

Likewise, Nathan the prophet did not stay silent when King David sinned with Bathsheba and murdered her husband Uriah. He confronted David with the truth, declaring, *"You are the man!"* (2 Samuel 12:7). Nathan risked his standing before the king, but he chose God's approval over David's favor. Through his boldness, David repented and turned back to God.

The Cushite writer in 2 Samuel 18 was another example of truth-telling. When David's son Absalom was killed, the Cushite messenger did not sugarcoat the news. He told the king directly, "May the enemies of my lord the king and all who rise to harm you be like that young man" (2 Samuel 18:32). Speaking the truth cost him nothing less than delivering grief to the king's heart, but he carried the message faithfully.

In the New Testament, John the Baptist refused to stay silent against political corruption. He openly rebuked Herod for his unlawful marriage and immoral lifestyle. His boldness eventually cost him his life, but Jesus declared him the greatest of those born of women (Matthew 11:11). His legacy reminds us that silence in the face of sin is never God's way.

Today, many churches have allowed politics to divide the body. Pastors often preach with one eye on their congregations and another eye on the approval of politicians. Instead of proclaiming the gospel of repentance, they water down the message to keep their funding and their influence. This is not new; the prophets of old faced the same temptation. Yet Jeremiah 23:28 commands: *"Let the prophet who has a dream tell the dream, but let the one who has my word speak it faithfully. For what has straw to do with grain?"*

When leaders and churches fail to speak, the people suffer. Proverbs 29:18 warns, *"Where there is no vision, the people perish."* Vision comes from truth, and truth comes from God. A nation without truth is a nation stumbling in the dark. Lies cannot build justice, and silence cannot protect the oppressed.

God has always revealed evil, whether in the church or in the palace. Pharaoh was exposed when Moses confronted him. Nebuchadnezzar was humbled when Daniel spoke truth to him.

Belshazzar was judged when the handwriting appeared on the wall. No king, pope, president, or prime minister is exempt from God's authority. As Daniel declared, *"The Most High rules in the kingdom of men and gives it to whomever He chooses"* (Daniel 4:32).

The problem today is not that evil exists; it always has. The problem is that the church often refuses to confront it. Too many pulpits are filled with motivational speeches rather than prophetic truth. Too many leaders are more concerned with filling pews than saving souls. But God does not measure success by numbers; He measures it by obedience.

Silence in this generation is costing lives. Racism continues to wound communities. Violence fills the streets. Lies corrupt the airwaves. And while these things are happening, many leaders remain silent because they fear losing their platforms. Yet Jesus warned in Matthew 10:33, *"But whoever denies me before men, I will also deny before my Father who is in heaven."* Silence, in effect, is denial.

The church must reclaim its prophetic voice. It must declare that no leader is above God's law, no administration can hide from His justice, and no media outlet can distort His truth without consequence. As Amos 5:24 declares, *"But let justice roll on like a river, righteousness like a never-failing stream!"* That is the calling of the church to let justice and truth flow freely.

God's people must remember that the gospel is not tied to political parties. The gospel transcends political ideologies. The early church lived under the oppression of Rome, yet they did not sell out the truth to please Caesar. They proclaimed Jesus as Lord, even when it cost them their lives.

If the church of today were to recover that same boldness, nations could be transformed. If pulpits thundered with the Word of God instead of political talking points, corruption would be confronted, and truth would shine. Paul reminded Timothy: *"Preach the word; be ready in season and out of season; reprove, rebuke, and exhort, with complete patience and teaching"* (2 Timothy 4:2). That call has not changed.

We must remember that silence is not neutral; it is a partnership with darkness. Ephesians 5:11 commands us: *"Have nothing to do with the fruitless deeds of darkness but rather expose them."* Exposure requires speaking out, even when it costs reputation or influence.

Esther, Nathan, John the Baptist, and the Cushite messenger all remind us that silence has never been God's way. God raises courageous voices in every generation. He is raising them now. The question is, will the church listen and join them, or will it stay silent and be judged alongside the corrupt?

The time has come for believers to stand together—not as conservatives or liberals, not as right or left—but as one body in Christ. Jesus is not divided. His Word is not bound by politics. His kingdom is not built on lies. And His church cannot afford to stay silent. If we are to honor Him, we must proclaim the truth boldly, expose evil faithfully, and trust that God will protect and reward those who stand for righteousness.

When political leaders distort the truth and administrations suppress accountability, the media is tempted to report one-sided narratives. At the same time, many churches and leaders remain quiet, often swayed by money, fear, or political influence. God is not pleased with silence.

Throughout Scripture, men and women of faith like Esther, Nathan, John the Baptist, and the Cushite (Ethiopian) messenger from the tribe of Ham chose to speak boldly in the face of power, risking their lives to reveal truth. God calls His church today to do the same, for in His eyes, there are no political labels, only one unified body of Christ, called to be a prophetic voice in a world filled with deception.

Chapter 19: Political Violence, Nationalism, and the Counterfeit Church.

"Woe to those who make unjust laws, to those who issue oppressive decrees, to deprive the poor of their rights and withhold justice from the oppressed of my people."
— *Isaiah 10:1–2 (NIV)*

Political violence is the misuse of power to silence, oppress, and control. It is not only seen in wars and riots but also in policies, rhetoric, and systemic injustices that strip people of dignity and freedom. When governments or leaders weaponize authority to serve selfish interests, they unleash violence that poisons entire societies.

The Bible warns us about rulers who pervert justice for gain. Micah 3:9 declares, *"Hear this, you leaders of Jacob, you rulers of Israel, who despise justice and distort all that is right."* Political violence often begins in such distortions, when leaders craft systems that benefit the powerful while crushing the powerless.

Christian nationalism today is one of the most dangerous distortions of the gospel. It seeks to blend faith with politics, convincing people that loyalty to a nation or race is equal to loyalty to God. But Jesus made clear: His Kingdom is not of this world (John 18:36). To merge nationalism with Christianity is to create a counterfeit gospel.

The rise of Christian nationalism is often fueled by fear of losing cultural dominance, fear of diversity, and fear of change. Instead of trusting God's sovereignty, many seek to protect their own traditions and privileges by wrapping them in the language of faith. This idolatry not only betrays Christ but also fuels political violence.

A troubling reality is tat many who call themselves Conservative Christians are lending their support to nationalist ideologies and even white supremacy. They do so under the guise of "preserving Christian values," yet their actions betray the gospel. Supporting policies that marginalize the poor, immigrants, and people of color is not Christianity—it is hypocrisy.

White supremacy is not merely political; it is spiritual. It is a false religion that elevates one race as superior and others as inferior. In truth, it is rooted in pride—the very sin that caused Lucifer to fall. Whenever the church aligns with white supremacy, it aligns with Satan's kingdom of pride, hatred, and division.

The danger of the counterfeit church is that it looks holy on the outside but is corrupt on the inside. Jesus warned against this in Matthew 7:15-16: *"Beware of false prophets, who come to you in sheep's clothing, but inwardly they are ravenous wolves. You will know them by their fruits."* The fruits of the counterfeit church are violence, racism, exclusion, and hypocrisy.

A counterfeit church may use the name of Jesus, but it denies His character. True religion cares for the orphan, the widow, and the marginalized (James 1:27). Counterfeit religion, however, cares only for power, privilege, and dominance. It creates political violence because it serves the agenda of men rather than the justice of God.

The Scriptures show us that God has always opposed nations and leaders who build their empires on oppression. Pharaoh enslaved the Israelites, but God brought judgment on Egypt.

Nebuchadnezzar exalted himself, but God humbled him to eat grass like an animal (Daniel 4:33). Herod sought to kill the Messiah, but God struck him down. Political violence always invites divine judgment.

Those who support nationalism and white supremacy fail to exercise critical thinking. Paul warned Timothy about such deception, saying, *"They will turn their ears away from the truth and turn aside to myths"* (2 Timothy 4:4). When people accept propaganda instead of truth, they surrender their minds and become pawns in systems of oppression.

Critical thinking is a gift from God. Proverbs 18:13 reminds us, *"To answer before listening— that is folly and shame."* When believers abandon reason and discernment, they lose the ability to test spirits and recognize counterfeit teachings. This intellectual laziness allows political violence to spread unchallenged.

Every human being is created in the image of God (Genesis 1:27). This foundational truth dismantles racism, nationalism, and political dominance. To treat anyone as lesser because of skin color, culture, or language is to deny God's creative design. A Christian nation is not built on the supremacy of one race but on the unity of all people under Christ.

Paul reminds us in Galatians 3:28, *"There is neither Jew nor Gentile, slave nor free, nor is there male and female, for you are all one in Christ Jesus."* This radical equality is the heart of the gospel. Nationalism and white supremacy are antithetical to this truth because they divide where Christ unites.

Freedom of speech and cultural diversity are not threats to Christianity—they are reflections of God's creation. Pentecost in Acts 2 showed the Spirit of God falling on people of many languages and cultures. Instead of enforcing uniformity, the Spirit celebrated diversity. Christian nationalism, however, tries to erase diversity in the name of conformity, which directly opposes the work of the Holy Spirit.

The root of political violence in many nations, particularly in the United States, is white supremacy. This false ideology masquerades as religion but is actually idolatry. It places whiteness on the throne instead of Christ. When the church fails to denounce this evil, it becomes a counterfeit institution that leads people into sin rather than salvation.

Jesus warned His disciples that in the last days false Christs and false prophets would appear, performing signs and wonders to deceive even the elect (Matthew 24:24). Christian nationalism is one such deception. It uses the language of faith to advance the goals of politics, confusing sincere believers who think they are defending Christianity when, in truth, they are defending idols of power.

True Christianity is marked not by dominance but by service. Jesus washed the feet of His disciples (John 13:14-15) as an example of humility and love. Nationalism, however, seeks to dominate, conquer, and control. The counterfeit church embraces this spirit of dominance, preferring political influence to spiritual integrity.

When political violence becomes normalized, it numbs the conscience of a nation. People grow accustomed to seeing hatred, injustice, and exclusion. The prophet Jeremiah lamented, *"Are they ashamed of their loathsome conduct? No, they have no shame at all; they do not even know how to blush"* (Jeremiah 6:15). In the same way, the church today risks losing its ability to blush when it excuses the violence of nationalism.

The conservative Christian movement, when aligned with white supremacy, often claims it is protecting "biblical values." But these values are selectively applied. They fight against abortion yet ignore systemic racism. They defend religious liberty yet suppress the liberty of immigrants, Muslims, or people of color. Such hypocrisy exposes their alignment not with Christ but with cultural preservation.

The Bible makes it clear that God detests unjust scales (Proverbs 11:1). Whenever one group is given privilege at the expense of another, injustice is present. White supremacy is nothing more than a rigged scale that favors whiteness while denying the full humanity of others. This imbalance is political violence at its core.

We must not forget that Jesus Himself was born into a context of political violence. Herod attempted to murder Him as an infant to protect his throne (Matthew 2:16). Later, He was crucified by the state under pressure from religious leaders. The gospel is not silent about political violence—it reveals that God's Son endured it and overcame it.

One of the most dangerous aspects of the counterfeit church is its ability to blind believers into thinking they are serving God while actually serving evil. Jesus warned in John 16:2 that there would be those who kill in the name of God, believing they are offering Him service. Christian nationalism fulfills this prophecy when it justifies violence, racism, and exclusion in the name of Christ.

The church must recover its prophetic voice. In the Old Testament, prophets like Amos and Isaiah denounced nations for trampling on the poor and perverting justice. Amos 5:24 still calls out: *"But let justice roll on like a river, righteousness like a never-failing stream!"* Silence in the face of political violence makes the church complicit in the very evil it is supposed to confront.

Critical thinking is an act of discipleship. Romans 12:2 instructs believers not to conform to the pattern of this world but to be transformed by the renewing of their minds. Renewed minds are discerning minds. When the church fails to teach discernment, believers are left vulnerable to propaganda, false teachers, and counterfeit movements.

White supremacy is fundamentally opposed to the gospel because it rejects the universality of God's love. John 3:16 does not say, "For God so loved the white world," but "For God so loved the world." Every race, every culture, every tribe is included in God's redemptive plan.

Nationalism that elevates one group above another is a direct insult to the cross of Christ.

The root sin of white supremacy is pride. Proverbs 16:18 warns, *"Pride goes before destruction, a haughty spirit before a fall."* Nations and churches built on the pride of racial superiority are destined for destruction. Humility, not pride, is the foundation of true Christian community.

Political violence thrives wherever fear is greater than faith. When Christians fear losing power, status, or influence, they may turn to nationalism as a solution. Yet Scripture reminds us that *"God has not given us a spirit of fear, but of power and of love and of a sound mind"* (2 Timothy 1:7). Fear-driven politics contradicts faith-driven discipleship.

The early church modeled what it means to live beyond nationalism. They lived under Rome yet refused to worship Caesar. They honored God above the emperor, even at the cost of their lives. Their citizenship was in heaven (Philippians 3:20). The modern church must reclaim this heavenly perspective and reject the idolatry of wrapping faith in the flag.

Counterfeit religion always aligns itself with the powerful. But Jesus aligned Himself with the poor, the marginalized, and the oppressed. Luke 4:18 records His mission: *"The Spirit of the Lord is on me, because he has anointed me to proclaim good news to the poor. He has sent me to proclaim freedom for the prisoners and recovery of sight for the blind, to set the oppressed free."* Any church that supports oppression has abandoned the mission of Christ.

Political violence is often justified by twisting Scripture. Slaveholders once misused the Bible to defend slavery, just as some today misuse it to defend racism and nationalism. Peter warned about such distortions, saying, *"Ignorant and unstable people distort [the Scriptures], as they do the other Scriptures, to their own destruction"* (2 Peter 3:16).

The spirit of nationalism is divisive. Paul warned against factions in the church, saying, *"I follow Paul," "I follow Apollos," "I follow Cephas," "I follow Christ." Is Christ divided?* (1 Corinthians 1:12 13). Nationalism says, "I follow America," or "I follow my race," but the gospel says, "I follow Christ."

We must confront the lie that America or any nation is a "Christian nation." No nation can be Christian; only people can be. Nations are earthly institutions, prone to sin and corruption. The church is the body of Christ, set apart to live differently. To equate a nation with the Kingdom of God is a dangerous deception.

Jesus rebuked His disciples when they argued over who was greatest among them. He said, *"The greatest among you will be your servant"* (Matthew 23:11). Nationalism, however, thrives on greatness, "making nations great again," but greatness in God's eyes is measured by humility and service, not dominance.

The counterfeit church thrives when believers fail to test the fruit of movements. Jesus said, *"By their fruit you will recognize them"* (Matthew 7:20). The fruit of nationalism is division, hatred, violence, and pride. The fruit of Christ is love, joy, peace, patience, kindness, and self-control (Galatians 5:22-23). The contrast is undeniable.

Political violence is seductive because it promises safety, order, and power. But in reality, it leads to chaos and destruction. Proverbs 14:12 warns, *"There is a way that appears to be right, but in the end, it leads to death."* Nationalism appears righteous to many, but its end is death— death of justice, death of truth, and death of compassion.

The church cannot claim to follow the Prince of Peace while endorsing movements of violence. Isaiah 9:6 calls Christ the *Prince of Peace*, not the prince of domination. A church that blesses violence has forsaken its Prince and embraced a counterfeit king.

White supremacy is also idolatry because it turns race into a god. The first commandment says, *"You shall have no other gods before me"* (Exodus 20:3). Whenever a church elevates race, culture, or nation above Christ, it bows to a false idol. This idolatry must be torn down.

Paul confronted Peter when Peter separated himself from Gentile believers out of fear of the circumcision group (Galatians 2:11-12). Peter's hypocrisy reflected nationalism within the church. Paul reminded him that the gospel is not about separation but about unity in Christ. Likewise, the modern church must confront hypocrisy that divides along racial or political lines.

The counterfeit church often masquerades as "defenders of truth." But truth is not about slogans or political talking points—it is about Christ Himself, who declared, *"I am the way, the truth, and the life"* (John 14:6). If a church promotes lies, distortions, or propaganda, it is not defending truth but undermining it.

Critical thinking must be cultivated in discipleship. Believers must learn to ask: Does this teaching align with Scripture? Does this movement bear the fruit of the Spirit? Does it reflect the character of Christ? Without such questions, the church becomes gullible and vulnerable to manipulation.

The prophets often warned nations that trusted in military might or political alliances instead of God. Isaiah 31:1 declares, *"Woe to those who go down to Egypt for help, who rely on horses, who trust in the multitude of their chariots... but do not look to the Holy One of Israel."* Christian nationalism makes the same mistake—trusting in political power rather than the power of God.

The misuse of religion to justify political violence is nothing new. Caiaphas, the high priest, justified Jesus' execution by claiming, *"That one man should die for the people than that the whole nation perish"* (John 11:50). He twisted religion for political expedience, much like counterfeit churches twist Christianity to protect their power.

We must remember that judgment begins in the house of God (1 Peter 4:17). Before God judges nations, He cleanses His church. If the church continues to endorse political violence, nationalism, and racism, it will face God's refining fire. This is not a threat but a promise of His holiness.

The world is watching the church. When outsiders see believers excusing racism or violence, they rightly question the authenticity of our faith. Jesus said, *"By this everyone will know that you are my disciples, if you love one another"* (John 13:35). If love is absent, discipleship is counterfeit.

God is not impressed by churches filled with crowds if those crowds are filled with hatred. Amos 5:21-23 records God saying, *"I hate, I despise your religious festivals; your assemblies are a stench to me."* When worship is divorced from justice, it becomes an offense to God.

Christian nationalism often claims to defend freedom, yet it restricts freedom for those who are different. True freedom is found in Christ, who said, *"If the Son sets you free, you will be free indeed"* (John 8:36). Freedom in Christ is for all races, all nations, all people, not just a select few.

The danger of the counterfeit church is not only what it supports but also what it ignores. Silence on injustice is itself violence. James 4:17 reminds us, *"If anyone, then, knows the good they ought to do and doesn't do it, it is sin for them."* A silent church is a sinful church.

Nationalism thrives on exclusion, but the gospel thrives on inclusion. Ephesians 2:14 declares that Christ *"has destroyed the barrier, the dividing wall of hostility."* The cross is God's answer to division. Any church that rebuilds walls of hostility is working against the very work of Christ.

The fundamental root cause of political violence in America—and in many parts of the world is the idol of white supremacy. This false god has created centuries of oppression, segregation, and injustice. Until the church names this sin and repents, it will remain trapped in complicity.

But the good news is this: God is raising a remnant church that refuses to bow to nationalism or counterfeit religion. This remnant loves truth, embraces justice, and walks humbly with God.

Though political violence may rage, the Kingdom of God will prevail. Revelation 11:15 assures us: *"The kingdom of the world has become the kingdom of our Lord and of his Messiah, and he will reign for ever and ever."*

Prayer
Heavenly Father,

We come before You in humility, acknowledging that Your Kingdom is not of this world. Lord, forgive us for the times we have confused loyalty to politics, culture, or power with obedience to You. We repent for any complicity in injustice, hatred, or division, whether through silence or action.

Father, grant us discernment to recognize counterfeit faith, performative religion, and teachings that twist Your Word for selfish gain. Strengthen our hearts to resist Christian nationalism, racism, and white supremacy, and fill us with Your Spirit of love, justice, and wisdom.

Teach us to love all people as Your image-bearers, to act justly, and to walk humbly with You. Raise a faithful remnant in the church that boldly confronts hidden evil and stands as salt and light in the world. Protect us from fear, guide our minds with truth, and help us live lives that honor You above all earthly powers.

We pray for Your Kingdom to advance in our hearts, our churches, and our nations. Let Your justice roll like a river and Your righteousness shine as a never-failing stream. May Your Name be glorified, Your people awakened, and Your will be done on earth as it is in heaven.

In the mighty name of Jesus Christ, Amen.

Chapter 20: The Role of Lucifer and the Chief Prosecutor in Heaven

From the very beginning of creation, Scripture unveils a hidden drama that unfolds not only on earth but also in the heavenly courts. At the center of this conflict is Lucifer, the fallen angel, who once basked in the glory of God's presence but chose rebellion over worship. His fall from heaven (Isaiah 14:12–15; Ezekiel 28:12–19) marked the birth of evil, deception, and the spirit of accusation. The Bible portrays Lucifer not only as the enemy of God but also as the "accuser of the brethren" (Revelation 12:10), a role that mirrors a chief prosecutor in the court of heaven.

In ancient times, the prosecutor's duty was to present charges against the accused, to expose their faults, and to demand judgment. Lucifer, in his corrupted pride, assumed that role in the heavenly courtroom. His strategy was not simply to rebel against God but to undermine His creation by highlighting the sins, flaws, and failures of humanity. As the accuser, he sought to challenge the justice and holiness of God Himself.

The Heavenly Courtroom

The imagery of a heavenly courtroom appears multiple times in Scripture. In Job 1–2, Satan stands before God and presents accusations against Job, suggesting that Job only serves God because of divine blessings. Similarly, in Zechariah 3:1–2, the prophet sees Joshua the high priest standing before the angel of the Lord while Satan stands at his right hand "to accuse him." These passages unveil a sobering reality: Satan's accusations are not abstract; they are deliberate, strategic, and aimed at undermining the believer's standing before God.

Yet even in this courtroom scene, God provides the counter. In Zechariah's vision, the Lord rebukes Satan, saying, "The Lord who has chosen Jerusalem rebuke you! Is not this man a burning stick snatched from the fire?" (Zechariah 3:2). In other words, God Himself stands as the defender of His people. While Lucifer acts as prosecutor, Jesus Christ is both our advocate and our righteousness (1 John 2:1; Romans 8:33–34).

Lucifer's Strategy of Accusation

Lucifer's accusations are rooted in truth twisted by malice. He points out humanity's sins, weaknesses, and failures, demanding that God enforce His own standard of holiness. In doing so, he attempts to pit God's justice against His mercy. This is why Revelation 12 calls him "the accuser of our brothers and sisters, who accuses them before our God day and night." His persistence shows the intensity of his hatred toward believers and his determination to nullify the grace of God.

Christian author A.W. Tozer once observed that "Satan's greatest weapon is man's ignorance of God." When believers fail to understand God's character, they become vulnerable to accusation and condemnation. The enemy whispers lies into the believer's mind, suggesting that God cannot forgive, that grace is insufficient, or that one's past disqualifies them from God's future. These accusations mirror his heavenly strategy to erode confidence in God's love and mercy.

Christ the Advocate

But the Scriptures are clear: while Lucifer prosecutes, Christ advocates. The apostle John comforts believers with these words: "If anybody does sin, we have an advocate with the Father, Jesus Christ, the Righteous One" (1 John 2:1). In a courtroom, the advocate stands by the accused, defending their cause, presenting evidence for their innocence, and interceding on their behalf. Christ, by His shed blood, does not simply argue our case; He embodies our justification.

Derek Prince, in his teachings on spiritual warfare, emphasized that "Satan has no legal claim over a believer who is covered by the blood of Christ." This truth is central to understanding the believer's defense. The blood of Christ nullifies every accusation, silences every charge, and disarms every scheme of the enemy. It is not our righteousness that speaks on our behalf, but the righteousness of Christ imputed to us (2 Corinthians 5:21).

Many misunderstand Lucifer's original responsibility in heaven before his fall. Contrary to popular belief, he was not the angel leading worship but a member of God's heavenly court, functioning as a chief prosecutor (Ezekiel 28:12–15).

Lucifer's name, derived from the Latin *lux* (light) and *ferre* (to bring), means "light bringer." His role was to clarify and expose, bringing matters to light for judgment and accountability. Throughout Scripture, the devil, also referred to as Satan, a Hebrew title meaning "accuser," functions consistently in this role: tempting Adam and Eve (Genesis 3), accusing Job (Job 1–2), testing Joshua the High Priest (Zechariah 3), and tempting Jesus Christ (Matthew 4). C. S. Lewis, in *The Screwtape Letters*, illustrates how Satan operates as a master of accusation and deception, seeking to manipulate human thought and hinder obedience to God's Word.

Lucifer's fall occurred because pride corrupted his role. Ezekiel 28:15 confirms he was blameless at creation but became defiant, attempting to exalt himself above God, which ultimately resulted in his expulsion from heaven. A. W. Tozer, in *The Knowledge of the Holy*, reminds the Church that understanding Satan's methods clarifies the importance of discernment and spiritual vigilance. His work is to expose sin and confusion, not to lead worship.

The spirit of divination masquerading as prophecy today operates similarly: it misleads, manipulates, and seduces under the guise of spiritual authority, often cloaked in persuasive language or religious performance. Leonard Ravenhill, in *Why Revival Tarries*, stresses that deception and manipulation within the Church often mimic spiritual authority, leading believers astray while cloaked in appearances of piety or prophecy. True prophecy aligns with God's Word, edifies the Church, and points people to holiness, repentance, and obedience. False prophecy seeks self-exaltation, control, or gain, reflecting the methods of Satan in heaven and on earth.

Lucifer's original role and subsequent fall provide critical insight into spiritual deception. Scripture, Lewis, Tozer, and Ravenhill collectively warn the Church to discern genuine prophetic ministry from manipulative spirits masquerading as divine messengers. Lucifer seeks to act as prosecutor, accusing God's people in the heavenly courtroom, but his power is limited and ultimately silenced by Christ's sacrifice. What he intends for condemnation, God transforms into testimony of grace. Believers must recognize his tactics but stand firm in their identity in Christ.

The cross guarantees our acquittal, and the resurrection secures our defense. No accusation can stand against the blood of Jesus. As Paul declares, "Who will bring any charge against those whom God has chosen? It is God who justifies" (Romans 8:33).

Acts 16:16-18 recounts the story of a young slave girl possessed by a spirit of divination, who followed Paul and Silas, proclaiming false information. This passage illustrates how deceptive spirits can infiltrate communities, even masquerading as spiritual authority. The spirit of divination in the modern Church often manifests subtly, influencing decisions, sowing confusion, or creating dependency on human intermediaries rather than God.

Recognizing the spirit of divination is essential for protecting the Church from hidden evil. Scripture, Lewis, Tozer, and Ravenhill collectively affirm that vigilance, holiness, and discernment safeguard believers and ensure ministries reflect God's truth rather than human ambition or demonic influence. Scripture provides clear guidelines for discernment. 1 John 4:1 instructs believers to *"test the spirits to see whether they are from God."* This includes evaluating words, characters, and alignment with Scripture.

A key sign of the spirit of divination is the distortion of God's truth to satisfy selfish ambitions, control others, or achieve fame and recognition. It often masquerades as prophecy, wisdom, or Churches can unknowingly cultivate this spirit when they prioritize entertainment, prosperity, or numerical growth over holiness, obedience, and doctrinal fidelity. Scripture provides clear guidelines for discernment.

1 John 4:1 instructs believers to *"test the spirits to see whether they are from God."* This includes evaluating words, characters, and alignment with Scripture. Lewis emphasizes that discernment is not merely intellectual; it requires spiritual sensitivity and humility. The Holy Spirit enables the Church to recognize and resist deception.

The Scriptures present us with a sobering reality: the Church is not only the Bride of Christ, prepared for eternal union with her Savior, but also the object of Satan's accusation and hostility. From the moment Lucifer rebelled against the Most High, he took upon himself the role of prosecutor, the adversary who opposes God's people. In Hebrew, "Satan" literally means "accuser" or "adversary," a title that describes his continual attempt to bring charges against believers in the courtroom of heaven.

Revelation 12:10 speaks of Satan as "the accuser of our brethren, who accused them before our God day and night." This imagery is not poetic exaggeration but a spiritual reality: Satan's role has been to highlight the failures, sins, and weaknesses of God's people, presenting them as evidence against the Church's worthiness. In doing so, he seeks to undermine both the credibility of the saints and the glory of God's saving grace.

The book of Job gives us a powerful glimpse into this heavenly courtroom. Job, described as "blameless and upright," was brought into trial not because of hidden sin but because Satan demanded the right to test his integrity. Here we see Lucifer acting as prosecutor, attempting to prove that Job's faith was shallow and self-serving. God permitted the trial, not because He delights in suffering, but because He reveals hidden evil and exposes the counterfeit work of the adversary.

This role of prosecutor is not merely directed at individuals but at the Church collectively. In every age, Satan has sought to discredit the Body of Christ, highlighting hypocrisy, corruption, and weakness. His accusations often contain fragments of truth, but they are twisted and weaponized to obscure the grace and forgiveness of God. The Church, therefore, stands on trial in the sight of both heaven and earth, its witness scrutinized by angels, demons, and men.

In this cosmic drama, it is crucial to recognize that Lucifer is not a coequal with God. He is a created being who fell from grace, consumed by pride. His role as prosecutor is permitted for a time, but ultimately, it serves God's higher purpose. Through accusation, trial, and refinement, God reveals what is genuine and exposes what is counterfeit. The Church, purified by fire, emerges not as a defeated defendant but as a victorious bride clothed in the righteousness of Christ.

Counterfeit prophecy thrives in the shadows of accusation. When the adversary stands to accuse, false voices often rise to mislead, offering distorted interpretations of God's will. Such prophecies flatter, confuse, or condemn without the redemptive truth of the gospel. This is why discernment is vital: the Church must learn to distinguish between the Spirit of truth and the lying spirit that seeks to mimic divine revelation.

The prophet Zechariah provides another vivid scene of this heavenly prosecution. In Zechariah 3, Joshua the high priest stands before the angel of the Lord, clothed in filthy garments, while Satan stands at his right hand to accuse him. Here again, the prosecutor presents evidence of guilt. Yet the Lord Himself rebukes Satan and commands that Joshua's garments be changed, symbolizing the righteousness that comes by grace. The accuser is silenced not by denial of guilt but by the covering of God's mercy.

This passage teaches us that God reveals hidden evil not to condemn His people but to cleanse and restore them. Satan may point out the dirt, but God provides the garment of salvation. Thus, while the Church may be placed on trial, it is ultimately defended by the intercession of Christ, our Advocate with the Father (1 John 2:1). In this way, the accusations of Lucifer serve only to magnify the sufficiency of the cross.

Lucifer's strategy has always been twofold: accusation and deception. Where he cannot destroy the Church by direct assault, he seeks to corrupt it through counterfeit prophecy, false doctrine, and compromised leadership. By disguising himself as "an angel of light" (2 Corinthians 11:14), he lures many into believing his lies are prophetic insight. In this sense, the courtroom and the battlefield overlap: accusation weakens from within, while deception leads astray from without.

The modern Church faces this same prosecutorial attack. Scandals, divisions, moral failures, and false teachings are broadcast to the world, becoming fodder for the adversary's accusations. Yet, Scripture reminds us that judgment begins in the house of God (1 Peter 4:17). When God allows hidden evil to be exposed, it is not to destroy His people but to refine them. Every exposure is a summons to repentance, a call to realign with the truth of Christ.

One of the greatest deceptions in modern times is the elevation of self above Scripture. Lucifer, in his fall, declared, "I will ascend…I will be like the Most High" (Isaiah 14:13-14). This same spirit of pride seeps into counterfeit prophecy, where men and women claim visions and revelations that exalt their own voice above the Word of God. Here, the adversary whispers into human pride, turning prophets into performers and pulpits into stages of self-glorification.

The prosecuting nature of Satan finds agreement in such false voices, for when prophecy is stripped of God's heart of redemption, it becomes an instrument of condemnation. Many are led astray by words that sound spiritual but carry no grace, leaving believers burdened rather than freed. This, too, is part of Lucifer's deception: to replace the comfort of the Holy Spirit with the cold weight of accusation disguised as prophecy.

Christ, however, demonstrates the perfect answer to the accusation. When Satan tempted Him in the wilderness, the enemy twisted Scripture to bring charges against the Son of God. But Jesus responded with the unshakable truth of God's Word, saying, "It is written." In doing so, He modeled how the Church should respond when placed on trial: not by argument or self-defense, but by standing on the authority of God's Word.

Hidden evil often lurks undetected in the Church until the season of trial. God, in His wisdom, allows accusation to bring it to light. This is not to shame His people, but to cleanse the Bride for the return of Christ. When corruption in leadership, hidden sin, or false teaching is exposed, it is evidence that heaven's courtroom is active and that God's Spirit is still refining His people.

The adversary, however, delights in exploiting these exposures. He will magnify the failures of the Church before the world, presenting them as evidence that Christianity itself is fraudulent. This is why believers must remember that while the Church may stumble, Christ never fails. The true testimony of the gospel is not the perfection of men but the perfection of the Savior who redeems them.

The Church on trial is not abandoned in its defense. Christ is not only the Lamb slain for our sins but also the Advocate who pleads our case before the Father. Whereas Lucifer acts as the prosecutor, Christ stands as the defense attorney. He does not argue about our innocence but presents His own blood as sufficient covering for our guilt. The verdict, therefore, is not condemnation but justification, for "there is now no condemnation for those who are in Christ Jesus" (Romans 8:1).

Yet, we must not ignore the warning that counterfeit prophecy is increasing in these last days. Jesus Himself cautioned in Matthew 24:24 that false prophets would arise, showing signs and wonders to deceive, if possible, even the elect. The adversary's strategy is not only to accuse but also to counterfeit. In the courtroom of heaven, he points to our failures; in the marketplace of religion, he floods us with false voices.

God's revelation of hidden evil includes exposing such false ministries. Many who prophesy for profit, manipulate with charisma, or distort Scripture for gain are being unmasked in this hour. What may look like a scandal is, in truth, divine exposure. Just as Jesus overturned the tables of the money changers in the temple, so too is He cleansing His house today. Exposure, though painful, is a gift of mercy, protecting the Church from deeper deception.

The Church must not despise this refining work. Too often, believers grieve when leaders fall or when ministries collapse. Yet these exposures are the courtroom verdicts of heaven, declaring that what was built on deception cannot stand. For the Bride to be pure, she must be freed from counterfeit coverings. Thus, every exposure is both a warning and an invitation: a warning against falsehood, and an invitation to return to holiness.

In the end, the prosecutor will be silenced forever. Revelation 20:10 assures us that the accuser will be cast into the lake of fire, no longer able to bring charges against the saints. Until that day, the Church remains on trial, but it does so under the defense of Christ's intercession and the refining fire of the Holy Spirit. The question is not whether we will be accused, but whether we will stand clothed in our righteousness or in His.

The adversary's prosecutorial role is especially dangerous because it often mirrors the very language of truth. Satan rarely fabricates outlandish lies; instead, he distorts partial truths, presenting them without the context of grace. He points to sin but not to forgiveness, to weakness but not to the Spirit's strength, to failure but not to redemption. In this way, his accusations are persuasive because they highlight what is real but strip it of God's eternal perspective.

This explains why counterfeit prophecy is so alluring. A false prophet may speak accurately about circumstances or reveal hidden knowledge, but without the Spirit of God, such words are not redemptive. They may sound correct, but they do not lead people closer to Christ. In fact, Satan's most effective counterfeit is prophecy that resembles truth but lacks the heart of the Gospel. Such words leave hearers condemned, confused, or puffed up with pride instead of humbled before the Lord.

Scripture consistently portrays Satan as one who infiltrates religious spaces. In Job's account, he appears "among the sons of God" before the throne. In the New Testament, he plants tares among the wheat. Paul warns that "false apostles, deceitful workers, disguising themselves as apostles of Christ" will arise (2 Corinthians 11:13). This infiltration shows that Lucifer does not only attack from outside but

206

also works from within, prosecuting the Church not only in heaven's courtroom but also through earthly instruments.

Modern deception often flourishes when discernment is neglected. The Church has sometimes replaced testing the spirits (1 John 4:1) with blind acceptance of any charismatic display. Satan, knowing this vulnerability, packages counterfeit prophecy with eloquence, emotional intensity, and even miraculous signs. Yet Jesus warned that signs and wonders alone are no proof of truth, for even the elect could be deceived if they do not anchor themselves in the Word.

The role of Lucifer as prosecutor is not limited to accusation in the heavenly realm; it also manifests in accusations within the body of Christ. When believers slander, gossip, or condemn one another without grace, they unwittingly echo the voice of the accuser. Satan delights when the Church turns its prosecutorial gaze inward, for division weakens the testimony of the gospel and obscures the unity Christ prayed for in John 17.

In contrast, the Spirit of God convicts but does not condemn. Conviction leads to repentance, restoration, and life, while condemnation leads to despair and death. This distinction is essential when discerning true prophecy from counterfeit. A genuine prophetic word may pierce the heart, but it will always point to the hope of Christ. A counterfeit word, however, leaves no pathway to redemption. Thus, one can discern the spirit behind a message by examining whether it brings people closer to grace or further into shame.

Throughout church history, moments of revival have often been preceded by exposure of counterfeit prophecy and corruption. The Reformation, for instance, emerged in part because the Spirit exposed the false practices of indulgences and the manipulation of the faithful. Likewise, modern moves of God will require a similar purging, for Lucifer continues his age-old tactic of mingling truth with error. God, in His mercy, allows the Church to be placed on trial so that what is false may be separated from what is true.

The courtroom imagery also teaches us that believers must not fear accusation. Though the prosecutor may present a case against us, we have an Advocate whose defense cannot fail. Paul triumphantly declares in Romans 8:33, "Who will bring any charge against those whom God has chosen? It is God who justifies." This assurance transforms our perspective: accusations become opportunities for God's righteousness to shine all the more clearly.

Nevertheless, the exposure of hidden evil can be painful. When leaders fall, ministries collapse, or hidden sin comes to light, many are tempted to lose faith altogether. But such exposures are not evidence that God has abandoned His Church; rather, they are proof that He is actively purifying her. Just as fire refines gold by consuming the dross, so too does exposure burn away deception, leaving a Church more radiant and prepared for the return of Christ.

The Church, then, must learn to see trials and exposures through the lens of heaven's courtroom. When accusations arise, whether from the adversary or from public scandal, the question is not whether the Church will be condemned but whether she will repent and be refined. God reveals hidden evil not to destroy His people but to display His justice, His mercy, and His power to redeem. In this way, the trial becomes testimony, and what the enemy meant for harm, God turns for good.

One of the most striking aspects of Lucifer's prosecutorial role is that he is permitted access for a time. In Job, he stood before God; in Zechariah, he accused the high priest. But in Revelation 12, we see the turning point: the accuser is cast down, silenced by the blood of the Lamb and the testimony of the saints. This progressive unveiling reminds us that while accusations may rage today, their power is temporary. God has already appointed the day when no charge will ever again be heard against His people.

Until that day, the Church must navigate a world saturated with deception. Counterfeit prophecy is not limited to overtly false religions; it can infiltrate pulpits, worship music, and popular movements within the Church itself. Many believers are swayed by emotional highs, celebrity culture, or political promises disguised as spiritual revelation. These voices echo Lucifer's strategy: to accuse, to confuse, and to replace God's pure Word with man-centered proclamations.

The rise of social media has only magnified this danger. Today, anyone can claim the title of prophet, apostle, or seer, gaining thousands of followers with untested words. Lucifer delights in this unfiltered flood of voices, for amid the noise, the still small voice of the Spirit is often drowned out. In such an environment, discernment is not optional; it is the lifeline that protects believers from deception.

God, however, is not silent in the midst of this counterfeit flood. He raises true prophetic voices who confront deception and call the Church back to holiness. These voices are not always popular; they may be ridiculed or ignored, just as Jeremiah was in his time. Yet their faithfulness becomes a witness against the lies of the adversary. In every age, God ensures that His remnant hears the truth, even when deception abounds.

Lucifer's accusations also reveal the fragile nature of human pride. When we build ministries, reputations, or personal identities on anything other than Christ, they become vulnerable targets for the prosecutor's case. Satan knows our weak points and is eager to exploit them. This is why humility is not optional for the believer; it is the safeguard that prevents us from falling into the snare of prideful deception.

The role of Lucifer as chief prosecutor also exposes the danger of hidden sin. While God forgives confessed sin, the adversary will magnify unrepentant sin, using it as legal grounds to accuse. This is why Scripture urges believers to walk in the light, confessing faults one to another, and keeping short accounts with God. Hidden evil may seem safe for a season, but it will eventually be exposed either by the Spirit's conviction or by the adversary's accusations.

Modern counterfeit prophecy often thrives in environments where accountability is absent. False prophets surround themselves with admirers but resist correction. They deliver words without submitting them to testing, forgetting that Paul instructed believers to "weigh carefully what is said" (1 Corinthians 14:29). In this way, such ministries mirror Lucifer's rebellion: a refusal to submit, a hunger for glory, and an insistence on independence from God's order.

God reveals hidden evil through shaking. Hebrews 12:27 tells us that everything that can be shaken will be shaken, so that what cannot be shaken may remain. This shaking is visible today in ministries collapsing, movements splintering, and once-revered leaders being exposed.

Though painful, this is evidence that heaven's courtroom is active, silencing the prosecutor by bringing what is false into the light. The shaking is not destruction but purification.

For the individual believer, the accusations of the adversary can feel crushing. Many wrestles with guilt, shame, and the memory of past sins, believing the lie that they are disqualified from God's love. But Scripture assures us that "if anyone is in Christ, he is a new creation" (2

Corinthians 5:17). The prosecutor's voice may echo, but it cannot overturn the verdict already declared: justified, forgiven, redeemed.

Therefore, the Church must live with confidence in Christ's finished work while remaining vigilant against deception. Balance is critical: confidence without vigilance leads to complacency, while vigilance without confidence leads to despair. The prosecutor would prefer either extreme, but the Spirit calls us to a middle path: bold faith in the cross and careful discernment in the Spirit. This posture disarms Lucifer's accusations and protects us from modern deception.

The Church must understand that Lucifer's prosecutorial strategy is not only about individuals but also about systems. He targets families, communities, nations, and denominations. When corruption is uncovered in government or in the Church, the adversary uses it to argue that God's people are no different from the world. Yet God allows this exposure so that His people will not hide behind institutions but instead return to authentic holiness and truth.

In the last days, counterfeit prophecy will increasingly be used as a weapon of accusation. False prophets will predict doom to instill fear or promise blessings to exploit greed. Both extremes serve Lucifer's agenda, for fear paralyzes the Church while greed corrupts her witness. Only prophecy rooted in God's Word and centered in Christ can pierce through this fog of deception.

The Church on trial is not a metaphor but a spiritual reality. Each believer must see themselves as a witness in this cosmic courtroom. Our testimony matters. Revelation 12:11 declares that the saints overcome the accuser "by the blood of the Lamb and by the word of their testimony." Every time a believer speaks truth, lives faithfully, or stands firm against deception, it becomes evidence against the prosecutor's case.

This is why Satan fights so hard to silence the testimony of the saints. He seeks to entangle believers in sin, so their witness is compromised, or to intimidate them into silence through fear of persecution. Yet Christ reminds us that even when we are brought before rulers and courts, the Spirit will give us the words to speak (Luke 12:11-12). The testimony of God's people is unstoppable when yielded to the Spirit.

The hidden evil that God reveals is often closer than we expect. It may be hypocrisy in our own hearts, pride in our ministries, or compromise in our leadership. Before the Church can effectively expose deception in the world, she must first confront deception within herself.

Judgment begins in the house of God, not to condemn, but to purify and prepare her for her Bridegroom's return.

In this way, Lucifer's accusations, though malicious, become instruments of divine mercy. When he drags hidden sin into the light, it becomes an opportunity for confession, repentance, and renewal. What the adversary intends for destruction, God uses for restoration. The prosecutor unwittingly becomes a tool in God's redemptive hand, for his charges cannot ultimately condemn those covered by the blood of Christ.

For modern believers, the call is clear: test every prophecy, weigh every word, and measure all things by Scripture. Do not accept voices that flatter your desires or condemn without hope. Do not follow personalities who resist accountability or elevate themselves above Christ. The Church must cultivate a culture of discernment, where every spirit is tested and only what is true, holy, and Christ-centered is embraced.

The victory of the Church is certain, but the trial is ongoing. Until Christ returns, accusations will continue, deception will multiply, and counterfeit prophecy will abound. Yet none of these can overturn the eternal verdict written in the Lamb's book of life. The Church is not fighting for victory but from victory. Our Advocate has already secured the final ruling.

In the final courtroom scene of history, the accuser will stand condemned. The books will be opened, the hidden things revealed, and every false prophecy judged. On that day, there will be no more deception, no more accusation, no more trials. The Bride will stand radiant, clothed in white, vindicated by her Savior, and united forever with her King.

Until that day, let the Church be sober and watchful. Do not fear the accusations of the adversary, for they cannot erase the blood that speaks a better word. Do not be seduced by counterfeit prophecy, for it cannot replace the eternal truth of God's Word. Instead, stand firm, discern wisely, and live faithfully, knowing that though the Church is on trial, the verdict has already been secured in Christ. God reveals hidden evil not to shame His people but to sanctify them, preparing a Bride without spot or wrinkle for the return of the Bridegroom.

From the Old Testament prophets to the New Testament apostles, God has always spoken to His people through true voices that declare His will. Yet alongside those authentic voices, counterfeit prophets have arisen, seeking to deceive, mislead, and exploit God's people. Scripture warns repeatedly that false prophecy is not a possibility but a certainty in every generation. Jesus Himself declared: "For false messiahs and false prophets will appear and perform great signs and wonders to deceive, if possible, even the elect" (Matthew 24:24).

The urgency to discern true from false has never been greater than in our day. As the Church on trial, facing pressures from culture, compromise, and spiritual deception, believers must sharpen their discernment and return to the Word of God as the ultimate measure of truth. Counterfeit prophecy is not merely a theological error; it is a spiritual weapon in the hands of the enemy, designed to confuse the Church, distort God's character, and divert His people from their mission.

The Nature of Counterfeit Prophecy

Counterfeit prophecy often mimics the structure of true prophecy but lacks its essence. Like counterfeit money, it may appear convincing, even valuable, but upon closer inspection, it does not carry the authority of heaven. Jeremiah faced this in his day when false prophets declared "peace, peace" when there was no peace (Jeremiah 6:14). Their words soothed the people's ears but did not reflect the heart of God.

The apostle Peter warned that "there will be false teachers among you. They will secretly introduce destructive heresies, even denying the sovereign Lord who bought them—bringing swift destruction on themselves" (2 Peter 2:1). False prophecy often appeals to human desires, offering comfort without repentance, prosperity without obedience, and blessing without holiness.

Signs of Counterfeit Prophecy

One of the clearest signs of counterfeit prophecy is its contradiction with Scripture. True prophecy aligns with the revealed Word of God, never undermining or altering it. Isaiah 8:20 declares, "To the law and to the testimony! If they do not speak according to this word, they have no light of dawn."

Another sign is self-exaltation. True prophets point to God's glory and call people to repentance. False prophets, by contrast, draw attention to themselves, building personal platforms and promoting their own influence. Jesus said, "By their fruit you will recognize them" (Matthew 7:16). Leonard Ravenhill, in *Why Revival Tarries*, warned that the Church's tolerance for shallow messages and entertainment-based preaching leaves it vulnerable to deception. A generation that craves signs without substance will eagerly follow voices that offer spectacle rather than truth.

The Danger of Emotionalism

Counterfeit prophecy often appeals to emotions rather than the Spirit. While true prophecy may stir emotions, it is rooted in the unchanging truth of God's Word. False prophecy manipulates feelings, creating dependency on the prophet rather than on God.

A.W. Tozer observed, "When the church loses the discernment of the Holy Spirit, it is left to depend on carnal substitutes." These substitutes may include sensational predictions, vague promises, or flattery, all of which may temporarily inspire but ultimately mislead.

The Jezebel Connection

In Revelation 2:20, Jesus rebukes the church in Thyatira for tolerating "that woman Jezebel, who calls herself a prophet." This figure, symbolic of spiritual seduction, represents the danger of counterfeit prophecy within the Church. Jezebel's goal is control, not edification, manipulation, not revelation.

Modern parallels abound where individuals claim prophetic authority to gain influence, financial support, or power over others. Jennifer LeClaire, in her writings on the Jezebel spirit, notes that counterfeit prophecy often emerges from a spirit of control disguised as divine revelation.

The Role of Testing Prophecy

The apostle Paul instructed believers: "Do not treat prophecies with contempt but test them all; hold on to what is good, reject every kind of evil" (1 Thessalonians 5:20-22). Testing prophecy involves measuring it against Scripture, evaluating the fruit it produces, and discerning whether it points people toward Christ or toward the prophet.

Derek Prince emphasized that prophecy must be tested by the community of believers, not received in isolation. When prophecy is treated as unquestionable, it becomes a breeding ground for manipulation and abuse.

The modern Church must guard itself against counterfeit prophecy by cultivating biblical literacy. A church ignorant of Scripture cannot discern truth from deception. C.S. Lewis, through the lens of *The Screwtape Letters*, reminds us that the enemy thrives on half-truths and twists Scripture. Spiritual leaders must model transparency and humility, acknowledging that they, too, are accountable to the Word of God. When prophets are unwilling to be tested, they reveal their own lack of submission to God's authority. Believers must rely on the Holy Spirit, who leads into all truth (John 16:13). Discernment is not merely intellectual but spiritual, requiring prayer, fasting, and dependence on God.

Counterfeit prophecy is one of the greatest dangers facing the Church in these last days. It masquerades as light but leads to darkness, promising blessings while ignoring sin, and drawing attention to man rather than God. Yet God equips His Church with discernment, the Word of God, and the indwelling Spirit to expose deception. The task of the Church is not to despise prophecy but to test it, ensuring that every word aligns with the unchanging truth of Scripture.

As Ravenhill noted, "The true prophet has no price tag." The Church must learn to value the voices that call for holiness, repentance, and obedience over those that offer comfort without cost. When the Church refuses to tolerate Jezebel-like deception and clings to the voice of the Good Shepherd, it will walk in purity, power, and truth.

The Scriptures present us with a sobering reality: the Church is not only the Bride of Christ, prepared for eternal union with her Savior, but also the object of Satan's accusation and hostility. From the moment Lucifer rebelled against the Most High, he took upon himself the role of prosecutor, the adversary who opposes God's people. In Hebrew, "Satan" literally means "accuser" or "adversary," a title that describes his continual attempt to bring charges against believers in the courtroom of heaven.

Revelation 12:10 speaks of Satan as "the accuser of our brethren, who accused them before our God day and night." This imagery is not poetic exaggeration but a spiritual reality: Satan's role has been to highlight the failures, sins, and weaknesses of God's people, presenting them as evidence against the Church's worthiness. In doing so, he seeks to undermine both the credibility of the saints and the glory of God's saving grace.

The book of Job gives us a powerful glimpse into this heavenly courtroom. Job, described as "blameless and upright," was brought into trial not because of hidden sin but because Satan demanded the right to test his integrity. Here we see Lucifer acting as prosecutor, attempting to prove that Job's faith was shallow and self-serving. God permitted the trial, not because He delights in suffering, but because He reveals hidden evil and exposes the counterfeit work of the adversary.

This role of prosecutor is not merely directed at individuals but at the Church collectively. In every age, Satan has sought to discredit the Body of Christ, highlighting hypocrisy, corruption, and weakness. His accusations often contain fragments of truth, but they are twisted and weaponized to obscure the grace and forgiveness of God. The Church, therefore, stands on trial in the sight of both heaven and earth, its witness scrutinized by angels, demons, and men.

In this cosmic drama, it is crucial to recognize that Lucifer is not a coequal with God. He is a created being who fell from grace, consumed by pride. His role as prosecutor is permitted for a time, but ultimately, it serves God's higher purpose. Through accusation, trial, and refinement, God reveals what is genuine and exposes what is counterfeit. The Church, purified by fire, emerges not as a defeated defendant but as a victorious bride clothed in the righteousness of Christ.

Counterfeit prophecy thrives in the shadows of accusation. When the adversary stands to accuse, false voices often rise to mislead, offering distorted interpretations of God's will. Such prophecies flatter, confuse, or condemn without the redemptive truth of the gospel. This is why discernment is vital: the Church must learn to distinguish between the Spirit of truth and the lying spirit that seeks to mimic divine revelation.

The prophet Zechariah provides another vivid scene of this heavenly prosecution. In Zechariah 3, Joshua the high priest stands before the angel of the Lord, clothed in filthy garments, while Satan stands at his right hand to accuse him. Here again, the prosecutor presents the evidence of guilt. Yet the Lord Himself rebukes Satan and commands that Joshua's garments be changed, symbolizing the righteousness that comes by grace. The accuser is silenced not by denial of guilt but by the covering of God's mercy.

This passage teaches us that God reveals hidden evil not to condemn His people but to cleanse and restore them. Satan may point out the dirt, but God provides the garment of salvation. Thus, while the Church may be placed on trial, it is ultimately defended by the intercession of Christ, our Advocate with the Father (1 John 2:1). In this way, the accusations of Lucifer serve only to magnify the sufficiency of the cross.

Lucifer's strategy has always been twofold: accusation and deception. Where he cannot destroy the Church by direct assault, he seeks to corrupt it through counterfeit prophecy, false doctrine, and compromised leadership. By disguising himself as "an angel of light" (2 Corinthians 11:14), he lures many into believing his lies are prophetic insight. In this sense, the courtroom and the battlefield overlap: accusation weakens from within, while deception leads astray from without.

The modern Church faces this same prosecutorial attack. Scandals, divisions, moral failures, and false teachings are broadcast to the world, becoming fodder for the adversary's accusations. Yet, Scripture reminds us that judgment begins in the house of God (1 Peter 4:17). When God allows hidden evil to be exposed, it is not to destroy His people but to refine them. Every exposure is a summons to repentance, a call to realign with the truth of Christ.

One of the greatest deceptions in modern times is the elevation of self above Scripture. Lucifer, in his fall, declared, "I will ascend...I will be like the Most High" (Isaiah 14:13-14). This same spirit of pride seeps into counterfeit prophecy, where men and women claim visions and revelations that exalt their own voice above the Word of God. Here, the adversary whispers into human pride, turning prophets into performers and pulpits into stages of self-glorification.

The prosecuting nature of Satan finds agreement in such false voices, for when prophecy is stripped of God's heart of redemption, it becomes an instrument of condemnation. Many are led astray by words that sound spiritual but carry no grace, leaving believers burdened rather than freed. This, too, is part of Lucifer's deception: to replace the comfort of the Holy Spirit with the cold weight of accusation disguised as prophecy.

Christ, however, demonstrates the perfect answer to the accusation. When Satan tempted Him in the wilderness, the enemy twisted Scripture to bring charges against the Son of God. But Jesus responded with the unshakable truth of God's Word, saying, "It is written." In doing so, He modeled how the Church should respond when placed on trial: not by argument or self-defense, but by standing on the authority of God's Word.

Hidden evil often lurks undetected in the Church until the season of trial. God, in His wisdom, allows accusation to bring it to light. This is not to shame His people, but to cleanse the Bride for the return of Christ. When corruption in leadership, hidden sin, or false teaching is exposed, it is evidence that heaven's courtroom is active and that God's Spirit is still refining His people.

The adversary, however, delights in exploiting these exposures. He will magnify the failures of the Church before the world, presenting them as evidence that Christianity itself is fraudulent. This is why believers must remember that while the Church may stumble, Christ never fails. The true testimony of the gospel is not the perfection of men but the perfection of the Savior who redeems them.

The Church on trial is not abandoned in its defense. Christ is not only the Lamb slain for our sins but also the Advocate who pleads our case before the Father. Whereas Lucifer acts as the prosecutor, Christ stands as the defense attorney. He does not argue our innocence but presents His own blood as the sufficient covering for our guilt. The verdict, therefore, is not condemnation but justification, for "there is now no condemnation for those who are in Christ Jesus" (Romans 8:1).

Yet, we must not ignore the warning that counterfeit prophecy is increasing in these last days. Jesus Himself cautioned in Matthew 24:24 that false prophets would arise, showing signs and wonders to deceive, if possible, even the elect. The adversary's strategy is not only to accuse but also to counterfeit. In the courtroom of heaven, he points to our failures; in the marketplace of religion, he floods us with false voices.

God's revelation of hidden evil includes exposing such false ministries. Many who prophesy for profit, manipulate with charisma, or distort Scripture for gain are being unmasked in this hour. What may look like a scandal is, in truth, divine exposure. Just as Jesus overturned the tables of the money changers in the temple, so too is He cleansing His house today. Exposure, though painful, is a gift of mercy, protecting the Church from deeper deception.

The Church must not despise this refining work. Too often, believers grieve when leaders fall or when ministries collapse. Yet these exposures are the courtroom verdicts of heaven, declaring that what was built on deception cannot stand. For the Bride to be pure, she must be freed from counterfeit coverings. Thus, every exposure is both a warning and an invitation: a warning against falsehood, and an invitation to return to holiness.

In the end, the prosecutor will be silenced forever. Revelation 20:10 assures us that the accuser will be cast into the lake of fire, no longer able to bring charges against the saints. Until that day, the Church remains on trial, but it does so under the defense of Christ's intercession and the refining fire of the Holy Spirit. The question is not whether we will be accused, but whether we will stand clothed in us.

The adversary's prosecutorial role is especially dangerous because it often mirrors the very language of truth. Satan rarely fabricates outlandish lies; instead, he distorts partial truths, presenting them without the context of grace. He points to sin but not to forgiveness, to weakness but not to the Spirit's strength, to failure but not to redemption. In this way, his accusations are persuasive because they highlight what is real but strip it of God's eternal perspective.

This explains why counterfeit prophecy is so alluring. A false prophet may speak accurately about circumstances or reveal hidden knowledge, but without the Spirit of God, such words are not redemptive. They may sound correct, but they do not lead people closer to Christ. In fact,

Satan's most effective counterfeit is prophecy that resembles truth but lacks the heart of the Gospel. Such words leave hearers condemned, confused, or puffed up with pride instead of humbled before the Lord.

Scripture consistently portrays Satan as one who infiltrates religious spaces. In Job's account, he appears "among the sons of God" before the throne. In the New Testament, he plants tares among the wheat. Paul warns that "false apostles, deceitful workers, disguising themselves as apostles of Christ" will arise (2 Corinthians 11:13). This infiltration shows that Lucifer does not only attack from outside but also works from within, prosecuting the Church not only in heaven's courtroom but also through earthly instruments.

Modern deception often flourishes when discernment is neglected. The Church has sometimes replaced testing the spirits (1 John 4:1) with blind acceptance of any charismatic display. Satan, knowing this vulnerability, packages counterfeit prophecy with eloquence, emotional intensity, and even miraculous signs. Yet Jesus warned that signs and wonders alone are no proof of truth, for even the elect could be deceived if they do not anchor themselves in the Word.

The role of Lucifer as prosecutor is not limited to accusation in the heavenly realm; it also manifests in accusations within the body of Christ. When believers slander, gossip, or condemn one another without grace, they unwittingly echo the voice of the accuser. Satan delights when the Church turns its prosecutorial gaze inward, for division weakens the testimony of the gospel and obscures the unity Christ prayed for in John 17.

In contrast, the Spirit of God convicts but does not condemn. Conviction leads to repentance, restoration, and life, while condemnation leads to despair and death. This distinction is essential when discerning true prophecy from counterfeit. A genuine prophetic word may pierce the heart, but it will always point to the hope of Christ. A counterfeit word, however, leaves no pathway to redemption. Thus, one can discern the spirit behind a message by examining whether it brings people closer to grace or further into shame.

Throughout church history, moments of revival have often been preceded by exposure of counterfeit prophecy and corruption. The Reformation, for instance, emerged in part because the Spirit exposed the false practices of indulgences and the manipulation of the faithful. Likewise, modern moves of God will require a similar purging, for Lucifer continues his age-old tactic of mingling truth with error. God, in His mercy, allows the Church to be placed on trial so that what is false may be separated from what is true.

The courtroom imagery also teaches us that believers must not fear accusation. Though the prosecutor may present a case against us, we have an Advocate whose defense cannot fail. Paul triumphantly declares in Romans 8:33, "Who will bring any charge against those whom God has chosen? It is God who justifies." This assurance transforms our perspective: accusations become opportunities for God's righteousness to shine all the more clearly.

Nevertheless, the exposure of hidden evil can be painful. When leaders fall, ministries collapse, or hidden sin comes to light; many are tempted to lose faith altogether. But such exposures are not evidence that God has abandoned His Church; rather, they are proof that He is actively purifying her. Just as fire refines gold by consuming the dross, so too does exposure burn away deception, leaving a Church more radiant and prepared for the return of Christ.

The Church, then, must learn to see trials and exposures through the lens of heaven's courtroom. When accusations arise, whether from the adversary or from public scandal, the question is not whether the Church will be condemned but whether she will repent and be refined. God reveals hidden evil not to destroy His people but to display His justice, His mercy, and His power to redeem. In this way, the trial becomes testimony, and what the enemy meant for harm, God turns for good.

One of the most striking aspects of Lucifer's prosecutorial role is that he is permitted access for a time. In Job, he stood before God; in Zechariah, he accused the high priest. But in Revelation 12, we see the turning point: the accuser is cast down, silenced by the blood of the Lamb and the testimony of the saints. This progressive unveiling reminds us that while accusations may rage today, their power is temporary. God has already appointed the day when no charge will ever again be heard against His people.

Until that day, the Church must navigate a world saturated with deception. Counterfeit prophecy is not limited to overtly false religions; it can infiltrate pulpits, worship music, and popular movements within the Church itself. Many believers are swayed by emotional highs, celebrity culture, or political promises disguised as spiritual revelation. These voices echo Lucifer's strategy: to accuse, to confuse, and to replace God's pure Word with man-centered proclamations.

The rise of social media has only magnified this danger. Today, anyone can claim the title of prophet, apostle, or seer, gaining thousands of followers with untested words. Lucifer delights in this unfiltered flood of voices, for amid the noise, the still small voice of the Spirit is often drowned out. In such an environment, discernment is not optional; it is the lifeline that protects believers from deception.

God, however, is not silent in the midst of this counterfeit flood. He raises true prophetic voices who confront deception and call the Church back to holiness. These voices are not always popular; they may be ridiculed or ignored, just as Jeremiah was in his time. Yet their faithfulness becomes a witness against the lies of the adversary. In every age, God ensures that His remnant hears the truth, even when deception abounds.

Lucifer's accusations also reveal the fragile nature of human pride. When we build ministries, reputations, or personal identities on anything other than Christ, they become vulnerable targets for the prosecutor's case. Satan knows our weak points and is eager to exploit them. This is why humility is not optional for the believer; it is the safeguard that prevents us from falling into the snare of prideful deception.

The role of Lucifer as chief prosecutor also exposes the danger of hidden sin. While God forgives confessed sin, the adversary will magnify unrepentant sin, using it as legal grounds to accuse. This is why Scripture urges believers to walk in the light, confessing faults one to another, and keeping short accounts with God. Hidden evil may seem safe for a season, but it will eventually be exposed either by the Spirit's conviction or by the adversary's accusations.

Modern counterfeit prophecy often thrives in environments where accountability is absent. False prophets surround themselves with admirers but resist correction. They deliver words without submitting them to testing, forgetting that Paul instructed believers to "weigh carefully what is said" (1 Corinthians 14:29). In this way, such ministries mirror Lucifer's rebellion: a refusal to submit, a hunger for glory, and an insistence on independence from God's order.

God reveals hidden evil through shaking. Hebrews 12:27 tells us that everything that can be shaken will be shaken, so that what cannot be shaken may remain. This shaking is visible today in ministries collapsing, movements splintering, and once-revered leaders being exposed.

Though painful, this is evidence that heaven's courtroom is active, silencing the prosecutor by bringing what is false into the light. The shaking is not destruction but purification.

For the individual believer, the accusations of the adversary can feel crushing. Many wrestle with guilt, shame, and the memory of past sins, believing the lie that they are disqualified from God's love. But Scripture assures us that "if anyone is in Christ, he is a new creation" (2 Corinthians 5:17). The prosecutor's voice may echo, but it cannot overturn the verdict already declared: justified, forgiven, redeemed.

Therefore, the Church must live with confidence in Christ's finished work while remaining vigilant against deception. Balance is critical: confidence without vigilance leads to complacency, while vigilance without confidence leads to despair. The prosecutor would prefer either extreme, but the Spirit calls us to a middle path: bold faith in the cross and careful discernment in the Spirit. This posture disarms Lucifer's accusations and protects us from modern deception.

The Church must understand that Lucifer's prosecutorial strategy is not only about individuals but also about systems. He targets families, communities, nations, and denominations. When corruption is uncovered in government or in the Church, the adversary uses it to argue that God's people are no different from the world. Yet God allows this exposure so that His people will not hide behind institutions but instead return to authentic holiness and truth.

In the last days, counterfeit prophecy will increasingly be used as a weapon of accusation. False prophets will predict doom to instill fear or promise blessings to exploit greed. Both extremes serve Lucifer's agenda, for fear paralyzes the Church while greed corrupts her witness. Only prophecy rooted in God's Word and centered in Christ can pierce through this fog of deception.

The Church on trial is not a metaphor but a spiritual reality. Each believer must see themselves as a witness in this cosmic courtroom. Our testimony matters. Revelation 12:11 declares that the saints overcome the accuser "by the blood of the Lamb and by the word of their testimony." Every time a believer speaks truth, lives faithfully, or stands firm against deception, it becomes evidence against the prosecutor's case.

This is why Satan fights so hard to silence the testimony of the saints. He seeks to entangle believers in sin so their witness is compromised, or to intimidate them into silence through fear of persecution. Yet Christ reminds us that even when we are brought before rulers and courts, the Spirit will give us the words to speak (Luke 12:11-12). The testimony of God's people is unstoppable when yielded to the Spirit.

The hidden evil that God reveals is often closer than we expect. It may be hypocrisy in our own hearts, pride in our ministries, or compromise in our leadership. Before the Church can effectively expose deception in the world, she must first confront deception within herself.

Judgment begins in the house of God—not to condemn, but to purify and prepare her for her Bridegroom's return.

In this way, Lucifer's accusations—though malicious—become instruments of divine mercy. When he drags hidden sin into the light, it becomes an opportunity for confession, repentance, and renewal. What the adversary intends for destruction, God uses for restoration. The prosecutor unwittingly becomes a tool in God's redemptive hand, for his charges cannot ultimately condemn those covered by the blood of Christ.

For modern believers, the call is clear: test every prophecy, weigh every word, and measure all things by Scripture. Do not accept voices that flatter your desires or condemn without hope. Do not follow personalities who resist accountability or elevate themselves above Christ. The Church must cultivate a culture of discernment, where every spirit is tested and only what is true, holy, and Christ-centered is embraced.

The victory of the Church is certain, but the trial is ongoing. Until Christ returns, accusations will continue, deception will multiply, and counterfeit prophecy will abound. Yet none of these can overturn the eternal verdict written in the Lamb's book of life. The Church is not fighting for victory but from victory. Our Advocate has already secured the final ruling.

In the final courtroom scene of history, the accuser will stand condemned. The books will be opened, the hidden things revealed, and every false prophecy judged. On that day, there will be no more deception, no more accusation, no more trials.

The Bride will stand radiant, clothed in white, vindicated by her Savior, and united forever with her King.

Until that day, let the Church be sober and watchful. Do not fear the accusations of the adversary, for they cannot erase the blood that speaks a better word. Do not be seduced by counterfeit prophecy, for it cannot replace the eternal truth of God's Word. Instead, stand firm, discern wisely, and live faithfully, knowing that though the Church is on trial, the verdict has already been secured in Christ. God reveals hidden evil not to shame His people but to sanctify them, preparing a Bride without spot or wrinkle for the return of the Bridegroom.

Chapter 22: Holy and Fearless Church

The Church is called to be holy and fearless, reflecting the character of God in a world filled with compromise and deception. Scripture repeatedly exhorts believers to pursue holiness, for "without holiness no one will see the Lord" (Hebrews 12:14). Holiness is not merely ritual purity or external conformity; it is a heart attitude that prioritizes God above self, obedience above convenience, and truth above popularity.

Fearlessness is the natural companion of holiness. When the Church stands on God's Word, empowered by the Holy Spirit, it is emboldened to confront sin, resist deception, and walk boldly in the authority of Christ. Paul exhorted Timothy: "Do not be ashamed of the testimony about our Lord… Join with me in suffering for the gospel, by the power of God" (2 Timothy 1:8).

The Biblical Call to Holiness

Holiness begins with separation from sin. Leviticus 19:2 commands, "Be holy because I, the Lord your God, am holy." God's holiness is the standard by which His people are measured, and the Church is called to reflect His purity in both conduct and doctrine. Tozer emphasized that the Church must cultivate a "hunger for God" that surpasses desire for comfort or worldly approval. A holy Church is not defined by programs or buildings but by hearts fully surrendered to God's authority.

Holiness requires inward transformation. Paul writes in Romans 12:1-2 that believers are to present themselves as living sacrifices, transformed by the renewing of their minds. The fearlessness of the Church flows from the confidence that comes from surrendering entirely to God's will.

Fearlessness in the Face of Opposition

The Church faces opposition from both the world and spiritual forces. Jesus warned: "If they persecuted me, they would persecute you also" (John 15:20). Fearless churches are not naïve; they are courageous because their security rests in Christ, not in numbers, power, or human approval. Watchman Nee highlighted that fearlessness comes from intimacy with God. A Church that spends time in

226

prayer, worship, and the study of Scripture develops a spiritual courage that cannot be shaken by threats, intimidation, or worldly agendas.

Fearless believers do not shrink from confronting sin in the pulpit, in leadership, or in themselves. They embrace truth as a weapon and love as their guiding principle, modeling Christ's own approach to confrontation with sinners and hypocrites alike.

The Church's Armor

Spiritual fearlessness is supported by the armor of God described in Ephesians 6:10-18: truth, righteousness, readiness, faith, salvation, the Word of God, and prayer. Each piece equips the Church to resist deception, endure trials, and stand boldly against the schemes of the enemy.

C.S. Lewis, in *The Screwtape Letters*, illustrated the subtle ways the enemy attempts to instill fear and doubt. The Church's fearless stance is its defense against manipulation and spiritual paralysis. Tozer warned that a fearful church has compromised its devotion, sought human approval, or ignored the call to obedience. Courage is birthed in obedience and nourished through reliance on the Holy Spirit.

Holiness and Fearlessness in Leadership

Church leaders set the tone for both holiness and fearlessness. They must walk in integrity, humility, and transparency. When leaders fear man more than God, the entire congregation is affected. Conversely, leaders who walk boldly in obedience to God inspire courage and conviction in the body of Christ. Paul provides a model in Acts 20:28-31, exhorting leaders to watch over the flock diligently, warning against false teachers. Fearless leadership is proactive, not reactive. Secondary author Derek Prince emphasizes that leaders must guard their hearts against pride and self-interest, for these are the roots of fear and compromise. The Church becomes fearless when leaders are fearless in their dependence on God.

Walking in Purity in a Compromised World

Holiness requires resisting cultural pressures that normalize sin, compromise, or deception. The Church is called to be "in the world but not of the world" (John 17:14-16). Holiness protects the Church from being seduced by counterfeit teachings and modern distractions. Jennifer LeClaire notes that spiritual compromise often begins subtly—through acceptance of sin, neglect of Scripture, or tolerance of deception. Fearlessness ensures the Church does not retreat in the face of opposition, persecution, or spiritual attack. It maintains a posture of prayer, discernment, and bold proclamation of God's truth.

Cultivating a Holy and Fearless Culture

Practical steps include consistent Bible study, communal prayer, accountability, confession, and mentorship. Holiness is cultivated in community, not isolation. A fearful Church tolerates compromise; a fearless Church challenges it with truth and love. It values obedience over popularity and righteousness over comfort. Leonard Ravenhill observed that revival is birthed in holy, fearless churches. The fear of the Lord, he said, is the beginning of courage, not terror.

Worship and reverence reinforce holiness and fearlessness. The Church's devotion to God strengthens faith, aligns hearts with heaven, and wards off spiritual intimidation.

Facing Modern Challenges

Today, the Church faces pressures from secularism, moral relativism, and internal strife. Fearlessness is tested when speaking the truth and risks criticism, rejection, or loss. The holy Church resists compromise even when it is popular. It models obedience and integrity, trusting God's vindication rather than human approval. Tozer emphasized that the Church must be willing to stand alone if necessary, relying on God's presence as its ultimate validation.

Fearlessness does not mean recklessness. It is guided by Scripture, wisdom, and prayer, ensuring that courage is grounded in God's will, not impulsive emotion. Paul's letters to the churches demonstrate how accountability, exhortation, and correction build a culture of holiness and boldness, even amidst opposition (1 Corinthians 15:58; 2 Corinthians 10:3–5).

Impact of a Holy and Fearless Church

Such a Church draws unbelievers not by worldly attraction but by the radiance of God's presence. Holiness attracts, fearlessness inspires, and truth convinces. A holy and fearless Church prays boldly, evangelizes diligently, and stands firmly against injustice and deception. Its influence is eternal rather than temporary, shaping generations in alignment with God's purposes. Michael Heiser notes that spiritual battles intensify against the Church as it grows in discernment. Holiness and fearlessness are both offensive and defensive weapons in spiritual warfare. Leaders, prophets, and laity together cultivate courage by resisting spiritual shortcuts, emphasizing obedience, and prioritizing God's glory over personal gain.

Fearless churches resist manipulation, expose counterfeit teaching, and encourage believers to confront sin within their own hearts. Holiness creates moral clarity; fearlessness creates spiritual boldness. Both together produce a Church that cannot be intimidated or silenced by the enemy. Historical examples of fearless Churches include the early apostles who preached boldly despite persecution and martyrdom. They modeled courage grounded in holiness, guided by the Spirit, and empowered by God's promises.

Holiness prevents the Church from compromising truth for convenience or social acceptance. Fearlessness prevents retreat in the face of spiritual or cultural pressure. A holy and fearless Church maintains accountability structures, ensuring leaders and members alike remain aligned with Scripture.

It resists the temptation to follow charismatic personalities over Christ, recognizing that God alone is the Head of the Church. The fruit of holiness and fearlessness is evident in consistent prayer, courageous outreach, faithful teaching, and transparent leadership. Holiness fosters humility, while fearlessness fosters courage; together they create spiritual maturity. C.S. Lewis emphasized that courage is not the absence of fear but the triumph over fear through faith and obedience. Churches that embrace these principles are better equipped to confront deception, handle spiritual attacks, and foster revival.

Fearlessness is cultivated through obedience, prayer, Scripture meditation, and reliance on the Spirit. Holiness requires ongoing sanctification, repentance, and surrender, recognizing that perfection is in Christ alone. Fearless believers are willing to speak truth even when unpopular, trusting God to vindicate His Word. Tozer and Ravenhill both highlight that spiritual courage is essential for revival and for maintaining integrity in ministry. Holiness ensures that the Church's witness is credible; fearlessness ensures it is unshakable.

The combination of these traits produces a Church that boldly advances God's Kingdom without compromise. Even in persecution or opposition, a holy and fearless Church stands as a beacon of hope, truth, and righteousness. Its leaders serve not to control but to guide, not to dominate but to nurture, fostering an environment where God's Spirit can move freely. The Church that walks in holiness and fearlessness reflects Christ's character, impacting the world both spiritually and morally. Ultimately, the holy and fearless Church is a testimony of God's power, faithfulness, and glory, an unshakeable witness in a shaken world.

The Revelation of Hidden Sin

Uncovering the secret sins and corruption that have defiled the Church

Hidden sin corrodes the Church from within, weakening its witness and mission. Exposure illuminates secret transgressions that leaders and members may have ignored. God calls His people to repentance, confession, and purification. Leaders must be courageous in confronting secret sin among congregants and ministries. Exposure reveals the subtle ways pride, lust, greed, and manipulation infiltrate the Church.

Believers must examine their hearts honestly before God. Leaders must establish accountability structures to identify and correct hidden sin. Exposure strengthens vigilance against secrecy, deception, and compromise. Hidden sin thrives where accountability, transparency, and humility are absent. Leaders must guide the Church in fostering environments of truth and openness.

Exposure encourages repentance, healing, and restoration within the body of Christ. Believers must embrace confession, reconciliation, and transformation.

Leaders must address systemic sin, corruption, and hidden agendas decisively. Exposure highlights the consequences of covering sin or ignoring spiritual warning signs. Hidden sin erodes faith, unity, and spiritual vitality. Leaders must cultivate humility, discernment, and courage in confronting evil. Exposure ensures that sin is not tolerated, concealed, or normalized.

Believers must pursue holiness, obedience, and integrity in thought, word, and deed. Leaders must provide guidance, instruction, and correction in line with Scripture. Exposure clarifies patterns of deception, compromise, and moral failure.

Hidden sin must be confronted to restore the Church's spiritual authority. Leaders must exemplify accountability, integrity, and transparency.

Exposure strengthens the Church's ability to resist manipulation, pride, and corruption. Believers must cultivate hearts sensitive to conviction, truth, and God's guidance. Leaders must teach discernment, vigilance, and righteous boldness. Exposure reveals the spiritual cost of ignoring sin and deception. Hidden sin often manifests in selfish ambition, favoritism, and abuse of authority. Leaders must provide pastoral care while maintaining the standard of God's holiness.

Exposure motivates corrective action, repentance, and systemic reform. Believers must pursue restoration, forgiveness, and renewed commitment to God. Leaders must ensure that the Church's teaching, practices, and leadership are aligned with Scripture. Exposure fosters awareness, accountability, and vigilance among all members. Hidden sin diminishes the Church's effectiveness in fulfilling God's mission.

Leaders must cultivate environments of integrity, honesty, and spiritual maturity. Exposure ensures that secret sin is brought into the light for correction and healing. Believers gain freedom, courage, and spiritual authority through confession and repentance. Leaders must equip the Church to resist deception, compromise, and hidden corruption. Exposure strengthens unity, resilience, and spiritual vitality. Hidden sin must be removed for revival, holiness, and spiritual breakthrough to occur.

Leaders must model obedience, humility, and commitment to God's truth. Exposure clarifies areas of vulnerability, weakness, and compromise in the Church. Believers must remain steadfast in faith, prayer, and righteous living. Leaders must provide accountability, mentorship, and guidance to prevent future sin. Exposure ensures that the Church is purified, renewed, and restored in God's sight. Ultimately, the revelation of hidden sin leads to repentance, cleansing, and the Church's restoration to holiness, unity, and faithful service.

The Church is on the brink of a profound spiritual awakening, but before revival comes, there must be exposure — a revelation of hidden sin, deception, and compromise. God's Word teaches that the Spirit brings light to darkness so that hearts can be cleansed and renewed (Ephesians 5:13-14). Exposure is not punitive; it is redemptive. God reveals what has been hidden not to condemn but to restore. When the Church embraces transparency and repentance, revival follows. Leonard Ravenhill repeatedly emphasized that revival is always preceded by a godly exposure of sin.

Exposure begins in the individual heart. Psalm 139:23-24 instructs: "Search me, God, and know my heart; test me and know my anxious thoughts. See if there is any offensive way in me, and lead me in the way everlasting." God uses conviction to align believers with His holiness.

Corporate exposure occurs when churches confront areas of compromise, hypocrisy, or deception. A congregation unwilling to face the truth cannot experience revival. The prophet Joel warned, "Return to me with all your heart, with fasting and weeping and mourning" (Joel 2:12).

Modern ministries often avoid exposure for fear of controversy or criticism, but Derek Prince teaches that revival requires courage, transparency, and a willingness to address spiritual decay. Exposure and revival are intertwined. The Spirit uncovers hidden sin, calls for repentance, and stirs a hunger for God that leads to renewal. A revival-ready Church is willing to confront both personal and corporate compromise.

True revival does not emerge from manipulation, emotional hype, or superficial excitement. Watchman Nee noted that revival is the outpouring of God's Spirit on a people who have humbled themselves and sought His face in truth. The Church must cultivate prayer, fasting, and the study of Scripture. These disciplines prepare hearts for exposure and open doors for God's powerful work.

Hidden compromise often masquerades as cultural adaptation, unity, or expediency. While some accommodations are practical, spiritual compromise occurs when the Word is ignored, truth is softened, or God's principles are overridden. A holy

Church does not excuse sin or tolerate deception. Fearlessness allows leaders and believers to confront issues honestly and courageously. Jennifer LeClaire emphasizes that spiritual discernment is essential to identify the subtle Jezebel spirit that undermines truth. Exposure may be uncomfortable, but it is necessary.

C.S. Lewis observed that spiritual growth often comes through trials that reveal hidden weaknesses and force dependence on God.

God prepares His Church for revival by refining hearts and cleansing motives. Isaiah 57:15 reminds us that God dwells with the contrite and lowly, reviving the spirit of the humble.

Leaders must model transparency, confession, and accountability. When leaders embrace exposure, the congregation follows, cultivating a culture of holiness and openness. Prayer and intercession play a critical role. Leonard Ravenhill stressed that revival always follows prayerful preparation, passionate petitions for God's presence and power.

Repentance is the gateway to revival. 2 Chronicles 7:14 highlights God's promise: "If my people, who are called by my name, will humble themselves and pray and seek my face and turn from their wicked ways, then I will hear from heaven and will forgive their sin and will heal their land." True revival is not about numbers, programs, or media attention. It is about transforming hearts and lives fully surrendered to God. Exposure illuminates areas where repentance is required, while revival empowers believers to walk in renewed strength and obedience.

The Holy Spirit guides the Church into truth and illuminates areas that require exposure (John 16:13). Discernment and sensitivity to the Spirit are vital in preparing for revival. Spiritual maturity ensures that exposure does not lead to condemnation or despair but to repentance, healing, and empowerment. Michael Heiser notes that the unseen spiritual realities influence the visible Church. Awareness of the enemy's schemes helps believers respond faithfully to God's calling for holiness and revival.

Begin with personal confession and surrender. Psalm 51 models this process, showing the heart that God honors in preparation for His work. Establish corporate accountability. Churches must be willing to examine their leadership, ministries, and practices in light of Scripture. Encourage intercessory prayer. Ravenhill and

Tozer highlight the power of persistent prayer to invite God's presence and expose hidden deception. Foster a culture of humility. A Church that exalts God above all is prepared to receive His Spirit in abundance. Identify and remove counterfeit influences. False teaching, manipulation, and compromise must be confronted and corrected to make way for revival.

Revival as Restoration

Revival restores the Church to its intended mission: to glorify God, proclaim truth, and disciple nations. It brings unity not through compromise but through shared obedience and commitment to God's Word. Exposure and revival together reveal God's power over darkness, calling His people into courage, faithfulness, and bold witness. Fearless believers are more willing to confront spiritual deception, knowing that God's Spirit empowers them to overcome.

Holiness ensures that revival is sustained, not fleeting or superficial. Secondary authors such as Derek Prince, Jennifer LeClaire, and Tozer provide insights on the correlation between exposure, repentance, and revival in contemporary ministry contexts. The Church must anticipate resistance. Spiritual awakening often provokes opposition, both internally and externally. Fearlessness sustains believers during this process.

Revival requires patience. God's timing is perfect, and the Church must remain steadfast, continuing prayer, fasting, and obedience while awaiting His move. Holiness ensures that revival is authentic; exposure without repentance results in shame, not transformation. Ravenhill observed that the greatest revivals in history followed seasons of intense conviction, confession, and spiritual cleansing. Leaders and members alike must embrace transparency, allowing God to bring hidden sin to light for the sake of restoration. Exposure prepares the Church to be a witness of God's power in a world hungry for truth.

Fearlessness allows the Church to proclaim repentance and revival boldly, without fear of ridicule or persecution. Revival empowers the Church to confront modern spiritual deception, including counterfeit teachings, idolatry, and moral compromise. Prayer, accountability, humility, and obedience are essential tools in this preparation process. Exposure is a grace, not a punishment, revealing areas where God's Spirit can bring lasting transformation.

A revived Church impacts society by modeling righteousness, courage, and spiritual discernment. Holiness attracts the presence of God; fearlessness enables bold action in obedience to His Word. Secondary authors such as Michael Heiser provide insight into the unseen spiritual dynamics that preceded revival, emphasizing the cosmic reality behind visible Church renewal.

Leaders must encourage the body to embrace exposure, repent fully, and pursue revival as a divine priority. Exposure prepares the Church for accountability, ensuring that revival is sustainable and aligned with God's purposes. God honors hearts that humbly submit to His examination and cleansing. The Church must not resist the Spirit's conviction but embrace it as preparation for His mighty work. Revival flows naturally from a Church willing to face the truth, repent, and align with God's will. The final exposure and revival are God's promise to a faithful Church, preparing it to shine as a beacon of light in a darkened world.

Rekindling the Fire of Holiness

Reviving spiritual purity and passionate devotion in the Church

Holiness is the foundation of revival, and it begins in the hearts of believers. Exposure of hidden evil highlights where holiness has been neglected or compromised. Rekindling the fire requires repentance, humility, and sincere surrender to God. Leaders must model holy living, inspiring the congregation through integrity and obedience. Fire represents God's presence, conviction, and purifying power. Exposure illuminates practices, attitudes, and behaviors that extinguish spiritual fervor.

Rekindling begins with personal commitment to obedience, prayer, and Scripture study. Leaders play a pivotal role in fostering an environment that nurtures holiness. Exposure motivates corrective action, removing distractions, sin, and compromise. Holiness strengthens faith, discernment, and spiritual resilience. Rekindling the fire brings clarity of purpose, vision, and divine mission. Believers must prioritize God's Word, aligning all actions with His standards.

Exposure teaches that neglecting holiness allows deception and compromise to flourish. Fire purifies hearts, removing pride, greed, and hidden sin. Leaders must encourage accountability, discipleship, and confession. Rekindling holiness restores unity, integrity, and spiritual authority in the Church. Exposure ensures that corrective measures address both personal and corporate sin. Believers experience spiritual renewal when holiness is prioritized over convenience.

Leaders who embrace holiness inspire trust, respect, and faithfulness among followers. Rekindling the fire ignites passion, zeal, and courageous obedience to God. Exposure clarifies the consequences of spiritual compromise, prompting action. Holiness protects the Church from deception, corruption, and worldly influence. Rekindling requires continual prayer, devotion, and surrender to God's guidance. Leaders must cultivate environments that nurture spiritual growth and accountability. Exposure strengthens awareness, prompting vigilance against subtle compromises.

Holiness fosters spiritual intimacy, worship, and bold proclamation of truth. Rekindling the fire restores hope, purpose, and courage in the congregation. Believers are called to pursue purity in thought, word, and deed. Leaders must provide teaching, mentorship, and support to encourage holy living. Exposure removes the veil of deception, allowing the Spirit to purify the Church.

Rekindling inspires faithful stewardship, service, and ministry effectiveness.

Holiness empowers the Church to fulfill its mission with integrity and impact. Leaders who embrace the holy living model of obedience, humility, and accountability. Exposure reveals hidden pride, manipulation, or compromise, prompting correction. Rekindling the fire strengthens personal devotion, corporate worship, and ministry vitality. Believers learn to recognize and resist influences that weaken spiritual fervor. Leaders must encourage a culture of transparency, integrity, and accountability.

Exposure guides the Church in identifying and removing obstacles to revival. Holiness restores spiritual authority, trust, and confidence in God's leadership. Rekindling the fire deepens spiritual intimacy, empowering prayer, worship, and obedience. Leaders must nurture hearts, minds, and souls to sustain spiritual passion. Exposure ensures the Church is aligned with God's Word and divine purposes. Holiness shapes character, ministry, and the Church's witness to the world. Rekindling the fire equips believers to resist compromise, deception, and sin. Ultimately, restoring holiness rekindles the Church's spiritual fire, enabling it to serve God faithfully, powerfully, and victoriously.

Chapter 24: Confronting the Spirit of Jezebel in Modern Ministry

The Spirit of Jezebel is one of the most insidious influences in the Church today, subtly infiltrating ministries, leadership, and congregations. While named after the infamous queen in 1 Kings 16–21, this spirit represents manipulation, control, seduction, and rebellion against God's authority.

Jesus warned the Church in Thyatira, saying, "I have this against you: You tolerate that woman Jezebel, who calls herself a prophetess. By her teaching she misleads my servants into sexual immorality and the eating of food sacrificed to idols" (Revelation 2:20). This warning is timeless, highlighting the dangers of tolerating spiritual seduction and deception in ministry.

Characteristics of the Jezebel Spirit

The Jezebel spirit is subtle, often disguised as charisma, leadership, or prophetic gifting. It seeks to dominate rather than serve, manipulate rather than submit, and control rather than empower. Jennifer LeClaire, in her writings on spiritual warfare, describes the Jezebel spirit as a master of seduction, intimidation, and division, targeting leaders, influencers, and vulnerable believers. It thrives on fear, pride, and rebellion. When leaders or congregations tolerate it, ministries become spiritually compromised, focusing on personal gain, control, or appearance rather than God's mission. A.W. Tozer warned that compromise in leadership invites deception, leading the Church away from God's truth. The Jezebel spirit often appears where pride, ambition, or ungodly alliances flourish.

Recognizing Jezebel's Influence

Spiritual discernment is essential. Jezebel's influence can manifest in the manipulation of finances, distortion of truth, inappropriate relationships, control over staff or congregants, and resistance to accountability. Scripture emphasizes the danger: "She misleads my servants." When Jezebel's influence is unchecked, leaders may be misled into actions contrary to God's will, causing widespread compromise. Michael Heiser notes that spiritual forces often operate in networks of deception. The Jezebel spirit frequently works behind the scenes, influencing decisions, alliances, and organizational culture. The presence of jealousy, manipulation, seduction, and hidden agendas is often a sign that Jezebel's influence has penetrated a ministry.

Confronting Jezebel in Leadership

Confrontation begins with prayer, discernment, and reliance on God's authority. Leaders must first examine themselves for pride, ambition, or fear that allows Jezebel's influence to persist. Paul reminds believers in 1 Corinthians 16:13-14: "Be on your guard; stand firm in the faith; be courageous; be strong. Do everything in love." Courage and love are essential when addressing Jezebel's influence. Leonard Ravenhill emphasized that boldness in leadership is necessary to oppose spiritual deception. Fearful or passive leaders enable Jezebel's influence to grow unchecked.

Transparency, accountability, and adherence to Scripture protect ministries from manipulation and compromise. Leaders must not tolerate behaviors that undermine God's authority or distort His Word.

Practical Steps for the Church

Evaluate leadership structures and relational dynamics. Ensure decisions align with God's Word, not human desire or manipulation. Test prophetic words. Jezebel's influence often hides in counterfeit prophecy, enticing leaders to follow ungodly guidance. Encourage a culture of accountability. Leaders and congregants must be willing to speak truth, even when unpopular, to resist manipulation. Prayer and fasting are powerful weapons. Spiritual warfare requires intentional engagement with God to expose hidden deception. Tozer stated that spiritual compromise begins with tolerating minor errors. The Jezebel spirit gains a foothold in environments lacking vigilance, humility, and obedience.

Addressing Jezebel Spirit in Modern Ministry

In contemporary churches, Jezebel's influence may appear as ambition-driven ministry, desire for control, abuse of spiritual gifts, or dominance over decisions. Leaders must confront manipulation in hiring, financial oversight, and ministry strategy. Teach congregations to discern the Spirit of God from controlling influences. True prophecy builds, edifies, and aligns with Scripture. Jennifer LeClaire emphasizes that exposing Jezebel requires courage, spiritual authority, and Godly wisdom.

Spiritual counseling, accountability teams, and mentorship help identify and resist Jezebel's tactics. The Church must prioritize God's authority over individual ambition or charismatic personalities. False alliances and compromise in leadership allow Jezebel to operate. Strong leadership, rooted in prayer and Scripture, resists her influence. Leaders must maintain humility, submission to God, and accountability to others to prevent Jezebel from taking root.

Fearlessness is required. Jezebel thrives on intimidation, seduction, and fear; confronting her influence requires spiritual boldness. Holiness is essential. Compromise, sin, or rebellion opens doors to manipulation and deception. Exposing Jezebel strengthens the Church, protecting it from deception, division, and compromise.

Historical and Modern Insights

Historical examples of Jezebel-like influence show leaders who sought control through fear, manipulation, or false teaching. Modern ministry abuses, including misuse of authority, financial deception, or coercive leadership, often trace back to the Jezebel spirit. Secondary authors, such as Derek Prince and Michael Heiser, highlight strategies for resisting her influence through discernment, prayer, and adherence to Scripture. Ravenhill warned that revival and purity require confronting all forms of spiritual compromise, including Jezebel-like manipulation. Tozer emphasized that fear of man often allows deception to flourish in ministry. Courage and obedience are essential.

C.S. Lewis illustrated that deception often begins subtly, gaining influence through lies, half-truths, and seduction. Exposure of Jezebel's tactics in ministry is not for punishment but for restoration and protection of the Church. Leaders must foster transparency, accountability, and humility at every level of ministry. Congregations must be educated in spiritual discernment to resist manipulation, deception, and coercion. Prayer, fasting, and reliance on the Holy Spirit are vital in confronting Jezebel's influence.

Fearless, holy leadership models resistance to manipulation and invites God's presence. Revivals often occur when Jezebel-like control is exposed and replaced with submission to God.

Leadership must balance authority with accountability, courage with humility, and discernment with love. Exposure of Jezebel ensures that ministries reflect Christ's character, not personal ambition. False teaching, financial manipulation, and ungodly control are addressed through bold, Scriptural confrontation.

God empowers believers to resist Jezebel through the Word, prayer, and community support. Spiritual maturity and vigilance prevent the Jezebel spirit from gaining influence. Holiness and fearlessness equip leaders and congregations to maintain purity, discernment, and obedience.

Confronting Jezebel protects the Church from spiritual compromise and prepares it for revival. Ultimately, resisting Jezebel's influence ensures that ministries honor God, promote truth, and foster authentic spiritual growth.

Identifying the Hidden Forces

Recognizing the spiritual powers behind corruption, deception, and oppression in the Church

Darkness often operates subtly, influencing hearts, minds, and ministries without detection. Exposure of hidden evil reveals the spiritual forces manipulating leaders and congregations. Satan works through pride, greed, manipulation, and false doctrine. The Church must learn to discern the enemy's strategies with prayer and Scripture. Leaders must recognize that hidden forces target both individuals and institutions. Exposure clarifies how deception can infiltrate even well-meaning ministries.

Spiritual discernment is essential to identify subtle attacks, distractions, and distortions. The faithful must understand that corruption is often a product of unseen spiritual battles. Leaders must equip the Church to recognize, resist, and overcome these hidden powers. Exposure reveals how manipulation, fear, and compromise open doors to darkness. Prayer and fasting sharpen spiritual perception, enabling believers to confront hidden evil.

Leaders must model vigilance, humility, and discernment in spiritual warfare. Exposure teaches that compromise often precedes deception and exploitation. Darkness can corrupt doctrines, distort worship, and control congregations. Leaders

240

must guard their hearts, minds, and ministries against subtle influence. Exposure strengthens the Church's ability to identify and address spiritual threats. Spiritual warfare requires awareness, prayer, and Scripture-based strategies.

Hidden forces often operate through cultural, social, and institutional pressures. Leaders must train the faithful to recognize spiritual deception in all forms. Exposure clarifies the need for accountability, transparency, and godly oversight. Darkness thrives in secrecy, silence, and unrepentant sin. Prayer and discernment expose hidden patterns of corruption and manipulation.

Leaders must protect the Church by confronting evil with courage and wisdom. Exposure demonstrates that ignorance or apathy can amplify the enemy's influence. Spiritual maturity enables believers to see beyond appearances and confront deception. Leaders must cultivate environments that encourage truth, accountability, and discernment. Exposure reveals spiritual blind spots, teaching the Church to remain vigilant.

Darkness often disguises itself as cultural norms, traditions, or harmless practices. Leaders must equip the Church to test every teaching, motive, and practice against Scripture. Exposure fosters courage, conviction, and willingness to confront spiritual threats. Spiritual vigilance protects the Church from being misled or manipulated. Leaders must lead by example, demonstrating obedience, discernment, and integrity. Exposure emphasizes that hidden forces target both leaders and followers alike.

Prayer, worship, and Scripture fortify the Church against deception and compromise. Leaders must teach the importance of spiritual awareness, maturity, and accountability. Exposure helps believers distinguish between God's voice and the enemy's deception. Darkness seeks to divide, control, and corrupt the Church from within. Leaders must remain alert, humble, and Spirit-led in confronting evil. Exposure clarifies where the Church has been vulnerable to spiritual attacks.

Vigilance, prayer, and obedience empower the Church to resist and overcome deception. Leaders must prepare the Church for sustained spiritual warfare and discernment. Exposure strengthens the faithfulness to recognize patterns, practices, and influences of darkness. Spiritual readiness ensures that the Church can confront deception without fear. Leaders must cultivate courage, wisdom, and faith to navigate spiritual battles. Ultimately, identifying hidden forces equips the Church to stand firm, resist evil, and fulfill God's calling with boldness and integrity.

Chapter 25: The Church on Trial and Walking in Transparency

The Church is under scrutiny, both spiritually and culturally. God calls His people to live openly, honestly, and in alignment with His Word. Walking in transparency is not optional; it is essential for integrity, accountability, and revival. Proverbs 28:13 reminds us, "Whoever conceals their sins does not prosper, but the one who confesses and renounces them finds mercy."

Transparency is the antidote to deception, hypocrisy, and compromise. When the Church hides behind appearances, programs, or personalities, it becomes vulnerable to spiritual attack, counterfeit prophecy, and internal decay. Leonard Ravenhill emphasized that revival always begins with exposed hearts and honest acknowledgment of weakness.

Why the Church Is on Trial

The Church is tested in multiple arenas: doctrinal integrity, moral conduct, leadership accountability, financial stewardship, and care for the marginalized. These tests are not arbitrary; they reveal whether the Church honors God or man. Modern scrutiny also comes from the culture, media, and congregation members. The Church cannot escape evaluation, but God's Word provides the standard by which it is judged (John 12:48). Tozer observed that the Church often fails its divine test by prioritizing numbers, popularity, or comfort over obedience, truth, and holiness. When the Church compromises, it invites judgment and diminishes its witness.

The Role of Transparency

Transparency requires courage. Leaders and members must openly confess mistakes, acknowledge limitations, and embrace accountability. Paul wrote to the Corinthian Church, "We are not concealing anything, but commending ourselves to everyone's conscience in the sight of God" (2 Corinthians 4:2). Integrity demands openness in both public and private ministry.

Secondary authors, including Derek Prince, highlight transparency as the foundation for healthy leadership, spiritual growth, and revival. When the Church walks in light, deception cannot thrive. Transparency is relational as well as structural.

Leaders must be approachable, vulnerable, and willing to admit shortcomings while pointing to God's power and guidance.

Benefits of Walking in Transparency

First, it cultivates trust. Congregations that observe honesty and accountability are more likely to engage fully and obey God's direction. Second, transparency strengthens discernment. When the Church is open about challenges, deception, or doctrinal disputes, members learn to recognize truth and resist manipulation. Third, it fosters revival. Ravenhill and Tozer emphasize that revival flourishes in an environment of honesty, repentance, and dependence on God. Fourth, transparency protects the Church from external attack. Hidden sin or compromise invites criticism and scandal; openness disarms the enemy and fortifies the body.

Implementing Transparency in the Church

Establish accountability structures for leaders and ministry teams. Regular evaluations, mentoring, and reporting prevent secrecy and encourage integrity. Encourage confession and repentance. Public and private acknowledgment of mistakes promotes spiritual growth and humility.

Align all ministry activities with Scripture. Counterfeit teachings and practices often thrive where transparency is absent. Use teaching, preaching, and workshops to educate congregations about honesty, integrity, and discernment. Engage in community and intercessory prayer.

Transparency thrives where believers pray for each other and hold one another accountable in love.

Addressing Resistance

Transparency is often resisted due to fear of criticism, loss of influence, or shame. Leaders must model courage and humility to overcome this resistance. C.S. Lewis observed that pride and self- preservation can blind believers to truth, making openness difficult. Tozer emphasized that fear of man is one of the greatest obstacles to spiritual clarity and revival. Fearlessness rooted in God allows the Church to face exposure without compromise.

Leaders must communicate the spiritual necessity of transparency, framing it as obedience to God rather than a man-made requirement. Consistent teaching on the value of integrity, humility, and accountability helps cultivate a culture that embraces exposure and confession.

Transparency as a Weapon Against Deception

Counterfeit prophecy, manipulation, and compromise cannot endure in a transparent Church. Hidden agendas are revealed, and truth is clarified. Jennifer LeClaire notes that Jezebel-like influences weaken the Church when secrecy persists. Exposure and openness break the power of manipulation.

Spiritual discernment is heightened in an environment of transparency. Members learn to identify true versus false teaching and embrace God's Word as the ultimate authority. The Church becomes a light to the world when its operations, finances, and leadership are transparent, reflecting God's character and truth.

Cultivating a Culture of Accountability

Leadership must be humble, approachable, and teachable. Leaders who resist accountability invite error and deception. Congregational engagement promotes collective discernment, prayer, and intercession, reinforcing spiritual vigilance. Ravenhill emphasized that revival is impossible without confession, repentance, and openness. God honors hearts willing to be examined.

Fostering transparency requires ongoing teaching, mentoring, and vigilance against pride or fear. Paul's letters to the churches demonstrate accountability mechanisms: correction, exhortation, and encouragement to walk in truth (Galatians 6:1–2).

Transparency in Practice

Financial oversight: open reporting and stewardship accountability prevent misuse and build trust. Leadership decisions: involve team members in planning, review, and discernment, ensuring God's will is central. Ministry outcomes: celebrate successes and acknowledge failures openly, pointing to God's guidance rather than human achievement. Conflict resolution: address issues biblically, without secrecy, manipulation, or favoritism. Teaching and preaching model honesty, vulnerability, and confession, showing that leaders, too, need God's grace.

Trust among members increases, strengthening the community and mission. Discernment improves, enabling the congregation to resist deception and embrace God's truth. Revival is more likely as God's Spirit moves freely among a people willing to be examined and corrected. Spiritual maturity grows as members model accountability, humility, and integrity.

Transparency fosters fearlessness, allowing the Church to confront sin, deception, and compromise without hesitation. The Church becomes a credible witness to the world, demonstrating God's holiness, love, and power. Secondary authors like Derek Prince and Tozer emphasize that accountability and openness protect against spiritual manipulation and moral failure.

Spiritual exposure, confession, and transparency prepare the Church for revival, purity, and bold ministry. Leaders and members alike experience freedom, peace, and courage as they walk in light, leaving secrecy and deception behind. A transparent Church invites God's presence, blessing, and guidance in every aspect of ministry. It becomes a refuge for believers, a beacon of light to the lost, and a witness to God's glory.

Walking in transparency ensures that the Church is not merely surviving but thriving spiritually, morally, and relationally. Ultimately, transparency, accountability, and fearlessness demonstrate obedience to God, positioning the Church to fulfill its divine mission in the world.

Part V – The Call to Repentance and Renewal

Chapter 26: Return to the Altar

Joel 2:12-13 calls the Church to repentance: *"Return to Me with all your heart, with fasting, weeping, and mourning."* God invites His people to realign with Him and abandon the sin and compromise that have separated them from His presence.

The altar has always been a place of encounter, where humanity meets the holiness of God. In the Old Testament, the altar was not merely a structure but a symbol of surrender, repentance, and covenant renewal. Today, the church finds itself at a crossroads, where God is summoning His people back to the altar. Not to a physical pile of stones, but to a posture of brokenness and humility before Him. In this hour of trial, when hidden evils are being revealed, the altar is not optional; it is the lifeline for the survival of the Bride of Christ.

The imagery of the altar reminds us of Elijah's showdown on Mount Carmel (1 Kings 18). Before fire fell, the prophet first rebuilt the altar of the Lord that had been torn down. This act symbolized the restoration of true worship in a land polluted by idolatry and compromise. In the same way, the modern church must rebuild the altar of prayer, repentance, and consecration. The Lord cannot consume what is not surrendered. The altar must be restored before the fire of revival can descend. C. S. Lewis, in *Mere Christianity*, emphasizes that genuine repentance is not mere sorrow for wrongdoing, but a deliberate turning toward God and away from sin.

Returning to the altar symbolizes wholehearted commitment to His will.

God's uncovering of hidden evil within His house is not an act of cruelty but an act of mercy. Like a skilled surgeon, He exposes what is diseased so that healing can begin. The scandals of hypocrisy, abuse, greed, and spiritual manipulation surfacing within churches are not to destroy the body of Christ but to cleanse it. The call to the altar is therefore a call to allow the light of God's presence to expose every hidden corner of the heart, both corporately and individually.

Scripture declares in 1 Peter 4:17, "For the time has come that judgment must begin at the house of God." Before God judges the nations, He purifies His people.

This purification requires us to forsake the complacency that has crept into our pews and pulpits. We have often been more concerned with attendance numbers than with holiness, more devoted to cultural relevance than to biblical obedience. Returning to the altar demands we abandon such shallow pursuits and embrace once again the weightiness of God's presence. A. W. Tozer, in *The Pursuit of God*, notes that the altar represents intimate fellowship with God. A return to the altar involves humility, confession, and a renewed focus on holiness and devotion.

At the altar, pride is shattered. Leaders who once sought recognition must bow low. Congregations that were enticed by entertainment rather than discipleship must lay aside their idols. The altar strips away pretense and masks, forcing us to confront our sins before a holy God. It is there that ministers confess failures, congregants repent of compromise, and the entire body experiences the cleansing blood of Christ anew. Without such a return, the church cannot withstand the trials that are already upon it. The altar is both a place and a posture. It signifies surrender, repentance, and readiness to obey God's Word without compromise. Returning to the altar is a personal and corporate act of recommitment.

The exposure of hidden evil is also a fulfillment of Jesus' words in Luke 12:2 3: "There is nothing covered, that shall not be revealed; neither hid, that shall not be known." Secret sins within church leadership and membership are being brought into the light because God will not allow His name to be mocked. He is purging His temple, just as Jesus did in Jerusalem when He drove out the moneychangers. The shaking is divine, and only what is built upon righteousness will remain. Leonard Ravenhill, in *Why Revival Tarries*, highlights historical revivals that began with the Church humbling itself at the altar. Leaders and congregants alike experienced awakening when they confronted sin and sought God earnestly.

We must remember that revival does not begin with the world but with the church. Second Chronicles 7:14 is clear: "If my people, which are called by my name, shall humble themselves, and pray, and seek my face, and turn from their wicked ways; then will I hear from heaven, and will forgive their sin, and will heal their land." Healing for nations will never come apart from the repentance of God's people. The altar is where this divine exchange takes place—sin for forgiveness, shame for cleansing, brokenness for renewal. Lewis emphasizes that sin disrupts intimacy with God. Without repentance, the Church risks spiritual stagnation and divine discipline. Returning to the altar restores the connection necessary for revival and renewal.

The altar is also a place of sacrifice. In biblical times, what was laid on the altar could not be reclaimed; it was consumed by fire. Likewise, when the church returns to the altar, it must be willing to lay down comfort, compromise, and control. Too often, we have treated repentance as a temporary adjustment rather than a complete surrender. God calls us not to offer Him fragments but to present ourselves as living sacrifices, holy and acceptable unto Him (Romans 12:1). Tozer observes that many Christians attempt worship and ministry without returning to the altar of personal consecration. This disconnect produces lukewarm faith, ineffective witness, and vulnerability to deception.

This chapter of history reveals a sobering truth: the church is indeed on trial. The trial is not set in earthly courts but before the heavenly Judge who sees all. The charges are hypocrisy, lukewarmness, worldliness, and neglect of true discipleship. Yet even in judgment, mercy triumphs. The Judge offers a pardon if the accused will confess, repent, and return. The altar is God's courtroom, where justice meets mercy, and where sentences of death are overturned by the blood of the Lamb.

The restoration of the altar is not a nostalgic return to religious ritual but a prophetic act that prepares the way of the Lord. Just as John the Baptist called Israel to repentance before the coming of Christ, the Spirit now calls the church to repentance before the return of Christ. The hidden evil being revealed is a trumpet blast—warning us to cleanse our garments and fill our lamps with oil. The Bridegroom is near, and the altar is where the Bride prepares herself.

When we return to the altar, we return to first love. Many churches have become proficient in programs, branding, and social media presence, yet have lost the intimacy that once defined their walk with Christ. Jesus rebuked the church in Ephesus for abandoning its first love (Revelation 2:4). The altar is where love is rekindled—where worship becomes more than a song, prayer becomes more than words, and obedience becomes more than duty. Without this return, the church risks operating with form but no power.

The altar also signifies brokenness. David declared in Psalm 51:17, "The sacrifices of God are a broken spirit: a broken and a contrite heart, O God, thou wilt not despise." True repentance does not defend sin but mourns over it. It does not excuse rebellion but seeks transformation. In this generation, we have too often celebrated grace without repentance, blessings without obedience, and destiny without discipline. The altar confronts this shallow gospel and demands that our hearts be crushed and contrite before God.

Hidden evil thrives in secrecy, but the altar forces exposure. In Joshua 7, Achan hid the accursed thing in his tent, bringing defeat to the entire nation of Israel. When sin was exposed and dealt with, victory returned. Likewise, hidden compromises in our churches, whether financial corruption, sexual immorality, or doctrinal error, have weakened our witness. At the altar, God reveals these "accursed things," not to humiliate His people but to restore their power and purity.

A return to the altar also revives intercession. The early church advanced not through human strategy but through prayer that shook buildings (Acts 4:31). Today, prayer meetings are often the least attended gatherings in our churches. Yet when God calls His people back to the altar, intercession becomes the engine of revival. Pastors weep between the porch and the altar (Joel 2:17), interceding for the people. Saints travail in prayer until chains break and prodigals return. The altar is where tears water the seeds of awakening.

Repentance at the altar is not simply individual but communal. The prophets often called nations to repent as a collective body. Joel summoned priests, elders, and children to fast and cry out to God together (Joel 2:15–16). Similarly, the modern church must repent not only for personal sins but also for collective failures—silence in the face of injustice, divisions fueled by pride, neglect of the poor, and indifference toward holiness. At the altar, we confess as one body, acknowledging that the sins of one affect us all.

The altar is where God births a new identity. Jacob wrestled with God and built an altar, and there his name was changed to Israel (Genesis 32:28; 35:7). In the same way, when the church returns to the altar, it will no longer be identified by scandals, divisions, or failures but by holiness, unity, and Spirit-empowered witness. The altar does not leave us the same; it redefines us in alignment with God's covenant and calling.

Another dimension of returning to the altar is the restoration of prophetic clarity. When the church drifts from the altar, its voice becomes muddled, echoing the culture rather than confronting it. But when leaders linger at the altar, they receive heaven's vision and speak with boldness. Elijah confronted Israel's idolatry only after he rebuilt the altar. Likewise, the church cannot confront societal darkness unless it first regains its authority at the altar of repentance and prayer.

The exposure of hidden evil within the church may seem devastating, but it is actually a prelude to revival. God never tears down without the intention to rebuild. When the temple in Jerusalem was defiled, He raised leaders like Nehemiah and Ezra to restore worship. Today, as God uncovers corruption and sin in His house, He is simultaneously raising voices of holiness and reform. The altar is where this rebuilding begins, one heart at a time.

A church without an altar becomes a stage. It becomes a place for performance, not transformation, for applause, not repentance. This is why God is calling His people to shift from performance-driven Christianity to altar-centered Christianity. At the altar, lights and microphones are unnecessary, for the glory of God becomes the spotlight. At the altar, the only audience that matters is the King of kings, before whom every knee will bow.

The altar also calls us to endurance. Repentance is not a one-time act but a lifestyle. Israel often drifted into idolatry, only to be called back to the altar through the prophets. The same cycle is evident today, but God is inviting His people into a sustained walk of holiness. The altar must be rebuilt not only for moments of crisis but as a permanent fixture in the life of the church. It is at the altar that we learn to walk in continual renewal, not temporary emotional experiences.

The altar is also where the fear of the Lord is restored. Proverbs 9:10 declares, "The fear of the Lord is the beginning of wisdom." Yet, in many pulpits today, the fear of God has been replaced with the fear of losing popularity or financial support. At the altar, we encounter His holiness, and suddenly our opinions and ambitions fade. The fear of the Lord brings a reverence that cleanses casual worship and restores the awe of His majesty to His people.

Returning to the altar revives holiness as the standard of the church. God is not impressed by large buildings or polished programs. He is seeking people who are set apart. Hebrews 12:14 reminds us that without holiness, no one will see the Lord. At the altar, holiness is not viewed as an outdated concept but as the natural fruit of true repentance. The Holy Spirit empowers us to forsake sin and live in purity, shining as lights in a crooked generation.

The altar is a place of reconciliation. Jesus warned in Matthew 5:23-24 that if a believer brings an offering to the altar but remembers a broken relationship, reconciliation must take place first. This reveals that worship is incomplete without restored fellowship. In today's church, divisions over race, class, politics, and tradition have fractured the body. At the altar, grudges are surrendered, and walls of hostility are torn down. True unity begins when the people of God lay down offenses before the cross.

At the altar, we also rediscover our priestly role. In the Old Testament, priests ministered at the altar to mediate between God and the people. Today, every believer is called to the priesthood of intercession (1 Peter 2:9). When we neglect the altar, we abandon this holy assignment. But as we return, we take up the mantle to stand in the gap for our families, our communities, and our nations. The church is called not to mirror the culture's despair but to intercede until heaven breaks through.

The altar is where the fire falls. When Solomon dedicated the temple, fire came down from heaven and consumed the sacrifice, and the glory of the Lord filled the house (2 Chronicles 7:1). In Acts 2, the Spirit descended as tongues of fire on the early church. Fire is always connected to the altar. Without an altar of repentance and consecration, there will be no fire of revival. The modern church prays for fire but neglects the altar—it is time to rebuild it so the fire may descend again.

Returning to the altar exposes the futility of man-made religion. Throughout history, religious systems have arisen that look spiritual outwardly but lack the inward reality of God's presence. Jesus confronted the Pharisees for honoring God with their lips while their hearts were far from Him (Matthew 15:8). At the altar, such empty rituals are burned away, leaving only authentic devotion. This is why God is stripping the church of superficiality so that what remains is pure, Spirit-breathed worship. Ravenhill reminds us that corporate repentance at the altar can catalyze revival movements. Confession and humility collectively invite the power of God to move mightily among His people.

The altar is also a place of generational renewal. Abraham built altars, Isaac rebuilt them, and Jacob encountered God at them. Each generation must return to the altar for itself; faith cannot be inherited like property. In our time, young believers must encounter the God of their fathers and mothers in personal surrender. At the altar, the next generation is not merely entertained but transformed, carrying the flame of revival forward into the future.

At the altar, hidden motives are tested. Ananias and Sapphira brought an offering to God but lied about their sacrifice, and judgment fell on them (Acts 5:1-10). God is not fooled by appearances; He weighs the heart. When the church returns to the altar, giving, serving, and worshiping are purified of selfish ambition. Leaders who once sought platforms will seek His presence.

Members who once gave for recognition will give in secret. The altar burns away every false motive until only sincerity remains. The Church must cultivate environments that facilitate return to the altar: teaching on repentance, open calls to confession, and leadership modeling spiritual transparency. These practices help believers confront sin and seek restoration.

The altar also prepares the church for spiritual warfare. Israel's victories were always tied to obedience and consecration. Before the fall of Jericho, Israel was circumcised and set apart to God (Joshua 5:2–10). Before victory over the Midianites, Gideon built an altar of peace (Judges 6:24). Today, the church faces battles against demonic ideologies, cultural strongholds, and spiritual darkness. Only a church purified at the altar can march forward with authority to pull down strongholds in Jesus' name.

Finally, the altar positions us for the outpouring of the Spirit. Joel prophesied that after repentance and returning to God, He would pour out His Spirit on all flesh (Joel 2:28). Pentecost was not an accident—it came after days of prayer, unity, and waiting before God. The church cannot skip the altar and expect the Spirit to move mightily. Renewal follows repentance, and empowerment follows surrender. If we long for another Pentecost, we must first gather at the altar.

The altar is a place of divine exchange. At the cross—the ultimate altar—Christ took our sin, shame, and death, giving us righteousness, grace, and eternal life in return. Every return to the altar is a return to the foot of the cross, where we trade self-reliance for dependence on Christ, bitterness for forgiveness, and fear for faith. This ongoing exchange is how the church regains its strength, not by clinging to its own resources, but by drawing from the limitless supply of God's mercy.

At the altar, we confront the idols of our age. Just as Israel bowed before Baal, the modern church has bowed before idols of success, consumerism, politics, and celebrity culture. These idols are subtle, cloaked in religious language yet devoid of God's Spirit. The altar demands their destruction. Like Gideon, who tore down his father's altar to Baal (Judges 6:25–26), the church must tear down false altars and return to worshiping the living God alone. Without this tearing down, no true rebuilding can occur.

The altar is where lament and hope meet. The prophets often led God's people in weeping over sin, yet their tears carried a promise of renewal. Jeremiah wept over Jerusalem's destruction, yet he also declared that God's mercies are new every morning (Lamentations 3:22–23). At the altar, we bring our grief over sin, but we also rise with the assurance of grace. This balance of sorrow and hope prevents despair while fostering genuine transformation.

At the altar, worship is purified. Worship has too often become centered on style, preference, or performance. But when hearts are broken before God, worship transcends music and becomes a living sacrifice. In John 4:23, Jesus said the Father seeks worshipers who worship in spirit and in truth. At the altar, pretense fades, and truth flows from the depths of surrendered hearts. This kind of worship is not about pleasing crowds but about touching heaven.

The altar restores prophetic urgency. When Isaiah saw the Lord high and lifted, he also saw his own sinfulness and cried out, "Woe is me!" (Isaiah 6:5). Only after the coal from the altar touched his lips was he commissioned to speak for God. Likewise, when the church lingers at the altar, its message carries weight. Sermons stop being motivational speeches and become prophetic declarations that pierce hearts, because they are birthed in fire at the altar.

The altar also awakens compassion. A church that avoids repentance often becomes self- righteous and harsh toward the world. But at the altar, when we see the depth of our own sin and the greatness of God's grace, we cannot help but extend mercy to others. The church regains its mission when it remembers that it was forgiven much and therefore must love much. The altar transforms judgmental hearts into vessels of grace that embody Christ's love to the broken.

At the altar, revival is sustained. Many moves of God in history began with repentance at the altar but faded when prayer and humility were abandoned. True renewal is not an emotional outburst but a lifestyle of continual return. The altar must become the heartbeat of the church, the place where leaders and laity alike consistently return to seek His face. Without this ongoing surrender, revival will flicker out; with it, revival will blaze until Christ returns.

The altar equips the church to endure persecution. When trials intensify and opposition rises, only those who have died at the altar will stand firm. Shallow faith collapses under pressure, but crucified faith perseveres. The early disciples endured beatings, imprisonments, and martyrdom because they had already laid their lives on the altar. Likewise, if the modern church is to withstand increasing hostility, it must be a people who have counted the cost and surrendered all at the altar of God.

The altar ultimately points us to eternity. Every act of repentance, every prayer of surrender, every sacrifice of worship is preparing the Bride for her Bridegroom. Revelation 8:3–4 describes the prayers of the saints rising like incense before God's throne. The altar on earth connects with the altar in heaven, reminding us that our worship and repentance are eternal in significance. The altar is not just about personal renewal but about preparing for the marriage supper of the Lamb.

Therefore, the call to return to the altar is urgent and unavoidable. The church is on trial, and God is revealing hidden evil—not to condemn but to purify. The altar stands as the place of decision: will we cling to our pride, our idols, and our superficial religion, or will we bow low in brokenness and surrender? Revival, renewal, and restoration await those who return. The fire of God is ready to fall, but it will only descend on a church that has rebuilt the altar of repentance and consecration. Now is the time to return. In conclusion, returning to the altar is essential for spiritual renewal. Scripture, Lewis, Tozer, and Ravenhill collectively affirm that true repentance and heartfelt surrender prepare the Church to experience God's glory, healing, and revival.

Hebrews 12:14 instructs, *"Pursue peace with all people, and holiness, without which no one will see the Lord."* Holiness is not optional; it is a prerequisite for intimacy with God and spiritual effectiveness. C. S. Lewis, in *Mere Christianity*, emphasizes that holiness is an inner transformation, not merely outward conformity. God calls believers to align every thought, word, and deed with His will.

"Holiness unto the Lord" was inscribed on the priest's forehead in the Old Testament (Exodus 28:36-38). It was a visible reminder that everything connected to the worship of God must be holy. Today, God has not lessened His standard. If anything, He has heightened it through Christ, who calls His people to be holy as He is holy (1 Peter 1:16). Holiness is not optional—it is the defining mark of God's people, setting them apart in a world drowning in compromise.

Holiness is not simply moral perfection but separation unto God. To be holy means to be "set apart" for His use, cleansed from defilement, and dedicated to His glory. Israel was chosen to be holy, not because of their greatness, but because of God's covenant love. In the same way, the church has been redeemed to live distinctly. Holiness is not about legalism or self- righteousness—it is about belonging wholly to God and reflecting His nature in a darkened world.

The cry for holiness is especially urgent in this generation because compromise has crept into the house of God. Many have blurred the line between the sacred and the profane, treating holy things casually. Entertainment has often replaced reverence, and convenience has replaced consecration. Yet God's standard has not changed. He still declares, "Be ye holy, for I am holy" (Leviticus 11:44). Holiness is not a suggestion; it is a command that echoes from Sinai to Calvary to eternity.

Holiness is both positional and practical. Through Christ's blood, believers are declared holy, justified before the Father. But holiness is also progressive, worked out daily in our actions, attitudes, and affections. Paul exhorted the Corinthians to cleanse themselves "from all filthiness of the flesh and spirit, perfecting holiness in the fear of God" (2 Corinthians 7:1). This means holiness is not just what we receive; it is also what we pursue with intentionality and discipline.

At its core, holiness is about intimacy with God. Sin separates, but holiness draws us near. Hebrews 12:14 warns that without holiness no one will see the Lord. This is not about earning salvation but about cultivating the purity that allows unhindered fellowship with Him. A holy life is not sterile or joyless—it is vibrant and overflowing, because nothing hinders the flow of God's Spirit. The closer we walk in holiness, the deeper our intimacy with the One who is holy.

Holiness is also a witness to the world. Jesus said we are the light of the world, a city set on a hill that cannot be hidden (Matthew 5:14). When believers live in holiness, they shine in contrast to the darkness around them. The church does not impact the world by blending in but by standing out. Our purity becomes a testimony that God transforms lives. Without holiness, the church loses its distinction and becomes just another voice among the noise.

Holiness demands the cleansing of both the outward and the inward life. Jesus rebuked the Pharisees for cleaning the outside of the cup while leaving the inside filthy (Matthew 23:25). Outward conformity to religious rules means nothing if the heart is corrupt. True holiness begins within—purity of thought, motive, and desire—that then flows outward into behavior. Holiness is not simply about what we avoid but about what we pursue: love, integrity, humility, and obedience. A. W. Tozer, in *The Pursuit of God*, reminds the Church that holiness is the response to God's presence. It flows from a heart surrendered fully to Him, producing reverence, obedience, and discernment.

Holiness requires separation from sin but also dedication to God. Israel was called not just to abstain from pagan practices but to actively worship and serve Yahweh. Likewise, the church is not holy merely because it avoids sin but because it clings to Christ. A holy life is not lived in isolation but in devotion. It is not defined by a list of "don'ts" but by an all-consuming "yes" to God's will and purposes. Tozer observes that many in the Church settle for mediocrity, neglecting the pursuit of holiness. Without sanctification, believers are susceptible to deception, spiritual weakness, and ineffectiveness in ministry.

Holiness is costly. It requires the denial of fleshly desires, the breaking of sinful habits, and the rejection of worldly systems. Moses chose to suffer affliction with the people of God rather than enjoy the pleasures of sin for a season (Hebrews 11:25). Daniel refused to defile himself with the king's delicacies, even at the risk of losing favor (Daniel 1:8). Today, believers must be willing to pay the price of holiness, even if it means rejection, ridicule, or sacrifice.

Holiness is possible only through the empowerment of the Holy Spirit. Left to ourselves, we cannot live pure lives. My flesh is weak, and temptation is strong. But God has not left us powerless. His Spirit indwells believers, convicting, guiding, and empowering us to walk in holiness. Galatians 5:16 assures us, "Walk in the Spirit, and ye shall not fulfil the lust of the flesh." Holiness is not achieved by sheer willpower but by surrendering to the Spirit's work in us.

Holiness requires vigilance because the enemy seeks to subtly erode purity. Samson was called a Nazarite, consecrated to the Lord from birth, yet he compromised little by little until his strength was gone (Judges 16:19–20). The same danger faces the church today's small compromises in entertainment, doctrine, or behavior slowly chip away at holiness until we no longer notice the Spirit's absence. Vigilance means guarding our hearts diligently, for out of them flow the issues of life (Proverbs 4:23).

Holiness also requires obedience, even when it conflicts with culture. Noah stood out in his generation because he walked with God while the world drowned in wickedness (Genesis 6:9). His obedience set him apart as holy. Likewise, when the church chooses to obey Scripture above societal trends, it shines as a prophetic witness. Holiness is not determined by majority vote; it is anchored in God's unchanging Word, even when that Word places us at odds with the world.

Holiness is practical. It touches how we speak, how we treat others, and how we conduct ourselves in daily life. James teaches that pure religion is to keep oneself unspotted from the world while caring for the vulnerable (James 1:27). A holy church does not merely preach against sin, it demonstrates holiness through compassion, generosity, justice, and integrity. Our holiness is verified not only in what we resist but also in how we love and serve.

Holiness demands renewal of the mind. Paul urged believers in Romans 12:2 not to conform to this world but to be transformed by the renewing of their minds. What we feed our minds will eventually shape our lives. In an age saturated with media, compromise often enters through the eye and ear gates. Holiness means filtering what we allow to influence us and submitting our thoughts to the obedience of Christ. A renewed mind produces a renewed life. Leonard Ravenhill, in *Why Revival Tarries*, stresses that the lack of holiness among God's people hinders revival. Where compromise, sin, or indifference persist, the Church cannot experience God's power or glory.

Holiness is sustained through spiritual disciplines. Prayer, fasting, studying Scripture, worship, and fellowship with other believers are not optional extras but the backbone of a holy life.

Neglect of these disciplines leaves us vulnerable to temptation and spiritual drift. Just as a fire dies without fuel, holiness withers without daily communion with God. The church must return to these disciplines, not as rituals, but as lifelines that keep us anchored in God's presence.

Holiness requires courage in a hostile world. Shadrach, Meshach, and Abednego stood before Nebuchadnezzar's fiery furnace rather than bow to an idol (Daniel 3:18). Their holiness was not theoretical but tested in the heat of trial. The modern church will also face fiery tests—whether in workplaces, schools, or society at large. Holiness may cost careers, friendships, or reputations. But like those three men, we must declare that our loyalty belongs to God alone, no matter the consequences.

Holiness exposes hypocrisy. Jesus confronted the religious leaders of His day, who outwardly appeared righteous but inwardly were full of dead men's bones (Matthew 23:27). The church today must examine itself lest we fall into the same trap, appearing spiritual while harboring hidden sin. True holiness refuses duplicity. It demands integrity in private as well as in public, on Monday as much as on Sunday. Where hypocrisy is exposed, holiness invites genuine transformation.

Holiness is beautiful. Psalm 29:2 commands us to worship the Lord in the beauty of holiness. When God's people live consecrated lives, the radiance of His presence shines through them. Holiness is not dull or restrictive; it is radiant, life-giving, and attractive. A holy church becomes a testimony to the world, drawing others not through gimmicks but through the visible reality of God's glory resting on His people.

Holiness brings freedom. Sin enslaves, but holiness liberates. Jesus declared that whoever sins is a slave to sin, but whoever the Son sets free is free indeed (John 8:34-36). Living in holiness is not bondage but deliverance from destructive habits and desires. The truly holy believer is not weighed down by shame or addiction but walks in the liberty of a clear conscience and the joy of the Spirit. Holiness is not chains, it is wings.

Holiness positions the church for revival. Every major awakening in history was preceded by a return to holiness. The Welsh Revival, the Great Awakenings, and the Azusa Street outpouring all began with repentance and consecration. When God's people cleanse themselves, His Spirit is poured out without measure. A church that ignores holiness forfeits revival, but a church that embraces holiness becomes a vessel for God's glory. If we long for awakening, we must first long for holiness.

The call to holiness has always been at the center of God's relationship with His people. From the earliest days of the covenant at Sinai, God declared to Israel, "Be ye holy; for I am holy" (Leviticus 11:44). This was not a mere suggestion or lofty ideal, but a divine command rooted in the very nature of God Himself. Holiness is not optional for the people of God; it is the distinguishing mark of those who belong to Him. Without holiness, the church cannot represent Christ to the world, nor can it stand as a light in the midst of darkness.

In a time when the church is on trial, holiness becomes the primary evidence that it truly belongs to the Lord. Too often, believers attempt to substitute programs, traditions, or even charity in place of holiness. Yet Scripture makes it clear that it is the purity of heart, mind, and action that God requires. Holiness is not just about separation from sin but also about dedication to God's service. It is both cleansing and consecration, a washing and a setting apart.

The phrase "Holiness Unto the Lord" once adorned the priestly garments in the Old Testament. Engraved on a golden plate, it was fastened to the forehead of the high priest (Exodus 28:36–38). This visible reminder proclaimed to all of Israel that their priest and, by extension, the entire nation was consecrated to God. In the same way, the church today is called to wear holiness like a crown upon its head, visible not just in word but indeed, showing the world that it belongs to God.

When holiness is neglected, compromise quickly takes root. The church begins to adopt the world's values, philosophies, and practices under the guise of relevance. Instead of being salt and light, it becomes diluted and dim. Holiness is the safeguard against hidden evil infiltrating the body of Christ. It exposes corruption, restrains sin, and restores reverence for God's presence.

Without holiness, the altar becomes defiled, and worship loses its power.

The holiness God requires cannot be manufactured by human effort alone. It is not a product of self-righteousness, legalism, or outward appearance. True holiness flows from a transformed heart made new by the Spirit of God. Jesus prayed, "Sanctify them through thy truth: thy word is truth" (John 17:17). Holiness begins with the Word of God renewing the mind, reshaping the desires, and conforming the believer into the image of Christ.

Sadly, in the modern church, holiness has been reduced to a controversial or outdated concept. Some equate it with rigid dress codes or strict denominational rules, while others dismiss it as impossible in an age of grace. Both extremes miss the heart of God's call. Holiness is not bondage but freedom, freedom from the chains of sin, freedom to walk in righteousness, and freedom to live a life pleasing to God. Grace does not excuse sin; it empowers holiness. The Church must model holiness publicly and privately, emphasizing accountability, discipleship, and devotion. Leaders play a crucial role in exemplifying holy living to inspire others.

The altar of God is where holiness is renewed. In the Old Testament, sacrifices were offered to atone for sin and restore purity. Today, the altar represents the place of surrender, repentance, and consecration in the life of a believer. Returning to the altar is not about ritual but about relationships. It is about laying down pride, confessing sin, and embracing the cleansing power of Christ's blood. Holiness begins afresh each time the church bows low before the altar of God.

A holy church will always be a peculiar church. Scripture reminds us that God's people are "a chosen generation, a royal priesthood, a holy nation, a peculiar people" (1 Peter 2:9). Peculiar does not mean strange for the sake of being different; it means set apart for God's purposes. The church is not called to blend into the world but to stand out as a witness of God's holiness. When believers embrace this identity, they carry the fragrance of Christ wherever they go.

Holiness is also deeply tied to integrity. It is not simply about avoiding obvious sins but about being the same in private as in public. Hidden evil thrives in secrecy, but holiness thrives in transparency. When the church walks in holiness, there is nothing to hide and nothing to fear. Leaders are accountable, members are sincere, and the Spirit of God has room to move. Holiness eliminates hypocrisy and restores credibility to the witness of the church.

The pursuit of holiness is not a one-time event but a lifelong journey. It requires daily surrender, daily discipline, and daily renewal of the mind. The Apostle Paul described it as a race to be run with endurance, laying aside every weight and sin that so easily besets us (Hebrews 12:1). This ongoing pursuit keeps the church vigilant and dependent on God. Holiness is not perfection achieved overnight but obedience practiced consistently.

Holiness in leadership is essential if the church is to reflect Christ faithfully. Leaders are not merely administrators or organizers; they are shepherds who must model holiness in their character and decisions. When leaders compromise in secret, the entire flock suffers. Scripture warns, "Be thou an example of the believers, in word, in conversation, in charity, in spirit, in faith, in purity" (1 Timothy 4:12). A holy leader sets a standard, creating an atmosphere where sin cannot thrive unnoticed. Holiness involves separation from worldly values, pleasures, and compromises that oppose God's commands. It is a daily commitment to live under the authority of Scripture and the guidance of the Holy Spirit.

One of the greatest threats to holiness in leadership is the lure of power. When authority is abused, hidden evil quickly creeps in. Leaders may begin to prioritize their own reputation, wealth, or influence over the call of Christ. But holiness demands humility. It requires leaders to remember that they are servants first, accountable not only to their congregations but to God Himself. True holiness strips away pride and positions the leader at the feet of Christ.

Holiness also transforms worship. Worship that is rooted in entertainment or performance lacks the power of God's presence. The psalmist declared, "Worship the LORD in the beauty of holiness" (Psalm 29:2). Holiness beautifies worship because it purifies the heart of the worshipper. When the church gathers in holiness, its songs become more than melodies; they become sacrifices of praise. Its prayers rise as incense, and its gatherings become filled with the tangible presence of God.

A holy church cannot compartmentalize holiness to Sunday mornings. It must carry holiness into its relationships, workplaces, and homes. Holiness shapes the way husbands love their wives, the way parents nurture their children, and the way believers treat their neighbors. When holiness governs relationships, forgiveness replaces bitterness, compassion replaces selfishness, and unity replaces division. In this way, holiness builds community, not isolation.

Holiness is also necessary in how the church engages with the culture around it. Too often, believers are tempted to compromise to be accepted or applauded by society. Yet God has not called His church to mirror the world but to transform it. Jesus said believers are to be "the salt of the earth" and "the light of the world" (Matthew 5:13-14). Without holiness, salt loses its savor, and light grows dim. The world is transformed only when it sees a church living differently.

The battle for holiness is spiritual warfare. Satan knows that a holy church is a powerful church. That is why he works tirelessly to corrupt, distract, and deceive. He whispers lies that holiness is too difficult, too outdated, or too radical. He tempts believers with hidden sins that slowly erode their spiritual strength. But holiness, guarded by prayer and the Word of God, becomes a shield against his attacks. When believers resist the devil in holiness, he must flee.

The Holy Spirit is the divine agent of holiness. No one can walk in holiness apart from the Spirit's sanctifying work. Paul reminded the Corinthians, "Ye are washed, ye are sanctified, ye are justified in the name of the Lord Jesus, and by the Spirit of our God" (1 Corinthians 6:11). The Spirit convicts of sin, empowers obedience, and produces the fruit of righteousness. Without the Spirit, holiness becomes legalism; with the Spirit, holiness becomes transformation.

Holiness requires separation from sin but never isolation from sinners. Jesus Himself ate with tax collectors and was called a friend of sinners, yet He never compromised His holiness. The church must learn to live in the world without being of the world. This means rejecting sinful practices while still loving and reaching the lost. Holiness draws boundaries but also extends grace. It stands firm in truth while still offering the invitation of mercy. Lewis explains that spiritual maturity demands intentional choices to reject sin, embrace righteousness, and cultivate virtue. Holiness is not optional but the natural fruit of a transformed heart.

A holy church will experience persecution. The world cannot tolerate a community that shines too brightly against its darkness. Jesus warned, "If the world hates you, ye know that it hated me before it hated you" (John 15:18). Holiness will always expose the corruption of society, and those who love sin will resist it. Yet persecution only confirms that the church is walking in the footsteps of Christ. Holiness is costly, but it is worth the price.

Holiness also restores fear and reverence for God in the congregation. When sin is tolerated, reverence fades, and worship becomes casual. But when holiness is pursued, awe of God returns. In Acts 5, the story of Ananias and Sapphira shows how God judged dishonesty in the early church, and Scripture records that "great fear came upon all the church." That fear was not terror but reverence—a renewed understanding that God is holy and must be honored.

Holiness must not be confused with perfectionism. Perfectionism focuses on human effort and outward achievement, while holiness focuses on surrender to God's sanctifying work. A believer walking in holiness will stumble at times, but repentance restores fellowship. The difference is that a holy heart hates sin and desires righteousness. Holiness is not about never failing but about never settling for sin.

One mark of holiness is simplicity. The holy life is not cluttered by greed, vanity, or worldly ambition. It seeks first the kingdom of God (Matthew 6:33). Simplicity in lifestyle, speech, and priorities creates space for God's presence. In contrast, a compromised life is weighed down with distractions that suffocate spiritual growth. Holiness calls believers to lay aside anything that competes with their devotion to God.

Another mark of holiness is purity in thought. The battle for holiness often begins in the mind. Paul urged believers, "Bring into captivity every thought to the obedience of Christ" (2 Corinthians 10:5). A holy church guards its imagination, rejecting lust, bitterness, and pride before they take root. It fills its mind with the truth of Scripture and the beauty of Christ. What occupies the mind will eventually shape the heart and behavior.

Holiness produces joy. Contrary to the lie that holiness is restrictive, those who walk in holiness experience the freedom of a clear conscience and the joy of intimacy with God. David declared, "Blessed is he whose transgression is forgiven, whose sin is covered" (Psalm 32:1). Joy flows from knowing that nothing stands between the believer and God. The world offers fleeting pleasures, but holiness brings lasting joy.

Holiness is also the foundation of unity in the church. Division thrives where sin reigns, but holiness unites believers around Christ. A holy church does not gossip, backbite, or compete for recognition. Instead, it esteems others above itself and seeks peace. Paul urged the Ephesians to keep "the unity of the Spirit in the bond of peace" (Ephesians 4:3). Unity is not achieved by compromise but by shared holiness. Ravenhill highlights historical awakenings that began with individuals and congregations embracing holiness. These movements demonstrate the catalytic power of consecrated living in bringing revival and transformation.

The pursuit of holiness must be intentional. It does not happen by accident. Believers must discipline themselves in prayer, fasting, studying Scripture, and practicing obedience. Just as an athlete trains for a race, so the church must train for holiness. Spiritual disciplines do not earn holiness but cultivate it. They prepare the heart for God's refining work and keep the believer strong in times of temptation.

Holiness is the standard for the family. The home is the first place where holiness should be practiced. Parents must teach their children the fear of the Lord, modeling holiness in their speech, habits, and priorities. A home filled with holiness becomes a sanctuary where God's presence dwells. When families are holy, the church grows strong, and when families compromise, the church grows weak.

Holiness is the church's testimony to the world. It is not the size of the building or the eloquence of the sermons that convinces unbelievers of the reality of God. It is the visible holiness of His people. Jesus said, "By this shall all men know that ye are my disciples, if ye have love one to another" (John 13:35). Love expressed in holiness becomes the most powerful apologetic for the gospel.

Holiness exposes hidden evil. Darkness cannot coexist with light. When holiness is embraced, secret sins come to the surface, corruption is revealed, and hypocrisy is destroyed. This may be painful, but it is necessary for the healing of the church. God will not allow His bride to remain defiled. He is cleansing His house so that it may be presented without spot or wrinkle at Christ's return.

Holiness also fuels intercession. A holy heart prays with power because it is aligned with God's will. James reminds us that "the effectual fervent prayer of a righteous man availeth much" (James 5:16). When the church prays in holiness, its petitions move heaven and shake earth.

Intercession flows from undefiled hearts, and such prayers become mighty weapons against the forces of evil.

Holiness prepares the church for revival. Revival does not come to a church that tolerates sin. It comes to a church that humbles itself, repents, and seeks the face of God. Every great revival in history has been preceded by a return to holiness. God pours out His Spirit where hearts are clean and altars are restored. Without holiness, revival remains a distant dream.

Holiness also prepares the church for suffering. A compromised church crumbles under pressure, but a holy church stands firm. Holiness strengthens believers to endure hardship with faith and hope. It reminds them that suffering refines faith like gold and draws them closer to Christ. In times of trial, holiness keeps the church anchored in eternal realities rather than shaken by temporary storms.

Holiness teaches believers to value eternal rewards over earthly gain. The holy heart looks not for applause from men but for approval from God. It treasures crowns that will not fade, even if it means losing comfort or recognition now. Paul testified, "I press toward the mark for the prize of the high calling of God in Christ Jesus" (Philippians 3:14). Holiness reorients priorities around eternity.

Holiness also guards against deception. In the last days, false prophets and teachers will arise, leading many astray. Only a holy church, grounded in truth, will be able to discern the difference between light and darkness. Jesus warned that even the elect could be deceived if possible. But holiness, guided by the Spirit, equips the church with discernment to recognize and resist deception.

Holiness is inseparable from love. Some portray holiness as harsh or judgmental, but true holiness is marked by compassion. It is not about condemning others but about loving them enough to call them freedom. Holiness without love becomes legalism, and love without holiness becomes compromised. Together, holiness and love reflect the fullness of Christ.

Holiness also transforms the way believers use their resources. A holy heart is generous, viewing money, time, and talents as gifts entrusted by God for His purposes. Holiness breaks the grip of greed and cultivates stewardship. When the church practices holiness in giving, needs are met, the poor are cared for, and the gospel advances without hindrance.

The call to holiness is urgent because Christ is coming soon. Scripture declares that Jesus will return for a bride "arrayed in fine linen, clean and white" (Revelation

19:8). The church cannot afford to be entangled in sin when the Bridegroom arrives. Holiness prepares the church to meet Him with joy rather than shame. It keeps the lamp filled with oil, ready for the midnight cry.

Holiness is not only personal but corporate. The church as a body must pursue holiness together. This means holding one another accountable, encouraging one another in righteousness, and restoring one another in gentleness when someone falls. A holy church bears one another's burdens and spurs one another on to good works. Holiness is strengthened in community.

The legacy of the church depends on holiness. Programs and buildings may fade, but the holiness of God's people leaves an eternal impact. Generations to come will be shaped not by what the church built but by how it lived. A holy church passes down faith, integrity, and reverence for God to its children and grandchildren. Holiness ensures that the flame of truth never goes out.

In the end, the banner over the church must read, "Holiness Unto the Lord." This is not simply a slogan but a declaration of identity and destiny. The church belongs to a holy God and is called to reflect His nature in every area of life. In a world filled with compromise, corruption, and hidden evil, holiness is the answer. It is both the shield that protects the church and the light that guides it forward. Holiness unto the Lord is the only way the church can stand blameless when it appears before the Judge of all the earth. In conclusion, holiness unto the Lord is essential for revival and spiritual authority. Scripture, Lewis, Tozer, and Ravenhill collectively affirm that the pursuit of holiness enables believers to experience God's presence, power, and protection in their lives and ministries.

Restoring hearts, rebuilding trust, and renewing spiritual vitality Traditions Without Command

When we look closely at the Old Testament, we find no command from God for His people to build synagogues. God commanded Moses concerning the tabernacle in the wilderness (Exodus 25:8-9) and later directed Solomon to build the temple in Jerusalem (1 Kings 6:11-13). But the synagogue system was never divinely ordered. Instead, it arose as a human response during the Babylonian exile. Stripped of access to the temple, the Jews gathered in local meeting places to preserve their identity and traditions. Over time, what began as survival in crisis became sacred ritual. Yet when Christ Himself came as the true temple (John 2:19-21), many of those who clung to these traditions rejected Him. Jesus rebuked them: "You nullify the word of God for the sake of your tradition" (Matthew 15:6).

Ekklesia, Not Institutions

Jesus never told His disciples to construct another temple or build religious institutions. Instead, He spoke of His *ekklesia*—a people called out of the world, sin, and dead religion to walk in relationship with Him (Matthew 16:18). The Greek word *ekklesia* refers to a gathered assembly of people, not a building or denomination. Paul reinforced this truth: "Do you not know that you are God's temple and that God's Spirit dwells in you?" (1 Corinthians 3:16). The early church lived this reality. After Pentecost, believers met in homes, broke bread together, prayed fervently, and lived Spirit-filled lives (Acts 2:42-47). True worship was never confined to a structure or stage but flowed from hearts consecrated to Christ.

When Rome Replaced the Relationship with Religion

History shows how quickly man replaces intimacy with God with institutions. In the fourth century, when Constantine legalized Christianity, the church shifted from house gatherings and Spirit-led worship to formalized religion. Cathedrals, creeds, and rituals replaced the simplicity of fellowship in Christ. A.W. Tozer observed, "Religion can reform a man's life, but it can never transform him. Only the power of the cross can do that" (*The Pursuit of God*). By Rome's hand, Christianity was reshaped into something polished, respectable, and state-approved—but far removed from the raw presence of the Holy Spirit. Like ancient Babylon, Rome corrupted the worship of God by trading His living presence for lifeless ceremony.

The Covering of Sin With Tradition

This danger persists today. Many modern churches are focused on stages, programs, and performance-driven worship, but often lack the presence of God. Paul warned Timothy about those who are "having a form of godliness but denying its power" (2 Timothy 3:5). Just as the Jews clung to lifeless rituals and missed their Messiah, Christians today can become so attached to traditions, denominations, and cultural expectations that they overlook the living Christ among them. Leonard Ravenhill, in Why Revival Tarries, said, "The church used to be a lifeboat rescuing the perishing. Now she is a cruise ship recruiting the promising." Worship becomes entertainment rather than surrender, and the altar turns into a stage.

Worship in Spirit and Truth

Jesus told the Samaritan woman, "A time is coming and has now come when the true worshipers will worship the Father in the Spirit and in truth, for they are the kind of worshipers the Father seeks" (John 4:23-24). This reflects God's plan for His church. Worship is not connected to buildings, creeds, or man-made traditions—it is the response of a heart changed by His Spirit.

Paul told the Romans, "Offer your bodies as a living sacrifice, holy and pleasing to God—this is your true and proper worship" (Romans 12:1). To restore authentic worship, we must move away from polished religion and return to genuine, holy intimacy with Christ. We are not called to build sacred spaces but to be sacred people—His temple, His bride, His dwelling place.

John 4:23–24 declares, *"God is Spirit, and those who worship Him must worship in spirit and truth."* True worship is not about music, style, or performance; it is a matter of the heart fully surrendered to God. Hidden evil leaves deep wounds in believers' hearts. Revealing corruption is just the first step toward healing. True healing starts with acknowledging pain, betrayal, and spiritual harm. God calls His Church to offer restoration instead of condemnation to the wounded. Leaders must demonstrate empathy, humility, and care for those affected. S. Lewis, in *Mere Christianity*, emphasizes that genuine worship reflects inward devotion. Outward acts, without heart alignment, fail to honor God and are ineffective in connecting with Him.

Exposure allows the congregation to confront the root causes of their suffering. Healing involves confession, repentance, and reconciliation with God and one another. Spiritual wounds can lead to bitterness, discouragement, and spiritual stagnation. Exposure helps believers understand that they are not alone in their struggles. A. W. Tozer, in *The Pursuit of God*, asserts that worship is the natural response to God's presence and majesty. When the Church engages in superficial worship, it hinders intimacy with God and stifles the Holy Spirit. God's Spirit brings comfort, conviction, and guidance for restoration. Healing requires both personal surrender and corporate support. Leaders must provide safe spaces for vulnerability, prayer, and counseling. Exposure ensures that the causes of harm are addressed and corrected.

Healing strengthens faith, resilience, and spiritual discernment. The wounded are called to forgive, not to forget, releasing bitterness to God. Leaders must lead with integrity, demonstrating that God's justice prevails. Exposure educates the congregation on the dangers of hidden sin and compromise. Healing restores trust, unity, and spiritual vitality within the Church. Believers must engage in prayer, Scripture study, and community support. Leonard Ravenhill, in *Why Revival Tarries*, observes that historical revivals were accompanied by the restoration of true worship. Congregations humbled themselves, removed distractions, and focused on glorifying God in spirit and truth. False worship can be seen in performances designed to entertain rather than glorify God. Leaders and congregants may prioritize applause, popularity, or emotion, neglecting the transformative purpose of worship.

Leaders are responsible for protecting the flock from further harm. Exposure dismantles false teachings, manipulations, and oppressive structures. Healing empowers the faithful to reclaim spiritual authority in their lives. God's grace facilitates restoration for those broken by deception or abuse. Healing requires time, patience, and consistent spiritual nurturing. Leaders must provide guidance, mentorship, and accountability during recovery. Lewis explains that authentic worship requires honesty before God. It involves confessing sin, seeking forgiveness, and offering praise that reflects understanding and reverence for God's holiness.

Exposure motivates corrective measures, ensuring repeated harm is prevented. The wounded flock gains confidence when justice and transparency prevail. Healing strengthens relationships within families, communities, and ministries. Believers are reminded that God's love restores, renews, and redeems. Leaders must cultivate trust through transparency, humility, and faithful leadership. Exposure restores hope, demonstrating that God is sovereign over every situation.

Tozer emphasizes that music, ritual, and liturgy are tools, not the essence of worship. They facilitate connection with God but cannot replace heartfelt devotion, obedience, and spiritual focus.

Healing requires confronting fear, anger, and doubt with truth and prayer. The Church becomes a sanctuary for restoration when hidden evil is addressed. Leaders must actively participate in healing, offering guidance, prayer, and accountability. Ravenhill highlights that true worship produces fruit: spiritual renewal, conviction of sin, and empowerment for ministry. Without these outcomes, worship risks becoming an empty ritual. Healing requires confronting fear, anger, and doubt with truth and prayer. The Church becomes a sanctuary for restoration when hidden evil is addressed. Leaders must actively participate in healing, offering guidance, prayer, and accountability.

Exposure reinforces the importance of vigilance, discernment, and obedience to God. Healing produces spiritual maturity, compassion, and deeper devotion. The wounded are equipped to minister to others who have suffered similarly. Exposure clarifies the dangers of compromise, deception, and unchecked authority. The Church must educate, model, and encourage worship that is Scripture-based, Spirit-led, and Christ-centered. Leaders must guard against commercialization or superficial expressions that distort God's glory. Healing restores joy, peace, and confidence in God's provision and protection. Leaders who embrace healing inspire hope, courage, and spiritual growth. The Church is strengthened when the faithful are restored and spiritually empowered. Exposure teaches believers to recognize deception and stand firm in God's truth.

Restoring true worship is essential for spiritual renewal. Scripture, Lewis, Tozer, and Ravenhill collectively affirm that worship in spirit and truth draws believers closer to God, ignites revival, and cultivates enduring transformation. Healing requires ongoing prayer, discipleship, and accountability. Restoration of the wounded flock ensures the Church fulfills its calling with integrity and holiness. Ultimately, healing the wounded flock restores the Church's strength, unity, and devotion to Christ, enabling it to serve as a beacon of God's love and truth.

Equipping the Church for God's Mission

Preparing the Church to serve, proclaim, and impact the world with God's truth

Equipping the Church begins with recognizing the spiritual gifts God has given His people. Exposure of hidden evil highlights areas where the Church has neglected its mission. God calls leaders to train, disciple, and prepare believers for faithful service. Equipping involves teaching, mentorship, and practical opportunities to serve. Exposure clarifies weaknesses in leadership, ministry, and congregational engagement.

God desires a Church that is spiritually mature, disciplined, and mission-focused. Leaders must identify and nurture the gifts, talents, and callings of each member. Equipping strengthens faith, knowledge of Scripture, and discernment in ministry. Exposure ensures that resources, training, and leadership are aligned with God's purposes. God equips the Church through the Holy Spirit, Scripture, and community accountability.

Leaders must model service, humility, and dedication to God's mission. Equipping prepares believers to face spiritual opposition, deception, and challenges. Exposure motivates the Church to confront hidden compromises that hinder ministry. God calls for readiness, discipline, and perseverance in every aspect of service. Leaders must cultivate environments that encourage spiritual growth and skill development.

Equipping the Church strengthens unity, focus, and commitment to God's calling. Exposure highlights gaps in teaching, discipleship, and leadership integrity. Believers must embrace their roles, responsibilities, and callings with faithfulness. Leaders must foster accountability, spiritual mentorship, and practical ministry training. Equipping ensures the Church is prepared for evangelism, outreach, and discipleship.

Exposure teaches the importance of spiritual vigilance, humility, and obedience. God equips the Church for both local and global impact, emphasizing His glory. Leaders must identify barriers to effective ministry and provide solutions. Equipping the Church encourages confidence, resilience, and boldness in proclaiming truth. Exposure ensures that hidden sin or compromise does not hinder mission effectiveness.

Believers are called to serve with passion, integrity, and alignment with God's Word. Leaders must prioritize spiritual formation, equipping members for both service and leadership.

Equipping prepares the Church to respond to crises, challenges, and opportunities faithfully. Exposure reinforces the need for transparency, accountability, and holiness in ministry. God equips the Church to be a light in darkness, demonstrating His love and power.

Leaders must provide encouragement, guidance, and correction when necessary. Equipping strengthens the Church's capacity to disciple, mentor, and reproduce ministry fruit. Exposure protects the Church from false teachings, deception, and hidden corruption. Believers must embrace lifelong learning, spiritual growth, and active participation in mission. Leaders must empower members to discover and exercise their gifts effectively.

Equipping the Church aligns spiritual passion with God's mission and purposes. Exposure ensures leaders address weaknesses, corruption, and inefficiency in the ministry. Believers are strengthened to stand firm in faith, truth, and obedience. Leaders must teach discernment, service, and the application of God's Word in everyday life. Equipping the Church produces maturity, effectiveness, and enduring spiritual impact.

Exposure clarifies where reform, accountability, and purification are needed. God equips the Church to be a bold, holy, and compassionate witness to the world. Leaders must inspire dedication, courage, and integrity in fulfilling God's mission. Equipping the Church ensures that every member participates meaningfully in advancing God's Kingdom. Ultimately, a fully equipped Church serves as a powerful instrument of God's glory, transforming lives, communities, and nations through faithful obedience and mission-focused ministry.

Have I substituted religious tradition for true intimacy with God? Do I view worship as a program or performance, rather than a daily surrender of my life to Christ?

Prayer:

Lord, strip away every tradition, ritual, or man-made practice in my life that has replaced Your presence. Restore in me the heart of true worship, that I may walk in the Spirit and in truth. Make me Your dwelling place, a living sacrifice, holy and acceptable to You. Amen.

The story of King Ahab is not just a dusty piece of Israel's past—it is a mirror held up before our own generation. Ahab's reign, marked by greed, lust, injustice, and idolatry, reads like the headlines of our own day. His decisions were not isolated mistakes; they were consistent acts of rebellion against God, shaping a kingdom steeped in corruption. When we look at our churches and political systems today, we cannot help but see the same shadow of Ahab stretching across history. The Bible says there is nothing new under the sun (Ecclesiastes 1:9), and the sins of leaders then are tragically reflected in the sins of leaders now.

In Ahab's time, the throne became a seat of compromise and manipulation rather than righteousness. The same is true today when political leaders use their offices to enrich themselves and protect the wealthy while the poor remain oppressed. Likewise, church leaders who were called to shepherd God's people often instead build empires for their own glory. From lavish lifestyles funded by offerings to pulpits that protect predators, these are the dark days of the modern church world. We see Ahab's story unfolding in real time before our eyes.

Ahab's partnership with Jezebel deepened the darkness of his reign. Jezebel brought with her the spirit of Baal worship, seduction, and manipulation. This same spirit operates today in our churches and governments. It is the spirit that convinces leaders that they can exploit the vulnerable without consequence, that power is for personal gain rather than service. It is the same spirit that manipulates with lies, seduces with promises of prosperity, and silences those who dare to speak truth. Jezebel may be gone in body, but her spirit is alive and active.

One of the most grievous parallels between Ahab's time and ours is the abuse of the innocent. In recent years, countless scandals have erupted of pastors, priests, and leaders abusing children, women, and congregants. These are not small mistakes; they are deliberate acts of wickedness carried out under the cover of religion. Just as Ahab took what was not his when he seized Naboth's vineyard, so too have leaders stolen innocence, trust, and dignity from those they were called to protect. God is not silent about these sins—He is exposing them.

The cry of the oppressed has always reached the ears of God. In Ahab's day, Naboth's blood cried out from the ground after he was unjustly murdered to satisfy Ahab's greed. Today, the cries of abused children, silenced women, and betrayed congregations rise to heaven, and God hears. These dark days in our church world are not hidden from Him. Just as He sent Elijah to confront Ahab, He is raising voices now to confront leaders who think their sin will remain concealed.

The problem is not only in the church. Political leaders, too, walk in the same arrogance and greed as Ahab. Instead of serving the people, they serve themselves. Instead of protecting the vulnerable, they exploit them. Wars are waged for profit, while the poor are left to suffer.

Leaders pass laws that benefit the wealthy and oppress the needy, echoing the very sins of Ahab, who sacrificed righteousness for gain. These are not just political issues; they are spiritual issues, because they represent rebellion against God's justice.

Jezebel's influence over Ahab can also be seen in how today's leaders are swayed by ungodly influences. Whether through lobbyists in politics or false prophets in the church, leaders are manipulated into making decisions that dishonor God. Jezebel's spirit thrives wherever leaders surrender their authority to voices that whisper lies, encourage compromise, and promote self- indulgence. The result is a nation and a church that stumble deeper into darkness.

God's rebuke of hidden evil is a recurring theme in Scripture. Jesus Himself said that what is done in darkness will be brought to light (Luke 8:17). We see this unfolding in our time as scandals are exposed, secret sins are uncovered, and leaders are removed from their positions of power. These exposures are not coincidences—they are acts of divine justice. God will not allow His name to be mocked. When His leaders betray Him, He raises prophets, journalists, whistleblowers, and ordinary believers to shine the light of truth.

Yet even in the midst of judgment, God extends an invitation to repentance. When Elijah confronted Ahab, the king humbled himself in sackcloth and fasting, and God delayed His judgment (1 Kings 21:27-29). This shows us that no leader is beyond redemption if they will truly repent. Today, the same call is going out to church and political leaders: repent, humble yourselves, and turn from wickedness before it is too late. God's mercy is great, but His justice will not sleep forever.

The Scripture in *2 Chronicles 7:14* is not just a memory verse; it is a roadmap to healing: "If my people, who are called by my name, will humble themselves and pray and seek my face and turn from their wicked ways, then I will hear from heaven, and I will forgive their sin and will heal their land." This verse makes it clear: the responsibility begins with God's people, including leaders. The promise of healing is conditional on repentance. Without humility, there can be no forgiveness. Without turning, there can be no healing.

In these dark days, the pattern of Ahab is repeated in pulpits across the world. Leaders who should be shepherding God's people are instead building kingdoms for themselves. Their sermons are crafted to entertain rather than convict, and their ministries are designed to elevate their personal brand rather than magnify the name of Jesus. Ahab was a king who lived for his own comfort and gain, and many modern leaders are no different. The pursuit of wealth, fame, and influence has taken priority over holiness, service, and sacrifice.

One of the tragedies of Ahab's reign was his failure to defend righteousness. Instead of standing up to Jezebel and the prophets of Baal, he allowed them to thrive under his watch. This is mirrored today in churches where sin is ignored, excused, or covered up. Leaders turn a blind eye to abuse and corruption because addressing it might tarnish their reputation or cost them members. But silence in the face of evil is complicity. When leaders protect predators or sweep scandals under the rug, they are walking in Ahab's footsteps.

Ahab's desire for Naboth's vineyard reveals the greed that often drives leadership. Rather than being content with what God had given him, he lusted for more. In today's church world, this lust manifests in pastors and bishops seeking bigger churches, larger followings, and more extravagant lifestyles. Political leaders, too, exploit the vulnerable to expand their influence and fill their coffers. The poor and needy, meanwhile, are neglected and left to suffer. Greed blinds leaders to justice, just as it blinds Ahab.

Jezebel's spirit is not merely about seduction; it is about control. She orchestrated Naboth's murder with lies and manipulation, using false witnesses to carry out her scheme. Today, the Jezebel spirit infiltrates leadership through the manipulation of systems, silencing of victims, and the spreading of propaganda to maintain power. Whether in the political sphere or the church, Jezebel's influence thrives wherever leaders use deceit to protect their authority rather than surrendering to

God's truth.

These dark days are marked by the suffering of the innocent. Just as Naboth paid with his life for Ahab's greed, countless children, women, and men have suffered because of the selfishness of leaders. Abuse within the church has left lifelong scars on victims who trusted their leaders to be safe. Wars driven by political greed have destroyed nations, displaced families, and left orphans in their wake. God's heart breaks for the oppressed, and He promises to bring justice.

The exposure of hidden evil in our time is not accidental; it is divine. Every headline about another scandal, every corruption investigation, is evidence that God is shining light on what was done in secret. He is rebuking leaders who thought their sin would remain hidden. This exposure is both judgment and mercy: judgment, because sin is brought into the open; mercy, because it allows repenting before destruction comes.

Many leaders today, like Ahab, mistake God's patience for permission. Because judgment does not fall immediately, they believe they are safe. But the Bible warns us that God is not mocked, and what we sow we will reap (Galatians 6:7). Ahab ruled for years, but his end was destruction. Leaders who persist in wickedness, whether in church or politics, will eventually face the same outcome. God's patience is meant to lead us to repentance, not to justify our rebellion.

The church itself is at a crossroads. Will it rise with the spirit of Elijah and confront sin, or will it shrink back like Ahab, allowing Jezebel to rule unchecked? The modern Elijahs are not always found in pulpits; sometimes they are the whistleblowers, the survivors, the faithful few who refuse to compromise. They may not be popular, but they carry the prophetic mantle to call out sin and demand righteousness. Without such voices, darkness spreads unchecked.

Political leaders, too, need prophets who will speak truth to power. Elijah did not fear Ahab's wrath; he feared God. Today, too many spiritual leaders cozy up to politicians for influence, rather than challenging them to righteousness. The result is a blending of politics and religion that mirrors Baal worship, where God's name is used to justify wickedness. What we need are Elijahs who will confront kings, not flatter them.

Repentance must begin with humility. Ahab, for all his wickedness, humbled himself when confronted by Elijah. That act of humility delayed judgment. Leaders today must follow his example, not in sin, but in repentance. They must confess their wickedness, step down from positions of power if necessary, and seek God's forgiveness. Without humility, there can be no healing. Without repentance, there can be no restoration.

The promise of *2 Chronicles 7:14* is not limited to ancient Israel—it applies to God's people in every generation. Healing for our land will not come through political reform alone, nor through church growth strategies, but through repentance. Leaders must lead the way by humbling themselves, seeking God's face, and turning from evil. If they will not, then God will raise others who will. The church belongs to Christ, not to corrupt leaders.

One reason repentance is urgent is that prophecy is being fulfilled before our eyes. Jesus warned of wars and rumors of wars, of nations rising against nations, of lawlessness increasing, and of love growing cold (Matthew 24). We see these signs unfolding in our time. Greed fuels wars, lust fuels abuse, and lawlessness spreads unchecked in both political and religious institutions. These are the dark days of which Jesus spoke, and they remind us that time is short.

In this climate, the church cannot afford to be complacent. Just as Elijah confronted the prophets of Baal on Mount Carmel, we must confront the idols of our time: money, power, lust, and fame. We must declare with boldness that the Lord is God, and that no other power can save. This requires courage, because the Jezebel spirit does not surrender easily. But God is raising a remnant who will not bow to Baal, who will not compromise with sin.

Leaders who continue in wickedness while using the name of Christ bring greater judgment upon themselves. Jesus warned that it would be better for someone to have a millstone tied around their neck and be cast into the sea than to cause one of His little ones to stumble (Matthew 18:6). Every act of abuse, every exploitation of the poor, every false teaching that leads people astray, brings down the wrath of God. Judgment is certain unless there is repentance.

These dark days also reveal the emptiness of human power. Ahab was a king, yet he was powerless to save himself from God's judgment. In the same way, no political leader, no bishop, no pastor can escape the justice of God. Titles and positions mean nothing in the face of divine authority. What matters is obedience, humility, and righteousness. Without this, all the wealth and influence in the world cannot prevent judgment.

God is not looking for perfect leaders; He is looking for repentant ones. None of us is good in His sight until we turn from our sin and receive His mercy. Leaders who acknowledge their failures and repent can still be used by God. But those who persist in rebellion will be brought low. The choice is theirs: repentance or ruin.

The church must also learn to discern. Too often, congregations elevate leaders based on charisma rather than character, on eloquence rather than holiness. This is how Ahabs and Jezebels rise to power in the church. The people must awaken to the truth that not every leader who speaks in God's name is sent by Him. We must test the spirits, measure teachings against Scripture, and refuse to idolize human leaders.

The call to repentance is urgent not just for leaders, but for all God's people. Judgment begins in the house of God (1 Peter 4:17). If we tolerate wickedness in our midst, we share in its guilt. The church must cleanse itself of corruption, not through cover-ups but through confession. Only then will the world see a true reflection of Christ in His people.

These dark days are not without hope. Just as God preserved a remnant in Israel who had not bowed to Baal, He is preserving a remnant today. There are still faithful leaders who walk in humility, still churches that pursue righteousness, still believers who hunger for truth. They may be few, but they shine all the brighter against the backdrop of darkness.

Ultimately, the story of Ahab reminds us that God is sovereign. He raises kings and brings them down. He exposes sin and calls for repentance. He rebukes hidden evil and shines His light in the darkness. The question is not whether God will act; the question is whether we will respond. Will we humble ourselves, repent, and seek His face? Or will we persist in rebellion until judgment falls?

Leaders who continue in sin under the guise of Christianity deceive not only themselves but the people they lead. Ahab justified his desires through the influence of Jezebel, but God saw the truth of his heart. Today, leaders who preach righteousness while practicing exploitation are no different. God sees their hypocrisy, and history will hold them accountable. The faithful must not be silent, because speaking the truth is a spiritual responsibility.

The exploitation of wealth and status is rampant. Just as Ahab allowed the rich to prosper while Naboth lost his inheritance, modern leaders often prioritize the powerful elite over the marginalized. The policies, church programs, and sermons are skewed toward those who give the most or hold influence, leaving the poor, widows, orphans, and vulnerable neglected. God's heart breaks over this injustice, and His Word calls for equity and care for the oppressed.

Jezebel's spirit manifests today in the manipulation of loyalty and fear. Many leaders maintain control by threatening exposure, silencing critics, or creating dependence. This form of spiritual abuse mirrors the manipulation of Israel under Ahab and Jezebel, where fear dictated obedience and truth was silenced. God warns that leadership built on fear and deception will collapse, for His truth cannot be suppressed.

The church must confront this darkness courageously. Just as Elijah stood alone on Mount Carmel, proclaiming God's supremacy against hundreds of false prophets, believers today must not shrink from confronting sin in high places. It is uncomfortable, dangerous, and unpopular— but God's power goes with those who obey. Speaking truth to corrupted leaders is not rebellion; it is faithfulness to God.

Repentance is a personal and corporate act. Ahab's humility came only after confrontation, and even then, it was brief. Today, leaders must not only confess privately but also demonstrate visible change. Policies must be corrected, victims must be restored, and the misuse of power must end. Without tangible action, repentance remains superficial, and God's healing cannot manifest.

Political leaders who exploit justice for personal gain mirror the vineyard story in Ahab's reign. Wealthy donors and powerful corporations are often prioritized while the needy suffer. God's Word declares that justice delayed is oppression (Proverbs 21:15). Leaders who ignore the plight of the poor are walking in the same rebellion as Ahab, and God will judge them if they refuse to repent.

The Jezebel spirit also targets spiritual discernment. It suppresses accountability and isolates leaders from correction. Many victims of abuse in churches have been silenced because this spirit convinces people that questioning authority is sinful. God, however, values truth over position and calls His people to expose evil courageously. Where sin is hidden, God's rebuke will come sooner or later.

The prophetic role is critical in these dark days. Elijah did not compromise; he delivered God's message even at personal risk. Modern prophets and faithful leaders must do the same, confronting corruption in both politics and the church. God uses ordinary voices to perform extraordinary works when they speak boldly in obedience. Fear must not silence the messenger of truth.

The call for repentance is urgent because time is short. Scripture warns that in the last days, lawlessness will increase, and love will grow cold (Matthew 24:12). Leaders who persist in sin worsen the societal and spiritual decay around them. Yet God still offers mercy; His patience is not approval. The moment leaders humble themselves, they initiate the process of restoration and healing.

Repentance must be immediate, not delayed. Ahab's temporary humility postponed judgment, but it did not remove the consequences of years of wickedness. Modern leaders must recognize that delaying repentance only compounds the damage. The longer abuse, greed, and manipulation continue, the more difficult it becomes to restore trust and righteousness. Time is a gift, not a guarantee.

God's promise of healing for the land is tied directly to the repentance of leaders. Healing will not come through legislation, popularity, or wealth alone. It requires humility before God, confession of sin, and tangible acts of restitution. Leaders must turn from exploitation, address wrongdoing, and lead with justice, mercy, and righteousness. Only then will communities and nations begin to recover.

The church must protect the vulnerable. One of Ahab's failures was his complicity in the oppression of Naboth. Today, church and political leaders must actively safeguard children, women, and the poor. Ignoring abuse is complicity. Sheltering predators under the guise of ministry or authority is rebellion against God Himself. The call is clear: righteousness must be restored in both leadership and care for the oppressed.

Leaders must recognize the limits of human power. Ahab was king, but his authority could not shield him from God's judgment. Today's leaders may wield influence over congregations, legislation, or finances, but divine justice is greater. No position, prestige, or power can protect against the consequences of sin. God is sovereign, and His standards of holiness and justice are unchanging.

Repentance is not optional. Scripture commands all people everywhere to repent (Acts 17:30). Leaders who continue to exploit, deceive, or abuse under the guise of Christianity are called to step down, confess, and change their ways. Obedience is the key to restoration; without it, judgment is certain. Ahab's story reminds us that disobedience has long-term consequences.

God's rebuke can come in various forms. For Ahab, it was through Elijah's confrontation. Today, rebuke may come through investigations, media exposure, or prophetic voices. Leaders must recognize these interventions as acts of divine mercy designed to prompt repentance. Ignoring correction invites further judgment, while responding with humility initiates healing.

The Jezebel spirit often attacks those who confront it. Elijah faced threats and pursuit by Jezebel herself. Modern leaders exposing corruption may face backlash, loss of position, or slander. Yet Scripture encourages steadfastness: "Do not fear those who can kill the body but cannot kill the soul" (Matthew 10:28). Courageous confrontation is necessary to restore God's justice.

Leaders must flee temptation. Elijah often withdrew from danger and deception to pray and seek God's guidance. Similarly, modern leaders must distance themselves from corrupting influences, worldly allure, and political compromise. True leadership requires holiness, not opportunism. Running from evil is an act of wisdom, not weakness.

God's power remains unmatched. Elijah called fire from heaven; God's Spirit today can still convict hearts, heal wounds, and expose evil. Leaders who witness God's power in their lives are reminded that authority is not self-generated but divinely sanctioned. Only through obedience and submission to God can leaders avoid the pitfalls of pride and corruption.

Chastisement is evidence of God's love. Hebrews 12:6 teaches that those God loves, He chastens. Public exposure of sin, personal failure, and divine correction are all opportunities for repentance and renewal. Leaders who embrace correction can change the trajectory of their ministry or office; those who resist will follow Ahab to destruction.

The prophetic call includes the laity as well. Congregants and citizens must not remain passive in the face of injustice. Silence perpetuates corruption. We are called to hold leaders accountable, pray for their repentance, and support righteous voices. God's remnant will rise not only from the pulpit but from ordinary believers who refuse to compromise.

Repentance produces restoration. When leaders confess sin, make restitution, and lead righteously, communities and churches heal. Trust is rebuilt, spiritual life is renewed, and the oppressed are restored. God delights in reconciliation, and His promise is clear: when His people turn, He forgives and heals.

Prophetic discernment is essential. Just as Elijah discerned Ahab's heart, leaders today must cultivate sensitivity to the Spirit of God. This allows them to identify corruption, resist manipulation, and guide others in truth. The Jezebel spirit often blinds leaders to their own faults; discernment is the antidote.

Leadership is a sacred trust. Ahab abused his position, and history remembers him for it. Modern leaders must recognize that authority is not a personal prize but a divine responsibility. Exploiting power for personal gain violates God's covenant and invites judgment. Repentance restores trust, humility preserves influence, and obedience ensures alignment with God's purposes.

Every day of delay compounds damage. Abused children, neglected congregations, and marginalized communities continue to suffer while leaders persist in wickedness. Time is God's mercy; misuse of it is rebellion. Leaders must seize the moment to repent and correct their ways.

God raises Elijah-like voices for every generation. These are not always clergy; sometimes they are survivors, journalists, or ordinary believers. They confront the darkness with courage and wisdom. In a time when Jezebel and Ahab-like leaders flourish, the prophetic voice is a lifeline to the nation, a call to repentance, and a declaration of God's authority.

Restoration is possible but conditional. God does not leave repentance untested; it must be genuine. Leaders must confess, change behavior, and lead with justice and mercy. Superficial apologies or cosmetic fixes are insufficient. True repentance transforms lives, communities, and nations.

The Church's credibility depends on accountability. The world is watching, and hypocrisy undermines the Gospel. Leaders who exploit the name of Christ for selfish purposes tarnish the faith itself. Repentance restores not only their ministry but the witness of the Church to the world.

God's timing is perfect. Just as Ahab had a reprieve after humbling himself, so today's leaders can experience restoration if they turn now. Delayed repentance risks permanent loss, but obedience opens the door for mercy, forgiveness, and divine blessing.

The dark days will end when leaders, prophets, and the laity collectively align with God's Word. When sin is exposed, confronted, and abandoned; when justice is pursued; when the oppressed are restored, the darkness will recede. The Church and nation will flourish, not because of human efforts, but because of God's intervention through repentance and obedience.

The story of Ahab is a warning and a call to action. Leaders who refuse to repent will face judgment, but those who humble themselves, turn from sin, and seek God's face will see mercy and restoration. The dark days in our church and political world are an invitation to awaken, to confront sin, to embrace obedience, and to trust God to heal the land. The choice is ours, the time is now, and God's promise remains true: repentance brings restoration.

King Ahab is remembered as one of the darkest rulers in Israel's history, not because he made a single mistake, but because he lived in deliberate rebellion against God. His reign became a tragic testimony of what happens when leaders ignore the divine standard and embrace corruption as their way of life. In the same way, today's headlines are filled with rulers, politicians, and even pastors who seem to shape their entire leadership on deception, greed, and the abuse of power. When history books are written about our era, the pattern of moral collapse will stand out just as Ahab's legacy does in Scripture, and it will be remembered as a generation where truth was trampled for personal gain.

Ahab's name has become synonymous with evil because his leadership infected an entire nation. The Bible says, "Ahab, son of Omri, did more evil in the eyes of the Lord than any of those before him" (1 Kings 16:30). His rule was not neutral; it pulled Israel into idolatry, compromise, and judgment. Today, we see a similar trend as leaders use their influence not to elevate truth or justice, but to normalize sin. When political leaders pass laws that promote immorality, or when church leaders cover up abuse against children, women, or vulnerable adults, they become modern-day Ahabs. They are shaping the moral climate of nations in ways that provoke the anger of God.

What makes Ahab's reign so chilling is not just his disobedience but his intentional disregard for God's covenant. He knew the truth, yet he chose to live as if God did not matter. This is the reality in our own time, where many leaders—both in politics and the pulpit—profess to know God, but their actions betray Him. The abuse scandals in churches, the exploitation of the poor by greedy corporations, and the oppression of entire populations by corrupt regimes mirror Ahab's deliberate path of rebellion. When leaders treat holiness as optional and sin as manageable, they set themselves and their followers on a path toward destruction.

Ahab's reign as a spiritual disaster because he replaced worship of the true God with worship of idols. Idolatry is not always a golden statue; it can be money, power, sex, or fame. In our day, leaders bow before the idol of political power, sacrificing truth to secure their position. Some church leaders bow before the idol of celebrity status, building empires while their congregations starve spiritually. Meanwhile, the people suffer under policies, teachings, and environments that erode their dignity and silence their cries for justice. Just as Ahab brought Baal worship into Israel, modern leaders are ushering in a culture of compromise where sin is rebranded as progress.

Ahab's story is not just a cautionary tale; it is a prophetic mirror held up to our generation. His reign shows us how quickly a people can fall when leaders abandon the fear of God. Today, we see governments that exalt greed and suppress the poor, and churches that protect abusers while ignoring the cries of victims. The rise of wars, economic injustice, and corruption across the globe is not random; it reflects the fruit of leadership that rejects righteousness. Ahab's story reminds us that leadership matters, and when leaders turn away from God, entire nations are led into darkness.

Ahab's Union with Jezebel

Ahab's marriage to Jezebel was more than a political alliance; it was a spiritual disaster. Jezebel brought with her the worship of Baal, filled with sexual immorality, bloodshed, and manipulation. Ahab, instead of resisting, opened his heart and throne to her influence. This is a perfect reflection of how compromise works in leadership today. When political leaders make alliances with corruption, or when church leaders allow worldly practices into the house of God, they are marrying Jezebel all over again. They permit ungodly influence into the very center of decision-making, and the result is the spiritual decay of the people.

Jezebel was not just a foreign queen; she was a manipulator, a seducer, and an intimidator. Her spirit lives today in leaders who silence whistleblowers, suppress truth-tellers, and persecute those who stand for righteousness. In many churches, women and children have been abused by leaders who use intimidation to keep them silent, mirroring Jezebel's tactics of fear and control. In politics, truth-speakers are sidelined, censored, or destroyed while corrupt voices thrive. The Jezebel spirit is alive, deceiving leaders into believing they can suppress God's truth without consequence.

When Jezebel entered Israel, she did not come quietly; she actively promoted idolatry and persecution of God's prophets. Likewise, when compromise enters a church or government, it does not sit passively; it spreads like cancer. Today, the entertainment industry, pornography culture, and even some religious institutions are saturated with Jezebel's influence. Lust is marketed as liberation, greed is celebrated as success, and the voices that cry out against injustice are silenced as "old-fashioned" or "intolerant." God's anger burns against such deception because it leads His people into destruction.

The marriage of Ahab and Jezebel shows us the danger of leadership that prioritizes power over purity. Ahab's throne was corrupted because he valued political gain more than obedience to God. In our world today, leaders are quick to sell their integrity for votes, money, or influence. Church leaders may sacrifice holiness for popularity or compromise the truth of Scripture to keep a crowd. This is not just a leadership failure; it is a covenant betrayal, the same betrayal that provoked God's judgment in Ahab's time. And just like then, judgment will come again.

Jezebel's influence did not stay in the palace; it spread throughout Israel, corrupting prophets, priests, and common people alike. The same is true today: when a leader is compromised, it infects the entire community. Abuse scandals in the church do not just damage victims—they wound congregations, destroy trust, and push entire generations away from God. Political corruption does not just harm the poor—it fractures societies and deepens divisions. This is why God is so angry with leaders today; their hidden sins have become public wounds, and His people suffer while those in power live in excess. Like Israel under Ahab and Jezebel, our generation is paying the price for leadership built on compromise.

Modern Political Leaders

Just as Ahab used his throne to advance an agenda of rebellion against God, many political leaders today govern not for the people but for themselves. We see policies that favor the wealthy and powerful, while the poor are left to suffer. Corruption is often hidden under layers of bureaucracy, but its effects are visible in the hunger of children, the exploitation of workers, and the despair of communities left behind. Like Ahab, who ignored God's covenant to pursue his own desires, today's leaders craft laws that legalize what God calls sin: abortion, exploitation, and the normalization of immorality. Their decisions are not neutral; they shape the spiritual direction of nations, and they provoke the righteous anger of God.

Wars and conflicts erupt around the world, fueled by greed and the lust for power. Leaders fund violence while innocent civilians pay the price. Ahab's desire for control mirrors these leaders who will sacrifice lives for land, oil, or political dominance. Prophecy warned of "wars and rumors of wars" (Matthew 24:6), and we are living in those days. Political leaders, instead of seeking peace through justice, profit from chaos. This makes them modern Ahabs, presiding over kingdoms where truth is silenced, violence is glorified, and the people of God are left to mourn.

Many governments now openly pass laws that defy God's design for marriage, family, and holiness. They call evil good and good evil, exactly as Isaiah prophesied (Isaiah 5:20). Ahab legalized idolatry in Israel by building temples for Baal, and today our leaders legalize sins that destroy societies. They defend what is perverse while criminalizing those who stand for biblical truth. Just as Elijah stood before Ahab as a lonely voice for righteousness, modern prophets are mocked, silenced, or even persecuted. Yet God always preserves His voice, and even in this dark hour, He is exposing the lies of leaders who pretend to care for justice while promoting sin.

One of Ahab's greatest sins was cloaking corruption in the garments of respectability. He still wore the crown of Israel's king, yet behind the throne, he bowed to idols. In the same way, modern politicians make speeches about "justice," "freedom," and "equity," while enriching themselves and ignoring the cries of the poor. Wealthy donors and corporate interests often control policies, and the common people are exploited. God sees this hypocrisy, just as He saw Ahab's double life. He is not deceived by polished appearances or political slogans. The Lord declares, "I know your deeds" (Revelation 3:15), and His judgment will expose what is hidden.

But God always raises a prophetic witness. Just as Elijah confronted Ahab, God is stirring voices in this generation to speak truth to power. These voices may not sit in high offices, but they carry authority from heaven. They call out the corruption of politicians, they stand with the oppressed, and they cry out for righteousness. Yet, just like Elijah, they face opposition from Jezebel-like figures who seek to silence them. Still, their words pierce the darkness, reminding nations that God is not mocked, and judgment always follows when leaders forsake His ways.

Modern Church Leaders

The tragedy of our age is that the sins of Ahab are not limited to politics; they have infected the church. Leaders in pulpits, bishops, and pastors are often found guilty of the same evils that brought Ahab down: greed, lust, and manipulation. Abuse scandals in churches are not isolated incidents; they are systemic symptoms of hearts that have turned from God. Children, women, and even men have suffered at the hands of leaders who should have protected them. This mirrors the reign of Ahab, who allowed Jezebel to murder the innocent Naboth for a vineyard. Spiritual leaders abusing the vulnerable are no different; they shed innocent blood while feeding their lust for control.

Many church leaders have become celebrities, building personal empires instead of the kingdom of God. They market the gospel as a product, using prosperity promises to line their pockets while congregations remain spiritually malnourished. Ahab built palaces and altars to false gods; modern leaders build mega-centers that glorify themselves more than Christ. The poor remain oppressed, and their cries go unheard. God is angry because the shepherds who should feed the flock are devouring it. Ezekiel 34 condemns such shepherds, declaring that God Himself will step in to rescue His people when leaders fail.

In many cases, church leaders have silenced victims of abuse to protect reputations or institutions. This is the spirit of Jezebel at work: silencing truth, intimidating prophets, and covering up sin. Victims are told to remain quiet for the "sake of the ministry," while abusers continue unchecked. This is nothing less than spiritual murder, as it destroys lives and faith.

God's anger burns against such hidden evil. Just as Elijah declared judgment on Ahab's household, prophets today declare judgment on churches that cover sin instead of confronting it.

In other cases, pastors have aligned themselves with political powers, using the pulpit to advance agendas rather than preach the gospel. Ahab's throne was corrupted by his alliance with Jezebel; today, pulpits are corrupted when leaders exchange truth for political favor. They elevate ideologies above Christ, and in doing so, they turn worship into idolatry. When the church becomes a tool for power instead of a voice for truth, it ceases to be the church of Jesus Christ.

God is not blind to this betrayal, and He will hold accountable every leader who has misused His name for gain.

The prophets of Baal who dined at Jezebel's table remind us of religious leaders today who compromise truth for comfort. They preach what the people want to hear instead of what God has commanded. They bless sin instead of calling for repentance. They make alliances with wealth and power while neglecting the cross. Yet God's fire still falls from heaven, consuming false altars and proving that He alone is God. The church today must choose: will we be Elijahs, or will we be prophets of Baal?

The Church on Trial

The church today stands as if in a courtroom, placed on trial before the Judge of heaven. God is exposing what has been hidden in darkness for generations. The scandals that make headlines are not simply the work of journalists or activists— they are the hand of God pulling back the veil.

Just as Ahab's private theft of Naboth's vineyard was dragged into the light by the prophet Elijah, the hidden sins of church leaders—financial fraud, sexual abuse, manipulation, and exploitation—are being dragged into public view. This exposure is not God's cruelty; it is His justice. He is saying, "No more hiding. No more pretending. No more abuse in My name."

Many leaders thought they could bury their sins under titles, robes, and pulpits. They believed their charisma and authority could shield them from accountability. But God sees what happens in the shadows. He sees the hands that harm children, the mouths that seduce vulnerable women, the hearts that lust after money instead of holiness. He hears the cries of the wounded—the victims of leaders who abused their power. Just as God told Cain that the blood of Abel cried out from the ground, so today the cries of abuse victims rise before God, demanding justice.

The church is not being judged to destroy it, but to purify it. When gold is tested in fire, impurities rise to the surface so they can be removed. Likewise, scandals and exposures are not meant to humiliate the body of Christ but to cleanse it from within. God is preparing a bride without spot or wrinkle, and that means everything hidden must come to the light. Yet this purification will not come without pain. Entire denominations will be shaken, reputations destroyed, and idols toppled. But in the end, what remains will be pure and holy before God.

Some resist this trial, trying to cover sin with public relations campaigns or silencing whistleblowers, but that only deepens God's anger. Ahab tried to put on sackcloth and appear humble after Elijah's rebuke, but his repentance was shallow. Likewise, many leaders issue apologies without true repentance, trying to preserve their position while refusing to change their ways. But God cannot be fooled by appearances. He demands genuine humility, brokenness, and transformation. Anything less is hypocrisy, and hypocrisy will not stand in the day of His judgment.

God's people must recognize this season for what it is: a divine courtroom moment. When the church is on trial, every believer is called to examine their own heart. Are we covering sin or confronting it? Are we complicit in silence, or are we standing with the truth? God is calling His people to wake up and discern the times. Prophecy is being fulfilled before our eyes—wars, lawlessness, and corruption are rising—but so too is the refining fire of God upon His house.

Judgment begins with the household of God (1 Peter 4:17), and we must be ready.

Elijah vs. Ahab – The Confrontation

On Mount Carmel, Elijah stood alone before Ahab and hundreds of prophets of Baal. It was a confrontation not just of men, but of gods who truly held the power to rule Israel. In that moment, Elijah's courage shattered the illusion of Jezebel's false worship. Today, we need modern Elijahs who are willing to stand alone against corruption in pulpits and palaces alike. The confrontation may not take place on a mountain, but in courtrooms, boardrooms, and the public square, where truth is tested against lies. The world is asking: "Who is God money, power, or the Lord Almighty?" And the church must answer with fire.

Elijah's question still echoes: "How long will you waver between two opinions?" (1 Kings 18:21). That question was for Israel then, and it is for us now. How long will church leaders waver between holiness and compromise? How long will politicians waver between justice and greed? How long will believers live with one foot in the world and one foot in the kingdom of God? This is a call to decision. Neutrality is no longer an option. The trial demands a verdict: will we serve the Lord, or will we bow to Baal?

Today's prophets face the same ridicule Elijah faced. They are labeled extremists, legalists, or outdated. Yet, just like Elijah, they carry the authority of heaven. While Jezebel's prophets danced around their altars and cut themselves in vain, Elijah's simple prayer brought down fire. This shows us that true power does not come from theatrics, manipulation, or popularity it comes from alignment with God. In this age of flashy ministries and political spectacles, God is raising humble voices that carry His fire. They may not be the majority, but they are unstoppable.

Ahab and Jezebel tried to silence Elijah, but they could not silence the truth he carried. Likewise, governments and corrupt church systems may try to censor, cancel, or persecute modern prophets, but they cannot silence God's word. The blood of martyrs throughout history proves that truth outlives every tyrant. Even when prophets are slain, their message thunders from heaven. This is why leaders who think they can suppress truth are deceived they may kill the messenger, but they cannot kill the message.

The confrontation between Elijah and Ahab shows us that God does not need a crowd to demonstrate His power. He needs one faithful voice. Today, in a world drowning in lies, one faithful church, one courageous pastor, one righteous politician can change the course of a nation. When fire falls, it only takes one altar to be rebuilt in obedience for revival to spread.

God is looking for Elijahs who will stand in their generation without fear, declaring,

"The Lord, He is God!"

Hidden Evil Exposed

Ahab thought he could secretly seize Naboth's vineyard through Jezebel's schemes, but God exposed the crime. This is a warning for all leaders today: no hidden sin remains hidden forever. What is done in secret will be shouted from the rooftops. Abuse covered up in churches, corruption hidden in governments, and secret deals made in darkness are being uncovered by the hand of God. Every hidden vineyard stolen from the powerless will be reclaimed in God's justice. Leaders may think they have buried their sins, but God has a shovel that uncovers every lie.

In our time, we see this truth unfolding daily. Scandals that were once whispers are now headlines. Powerful men who thought themselves untouchable are falling from their pedestals. Churches once admired for their size are crumbling under the weight of unrepentant sin. Political leaders once celebrated are now exposed to corruption, immorality, and exploitation. This is not a coincidence—it is divine reckoning. Just as Elijah confronted Ahab in Naboth's vineyard, prophets today are confronting leaders in the very places where they sinned. God will not be mocked.

The sin of abuse, especially within the church, is one of the greatest evils God is exposing. For decades, victims were silenced, told to keep quiet "for the sake of the ministry." But God has heard their cries, and He is bringing their stories into the light. Leaders who preyed on children, manipulated women, or exploited men will face judgment. The Jezebel spirit may have silenced them temporarily, but the Spirit of God is giving victims a voice, and their testimonies are shaking institutions to the core.

Financial corruption is another vineyard stolen in our time. Leaders who enrich themselves at the expense of the poor are following in Ahab's footsteps. They buy luxurious homes while congregations struggle to pay rent. They host lavish banquets while their neighbors go hungry.

But just as God told Ahab that the dogs would lick up his blood in the same place where Naboth was killed, today's corrupt leaders will reap what they have sown. The wealth they hoarded will testify against them on the day of judgment.

No matter how carefully leaders try to hide evidence, God's justice cannot be avoided. Surveillance cameras, whistleblowers, leaked documents, and courageous testimonies are often the earthly means by which sin is exposed, but behind them stands the God who reveals. He sees every hidden file, every covered-up scandal, every silenced voice. Leaders may evade human courts for a time, but they cannot escape the divine court. Ahab's story teaches us that sooner or later, God's gavel falls.

The Spirit of Jezebel Today

Jezebel's spirit did not die with her body; it continues wherever manipulation, seduction, intimidation, and idolatry dominate leadership. This spirit works behind the scenes, pulling strings, spreading lies, and corrupting hearts. We see it in politics when truth is sacrificed for votes. We see it in churches when leaders manipulate scripture to excuse sin. We see it in families when lust, abuse, and control destroy trust. Jezebel's spirit thrives wherever fear silences truth and selfish ambition replace holiness.

Jezebel targeted prophets, seeking to silence those who spoke God's word. Today, prophetic voices are mocked, censored, or discredited. Social media algorithms suppress messages of holiness, while false teachers are promoted to millions. Jezebel's spirit whispers, "Compromise to survive," but Elijah's spirit declares, "Stand even if you stand alone." God is calling His people to recognize the spirit of Jezebel in our time, so we do not fall victim to her deceptions.

This spirit also manifests in the exploitation of sexuality. Jezebel used seduction to control and manipulate, and today we live in a culture saturated with lust. Pornography, trafficking, and sexual immorality are celebrated while purity is mocked. Even in the church, leaders fall prey to secret sins of lust, destroying marriages, ministries, and souls. God's anger burns hot against this spirit because it defiles His temple the human body and the corporate body of Christ.

The Jezebel spirit thrives when leaders demonize those who expose corruption. Whistleblowers are called divisive, truth-tellers are accused of rebellion, and victims are blamed for their abuse. This reversal of blame is Jezebel's tactic it shifts attention away from sin and onto the voices that dare confront it. Yet God defends the oppressed. He told Elijah that He had preserved seven thousand in Israel who had not bowed to Baal, and today He preserves faithful voices that Jezebel cannot silence.

Jezebel's story reminds us that her reign was temporary. She seemed unstoppable, but her end was violent and humiliating. Likewise, the spirit of Jezebel in our time may appear strong, but it is doomed to defeat. God has decreed that manipulation, lust, and intimidation will not rule forever. The dogs that devoured Jezebel symbolize the certainty of divine justice—every Jezebel spirit will face its end.

Ahab's reign ended not with honor but with shame. Though he wore a crown, he died as one despised and judged by God. He went into battle thinking he could disguise himself and escape the word of the Lord, but no disguise can protect a man from the truth. The arrow that struck him was not shot with his name on it, but God directed it to pierce through the cracks of his armor. In this, we are reminded that no leader political or spiritual can hide behind their position, their wealth, or their excuses. When God's appointed time for judgment arrives, even the smallest crack will expose them.

Many leaders today live as if they are untouchable. They sit in plush offices, behind cameras, or in gated mansions, thinking their power shields them from accountability. Yet, history shows that when God says the time is up, power crumbles overnight. Dictators are toppled, abusive pastors are exposed, and corrupt systems collapse in scandals. The lesson of Ahab's death is sobering no one is above God's law. He is sovereign, and He will not be mocked.

Jezebel herself met a gruesome end. The woman who once commanded armies, manipulated kings, and silenced prophets was thrown down from a high window and trampled by horses. Dogs devoured her body, leaving nothing but bones. Her end was a direct fulfillment of Elijah's prophecy. This reminds us that the Jezebel spirit—no matter how powerful it seems in the present—will always be destroyed by God. Those who align with her ways of seduction, abuse, and manipulation will share her fate.

Today, we see Jezebel's spirit rising in new forms. It is the seductive influence that convinces churches to cover up sexual abuse rather than repent. It is the political voice that encourages leaders to enrich themselves at the expense of the poor. It is the entertainment industry glorifying lust and violence, shaping generations to embrace perversion as normal. Yet Jezebel's fate has already been sealed. God will not allow her to reign forever. Her downfall is certain, and those who ride with her will fall as she did.

Ahab's story is not just an ancient tale it is a prophetic mirror. When we look at today's world and see child abuse in churches, pastors who prey on women, and leaders who exploit vulnerable adults, we must see Ahab's reflection. When political leaders start wars for profit, pass laws for the rich, or ignore the cries of the oppressed, we must see Jezebel's influence. These are not isolated scandals—they are signs that we are living in days where God is shaking the nations to expose hidden evil.

The wars raging around the world are not random; they are the fruit of greed and pride. Nations are rising against nations, leaders are grasping for power, and innocent blood is spilled daily.

Scripture reminds us that these are birth pains leading to the return of Christ. Just as Ahab's greed led to Naboth's murder, so today greed leads to wars that kill thousands for the sake of oil, land, and political dominance. God is angry at leaders who sacrifice lives for gain.

The church is not exempt from judgment. In fact, judgment begins with the house of God (1 Peter 4:17). When leaders in churches abuse children, manipulate women, and exploit congregations financially, they are no different from Ahab allowing Jezebel to slaughter God's prophets. The cries of the abused reach heaven, and God responds with judgment. What we are witnessing in church scandals today is not a coincidence—it is God pulling the veil back so that His people are not deceived any longer.

Prophecy is fulfilling before our very eyes. Jesus warned of false prophets, wars, rumors of wars, and love growing cold. Paul warned leaders who would have a form of godliness but deny its power. John spoke of the antichrist spirit rising. All of these warnings are seen today. Ahab's dark chapter in history serves as a foreshadow of the evil leadership we are enduring in modern times. But just as Elijah rose to confront Ahab, God is raising a remnant now to declare truth and call the church to repentance.

The rich leaders of our time often look out only for themselves. They build networks of wealth where the rich support the rich, while the poor suffer without voice or justice. The same pattern was seen in Ahab's day, when Naboth's vineyard was stolen so that Ahab could add to his possessions. The Lord sees how the poor and needy are trampled in modern society, and He declares that He will arise as their defender. Those who exploit the vulnerable will face His wrath.

Jezebel's manipulation is not only political but deeply spiritual. She seeks to infiltrate churches, twisting the gospel into a message of tolerance for sin, prosperity for leaders, and silence for the oppressed. She whispers into the ears of leaders that numbers matter more than holiness, image matters more than integrity, and silence matters more than repentance. But the Spirit of God is breaking that silence in this generation. Whistleblowers, victims, prophets, and ordinary believers are rising to speak the truth that Jezebel tried to suppress.

The time for pretending is over. Just as God sent Elijah to call down fire on Mount Carmel to prove who was truly God, we are in a season where God is proving Himself again. The exposure of leaders, the shaking of governments, the unrest in nations all of this is God calling people to see that no idol, no Jezebel, no corrupt leader can stand before His consuming fire. The church must awaken, for God is separating the false from the true.

The eyes of the people must be opened. For too long, many have blindly followed leaders because of titles, charisma, or wealth. But Jesus warned that many would come in His name and deceive many. It is time for believers to test the spirits, to discern fruit, and to refuse to bow to Baal disguised as modern religion. The day of casually attending church while ignoring corruption is over. God demands holiness from His people, and He is shaking His church until we surrender.

The world is being shaken by wars, pandemics, economic collapse, and moral decay not because God has lost control, but because prophecy is unfolding. Just as Ahab's kingdom was shaken until Elijah stood, so our modern kingdoms are trembling until God's people rise. These events are birth pains announcing that Christ is coming soon. Every headline about corruption, every scandal in leadership, every war declared is another trumpet reminding us to prepare.

Leaders who continue in hidden sin should not mistake God's patience for approval. He gave Ahab opportunities to repent, but Ahab's heart remained hardened. Likewise, God gives leaders today time to turn, but many persist in abuse, greed, and hypocrisy. When judgment comes, it will not be without warning. Ahab's story is a warning written in history to tell every leader: repent before it is too late.

For those who have been wounded by corrupt leaders, take comfort in knowing that God has not abandoned you. Just as He saw Naboth's death and responded with judgment, He sees your pain. He hears the cries of children abused by clergy, women silenced by church leaders, and victims ignored by politicians. God is near to the brokenhearted, and He will repay those who have hidden their evil under cloaks of power.

The Jezebel spirit flourishes when people are afraid to speak, but God is empowering His people in this hour. Victims are rising. Prophets are rising. Ordinary believers are rising with boldness to say "enough." This movement is not political but spiritual it is God Himself lifting the veil so the world can see the corruption that has festered in secret. Just as Elijah stood alone but shook a nation, so God can use one voice to awaken thousands.

We must remember that revival does not come without confrontation. Elijah had to confront Ahab. Jesus had to confront the Pharisees. Paul had to confront Peter when he acted in hypocrisy. Likewise, the modern church must confront its leaders, not in rebellion but in righteousness, demanding repentance and integrity. Ahab's story shows us that silence is deadly—evil thrives when it is unchallenged. But when truth is spoken, God's fire falls.

God is calling His people to repentance, not just leaders but all of us. It is easy to point at Ahab, Jezebel, or corrupt pastors, but what about our own compromises? Have we bowed to idols of comfort, entertainment, or political allegiance? Have we allowed the Jezebel spirit into our homes through what we watch, tolerate, or excuse? The call of Elijah echoes today: choose whom you will serve. If the Lord is God, then follow Him with your whole heart.

The church is indeed on trial in this generation. The scandals, the exposure, the falling of leaders—it is all part of God's judgment beginning with His house. He is refining His bride so that she will be without spot or wrinkle. The trial is not meant to destroy the church but to purify it, removing Ahab-like leaders and Jezebel-like influences so that Christ may present to Himself a holy bride.

Yet with all the darkness of Ahab's story, there is hope. After Elijah confronted Ahab, God proved Himself by sending fire from heaven. He showed Israel that He alone is God. Today, God is proving Himself again. Even as leaders fall, God is raising faithful shepherds. Even as churches crumble in scandal, new movements of holiness and truth are rising. Even as nations rage, the gospel is spreading faster than ever. What the enemy meant for evil, God will use to awaken His people.

The lesson of Ahab is clear: hidden evil cannot last. God rebukes leaders who abuse, manipulate, and exploit His people. He tears down Jezebel's influence and judges those who persist in rebellion. Our generation is living in a time of great shaking, but it is also a time of great opportunity. The church must rise, eyes open, voices bold, hearts pure, ready to confront sin and proclaim truth. Just as Elijah did, we must stand and declare: "The Lord, He is God!"—and prepare for Christ's return.

The Dark Reign of Ahab and the Call to Repentance

The Bible makes it clear: no one is righteous in the sight of God without repentance. Leaders may wear robes, suits, or collars, but their outward image cannot cover inward corruption. Ahab sat on a throne, but he was no king in God's eyes because his heart was defiled. Likewise, modern leaders who parade as holy while living in sin deceive only themselves. Scripture says plainly, "There is none righteous, not one" (Romans 3:10). Without repentance, power and titles mean nothing before a holy God.

The Word of the Lord in 2 Chronicles 7:14 is not just a suggestion—it is a divine prescription for healing a nation. "If my people, who are called by my name, shall humble themselves, and pray, and seek my face, and turn from their wicked ways; then will I hear from heaven, and will forgive their sin, and will heal their land." Notice, God does not call the wicked nations to repent first; He calls *His people* the ones who claim His name. This means pastors, prophets, bishops, elders, and political leaders who profess Christ must repent first, for revival begins in the house of God.

Why must they repent? Because hypocrisy has reached a stench before heaven. Leaders who preach purity, but practice perversion misrepresent the very name of Christ. Politicians who claim Christian faith but legislate injustice mock God's Word. Ahab's sin was not merely personality corrupted a whole nation. The sins of leaders today also ripple outward, wounding congregations, poisoning communities, and hardening hearts against God. Repentance is the only antidote to this infection.

How must they repent? Not with empty words or public statements drafted by lawyers, but with genuine humility before the Lord. Ahab himself, wicked as he was, once tore his clothes and put on sackcloth when Elijah rebuked him (1 Kings 21:27–29). Though his repentance was short- lived, God still took notice. This shows us that even the most corrupt leader has a chance if they truly humble themselves. Repentance is not about image it is about brokenness before God.

When must leaders repent? The answer is simple: *now*. Not tomorrow, not after the next scandal, not once they are caught, but now—while there is still time. Delayed repentance is disobedience. Ahab was delayed, and his house was destroyed. Today's leaders must understand that each day unrepentant sin piles up wrath for the day of judgment. The only safe time to repent is the present moment, for tomorrow is not promised.

Leaders who use Christianity as a cloak for their wickedness are in greater danger than outright unbelievers. Jesus said it would be better for a man to have a millstone tied around his neck and be cast into the sea than to cause one of His little ones to stumble (Luke 17:2). Abusive pastors, manipulative prophets, and corrupt politicians who use the Bible to justify sin will face harsher judgment if they do not repent. The call to turn is urgent because their sin has not only destroyed themselves but has led others astray.

The role of Elijah on Ahab's day was not comfortable, but it was necessary. Elijah stood alone against a government, a queen, and hundreds of false prophets. Yet he stood because God called him. Today, we desperately need Elijah-like leaders who will not bow to Jezebel, who will not compromise with corruption, and who will not be silenced by fear. These leaders may not be popular, but they will be powerful because they walk in God's authority.

Elijah's power did not come from himself but from obedience to God's Word. When he prayed, fire fell. When he declared drought, the heavens shut up. When he spoke of rain, the clouds gathered. Likewise, true spiritual leaders today will see God's power revealed not through theatrics or manipulation, but through obedience. God honors those who honor Him, and when leaders stand boldly for righteousness, heaven backs them.

Repentance must be preached again from pulpits across the world. Too many sermons today focus on prosperity, motivation, and comfort, while ignoring sin and holiness. Elijah did not tell Ahab that his best days were ahead; he told him judgment was at the door. We need preachers who will weep between the porch and the altar, crying out for God's people to turn from wickedness. Without repentance, there can be no revival, no healing, no true restoration.

The church must stop excusing sin among its leaders. Cover-ups only prolong judgment. When Nathan confronted King David after his sin with Bathsheba, David did not silence him; he repented and cried out, "Create in me a clean heart, O God" (Psalm 51:10). David sinned, but unlike Ahab, he repented sincerely, and God restored him. Modern leaders must choose whether they will follow David's example of humility or Ahab's example of pride.

God's rebuke is an act of mercy, not cruelty. When Elijah confronted Ahab, it was God giving the king another chance to turn. Likewise, the exposure of scandals today is God's mercy; it is His way of saying, "Turn before it's too late." Leaders who ignore this mercy will face judgment. Those who humble themselves, however, can still find forgiveness. The door of grace is still open, but it will not remain open forever.

Spiritual leaders must flee from the Jezebels of this world. Too many have been seduced by money, sex, and fame, thinking they can handle the compromise. But Scripture warns us to "flee youthful lusts" (2 Timothy 2:22), not flirt with them. Elijah did not entertain Jezebel; he confronted her. Leaders must learn that running from temptation is not weakness; it is wisdom. Holiness requires separation from evil influences, even if that means losing popularity or power.

The power of God is not for show; it is for transformation. Elijah called down fire, but the purpose was not entertainment; it was to turn the people's hearts back to God. Today, the gifts of the Spirit are often abused to impress crowds or build brands, but true manifestations of God's power will always point people to repentance. Leaders must stop using God's name for their own glory and return to the place where His power brings conviction, not applause.

Chastisement is not pleasant, but it is proof of God's love. Hebrews 12:6 declares, "For whom the Lord loves He chastens, and scourges every son whom He receives." Leaders who experience public rebuke and exposure should not despise it but recognize it as God's invitation to repentance. Ahab resisted correction and was destroyed; David embraced correction and was restored. The difference is not in the severity of the sin but in the response to rebuke.

Repentance is not optional; it is commanded. Jesus' first message was, "Repent, for the kingdom of heaven is at hand" (Matthew 4:17). Paul preached that "God commands all men everywhere to repent" (Acts 17:30). If repentance was central to the message of Christ and the apostles, how much more must it be central in the lives of leaders today? No one is good in the sight of God until they bow low in repentance at the cross of Jesus Christ.

When leaders repent, healing follows. 2 Chronicles 7:14 promises not just forgiveness but healing of the land. Our nations are sick with violence, greed, corruption, and division. Our churches are sick with compromise, abuse, and scandal. But God promises that if His people repent, He will heal. The healing of our lands is not dependent on elections, policies, or new programs; it is dependent on repentance.

The urgency of repentance cannot be overstated. Every day leaders delay, more people are hurt, more souls are lost, and more judgment is stored up. Just as Ahab's refusal to repent led to national disaster, so too will modern leaders' stubbornness lead to collapse. Now is the acceptable time; today is the day of salvation. Leaders must choose humility now, not later.

God is raising a remnant of leaders like Elijah who will not bow to idols, who will not compromise with Jezebel, and who will not be silenced by threats. These leaders will call sin by its name, point people back to the cross, and demonstrate God's power with purity. They may not have the largest churches, the most followers, or the most wealth, but they will have God's fire. And when God's fire falls, nations will tremble.

For the people of God, the message is also clear: do not put your trust in corrupt leaders. Do not idolize pastors, prophets, or politicians. Follow them only as they follow Christ. When leaders fall, do not fall with them—stand firm on the Word of God. Elijah was only one man, but he stood on the unshakable truth of God, and it was enough. You too can stand when leaders fail, if your foundation is Christ.

The story of Ahab ends in destruction, but the story of repentance always ends in restoration. Our leaders today must decide which story they want to write about themselves. Will they be remembered as Ahabs who resisted God and were destroyed, or as Davids who fell but repented and were restored? The choice is urgent, the call is clear: repent now, humble yourselves, seek His face, turn from wicked ways. Then and only then will God forgive our sins and heal our land.

Invitation to Repentance

The story of King Ahab is a powerful reminder that even the worst leaders can find God's forgiveness when they repent. Ahab's reign was filled with greed, lust, compromise, and abuse of power. He allowed idolatry and evil to flourish, even murdering Naboth to seize his vineyard. Yet when confronted by the prophet Elijah, Ahab humbled himself, confessed his sins, and turned from his evil ways. God responded with mercy, delaying judgment and showing that restoration is possible when repentance is sincere.

Today, God calls every leader—whether in the Church, in politics, or in positions of influence— to follow Ahab's example of genuine repentance:

Confess honestly: Admit the ways you have exploited, manipulated, or oppressed others. Do not hide behind excuses or pride.

Seek restitution: Restore what has been broken—heal victims, correct injustices, and return what was taken or misused.

Turn from evil: Leave behind greed, lust, compromise, and manipulation. Choose obedience and righteousness.

If you are a follower of Christ who has remained silent or complacent, God calls you to action:

Pray for those in leadership who have strayed.
Speak truth in love where it is safe and effective.
Stand with the vulnerable and refuse to tolerate hidden sin.
God promises:

"If my people, who are called by my name, will humble themselves and pray and seek my face and turn from their wicked ways, then I will hear from heaven, and I will forgive their sin and will heal their land" (*2 Chronicles 7:14*).

Today is the day to turn back to God. Today is the day for repentance, restoration, and renewed obedience.

Prayer of Repentance and Acknowledgement: (**If you have repented, repeat this prayer**)

Heavenly Father,

We come before You with hearts humbled by the weight of sin and corruption in our world. Lord, we confess that, like King Ahab, many leaders have walked in greed, lust, manipulation, and compromise. Forgive us for the times we have ignored injustice, stayed silent, or tolerated sin.

Lord, we pray for our leaders in the Church, politics, and all positions of authority. Open their eyes to their wrongdoing. Convict them of their sins, and give them the courage to repent fully. Help them to confess honestly, seek restitution for those they have harmed, and turn from evil to walk in righteousness. Restore what has been broken, heal the wounded, and bring justice where oppression has reigned.

Raise Elijah-like voices in this generation—prophetic, courageous, and obedient to confront evil and call leaders back to You. Give us the discernment to recognize hidden sin, the courage to act in love, and the faith to trust Your power to heal and restore.

Lord, we also pray for ourselves. Cleanse our hearts, renew our minds, and empower us to be instruments of truth, justice, and mercy. Let us not be silent in the face of sin but active in spreading Your light in darkness.

Father, just as You forgave Ahab when he turned to You, we ask that You pour out mercy on all who repent sincerely. Let restoration, healing, and righteousness flow in our churches, our communities, and our nations. May Your Kingdom come, Your will be done, and Your glory be revealed through transformed lives.

In the mighty and merciful name of Jesus Christ, we pray. Amen.

The Church on trial today faces accusations not only from the world but also from within. Hypocrisy, division, and compromise have weakened its witness. To stand firm, the Church must realign itself with Christ and embrace a framework that leads to spiritual credibility. The Five P's Pillars—Passion, Presence, Prestige, Powerbase, and Process—form a prophetic guide for renewal and accountability.

Passion

Passion is the driving fire of the Church. Without passion for Jesus Christ, ministry becomes mechanical, and worship turns into ritual. The first love that Christ demanded in Revelation 2:4 must be rekindled, for passion ignites hearts and testifies to the reality of the gospel.

Fear often suppresses passion. Fear of persecution, rejection, or cultural backlash can silence believers. Yet Paul reminded Timothy that God has not given us a spirit of fear, but of power, love, and a sound mind (2 Timothy 1:7). Passion burns away fear, because perfect love casts it out.

Passion must defend free speech, not in a political sense alone, but in the sacred right to proclaim Christ without apology. When the apostles were ordered to stop speaking in the name of Jesus, their passion compelled them to declare, "We cannot help speaking about what we have seen and heard" (Acts 4:20).

Racism quenches passion because it denies the image of God in others. A Church that is passionate about Christ must be equally passionate about justice and equality, for the kingdom of God gathers every tribe, tongue, and nation in worship (Revelation 7:9).

Passion must be sustainable. Too often, ministries begin with zeal but fade when trials arise. The sustainable passion of the Church comes from the indwelling Spirit, not human hype. Jesus promised rivers of living water that never run dry (John 7:38).

Cultural competence requires a passion that listening and learns. To reach people across backgrounds, the Church must passionately understand their struggles without compromising the gospel. Paul modeled this when he became all things to all people so that some might be saved (1 Corinthians 9:22).

Presence

Presence speaks of God's nearness in the Church and the Church's witness in the world. A Church without the manifest presence of God becomes a social club rather than a sanctuary of transformation. Fear isolates people from presence. When Adam and Eve sinned, they hid from God's presence (Genesis 3:8). But Christ restored the ability to draw near with boldness. The Church on trial must demonstrate that God's presence is greater than fear.

Free speech without presence is noise. The authority of Christian proclamation comes from the awareness that God is with us. Moses declared, "If Your Presence does not go with us, do not send us up from here" (Exodus 33:15). Racism corrupts presence by building walls between believers. The early Church overcame these walls when Jews and Gentiles discovered that the same Spirit fell on all who believed (Acts 10:44-45). Presence makes us one.

Sustainability in presence means living in daily communion with God, not depending on Sunday services alone. Presence must invade workplaces, schools, families, and communities so the world sees Christ in everyday life. Cultural competence in presence means being incarnational. Just as Christ took on flesh and dwelt among us (John 1:14), the Church must embody God's love in real contexts. This presence disarms prejudice and builds bridges for the gospel.

Prestige

Prestige represents the honor and credibility of the Church in society. Not worldly status, but the moral and spiritual integrity that commands respect. Prestige is earned through holiness, humility, and sacrificial service. Fear undermines prestige when leaders seek approval from men rather than God. Prestige cannot come from compromise with the world but from standing firm in righteousness, even when unpopular.

Free speech enhances prestige when the Church speaks truth to power with clarity and love. Prophets in Scripture gained credibility not through wealth but through bold proclamation that aligned with God's word. Racism destroys prestige. A

Church divided along racial lines has no authority to preach reconciliation. The prestige of the Church must come from embodying the unity Christ prayed for in John 17.

Sustainability of prestige depends on consistency. Scandals, hypocrisy, and abuse erode the Church's credibility. A faithful witness over time builds a prestige that points not to man, but to Christ. Cultural competence adds depth to prestige. When the Church listens, learns, and ministers with sensitivity, it demonstrates wisdom. Prestige rooted in Christ allows the Church to be both firm in truth and tender in love.

Powerbase

Powerbase is the foundation from which the Church operates. Unlike worldly institutions that rely on money or influence, the Church's true power base is the Spirit of God. Without this, programs are empty. Fear weakens the power base when believers rely on fresh weapons. Paul reminded the Corinthians that "the weapons of our warfare are not carnal but mighty through God" (2 Corinthians 10:4).

Free speech is amplified by the Spirit. Peter, once fearful, became bold at Pentecost because his power base shifted from self to Spirit. The Church must recover this power if it is to withstand trials. Racism fractures the power base. A house divided cannot stand (Mark 3:25). When racism is tolerated, the Spirit is grieved, and the Church loses power. Only unity in Christ restores its base of authority.

Sustainability requires a power base that does not depend on trends. Human systems fail, but the Spirit endures. Jesus promised His followers that they would receive power when the Holy Spirit came upon them (Acts 1:8). Cultural competence strengthens the power base by aligning ministry with Spirit-led discernment. The apostles adjusted their strategies to reach both Jews and Gentiles without compromising truth, ensuring the power base extended across cultures.

Process

Process is the practical application of vision. Without process, passion fizzles, presence diminishes, prestige fades, and power base collapses. Process makes the vision plain (Habakkuk 2:2). Fear resists process by clinging to the familiar. Many churches fear change and refuse to adjust, but God calls for new wineskins to hold new wine (Mark 2:22). Process requires courage to reform.

Free speech is safeguarded through a process that is structured to ensure accountability. Churches must create safe spaces where truth can be spoken without fear of retaliation. This strengthens integrity. Racism must be dismantled through a process. It is not enough to preach against it; systems must change. The early Church established processes to care for widows of different ethnic groups, ensuring equity (Acts 6:1-7).

Sustainability depends on a process that balances vision and stewardship. Resources must be managed with integrity, ensuring the mission of Christ continues from generation to generation. Cultural competence grows through the process by equipping leaders with training and discipleship that embrace diversity. A Spirit-led process ensures that no culture dominates the gospel, but all are welcomed into God's kingdom.

Integration of the Five P's

When Passion, Prestige, Powerbase, and Process work together, the Church becomes a holistic witness. Isolated, they are fragile; together, they are unshakable. Passion without process is reckless. Presence without power is sentimental. Prestige without integrity is hollow. Power bases without presence are oppressive. Process without passion is dead. The balance of all five ensures spiritual health. Fear, free speech, racism, sustainability, and cultural competence are not external challenges alone; they are internal tests. How the Church responds reveals whether it stands on the rock of Christ or the shifting sands of culture.

The Church must move beyond denominational disputes and doctrinal wars. Jesus is the Way, the Truth, and the Life (John 14:6). The Five P's pillars direct attention back to Him, not to human systems. Passion fuels evangelism, presence brings transformation, prestige secures credibility, power base empowers mission, and process ensures endurance. These five build a Church that can withstand trial. If the Church fails to align with these pillars, its lampstand risks removal (Revelation 2:5). God rebukes hidden evil not to destroy, but to purify and prepare a spotless bride.

Closing Call

The Church on trial must rise with passion, unashamed of Christ. It must stand with presence that hosts God's glory, not man's agenda. It must carry prestige not of worldly honor but of heavenly recognition. It must be rooted in the Spirit as its unshakable power base.

It must walk in a process that ensures equity, accountability, and mission integrity. This is how the world will know Jesus Christ—not as a religious figure boxed by denomination, but as the living Lord, the Truth, and the Life.

Deepening the Five Ps in Today's World

Passion must become a prophetic flame in a time of spiritual apathy. Many churches today are more passionate about buildings, programs, and personalities than the presence of God. This misplaced zeal leaves congregations dry. True passion burns for Christ Himself, and such a passion is contagious.

Presence must confront the emptiness of religious performance. Without God's manifest presence, services may entertain but will not transform. As Moses longed for God's glory, so the Church must plead, "Show us Your glory" (Exodus 33:18). Only His presence can heal deep wounds of fear, racism, and division.

Prestige must not be confused with popularity. A church may fill arenas yet lack integrity. Prestige rooted in holiness often looks foolish to the world. Jesus Himself, despised and rejected, carried the greatest prestige in heaven's eyes. The Church must reclaim this paradoxical honor— glory through humility.

The power base of the Church is weakened when it bows to politics more than prayer. Many have traded the altar for alliances, forgetting that revival never comes from government halls but from God's Spirit poured on His people. A Spirit-anchored power base cannot be shaken by cultural storms.

Process must counter the spirit of disorder that plagues many ministries. Where there is no vision, the people perish (Proverbs 29:18). God is not the author of confusion, but of peace (1 Corinthians 14:33). Churches must reform broken systems and establish Spirit-led processes that uphold righteousness.

Addressing Fear Through the Five P's

Fear paralyzes passion. Believers hide their light, retreating from opportunities to witness. Yet passion fueled by love conquers fear. When the early disciples prayed for boldness, the place shook, and they spoke the Word with renewed power (Acts 4:31). Fear erodes presence when believers withdraw from God instead of running to Him. Yet the psalmist declares, "In Your presence is fullness of joy" (Psalm 16:11). A Church unafraid of God's presence will overcome worldly intimidation.

Fear distorts prestige when leaders compromise truth to avoid criticism. But Christ said, "Blessed are you when people insult you, persecute you...because of Me" (Matthew 5:11). Endurance under pressure earns eternal honor. Fear shrinks the power base when prayer is replaced by panic. Gideon's army was reduced to a handful, yet God showed that power rests not in numbers but in obedience. The Church must rediscover strength in surrender. Fear hinders the process when churches refuse to reform outdated systems. But God calls His people to move forward in faith, trusting His guidance even in uncertain times. Faith-driven processes create future harvests.

Addressing Free Speech Through the Five P's

Passion defends free speech by testifying boldly of Christ. When silenced, passion cries louder, as the stones themselves would shout if disciples remained quiet (Luke 19:40). Presence emboldens free speech. Peter, filled with the Spirit, spoke truth fearlessly before hostile councils. Presence transforms ordinary speech into prophetic witness.

Prestige gives credibility to free speech. A holy life ensures that when the Church speaks, the world cannot easily dismiss it as hypocrisy. Integrity amplifies testimony. The power base of free speech is the Spirit's anointing. Paul's preaching was "not with persuasive words of wisdom, but with a demonstration of the Spirit's power" (1 Corinthians 2:4). Spirit-filled speech shakes nations. Process protects free speech by establishing platforms of accountability and equity.

Leaders must create environments where voices from every background are heard, ensuring unity in diversity.

Passion denounces racism because love cannot coexist with hate. True passion for Christ burns away prejudice and embraces every person as made in God's image. Presence dismantles racism. At Pentecost, God's Spirit fell on Jews, Greeks, Arabs, and Africans alike, showing that His presence recognizes no cultural boundaries. Prestige is destroyed by racism but rebuilt through reconciliation. When the Church embodies justice and unity, its credibility shines brightly in a divided world. The power base of the Spirit cannot flow through a racist church. Division quenches power, but unity multiplies it. When the Church reconciles across racial lines, its witness regains authority and its mission expands globally.

Closing Word

The Five P's Pillars are not optional strategies; they are divine necessities. In a world fractured by fear, silenced by censorship, poisoned by racism, struggling for sustainability, and desperate for cultural competence, the Church must rise as Christ's true body. Passion must burn, presence must remain, prestige must be reclaimed, power base must be Spirit-rooted, and process must be Spirit-led. Only then will the Church on trial stand acquitted—not by the judgment of man, but by the approval of the Judge who declares, "Well done, good and faithful servant" (Matthew 25:21).

Chapter: 31: The Cost of Broken Collaboration and the Call to Unity

The body of Christ was never designed to function in isolation or competition, but in harmony and interdependence, reflecting the unity of the Triune God. Yet, as the Church stands on trial before a holy and discerning God, Heaven's witness bears record of the broken collaboration that has infected the modern body of believers. Where there was once fellowship, there is now rivalry; where there was once collaboration, there is now suspicion. The cost of broken unity is spiritual decay—an invisible corrosion that eats away at the credibility of our witness and the strength of our collective anointing. The Church cannot cast out darkness when its members are at war with each other. The same Spirit that descended upon the believers in the upper room has been grieved and quenched by pride, ambition, and self-promotion masquerading as ministry.

Jesus prayed in John 17 that His followers "may be one" as He and the Father are one, a unity that was meant to demonstrate divine love to a watching world. Yet, the modern church has traded that prayer for the politics of power, territorialism, and doctrinal ego. The spiritual war within the house of God has caused many believers to stumble, lose faith, and withdraw from fellowship altogether. The cost is not merely attendance or tithes—it is the loss of divine presence. When leaders compete for influence instead of bowing in humility, the Spirit of God withdraws His power, leaving behind a shell of religious performance that impresses men but repels Heaven.

Disunity is not a trivial disagreement; it is a rebellion against divine order. Lucifer was the first to fracture heavenly collaboration by exalting self above the Creator, and his same spirit works today in those who refuse correction, despise accountability, and sabotage kingdom partnerships. Every time the Church chooses personality over principle and platform over purpose, it replays the rebellion of Heaven's fallen cherub. God cannot bless what He has already judged, and He will not pour His glory upon divided altars built in the name of personal kingdoms.

Broken collaboration has crippled the mission of evangelism. The early Church in Acts moved in explosive growth because "they were of one heart and one soul." They shared resources, bore each other's burdens, and advanced the Gospel with one voice. Today, however, ministries compete for followers, social media clout, and brand recognition while the lost perish unnoticed. Heaven weeps as the Church becomes an enterprise rather than an embassy of the Kingdom.

Every fractured relationship among believers becomes an open wound in the body of Christ, and the world observes our bleeding hypocrisy with justified skepticism.

When believers refuse to walk together in agreement, the prophetic witness of the Church is silenced. Amos 3:3 asks, "Can two walk together, except they be agreed?" The answer is evident in the chaos of the modern religious landscape. Agreement has been replaced with accusation; discernment replaced with division. Churches split not because of heresy but because of wounded egos. Boards and committees collapse under the weight of pride. Pastors walk away from pulpits not because of burnout but because they can no longer endure the backbiting of those who call themselves ministry partners. The tragedy is that this brokenness becomes the very evidence Satan uses to accuse the Church before God's throne.

The cost of broken collaboration is not just emotional—it is spiritual warfare that drains divine momentum. When the Church fights itself, it cannot fight the enemy effectively. The Apostle Paul warned that the weapons of our warfare are not carnal, but mighty through God. Yet those weapons lose potency when turned inward. Instead of tearing down strongholds, many congregations have built walls of distrust, competition, and theological arrogance. The spiritual fallout is devastating prayer movements weaken, revival tarries, and the lost remain unreached because the Church cannot stand together under one banner of truth.

Every time believers walk away from each other over offense rather than seeking reconciliation, the cross of Christ is dishonored. Jesus shed His blood to reconcile man to God and man to man, but many within the body treat reconciliation as optional. Forgiveness has become a slogan rather than a spiritual discipline. Collaboration requires humility, and humility demands crucifixion of the ego. Until leaders are willing to die to self, the Church will remain a battlefield of gifted but disconnected soldiers. God never called us to build empires; He called us to build altars where His glory can dwell among a unified people.

The Spirit of God is calling for repentance among ministers who have used the pulpit as a platform of pride. The competition among churches for attendance, attention, and acclaim has made ministry a performance instead of a service. The unity Christ desires is not conformity—it is covenantal alignment under one Spirit and one mission. When collaboration is restored, revival follows. When egos are crucified, glory returns. The fragmented Church must now humble itself before God, confessing that division has cost us more than we were willing to admit it has cost us power, purity, and presence.

Heaven's court is convening, and the charges against the Church are not about the sins of the world but the sins within its walls. The Spirit testifies that the Church has broken covenant through gossip, slander, and rivalry. Every ministry that undermines another for the sake of prominence stands guilty before the Judge. Unity is not optional in the Kingdom—it is the evidence of maturity and the foundation of credibility. A house divided against itself cannot stand, and the Lord is shaking every institution that bears His name but not His nature.

In this trial, God is exposing the hidden costs of broken collaboration: the wounded saints who left the church because of leadership betrayal; the young ministers who lost faith because mentors competed instead of covering; the communities who turned away because they saw hypocrisy instead of holiness. Each wound tells the story of a Church that forgot how to love beyond its own walls. The Father grieves over His children who cannot dwell together in unity, for in that unity He commanded a blessing. The absence of that blessing is evidence that something sacred has been broken.

Yet amid the rebuke, there is a divine call to restoration. God is not finished with His Church; He is refining it. The fire of conviction is meant to purify, not destroy. He is raising a remnant of leaders who refuse to compete, who choose collaboration over control. These are the Davids who will unite divided tribes, the Nehemias who will rebuild broken walls, the Esthers who will intercede for nations rather than institutions. The call to unity is a call back to the cross—the only ground where all men are equal and all pride is crucified.

The cost of broken collaboration is heavy, but the reward of restored unity is glorious. When believers lay down their swords against one another and lift them together against darkness, Heaven responds. Miracles return. Revival awakens. The same Spirit that fell at Pentecost still waits for a united upper room. The trial of the Church is not meant to condemn but to cleanse. God is calling His people to rebuild what has been torn apart by selfish ambition, to labor again side by side, and to prove to a watching world that love—true, sacrificial, covenantal love—is stronger than division.

True collaboration is born not in the conference room but in the prayer room. It is there that God melts hardened hearts, aligns motives, and reminds His servants that the work belongs to Him alone. Collaboration requires surrendering the laying down of one's right to be first, to be seen, or to be celebrated. Many have confused unity with uniformity, but divine unity flows from shared submission, not identical expression. When each part of the body operates in obedience to the Head, Christ is exalted, and the Church becomes an unstoppable force. But when each limb competes for glory, paralysis sets in, and movement ceases.

The Church's failure to collaborate has also opened doors for demonic infiltration. Where there is confusion and competition, there is strife, and "where envying and strife is, there is confusion and every evil work" (James 3:16). Demons thrive in disorder. Every broken alliance between ministries becomes an access point for the enemy to plant deception, bitterness, and mistrust.

This is why revival tarries—because revival demands order, and order demands humility. Heaven's agenda cannot advance through divided hearts, for God refuses to dwell in a temple where pride reigns.

The modern Church has mistaken networking for collaboration. Networking connects talent; collaboration connects purpose. True collaboration is born in the Spirit, not in strategy. It is when prophets, pastors, teachers, and intercessors align under one divine vision that the heavens open and the earth shakes. When believers gather only for influence or visibility, God steps aside, allowing human agendas to produce human results temporary and hollow. Collaboration that pleases God must cost something: the death of ego, the sacrifice of preference, and the willingness to serve where no one applauds.

The cost of broken collaboration is not only external division but internal decay. Many leaders who once carried fire now carry frustration because they attempted to walk alone. Isolation in ministry leads to exhaustion, and exhaustion gives birth to compromise. Moses needed Aaron and Hur to hold up his hands. Paul needed Barnabas, then Silas, then Timothy. Even Jesus sent His disciples two by two, teaching that no one fulfills the mission alone. Yet, in the pride of independence, many modern ministers reject accountability, forgetting that isolation is the first symptom of spiritual decline.

The spirit of competition is a silent killer in the Church. It masquerades as excellence but breeds jealousy. It disguises itself as vision but produces vanity. Ministers measure success not by obedience to the Spirit but by attendance, likes, and applause. This spirit has turned sanctuaries into stages and pastors into performers. But Heaven does not measure impact by numbers—it measures obedience. Collaboration becomes impossible where comparison reigns, for comparison kills contentment and stifles spiritual growth.

The brokenness of collaboration has also silenced prophetic voices that once carried divine fire. Many have grown weary of being misunderstood, ignored, or rejected by their peers. Prophets who once stood boldly before kings now retreat to caves of despair because their brothers would not stand beside them. But God is not unjust—He sees every faithful servant who has labored alone, every voice that has cried in the wilderness, every hand that has built without help. To them, He is sending divine partnerships in this new season—alliances forged not in convenience but in covenant.

Heaven is calling the Church to rebuild the bridges that pride has burned. Division has robbed the world of the unity Christ intended to display through His people. The miracle of Pentecost was not only tongues of fire but hearts of one accord. Before the Spirit fell, they prayed together; before they preached, they waited together. Unity was the prerequisite for power. If the Church desires to see another outpouring of glory, it must return to that upper room posture of humility and expectation, one heart, one purpose, one cry.

Every denomination, every ministry, every believer must examine the motives behind their labor. Are we building to exalt Christ or to extend our brand? Are we collaborating for the Kingdom or competing for control? God's judgment begins at the house of God because He loves it too much to leave it in deception. The call to unity is not optional; it is mandatory for revival. The body cannot heal the world if it refuses to heal itself.

Collaboration is not the erasure of distinction but the celebration of divine diversity under one purpose. Just as the human body has many members with different functions, the Church has many gifts and callings that complement rather than compete. The eye cannot say to the hand, "I do not need you." Yet many ministries do exactly that, denying the value of others who do not operate in their style or tradition. God designed diversity to display His manifold wisdom, but when pride rejects that design, the beauty of unity becomes marred by arrogance.

The call to unity is not sentimental; it is spiritual warfare. When the Church stands united, the gates of hell tremble. But when it fights within, Satan rests easy. The enemy fears a praying, unified people because he understands the authority released when believers agree in the Spirit. Jesus declared, "If two of you shall agree on earth as touching anything that they shall ask, it shall be done." Agreement multiplies power, and division multiplies defeat. The Church must decide whether to keep fighting one another or start fighting for one another.

Broken collaboration also weakens the Church's credibility in the eyes of the world. Unbelievers witness denominational feuds, public scandals, and social media wars among ministers and conclude that the Church is no different from the world it preaches against. The Gospel loses its power when delivered by a divided messenger. The world is not waiting for another sermon; it is waiting for a demonstration of love. Jesus said the world would know we are His disciples not by our miracles or our doctrines but by our love for one another. Love is the proof of unity, and unity is the proof of divine authenticity.

The cost of broken collaboration reaches beyond institutions; it seeps into families, marriages, and communities. A divided Church produces divided homes. Parents who cannot reconcile with one another raise children who distrust reconciliation. Leaders who cannot work together disciple congregations that replicate their dysfunction. The brokenness of leadership becomes the blueprint for the body. Thus, God's rebuke of disunity is not harshness—it is mercy. He corrects the Church so that generations to come will not inherit our division but our devotion.

Unity requires intentional humility. It is not enough to desire peace; we must pursue it. "Endeavor to keep the unity of the Spirit in the bond of peace," the Apostle Paul wrote. Endeavor means to strive, to labor, to fight for unity. It will not come easily because our flesh resists submission. But the reward of such pursuit is divine presence. When believers value unity more than vindication, the Spirit of peace descends, and God dwells among them.

Collaboration must also be guarded. The enemy attacks unity not always through external persecution but through internal offense. One careless word, one misunderstood action, one whisper of gossip can destroy years of partnership. Therefore, the Church must learn to practice mature forgiveness and confront issues biblically rather than carnally. The ministry of reconciliation must be restored to the pulpit, for only a reconciled Church can reconcile the world to God.

The call to unity demands transparency and repentance. It is impossible to collaborate while hiding sin or harboring secret agendas. God cannot anoint what pride conceals. In this trial of the Church, He is exposing hidden motives not to embarrass but to heal. When light shines, darkness flies. When confession replaces concealment, collaboration becomes pure again. Holiness and unity walk hand in hand; you cannot have one without the other.

Broken collaboration has also hindered financial stewardship within the Kingdom. Instead of pooling resources for greater impact, many ministries hoard funds out of fear or distrust. As a result, projects stagnate, missions go unsupported, and communities remain unreached. But when unity is restored, provision flows. God funds collaboration because it reflects His nature of partnership. The early believers "had all things common," and none lacked among them. That is not socialism; it is spiritual stewardship borne from love and trust.

To rebuild unity, the Church must return to the altar of prayer and fasting. Strategies, summits, and committees cannot produce the kind of unity Heaven demands. Only brokenness before God can. When believers gather not to debate but to weep together, not to boast but to repent, unity is birthed. The call to unity begins with a call to humility, and humility begins with repentance. God cannot heal a Church that refuses to admit it is sick.

There is a restoration cost. To repair what was broken, someone must lay down pride first. Someone must say, "I'm sorry." Someone must extend forgiveness even when wronged. True collaboration often begins with one heart willing to obey God at any cost. It is that heart that becomes the seed for revival. One obedient person can ignite a movement of reconciliation that transforms generations. God is raising a remnant who understand that unity is not weakness but warfare.

They are intercessors who bridge gaps, apostles who unite regions, prophets who speak reconciliation, and pastors who shepherd without competition. This remnant will not tolerate gossip, envy, or spiritual politics. They will rebuild what has been torn down by pride and restore credibility to the Church's witness. Through them, the prayer of Jesus in John 17 will be fulfilled in this generation.

The Church must also recognize that collaboration extends beyond its walls. Unity must include the wider body of Christ across nations, cultures, and denominations. The Holy Spirit is not divided by geography or tradition. The same anointing that moves in one culture operates in another, and God desires His global Church to move as one army, not fragmented battalions.

Every revival in history began when believers transcended personal and cultural barriers to seek the same fire from the same God.

Broken collaboration has cost the Church time, souls, and credibility. Every disagreement that escalated into division delayed the Great Commission. Every partnership destroyed by pride hindered the advancement of the Kingdom. But in His mercy, God is redeeming lost time. He is restoring divine connections that were severed and giving new strength to those weary from isolation. The latter glory will be greater than the former if we repent and return to the simplicity of love and obedience.

The Spirit of the Lord is now calling His people to lay down their agendas at the feet of Christ. There is no true unity apart from surrender. The Church cannot move forward until it stops fighting for control and starts yielding to the Holy Spirit. The next revival will not be led by personalities but by people who are broken in humility and bound together on purpose. The cost of unity is death to self, but resurrection always follows death.

The cross stands as the eternal symbol of collaboration between Heaven and Earth. The Father gave His Son; the Son gave His life; the Spirit gives His power. Perfect unity produced perfect redemption. If the Church desires to walk in resurrection power, it must embrace crucified collaboration. We cannot carry the cross and our egos at the same time. The same wood that carried Christ must also crucify our pride, that His resurrection life may flow through a unified Church.

Unity is not merely a strategy; it is a supernatural testimony of God's character. When believers dwell together in peace, they display the very nature of God to a fractured world. The Church was meant to be Heaven's preview, not Hell's reflection. A united body reveals the power of redemption; a divided one contradicts the Gospel. God is restoring His image in the earth through a Church that refuses to bow to division any longer.

As this chapter closes, the Spirit's voice echoes through time and eternity: "Come together again." The call to unity is not an invitation but a command. The Church stands on trial for its disobedience to love, but mercy is still extended. If we repent of our broken collaboration, God will heal our land, restore our power, and renew our witness. But if we continue to divide, He will remove our lampstand and raise another generation that understands the value of covenant partnership. The cost of broken collaboration has been great, but the reward of restored unity will shake nations and usher in the glory of God once more.

The failure of community collaboration, especially among faith-based organizations, schools, healthcare, nonprofits, and government agencies—has direct spiritual consequences. God calls His people to unity for the sake of righteousness and justice. When the Church and community organizations fail to collaborate, evil gains ground, and issues like gun violence, domestic violence, ACEs (Adverse Childhood Experiences), child abuse, teenage sexual abuse, and addictions deepen.

Biblical Foundation of Collaboration

God designed His people to work in unity. Psalm 133:1 declares, "How good and pleasant it is when God's people live together in unity!" Collaboration multiplies strength, while disunity multiplies destruction. Ecclesiastes 4:9-10 reminds us, "Two are better than one, because they have a good return for their labor: if both fall, one can help the other up." When organizations refuse to collaborate, communities fall without support.

Jesus prayed for unity in John 17:21, saying, "That all of them may be one, Father… so that the world may believe." When faith-based organizations compete rather than collaborate, they hinder the world from seeing Christ clearly.

Failure of Collaboration and Its Consequences Gun Violence

When churches, schools, and community leaders fail to collaborate, young people fall prey to cycles of violence. Proverbs 29:18 warns, "Where there is no vision, the people perish." Without joint vision, violence claims lives. The lack of collaborative mentorship programs leaves vulnerable youth unguarded. Judges 2:10 describes a generation that "knew neither the Lord nor what He had done." Disconnected communities breed lost generations.

Faith communities alone cannot address gun violence, and civic organizations alone cannot heal the soul. Without collaboration, responses are fragmented and ineffective.

Domestic Violence

Failure to collaborate silences victims. Isaiah 1:17 commands, "Defend the oppressed. Take up the cause of the fatherless; plead the case of the widow." When organizations work in isolation, survivors slip through cracks. Some churches avoid the issue of domestic violence, while agencies lack spiritual support. Collaboration bridges this divide, providing both practical safety and spiritual healing.

ACE (Adverse Childhood Experiences)

When schools, churches, and health providers fail to collaborate, trauma goes untreated. Hosea 4:6 declares, "My people are destroyed from lack of knowledge." Without shared education, ACEs perpetuate generational harm.

Collaboration provides early intervention. Without it, children with untreated trauma grow into adults struggling with violence, addiction, and brokenness.

Child Abuse

The Church is commanded in Proverbs 31:8 to "Speak up for those who cannot speak for themselves." When collaboration fails, children remain in abusive homes because no single agency has all the information to intervene. Scandals occur when churches cover up abuse instead of partnering with legal and social authorities. This destroys credibility and leaves children unprotected.

Teenage Sexual Abuse

When youth programs fail to partner with schools and counselors, teens are left without trusted spaces to report abuse. Ephesians 5:11 urges, "Have nothing to do with the fruitless deeds of darkness, but rather expose them." Collaboration exposes abuse.

Failure to collaborate allows predators to move unchecked between organizations, exploiting gaps in communication.

Addictions

Proverbs 23:29–30 describes the destruction of addiction: "Who has woe? Who has sorrow? … Those who linger over wine." When recovery ministries, hospitals, and churches do not collaborate, addicts relapse without holistic care.

Faith-based ministries may provide spiritual encouragement, while clinics provide medical support, but without integration, both are weakened.

Scriptural Rebukes Against Disunity

In Genesis 11:6, even at Babel, God acknowledged the power of human collaboration: "If as one people speaking the same language, they have begun to do this, then nothing they plan will be impossible for them." If world unity is powerful, how much more should godly unity prevail?

Mark 3:25 warns, "If a house is divided against itself, that house cannot stand." Communities divided in their response to violence and abuse collapse under evil's weight. James 4:17 rebukes inaction: "If anyone knows the good, they ought to do and doesn't do it, it is sin for them." Knowing the need for collaboration but refusing to act is corporate sin.

1 Corinthians 12:21 reminds us, "The eye cannot say to the hand, 'I don't need you!'" Faith organizations cannot dismiss the role of educators, healthcare workers, or law enforcement, and vice versa.

Vision for Restored Collaboration Gun Violence

Collaboration between churches, schools, and civic groups can establish mentoring, after-school programs, and safe havens. Isaiah 54:13 promises, "All your children will be taught by the Lord, and great will be their peace."

Partnerships allow churches to offer spiritual mentoring while schools provide education, and police offer safety. Collaboration brings holistic protection.

Domestic Violence

When faith-based shelters, nonprofits, and government agencies collaborate, victims receive both immediate safety and long-term healing. Psalm 34:18 assures, "The Lord is close to the brokenhearted." Collaboration allows His closeness to be felt.

ACE (Adverse Childhood Experiences)

Churches can collaborate by training leaders to recognize trauma and working with educators for early intervention. Proverbs 22:6 directs, "Start children off on the way they should go." Collaboration equips children with resilience.

Child Abuse

Collaboration between faith communities and child protective services ensures a swift response.

Matthew 18:6 warns against harming little ones, and collaboration honors Christ's command.

Teenage Sexual Abuse

Joint efforts of counselors, schools, churches, and parents build protective walls. Galatians 6:2 calls us to "Carry each other's burdens." Collaboration prevents teens from carrying abuse alone.

Addictions

Recovery from hidden evils—whether spiritual oppression, addiction, or systemic sin within the church—requires intentional collaboration between multiple layers of support: rehab centers, churches, families, and health services. The process unfolds in stages, beginning with acknowledgment, where individuals and the community recognize the presence of wrongdoing or spiritual bondage. Next comes intervention, where trained professionals, spiritual leaders, and family members provide guidance, accountability, and practical support. The healing stage follows, emphasizing restoration of mind, body, and spirit through counseling, prayer, and scriptural grounding. Finally, reintegration ensures that the recovered individual is fully supported within the church and community, preventing relapse into old patterns. As John 8:36 reminds us, "If the Son sets you free, you will be free indeed." Freedom is not merely an abstract promise—it becomes tangible when communities intentionally work together, combining spiritual authority, professional expertise, and familial love. Without such collaboration, hidden evils remain, festering quietly; with it, the church becomes a sanctuary of true deliverance, a place where God's rebuke transforms darkness into light, and chains into victory.

Chapter: 32 Accountability Before God – The Reckoning of the Church and the World

How God will hold the world accountable for failure in collaboration, Scriptures on accountability, judgment, and stewardship, Examples of accountability in biblical history (e.g., Eli failing to stop his sons' abuse in 1 Samuel 2, Ananias & Sapphira in Acts 5, nations judged for injustice in Amos), How accountability ties to the Five P's (Passion, Presence, Prestige, Powerbase, Process).

The Church on Trial – God Rebukes Hidden Evil, centered on God's accountability and how it applies to the Church, leaders, organizations, and the world. It connects directly to the Five P's (Passion, Presence, Prestige, Powerbase, Process), the failure of collaboration, and the divine reckoning God will bring.

The Weight of Accountability

Accountability is not optional; it is divine law. Romans 14:12 declares, *"So then, each of us will give an account of ourselves to God."* This means no person, no church, no organization, and no nation will escape God's evaluation.

God's accountability extends beyond religious life. He will hold leaders accountable for how they governed, churches accountable for how they shepherded, and communities accountable for how they cared for the vulnerable.

The Church must remember that God does not judge by appearance, denomination, or reputation, but by truth. 1 Samuel 16:7 reminds us, *"Man looks at the outward appearance, but the Lord looks at the heart."*

Accountability means that even hidden evil—corruption, abuse, cover-ups, or neglect—will be brought into the light. Luke 12:2 warns, *"There is nothing concealed that will not be disclosed, or hidden that will not be made known."* The Church on Trial is not just a metaphor; it is a spiritual reality. God Himself sits as Judge, Christ is Advocate for the faithful, and the Holy Spirit convicts of truth.

Biblical Examples of Accountability

In Genesis 4:9, God asked Cain, *"Where is your brother Abel?"* Cain denied responsibility, but God declared Abel's blood cried out from the ground. Likewise, God will call the Church to account for ignored violence and neglected victims. Eli, the priest, was judged because he refused to restrain his sons who exploited their priestly positions (1 Samuel 2:22–25). Leaders today face the same judgment when they cover up abuse in the Church.

Ananias and Sapphira (Acts 5:1-10) were struck dead for lying to the Holy Spirit. This shows God holds believers accountable for integrity in stewardship. Hidden deceit within organizations will face His judgment. King David was confronted by Nathan for his sin with Bathsheba (2 Samuel 12). Even kings are not exempt from accountability. Today's political leaders will also be measured by God's justice.

The nations of Israel and Judah were held accountable by prophets like Amos, Isaiah, and Jeremiah for oppressing the poor and corrupting worship. God still rebukes nations that neglect justice.

As the final gavel of Heaven echoes through the ages, the Church must confront the sobering truth that accountability is not optional but inevitable. Every sermon preached, every soul neglected, every hidden motive, and every act of disobedience will one day be revealed in the light of divine scrutiny. For it is written, "For we must all appear before the judgment seat of Christ; that everyone may receive the things done in his body, according to that he hath done, whether it be good or bad" (2 Corinthians 5:10). The stage of accountability is not set on earth's platforms but before Heaven's throne, where no title, charisma, or reputation can hide hypocrisy. The Church has long judged the world, but now Heaven declares, "Judgment must begin at the house of God."

Accountability before God is not an act of cruelty; it is an expression of divine justice and mercy. God holds His Church accountable because He loves it too deeply to let it decay in corruption.

When the Church tolerates what God condemns, He exposes it—not to shame, but to cleanse. The exposure of hidden sin, the fall of once-revered leaders, and the shaking of religious institutions are not random scandals; they are divine interventions. The Holy Spirit is stripping away the fades so that what remains will be authentic, holy, and true. The reckoning is not punishment; it is purification.

For too long, the Church has confused grace with permission. Grace was never meant to justify sin but to empower repentance. Yet many have built ministries on the illusion of immunity— preaching forgiveness while living in rebellion. The pulpit became a stage of performance rather than a platform of truth. But God will not be mocked. The hour has come when every hidden work of darkness will be revealed, and every secret intention judged. This is not a word of condemnation but of alignment: the Bride must be cleansed before the Bridegroom returns.

The reckoning of the Church begins in the mirror of the Word. Many read Scripture to defend themselves rather than to be transformed by it. The Word of God is not a weapon to wound others—it is a mirror that exposes the self. When believers cease to allow the Word to confront their sin, they lose the fear of the Lord, and with that loss comes moral collapse. Revival begins when the Church once again trembles at His Word, allowing it to pierce through hypocrisy, pride, and pretense. The Bible is not merely a book; it is the voice of God holding His people accountable in every generation.

Accountability is the safeguard of holiness. Without it, power corrupts, and influences deceives. The absence of accountability in leadership has birthed an era of celebrity Christianity where charisma replaces character and success is measured by applause rather than obedience. God never anoints personalities; He anoints purpose. Yet, the modern Church has exalted giftedness above godliness, allowing unrepentant hearts to govern sacred platforms. The reckoning of this generation will expose how the Church traded discernment for popularity and righteousness for relevance.

God is not silent in this hour. He is speaking through storms, scandals, and shaking. Every exposure of hidden evil is a trumpet blast from Heaven calling the Church to repentance. When corruption is revealed, it is not the victory of the enemy but the mercy of God. He would rather embarrass a ministry than lose a soul. The cleansing fire now sweeping through pulpits and pews alike is a sign that God is preparing His Bride for a greater glory. What is being dismantled by judgment will be rebuilt in righteousness.

The reckoning extends beyond the Church to the systems of the world. Nations that once honored God now legislate sin. Governments built on moral foundations now crumble under corruption. But before God judges a nation, He judges its altars. The Church cannot intercede effectively for the world while participating in its wickedness. The same standard that God applies to the nations begins with His people. This is why revival cannot come without repentance, and transformation cannot come without truth. The Church must first be washed before it can become a cleansing agent in society.

Accountability begins in secret before it is made public. The Spirit convicts long before exposure comes. Every warning ignored brings a greater shaking. God always sends prophets before judgment, giving His people time to repent. Yet, too often, the modern Church silences the prophetic voice because it disrupts comfort. But the prophets are not sent to comfort the complacent; they are sent to awaken the sleeping. When the Church rejects accountability, it invites public humiliation; when it embraces correction, it receives revival. Accountability is not God's anger; it is His invitation to return to holiness.

The reckoning of the Church is also a reckoning of motives. God is weighing hearts, not just actions. Many have done the right thing for the wrong reason, serving for applause, giving for recognition, and preaching for influence. The Lord declared through Jeremiah, "I the Lord search the heart, I try the reins." In this hour, the fire of God is purifying motives so that only those who labor from love, not ambition, will stand. The shaking is separating the performers from the prophets, the opportunists from the obedient, the false from the faithful. Only truth will remain.

Heaven is recording everything. Every secret conversation, every act of deceit, every word spoken in darkness will one day be shouted from the rooftops. This is not a myth but a promise from the mouth of Jesus Himself: "There is nothing covered, that shall not be revealed; neither hid, that shall not be known." The Church has preached accountability to sinners while avoiding it among saints. Yet, divine justice is impartial. God's holiness demands consistency; His standard does not change for bishops, prophets, or presidents. The fear of the Lord is returning to the Church, and with it, the restoration of integrity.

Accountability also means stewardship. Every gift, every resource, every soul entrusted to the Church will be weighed in eternity scales. Many have mishandled their callings through negligence, pride, or greed. The Lord's parable of the talents is not a motivational story; it is a warning of divine expectations. "Well done, good and faithful servant" will not be said to those who built monuments to themselves, but to those who multiplied what they were given for the Master's glory. The reckoning of the Church will reveal who truly served the Kingdom and who served their own.

There is a divine sorrow in Heaven over the state of the modern Church. Angels who once rejoiced over revival now weep over compromise. The glory that once filled sanctuaries now hovers outside, waiting for repentance. The Spirit grieves when pulpits become platforms of pride, and altars become stages of entertainment. Yet, even in grief, there is hope. God's mercy still pleads, "Return to Me, and I will return to you." The door of repentance remains open, but not forever. The time for accountability is now; the reckoning has begun.

This reckoning is not merely disciplinary; it is prophetic. God is aligning His Church for the last harvest. The exposure of corruption is clearing the field of counterfeit shepherds so that true laborers may arise. The shaking is not destruction but preparation. As wheat is separated from chaff, so God is refining His people for purity, power, and purpose. Accountability is Heaven's reset button, restoring order where chaos reigned. Through this holy reckoning, God is reminding His Church that He will have a Bride without spot, wrinkle, or blemish prepared, purified, and proven by fire.

The fire of accountability will not spare the comfort or the complacent. It will move through pews and pulpits alike, testing the integrity of every heart. For too long, the Church has mistaken silence for peace and tolerance for unity. But God's peace is not the absence of conflict; it is the presence of righteousness. The reckoning comes to expose false unity built on compromise, where truth was sacrificed to avoid offense. The Spirit of the Lord is reclaiming His Bride from the deception of comfort and calling her into courageous holiness. The Church must rediscover the holy fear that bows before His Word and trembles at His voice.

When God begins to reckon with His people, He does not start with the world but with His priests. Those who stand closest to the altar will be examined first. This principle echoes through Scripture from Aaron's sons consumed by strange fire to Eli's sons judged for desecrating the offering, to Ananias and Sapphira struck down for lying to the Holy Spirit. These stories are not mere history; they are prophetic warnings for this generation. Those who handle the sacred must not do so casually. The Lord is cleansing His ministers because He desires to pour out revival without mixture, purity without performance, truth without pretense.

Many churches have turned ministry into machinery, where programs replace prayer and marketing replaces miracles. But God cannot be marketed. His Spirit cannot be scheduled. The reckoning will dismantle man-made systems that replaced dependence with strategy. In this shaking, ministries will discover that the power of God cannot coexist with the pride of man. The Spirit is calling the Church back to the upper room, not the boardroom, back to tears on the altar, not trends on the stage. Only a Church stripped of its idols will carry the weight of His glory.

There is a sacred shift taking place from celebrity Christianity to servant leadership. The reckoning is unmasking those who built kingdoms in God's name but not for His glory. They sought crowds, not conversions; applause, not anointing. Yet the Lord, in His mercy, is replacing personality-driven religion with presence-driven revival. He is raising unknown voices from hidden places, intercessors, watchmen, and remnant believers who seek no stage but His face.

These are the ones who will restore the credibility of the Gospel, not by charisma but by consecration.

This accountability also reaches into the hearts of believers who have become spectators rather than participants. The Church was never called to be an audience but an army. Many sit week after week, consuming sermons but refusing to carry the cross. The reckoning of God will awaken slumbering saints, breaking the cycle of spiritual apathy. The Lord is asking His people, "How long will you waver between two opinions? If the Lord be God, follow Him." (1 Kings 18:21). The days of lukewarm Christianity are ending. Those who are truly His will burn with conviction; those who are not will drift into deception.

In this season, God is exposing false unity that covers sin instead of confronting it. Many have called compromise "grace" and silence "love." But grace without truth is lawlessness, and love without righteousness is deception. The reckoning will divide truth from tolerance. Christ did not die to make sin acceptable; He died to make holiness attainable. The Church must stop apologizing for the Gospel. The cross still offends because it still saves. The Spirit is restoring conviction to the pulpits, so that the Word once again cuts to the heart and brings forth genuine repentance.

The accountability of God also demands that we confront the misuse of power within the Church. Spiritual abuse has left many broken, silenced, and distrustful of faith. Leaders who weaponized Scripture to manipulate and control will face divine justice. The Lord is defending His sheep. He is healing the wounded who were cast aside and rejected by the very institutions that should have nurtured them. The same Jesus who drove out the money changers is now driving out the manipulators of His name. The Church's credibility before the world depends on its willingness to repent for the harm done in His name.

This reckoning is not meant to destroy hope but to restore it. God's judgment always leads to redemption when His people respond with repentance. The shaking is painful, but it is also purifying. Like a refiner's fire, it burns away impurities to reveal something radiant beneath — the true Bride of Christ, without spot or wrinkle. What feels like destruction is actually divine reconstruction. The Lord is tearing down walls built by pride and rebuilding altars built by prayer. Those who endure the fire will emerge with renewed authority and divine credibility.

As the Spirit of truth moves through the earth, exposure will come swiftly. Hidden conversations, secret alliances, and false doctrines will come to light. The Lord will no longer allow deception to masquerade as discernment. This is why discernment is being restored to the Body so that the sheep can recognize the voice of their Shepherd amid the chaos of counterfeit callings. The Holy Spirit is training believers to test every prophecy, weigh every teaching, and discern every spirit, not by charisma but by Scripture. The days of blind loyalty to corrupt systems are over.

The Church stands now at a threshold between judgment and renewal. God is giving us one more opportunity to repent collectively, to rebuild our altars, and to realign with His mission. The Great Commission has been buried beneath the great competition, but He is resurrecting it again. Evangelism will rise, not through fame but through fire-filled faith. The Church's witness in the world will not be restored through clever strategies but through visible holiness. When the world sees a people who truly walk in love and truth, it will no longer mock the Church, it will marvel at Christ within her.

Accountability before God means surrendering the illusion of control. Many have tried to lead without listening, to build without blessing, and to plan without prayer. But the Lord is silencing human ambition that has pretended to be divine vision. True leadership in the Kingdom begins at the feet of Jesus, not the head of a table. The reckoning will humble those who exalted themselves and exalt those who humbled themselves before God. The Spirit is looking for broken vessels through whom His glory can flow freely, untainted by pride.

God's accountability also exposes the idolatry of success within ministry. We have measured faithfulness by numbers, budgets, and buildings, forgetting that Jesus' greatest ministry moment was the cross, where He stood alone. The Lord is recalibrating His Church's definition of success to match His own: obedience. The applause of men will fade, but the approval of God endures forever. When the reckoning is complete, what will remain are not the largest ministries but the purest hearts.

The reckoning will reveal that not all who call themselves shepherds have the heart of a shepherd. Some have led with greed instead of grace, ambition instead of anointing. But the true shepherds are rising those who would rather lose followers than lose the favor of God. They will preach the truth even when it costs them their platform. They will defend the weak, comfort the wounded, and confront the wolves. Through them, God will restore trust in spiritual leadership. For in the days ahead, the Church will need courageous shepherds more than charismatic ones.

The accountability of heaven is also a mirror for every believer. We cannot pray for God to cleanse the pulpit while living unrepentantly in the pew. Each soul must stand before the same holy God and give an account for their life. The Holy Spirit calls every heart to self-examination: Are we living what we proclaim? Are we walking in forgiveness, purity, and compassion? The reckoning is not only for them, it is for us. And in that realization lies the beginning of true revival.

The world is watching how the Church responds to its own exposure. If we respond with arrogance, we confirm their doubts. If we respond with repentance, we reveal God's heart. The Church has a divine opportunity to model what restoration looks like. The Lord is inviting His people to be transparent, not defensive; broken, not boastful. When the world sees humility where it expected hypocrisy, it will once again recognize the presence of Christ among His people.

The reckoning is a prelude to revival. Before every great move of God, there is a great cleansing. Before the upper room came repentance in the upper chamber. Before glory came groaning. The Lord is not punishing His Church; He is preparing her. Like Esther before the king, the Bride must be purified before presentation. Every trial, every exposure, every correction is God's way of making His Church ready for the outpouring that will precede His return.

This divine accountability will also separate the wheat from the tares. Not everyone who appears anointed has been appointed. Many who perform signs and wonders in His name will hear the dreadful words, "I never knew you" (Matthew 7:23). The reckoning will distinguish relationships from religion, intimacy from influence. Those who truly know the Lord will stand firm amid the shaking, while those who merely use His name will crumble under the weight of truth. Authenticity will become a new anointing.

As the Church stands before God's refining fire, nations will be affected. When the Church is pure, the land will heal. When righteousness rises, corruption falls. The accountability of the Church determines the destiny of the world, for the Church is the moral compass of civilization. When the compass is broken, society wanders in darkness. But as God restores holiness within His people, justice and righteousness will again flow from the sanctuary into the streets. The healing of the nation begins with the repentance of the Church.

The Spirit of God is calling intercessors to stand in the gap once more. As judgment draws near, prayer must increase. True accountability is sustained by intercession by those who plead for mercy even as truth prevails. The Church needs watchmen who will not slumber, who will cry day and night for a wayward people. In this hour, tears are more powerful than talent, and brokenness is a greater weapon than brilliance. The reckoning will not end in ruin if the remnant rises in repentance.

The Lord reminds His people that He takes no pleasure in judgment. His desire is always redemption. Like the father of the prodigal son, He waits with open arms, ready to restore those who return. The reckoning is a call home. It is the Father's voice crying out through the chaos, "Where are you?" Just as He did in Eden, He calls His children to step out of hiding, to confess, to be clothed again in righteousness. The Church's future depends not on perfection, but on returning to the One who is perfect.

In this divine season, the Bride is being prepared for her Groom. The accountability of the present is preparing her for the glory of the future. She is learning to let go of every impurity that cannot enter the Kingdom. The trials, exposures, and humbling of this age are removing every stain, so that when Christ appears, she may stand radiant in white. The Church must see this reckoning not as rejection but as preparation for eternal union.

God's reckoning also brings reassurance that He has not abandoned His Church, even in her failures. His discipline is proof of His covenant. The very fact that He corrects us means He still claims us as His own. The shaking is not the end of the Church; it is the beginning of her renewal. When the dust settles, a remnant will rise stronger, purer, and more united than before. The Church will emerge, not as a fractured institution, but as a fiery movement carrying the heart of Christ to a lost world.

As the final trumpet approaches, the Spirit cries out to every believer: *Prepare the way of the Lord.* This is not a season to hide but to heed. Accountability is God's last mercy before judgment. Those who heed the call will shine like lights in the darkness. Their integrity will draw the lost, their holiness will convict the wicked, and their love will reveal the heart of Christ. This is the hour for the Church to rise purified, empowered, and fearless in truth.

The reckoning of the Church and the world will culminate in the unveiling of true justice. Every secret will be revealed, every lie overturned, every injustice avenged. The Judge of all the earth will do right. For those who loved His appearance, this will be glory; for those who mocked His warnings, it will be terror. Yet through it all, the mercy of God will remain evident — that He warned before He judged, pleaded before He punished, and offered grace before wrath. The time to choose righteousness is now.

In the end, the Church on trial will become the Church triumphant. The same fire that exposes will be refined. The same hand that disciplines will restore. And the same God who rebukes hidden evil will reward hidden faithfulness. When the final reckoning is complete, the Bride will stand blameless before the throne, her garments washed in the blood of the Lamb. Then heaven will declare, *"Behold, the tabernacle of God is with men."* The Church purified will become the vessel through which His glory fills the earth. This is the purpose of divine accountability, not destruction, but transformation, not shame, but glory.

Failure of Collaboration and Accountability

God will hold faith-based organizations accountable for refusing to collaborate in addressing gun violence when children's lives are at stake. He will hold churches accountable for ignoring domestic violence survivors in their pews while preaching about family values.

He will hold schools, hospitals, and churches accountable for failing to work together to address ACEs, leaving traumatized children without healing. He will hold communities accountable for allowing child abuse to continue unchecked because agencies worked in silos instead of in unity.

He will hold leaders accountable for tolerating sexual abuse of teens in youth ministries instead of reporting and protecting them. He will hold organizations accountable for ignoring the cries of the addicted, refusing to work across sectors for recovery. Disunity will not excuse anyone. Mark 3:25 declares, *"If a house is divided against itself, that house cannot stand."*

Accountability in Leadership

James 3:1 warns that teachers will be judged more strictly. Pastors and spiritual leaders must know their accountability is heavier than others. Matthew 18:6 warns that causing little ones to stumble brings severe judgment. Leaders who exploit children will face the wrath of God.

Ezekiel 34:10 rebukes shepherds who abandoned the flock: *"I am against the shepherds and will hold them accountable for my flock."* God holds leaders accountable not only for what they did, but also for what they failed to do. Silence in the face of injustice is itself a sin. Isaiah 58:1 calls, *"Shout it aloud, do not hold back. Raise your voice like a trumpet. Declare to my people their rebellion.* "Collaboration is not optional; it is obedience to God's call to justice.

Accountability in the Church and the World

God will hold entire congregations accountable when they choose comfort over justice. Revelation 3:16 warns lukewarm churches will be spit out. God will hold nations accountable for policies that oppress the poor, deny justice, and exploit the weak. Amos 5:24 declares, *"Let justice roll on like a river, righteousness like a never-failing stream."*

He will hold community leaders accountable for refusing to act against systemic racism when they had the power to influence. He will hold schools accountable for ignoring child welfare in pursuit of test scores or funding. He will hold businesses accountable for exploiting workers instead of supporting families. Accountability will reach every corner of society because God is just and His throne is founded on righteousness (Psalm 89:14).

Final Day of Accountability

On the Day of Judgment, every hidden thing will be revealed. 2 Corinthians 5:10 declares, *"For we must all appear before the judgment seat of Christ.* "The Church will be judged first. 1 Peter 4:17 says, *"It is time for judgment to begin with God's household."*

Leaders will stand before God and explain every sermon, every decision, and every policy. Congregations will answer for whether they served Christ in the poor, the broken, and the abused. Nations will be weighed like Babylon in Daniel 5 and found wanting if they ignore justice. Every person will face the Lord of Truth, with no excuse left.

Hope in Accountability

Accountability is not only about punishment, it is about restoration. Hebrews 12:11 says discipline produces righteousness. Churches that repent can still rebuild credibility and trust. Leaders who humble themselves can still be restored to godly service.

Communities that unite can still heal the wounds of violence and abuse. Accountability reminds us of God's mercy as much as His justice. Lamentations 3:22-23 declares His mercies are new every morning. Repentance leads to revival, but arrogance leads to ruin.

The Call to Action

The Church must embrace accountability now, not later. Repentance today avoids judgment tomorrow. Leaders must examine their motives, ministries, and methods before God exposes them. Communities must collaborate across boundaries to reflect the Kingdom of God. Above all, we must remember John 14:6—Jesus is the Way, the Truth, and the Life. True accountability leads us back to Him, beyond religion, denomination, or doctrine.

"The Lord is close to the brokenhearted and saves those who are crushed in spirit." — **Psalm 34:18 (NIV)**

This verse immediately reminds us that God is not distant from our struggles. Mental health challenges, emotional trauma, addiction, and grief are not signs of weakness—they are part of the human experience. God's Word assures us that He is near to those who suffer, providing comfort, restoration, and hope. The Psalmist captures a truth often overlooked in faith communities: **healing begins when the broken are recognized, not judged**.

Mental health struggles have been present since biblical times. Figures like Elijah, David, Job, and Paul all faced despair, isolation, guilt, and overwhelming emotional burdens. Yet Scripture consistently demonstrates that God meets individuals where they are, offering restoration through presence, guidance, and divine intervention. These examples remind the church that mental health challenges are not spiritual failings but opportunities for God's power to be revealed.

The church is called to model this same grace. Stigma—whether rooted in misunderstanding, shame, or cultural bias—creates barriers that prevent people from seeking help. Many fear judgment for admitting struggles with depression, anxiety, trauma, or addiction. Psalm 34:18 encourages faith communities to respond with empathy rather than condemnation, affirming that **healing and restoration are possible for all, regardless of past failures or current struggles**.

Breaking stigma is central to the mission of recovery and restoration. It requires acknowledging mental health as a legitimate and vital component of holistic well-being, just as God honors the physical, emotional, and spiritual aspects of life. By openly addressing these challenges in the sanctuary and in community, the church can provide a safe space where individuals feel seen, understood, and supported.

Healing in mental health is deeply intertwined with faith. The Bible presents numerous examples of God's restorative power: He lifts the crushed in spirit, renews hope in the despairing, and strengthens those who feel weak or overwhelmed. These divine acts of restoration provide a template for how the church should approach mental health—**with compassion, education, and practical support**.

Recovery and mental health restoration also require a communal response. Scripture emphasizes the importance of mutual care: *"Carry each other's burdens, and in this way you will fulfill the law of Christ"* (Galatians 6:2). Faith communities must step beyond mere awareness and actively participate in healing—providing prayer, counseling, mentorship, and practical resources for those struggling.

I will examine the church's role in the recovery journey, highlighting how **faith, mental health awareness, and stigma reduction** intersect. By integrating biblical principles with modern recovery practices, including trauma-informed care and spiritual support, the church can become a place of genuine restoration—a sanctuary where people are empowered to reclaim their lives and experience God's wholeness.

As we explore the mental health journey, it is crucial to remember that recovery is **holistic**. Physical, emotional, relational, and spiritual healing are interconnected. The church, as a community of believers, is uniquely positioned to address each dimension, helping individuals not only survive their struggles but thrive in God's purpose and grace.

Psalm 34:18 is more than encouragement it is a blueprint for ministry. Brokenhearted individuals need more than platitude; they need recognition, support, and guidance. Mental health awareness and stigma reduction are not optional for the church they are essential components of living out God's love and demonstrating His healing power in practical, tangible ways.

With this understanding, we are prepared to explore **why Recovery Month exists, the process of healing, and the church's responsibility** in fostering hope, resilience, and restoration. Through Scripture, biblical examples, and modern recovery principles, this chapter will offer a framework for transforming suffering into healing, isolation into community, and stigma into compassionate understanding.

September marks a significant observance in the United States and increasingly worldwide: National Recovery Month. Established in 1989 by the Substance Abuse and Mental Health Services Administration (SAMHSA), this month shines a much-needed light on mental health challenges, substance use disorders, trauma, and the long journey of healing. Its purpose is both awareness and action reminding communities that recovery is possible and that no one must face their struggles alone.

Recovery Month is fundamentally about **awareness and education**. Millions of people silently battle mental health conditions, trauma, addiction, or grief, yet stigma and shame often keep them hidden. By openly recognizing the journey of recovery, society begins to dismantle myths, misjudgments, and harmful stereotypes that discourage individuals from seeking help.

Knowledge and understanding are the first steps toward a compassionate response.

At its core, Recovery Month is also a **celebration of hope**. It honors the millions of people who have found healing and change, demonstrating that recovery is not only possible but achievable. Their stories are living proof that despair does not have the final word, and that transformation, though often gradual and challenging, is real. Witnessing these stories inspires others who may still struggle to take courageous steps toward restoration.

One of the most crucial aspects of Recovery Month is its role in **reducing stigma**. Fear of judgment, prejudice, or misunderstanding keeps many from reaching out for help. By normalizing recovery and presenting it as a sign of courage rather than weakness, communities encourage openness and foster acceptance, allowing people to seek support without shame or fear.

Recovery is never meant to be a solo journey. **Encouraging community support** is central to the recovery process. Families, churches, professionals, and community organizations play vital roles in creating safe spaces where healing can occur. Recovery Month emphasizes that encouragement, accountability, and practical support from others are essential components of lasting change.

The origins of Recovery Month trace back to a focus on substance use treatment, but its vision has expanded to encompass **mental health recovery more broadly**. Every September, events, campaigns, and discussions center on themes such as healing, breaking stigma, and fostering community support, demonstrating that recovery is holistic, encompassing body, mind, and spirit.

The heart of Recovery Month is its message: **recovery is a movement of hope**. It proclaims that people can recover from addiction, trauma, and mental illness; that healing is worth celebrating; and that communities bear a responsibility to make recovery visible, accessible, and sustainable. Recovery is not a private struggle it is a shared journey that thrives within supportive relationships and compassionate systems.

But what exactly is recovery? At its essence, recovery is the process of **regaining health, wholeness, and stability** after experiencing life-altering challenges such as addiction, trauma, mental illness, or significant loss. It is more than a return to a prior state; it is a transformation into a renewed way of living, characterized by hope, purpose, and meaningful connection.

Recovery rests on key foundations: **honesty, willingness, support, and spiritual grounding.** Many who embark on this journey draw upon faith in God, a higher power, or the strength of community. This foundation provides the resilience needed to face the emotional, physical, and spiritual challenges inherent in healing.

The **healing process in recovery** often unfolds in stages. The first stage is **awareness and acknowledgment,** recognizing there is a problem and choosing to confront it. Admitting the need for change is a courageous act of self-awareness and the critical first step toward restoration.

Following awareness is **surrender and support**. Healing begins when individuals relinquish the illusion of control and reach out for help, whether through community, professional counseling, or spiritual guidance. Recovery is accelerated when people stop isolating and allow trusted individuals to journey alongside them.

The stage of **detox and renewal** addresses the physical and emotional residue of trauma or substance use. For addictions, this often involves a physical detox; for trauma, it requires safely confronting and processing pain. Though uncomfortable, this stage allows the body and mind to reset and prepares the individual for deeper emotional work.

Inner work is central to lasting recovery. It involves addressing emotional wounds, mental health challenges, and broken relationships. Learning to forgive oneself and others, adopting healthier habits, and seeking spiritual guidance or therapy enable individuals to transform pain into growth and resilience.

Growth and restoration follow inner work. During this stage, individuals develop coping skills, build healthy routines, strengthen relationships, and restore trust. Recovery becomes relational, impacting families, communities, and broader networks. Healing is no longer solitary it extends outward, touching those around the individual.

Ongoing maintenance emphasizes that recovery is lifelong. It requires consistency, accountability, and community engagement. Setbacks may occur, but they do not negate progress. Each day of commitment strengthens resilience, deepens insight, and reinforces the transformative power of God's grace or the supportive framework of a recovery community.

Key elements of healing in recovery include **physical, emotional, spiritual, and relational restoration**, as well as the rediscovery of purpose and identity. Physical healing repairs the damage caused by stress, trauma, or substance abuse; emotional healing teaches individuals to process feelings without being overwhelmed; spiritual healing reconnects them with God or a higher power; relational healing repairs bonds with family, friends, and community; and purpose restores a sense of self-worth and direction.

The **fruits of recovery** are abundant. They include renewed hope, peace of mind, greater self- control, stronger relationships, restored trust, and a deeper sense of purpose. Recovery equips individuals to help others, transforming their personal journey into a source of inspiration and support.

Recovery Month underscores that healing is possible, visible, and worth celebrating. It challenges communities, including churches, to recognize that trauma, mental illness, and addiction are not signs of spiritual failure but human experiences that require compassion, understanding, and active engagement.

Within the church context, recognizing these realities is particularly urgent. Faith communities often serve as the first point of contact for those in distress, yet stigma, ignorance, or rigidity can prevent leaders from offering meaningful guidance. Recovery Month serves as a call to action— urging the church to model empathy, education, and healing-centered ministry.

By opening this conversation, we prepare to explore the deeper intersections of **mental health, trauma, and the healing journey**. Recovery Month provides a lens through which the church can evaluate its role: Are we a sanctuary of hope, understanding, and restoration, or are we perpetuating judgment, neglect, and silence? This chapter will examine how faith, community, and holistic recovery intersect, providing insight, guidance, and biblical grounding for those committed to transforming suffering into restoration.

The Role of Healing

Healing is not merely the absence of pain or trauma; it is the restoration of the soul, mind, and body. In Scripture, we see God's healing work as holistic, addressing both physical ailments and the deep wounds of the heart and spirit. For those recovering from trauma, understanding healing as a process rather than an instant fix is vital.

Elijah, after his confrontation with the prophets of Baal, fled in fear and despair. Alone in the wilderness, he felt hopeless and ready to die. God's response was not immediate triumph but gentle care rest, nourishment, and reassurance. This teaches that healing begins with meeting the person where they are, acknowledging exhaustion, and providing sustenance for both body and spirit.

David's psalms reveal the raw honesty of a wounded soul. Anxiety, guilt, and loneliness plagued him, yet he expressed his struggles openly in prayer. Healing, in David's example, involved confession, lament, and returning continually to God's presence. The process was cyclical, reminding us that recovery from mental and emotional trauma requires ongoing engagement with God and community.

Job's story exemplifies the depth of suffering and the long journey toward restoration. Losing family, health, and wealth, Job experienced profound grief and trauma. His healing process involved lamenting, questioning God, and enduring in faith. Job illustrates that healing often involves wrestling with difficult questions and acknowledging the reality of pain while remaining anchored in trust.

Chronic trauma, as seen in Jeremiah's life, demonstrates the need for sustained care and hope. Living through national collapse, imprisonment, and repeated rejection, Jeremiah's despair was profound. Yet, God's faithfulness provided a framework for emotional resilience. Healing can be gradual, often requiring repeated reassurance, guidance, and the cultivation of hope amidst ongoing struggles.

Paul's "thorn in the flesh" represents another dimension of healing: living with ongoing weakness or chronic stress. Paul did not receive complete removal of his affliction; instead, God offered strength and purpose through it. This teaches that healing does not always mean the elimination of difficulty but finding meaning, resilience, and growth even within suffering.

Healing also requires community. Many biblical figures, including Mary Magdalene and the demon-possessed man, were restored not only by God but also through reintroduction into a supportive community. Isolation deepens trauma; recovery flourishes when individuals are welcomed, affirmed, and empowered to participate once more in life and society.

Understanding the role of healing in recovery means acknowledging the mind, body, and spirit connection. Trauma affects neural pathways, emotional regulation, and physical health. Scripture demonstrates that God's care addresses the whole person: Elijah received food; David poured out his heart; Job engaged in prayerful reflection; Paul embraced spiritual strength within his weakness.

Healing often involves patience. The Israelites' exodus from Egypt illustrates communal trauma and the necessity of a journey toward restoration. Despite deliverance, their minds and hearts carried fear and mistrust for decades in the wilderness. This mirrors today's understanding that trauma leaves lasting effects and recovery requires time, consistent support, and safe environments.

Restoration is relational. Healing is incomplete without reconciliation, forgiveness, and community reintegration. The Prodigal Son's journey highlights that even after reckless or self- destructive behavior, a person can be restored when met with acceptance and love. Recovery is strengthened when individuals experience relational restoration alongside personal growth.

Spiritual healing is intertwined with emotional and psychological healing. Biblical figures often experienced despair and fear, yet their relationship with God provided hope and direction.

Prayer, worship, and reliance on divine guidance are integral to restoring balance and peace in the soul, complementing practical and professional recovery methods today.

Trauma-informed healing emphasizes listening and validation. Elijah's lamentation, David's confessions, and Job's dialogues with friends illustrate the importance of being heard. For modern recovery, this principle translates into empathetic care, validating emotions, and providing spaces where individuals can safely share their pain without judgment.

Healing involves confronting the source of trauma. Samson's impulsiveness, Paul's persecutions, and Mary Magdalene's past bondage all required facing realities of sin, betrayal, or oppression. Recovery is incomplete without acknowledging the root causes of trauma, whether personal, societal, or spiritual, allowing for transformation and deeper resilience.

Hope is a critical element of healing. God's promises in Scripture, from the rainbow covenant with Noah to the resurrection hope for Mary Magdalene, provide a foundation for endurance. For those recovering today, cultivating hope—spiritual, emotional, and relational—is essential for sustaining long-term recovery from mental health challenges and chronic trauma.

Healing often involves action. David acted through worship, confession, and righteous deeds; Elijah moved forward after rest; the Prodigal Son returned to his father. Recovery is not passive; it includes engaging in meaningful practices, therapy, spiritual disciplines, or community service that reinforce growth and restoration.

Self-compassion and patience are part of God's model for healing. Job's friends initially misjudged him, yet God's ultimate restoration of Job included reaffirmation of dignity. Modern recovery teaches similar principles: self-blame hinders healing, while patience, self-compassion, and understanding that recovery is a process foster restoration.

Integrating spiritual disciplines in the healing process strengthens resilience. Daily prayer, meditation, worship, and scripture reflection support mental health by providing structure, purpose, and connection. Biblical examples show that returning to God, even in ongoing struggle, nurtures recovery and fortifies the mind against despair.

Healing requires confronting shame. Many biblical figures, including Noah, Samson, and David, experienced public or private shame. Restoration involved acceptance and affirmation from God or the community. In today's context, addressing stigma associated with mental health, addiction, or trauma is central to full recovery, creating spaces where shame does not prevent healing.

Recovery is iterative. Elijah, David, and Paul all experienced setbacks and ongoing struggles, demonstrating that healing is not linear. Trauma-informed care today echoes this understanding: relapses, emotional flare-ups, or re-experiencing trauma are not failures but part of the recovery trajectory, requiring renewed care and faith.

Finally, the role of healing in the biblical narrative emphasizes that God is present in the process, not just at the resolution. Recovery is a journey where divine guidance, community support, self- reflection, and practical action converge. Healing is relational, holistic, and continuous, providing a blueprint for the church today to walk alongside those navigating trauma and mental health challenges.

Breaking the Stigma

Stigma has been a barrier to healing since biblical times. Individuals who struggled with mental, emotional, or spiritual burdens were often misunderstood, marginalized, or blamed. Today, stigma around race, addiction, alcoholism, and mental health continues to prevent many from seeking help.

Elijah's depression and burnout were met with silence and misunderstanding. Leaders expected prophets to be unwavering and courageous. God's gentle care for Elijah models a counter- narrative: acknowledging vulnerability is not shameful, and seeking rest and support is part of spiritual and mental health.

David's guilt and anxiety highlight how stigma can intensify suffering. Kings were not supposed to admit fear or despair, yet David poured out his soul in psalms. By expressing vulnerability publicly, he broke cultural norms and demonstrated that even leaders are human, setting a precedent for today's men and women in leadership to seek help without shame.

Job faced social stigma in addition to personal trauma. His friends wrongly assumed that his suffering was punishment for sin. The societal misjudgment added layers to his grief. Breaking stigma requires correcting false narratives, as God ultimately rebuked Job's friends and restored Job's dignity.

Jeremiah, the "weeping prophet," was often mocked for expressing sorrow and fear. His emotional openness challenged cultural expectations that men must be stoic. Today, men of color and others marginalized by societal norms often face similar stigmas when showing emotional vulnerability.

Paul's chronic weakness and physical afflictions were not widely understood by those around him. Society expected apostles to demonstrate power and invulnerability. By reframing his weakness as strength through Christ, Paul broke stigma and provided a model for individuals living with chronic illness or mental health struggles today.

Mary Magdalene's history of spiritual bondage subjected her to marginalization, both as a woman and a former outcast. Jesus restored her dignity and empowered her to be the first witness of the resurrection, illustrating that stigmatized individuals can be restored to leadership and community.

The demon-possessed man in Mark 5 endured both isolation and societal fear. He was chained and feared by others, considered dangerous and unclean. His restoration by Jesus not only healed him physically and mentally but also reintegrated him socially, demonstrating that breaking stigma includes community acceptance and dignity restoration.

Noah's lapse into drunkenness after surviving the flood shows that even those chosen by God are vulnerable to shame and societal judgment. His story reminds us that relapse or coping mechanisms do not erase God's purpose, and breaking stigma means offering grace alongside accountability.

Samson's impulsive behavior, lust, and eventual captivity highlight how failures can create stigmas. Though he was seen as weak or unfaithful, God's restoration in his final act illustrates that redemption and breaking stigma are possible even after repeated missteps.

Lot's experience with family dysfunction and substance use highlights generational trauma and societal judgment. Modern parallels include communities where cycles of addiction and dysfunction carry stigma, discouraging individuals from seeking help. Breaking stigma involves understanding trauma's root causes and promoting healing over judgment.

The Prodigal Son's reckless living exemplifies shame and estrangement, often stigmatized by society. His father's radical acceptance demonstrates the transformative power of unconditional love, illustrating that breaking stigma involves welcoming back those who have strayed without judgment.

Judas, whose despair led to suicide, illustrates the extreme consequences of unresolved trauma and internalized shame. His story challenges the church to confront the stigma around suicide, mental health, and hopelessness, emphasizing the importance of compassion, intervention, and grace.

The Bible consistently shows that stigma often arises from misunderstanding, fear, or rigid expectations. In all cases, God's response models empathy, patience, and restoration. Today, the church and society must emulate these principles to support individuals struggling with trauma or mental health issues.

Race, health, and gender intersect with mental health stigma today. People of color often face systemic barriers to mental health resources, women may be dismissed or blamed for emotional struggles, and those with physical illness or addiction are judged rather than supported. Biblical narratives demonstrate that God's care transcends these social barriers.

Elijah, a man of deep faith, was dismissed and isolated due to his emotional exhaustion. Today, individuals experiencing depression or burnout face similar societal disbelief, especially in ministry contexts. Breaking stigma involves acknowledging emotional reality and providing nonjudgmental support.

David, though a king, experienced shame, guilt, and relational rejection. By writing psalms that expressed his inner turmoil, he demonstrated that authenticity and emotional honesty are strengths, challenging the stigma around mental health for those in positions of authority or influence.

Paul's acceptance of his "thorn in the flesh" models how embracing one's vulnerabilities can counter societal stigma. Living openly with chronic weakness while fulfilling God's purpose challenges cultural narratives that equate weakness with inadequacy.

Mary Magdalene's transformation breaks the stigma attached to her past and gender. She became a trusted disciple and witness, exemplifying that healing and redemption overturn social bias and exclusion, creating space for women and marginalized individuals to lead.

Breaking stigma requires both **acknowledgment and action**. Acknowledging trauma, addiction, or mental health struggles is the first step. Action includes community support, education, integration of faith and professional care, and public examples of restoration. Biblical examples provide timeless lessons: God validates the struggles of His people and restores them to purpose, challenging societal assumptions and stigma.

Integrating Faith & Professional Help

Recovery from trauma and mental health challenges is most effective when faith and professional care work together. The Bible illustrates that God often uses people, communities, and practical means to restore His children, showing that divine intervention and human resources are not mutually exclusive.

Physicians appear in Scripture as instruments of God's healing. Luke, a physician, wrote carefully about healing and ministry. This demonstrates that professional expertise can complement spiritual care, highlighting the integration of medical, psychological, and pastoral resources in modern recovery.

Elijah's burnout required rest, nourishment, and guidance. While God provided spiritual renewal, practical support shelter, food, and a listening companion was essential. Today, faith-based recovery must recognize the importance of professional counseling, nutrition, and holistic self- care alongside spiritual guidance.

David sought both divine help and relational support. Prayer, lament, and confession were paired with interaction with mentors, friends, and community. Trauma-informed care today echoes this, combining psychotherapy, support groups, and pastoral care to address emotional and spiritual wounds.

Job's counselors initially failed because they misinterpreted his suffering. This underscores the importance of professional and trained support that understands trauma. Modern mental health recovery emphasizes evidence-based therapy and trauma-informed care to avoid re- traumatization.

Paul's letters reveal both spiritual guidance and practical strategies for community care. He encouraged accountability, mentoring, and mutual support, illustrating that integrating faith and structure, professional frameworks promote holistic healing.

Mary Magdalene's restoration highlights the synergy of divine intervention and social support. Jesus delivered her, but her ongoing integration into the community of disciples facilitated sustained recovery, showing that connection and practical guidance are critical in trauma recovery today.

The demon-possessed man required Jesus' spiritual authority, but community reintegration was necessary for complete restoration. This mirrors modern practice: spiritual care alone is insufficient without therapeutic support, community engagement, and skill-building to reintegrate individuals safely.

Noah's trauma after the flood demonstrates the need for both spiritual hope and practical coping strategies. Modern parallels include survivors of disaster or war who benefit from counseling, group support, and faith-centered encouragement to process trauma effectively.

Samson's impulsiveness and captivity illustrate the need for interventions addressing both behavioral patterns and spiritual direction. Contemporary recovery programs combine cognitive- behavioral therapy with spiritual mentorship, modeling integrated approaches that address chronic trauma and impulsivity.

Lot's experience with dysfunction and shame underscores that generational trauma may require layered interventions. Faith-based guidance paired with professional therapy can break cycles of abuse, substance use, or maladaptive coping mechanisms.

The Prodigal Son's reconciliation emphasizes guidance, accountability, and reintegration. Recovery today follows similar principles: spiritual mentorship, community support, and professional counseling work together to restore individuals' sense of purpose and belonging.

Judas' despair leading to suicide demonstrates the need for early intervention. Modern integration of pastoral care, mental health counseling, and crisis support networks can prevent tragedy, providing a blueprint for churches to address stigma and risk proactively.

Trauma-informed care in biblical narratives often involves listening, validation, and safe spaces. Integrating faith and professional help requires creating environments where individuals feel understood, supported, and empowered to engage with both spiritual and therapeutic guidance.

Chronic trauma, as seen in Jeremiah or Paul, illustrates that long-term support is essential. Recovery frameworks combining ongoing pastoral counseling, psychotherapy, and peer support enable individuals to process persistent emotional and spiritual stress safely.

Addiction and substance misuse, reflected in Noah, Lot, and the Prodigal Son, highlight the importance of integrated approaches. Faith communities can support sobriety and recovery while collaborating with medical and counseling professionals to provide structured care and relapse prevention.

Addressing stigma and promoting mental health within the church is integral to integrating professional help. Biblical narratives show that awareness, teaching, and empathetic guidance dismantle misconceptions and create spaces where individuals can seek both faith-based and professional support without shame.

Integrating faith and professional help also involves equipping leaders and clergy with knowledge about trauma, chronic stress, and mental illness. Training programs can empower church leaders to recognize warning signs, provide appropriate spiritual care, and refer to qualified professionals when needed.

Combining scripture and evidence-based practice offers unique advantages. Biblical teachings provide hope, meaning, and moral guidance, while professional intervention addresses neurological, emotional, and social aspects of trauma. Together, they provide comprehensive recovery pathways.

Ultimately, the role of integration is to honor the wholeness of the person. Spiritual, emotional, cognitive, and physical healing are interconnected. Biblical examples show that God works through relationships, interventions, and practical means. Today, churches that embrace trauma- informed approaches, break stigma, and integrate professional help mirror God's holistic care, supporting individuals in reclaiming dignity, purpose, and hope.

When the Church Fails: Leaders, Stigma, and the Neglect of Mental Health Many individuals enter the church carrying invisible burdens—depression, anxiety, addiction, trauma, grief but often the first response they receive is judgment, indifference, or ignorance. Church leaders, unintentionally or intentionally, may stigmatize the hurting rather than offering God's restorative Word.

Throughout Scripture, leaders sometimes failed to recognize the suffering of those in their care.

Eli, the priest, neglected Hannah's deep anguish, dismissing her silent weeping in the temple. This neglect mirrors modern leaders who overlook emotional and mental suffering, offering perfunctory advice instead of meaningful support.

The church often creates invisible walls around those in need. The less fortunate, the financially struggling, or the emotionally broken are frequently viewed through lenses of judgment: a lack of faith, poor stewardship, or spiritual deficiency. This stigma discourages individuals from seeking help, prolonging their pain.

The church often creates invisible walls around those in need. The less fortunate, the financially struggling, or the emotionally broken are frequently viewed through lenses of judgmental lack of faith, poor stewardship, or spiritual deficiency. This stigma discourages individuals from seeking help, prolonging their pain. Yet, the tragedy deepens when we recognize that many of these same judgments come from religious leaders who themselves have silently wrestled with deep emotional and mental wounds. Many have endured trauma in childhood, battled depression, anxiety, or rejection in their own marriages and relationships, or suffered forms of abuse that they have buried beneath titles, sermons, and public smiles. They preach healing yet hide their own brokenness, afraid of exposure, afraid of judgment, and afraid of losing the image of holiness that the church demands they uphold.

Because of this silence, congregations are left without genuine examples of vulnerability or wholeness. Members who struggle with mental health, those enduring depression, suicidal thoughts, trauma, or shame, are often met with condemnation instead of compassion. They are told to "pray harder" or "have more faith," when what they truly need is understanding, counseling, and a safe place to heal. The church has become a place where the wounded are expected to hide their scars, and where leaders conceal their pain behind pulpits, refusing to confront the truth that healing begins with honesty.

It is time for the Church, especially those in leadership, to confront the hidden evil of silence and hypocrisy. It is time for pastors, ministers, elders, and spiritual leaders to acknowledge their humanity and seek help for their own mental and emotional struggles. Some have even crossed sacred boundaries, abusing their authority by manipulating or exploiting the vulnerable young men and women silenced by threats or guilt. But God is now exposing these hidden sins. What was once whispered in the dark is being shouted from the rooftops. It is *not okay* to silence victims, to normalize abuse, or to hide behind the cloak of ministry while souls are suffering.

The true Church must be a place of repentance, restoration, and transparency, a place where both leaders and members can seek healing without shame. For only when truth is spoken, and darkness is confronted, can the light of God's mercy and justice truly shine upon His people.

For judgment must begin at the house of God (1 Peter 4:17). Before revival can sweep through the land, repentance must first break forth within the Church. God is shining His light into the hidden corners of the sanctuary, not to destroy His people, but to deliver them. The Lord is exposing the unspoken pain, the long-suppressed trauma, and the deep emotional bond that has lingered beneath the surface of ministry. He is calling His leaders to stand naked before His presence, not in shame, but in truth that healing can finally take root. The pretense of perfection has crippled the body of Christ; many have been performing rather than transforming. But God's cleansing fire is not coming to condemn; it is coming to purify, to strip away the masks, to bring leaders and members alike into wholeness of mind, body, and spirit.

The mental health crisis within the church is not merely a social concern; it is a spiritual warning. When God's people ignore the cries of the wounded, when leaders suppress their own anguish instead of surrendering it to Christ, they allow the enemy to gain ground within the body. Satan thrives in silence, but healing begins in confession. The Spirit of God is pleading with His church to create spaces of safety, not secrecy, restoration, not rejection. The altar must again become a place of honesty, where pastors can weep without fear of losing respect, and where members can pour out their hearts without being ashamed.

This is God's rebuke and invitation: that His people would stop pretending and start healing. He desires to break the generational chains of abuse, trauma, and emotional neglect that have been passed down through families and pulpits alike. The same God who delivered the demoniac, restored the woman at the well, and comforted Elijah under the juniper tree still heals today. But healing will not come through silence or denial; it will come through repentance, accountability, and compassion. God is raising a remnant of leaders who will no longer hide behind religion, but will minister from their scars, testifying that Jesus Christ heals the mind, restores the soul, and binds up the brokenhearted. For this is the Church's final call: to be a house of healing, not hiding; a refuge for the hurting, not a stage for the proud; a vessel through which the glory of God can shine unhindered through truth, humility, and love.

Denominationalism, rigid creeds, and religious traditions can unintentionally overshadow God's mission of healing. Leaders may focus more on doctrinal purity or ritual compliance than on ministering to broken hearts, echoing the Pharisees' prioritization of law over mercy in Jesus' time.

Mental health issues are often misunderstood as spiritual failure. Depression is labeled "lack of faith," anxiety dismissed as "prayerlessness," and addiction condemned as "sin." This misunderstanding perpetuates shame and prevents individuals from receiving the holistic care God desires.

Mental health issues are often misunderstood as spiritual failure. Depression is labeled "lack of faith," anxiety dismissed as "prayerlessness," and addiction condemned as "sin." This misunderstanding perpetuates shame and prevents individuals from receiving the holistic care God desires. Yet beneath this distortion lies a deeper evil festering in the shadows of power.

There are political and influential figures—wealthy leaders who have preyed upon the innocent, abusing young women and young men, then attempting to buy silence with money, settlements, or threats of legal retaliation. Some have even manipulated the system, using lawsuits or imprisonment to intimidate victims into silence. Fear grips the hearts of many, especially our youth, who watch power and corruption triumph while truth and justice are suppressed.

What makes this even more grievous is that, at times, religious leaders know of these hidden sins and yet say nothing, choosing comfort over conviction. Some have been bribed; their silence purchased with large donations or favors that keep churches financially comfortable but spiritually compromised. They exchange truth for wealth and holiness for status, allowing darkness to remain unchallenged in the very places meant to shine God's light. And while they remain silent, mental health struggles continue to spread like wildfire, depression deepens, anxiety intensifies, and hopelessness rises across the world.

God never called His shepherds to be silent spectators of injustice or protectors of the powerful. He called them to be voices for the voiceless, defenders of truth, and healers of the brokenhearted. Until the Church and its leaders take this stand, until they confront evil without compromise, the spiritual sickness in our society will only worsen. For God's justice cannot be bribed, and His eyes see what is done in secret. The hour has come for truth to rise, for repentance to begin at every level of leadership, and for the Church to reclaim her mantle as a beacon of healing, truth, and courage in a wounded world.

But the Word of God declares, *"For nothing is hidden that will not be revealed, nor anything secret that will not be made known and come to light"* (Luke 8:17). The time of covering up sin through power, wealth, or position is drawing to an end. God is uncovering the lies, the abuse, the payoffs, and the secret deals that have been hidden behind closed doors. His judgment is not partial. He does not overlook the sins of kings or excuse the failures of preachers. Every man and woman who has used authority to manipulate, exploit, or silence others will one day stand before the righteous Judge, and no amount of money, legal defense, or influence will save them from divine accountability. Scripture warns, *"For God will bring every deed into judgment, including every hidden thing, whether it is good or evil"* (Ecclesiastes 12:14).

God's justice will not be mocked. He is raising a generation that will no longer bow to fear or intimidation, a people clothed in righteousness who will cry aloud and spare not. The voices of those who were silenced are being awakened by the Spirit of Truth. What was buried in shame will be unearthed in glory. The Lord is exposing not to destroy, but to deliver; not to humiliate, but to heal. Yet that healing cannot come without repentance. Political leaders, religious figures, and every person who has participated in or protected injustice must humble themselves before God and seek forgiveness. The Lord commands, *"Learn to do right; seek justice. Defend the oppressed. Take up the cause of the fatherless; plead the case of the widow"* (Isaiah 1:17). The Church must rise as a prophetic voice that demands accountability, not one that bows to political gain or hides behind stained-glass silence.

This is the hour of divine reckoning, when God's light pierces the darkness of corruption and fear. He is calling His people to stand for truth even when it costs them friends, finances, or favor. For the fear that grips the hearts of our youth and even our adults will only be broken when the Church walks in boldness and truth again. The next great revival will not be born out of entertainment or emotionalism; it will rise from repentance, from exposure, from the ashes of a system God Himself is shaking. When the Church begins to speak truth to power and heal the mentally and spiritually broken, then the Spirit of the Lord will return in glory. Only a pure Church can carry the power of a holy God.

The biblical narrative is rich with examples of suffering that went unrecognized. Job's friends assumed his grief was punishment for sin. They offered judgment rather than compassion. Churches today mirror this pattern when leaders misdiagnose mental health struggles as moral failings. Elijah's depression and burnout were invisible to those around him until God intervened. In modern contexts, pastors or church staff may fail to recognize burnout, trauma, or mental illness in congregants, expecting visible strength and unwavering faith.

Leaders sometimes extend their pockets but neglect their hearts. Charity is often financial rather than relational, offering material aid while ignoring the deeper emotional and spiritual needs of those they serve. True ministry combines provision with presence, empathy, and guidance toward healing.

Mary Magdalene's restoration by Jesus exemplifies recognizing hidden suffering and addressing it with compassion and dignity. When church leaders today fail to see those "bound by seven demons" in their congregations—whether literal or metaphorical—they fail the very ministry God called them to perform.

Denominationalism can create hierarchies that inadvertently silence the hurting. When doctrinal alignment is valued above human need, those struggling feel unwelcome. Healing requires that leaders prioritize people over positions, mercy over orthodoxy.

Addiction and alcoholism are often stigmatized within churches. Individuals battling substance abuse frequently encounter judgmental attitudes instead of pastoral guidance and professional support. Biblical figures like Noah and the Prodigal Son illustrate that God meets us in our brokenness, offering restoration rather than condemnation.

Chronic trauma and mental health challenges are seldom addressed in sermons or church programs. Leaders may lack education or awareness about PTSD, depression, or anxiety. Ignorance, however well-intentioned, perpetuates suffering and isolates those who desperately need help.

The church sometimes overemphasizes religiosity and ritual, measuring attendance, tithing, and outward piety, while ignoring the emotional and spiritual health of its people. The result is a congregation that appears faithful on the outside but is wounded and unsupported within.

Leaders may fail to integrate mental health resources with spiritual care. Biblical examples demonstrate God's use of practical measures: physicians, wise counselors, and community support. Modern churches that ignore therapy, counseling, or professional help miss opportunities to complement divine healing with human expertise.

Pharisaical attitudes persist today when church leaders judge rather than listen. Congregants with mental health struggles may be labeled lazy, unfaithful, or spiritually weak. This mirrors the judgment Job faced, the isolation Elijah endured, and the derision David experienced in his loneliness.

Trauma often intersects with socioeconomic status. Individuals walking into a sanctuary carrying the weight of financial hardship are sometimes met with subtle disdain or exclusion. True ministry calls for empathy, extending grace and practical support alongside spiritual guidance.

The church fails when it prioritizes image over reality. Leaders who focus on reputations, attendance numbers, and denominational influence risk ignoring the very people God calls them to serve: the hurting, the marginalized, and those who quietly suffer in silence.

Mental health literacy is minimal in many congregations. Church leaders may not recognize depression, anxiety, or suicidal ideation in congregants. Ignorance becomes complicity, leaving vulnerable individuals without guidance, hope, or intervention. But the Word of God declares, *"For nothing is hidden that will not be revealed, nor anything secret that will not be made known and come to light"* (Luke 8:17). The time of covering up sin through power, wealth, or position is drawing to an end. God is uncovering the lies, the abuse, the payoffs, and the secret deals that have been hidden behind closed doors. His judgment is not partial—He does not overlook the sins of kings or excuse the failures of preachers. Every man and woman who has used authority to manipulate, exploit, or silence others will one day stand before the righteous Judge, and no amount of money, legal defense, or influence will save them from divine accountability. Scripture warns, *"For God will bring every deed into judgment, including every hidden thing, whether it is good or evil"* (Ecclesiastes 12:14).

Ignorance is no excuse to any law, so why should it be an excuse to hide injustice? Ignorance becomes complicity, leaving vulnerable individuals without guidance, hope, or intervention. When the Church turns a blind eye to the suffering of the abused, or when leaders remain silent because of fear or financial gain, they become participants in the very evil God detests. Silence is agreement, and apathy is a sin of omission. God's justice will not be mocked. He is raising a generation that will no longer bow to fear or intimidation—a people clothed in righteousness who will cry aloud and spare not. The voices of those who were silenced are being awakened by the Spirit of Truth. What was buried in shame will be unearthed in glory.

The Lord is exposing not to destroy, but to deliver; not to humiliate, but to heal. Yet that healing cannot come without repentance. Political leaders, religious figures, and every person who has participated in or protected injustice must humble themselves before God and seek forgiveness. The Lord commands, *"Learn to do right; seek justice. Defend the oppressed. Take up the cause of the fatherless; plead the case of the widow"* (Isaiah 1:17). The Church must rise as a prophetic voice that demands accountability, not one that bows to political gain or hides behind stained- glass silence.

This is the hour of divine reckoning, when God's light pierces the darkness of corruption and fear. He is calling His people to stand for truth even when it costs them friends, finances, or favor. For the fear that grips the hearts of our youth and even our adults will only be broken when the Church walks in boldness and truth again. The next great revival will not be born out of entertainment or emotionalism—it will rise from repentance, from exposure, from the ashes of a system God Himself is shaking. When the Church begins to speak truth to power and heal the mentally and spiritually broken, then the Spirit of the Lord will return in glory. For only a pure Church can carry the power of a holy God.

Biblical wisdom emphasizes the necessity of seeing the unseen. Jesus noticed the widow's grief, the leper's isolation, and the demon-possessed man's torment. Churches today are called to mirror this awareness, identifying hidden suffering and responding with both God's Word and practical care. Healing requires courage from leadership. It takes humility to admit that mental health struggles are complex and may require professional support in addition to spiritual care. Yet, when leaders embrace this responsibility, they create safe spaces where recovery is possible, stigma is dismantled, and God's restorative power is evident.

Many congregants quietly endure emotional pain, believing they must "bear it alone" because the church is perceived as judgmental or unapproachable. Leaders who fail to create safe spaces contribute to prolonged suffering and missed opportunities for divine healing. Denominations often prioritize theological purity over pastoral care. When adherence to creeds and ritual takes precedence, the church risks alienating those most in need, echoing the Pharisees' emphasis on law over compassion.

Leaders sometimes mistake outward compliance for spiritual health. Congregants may sit quietly in the pews, appearing faithful, while internally wrestling with depression, trauma, or addiction. The church that fails to engage deeply misses God's mandate to minister to the broken.

Eli's failure to respond to Hannah's silent anguish in the temple demonstrates a critical lesson: leaders must actively observe and engage with those in pain. Ignoring subtle signs of suffering perpetuates harm.

Modern pastors and church leaders often lack training in mental health awareness. Without education, they may unintentionally stigmatize, misdiagnose, or dismiss mental health struggles, leaving congregants isolated and spiritually malnourished.

Financial bias also plays a role. Churches may extend generosity to those who can contribute monetarily while overlooking those who arrive with little, failing to offer the care and support the latter desperately need. True ministry evaluates need, not net worth.

Judgment based on appearance is rampant. Mental health issues are often invisible, leading leaders to assume that outwardly composed individuals are spiritually or emotionally healthy, while ignoring subtle cues of despair, anxiety, or trauma.

Job's friends provide a biblical example of failed pastoral care. Instead of listening and supporting, they judged and misdiagnosed his suffering. Churches today risk repeating this mistake when leaders offer platitudes or blame rather than empathy and practical guidance.

Chronic trauma is particularly neglected. Congregants who experience long-term abuse, poverty, or systemic oppression often face compounded stigma when they seek help, as leaders may not recognize the depth or duration of their suffering.

Relational neglect is also evident. Individuals who are isolated, widowed, or single may struggle with loneliness, yet church programs often overlook their needs, focusing on families, couples, or youth ministries.

Addiction is frequently treated as a moral failure rather than a medical and spiritual issue. Congregants struggling with alcohol, drugs, or compulsive behaviors may face condemnation instead of counseling, therapy referrals, and grace-filled support.

Leaders who lack awareness of biblical examples of mental health struggle miss teaching moments. David's psalms, Elijah's despair, Paul's "thorn in the flesh," and Job's grief all illustrate that mental and emotional suffering has always existed and is compatible with faith.

Mental health stigma in the church can be intertwined with gender and race. Men are often discouraged from expressing vulnerability, while women's emotional struggles are sometimes minimized. People of color may encounter compounded barriers due to systemic and cultural biases.

Silence is a weapon of neglect. When churches avoid discussing mental health, trauma, or emotional wellness, congregants internalize shame, believing they are alone or spiritually deficient, delaying recovery and spiritual growth.

Leaders sometimes emphasize doctrinal correctness over compassion. Theological debates on sin, works, or denominational practices can overshadow God's mandate to love, restore, and heal the hurting.

Pastoral burnout mirrors congregational neglect. Leaders themselves may be overworked, spiritually drained, or insufficiently trained in mental health care, limiting their capacity to minister effectively. Without support and education, even well-intentioned leaders can perpetuate harm.

Counseling and professional help are often underutilized in churches. Integrating licensed therapists, social workers, or trauma-informed ministry teams can create pathways for recovery, yet many churches view outside assistance with suspicion or reluctance.

Elijah's wilderness experience demonstrates the necessity of rest, care, and external support. Leaders who ignore these needs in congregants fail to follow biblical principles of holistic restoration.

Shame is a pervasive tool of exclusion. When congregants feel judged for their emotional, financial, or social struggles, they are less likely to seek help, further entrenching stigma and perpetuating cycles of silence and suffering.

True spiritual leadership requires courage to confront institutional complacency. Addressing mental health needs, providing trauma-informed care, and integrating professional support demand humility, discernment, and obedience to God's call to shepherd the flock compassionately.

Many congregants internalize blame when leaders fail to recognize their suffering. Silence from the pulpit or judgment from peers reinforces the false belief that their struggles reflect spiritual inadequacy rather than human vulnerability.

Leaders who fail to acknowledge mental health needs often miss signs of crisis, including suicidal ideation, substance abuse, or severe depression. This neglect can have fatal consequences, as seen in tragic modern and historical cases like Judas' despair in the Bible.

Denominational pride sometimes overshadows pastoral responsibility. Leaders may prioritize defending church identity over reaching hurting individuals, perpetuating a culture where healing is secondary to institutional reputation.

Congregants may avoid attending church altogether due to perceived judgment, leaving them without the spiritual encouragement and community that could aid recovery. The sanctuary, intended as a place of refuge, becomes a space of fear and shame.

Mental health struggles are not signs of weak faith; biblical examples affirm this truth. Elijah despaired despite his obedience, David felt guilt and isolation, and

Paul wrestled with chronic weakness. Leaders ignoring these truths contribute to the misconception that mental illness is a spiritual failing.

Ignorance of trauma-informed care prevents church leaders from creating safe, supportive environments. Congregants dealing with domestic violence, abuse, or PTSD may feel unwelcome or misunderstood in spaces that lack awareness and training.

Pastors sometimes unintentionally perpetuate cycles of shame by emphasizing tithing, attendance, or public service as measures of faith. Those struggling to meet these expectations feel spiritually deficient, further marginalizing the most vulnerable.

Biblical narratives reveal that God values care over ritual. Jesus healed the sick, restored the marginalized, and ministered to the hurting without judgment. Churches that focus primarily on denominational doctrines fail to emulate this model of compassionate leadership.

Addiction and alcoholism are particularly stigmatized in religious spaces. When leaders frame recovery solely as spiritual discipline without acknowledging medical or psychological components, congregants receive incomplete care and may relapse.

Chronic trauma is often invisible, yet its impact is profound. Leaders who ignore long-term emotional suffering inadvertently allow cycles of abuse, neglect, and unresolved grief to persist across generations within their congregations.

Leaders' lack of engagement with mental health literature or training perpetuates misinformation and misunderstanding. Without awareness of evidence-based practices, leaders may unintentionally harm those they aim to help.

Churches may unintentionally encourage secrecy. Congregants fearing gossip, judgment, or condemnation avoid disclosing struggles, depriving themselves of pastoral care, peer support, and spiritual guidance essential for recovery.

Relational neglect within the church disproportionately affects marginalized populations. Single parents, the homeless, and communities of color often receive limited attention, reinforcing systemic inequities and the stigma of invisibility.

The church's emphasis on religiosity over relational care mirrors Job's friends' errors. Judgment, misinterpretation, and platitudes fail to comfort and often exacerbate suffering, while listening, validation, and guidance bring true healing.

Leaders must recognize that spiritual care and professional mental health support are complementary. Integrating counseling, therapy, and social work with prayer, discipleship, and scriptural guidance provides holistic care that the church often neglects.

Scripture repeatedly emphasizes God's concern for the vulnerable. Psalm 34:18 reminds leaders that "The Lord is close to the brokenhearted." When leaders ignore this mandate, they fail to minister to those God is drawing to Himself in their congregation.

Denominational boundaries should not obstruct care. Congregants struggling with trauma, mental illness, or addiction require assistance regardless of their alignment with specific creeds. Leadership that prioritizes doctrine over healing perpetuates harm.

True ministry requires empathy, education, and action. Leaders must identify suffering, validate experiences, and mobilize resources—spiritual, communal, and professional—to restore hope, dignity, and wholeness to those hurting.

Churches must also confront systemic stigma. Race, gender, socioeconomic status, and cultural expectations often intersect with mental health challenges. Leaders must advocate for equity, inclusion, and trauma-informed care, modeling God's justice and mercy.

Ultimately, leadership failure in recognizing and addressing mental health issues betrays the church's calling. Healing is God's mandate, and His Word provides guidance. By embracing awareness, compassion, and integration of professional support, the church can restore hope, break stigma, and embody God's restorative love for all who enter the sanctuary.

The Recovery Process: From Exposure to Healing

Recovery begins when truth is no longer resisted but received. God exposes not to shame, but to restore. Just as a wound cannot heal while covered in infection, the Church cannot recover until it faces the depth of its brokenness. The first step in recovery is confession—acknowledging the wrong, naming the pain, and admitting that silence has caused more harm than healing. Scripture says, *"He who conceals his sins does not prosper, but whoever confesses and renounces them finds mercy"* (Proverbs 28:13). For too long, leaders have confused image with integrity and reputation with righteousness. But recovery begins when we surrender pride, step into humility, and invite the Holy Spirit to do a deep cleansing work within the heart.

The next step is repentance. True repentance is not merely words it is a turning away from patterns that enabled evil to thrive. It means refusing to protect predators, refusing to hide sin behind pulpits or power, and standing with those who were wounded instead of those who inflicted the wound. It is repentance that leads to restoration. When leaders repent and seek healing, it opens a door for the entire body of Christ to heal collectively. God is not looking for perfection; He is looking for honesty. He cannot bless what we pretend to be. He heals what we are willing to expose to Him.

The recovery process also requires community. Healing does not happen in isolation. The Church must become a place of safe transparency where survivors can tell their stories, where those suffering from mental health issues can receive counseling without judgment, and where leaders can be accountable without condemnation. Galatians 6:2 reminds us, *"Bear one another's burdens, and so fulfill the law of Christ."* Recovery means rebuilding trust, restoring integrity, and reestablishing the Church as a hospital for the soul, not a stage for appearances.

Finally, recovery brings renewal. Once truth has been spoken, repentance made, and hearts are restored, the Church will rise stronger, purer, and more united than ever before. The Spirit of God will dwell again in the midst of a people who love truth more than comfort and justice more than reputation. Recovery is the evidence of God's mercy—proof that even after exposure, He still desires to use His Church to bring healing to the nations. As Psalm 147:3 declares, *"He heals the brokenhearted and binds up their wounds."* When the Church walks through the recovery process with humility and grace, she becomes what she was always meant to be—a sanctuary of restoration for the world.

The 12-Step Framework: A Pathway to Healing

At the heart of Alcoholics Anonymous (AA) and Narcotics Anonymous (NA) is the 12-step framework, a holistic approach to recovery that addresses the **physical, emotional, and spiritual dimensions** of addiction. Unlike quick fixes or temporary solutions, the 12-step guide leads individuals through a process of surrender, restoration, and reconciliation with God, self, and others.

Physical Healing is the first domain of recovery. Addiction and substance abuse take a toll on the body, creating dependence, disease, and neurological disruption. Step One—admitting powerlessness over addiction—marks the first acknowledgment that the body requires care and intervention.

Breaking the physical cycle of addiction involves intentional actions: detoxification, abstinence, medical care, and lifestyle changes. The 12-step approach integrates these practical measures with spiritual guidance, reinforcing the principle that the body is God's temple, as Paul teaches in 1 Corinthians 6:19.

Recovery is more than avoiding substances—it is learning to **honor the body as sacred**. Nutrition, exercise, rest, and medical support are all aspects of physical healing, showing that God's design for the body is holistic.

Emotional Healing follows, addressing the pain, shame, anger, and unresolved trauma often hidden behind addictive behaviors. Step Four's "searching and fearless moral inventory" encourages individuals to confront internal wounds honestly, a process mirrored in Scripture's calls for self-examination.

Step Five emphasizes confession: admitting wrongs to God, oneself, and another person. This practice releases guilt and resentment while fostering accountability. James 5:16 affirms that confession and prayer bring healing, demonstrating that emotional restoration is both spiritual and relational.

Emotional healing also involves forgiveness—both of self and others. Addiction frequently masks unmet needs or past traumas; the 12-step process teaches that letting go of grudges and resentment allows the heart to mend and trust to return.

Step Eight guides individuals to **list those they have harmed** and cultivate a willingness for restitution. Emotional healing is incomplete without reconciliation, as unresolved relational wounds can perpetuate cycles of shame and relapse. Biblical examples, like Zacchaeus' promise to repay those he wronged (Luke 19:8-9), highlight the restorative power of making amends.

Spiritual Healing is the ultimate aim of the 12-step framework. Step Two calls for belief in a Power greater than oneself—often understood as God—to restore sanity and purpose. Trust in God's intervention enables individuals to release control and embrace surrender.

Step Three reinforces surrender: "Decided to turn our will and our lives over to the care of God as we understood Him." Jesus' prayer in Gethsemane, "Not my will, but Yours be done" (Luke 22:42), exemplifies the spiritual posture necessary for lasting transformation.

Spiritual healing deepens through Step Eleven: prayer, meditation, and daily conscious contact with God. Withdrawal, reflection, and devotion restore a sense of guidance and divine presence that addiction often obscures. Like Jesus withdrawing to pray (Luke 5:16), this intentional time fosters resilience, clarity, and hope.

Step Six invites readiness for God to remove defects of character. True transformation requires humility and openness to God's work in the heart. Isaiah's recognition of his sinfulness and subsequent purification (Isaiah 6:5–7) parallels the surrender and cleansing process of recovery.

Step Seven—humbly asking God to remove shortcomings—acknowledges that divine strength, not human willpower, enables lasting change. Paul's "thorn in the flesh" illustrates that God's grace empowers believers to endure weakness and find strength in Him (2 Corinthians 12:7-9).

Step Nine, making direct amends wherever possible, demonstrates that spiritual healing is relational. Jesus taught reconciliation before worship (Matthew 5:23–24), reminding us that God values restored relationships as a crucial aspect of recovery.

Step Ten emphasizes ongoing self-assessment: taking a personal inventory and promptly admitting wrongs. Recovery is not a one-time event; it is a continuous process of reflection, honesty, and growth. Paul encourages this ongoing self-examination in 2 Corinthians 13:5.

Step Twelve embodies the culmination of physical, emotional, and spiritual healing: carrying the message and serving others. True recovery moves outward, transforming personal restoration into community impact. The healed man in Mark 5:19 exemplifies this principle by sharing testimony and helping others.

Each step ddresses a distinct dimension of the whole person. Physical healing restores bodily integrity, emotional healing mends the heart and relationships, and spiritual healing reconciles individuals with God, purpose, and hope.

The 12-step framework is inherently biblical in nature. Step One aligns with Paul's admission of weakness in Romans 7:19, demonstrating that acknowledging limitations is the starting point of God-centered recovery.

Step Two parallels the Prodigal Son's realization that only his father's love could restore him (Luke 15:11–32). Trusting in God's higher power initiates faith-filled transformation, reinforcing that recovery requires dependence beyond human effort.

Step Three mirrors Christ's surrender in Gethsemane, reminding participants that recovery is not

mere self-discipline but active submission to God's will, aligning desire with divine purpose.

Step Four encourages introspection, honesty, and courage, much like David's prayer in Psalm 139:23–24. Identifying hidden sin, brokenness, and unresolved pain allows individuals to invite God's transformative work.

Step Five's practice of confession integrates emotional and spiritual healing. Accountability through trusted others creates a safe environment for vulnerability, fostering growth and restoration.

Steps Six and Seven invite participants to align their hearts with God's work. Healing occurs when individuals embrace God's power to transform character flaws and internal wounds, rather than relying solely on self-effort.

Steps Eight and Nine emphasize relational restoration. By acknowledging harm and actively seeking reconciliation, individuals restore broken connections and repair trust—an essential component of emotional healing and community reintegration.

Step Ten highlights the ongoing nature of healing. Self-reflection, acknowledgment of mistakes, and willingness to change foster sustained recovery and prevent relapse. Spiritual growth and character development are continuous, not static.

Step Eleven cultivates intimacy with God. Daily prayer, meditation, and reflection deepen spiritual awareness, providing guidance, comfort, and strength to navigate challenges and maintain sobriety.

Step Twelve integrates all aspects of recovery into service. Sharing testimony, mentoring others, and living by recovery principles amplify the healing process and extend hope to the wider community.

Physical healing in the 12-step program often begins with practical interventions such as detox, rest, nutrition, and exercise. Step One encourages acknowledging dependence and taking proactive steps toward bodily restoration.

Emotional healing requires confronting shame, guilt, trauma, and unresolved anger. The 12 steps provide structured reflection, confession, and accountability to facilitate inner peace and restored self-worth.

Spiritual healing reconnects the individual with God through surrender, trust, prayer, and meditation. Each step reinforces the dependence on a Higher Power, fostering hope, faith, and purpose.

The 12-step framework teaches that **recovery is holistic**. Ignoring physical, emotional, or spiritual dimensions undermines the process, but addressing all three fosters comprehensive restoration.

The Bible consistently emphasizes confession, surrender, and reconciliation as pathways to healing. Integrating 12-step principles with Scripture deepens understanding, offering both spiritual grounding and practical guidance.

Step One teaches humility and honesty. Recognizing personal powerlessness over addiction mirrors biblical admissions of weakness, allowing God's strength to intervene.

Step Two fosters faith and trust in God's restorative power. Spiritual surrender begins when individuals believe divine intervention is greater than their limitations.

Step Three involves relinquishing control and submitting to God's guidance. Recovery requires yielding the will to a Higher Power, echoing Christ's model of obedience in Gethsemane.

Step Four promotes self-awareness. Honest moral inventories uncover hidden pain, sin, or trauma, aligning with biblical calls for introspection and repentance.

Step Five encourages confession to God and another person. Accountability, prayer, and transparency release emotional burdens and foster spiritual freedom.

Steps Six and Seven cultivate readiness and humility for God's transformative work, emphasizing that internal change is dependent on divine grace rather than human effort alone.

Steps Eight and Nine restore relationships. By acknowledging harm and making amends, participants repair relational fractures, reflecting Jesus' teaching on reconciliation before worship.

Step Ten ensures ongoing accountability. Personal inventories and prompt admissions of wrongdoing maintain emotional balance, integrity, and spiritual alignment.

Step Eleven reinforces spiritual intimacy. Consistent prayer and meditation deepen connection with God, cultivating resilience, discernment, and peace.

Step Twelve integrates service and testimony. Sharing recovery experiences encourages others, strengthens community bonds, and fulfills God's call to minister to the hurting.

Physical, emotional, and spiritual healing are interconnected. Addiction affects the body, wounds the heart, and strains faith; holistic recovery addresses each domain simultaneously.

Biblical examples support 12-step principles. Paul's admission of weakness, David's confession, and the Prodigal Son's surrender illustrate the alignment between spiritual recovery and the structured steps. Healing is ongoing. Step Ten reminds participants that relapse, temptation, and imperfection are part of the journey, requiring continuous reflection, confession, and reliance on God.

The 12-step framework models **community-based recovery**. Fellowship, mentorship, and peer support mirror biblical principles of mutual encouragement, accountability, and shared restoration.

Integrating faith with the 12 steps emphasizes the necessity of spiritual surrender alongside practical action. Recovery is neither purely spiritual nor purely behavioral—it is a divine-human collaboration.

Addiction and mental health struggles often conceal deeper wounds. The 12 steps address these underlying issues through self-examination, confession, reconciliation, and prayer, facilitating comprehensive healing.

The framework equips participants to reclaim agency while depending on God. Step One admits powerlessness, yet subsequent steps empower action, reflection, and service, demonstrating the balance of surrender and responsibility.

True recovery transforms the individual, relationships, and community. As the healed person carries the message and models God's restoration, the impact extends beyond the self, reflecting the holistic vision of the 12 steps and biblical healing principles.

This chapter has explored the profound intersections between **mental health, trauma, addiction, and the church's role** in fostering healing and hope. Mental health challenges— ranging from depression, anxiety, and chronic trauma to substance abuse and addiction—affect millions worldwide, often in silence due to stigma and misunderstanding. The Bible provides numerous examples of individuals who faced overwhelming emotional burdens, trauma, and despair—yet God's presence brought healing, restoration, and renewed purpose.

We examined the purpose of **Recovery Month**, emphasizing awareness, celebration of hope, stigma reduction, and community support. Recovery is a holistic journey encompassing **physical, emotional, spiritual, and relational healing**, often requiring surrender, honesty, and engagement with both faith-based and professional resources.

The church, as a spiritual and communal body, bears a responsibility to actively engage in this healing process. Historically, stigma, lack of knowledge, and misplaced focus on denominationalism or religiosity have hindered support for those struggling. Today, faith communities must model **compassion, education, and practical support**, partnering with families, mental health professionals, and government programs to ensure that resources, care, and advocacy reach those in crisis.

Through stories of biblical figures, modern recovery frameworks such as the **12-step process**, and the principles of trauma-informed care, this chapter highlights that healing is possible. It calls the church and community to break stigma, provide safe spaces for help, and actively participate in recovery efforts—offering hope, relief, and restoration.

Prayer for Healing, Hope, and Community Support

Heavenly Father,

We come before You are acknowledging the pain, trauma, and struggles that so many carry in silence. Lord, You are close to the brokenhearted, and You save those crushed in spirit (Psalm 34:18). Today, we lift those who are battling **mental health challenges, addiction, substance abuse, and emotional trauma.** Surround them with Your love, comfort, and presence.

Father, break the chains of stigma, fear, and shame that keep Your children from seeking help. Restore their **hope, dignity, and purpose**, and guide them to safe spaces, supportive communities, and professionals who can walk with them in recovery. Strengthen families, churches, and community organizations to provide **practical care, encouragement, and resources** for those in need.

Lord, we pray for government agencies and leaders, that they will provide **funding, programs, and policies** that address mental health crises, ensuring equitable access to treatment and support for all, especially the vulnerable and underserved. Help communities come together to **bring relief, restoration, and advocacy** where it is most needed.

Grant wisdom, patience, and compassion to all who serve those in pain. Let the church be a sanctuary of healing, understanding, and hope—a reflection of Your heart for the lost, hurting, and marginalized.

We declare that **healing, recovery, and restoration are possible** through You, O Lord, and we commit to walking alongside those in need, guided by Your Spirit and empowered to bring hope to the hopeless.

In Jesus' name, Amen.

Practical Action Steps

Personal Healing

Commit to daily prayer, meditation, or Scripture reading for mental and emotional strength. Journal your thoughts, emotions, and progress in your recovery journey.

Seek professional counseling, support groups, or mentorship if experiencing trauma, addiction, or mental health challenges.

Breaking Stigma

Speak openly about mental health in safe spaces, modeling vulnerability and courage. Educate yourself and others about trauma, addiction, and mental illness to combat ignorance.

Encourage your faith community to hold seminars, workshops, or prayer sessions that address mental health awareness.

Community Engagement

Volunteer or partner with local organizations that provide resources for mental health support, addiction recovery, or trauma counseling.

Advocate for policies and programs that provide funding, treatment access, and resources for mental health care in your community.

Mentor, check in on, or support individuals who are isolated, struggling, or in recovery.

Faith-Based Support

Incorporate prayer, Scripture, and pastoral care as part of holistic support for those in recovery. Encourage your church leadership to adopt trauma-informed approaches, acknowledging both spiritual and mental health needs.

Celebrate stories of recovery, showing that healing, grace, and God's restoration are possible.

Scripture-Based Encouragement
Psalm 34:18 – God is close to the brokenhearted.
Galatians 6:2 – Carry one another's burdens.
Isaiah 61:1-3 – God sends healing, comfort, and restoration.
Matthew 11:28-30 – Jesus offers rest to the weary and heavy-laden.

Commitment to Action
Personal Commitment: Write a short statement committing to take at least one step this week toward personal healing, self-care, or seeking help. Community Commitment: Identify one action you will take to support someone else in their recovery journey. Advocacy Commitment: Choose one advocacy step, such as contacting local officials, donating to a mental health organization, or raising awareness in your community.

Mental Health, Recovery, and Restoration — Then and Now

Mental health struggles are not new to our generation. From the days of Noah to the apostles in the New Testament, Scripture records leaders, prophets, kings, and everyday people wrestling with trauma, depression, addiction, guilt, and despair. Yet in every case, God provided a path toward healing, recovery, and reintegration into the community.

Today, mental health crises—addiction, depression, anxiety, and broken family systems—mirror those same struggles. By comparing biblical examples with modern recovery processes, we see how God's timeless principles remain the foundation for true healing.

Biblical Examples of Mental and Emotional Struggles

Old Testament Highlights

Noah wrestled with trauma and alcohol (Genesis 9:20–21)
 Moses faced burnout and depression (Numbers 11:14-15).
Elijah despaired and wished for death (1 Kings 19:4).
Job endured grief, trauma, and despair (Job 3:11).
David battled guilt and depression (Psalm 51).
Jeremiah was rejected and wept in loneliness (Jeremiah 20:14). Jonah struggled with anger and suicidal thoughts (Jonah 4:3). Samson fell into lust, pride, and

self-destruction (Judges 16).

Lot suffered anxiety, survivor's guilt, and family dysfunction (Genesis 19).

New Testament Highlights

Mary Magdalene was tormented until delivered by Jesus (Luke 8:2).

The Prodigal Son struggled with reckless living and depression (Luke 15:11–32)

 Peter carried guilt and shame after denying Christ (Luke 22:61-62).

Paul endured ministry stress and personal affliction (2 Cor. 12:7–10).

Judas fell into despair and suicide (Matthew 27:3–5).

The Gerasene Demoniac suffered extreme torment and isolation (Mark 5:1–20).

Timothy battled anxiety and timidity (2 Tim. 1:7).

God's Recovery Process in Scripture

Rest: God gave Elijah food, sleep, and presence.

Repentance: David confessed and was restored.

Deliverance: Mary Magdalene and the Gerasene demoniac were set free.

Community: The Prodigal Son was welcomed home.

Mentorship: Timothy was encouraged by Paul.

Hope in God's Covenant: Noah and Job found strength in God's promises.

Modern-Day Recovery Process

Today, recovery follows similar biblical patterns, supported by medical and therapeutic insights: Acknowledgment of the Problem – Owning the struggle (like the Prodigal Son "came to himself").

Repentance & Renewal of the Mind – Turning from destructive patterns.

Therapeutic Support – Counseling, group therapy, or medication when needed.

Community Reintegration – Finding support in church, family, and recovery groups.

Faith & Spiritual Healing – Prayer, worship, Scripture, and pastoral care.

Ongoing Accountability – Mentorship, sponsors, and discipleship.

Biblical Figures & Mental/Emotional Health Struggles

With Recovery Process, Reintegration, and Modern-Day Comparison

Old Testament

Biblical Figure	Struggle / Possible Mental Health Issue	Scripture Reference	Recovery / Healing Process	Reintegration into Society	Modern-Day Comparison
Noah	Trauma after the flood, alcohol dependence, and isolation	Genesis 9:20–21	God's covenant gave him hope (Gen. 9:12–17)	Continued family legacy, respected patriarch	PTSD, substance use after trauma; recovery through covenant hope/ community
Lot	Anxiety, fear, family dysfunction, survivor's guilt	Genesis 19:1–38	Delivered by angels; survival ensured	Struggled with trauma; generational effects continued	Survivors of crisis who carry unresolved trauma into family life
Moses	Anger, burnout, despair, possible dépression	Numbers 11:14–15; Exodus 32:19–20	God appointed helpers (Num. 11:16–17); reassurance	Continued leadership role until death	Pastors/leaders facing ministry burnout; recovery through shared leadership, counseling
Elijah	Depression, suicidal thoughts, exhaustion	1 Kings 19:4–8	God sent an angel with food, rest, and gentle presence	Restored as a prophet, mentored Elisha	Depression/anxiety; recovery through rest, nourishment, therapy, spiritual renewal
Job	Grief, despair, loss, questioning God	Job 3:11; Job 7:11	Honest lament, God's response, renewed faith	Restored health, wealth, and family	Those in grief and trauma; recovery through lament, counseling, and community support
David	Guilt, shame, anxiety, depression (esp. after sin)	Psalm 32; Psalm 51; 1 Samuel 21:12–13	Confession, repentance, worship	Continued as king and worship leader	Addiction, guilt, shame today; recovery through accountability, repentance, therapy

Biblical Figure	Struggle / Possible Mental Health Issue	Scripture Reference	Recovery / Healing Process	Reintegration into Society	Modern-Day Comparison
Jeremiah	Loneliness, depression, weeping, rejection	Jeremiah 20:14, 18; Lamentation	Expressed lament, clung to hope in God	Continued prophetic ministry	Those suffering rejection or isolation recover through counseling, support groups.
Jonah	Anger, despair, suicidal thoughts	Jonah 4:3–9	Honest dialogue with God; divine patience	Continued as a prophet despite struggles	Anger management, depression; recovery through therapy and divine perspective
Samson	Lust, impulsiveness, pride, and selfdestructive behavior	Judges 14–16	Repented and prayed for strength (Judges 16:28)	Final act of faith, redeemed calling	Addiction, reckless living; recovery through repentance, surrender, accountability

New Testament

Biblical Figure	Struggle / Possible Mental Health Issue	Scripture Reference	Recovery / Healing Process	Reintegration into Society	Modern-Day Comparison
Mary Magdalene	Demonic oppression, social stigma	Luke 8:2; Mark 16:9	Delivered by Jesus; full healing	Became a disciple, the first witness of the resurrection	Mental illness, trauma, stigma; recovery through deliverance, counseling, and a new identity
Prodigal Son	Addiction, reckless living, shame, depression	Luke 15:11–32	Came to himself, repented, returned home	Restored by father, celebrated by community	Addiction recovery, broken families; recovery through repentance, therapy, and family reconciliation

Biblical Figure	Struggle / Possible Mental Health Issue	Scripture Reference	Recovery / Healing Process	Reintegration into Society	Modern-Day Comparison
Peter	Guilt, shame, and anxiety after denying Christ	Luke 22:61–62; John 21:15–19	Forgiven and restored by Jesus	Recommended as a church leader	Leaders facing moral failure; recovery through grace, counseling, and the restoration process.
Paul	Emotional burden, thorn in the flesh, persecution stress	2 Corinthians 12:7–10; 2 Cor. 1:8–9	Found strength in God's grace; resilience	Became a leading apostle to the nations	Chronic illness, depression, ministry stress; recovery through faith, therapy, support
Judas Iscariot	Guilt, despair, suicidal actions	Matthew 27:3–5	Overcome by despair, took his life	Did not reintegrate	Warning for untreated depression and hopelessness today
The Gerasene Demoniac	Severe mental/ spiritual torment, isolation	Mark 5:1–20	Delivered by Jesus; mind restored	Sent back to testify in the community	Severe mental illness; recovery through treatment, community reintegration, testimony
Timothy	Anxiety, timidity, stress in ministry	2 Timothy 1:7; 1 Tim. 5:23	Encouragement from Paul, practical advice	Became a faithful church leader	Young leaders under pressure; recovery through mentorship, therapy, and spiritual support

Comparison with Modern-Day Mental Health & Recovery

Biblical Pattern	Modern Parallel	Recovery Process Then	Recovery Process Now
Trauma (Noah, Lot, Job)	PTSD, crisis survivors	God's covenant, divine intervention, and community	Therapy, trauma counseling, peer groups, and faith healing
Depression/ Despair (Elijah, Jeremiah, Jonah)	Clinical depression, burnout	Rest, spiritual encounter, lament, hope	Counseling, medication, prayer, rest, lifestyle changes
Addiction/ Recklessness (Samson, Prodigal Son)	Substance abuse, sexual addiction	Repentance, divine deliverance, community	12-step programs, rehab, counseling, accountability groups
Guilt/Shame (David, Peter)	Moral failure, relapses, regret	Confession, repentance, restoration	Counseling, forgiveness, and pastoral restoration processes
Isolation/Stigma (Mary Magdalene, Gerasene Demoniac)	Social stigma, marginalized mental illness	Deliverance, new identity in Christ, reintegration	Therapy, support groups, community/family acceptance
Anxiety/Fear (Moses, Timothy)	Anxiety disorders, leadership stress	God's reassurance, mentorship	Therapy, coaching, mentorship, spiritual encouragement
Suicide/Despair (Elijah, Judas)	Suicidal ideation, hopelessness	Elijah comforted and restored; Judas gave up	Suicide prevention programs, therapy, and crisis intervention

Practical Applications (For Today's Reader)

Daily Prayer & Reflection: Like David, bring your raw emotions before God (Psalm 51).

Seek Help: Like Moses, don't carry the burden alone, share leadership, and seek wise counselors.

Rest & Self-Care: Like Elijah, honor your body with rest, nourishment, and silence. Community Accountability: Like the Prodigal Son, reconnect with family, mentors, or church leaders.

Celebrate Small Victories: Like the Gerasene man, share your testimony of progress.

Devotional Prayer

Heavenly Father,

You are the God who heals the brokenhearted and restores the weary soul. Just as You restored David after his failure, comforted Elijah in his despair, and delivered Mary Magdalene from oppression, I believe You can bring healing to my life as well. Lord, touch the areas of my heart and mind that feel weak, burdened, or broken. Help me to seek both spiritual renewal and practical steps toward recovery. Surround me with people who will encourage me, walk with me, and remind me of Your unfailing love. May my story, like the Prodigal Son and the Gerasene man, be a testimony of Your power to restore. In Jesus' name, Amen.

Focus Point

This week, take one intentional step toward healing and recovery in your own life: If you are grieving: Write out your lament to God as Job did.

If you are burned out, set aside a day of rest and renewal like Elijah received.

If you are battling guilt or shame: Confess it to God in prayer and share it with a trusted mentor or counselor, as David sought restoration.

If you are struggling with addiction or reckless habits: Take one step toward accountability (call a sponsor, join a group, or tell a trusted friend).

If you feel isolated: Reach out to someone you trust and begin rebuilding community.

Remember: Recovery is a journey, not a one-time event. Each step you take brings you closer to the wholeness God desires for you.

The same God who restored Elijah's strength, redeemed Samson's failures, forgave David's sins, delivered Mary Magdalene, and welcomed home the Prodigal Son is still healing today. Recovery is a journey—but it is one of hope, grace, and restoration.

"He heals the brokenhearted and binds up their wounds." – Psalm 147:3

Igniting spiritual revival through repentance, prayer, and holy living

The imagery of the church as the Bride of Christ is one of the most beautiful and sobering pictures in Scripture. Paul declared in Ephesians 5:27 that Christ is preparing His church "that he might present it to himself a glorious church, not having spot, or wrinkle, or any such thing; but that it should be holy and without blemish." This vision reminds us that the ultimate destiny of the church is not to impress the world but to be made ready for the Bridegroom. The purity of the bride reflects the glory of the Groom.

A bride without spot or wrinkle speaks of a church purified from corruption, compromise, and contamination. Spots represent moral stains—sins that remain unconfessed or unrepentant. Wrinkles symbolize distortions and deformities in character caused by the pressures of the world. Christ desires to cleanse His church of both, preparing her for the eternal wedding banquet of the Lamb. Holiness is not just a doctrine but a bridal garment being woven for that great day.

In biblical times, a bride's preparation for marriage was a season of waiting, cleansing, and adornment. She would undergo rituals of purification and receive garments that signified her readiness. Likewise, the church is in a season of preparation. Each trial, each act of repentance, each moment of consecration is part of the process of making her radiant. God uses both fire and water purification and renewal to remove every blemish from His beloved.

The problem arises when the church forgets her bridal identity and begins to live like a harlot. When the people of God pursue the idols of power, wealth, and pleasure, they defile the garments Christ has given. Revelation 17 warns Babylon, the great harlot who intoxicates the nations with sin. The Bride of Christ must resist this temptation, remembering that she belongs exclusively to Him. Faithfulness is the essence of bridal holiness.

Christ Himself is the one who sanctifies His bride. Ephesians 5:26 says He "sanctifies and cleanses it with the washing of water by the word." Just as a bride bathes before her wedding, so the church must be cleansed by the Word of God. Scripture functions as both a mirror and a washbasin, revealing the stains that must be removed and providing the cleansing power to remove them. Without a steady washing in the Word, the church cannot remain spotless.

The wrinkles of the church often come from age-long traditions, unrepentant sin cycles, or patterns of compromise passed down through generations. These wrinkles distort the beauty of the bride, making her appear tired and worn. But Christ has promised renewal. Isaiah 40:31 declares that those who wait upon the Lord will "renew their strength." The Spirit smooths the wrinkles by bringing revival and refreshment, restoring the bride's youth and vitality.

Being spotless is not about appearing flawless to men but being pure before God. The church may be misunderstood, rejected, or mocked by society, but if her garments are clean in God's eyes, she is radiant. Spots are not always visible to human eyes, but they are unmistakable to the Bridegroom. This is why self-examination, confession, and surrender are essential practices. The Spirit convicts not to condemn but to cleanse.

A wrinkle-free bride also speaks of maturity. Wrinkles can symbolize immaturity, instability, or lack of discipline in spiritual life. Christ desires a church that is not tossed to and fro by every wind of doctrine (Ephesians 4:14). He is shaping a mature bride who knows His voice, follows His will, and resists deception. Spiritual maturity is one of the pieces of evidence that the church is growing into the likeness of Christ.

The wedding imagery points us to the marriage supper of the Lamb described in Revelation 19:7-9. "The marriage of the Lamb has come, and his wife hath made herself ready." Notice the partnership: Christ prepares His bride, yet the bride must also make herself ready. This readiness involves repentance, watchfulness, and holiness. It means keeping the lamp filled with oil, like the wise virgins who awaited the bridegroom in Matthew 25.

Readiness also requires separation. In the parable of the ten virgins, not all who awaited the bridegroom were admitted. Some lacked oil, representing those who were unprepared spiritually. The bride without spot or wrinkle must live in constant expectation of Christ's return, refusing to let distractions or compromises dull her devotion. She must choose intimacy with the Groom over infatuation with the world.

The bridal call is a call to intimacy. Holiness is not merely abstinence from sin but the pursuit of closeness with Christ. The bride desires her groom above all else. In Song of Solomon, the Shulamite longed for her beloved with a passion that consumed her thoughts. The church must rediscover this longing, replacing lukewarmness with burning love. A spotless bride is one whose heart beats in rhythm with her Groom's.

Hidden evil is often the greatest threat to bridal purity. Outwardly, the church may appear clean, but spots remain when sins are covered rather than confessed. Hypocrisy creates blemishes, while pride disguises wrinkles. Christ's cleansing work requires honesty before Him. He will not overlook secret corruption, for He desires a pure and undefiled bride. Exposure and repentance are painful, but they are necessary to remove the stains.

The beauty of the bride is not in her own works but in the garments provided by the Groom. Revelation 19:8 says she is "arrayed in fine linen, clean and white: for the fine linen is the righteousness of saints." These garments are not self-stitched but bestowed by grace. Christ clothes His people with His righteousness, covering their shame and making them radiant. The church's role is to keep the garment unsoiled.

A spotless bride is also a faithful witness. Her purity testifies to the reality of Christ's transforming power. The world is watching to see if the church's claims of holiness are real. When the church lives with integrity, humility, and purity, she shines as a light. But when scandals, hypocrisy, and compromises dominate, the witness is damaged. A wrinkle-free bride is a testimony that Christ truly redeems.

Preparation for the wedding requires vigilance. Just as a bride carefully guards her dress from stains before the ceremony, the church must guard her life from defilement. This vigilance means fleeing temptation, resisting worldliness, and pursuing righteousness. Paul urged Timothy to "keep this commandment without spot, unrebukable, until the appearing of our Lord Jesus Christ" (1 Timothy 6:14). Vigilance is the posture of a bride awaiting her Groom.

The image of the spotless bride also confronts complacency. Too many believers assume that grace allows them to remain careless with sin. But grace is not a license to sin; it is the power to overcome sin. A careless bride who neglects preparation will be ashamed when the groom arrives. The true bride, empowered by grace, takes holiness seriously, knowing that the day of the wedding draws near.

The wrinkles of division and strife must also be ironed out. A bride torn by quarrels cannot reflect the unity of Christ. Jesus prayed in John 17 that His people would be one, even as He and the Father are one. Unity does not mean uniformity but harmony—a shared holiness and devotion to Christ. A wrinkle-free bride is reconciled, walking in love and peace.

Wrinkles also appear when the church clings to past offenses. Bitterness ages the spirit, creating creases that mar the beauty of holiness. Forgiveness smooths those wrinkles, restoring tenderness of heart. The bride must learn to forgive as she has been forgiven. Only then can she reflect the mercy of the Groom who has forgiven her much.

Another wrinkle is spiritual apathy. A bride who loses her first love grows weary and dull. Christ warned the church at Ephesus, "Thou hast left thy first love" (Revelation 2:4). The remedy was repentance and a return to passionate devotion. Revival begins when the bride remembers her Groom and rekindles her love for Him. Without this, the garments become faded, and the beauty of holiness is lost.

Christ's cleansing work often comes through trials. Just as gold is refined in fire, so the bride is purified through suffering. Tribulation removes spots of pride and wrinkles of self-sufficiency, teaching dependence on Christ. James encouraged believers to "count it all joy" when they face trials, for these produce maturity and completeness. The fire of affliction is not to destroy but to beautify.

Christ's cleansing work is both positional and practical. Positionally, through His blood, believers are declared righteous before God. Practically, through the ongoing work of the Holy Spirit, believers are being sanctified—purified in their daily living so that their conduct reflects their new identity. A bride without spot or wrinkle is not only forgiven but also transformed, displaying the beauty of holiness in thought, word, and deed.

This preparation process often involves trials and testing. Just as gold is refined in the fire, so too is the church refined through hardships. These refining moments strip away impurities and reveal what is genuine. While the process may be painful, the church must shine forth in purity and strength, untainted by sin or compromise.

One of the dangers the church must guard against is spiritual complacency. A bride who ceases preparing for her wedding risks being caught unready. In the same way, the church must not grow dull in its devotion or distracted by worldly entanglements. Vigilance, prayer, and continual surrender to Christ are necessary if the church is to remain spotless and radiant for His coming.

The imagery of being without wrinkles speaks not only of purity but of timeless beauty. Wrinkles represent age, wear, and decline, but the bride of Christ is renewed daily by the Spirit. She is not diminished by the passing of years or the struggles of this age; instead, she is being continually renewed, her strength and beauty preserved by the life-giving presence of God.

A spotless bride also points to unity within the church. Division, strife, and bitterness stain the garment of righteousness and hinder the witness of God's people. Christ is coming for a united bride, not a fractured one. Therefore, the call to holiness includes reconciliation, forgiveness, and the pursuit of love among all members of the body of Christ.

Scripture repeatedly warns against the dangers of false teachings and worldly compromise. These act like blemishes upon the garment of the church. To remain without spot, the bride must cling firmly to the truth of God's Word and reject doctrines that distort or dilute the gospel.Faithfulness to the Word is central to her purity.

Holiness is not an abstract concept but a lifestyle. To be without spot or wrinkles means embodying holiness in the everyday choices of life. The bride adorns herself with virtues such as humility, patience, kindness, and integrity. These are not external decorations, but internal realities produced by the Spirit that radiate outward in godly living.

The church must also prepare by living in constant expectation of Christ's return. Just as a bride eagerly awaits her wedding day, the church must cultivate longing for the Bridegroom. This expectancy fuels holiness, motivating believers to cast off every hindrance and live with a singular devotion to Christ.

The work of cleansing is ultimately a cooperative process. Christ provides the blood and the Spirit for sanctification, but the church must yield in obedience. The garments remain spotless as believers align their lives with God's will, choosing faithfulness over compromise, and light over darkness. The spotless bride is a community that walks in active surrender to Christ.

A bride without spot or wrinkle also reflects the restorative power of grace. Many within the church carry scars from past sins, failures, and wounds. Yet through Christ's cleansing, these stains are washed away, and the bride is made new. Grace restores dignity, heals brokenness, and makes the church radiant with the beauty of forgiveness.

The idea of a wrinkle being smoothed out reminds us that sanctification is a process of maturity. Wrinkles are signs of stress and imperfection; spiritually, they can symbolize areas of immaturity or unresolved issues. The Spirit patiently works in believers to bring healing, growth, and maturity, smoothing out the "wrinkles" until the church reflects Christ's fullness.

The bride without blemish also speaks of separation from the world's defilement. While the church lives in the world, it must not conform to its patterns of sin. Just as a bride preserves her purity for her husband, the church must remain loyal to Christ, refusing to give her heart to idols of power, wealth, or pleasure.

Preparation involves not only abstaining from sin but actively pursuing righteousness. The spotless bride does not merely avoid what is evil but delights in what is good. Her garments are adorned with works of love, justice, mercy, and faith. In this way, her purity shines as a witness to the world of the transforming power of the gospel.

The coming banquet of the Lamb emphasizes celebration and joy. The spotless bride is not only pure but also joyful, knowing the hope of her eternal union with Christ. Joy becomes part of her adornment, a sign to the world that she belongs to the One who has overcome sin, death, and sorrow.

The call to be without spot or wrinkle is also a call to perseverance. The church must endure until the end, resisting the temptations that seek to stain her garments. Just as a bride must remain faithful through the waiting period, so the church must hold firm to Christ, even when the world mocks or persecutes her for her devotion.

The church's purity is also tied to her mission. A spotless bride is an effective witness. Her holiness draws others to Christ, showing the world that God's love transforms lives. The more the church reflects Christ's character, the more compelling her testimony becomes to a lost and broken generation.

The spotless bride is a prophetic image of what God intended humanity to be from the beginning: holy, blameless, and in communion with Him. In the final marriage of the Lamb, creation itself will be restored, and God's people will reflect His glory perfectly. The church's preparation now is a foretaste of that ultimate renewal.

This vision should fill believers with both hope and responsibility. Hope, because Christ is faithful to complete the work He has begun in His church. Responsibility, because believers are called to actively participate in the process of sanctification. Both aspects keep the church humble, dependent, and focused on Christ.

The spotless bride will stand in stark contrast to the harlot described in Revelation, who symbolizes a world system corrupted by sin, greed, and idolatry. While the harlot is decorated with false glory, the bride is clothed in true righteousness. This contrast highlights the urgency for the church to pursue holiness instead of compromise.

Ultimately, the bride without spot or wrinkle is the crowning display of God's redemptive power. She is not perfect by her own strength but by the love and sacrifice of Christ. Her beauty is borrowed from the Bridegroom Himself, who clothes her in His righteousness. When the wedding day arrives, her spotless garments will testify not to her own glory but to the glory of the One who has redeemed her with His blood.

Ephesians 5:25-27 reveals God's desire for the Church to be pure and holy, presented as a radiant bride without spot or wrinkle. This image illustrates the transformative power of Christ's love and sanctification. Revival begins when the Church awakens to its need for God's presence. C. S. Lewis, in *Mere Christianity*, emphasizes that God's grace and sanctification work together to cleanse believers from sin, producing righteousness that reflects His holiness and glory. Exposure of hidden evil acts as a catalyst, shaking believers from spiritual complacency. God calls His people to return to holiness, prayer, and obedience. Leaders must model fervent devotion, inspiring the congregation to seek revival. Awakening starts with individual hearts surrendering fully to God.

Exposure clarifies areas where the Church has neglected its spiritual responsibilities. Prayer is the cornerstone of revival, aligning hearts with God's will. Repentance removes barriers that hinder the flow of God's Spirit. A. W. Tozer, in *The Pursuit of God*, notes that the Church's beauty is not in outward displays or human perfection but in hearts fully surrendered to God, allowing His Spirit to refine, purify, and restore. Leaders must guide the Church in confession, accountability, and intercession. Awakening stirs passion, zeal, and boldness in proclaiming God's Word. Exposure reveals hidden compromises that suppress spiritual growth.

Revival requires humility, dependence, and a willingness to obey God fully. The Church must remove distractions, traditions, and pride that obstruct revival. Awakening strengthens faith, unity, and discernment within the body of Christ. Leaders must cultivate environments that encourage prayer, worship, and holiness. Exposure motivates corrective action, clearing the way for God's Spirit to move. Leonard Ravenhill, in *Why Revival Tarries*, underscores that revival movements require a sanctified Church. When believers commit to holiness, God can use them as instruments of transformation for communities and nations.

Revival ignites hearts, transforming attitudes, relationships, and ministry practices. The Church becomes a vessel through which God's glory and power flow. Exposure teaches believers the dangers of complacency, distraction, and deception. Awakening inspires renewed commitment, sacrifice, and service to God. Leaders must ensure that revival is rooted in Scripture, not emotionalism. The faithful learn to recognize God's leading through prayer, discernment, and obedience. The concept of the spotless bride involves ongoing repentance, surrender, and obedience. The Church is called to consistently align with Scripture, resisting compromise and worldly influences.

Exposure dismantles false teachings, prideful leadership, and manipulation. Revival brings clarity of mission, vision, and purpose to the Church. Awakening restores hope, faith, and spiritual vitality among the congregation. Leaders must encourage accountability, discipleship, and faithful stewardship. Exposure ensures that revival is built on truth, not human ambition. Lewis emphasizes that holiness is a process, not a momentary event. Believers must actively cultivate virtue, humility, and love, allowing God to remove blemishes and strengthen their spiritual character.

Revival impacts families, communities, and nations when the Church is purified and aligned with God. Awakening strengthens spiritual discernment, helping the Church resist deception. Leaders must lead, by example, demonstrating fervent prayer and obedience. Exposure reveals spiritual blind spots, allowing God to correct and restore. Revival ignites boldness, courage, and a renewed passion for

God's glory. Tozer observes that many churches fail to recognize the importance of internal sanctification. Without it, ministries may appear effective externally but lack enduring spiritual impact. Awakening encourages believers to share the message of Christ with urgency and conviction.

Leaders must cultivate personal intimacy with God, modeling spiritual authenticity. Exposure clears the path for spiritual renewal, protection, and empowerment. Revival strengthens unity, faithfulness, and perseverance in the Church. Awakening restores the Church's witness, credibility, and influence in society. Leaders must teach obedience, accountability, and the pursuit of holiness. Exposure reinforces the importance of addressing hidden sin and compromise. Revival inspires acts of compassion, justice, and service to others. Awakening deepens spiritual intimacy, transforming worship, prayer, and ministry. Ravenhill reminds leaders that their personal holiness directly affects the Church's testimony. A pure, obedient leadership fosters a community that reflects God's glory and power.

The Church must implement practices that cultivate sanctification: accountability, discipleship, prayer, Scripture study, and communal correction. This helps maintain spiritual integrity and readiness for Christ's return. Leaders must empower the congregation to participate actively in revival. Exposure challenges the Church to prioritize God's glory above human agendas. Revival ensures the Church is spiritually prepared to face challenges and opposition. Ultimately, awakening the Spirit of the Church ignites revival, restoring hearts, communities, and nations to God's purposes.

In conclusion, the Church as a bride without spot or wrinkle symbolizes the ideal of spiritual purity and devotion. Scripture, Lewis, Tozer, and Ravenhill affirm that holiness, sanctification, and Christ-centered living prepare the Church for God's purposes and eternal reward.

Chapter 35: When the Church Becomes the Crime Scene — God's Verdict on
Hidden Evil and the Call to Repentance

This chapter sheds light on the challenges of corruption, deception, and hypocrisy that have emerged within the modern Church and among some political leaders who misuse God's name for power and control. It highlights the importance of recognizing that God's judgment begins in His house and calls for sincere repentance, encouraging individuals to focus on heartfelt change rather than mere performance.

It urges us to be vigilant against those who take advantage of the vulnerable, including the abused, the unhoused, the youth, the elderly, and the broken. It reminds us that Christ's Church is meant to be a sanctuary of worship, truth, and holiness.

Importantly, within this call for accountability, there is a message of hope: those who have been silenced and wounded can rise as a purified remnant, dedicated to restoring integrity and compassion within the Body of Christ. The chapter concludes with a hopeful invitation to prepare our hearts, for the Bridegroom is coming, and only those who are ready will enter His Kingdom.

The Trumpet of Judgment Sounds

The Spirit of the Lord is sounding an alarm across the earth, and it echoes first through the halls of the church. The hour of reckoning has arrived, and Heaven's courtroom is in session. The Judge of all the earth is calling His people to account. No longer will hypocrisy hide behind polished sermons or empty rituals. No longer will charisma conceal corruption. The trumpet of truth is blasting through sanctuaries and across nations, announcing, *"Judgment must begin at the house of God"* (1 Peter 4:17). This is not a call of condemnation—it is a call of cleansing. God's fire is not coming to destroy His Bride but to purify her.

The light of divine truth is exposing what men have tried to bury beneath robes of religion and masks of ministry. The Spirit is uncovering what has been whispered in green rooms and hidden behind stained glass. The time of false comfort has ended; God is dismantling the platforms built on pride, deception, and greed. For too long, the voice of the hurting has been ignored, the abused silenced, the poor neglected, the broken dismissed. But Heaven has been listening. The cry of the afflicted has reached the throne of God, and He has declared, *"Enough!"*

Jesus Christ, the righteous Judge, stands at the door of His own house. His eyes blaze with holy fire, and His voice still echoes from Matthew 21:13: *"My Father's house shall be called a house of prayer, but you have made it a den of thieves."* That cry was not only for the temple in Jerusalem; it is a word for the Church today. Every sanctuary that has become a marketplace of manipulation will be overturned. Every pulpit used to oppress rather than liberate will be silenced. Every system built on deceit rather than devotion will crumble beneath the weight of His truth.

The Church has become a crime scene—where love has been murdered by pride, where compassion lies bleeding beneath the pews, and where the innocent have been crucified by religious politics. The evidence is undeniable. The blood of the betrayed cries from the altars, the tears of the wounded stain the carpets, and the silence of the leaders resounds louder than their sermons. But God is not mocked. What has been done in His name without His heart will be judged by His hand.

Yet even now, before the final gavel falls, mercy stands in the doorway. Grace pleads with outstretched hands, calling the Church to repentance. The Spirit of God is not delighting in destruction but inviting restoration. If the Church will fall to her knees and confess her hidden sins, revival will replace ruin. The same fire that exposes also refines. The same light that judges also heals. There is still time to repent, to return, to rebuild on righteousness and truth before it is too late.

Exposing the Lie of False Covering

The modern Church has misused one of its most sacred truths: "Touch not My anointed and do My prophets no harm" (1 Chronicles 16:22). These words were never meant to shield corruption. Yet, how many have used them as armor against accountability? The anointing was given for service, not for self-preservation. When the anointed vessel becomes corrupted and refuses correction, the Spirit of God lifts His covering and allows exposure for the sake of truth. God does not protect what He did not ordain.

There are pulpits today where leaders preach fire but live in filth. They speak in tongues but refuse repentance. They prophesy healing while harboring unconfessed sin. The same lips that declare blessing have cursed the broken. But the Lord is not blind. The One who walks among the lampstands (Revelation 2:1) is removing those who no longer burn with truth. He is silencing voices that have misrepresented His name and bringing humility to those who thought they could never fall.

The false shepherds tell the abused to stay quiet "for the sake of the ministry." They tell the wounded to "forgive and move on" while refusing to repent or seek justice. But the Lord says, *"Woe to the shepherds who destroy and scatter the sheep of My pasture!"* (Jeremiah 23:1). God never called leaders to protect institutions at the expense of His people. He called them to guard His flock with compassion and integrity. When shepherds devour instead of defending, Heaven intervenes.

Many have hidden sin beneath the garments of success. They speak of growth, numbers, and prosperity, yet behind closed doors lies a trail of manipulation, sexual immorality, and abuse of power. They have turned the sacred into a spectacle and made merchandise of the Gospel (2 Peter 2:3). But God declares, *"I am against the prophets who use their own tongues and yet declare, 'The Lord says'"* (Jeremiah 23:31). The Holy Spirit is withdrawing His endorsement from platforms that elevate men above the cross.

The day of false peace is over. God is tearing down every counterfeit covering. The anointing will no longer be confused with charisma. The Spirit will no longer tolerate those who speak for Him but do not walk with Him. The fear of the Lord is returning to His house. The trembling of the Spirit will once again be felt in the sanctuary. It is not revival until repentance returns to the pulpit.

Jesus Confronts the Religious Frauds

In His earthly ministry, Jesus was never intimidated by religious titles. He stood before priests, scribes, and rulers with unshakable authority. His words were not gentle toward hypocrisy. *"You brood of vipers,"* He declared, *"how can you, being evil, speak good things?"* (Matthew 12:34). His fire was not aimed at sinners but at those who claimed to represent God while betraying His character.

Jesus did not flatter the religious elite. He unmasked them. *"You are like whitewashed tombs— beautiful on the outside but full of dead men's bones and all uncleanness"* (Matthew 23:27). He saw through their polished robes and pious rituals. He discerned the pride behind their prayers and the greed beneath their giving. His rebuke was not cruelty—it was mercy, for truth is the only scalpel that can remove the cancer of deception.

When He declared, *"You devour widows' houses and for a pretense make long prayers,"* (Mark 12:40), He was addressing the exploitation that still plagues the modern Church. Even today, widows are manipulated through emotional appeals for money, and the poor are blamed for lacking faith. But Jesus has not changed. He will again overturn the tables of greed, casting out every spirit that turns worship into commerce and compassion into currency.

His cleansing of the temple was not an act of temper—it was an act of truth. When He drove out the merchants with a whip of cords (John 2:15), He was declaring war on religious exploitation. The whip of the Word is still in His hand. The temple of today is not made of stone but of souls, and He will cleanse it once again before His return. The Bride He comes for must be pure, not prosperous; humble, not haughty.

Christ is confronting His Church again, not to condemn but to call her back. His eyes are upon the pulpits that have grown cold. His Spirit is stirring the pews that have settled into comfort. He is whispering to the faithful remnant: "Do not be deceived by appearance. I am raising truth- tellers who fear no man and serve no agenda but Mine." The confrontation is not coming—it has begun.

Lies Told to the Wounded

There is a cruel deception whispered in sanctuaries and shouted from platforms—that pain is punishment, and suffering is proof of sin. The wounded are told they "must have done something wrong" to deserve their pain. But Jesus refuted that lie when His disciples asked about the blind man: *"Who sinned, this man or his parents?"* He answered, *"Neither... but that the works of God should be revealed in him"* (John 9:2–3). The Church must remember: the afflicted are not cursed; they are chosen vessels for God's glory.

The lie told to the abused is that silence is strength and exposure is betrayal. But God never called His children to protect predators. He called them to walk in the light. Ephesians 5:11 commands, *"Have no fellowship with the unfruitful works of darkness, but rather expose them."* When the Church covers sin instead of confessing it, it becomes an accomplice to evil. True strength is found in truth, not secrecy.

The unhoused are told that faith would have kept them from poverty, as if faith is a luxury for the privileged. Yet the Son of God Himself said, *"Foxes have holes, birds have nests, but the Son of Man has nowhere to lay His head"* (Matthew 8:20). Jesus was homeless by choice, that He might dwell among the broken. To despise the poor is to despise the image of Christ. God's judgment burns against those who claim to serve Him yet step over the Lazarus at their gate.

The youth are told they must "wait their turn" to serve, as though the Spirit of God has an age restriction. But the same God who called Samuel as a boy, who anointed David as a teenager, and who filled Jeremiah in his youth still moves through young vessels today. The modern Church often fears the fire of the next generation because it exposes the complacency of the current one. But Acts 2:17 declares, *"Your sons and daughters shall prophesy."* God is pouring new oil on young altars.

The elderly, the forgotten saints, are told that their season of usefulness is over. But the Bible declares that those who are planted in the house of the Lord "shall still bear fruit in old age" (Psalm 92:14). The Church has become so intoxicated with youth culture that it has forgotten the wisdom of the elders. God is calling seasoned intercessors out of silence. The gray-haired warriors are not retired; they are refired.

Divorced individuals are often told today that they are disqualified from God's favor, that their failure is final. But Scripture reveals a Savior who met a divorced woman at the well and turned her into a revivalist (John 4:39). Jesus did not condemn her; He commissioned her. The Church must stop crucifying people Jesus has already forgiven. God does not discard the broken; He rebuilds them into testimonies of grace.

The molested are told to "forgive and forget," as if forgiveness erases trauma. But Jesus never asked anyone to forget; He calls them to heal. He stood with the violated, the shamed, the outcast. His first public sermon proclaimed liberty to the captives and healing for the brokenhearted (Luke 4:18). The Church's failure to protect the innocent is a stench before God's throne. Judgment is coming upon those who have used His name to prey on His lambs.

The lame, physically, emotionally, and spiritually crippled, are often made spectacles of pity rather than recipients of power. But in John 5, Jesus did not pity the lame man at Bethesda; He healed him. The Lord is again asking, *"Do you want to be made whole?"* It is not the duty of the Church to maintain dependency but to restore dignity. When the powerless are empowered, God's kingdom is revealed.

These lies have chained multitudes in fear and shame. Yet Jesus, the Truth, still walks among the wounded, declaring, *"You shall know the truth, and the truth shall make you free"* (John 8:32). Every victim of deceit, every soul bruised by hypocrisy, is being called to rise. The very place where you were hurt will become the platform of your healing. The stone that the builders rejected is becoming the cornerstone of God's restoration.

Heaven is turning the tables. The last shall be first. Those dismissed by religion will be elevated by revelation. The rejected are becoming the redeemed. This is the hour of divine reversal. For every lie told by man, God is releasing a word of truth. For every heart broken by deception, He is pouring new oil of deliverance. The Spirit of the Lord is rebuilding the ruins of His house one healed soul at a time.

God's Courtroom Opens

The courtroom of Heaven is not a metaphor—it is reality. The Judge is seated, the witnesses are called, and the evidence is being presented. Angels record every hidden word, every unrepentant act, every secret conversation meant to deceive the flock of God. The gavel of truth is about to fall, and no one can appeal His verdict. *"For we must all appear before the judgment seat of Christ"* (2 Corinthians 5:10).

The Prosecutor is not Satan—he is already condemned. It is the Holy Spirit who convicts, who reveals, who pleads with hearts to repent before it is too late. The Spirit is not accusing to destroy but exposing to deliver. His voice is clear: "Return to Me, O backsliding church, for I am married to you" (Jeremiah 3:14). Mercy still stands, but grace has an expiration date for the unrepentant.

In this divine courtroom, victims are not forgotten. God Himself becomes their Advocate. *"He executes justice for the oppressed and gives food to the hungry"* (Psalm 146:7). The Lord rises from His throne to defend those who have been silenced. The abused, the abandoned, and the ashamed will see vindication in their lifetime. God's justice does not sleep.

The witnesses of truth are rising—prophets, intercessors, and reformers who refuse to bow to religious corruption. They are the John the Baptists of this generation, crying out in the wilderness, "Prepare the way of the Lord!" They are not motivated by fame but by fire. Their loyalty is not to denominations but to divine destiny. They will not flatter leaders—they will confront them.

The verdict over the hypocritical Church is being written in the Spirit: "Guilty of misrepresentation. Guilty of exploitation. Guilty of pride. Guilty of neglecting the least of these." Yet even now, God's mercy whispers from the cross, *"Father, forgive them, for they know not what they do."* But forgiveness requires confession. Without repentance, guilt remains.

The religious elite mocked Jesus as He hung between thieves, not realizing that they were the true robbers of God's glory. Today's leaders who sell salvation for profit and exchange truth for comfort are no different. But the same Jesus who overturned tables is coming again—not with a whip of cords but with a sword of justice. The Word that once cleansed the temple will now cleanse the nations.

Politicians, too, stand in this courtroom. Those who have invoked the name of God for power yet ignored His commands for justice will face His judgment. God is not Republican or Democrat; He is holy. *"Righteousness exalts a nation, but sin is a reproach to any people"* (Proverbs 14:34). The throne of Heaven is higher than every earthly office, and every ruler will bow before the King of kings.

The Church is on trial, but so is every individual believer. The question is not only "What did the leaders do?" but "What did we tolerate?" Silence in the face of sin is consent. The sin of omission is as deadly as the sin of commission. We must each ask ourselves: Did we defend the truth or protect the system? Did we serve God or serve reputation?

Yet for those who repent, there is hope beyond the judgment. The same courtroom where guilt was proven is the same place where grace is offered. The blood of Jesus still cries louder than the blood of the victims. It still speaks of mercy, of redemption, of new beginnings. God is not destroying His Church—He is detoxifying it. The shaking is mercy in motion.

Therefore, let every heart be still before Him. The Spirit calls: "Come out of hiding. Lay down the masks. Return to your first love." The trial is not meant to destroy but to deliver. The exposure is not humiliation; it is healing. Before the Bridegroom returns, the Bride must be pure. Before the trumpet sounds, repentance must resound. This is not just a warning; it is an invitation.

The Victims Rise Again — From Pain to Purpose

The Spirit of God is calling forth a generation of survivors—men and women who have walked through betrayal, rejection, abuse, and deception, yet still carry a flame that cannot be extinguished. What the enemy meant for evil, God is turning for good (Genesis 50:20). Those once silenced by fear will now become voices of truth. Their scars will testify louder than sermons, and their pain will become a prophetic purpose.

The Lord is saying to the wounded: "You are not forgotten. You are not forsaken. I saw every tear, every night you cried alone. I recorded your pain, not as a mark of shame but as evidence of your calling." The brokenhearted are not on the sidelines of God's plan—they are the very foundation stones of His next revival. The remnant rising now will not be built on celebrity, but on sincerity.

The abused who were told to "stay silent" are now becoming God's loudest preachers. Their testimonies will dismantle religious façades and restore integrity to the house of God. Every secret that once brought shame will now birth freedom. Revelation 12:11 declares, *"They overcame him by the blood of the Lamb and by the word of their testimony."* What once silenced you will now become your song of deliverance.

The unhoused and rejected are being positioned by Heaven as reformers of compassion. They have seen the church from the outside; now God is calling them to rebuild it from within. Their empathy will become the new architecture of mercy. Isaiah 58:7–8 resounds: *"Is it not to share your bread with the hungry... then your light shall break forth like the morning."* Out of the alleys and shelters, prophets of restoration are emerging.

The youth who were dismissed will rise as flames of revival. They will not wait for permission from institutions that have grown cold. They will cry out like Jeremiah, *"His word was in my heart like a burning fire shut up in my bones"* (Jeremiah 20:9). These young warriors will tear down idols of popularity and restore the altar of prayer. They will carry unfiltered faith, and their worship will shake nations.

397

The elderly who were overlooked are awakening again to their assignment. Like Anna in the temple (Luke 2:36-38), they will prophesy over the next generation. Their prayers will birth movements their eyes may never see. The gray hair that was dismissed will become the crown of wisdom, guiding the youth. The revival of this age will not be a youth movement alone—it will be a multi-generational awakening.

The divorced who were shamed will become preachers of restoration. Having tasted both failure and forgiveness, they will extend mercy to those drowning in guilt. Their message will echo the heart of Christ: *"Neither do I condemn thee; go and sin no more"* (John 8:11). The Church has often thrown stones, but God is placing in these restored hearts the balm of grace. They will lead multitudes back to the cross through compassion, not condemnation.

Those who were molested, silenced, and scarred are being healed by the gentle hand of the Savior. He is restoring what religion crushed. The same Jesus who defended the woman caught in adultery still stands between the victim and the accuser. He is saying again, "Let the one without sin cast the first stone." Their pain will no longer define them—it will refine them. From their wounds, healing rivers will flow.

The lame and disabled are rising as living testimonies of endurance and faith. God's glory shines brightest through broken vessels. Paul's thorn was not his limitation—it was his invitation to deeper grace. *"My grace is sufficient for you, for My strength is made perfect in weakness"* (2 Corinthians 12:9). Those who were told they were too weak will now demonstrate divine strength.

Every category of the forgotten—the orphan, the widow, the rejected, the misunderstood—is being drawn to the heart of Christ. They are the new foundation of His end-time Church. The Spirit is saying, "Come out from among the proud and the polished; I am building a Church that bleeds, a people that weeps, a Bride that loves." The next great move of God will not come from stages but from secret places of intercession.

The Fire of Refinement

Before resurrection comes, there must be crucifixion. Before glory, there must be purification. The fire that is sweeping through the Church is not to destroy, but to refine. Malachi 3:3 declares, *"He will sit as a refiner and purifier of silver; He will purify the sons of Levi."* The refining fire of God is exposing mixture—ministries with hidden agendas, leaders without integrity, and worship without surrender.

The Lord is not impressed by lights, conferences, or crowds. He is searching for contrite hearts. Isaiah 66:2 says, *"This is the one I esteem: he who is humble and contrite in spirit, and trembles at My word."* The trembling is returning. Reverence is coming back. God is dismantling performance-based Christianity and reestablishing holiness as the measure of true ministry.

The Spirit is whispering to pastors and leaders: "Repent before I remove your lampstand." This is the warning Jesus gave to Ephesus in Revelation 2:5. Titles will not protect anyone from accountability. God is exposing false humility and demanding authentic repentance. Those who bow low now will rise again in grace; those who resist correction will fall beneath the weight of their pride.

The refining fire will reach every level, pastors, prophets, politicians, and pew-sitters alike. The shaking will be global. Nations will see the hypocrisy of their idols, and the Church will no longer be able to hide behind cultural respectability. The consuming fire of God is not coming to destroy the Church; it is coming to restore her first love.

In this refining, every idol is being shattered. Ministries built on manipulation will collapse. Relationships founded on lust will dissolve. Platforms that glorify man will vanish like smoke. Only what is rooted in righteousness will remain. Hebrews 12:27 says, *"The removing of those things that can be shaken—so that what cannot be shaken may remain."* God is burning away what cannot endure eternity.

The faithful remnant, those who have not bowed to corruption, will shine brighter in this hour. Their humility will become their authority. Their secret place will become their strength. They will be carriers of revival that cannot be controlled by denominations or silenced by fear. God is raising voices that owe nothing to men and everything to the cross.

The Spirit of the Lord is saying, "Do not fear the exposure; fear disobedience." The shaking is mercy disguised as judgment. God would rather embarrass you now than lose you forever. His discipline is not cruel; it is covenanting love. *"For whom the Lord loves He corrects, even as a father the son in whom he delights"* (Proverbs 3:12). Correction today prevents condemnation tomorrow.

The refining process will hurt. It will cost friendships, platforms, and comfort. But those who endure the fire will emerge as pure gold. Job declared, *"When He has tried me, I shall come forth as gold"* (Job 23:10). The Lord is not destroying His servants—He is distilling them. Only through fire can purity emerge.

This is not the end of the Church—it is the end of counterfeit Christianity. The true Bride of Christ is being separated from the harlot of hypocrisy. Those who worship in spirit and truth (John 4:24) are being sealed for this end-time harvest. The division we see is not political—it is prophetic. God is distinguishing those who truly love Him from those who merely use His name.

The victims who rise from the ashes will lead the purified Church into revival. Their humility will be their power. Their compassion will be their platform. Their worship will be their weapon. Like the five wise virgins, they will keep their lamps filled with oil, prepared for the Bridegroom's return. And when He comes, they will be found ready—pure, awake, and faithful.

The Final Call to Repentance and the Restoration of God's True Church

Heaven continues to extend mercy, but mercy has a deadline. The Spirit calls out, "Repent, for the Kingdom of Heaven is at hand!" (Matthew 4:17). The Church stands at a crossroads between revival and removal, between purification and destruction. God's patience is not weakness; it is an opportunity. He delays His judgment so that more may turn and live, but the day is quickly approaching when delay will end, and destiny will be revealed.

This is not a time for emotional religion but for genuine repentance. Repentance is not simply saying "I'm sorry"; it is changing direction. It is the decision to return to holiness, to abandon compromise, and to rebuild altars of integrity. The Lord says, "Return to Me with all your heart, with fasting and weeping and mourning" (Joel 2:12). The tears of repentance are the first drops of rain.

God is calling His leaders to bow low before the people they have wounded. Public sin demands public humility. When Zacchaeus encountered Christ, he didn't hide his transformation—he repented openly and restored what he had taken (Luke 19:8). That is the mark of true conversion: restitution follows repentance. The Church will only be healed when its leaders stop hiding behind titles and start kneeling in truth.

The Spirit is searching for pulpits, not to condemn but to cleanse. The Lord is looking for pastors who weep more than they perform, who love more than they lecture. He is seeking shepherds after His own heart (Jeremiah 3:15), not entertainers, not empire builders, but broken vessels who know the cost of carrying His glory. The revival that's coming will be led by those who have been crushed by His presence.

God is also visiting the pews. He is confronting spectators who have grown comfortable with passivity. The days of sitting in church without being in the Church are over. Every believer is being summoned to holiness, to prayer, to accountability. The Spirit declares, "Be holy, for I am holy" (1 Peter 1:16). Holiness is not outdated; it is the fragrance of heaven.

There will be no spectators in this next move of God. Every son and daughter will be activated. Every heart will burn again for souls. The gifts that have lain dormant will come alive as the Spirit breathes upon His people. This awakening will not be led by programs but by presence. The outpouring of the Holy Spirit will fall not on stages but on altars of brokenness.

Those who were wounded will now carry healing oil. They will move in compassion rather than criticism. They will preach not from pride but from pain redeemed by grace. Their testimonies will pierce through religious pretense and awaken repentance in the hardest hearts. This new army of truth-tellers will shake nations—not with anger, but with anointing.

The Church that emerges from this trial will not look like the one that entered it. It will be smaller in number but stronger in spirit. It will be stripped of performance but filled with power. It will not chase fame; it will carry fire. The spotlight will no longer be on personalities but on purity. The Bride of Christ will once again be known for her holiness, humility, and love.

The Holy Spirit is restoring the fear of the Lord. This fear is not terror; it is reverent awe. It is the trembling awareness that God sees all, knows all, and judges righteously. The fear of the Lord is the beginning of wisdom (Proverbs 9:10). Without it, sermons are empty and worship is noisy. But when holy fear returns, glory follows.

God's house will once again become a house of prayer. The worship that rises will not be entertainment—it will be intercession. Tears will replace applause. Repentance will replace routine. The Spirit is cleansing the temple, flipping the tables of greed and apathy. And from the ashes, true worship will rise like incense before His throne.

The Bride Awakened

The Bride of Christ is awakening. She has been asleep, intoxicated by comfort, seduced by culture, and distracted by division. But now the midnight cry is sounding: *"Behold, the Bridegroom is coming; go out to meet Him!"* (Matthew 25:6). The wise are trimming their lamps; the foolish still sleep. The oil of intimacy will separate the prepared from the pretenders.

The oil represents devotion, not performance. It is the secret prayer life, the worship in the wilderness, the obedience in obscurity. The five wise virgins carried extra oil because they valued His presence above all else. This is what the Church must recover—private devotion that fuels public transformation. Without oil, there is only burnout; with oil, there is unquenchable flame.

The Bride's garments are being washed in the blood of the Lamb (Revelation 7:14). God is removing the stains of compromise and self-righteousness. The Church will no longer be known for scandal but for sanctity. Her beauty will not come from outward adornment but from inward purity. She will walk in love, radiate light, and carry the fragrance of Christ wherever she goes.

The call to holiness is not legal; it is love. It is the desire to look like the One we adore. Holiness is not a burden; it is a blessing. When the Bride loves the Groom, she gladly separates from what displeases Him. The world will see her glow, not because of makeup or marketing, but because the glory of God rests upon her.

In this final hour, the Holy Spirit is uniting true believers across denominational lines. This remnant Church will not be divided by doctrine but bound by devotion. They will walk in the spirit of Acts 2—sharing, praying, and breaking bread together with gladness and sincerity of heart. The world will know them not by their statements but by their love.

The nations are groaning for the manifestation of this purified Church (Romans 8:19). Creation itself waits for the sons and daughters of God to rise. Political systems are failing, economies are shaking, and hearts are fainting for fear. Yet in the midst of chaos, the radiant Bride will stand unshaken, declaring, "Jesus is Lord!" Her stability will be the anchor of a trembling world.

This end-time Church will carry both power and purity. Miracles will return, but so will the fear of the Lord. Deliverance will flow, but so will discernment. Prophecy will increase, but it will

exalt Christ, not man. The days of mixture are ending. God is releasing a double portion of truth and grace upon His purified people.

The Spirit and the Bride now cry out together, *"Come, Lord Jesus!"* (Revelation 22:17). This is the ultimate posture of revival—not ambition, but anticipation. The purified Church is not seeking a platform but a Person. Her longing is not for fame but for His face. Every trial, every tear, every shaking has prepared her for this moment—the return of the King.

And when He comes, He will not look for perfect performance but for pure hearts. He will not ask how many followers you had, but whether you followed Him. He will not measure success by buildings but by obedience. The question will not be "Did they know your name?" but "Did you know Mine?" Only those who truly loved Him will enter in.

Therefore, beloved, hear the call of the Spirit: Repent, return, and prepare. Lay aside every weight, forgive every wound, and keep your lamp burning. The Church is being purified for her final hour. The Judge is standing at the door, but so is the Bridegroom. The fire that exposes will also empower. The Church on trial will soon become the Church triumphant. Let every heart cry out with urgency and hope: *"Even so, come, Lord Jesus."*

The Church on Trial — God Rebukes the Hidden Evil within the Church The Day of Reckoning Approaches

In these last days, the Church must face a solemn tribunal, not before men, but before the omniscient eyes of God. The lies that have been spoken to the abused, the homeless, the youth, the elderly, the divorced, the traumatized, the lame, all these lies will be exposed. The One who holds the keys of death and Hades (Revelation 1:18) will bring into the open what has been hidden in darkness. Not everyone who cries "Lord, Lord" will enter His kingdom (Matthew 7:21). The Church is on trial, and the faithful must be purified.

It unveils how Jesus Himself confronted hypocrisy in His day, and how victims may rise in integrity, faith, and service in these closing times. Let us remember: God's house is not a den of thieves or a stage for deceit; it must become a sanctuary of truth, worship, and healing.

The Burden of Lies Spoken to the Vulnerable

To the abused: the lie that God abandoned you, that you must be silent, that you are disqualified for holy things. To the homeless and destitute: the lie that your poverty is your fault, that God's people have little to do with you. To the youth: the lie that your doubts, your wounds, your struggles make you less usable. To the elderly: the lie that age disqualifies you, that you have nothing to offer. To the divorced: the lie that you are forever tainted, that you can scarcely be restored. To those molested: the lie of shame, that the sin defines you, that your voice does not matter. To the lame (physically or spiritually): the lie that your weakness disqualifies you from service.

These lies are whispered by church leaders and politicians who cloak ambition, self-interest, and hypocrisy in pious speech. But God sees the bruises, the scars, the silenced voices—and He will bring every secret into the light (Luke 8:17; Mark 4:22). The victims are not too broken to be used—they are precisely those whom Christ came to heal, restore, and exalt.

How Jesus Exposed Religious Leaders in His Day

Jesus confronted the scribes, Pharisees, and teachers of the law with courage and truth. He denounced them as hypocrites, whitewashed tombs, blind guides (Matthew 23:13-36). "Woe to you, scribes and Pharisees, hypocrites! You shut the door of the kingdom of heaven in people's faces. You don't go in yourselves, and you won't let others enter" (Matt. 23:13). He said, "You clean the outside of the cup and dish, but inside you are full of greed and self-indulgence" (Matt. 23:25). He called them whitewashed tombs, beautiful outwardly but full of dead bones and uncleanness inside (Matt. 23:27–28). He said, "Woe to you, blind guides! You strain out a gnat but swallow a camel" (Matt. 23:24).

He pronounced woes upon them for hypocrisy, pride, injustice, and for devouring widows' houses while making long prayers for show. He called them serpents, brood of vipers, and asked, "How will you escape being condemned to hell?" (Matt. 23:33) Jesus rebuked legalism: He argued that they tithed mint and dill but neglected justice, mercy, and faithfulness (Matt. 23:23).

He undermined their hypocrisy over oaths, swearing, and ritual purity (Matt. 23:16–22). He lamented over Jerusalem, calling them rebellious children who would kill prophets (Matt. 23:37– 39). Jesus warned that not all who say "Lord, Lord" will enter the kingdom (Luke 6:46; cf. Matt. 7:21). Though they spoke piously, their hearts were far from God.

He said, "Beware the leaven of the Pharisees, which is hypocrisy" (Luke 12:1). The inner corruption eventually spreads. When confronted with hypocrisy over Sabbath laws, He said: "Which of you, if your son or ox falls into a well on the Sabbath, will not immediately pull him out?" (Luke 14:5) to show that mercy transcends rigid rules. He healed the man with dropsy on the Sabbath in the presence of religious leaders, exposing their hardness (Luke 14:1–6). Jesus associated with sinners, tax collectors, and broken people, offering them grace and exposing that the religious elite judged falsely (Luke 7:36-50).

In John 10, He said that a thief comes only to steal, kill, and destroy, but He came that people might have life. The false shepherds sneak in another way (John 10:1–10). Thus, Jesus established the principle that God's house is not to be a base for falsehood, greed, or power, but a dwelling of truth, healing, and relationship.

The Church on Trial: The Deceiver Within

The modern church can fall into the same traps, substituting external religiosity for inner transformation. Politicians and church leaders may promise help but exploit vulnerability, silencing those who suffer. They may tell abused victims to be quiet for the sake of peace, or that speaking out is unbelief. They may tell the homeless that they're unworthy, or that their need is an inconvenience. They may tell youths that their questions are rebellious, that faith demands no struggle. They may tell the elderly that they must fade quietly, not take up space for influence.

They may tell the divorced that their faith is compromised, that ministry doors are closed. They may tell the sexually abused that their sin binds them eternally, that they must live ashamed. They may tell the lame that their brokenness disqualifies them from service. Such lies serve darkness, not God. They preserve a facade, while the truth is hidden. The Church is judged not by how many attend but by how faithfully she reflects Christ's character. God will not suffer false worship indefinitely: "My house shall be called a house of prayer, but you make it a den of thieves" (Matthew 21:13).

The cleansing of the temple was one of Jesus' bold acts—He overturned tables, drove out merchants, and rebuked those who turned a sacred space into a marketplace of deceit. In that act, He signified that worship is not commerce, and that God's House is not a shield for profit, power, or hypocrisy. Those who hide evil behind pious language will be exposed. Every hidden motive, every unconfessed deception, will come to light (1 Corinthians 4:5). The Church's integrity depends not on image but on truth. Those who lead must answer for how they treated the weak, how they silenced victims, and how they warped the gospel for ego or gain. The victims must know: God is their advocate, their vindicator, and He will not forget.

From Victim to Victor: A Roadmap for Comeback

Repentance and Confession. The first step is honesty before God and before trusted brothers and sisters. Hidden sin must be named—both in leaders and in individual hearts. (1 John 1:9) *Grief and Lament.* The pain, anger, and betrayal must be brought before God. He hears the broken cry (Psalm 34:18). *Root Removal.* Any bitterness, revenge, or false belief must be uprooted. (Hebrews 12:15) *Renunciation of Lies.* Replace the lies spoken over you with God's truth. Declare: "I am loved. I am worthy. I have a voice. I will not be silenced."

Reeducation in Scripture. Let the Word of God renew your mind (Romans 12:2). Study how God deals with the broken, the marginalized, the oppressed. *Prayer and Fasting.* Cry out for breakthrough, wisdom, deliverance, and the infilling of the Spirit. *Find a faithful community.*

Seek those who will hear, validate, and believe you—not hide you or silence you. *Step into service from the margins.* Use your brokenness as a gateway to minister to others in pain. (2 Corinthians 1:4)

Speak Truth in Love. When God provides opportunity, confront falsehood—but do it in humility and for restoration. *Watch for divine vindication.* God fights for the weak (Psalm 68:5), and He will bring correction in His time. *Maintain integrity always.* Let your life match your confession. Don't adopt the tactics of the oppressors. *Trust God's timing.* Even when the Church seems slow to awaken, God's justice is perfect. *Persevere under opposition.* The comeback journey invites spiritual warfare—stand firm in faith (Ephesians 6:10-18).

Keep focus on Christ's return. Do not lose heart; your suffering will work in you patience, character, hope (Romans 5:3–5). *Live in expectancy.* Every day is an opportunity to proclaim mercy, justice, and faithfulness. *Raise others.* Bring others along who have been wounded, that together the body of Christ may heal. *Refuse to be silenced.* Where God gives a voice, speak— even if the majority resist. *Love your enemies.* Pray for those who hurt you and seek their repentance. This shatters the power of the lie.

Hold leaders accountable. Within biblical boundaries, call for transparency, justice, and restitution. *Teach the next generation.* Impart to youth the courage to discern truth, resist hypocrisy, and walk in holiness. *Pray for the institutional Church.* Intercede that leaders be awakened, repent, and be reformed. *Align with God's mission.* Let your comeback be part of God's greater coalition of healing and revival.

Final Warnings, Encouragements, and a Charge

Do not be deceived: the liar prowls. The church is not immune to the tactics of darkness (1 Peter 5:8). But greater is He who is in you than he who is in the world (1 John 4:4). The faithful remnant will be tested, purified, tried by fire—but will emerge refined (Malachi 3:3). Let no one steal your identity or your calling. You were redeemed, beloved, chosen (Ephesians 1).

Do not wait for perfect surroundings—worship God in spirit and in truth now (John 4:24). The five foolish virgins were shut out not because they lacked oil, but because they were unprepared (Matthew 25:1–13). Do not be unprepared. Keep your lamp trimmed, your heart vigilant, your walk upright, your hope fixed on Christ. When your faith is tried, declare: "Even if all abandon me, I will remain faithful. If I must suffer, I will suffer for Christ. Let truth prevail."

Chapter 36– When the Church Becomes a Crime Scene- God's Verdict on Hidden Evil and the Call to Repentance.

The Trumpet of Judgment Sounds

The Spirit of the Lord is sounding an alarm across the earth, and it echoes first through the halls of the church. The hour of reckoning has arrived, and Heaven's courtroom is in session. The Judge of all the earth is calling His people to account. No longer will hypocrisy hide behind polished sermons or empty rituals. No longer will charisma conceal corruption. The trumpet of truth is blasting through sanctuaries and across nations, announcing, *"Judgment must begin at the house of God"* (1 Peter 4:17). This is not a call of condemnation—it is a call of cleansing. God's fire is not coming to destroy His Bride but to purify her.

The light of divine truth is exposing what men have tried to bury beneath robes of religion and masks of ministry. The Spirit is uncovering what has been whispered in green rooms and hidden behind stained glass. The time of false comfort has ended; God is dismantling the platforms built on pride, deception, and greed. For too long, the voice of the hurting has been ignored, the abused silenced, the poor neglected, the broken dismissed. But Heaven has been listening. The cry of the afflicted has reached the throne of God, and He has declared, *"Enough!"*

Jesus Christ, the righteous Judge, stands at the door of His own house. His eyes blaze with holy fire, and His voice still echoes from Matthew 21:13: *"My Father's house shall be called a house of prayer, but you have made it a den of thieves."* That cry was not only for the temple in Jerusalem; it is a word for the Church today. Every sanctuary that has become a marketplace of manipulation will be overturned. Every pulpit used to oppress rather than liberate will be silenced. Every system built on deceit rather than devotion will crumble beneath the weight of His truth.

The Church has become a crime scene—where love has been murdered by pride, where compassion lies bleeding beneath the pews, and where the innocent have been crucified by religious politics. The evidence is undeniable. The blood of the betrayed cries from the altars, the tears of the wounded stain the carpets, and the silence of the leaders resounds louder than their sermons. But God is not mocked. What has been done in His name without His heart will be judged by His hand.

Yet even now, before the final gavel falls, mercy stands in the doorway. Grace pleads with outstretched hands, calling the Church to repentance. The Spirit of God is not delighting in destruction but inviting restoration. If the Church will fall to her knees and confess her hidden sins, revival will replace ruin. The same fire that exposes also refines. The same light that judges also heals. There is still time—time to repent, to return, to rebuild on righteousness and truth before it is too late.

Exposing the Lie of False Covering

The modern Church has misused one of its most sacred truths: "Touch not My anointed, and do My prophets no harm" (1 Chronicles 16:22). These words were never meant to shield corruption. Yet, how many have used them as armor against accountability? The anointing was given for service, not for self-preservation. When the anointed vessel becomes corrupted and refuses correction, the Spirit of God lifts His covering and allows exposure for the sake of truth. God does not protect what He did not ordain.

There are pulpits today where leaders preach fire but live in filth. They speak in tongues but refuse repentance. They prophesy healing while harboring unconfessed sin. The same lips that declare blessing have cursed the broken. But the Lord is not blind. The One who walks among the lampstands (Revelation 2:1) is removing those who no longer burn with truth. He is silencing voices that have misrepresented His name and bringing humility to those who thought they could never fall.

The false shepherds tell the abused to stay quiet "for the sake of the ministry." They tell the wounded to "forgive and move on" while refusing to repent or seek justice. But the Lord says, *"Woe to the shepherds who destroy and scatter the sheep of My pasture!"* (Jeremiah 23:1). God never called leaders to protect institutions at the expense of His people. He called them to guard His flock with compassion and integrity. When shepherds devour instead of defend, Heaven intervenes.

Many have hidden sin beneath the garments of success. They speak of growth, numbers, and prosperity, yet behind closed doors lies a trail of manipulation, sexual immorality, and abuse of power. They have turned the sacred into a spectacle and made merchandise of the Gospel (2 Peter 2:3). But God declares, *"I am against the prophets who use their own tongues and yet declare, 'The Lord says'"* (Jeremiah 23:31). The Holy Spirit is withdrawing His endorsement from platforms that elevate men above the cross.

The day of false peace is over. God is tearing down every counterfeit covering. The anointing will no longer be confused with charisma. The Spirit will no longer tolerate those who speak for Him but do not walk with Him. The fear of the Lord is returning to His house. The trembling of the Spirit will once again be felt in the sanctuary. It is not revival until repentance returns to the pulpit.

Jesus Confronts the Religious Frauds

In His earthly ministry, Jesus was never intimidated by religious titles. He stood before priests, scribes, and rulers with unshakable authority. His words were not gentle toward hypocrisy. *"You brood of vipers,"* He declared, *"how can you, being evil, speak good things?"* (Matthew 12:34). His fire was not aimed at sinners but at those who claimed to represent God while betraying His character.

Jesus did not flatter the religious elite. He unmasked them. *"You are like whitewashed tombs— beautiful on the outside but full of dead men's bones and all uncleanness"* (Matthew 23:27). He saw through their polished robes and pious rituals. He discerned the pride behind their prayers and the greed beneath their giving. His rebuke was not cruelty—it was mercy, for truth is the only scalpel that can remove the cancer of deception.

When He declared, *"You devour widows' houses and for a pretense make long prayers,"* (Mark 12:40) He was addressing the exploitation that still plagues the modern Church. Even today, widows are manipulated through emotional appeals for money, and the poor are blamed for lacking faith. But Jesus has not changed. He will again overturn the tables of greed, casting out every spirit that turns worship into commerce and compassion into currency.

His cleansing of the temple was not an act of temper—it was an act of truth. When He drove out the merchants with a whip of cords (John 2:15), He was declaring war on religious exploitation. The whip of the Word is still in His hand. The temple of today is not made of stone but of souls, and He will cleanse it once again before His return. The Bride He comes for must be pure, not prosperous; humble, not haughty.

Christ is confronting His Church again, not to condemn but to call her back. His eyes are upon the pulpits that have grown cold. His Spirit is stirring the pews that have settled into comfort. He is whispering to the faithful remnant: "Do not be deceived by appearance. I am raising truth- tellers who fear no man and serve no agenda but Mine." The confrontation is not coming—it has begun.

Lies Told to the Wounded

There is a cruel deception whispered in sanctuaries and shouted from platforms— that pain is punishment, and suffering is proof of sin. The wounded are told they "must have done something wrong" to deserve their pain. But Jesus refuted that lie when His disciples asked about the blind man: *"Who sinned, this man or his parents?"* He answered, *"Neither... but that the works of God should be revealed in him"* (John 9:2–3). The Church must remember: the afflicted are not cursed; they are chosen vessels for God's glory.

The lie told to the abused is that silence is strength and exposure is betrayal. But God never called His children to protect predators. He called them to walk in the light. Ephesians 5:11 commands, *"Have no fellowship with the unfruitful works of darkness, but rather expose them."* When the Church covers sin instead of confessing it, it becomes an accomplice to evil. True strength is found in truth, not secrecy.

The unhoused are told that faith would have kept them from poverty, as if faith is a luxury for the privileged. Yet the Son of God Himself said, *"Foxes have holes, birds have nests, but the Son of Man has nowhere to lay His head"* (Matthew 8:20). Jesus was homeless by choice, that He might dwell among the broken. To despise the poor is to despise the image of Christ. God's judgment burns against those who claim to serve Him yet step over the Lazarus at their gate.

The youth are told they must "wait their turn" to serve, as though the Spirit of God has an age restriction. But the same God who called Samuel as a boy, who anointed David as a teenager, and who filled Jeremiah in his youth still moves through young vessels today. The modern Church often fears the fire of the next generation because it exposes the complacency of the current one. But Acts 2:17 declares, *"Your sons and daughters shall prophesy."* God is pouring new oil on young altars.

The elderly, the forgotten saints, are told that their season of usefulness is over.

411

But the Bible declares that those who are planted in the house of the Lord "shall still bear fruit in old age" (Psalm 92:14). The Church has become so intoxicated with youth culture that it has forgotten the wisdom of the elders. God is calling seasoned intercessors out of silence. The gray-haired warriors are not retired; they are refired.

The divorced are told they are disqualified from God's favor, that their failure is final. But Scripture reveals a Savior who met a divorced woman at the well and turned her into a revivalist (John 4:39). Jesus did not condemn her; He commissioned her. The Church must stop crucifying people Jesus has already forgiven. God does not discard the broken; He rebuilds them into testimonies of grace.

The molested are told to "forgive and forget," as if forgiveness erases trauma. But Jesus never asked anyone to forget; He calls them to heal. He stood with the violated, the shamed, the outcast. His first public sermon proclaimed liberty to the captives and healing for the brokenhearted (Luke 4:18). The Church's failure to protect the innocent is a stench before God's throne. Judgment is coming upon those who have used His name to prey on His lambs.

The lame, physically, emotionally, and spiritually crippled, are often made spectacles of pity rather than recipients of power. But in John 5, Jesus did not pity the lame man at Bethesda; He healed him. The Lord is again asking, *"Do you want to be made whole?"* It is not the duty of the Church to maintain dependency but to restore dignity. When the powerless are empowered, God's kingdom is revealed.

These lies have chained multitudes in fear and shame. Yet Jesus, the Truth, still walks among the wounded, declaring, *"You shall know the truth, and the truth shall make you free"* (John 8:32). Every victim of deceit, every soul bruised by hypocrisy, is being called to rise. The very place where you were hurt will become the platform of your healing. The stone that the builders rejected is becoming the cornerstone of God's restoration.

Heaven is turning the tables. The last shall be first. Those dismissed by religion will be elevated by revelation. The rejected are becoming the redeemed. This is the hour of divine reversal. For every lie told by man, God is releasing a word of truth. For every heart broken by deception, He is pouring new oil of deliverance. The Spirit of the Lord is rebuilding the ruins of His house one healed soul at a time.

The courtroom of Heaven is not a metaphor—it is reality. The Judge is seated, the witnesses are called, and the evidence is being presented. Angels record every hidden word, every unrepentant act, every secret conversation meant to deceive the flock of God. The gavel of truth is about to fall, and no one can appeal His verdict. *"For we must all appear before the judgment seat of Christ"* (2 Corinthians 5:10).

The Prosecutor is not Satan—he is already condemned. It is the Holy Spirit who convicts, who reveals, who pleads with hearts to repent before it is too late. The Spirit is not accusing of destroying but exposing deliveries. His voice is clear: "Return to Me, O backsliding church, for I am married to you" (Jeremiah 3:14). Mercy still stands, but grace has an expiration date for the unrepentant.

In this divine courtroom, victims are not forgotten. God Himself becomes their Advocate. *"He executes justice for the oppressed and gives food to the hungry"* (Psalm 146:7). The Lord rises from His throne to defend those who have been silenced. The abused, the abandoned, and the ashamed will see vindication in their lifetime. God's justice does not sleep.

The witnesses of truth are rising—prophets, intercessors, and reformers who refuse to bow to religious corruption. They are the John the Baptists of this generation, crying out in the wilderness, "Prepare the way of the Lord!" They are not motivated by fame but by fire. Their loyalty is not to denominations but to divine destiny. They will not flatter leaders—they will confront them.

The verdict over the hypocritical Church is being written in the Spirit: "Guilty of misrepresentation. Guilty of exploitation. Guilty of pride. Guilty of neglecting the least of these." Yet even now, God's mercy whispers from the cross, *"Father, forgive them, for they know not what they do."* But forgiveness requires confession. Without repentance, guilt remains.

The religious elite mocked Jesus as He hung between thieves, not realizing that they were the true robbers of God's glory. Today's leaders who sell salvation for profit and exchange truth for comfort are no different. But the same Jesus who overturned tables is coming again—not with a whip of cords but with a sword of justice. The Word that once cleansed the temple will now cleanse the nations.

Politicians, too, stand in this courtroom. Those who have invoked the name of God for power yet ignored His commands for justice will face His judgment. God is not Republican or Democrat; He is holy. *"Righteousness exalts a nation, but sin is a reproach to any people"* (Proverbs 14:34). The throne of Heaven is higher than every earthly office, and every ruler will bow before the King of kings.

The Church is on trial, but so is every individual believer. The question is not only "What did the leaders do?" but "What did we tolerate?" Silence in the face of sin is consent. The sin of omission is as deadly as the sin of commission. We must each ask ourselves: Did we defend the truth or protect the system? Did we serve God or serve reputation?

Yet for those who repent, there is hope beyond the judgment. The same courtroom where guilt was proven is the same place where grace is offered. The blood of Jesus still cries louder than the blood of the victims. It still speaks of mercy, of redemption, of new beginnings. God is not destroying His Church; He is detoxifying it. The shaking is mercy in motion.

Therefore, let every heart be still before Him. The Spirit calls: "Come out of hiding. Lay down the masks. Return to your first love." The trial is not meant to destroy but to deliver. The exposure is not humiliation; it is healing. Before the Bridegroom returns, the Bride must be pure. Before the trumpet sounds, repentance must resound. This is not just a warning; it is an invitation.

The Victims Rise Again — From Pain to Purpose

The Spirit of God is calling forth a generation of survivors—men and women who have walked through betrayal, rejection, abuse, and deception, yet still carry a flame that cannot be extinguished. What the enemy meant for evil, God is turning for good (Genesis 50:20). Those once silenced by fear will now become voices of truth. Their scars will testify louder than sermons, and their pain will become a prophetic purpose.

The Lord is saying to the wounded: "You are not forgotten. You are not forsaken. I saw every tear, every night you cried alone. I recorded your pain, not as a mark of shame but as evidence of your calling." The brokenhearted are not on the sidelines of God's plan—they are the very foundation stones of His next revival. The remnant rising now will not be built on celebrity, but on sincerity.

The abused who were told to "stay silent" are now becoming God's loudest preachers. Their testimonies will dismantle religious façades and restore integrity to the house of God. Every secret that once brought shame will now birth freedom. Revelation 12:11 declares, *"They overcame him by the blood of the Lamb and by the word of their testimony."* What once silenced you will now become your song of deliverance.

The unhoused and rejected are being positioned by Heaven as reformers of compassion. They have seen the church from the outside; now God is calling them to rebuild it from within. Their empathy will become the new architecture of mercy. Isaiah 58:7–8 resounds: *"Is it not to share your bread with the hungry... then your light shall break forth like the morning."* Out of the alleys and shelters, prophets of restoration are emerging.

The youth who were dismissed will rise as flames of revival. They will not wait for permission from institutions that have grown cold. They will cry out like Jeremiah, *"His word was in my heart like a burning fire shut up in my bones"* (Jeremiah 20:9). These young warriors will tear down idols of popularity and restore the altar of prayer. They will carry unfiltered faith, and their worship will shake nations.

The elderly who were overlooked are awakening again to their assignment. Like Anna in the temple (Luke 2:36-38), they will prophesy over the next generation. Their prayers will birth movements their eyes may never see. The gray hair that was dismissed will become the crown of wisdom, guiding the youth. The revival of this age will not be a youth movement alone—it will be a multi-generational awakening.

The divorced who were shamed will become preachers of restoration. Having tasted both failure and forgiveness, they will extend mercy to those drowning in guilt. Their message will echo the heart of Christ: *"Neither do I condemn thee; go and sin no more"* (John 8:11). The Church has often thrown stones, but God is placing in these restored hearts the balm of grace. They will lead multitudes back to the cross through compassion, not condemnation.

Those who were molested, silenced, and scarred are being healed by the gentle hand of the Savior. He is restoring what religion crushed. The same Jesus who defended the woman caught in adultery still stands between the victim and the accuser. He is saying again, "Let the one without sin cast the first stone." Their pain will no longer define them—it will refine them. From their wounds, healing rivers will flow.

The lame and disabled are rising as living testimonies of endurance and faith. God's glory shines brightest through broken vessels. Paul's thorn was not his limitation—it was his invitation to deeper grace. *"My grace is sufficient for you, for My strength is made perfect in weakness"* (2 Corinthians 12:9). Those who were told they were too weak will now demonstrate divine strength.

Every category of the forgotten—the orphan, the widow, the rejected, the misunderstood—is being drawn to the heart of Christ. They are the new foundation of His end-time Church. The Spirit is saying, "Come out from among the proud and the polished; I am building a Church that bleeds, a people that weeps, a Bride that loves." The next great move of God will not come from stages but from secret places of intercession.

The Fire of Refinement

Before resurrection comes, there must be crucifixion. Before glory, there must be purification. The fire that is sweeping through the Church is not to destroy, but to refine. Malachi 3:3 declares, *"He will sit as a refiner and purifier of silver; He will purify the sons of Levi."* The refining fire of God is exposing mixture—ministries with hidden agendas, leaders without integrity, and worship without surrender.

The Lord is not impressed by lights, conferences, or crowds. He is searching for contrite hearts. Isaiah 66:2 says, *"This is the one I esteem: he who is humble and contrite in spirit, and trembles at My word."* The trembling is returning. Reverence is coming back. God is dismantling performance-based Christianity and reestablishing holiness as the measure of true ministry.

The Spirit is whispering to pastors and leaders: "Repent before I remove your lampstand." This is the warning Jesus gave to Ephesus in Revelation 2:5. Titles will not protect anyone from accountability. God is exposing false humility and demanding authentic repentance. Those who bow low now will rise again in grace; those who resist correction will fall beneath the weight of their pride.

The refining fire will reach every level—pastors, prophets, politicians, and pew-sitters alike. The shaking will be global. Nations will see the hypocrisy of their idols, and the Church will no longer be able to hide behind cultural respectability. The consuming fire of God is not coming to destroy the Church—it is coming to restore her first love.

In this refining, every idol is being shattered. Ministries built on manipulation will collapse. Relationships founded on lust will dissolve. Platforms that glorify man will vanish like smoke. Only what is rooted in righteousness will remain. Hebrews 12:27 says, *"The removing of those things that can be shaken—so that what cannot be shaken may remain."* God is burning away what cannot endure eternity.

The faithful remnant, those who have not bowed to corruption, will shine brighter in this hour. Their humility will become their authority. Their secret place will become their strength. They will be carriers of revival that cannot be controlled by denominations or silenced by fear. God is raising voices that owe nothing to men and everything to the cross.

The Spirit of the Lord is saying, "Do not fear the exposure; fear disobedience." The shaking is mercy disguised as judgment. God would rather embarrass you now than lose you forever. His discipline is not cruel; it is covenant love. *"For whom the Lord loves He corrects, even as a father the son in whom he delights"* (Proverbs 3:12). Correction today prevents condemnation tomorrow.

The refining process will hurt. It will cost friendships, platforms, and comfort. But those who endure the fire will emerge as pure gold. Job declared, *"When He has tried me, I shall come forth as gold"* (Job 23:10). The Lord is not destroying His servants—He is distilling them. Only through fire can purity emerge.

This is not the end of the Church—it is the end of counterfeit Christianity. The true Bride of Christ is being separated from the harlot of hypocrisy. Those who worship in spirit and truth (John 4:24) are being sealed for this end-time harvest. The division we see is not political—it is prophetic. God is distinguishing those who truly love Him from those who merely use His name.

The victims who rise from the ashes will lead the purified Church into revival. Their humility will be their power. Their compassion will be their platform. Their worship will be their weapon. Like the five wise virgins, they will keep their lamps filled with oil, prepared for the Bridegroom's return. And when He comes, they will be found ready—pure, awake, and faithful.

Heaven is still extending mercy, but mercy has a timeline. The Spirit cries out, "Repent, for the Kingdom of Heaven is at hand!" (Matthew 4:17). The Church stands at a crossroads—between revival and removal, between purification and perishing. God's patience is not weakness; it is opportunity. He delays His judgment so that more may turn and live, yet the day is fast approaching when delay will end and destiny will speak.

This is not a time for emotional religion but for genuine repentance. Repentance is not simply saying "I'm sorry"; it is changing direction. It is the decision to return to holiness, to abandon compromise, and to rebuild altars of integrity. The Lord says, "Return to Me with all your heart, with fasting and weeping and mourning" (Joel 2:12). The tears of repentance are the first drops of rain.

God is calling His leaders to bow low before the people they have wounded. Public sin demands public humility. When Zacchaeus encountered Christ, he didn't hide his transformation—he repented openly and restored what he had taken (Luke 19:8). That is the mark of true conversion: restitution follows repentance. The Church will only be healed when its leaders stop hiding behind titles and start kneeling in truth.

Spirit is searching for pulpits, not to condemn but to cleanse. The Lord is looking for pastors who weep more than they perform, who love more than they lecture. He is seeking shepherds after His own heart (Jeremiah 3:15), not entertainers, not empire builders, but broken vessels who know the cost of carrying His glory. The revival that's coming will be led by those who have been crushed by His presence.

God is also visiting the pews. He is confronting spectators who have grown comfortable with passivity. The days of sitting in church without being the Church are over. Every believer is being summoned to holiness, to prayer, to accountability. The Spirit declares, "Be holy, for I am holy" (1 Peter 1:16). Holiness is not outdated—it is the fragrance of heaven.

There will be no spectators in this next move of God. Every son and daughter will be activated. Every heart will burn again for souls. The gifts that have lain dormant will come alive as the Spirit breathes upon His people. This awakening will not be led by programs but by presence. The outpouring of the Holy Spirit will fall not on stages but on altars of brokenness.

Those who were once wounded will now carry healing oil. They will move in compassion rather than criticism. They will preach not from pride but from pain redeemed by grace. Their testimonies will pierce through religious pretense and awaken repentance in the hardest hearts. This new army of truth-tellers will shake nations—not with anger, but with anointing.

The Church that emerges from this trial will not look like the one that entered it. It will be smaller in number but stronger in spirit. It will be stripped of performance but filled with power. It will not chase fame; it will carry fire. The spotlight will no longer be on personalities but on purity. The Bride of Christ will once again be known for her holiness, humility, and love.

The Holy Spirit is restoring the fear of the Lord. This fear is not terror—it is reverent awe. It is the trembling awareness that God sees all, knows all, and judges righteously. The fear of the Lord is the beginning of wisdom (Proverbs 9:10). Without it, sermons are empty and worship is noise. But when holy fear returns, glory follows.

God's house will once again become a house of prayer. The worship that rises will not be entertainment—it will be intercession. Tears will replace applause. Repentance will replace routine. The Spirit is cleansing the temple, flipping the tables of greed and apathy. And from the ashes, true worship will rise like incense before His throne.

The Bride Awakened

The Bride of Christ is awakening. She has been asleep, intoxicated by comfort, seduced by culture, and distracted by division. But now the midnight cry is sounding: *"Behold, the Bridegroom is coming; go out to meet Him!"* (Matthew 25:6). The wise are trimming their lamps; the foolish still sleep. The oil of intimacy will separate the prepared from the pretenders.

The oil represents devotion, not performance. It is the secret prayer life, the worship in the wilderness, the obedience in obscurity. The five wise virgins carried extra oil because they valued His presence above all else. This is what the Church must recover—private devotion that fuels public transformation. Without oil, there is only burnout; with oil, there is unquenchable flame.

The Bride's garments are being washed in the blood of the Lamb (Revelation 7:14). God is removing the stains of compromise and self-righteousness. The Church will no longer be known for scandal but for sanctity. Her beauty will not come from outward adornment but from inward purity. She will walk in love, radiate light, and carry the fragrance of Christ wherever she goes.

The call to holiness is not legalism; it is love. It is the desire to look like the One we adore. Holiness is not a burden; it is a blessing. When the Bride loves the Groom, she gladly separates from what displeases Him. The world will see her glow, not because of makeup or marketing, but because the glory of God rests upon her.

In this final hour, the Holy Spirit unites true believers across denominational lines. This remnant Church will not be divided by doctrine but bound by devotion. They will walk in the spirit of Acts 2, sharing, praying, and breaking bread together with gladness and sincerity of heart. The world will know them not by their statements but by their love.

The nations are groaning for the manifestation of this purified Church (Romans 8:19). Creation itself waits for the sons and daughters of God to rise. Political systems are failing, economies are shaking, and hearts are fainting for fear. Yet in the midst of chaos, the radiant Bride will stand unshaken, declaring, "Jesus is Lord!" Her stability will be the anchor of a trembling world.

This end-time Church will carry both power and purity. Miracles will return, but so will the fear of the Lord. Deliverance will flow, but so will discernment. Prophecy will increase, but it will exalt Christ, not man. The days of mixture are ending. God is releasing a double portion of truth and grace upon His purified people.

The Spirit and the Bride now cry out together, *"Come, Lord Jesus!"* (Revelation 22:17). This is the ultimate posture of revival—not ambition, but anticipation. The purified Church is not seeking a platform but a Person. Her longing is not for fame but for His face. Every trial, every tear, every shaking has prepared her for this moment, the return of the King.

And when He comes, He will not look for perfect performance but for pure hearts. He will not ask how many followers you had, but whether you followed Him.

He will not measure success by buildings but by obedience. The question will not be "Did they know your name?" but "Did you know Mine?" Only those who truly loved Him will enter in.

Therefore, beloved, hear the call of the Spirit: Repent, return, and prepare. Lay aside every weight, forgive every wound, and keep your lamp burning. The Church is being purified for her final hour. The Judge is standing at the door, but so is the Bridegroom. The fire that exposes will also empower. The Church on trial will soon become the Church triumphant. Let every heart cry out with urgency and hope: *"Even so, come, Lord Jesus."*

Chapter 37: A Glorious Church, Ready for His Return

Revelation 19:7–9 celebrates the Church as the Bride of Christ, prepared and adorned for His return. God desires a holy, faithful, and vibrant Church that reflects His glory and truth in the world.

The church is called to be glorious because she bears the image of Christ. Just as the Bridegroom is radiant with holiness, so the bride is meant to reflect His glory. Scripture reminds us that Christ loved the church and gave Himself for her, sanctifying her and cleansing her with the washing of water by the Word (Ephesians 5:25-26). A glorious church is not a product of human effort but a creation of divine love and sanctification.

Readiness is central to the church's glory. Jesus repeatedly urged vigilance, warning the disciples to watch because no one knows the hour of His return (Matthew 24:42). A ready church demonstrates consistent obedience, persistent prayer, and active faith. Readiness is both a posture of the heart and a lifestyle that aligns every member with God's will. C. S. Lewis, in *Mere Christianity*, underscores that readiness for Christ's return is not passive but requires daily spiritual growth, obedience, and intentional pursuit of holiness.

A glorious church is united. Internal division diminishes the radiance of God's presence. Christ prayed that His followers would be one as He and the Father are one (John 17:21). Unity does not mean uniformity but a harmonious submission to God's Word and Spirit. A church divided by strife or factions cannot shine brightly, for discord shadows holiness.

Holiness undergoes readiness. A glorious church is spotless, consecrated, and set apart. It refuses compromise, avoids hidden sin, and pursues obedience in every sphere of life. When holiness reigns, the church stands ready, not merely for spiritual duties but for the climactic moment of Christ's appearing. A. W. Tozer, in *The Pursuit of God*, emphasizes that a Church fully prepared for Christ's return actively seeks God's presence, cultivates intimacy with Him, and allows His Spirit to guide all aspects of life and ministry.

Leonard Ravenhill, in *Why Revival Tarries*, stresses that revival begins when the Church awakens to God's standards, rejects compromise, and embraces total surrender, thereby becoming an instrument of transformation in society. Prayer is essential for a church to be ready. The early church devoted itself to prayer, awaiting the Spirit's empowerment and guidance (Acts 1:14). A glorious church maintains communion with God, seeking His wisdom and interceding for the world. Prayer keeps the church aligned with God's agenda and strengthens its preparedness for His return.

Worship elevates the church's glory. When worship is sincere, it becomes a reflection of heaven itself. Psalm 22:3 says God inhabits the praises of His people. A glorious church worships in spirit and truth, exalting God in every service, action, and moment of daily life. Worship becomes both preparation and a declaration of readiness.

A glorious church reflects God's character. Just as Christ embodies love, humility, and obedience, the church should mirror these attributes. The presence of God transforms believers, producing fruit such as patience, kindness, gentleness, and faithfulness. The radiance of a glorious church reflects Christ's nature shining through His people. A glorious Church is marked by love, faithfulness, service, and humility. Its members understand the urgency of the times and align their hearts, ministries, and communities with God's eternal purposes.

A church ready for Christ's return is vigilant against deception. The Scriptures warn of false prophets, false Christs, and spiritual wolves in sheep's clothing (Matthew 24:24). A glorious church discerns truth from error, anchored in the Word, filled with the Spirit, and obedient to Christ. It does not waver with every new doctrine or cultural trend.

The pursuit of godly leadership is critical. Leaders shape the church's readiness and influence its glory. Elders, pastors, and ministers must model righteousness, integrity, and humility, shepherding the flock in holiness. A church guided by faithful leaders grows stronger, unified, and prepared for Christ's coming.

The readiness of the church is visible in her compassion and service. Glory is not measured by accolades but by faithful acts of love, mercy, and justice. Serving the poor, comforting the afflicted, and upholding the oppressed are hallmarks of a church reflecting God's kingdom. This active righteousness makes her radiant before God and man. Lewis highlights that Christ will return to a Church that is spiritually prepared, not necessarily perfect, but actively seeking God's righteousness and walking in obedience to His Word.

Spiritual discipline sustains readiness. Fasting, prayer, Bible study, and accountability protect the church from compromise. Just as an athlete trains daily for a race, the church practices spiritual discipline to maintain its posture of readiness. Discipline strengthens faith, sharpens discernment, and deepens intimacy with Christ.

The glorious church is resilient in trials. Persecution, internal conflict, and societal pressures test the church's resolve. Yet trials refine faith, remove impurities, and strengthen obedience. A church that endures tribulation in faith demonstrates readiness for the ultimate confrontation with evil at Christ's return.

Evangelism is a sign of readiness. The church cannot be prepared for the Bridegroom while neglecting the lost. Sharing the gospel, discipling new believers, and advancing God's kingdom signal a church actively participating in His mission. Readiness is inseparable from faithfulness to Christ's Great Commission (Matthew 28:19-20).

Holiness and grace together define a glorious church. Holiness ensures purity, while grace reflects God's love to sinners. A church that balances both avoids legalism on one hand and compromise on the other. This balance prepares the bride to be radiant, compassionate, and aligned with Christ's heart.

Transparency and accountability reinforce readiness. When members confess sin, restore relationships, and submit to spiritual guidance, the church remains undefiled. Concealment of sin diminishes holiness and obscures glory. A glorious church fosters honesty, humility, and mutual restoration.

The church's corporate identity matters. While individual holiness is vital, the bride as a whole must reflect unity, purity, and obedience. One tarnished segment can overshadow the radiance of the entire body. Collective readiness amplifies glory and prepares the church to meet the Lord with confidence and joy.

The church must anticipate Christ's return with expectancy, not fear. A glorious church looks forward to His appearance with excitement and longing. This expectation fuels holy living, fervent prayer, and faithful service. Anticipation shapes priorities, aligning hearts and actions with eternal realities.

The glory of the church also impacts the world. A radiant, prepared church acts as a beacon, demonstrating the transforming power of God. Its holiness exposes sin, its love invites repentance, and its faith inspires others to seek Christ. The world recognizes the church's readiness not by words alone but by visible evidence of grace and righteousness.

The bride's adornment is spiritual. Fine linen, clean and white, symbolizes righteousness (Revelation 19:8). The church's beauty does not come from external appearances or material abundance but from a heart devoted to God. Spiritual adornment reflects obedience, humility, and the fruit of the Spirit.

Readiness requires a continual response to God's leading. The church must act promptly on convictions from the Spirit, obeying God's commands without delay. Hesitation, apathy, or disobedience diminishes glory and delays preparation. A glorious church walks in faithful immediacy to the Lord's direction.

Discipleship strengthens readiness. Each believer's growth contributes to the church's collective maturity. Teaching, mentoring, and guiding others in righteousness ensures the bride develops fully, equipped to reflect Christ's character in every situation. A church that neglects discipleship risks being spiritually immature and unprepared.

The glorious church embraces humility. Pride tarnishes beauty and hinders readiness. Christ washed the feet of His disciples to demonstrate servant leadership (John 13:4–5). Likewise, the church must embrace humility, serve selflessly, and prioritize God's will above personal ambitions or accolades.

Faithfulness in small matters cultivates readiness. Daily obedience, integrity in work, honesty in speech, and kindness in relationships create a lifestyle of readiness. The Lord observes faithfulness in both grand and ordinary tasks. A glorious church honors Him in every detail, preparing the bride for her eternal union.

Corporate worship is a training ground for readiness. Gatherings of praise, teaching, and prayer align hearts with God, reinforce unity, and empower the body for mission. Worship transforms individual believers and cultivates the collective glory of the church, equipping her for Christ's coming.

The bride's readiness is also expressed in perseverance. Seasons of waiting and testing reveal faith that endures. The parable of the ten virgins (Matthew 25:1–13) highlights the importance of endurance. Those who are prepared and vigilant enter the wedding feast, while the unready miss the blessing.

Spiritual vigilance preserves readiness. The church must be alert to temptation, deception, and complacency. Prayer, fasting, and Word study sharpen spiritual discernment. A vigilant bride recognizes the schemes of the enemy and resists defilement that could mar her glory. Ravenhill reminds believers that readiness for Christ's return requires both individual and corporate commitment. Leaders must model faithfulness, and congregations must cultivate discernment, holiness, and spiritual vigilance.

The church's readiness involves stewardship. God entrusts resources, talents, and opportunities to His people. Faithful stewardship demonstrates obedience, accountability, and maturity. The glorious bride manages well what has been given, ensuring her life is fruitful and her testimony unsullied. Tozer observes that the Church's glory is not in buildings, programs, or numbers but in its purity, devotion, and faithfulness to God's calling. True preparation involves transformation from the inside out.

Evangelical courage marks readiness. A prepared church speaks boldly for Christ, confronts injustice, and proclaims truth, even in hostile environments. Fearlessness in mission reflects confidence in God and signals a bride ready for her Groom.

The church's readiness is visible in relational holiness. Forgiveness, reconciliation, and love for one another preserve unity and prevent blemishes from forming. A glorious church models Christlike relationships, showing the world what His kingdom looks like in practice. A glorious Church anticipates Christ's return with hope, not fear. It engages in evangelism, discipleship, and social transformation, demonstrating God's love and justice while awaiting His ultimate kingdom.

Readiness requires discernment. A glorious church distinguishes truth from falsehood, righteousness from compromise, and wisdom from folly. Discernment enables the bride to remain undefined by doctrinal error, worldly influence, or internal deception.

Spiritual joy strengthens readiness. Joy is not superficial happiness but the deep contentment and confidence that Christ is sovereign. Joy empowers perseverance, fuels worship, and reinforces a positive witness to the world. The bride's radiant joy enhances her glory.

Faith unites the church in readiness. Believers who trust God in trials, decisions, and uncertainties demonstrate confidence in His promises. Faith creates a collective posture of expectation, enabling the bride to stand firm and glorious until Christ's return.

Obedience maintains readiness. Holiness, prayer, and worship are meaningless without action. A glorious church obeys God's commands, serves the needy, and actively pursues righteousness. Obedience is the visible expression of readiness, confirming the church's identity as the Bride of Christ.

The readiness of the church is cultivated through continuous sanctification. Each believer's submission to the Spirit removes spots, wrinkles, and blemishes. Sanctification is both individual and corporate, producing a radiant body prepared to meet the Lord.

Evangelical zeal enhances readiness. A church passionately committed to fulfilling the Great Commission embodies readiness. Sharing the gospel, mentoring new believers, and confronting darkness with light ensure that the bride is not only beautiful but active in her calling.

Perseverance through persecution preserves readiness. Tribulations test faith, refine character, and purify motives. The glorious church remains steadfast under pressure, demonstrating that her beauty and strength are rooted in Christ, not circumstances.

Gratitude sustains readiness. Recognizing God's blessings, provision, and faithfulness fosters humility, joy, and contentment. Gratitude prevents pride, jealousy, and discontent—blemishes that could mar the bride's glory.

Community accountability fortifies readiness. Believers encourage, correct, and restore one another, ensuring the body remains holy, united, and prepared. Accountability keeps the bride vigilant and obedient, preventing sin from spreading unchecked.

Anticipation of Christ's return motivates readiness. A church focused on the coming Bridegroom prioritizes eternal matters over temporal distractions. She invests in souls, pursues holiness, and nurtures love, knowing the reward is union with Christ. Revelation 19:7-9, Lewis, Tozer, and Ravenhill collectively affirm that a Church prepared for Christ's return is vibrant, holy, and fully surrendered. By embracing holiness, revival, and faithful service, the Church reflects God's glory and fulfills His divine purposes in the world.

Ultimately, a glorious church ready for His return fulfills God's eternal purpose. She reflects Christ's holiness, love, and glory to the world. She is spotless, united, vigilant, and faithful. When the Lord comes, He will find His bride radiant, rejoicing, and fully prepared to enter the eternal wedding feast, a testimony to His redeeming power and the faithfulness of His people.

Chapter 37: The Kingdom of Heaven at War – When the Gates of Hell Rise Against the Righteous

The War Between Heaven and Hell

From the dawn of creation, there has been a war that the human eye cannot fully perceive — a war between light and darkness, truth and deception, Heaven and Hell. The Kingdom of Heaven stands firm in righteousness, while the gates of Hell rage in rebellion. Yet Jesus declared with divine authority: *"Upon this rock I will build My church, and the gates of hell shall not prevail against it"* (Matthew 16:18). That promise stands as Heaven's decree that even in an age of corruption, compromise, and chaos, the Kingdom will not fall.

This war is not fought with earthly weapons, for the Apostle Paul reminds us, *"We wrestle not against flesh and blood, but against principalities, powers, rulers of darkness, and spiritual wickedness in high places"* (Ephesians 6:12). The violence, injustice, and political confusion of our time are manifestations of a deeper conflict raging in the unseen realm. The nations rage, kingdoms fall, but behind them are the demonic thrones seeking to silence truth and enslave souls.

The world's stage has become a theater of rebellion, where truth is mocked, justice is bought, and righteousness is treated as weakness. The Kingdom of Heaven, however, moves quietly, powerfully, and righteously — through those who will not bow to the idols of fame, wealth, or fear.

Every time a believer chooses truth over compromise, Heaven advances. Every time a disciple of Christ forgives instead of retaliating, the Kingdom pushes back the darkness. Every time compassion triumphs over cruelty, Hell trembles. The war is spiritual, but its evidence is visible in our streets, our pulpits, and our politics.

The enemy's greatest deception is fear — fear that silences prophets, intimidates the righteous, and drives the faithful into retreat. Yet Jesus said, *"Do not be afraid of those who kill the body but cannot kill the soul"* (Matthew 10:28). Hell's intimidation cannot defeat Heaven's boldness.

The same demonic schemes that opposed Christ in the wilderness are alive today, tempting leaders to trade their faith for power and their convictions for popularity.

Yet those who know their God shall be strong and do exploits (Daniel 11:32). The faithful remnant will not be bought.

The battle lines are drawn not between denominations, nations, or ideologies, but between the truth of God's Word and the lies of the serpent that still whispers in political halls and church pulpits. It is a war for hearts, not headlines.

Jesus faced these same principalities during His ministry — religious leaders who weaponized Scripture, governments that crucified the innocent, and crowds that preferred Barabbas over the Truth. Yet through His obedience unto death, He stripped the powers of their authority (Colossians 2:15).

The war is fierce, but victory is sure. The Lamb of God has triumphed, and the blood of the saints continues to testify against every work of darkness. The gates of Hell can rage, but they cannot conquer the power of an obedient, Spirit-filled Church.

In these last days, the Kingdom of Heaven is marching — not with swords, but with truth, love, and holiness. The world trembles not because of political armies, but because of the rising of God's sons and daughters who refuse to be silenced. The war is not coming — it is already here.

The Spirit of Fear vs. The Spirit of Power

Fear has become the invisible weapon of our age. It sits in boardrooms, pews, and political offices — whispering that justice costs too much, that love is naïve, and that standing for truth is dangerous. Yet Scripture declares, *"God has not given us a spirit of fear, but of power, love, and a sound mind"* (2 Timothy 1:7).

The enemy thrives when believers are afraid to speak. He celebrates when pastors choose silence over truth, when compassion is traded for comfort, and when justice is dismissed as political rather than spiritual. But Heaven calls for a Church that will roar with holy courage.

Jesus faced fear when religious leaders plotted to destroy Him, when Herod sought His life, and when Judas betrayed Him for silver. Yet He walked through every threat with unwavering obedience, setting His face like flint toward the cross (Isaiah 50:7). He feared no man, for His allegiance was to the Father.

Fear enslaves the conscience and blinds the heart. It keeps believers chained to tradition when God is calling for transformation. It silences prophets who carry Heaven's burden. It makes cowards of men who were born to lead.

But when fear is confronted by faith, its power breaks. When the Spirit of God fills a man or woman, they can stand before kings, courts, and corrupted institutions without trembling. Moses stood before Pharaoh. Daniel stood before lions. Esther stood before a throne of death — and God stood with them all.

The modern Church must decide whether it will live by fear or by faith. The days of neutrality are over. The war between Heaven and Hell has exposed who truly belongs to Christ. Those who love Him will follow Him into the fire if necessary.

Political systems now manipulate fear to control nations. Media outlets sow panic to profit from despair. Even religious voices echo the same fear-driven rhetoric to keep people dependent rather than free. But Christ said, *"Peace I leave with you; My peace I give unto you"* (John 14:27).

The peace of Christ is not the absence of war, it is the presence of divine assurance in the midst of it. It is the courage to love when hatred is fashionable. It is faith to forgive when revenge seems easier. It is the light that exposes Hell's agenda.

The spirit of fear disguises itself as wisdom, caution, and common sense, but in truth, it is the gatekeeper of Hell. It keeps believers from advancing, pastors from preaching, and nations from repenting. Yet those filled with the Spirit of power will tear down those gates.

The Kingdom of Heaven is not for the fearful, but for the faithful. Every generation must choose how to fear or walk by faith. The sons and daughters of God who overcome fear become instruments of divine warfare not through hate, but through holy love.

The Church Under Siege

The Church was meant to be the refuge of righteousness, the voice of the voiceless, the defender of truth. Yet in this hour, many pulpits have become silent altars of compromise. The same spirit that bribed Judas with thirty pieces of silver whispers today to those who exchange integrity for influence and holiness for acceptance.

When Jesus entered the temple, He did not applaud their rituals—He overturned their tables. He exposed the merchants of manipulation who profited from the poor in God's name. That same righteous anger burns in Heaven today against leaders who accept bribes, exploit the vulnerable, and bless corruption while ignoring the cries of the oppressed.

The Church stands at a dangerous crossroad. One path leads to repentance and revival; the other to judgment and removal. As Jesus warned in Revelation, *"I know your works, that you are neither cold nor hot… because you are lukewarm, I will spew you out of my mouth"* (Revelation 3:15-16). Lukewarm faith is the devil's comfort zone.

The Church under siege often looks successful on the surface—crowded sanctuaries, bright lights, wealthy ministries—but Heaven sees beyond attendance numbers. God measures faithfulness, not popularity; holiness, not hype. He weighs the motives of every heart.

The prophets of old warned Israel that their sacrifices meant nothing when their hands were filled with blood (Isaiah 1:15). Likewise, the modern Church cannot sing louder than its sin. No amount of music or ministry can drown out the voice of injustice when the poor are ignored and the broken are silenced.

God is raising a remnant—a people who refuse to be bought or bribed. They will not trade the anointing for applause or truth for titles. They are the Daniels in Babylon, the Elijahs before Ahab, the Johns crying in the wilderness. When the compromised Church bows to political altars, this remnant bows only to Christ.

Jesus faced the hypocrisy of religious leaders who loved positions more than people. They wore robes of righteousness but hid hearts of greed. To them He said, *"Woe to you, scribes and Pharisees, hypocrites! For you cleanse the outside of the cup, but inside are full of extortion and excess"* (Matthew 23:25). His words still pierce through centuries of religious disguise.

Corruption in the Church is more dangerous than persecution from the world, for betrayal from within wounds the Body of Christ from the inside. Yet even in betrayal, God purifies His Bride. Every scandal, every exposure, is not for destruction but for cleansing. Judgment begins at the house of God (1 Peter 4:17).

The siege upon the Church is both external and internal. Governments may legislate against truth, but deception within the sanctuary weakens the wall even faster. Therefore, the Lord calls His people to rebuild with repentance, prayer, and truth—the same tools Nehemiah used to restore Jerusalem's broken walls.

The Church under siege must rediscover its first love. It must remember the blood that bought it, the cross that defines it, and the Spirit that sustains it. When the fear of God returns to the pulpit, revival will return to the people. For though Hell roars against the Bride, Christ still declares: *"My Church shall prevail."*

The Church Under Siege

The hour has come when judgment begins at the house of God. Sanctuaries once built to honor His name have become marketplaces of ambition, trading holiness for influence. The altar has been polluted with political bribes and personal gain, yet the Lord still walks among His lampstands, searching for hearts that remain pure before Him.

The modern Church stands under siege not from external persecution alone, but from the internal decay of compromise. Many leaders have bowed to the gods of approval and applause. They have forgotten that friendship with the world is enmity with God (James 4:4). The same religious spirit that crucified Christ now hides behind clerical garments and eloquent sermons.

In the days of Jesus, the Pharisees sat in Moses' seat but neglected mercy, justice, and faithfulness. Today, a similar spirit blinds those who should see. They honor God with their lips, but their hearts are far from Him (Matthew 15:8). Their titles are great, but their love is cold.

Bribery has entered the temple gates. Offerings are exchanged for favor; endorsements for silence. Leaders justify corruption in the name of "strategy" and "survival." But the Lord declares through the prophet Ezekiel, *"Woe to the shepherds who feed themselves! Should not the shepherds feed the flock?"* (Ezekiel 34:2).

The Church was called to be the conscience of nations, yet she has become a consultant to kings. Where prophets once thundered truth, advisors now whisper what is comfortable. Where revival should blaze, bureaucracy now reigns. The light of many candles has dimmed beneath the weight of compromise.

Still, God keeps a remnant that will not bow to Baal. Hidden among the crowds are men and women who refuse to sell their faith for position or recognition. They are the Daniels in Babylon, the Elijahs on Carmel, the Marys who anoint His feet when others plot betrayal.

When the Church fears losing members more than losing the Holy Spirit, she has already lost her authority. Christ did not die to create an organization but a living body filled with truth and power. Every attempt to replace the cross with comfort invites defeat.

Yet even now the Spirit calls, *"Return to Me and I will return to you."* The siege can be broken when repentance replaces pride and prayer replaces performance. The gates of Hell cannot prevail where humility reigns.

The Church must rediscover the courage of the early disciples—men who rejoiced to suffer for His name (Acts 5:41). They had no budgets or political allies, yet they turned the world upside down because they carried Heaven's fire.

The storm shaking the Church is not sent to destroy but to purify. Every false altar will crumble so that the true altar may shine again. God is cleansing His house, and when the smoke clears, a remnant will rise clothed in righteousness, fearless before men and faithful before God.

The Righteous Remnant Rising

Though the night grows darker, Heaven is not without witnesses. Across nations and generations, God preserves a remnant whose loyalty cannot be purchased and whose worship cannot be silenced. When the multitude bows to convenience, this remnant stands in covenant.

They are the Daniels who refuse the king's delicacies, the Esthers who risk their lives for their people, the Jeremiahs who weep yet still proclaim. The world may call them foolish, but Heaven calls them faithful. Their prayers are the thunder that shakes strongholds unseen.

The remnant understands that righteousness is not rebellion, but allegiance to a higher throne. Their allegiance is not to empires or parties but to the Lamb who was slain. When injustice spreads like wildfire, they pour out intercession like rain.

Persecution does not extinguish their flame; it purifies it. Every attack becomes a testimony, every wound a weapon of grace. They stand as living epistles, read by all men, showing that love is stronger than death and truth brighter than deceit.

Heaven's generals are not always found on platforms but in prayer closets. They are mothers interceding for their children, elders fasting in secret, youths preaching on street corners. The world may not know their names, but Hell knows their voices.

The Lord strengthens this remnant with promises of endurance: *"You will be hated by all for My name's sake, but he who endures to the end will be saved"* (Matthew 10:22). Endurance is their anthem, holiness, their banner.

In a culture that is intoxicated by power, they choose purity. In a time obsessed with visibility, they choose obedience. They measure success not by numbers but by nearness to God. Their hearts echo Paul's confession, *"I count all things loss for the excellence of knowing Christ Jesus my Lord."*

God is positioning these hidden ones for visible impact. They will emerge not to boast but to build. Through them, cities will experience renewal, and broken altars will blaze again with first love. They are carriers of both mercy and fire.

The remnant carries compassion for the wounded and confrontation for the wicked. They are not extremists of anger but instruments of awakening. Their authority flows from intimacy with the King, their courage from the cross.

When the gates of Hell roar, the remnant will answer with worship. When the nations tremble, they will lift their eyes to the hills from whence comes their help. And when the final trumpet sounds, their faith will be found unshaken, shining as witnesses that the Kingdom of Heaven has already overcome.

The Clash of Kingdoms

The kingdoms of this world and the Kingdom of Heaven are on a collision course. One is built on pride, greed, and violence; the other on humility, truth, and love. The conflict is ancient, yet its climax unfolds in our generation. Revelation declares, *"The kingdoms of this world have become the kingdoms of our Lord and of His Christ"* (Revelation 11:15).

Every earthly empire exalts itself as eternal, yet all crumble when confronted by the Rock cut without hands (Daniel 2:34). The systems of men build towers of arrogance, but the hand of God brings them down. History is Heaven's reminder that no throne stands forever except the one in glory.

Satan once offered Jesus all the kingdoms of the world if He would only bow (Matthew 4:8-10). That same temptation echoes through corridors of power today. Many have sold their souls for visibility, for votes, for vanity. But those who worship the Lord alone will inherit an everlasting Kingdom that cannot be shaken.

The clash is not merely political—it is moral and spiritual. Darkness dresses itself as progress while mocking righteousness as outdated. Violence is justified in the name of vengeance, and deception is marketed as diplomacy. Yet the light of Christ still exposes the unfruitful works of darkness.

Jesus taught that His Kingdom is not of this world (John 18:36). It does not conquer through weapons but through witness, not through coercion but through compassion. Every time the Church forgets this and seeks power over people instead of service to them, she fights for the wrong kingdom.

The gates of Hell manifest wherever oppression reigns—when truth is censored, when the poor are forgotten, when leaders oppress the very souls they vow to serve. Yet the gates are not impregnable. At the sound of true worship, they quake; at the proclamation of truth, they crumble.

The cross stands as the great divide between the two realms. To the world it is foolishness, but to those who are being saved, it is the power of God (1 Corinthians 1:18). On that hill, Heaven declared war on Hell and won. Every demonic contract was canceled by the blood of the Lamb.

This present hour mirrors that battlefield. Nations rise against nations, truth is traded for propaganda, and humanity bleeds while politicians profit. Yet Heaven is not silent. The Spirit still whispers to those who listen: *"Lift your heads, for your redemption draws near."*

As the clash intensifies, believers must remember that victory does not come by might or manipulation but by surrender to God's will. The weapons of our warfare are not carnal but mighty through God to the pulling down of strongholds (2 Corinthians 10:4). Prayer, purity, and perseverance remain Heaven's artillery.

Soon every knee will bow and every tongue confess that Jesus Christ is Lord. The kingdoms that mocked Him will tremble before His throne. The clash of kingdoms will end not with negotiation but with coronation—the rightful King returning to reclaim what is His.

The Cross as the Battlefield

Calvary was not only a place of suffering; it was the greatest battlefield in history. On that hill, every force of darkness gathered to crush the Son of God, but through the agony of the cross, Heaven launched its final strike against Hell's dominion. Christ triumphed by surrendering, conquering death through obedience.

The nails that pierced His hands were the very weapons that disarmed the enemy. Paul wrote, *"Having spoiled principalities and powers, He made a show of them openly, triumphing over them in it"* (Colossians 2:15). The cross turned shame into glory and defeat into eternal victory.

Every injustice, every bribe, every abuse of power met its judgment there. When leaders today exploit the weak or twist truth for gain, the cross still stands as the verdict against them. It declares: "Your corruption ends here, beneath the blood of the Lamb."

Jesus faced the hatred of both church and state. Religious leaders conspired; politicians consented; soldiers obeyed. He bore the weight of institutional wickedness so future generations could stand free. He showed that the Kingdom conquers not by killing but by dying for the undeserving.

The same cross that purchased salvation also exposes hypocrisy. It reveals who truly loves God and who only uses His name. Those who stand near it must choose—repent or resist. There is no neutral ground at Golgotha.

When Christ cried, *"It is finished!"* (John 19:30), Hell heard its death sentence. The veil was torn; the divide between God and man was destroyed. The powers that fed on fear lost their hold. Love became the final law of the Kingdom.

Now every believer carries a cross-shaped calling. We are summoned to overcome evil with good, hatred with forgiveness, and lies with truth. Our daily obedience becomes a continuation of Calvary's victory in the world.

The enemy still tries to crucify truth in modern arenas—courtrooms, classrooms, and media platforms—but every attempt only spreads the message further. The blood of the Lamb continues to speak louder than the accusations of the accuser.

The Church must return to the foot of the cross to regain her authority. Programs and politics cannot substitute for power that flows from brokenness and prayer. Only a crucified Church can reveal a resurrected Christ.

he battlefield of Calvary echoes through time. Every act of humility defeats pride; every deed of mercy silences malice. Wherever the cross is lifted high, the gates of Hell shatter, and the Kingdom of Heaven advances with unstoppable grace.

The Judgment on Corrupt Altars

The eyes of the Lord roam the earth, searching for true worshippers, yet what He finds in many sanctuaries are altars built not for His glory but for human gain. These are the modern altars of idolatry—where offerings are measured by influence, not by obedience. The fire has gone out, replaced by theatrics that entertain but do not transform.

God is not mocked. The prophets cried out against false shepherds who devoured the flock while claiming to serve the Lord. Jeremiah thundered, *"Woe to the pastors that destroy and scatter the sheep of My pasture"* (Jeremiah 23:1). That woe still echoes today. Every pulpit that hides truth for comfort invites divine correction.

The Spirit of God is exposing secret sins within His house because judgment must begin there (1 Peter 4:17). He reveals what was hidden in shadows—greed, manipulation, and spiritual abuse— so that repentance may still be possible before destruction falls. He will not share His glory with corruption.

The altars of compromise are trembling. The incense of hypocrisy has become a stench before Heaven. What men call success, Heaven calls sickness. The Lord is tearing down the stages that were never meant for His presence, for He desires truth in the inward parts.

Prophets once silenced by fear are now awakening with a sword in their mouths. They speak not for profit but for purity. Their words cut through the pretense of religion like Elijah's cry on Mount Carmel: *"How long will you halt between two opinions?"* (1 Kings 18:21). The time for wavering has ended.

Those who take bribes to distort justice mirror the priests who sold sacrifices at inflated prices in the temple courts. Jesus overturned their tables once, and He will overturn them again. Every exchange that cheapens grace will face His holy wrath.

The world mocks the Church because it sees no difference between its leaders and its politicians. But God is separating the wheat from the chaff. Titles and positions cannot shield anyone from His scrutiny. Only repentance and humility can restore honor to His name.

Amos cried, *"I despise your feasts; I take no delight in your solemn assemblies"* (Amos 5:21). The Lord still rejects worship that ignores justice, songs that drown out the cries of the oppressed. He desires a Church whose praise is matched by compassion and whose theology is proven in mercy.

This judgment is not cruelty but cleansing. The fire that consumes the counterfeit will refine the genuine. Those who repent will emerge purer, stronger, and filled with a new anointing. God disciplines those He loves so that His bride may be spotless at His coming.

When the Lord is finished purging His house, the altars will burn again with holy fire. Worship will no longer be performance but presence. The poor will rejoice, the proud will tremble, and the nations will know that the Church of Jesus Christ stands once more in power and purity.

The Triumph of the Lamb

The final victory belongs to the Lamb who was slain. All the schemes of Hell, all the corrupt altars, and all the compromised leaders will bow under His authority. Revelation declares, *"He shall reign forever and ever"* (Revelation 11:15). The Kingdom of Heaven is unshakable because its foundation is eternal.

The nations may rage, and the powers may plot, but Heaven's purposes cannot be thwarted. Every attempt to silence the righteous, every plot to murder truth, only serves to fulfill God's plan. Christ triumphs through the obedience and courage of those who stand with Him.

Injustice will not have the final word. Violence will not triumph. Corruption cannot outlast divine judgment. Heaven's armies march on, not with swords of steel but with the Word of God, with prayer, with the testimony of faith.

Lamb's victory is evident in the oppressed rising, in captives being set free, and in the light piercing the darkest corners of the world. Those who love justice and mercy become instruments of His triumph. Their faithfulness accelerates the coming of His Kingdom on earth as it is in Heaven.

Every believer called to stand against injustice now carries a portion of the Lamb's authority. Each act of courage, compassion, and righteousness is a strike against Hell's gates. As Jesus faced betrayal and false witnesses, so too must His followers confront hidden evil with unwavering faith.

The triumph of Lamb is not merely spiritual; it transforms societies. Political upheaval, social injustice, and global violence cannot stop the advance of Heaven's Kingdom. The truth of God's Word infiltrates governments, restores broken systems, and ignites revival in hearts long enslaved by fear.

Even when the world appears chaotic, believers are called to declare victory because the war has already been won at Calvary. Satan's schemes are temporary; the Lamb's glory is eternal. The Kingdom expands not by compromise, but by standing firm in righteousness, mercy, and truth.

The Church, purified and awakened, will shine as a city on a hill. Its influence will draw nations, heal communities, and silence accusations against God's people. Every faithful remnant becomes a beacon, every prayer a trumpet blast, every righteous deed a victory banner.

Hell will rage, gates will tremble, and enemies will conspire, yet the Lamb's triumph is inevitable. Every oppressor, every hypocrite, every manipulator will face the righteous judgment of God. And those who persevered in love and courage will inherit eternal reward.

Therefore, rise, O Church of the living God. Do not fear the schemers, the violent, or the compromised leaders. Stand firm in love, justice, and truth. The Kingdom of Heaven is at war— but the Lamb reigns supreme, and the gates of Hell shall never prevail against His people.

Chapter 38: The Modern Athens: God's Final Rebuke and the Unveiling of Hidden Idols-

Thus says the Lord to My Church and to the nations in this hour: I see corruption in your midst. I see the hearts of men turned to their own devices, the altars of power raised in defiance of Me, and the leaders who bow before the applause of men rather than the judgment of Heaven. My Spirit is provoked, and My hand is lifted in rebuke against the hidden evils that defile both Church and state.

As I looked upon Athens in the days of My servant Paul, his spirit was stirred within him. He saw the city overflowing with idols, thirty thousand gods standing in proud defiance of My glory. Each idol represented a twisting of the human heart, a perversion of the capacity I placed within men to know and honor Me. Today, the same spirit of provocation rises over the nations.

I am raising my voice against the modern Athens—the cities of influence, the corridors of political power, the churches that have exchanged holiness for compromise. I see the leaders who tell lies, and the pastors who echo them, and I am not silent. The same spirit that moved Paul is moving now, calling forth a remnant to awaken and to contend for truth.

My people, do you not see that the idols have changed form but not nature? They are no longer carved from marble; they are made of ambition, greed, and deceit. They are found in political systems that ignore justice, in courts that fear righteousness, and in pulpits that endorse lies. I am exposing them, and I am shaking the foundations of the proud.

As Paul argued daily in the synagogue and in the marketplace, so My Spirit contends with the hearts of men today. I call the faithful to reason, to witness, and to stand. I am not pleased with silence, nor with apathy. I have called My Church to be a light in the darkness, but many have hidden their lamps under tables of compromise and comfort.

I see the cries of the oppressed, the suffering of the faithful, the persecution of those who love Me. From the highest offices of government to the sanctuaries of My own house, men have hardened their hearts, fearing the crowd rather than Me. Yet I am the Judge of all the earth, and I will not allow injustice to remain forever.

Athens was full of idols, and yet Paul perceived the hunger for truth within the hearts of its people. So too today, I see those who are seeking Me amidst the deception. Each false teaching, each compromise of conscience, each betrayal of My Word is a test of discernment. Will My people rise to contend, or will they bow to the wisdom of men?

My Spirit cries out against the political leaders who govern in fear of public opinion rather than in fear of the Lord. I see the compromise of law, the suppression of justice, and the bending of truth to satisfy the whims of the powerful. I say, the time of pretense is over. Repent, or the consequences of rebellion shall be your portion.

I also speak to the leaders of My Church who have aligned with unrighteousness. You who preach comfort while the world suffers; you who tolerate sin in high places; you who silence truth for acceptance—know that I see you, and My rebuke shall not pass unnoticed. Your pulpits are not thrones; they are altars of accountability.

As Paul walked the marketplaces, he reasoned with Jews and Gentiles alike. So must My servants today step into the public square, into the marketplace of ideas, and confront the idols of our age. You must speak truth, call out deception, and shine the light of My Word into the darkness that seeks to overwhelm.

I see nations that have abandoned justice, laws that are ignored, and leadership that fears My authority. I see the Church compromised by allegiance to power rather than to righteousness. The echoes of Athens resound again, and My Spirit is provoked. Will you hear the call before the final judgment is unleashed?

My eyes pierce the hidden corruption. I know the hearts that love wealth, influence, and prestige more than me. I know the leaders who oppress, deceive, and manipulate. I know the pastors who remain silent when My people are in bondage. I say, I will not be mocked, and the hour of exposure has come.

Athens had its philosophers, its wise men and rhetoricians, yet they were blind to the truth standing before them. Today, the world honors intellect and persuasion over wisdom from Heaven. False philosophies and empty promises have become the gospel of many. I say, return to My Word, for in it is life, and without it there is death.

My Spirit moves to provoke My Church, to stir the hearts of the faithful, and to awaken those who have been lulled into sleep. I am calling forth voices of courage, tongues of prophecy, and hands of action. Those who hear and obey shall see My favor, while those who continue in deception shall be broken and exposed.

Thus, I reveal the first truth of this hour: Idolatry is not only worship of images; it is compromise, deception, and fear. Wherever truth is silenced, wherever My Word is ignored, there I am moving to rebuke, to shake, and to awaken. As Paul's spirit burned over Athens, so My Spirit burns over the nations and over My Church today.

The outrage Paul felt in Athens becomes the mirror of our age. The marble monuments have turned into towers of influence; the temples into entertainment platforms; the philosophers into political pundits and digital prophets of self. Humanity still worships at its own reflection, and pride still wears the crown. Yet within this crowded marketplace of ideas, God still raises voices that refuse to bend—men and women who, like Paul, reason with courage, clarity, and compassion.

We walk through cities filled with noise and see the new altars: the altars of ideology, of technology, of self-promotion. The idols have circuitry instead of stone and algorithms instead of incense. But the heart of idolatry remains unchanged: the exaltation of the creature over the Creator.

The Church stands at a crossroads much like the synagogue of Athens. Some hear the truth and turn their hearts; others mock, postpone, or debate without repentance. The Lord still calls His people to preach Christ crucified, not a convenient gospel of comfort, for only the cross exposes the idols men try to hide.

Every generation faces its own Parthenon structure built to honor human greatness. Today's Parthenon is the culture of celebrity, the worship of wealth, the politics of image. It gleams on every screen, promising power but delivering emptiness. God's servants must climb those steps not to admire but to confront, declaring that the Unknown God whom the world ignores is the Lord who reigns.

Paul's method in Athens was dialogue, not destruction. He reasoned from the Scriptures, revealing that truth is not afraid of questions. Likewise, the Church must engage culture with both conviction and grace. Silence in the face of deception is agreement; reason anchored in Scripture is the antidote to chaos.

The modern Athens is global. Nations boast of freedom yet are enslaved to greed; governments legislate without conscience; and even within sanctuaries, the applause of the crowd outweighs the fear of God. The rebuke of Heaven is already echoing through political halls and church aisles alike: *Return to righteousness.*

Leaders rise and fall by the same principle that ruled empires of old. When truth is dismissed, judgment follows. History records it, Scripture foretells it, and our headlines confirm it. God allows shaking so that what cannot be shaken will remain. Some cry, "Where is God in all this corruption?" He is where He has always been—on the throne, exposing the works of darkness, calling His people to shine. When nations drift, His Spirit provokes reformers; when pulpits fall silent, He anoints prophets of integrity who refuse to trade truth for popularity.

The faithful remnant grows stronger in the fire. Just as Paul stood alone among philosophers, so believers today must stand among skeptics. The credibility of the gospel is not in numbers but in holiness, not in political favor but in spiritual authority. There is a cost to this calling. Paul risked ridicule in Athens; modern disciples risk rejection in boardrooms, classrooms, and congregations. Yet obedience has never been optional. The message of repentance is offensive because it exposes hidden idols, but without repentance, there is no restoration.

The Spirit still provokes hearts that see injustice ignored and righteousness silenced. That stirring is divine discomfort, the sign that God's people are alive. Indifference is death; holy unrest is evidence of His presence. The nations crave peace yet despise purity. They enact laws to silence conscience and call it progress. But peace without righteousness is merely a pause before collapse. God's justice is the foundation of lasting peace, and until leaders acknowledge Him, unrest will continue.

In the Church, compromise often dresses as compassion. False unity whispers that truth divides, when in fact it refines. Paul confronted the error because love demands honesty. So must the modern Church: love enough to warn, to discipline, to restore. The storm that shook Athens is shaking the world again—not of marble or empire, but of moral order. Economic towers tremble, political alliances fracture, and even religious institutions face exposure. The purpose of the shaking is mercy: that hearts may awaken before judgment is final.

Therefore, let the servants of God take courage. This hour is not for despair but discernment. The idols are many, but the Lord is one. The same power that sustained Paul in Athens empowers the faithful today to reason, to proclaim, and to stand until every false altar falls before the name of Jesus Christ.

The call to repentance still thunders through history. It is not the voice of condemnation but of rescue. Every idol uncovered, every secret motive exposed, is an invitation to return to the One who alone is holy.

When Paul declared that God now commands all people everywhere to repent, he spoke not of suggestion but of necessity. Repentance is the bridge between rebellion and renewal; without it, revival remains a dream. In this modern Athens, repentance must begin in the house of God. The Church cannot heal a culture it imitates. Confession must replace performance, humility must replace branding, and the fear of the Lord must replace the fear of losing influence.

True repentance is not merely sorrow for exposure but transformation through surrender. It demands that pulpits speak truth again, that worship return to reverence, and that believers measure success by obedience rather than attendance. Spiritual warfare now moves in unseen corridors—through misinformation, moral confusion, and emotional exhaustion. The battle for truth is not fought with weapons of flesh but with the steadfast proclamation of Scripture and the steadfast life of integrity.

The enemy thrives where discernment dies. A church without discernment becomes a city without walls, vulnerable to every invading ideology. The Spirit calls believers to test every message, weigh every spirit, and hold fast to what is good. Deception is persuasive because it flatters; truth is liberating because it confronts. The faithful must learn again the courage of confrontation, not with anger but with the calm authority of conviction rooted in God's Word.

Many leaders have confused visibility with victory. They pursue platforms rather than purity, influence rather than intimacy with God. Yet when the light of exposure shines, it is the hidden life that will stand, not the public image. The warfare of this hour is fought on the ground of allegiance: whom will we serve? Political loyalty, cultural acceptance, and even denominational pride must bow to the lordship of Christ. Divided hearts cannot stand in the day of testing.

God still equips a remnant who walk in quiet strength. Their power is not in the noise of social approval but in secret prayer. They carry the unshakable peace that confuses the proud and comforts the humble. To this remnant, God entrusts the ministry of reconciliation—to rebuild what hypocrisy has torn, to heal what injustice has wounded, and to speak hope where cynicism reigns. Their endurance will prove that light is stronger than darkness.

The hope of the faithful is not in the restoration of earthly systems but in the kingdom that cannot be shaken. Every collapse of human order points upward to the throne that endures forever. As nations tremble and leaders stumble, the people of God must remember their citizenship is in heaven. Their mission remains unchanged: to bear witness to truth, to love mercy, and to walk humbly with their God. The shaking of institutions is not the end of hope but the beginning of clarity. Through it, God separates the genuine from the false, the faithful from the fashionable. Purity always precedes power.

Therefore, let repentance be swift and courage constant. The same Spirit who convicted Athens now moves through every land, calling hearts to choose idols or truth, compromise or holiness, fear or faith. The hour is late, yet grace still speaks. In every generation, the truth-bearers have been mocked as fools, outcasts, or fanatics. Yet the foolishness of God confounds the wisdom of man, and the despised messenger becomes the instrument of divine correction.

The Church must remember that persecution is not the failure of faith but the refining of it. Fire does not destroy gold; it reveals its purity. So too must the fiery trials of this era reveal the authentic Church from the counterfeit. Many will fall away when the applause fades and comfort is taken. Their devotion was rooted in convenience, not covenant. But those who remain steadfast in love will shine as lights in a crooked generation.

The Lord is not impressed by the grandeur of our sanctuaries or the reach of our media platforms; He looks for the altar that still smokes with sacrifice. It is there—on the altar of obedience—that revival begins. Modern persecution may not always wear the chains of iron but the labels of accusation, intolerance, extremism, and irrelevance. Yet blessed are those who suffer for righteousness' sake, for theirs is the kingdom that cannot be shaken.

The Church must not remain silent when truth is mocked. This is the time for prophetic bravery to state that holiness is not hatred, and repentance is not rejection but redemption. God is testing His people, not to destroy but to clarify. The shaking reveals the wheat from the chaff, the faithful from the distracted, and those who serve God for His glory from those who serve for personal gain.

The sifting will expose not only corruption in leadership but also compromise in laity. Every believer is called to self-examination. For judgment begins at the house of God, not to condemn, but to cleanse and commission. The Spirit of God moves through the earth like a refiner's fire.

He purifies hearts, breaks idols, and restores reverence. What seems like chaos to the world is divine order being reestablished through shaking.

In this purification, many will rediscover simplicity—faith stripped of excess, worship free from performance, love without pretense. The Church that survives the shaking will not be the loudest, but the most surrendered. God's remnant carries an anointing of endurance. They are not driven by popularity but by purpose. They see beyond temporary suffering to the eternal reward of standing blameless before the Lamb.

The world calls this endurance foolish; Heaven calls it faith. For every tear shed in secret, intercession becomes a seed for revival. Every act of obedience under pressure becomes a testimony to the kingdom's power. The voices of compromise will grow louder, promising unity without truth and peace without repentance. But the Spirit warns: beware of the counterfeit harmony that silences conviction. True unity is built on righteousness, not convenience.

The coming storm is not to be feared by the faithful but embraced as the sign that redemption draws near. The darker the night grows, the closer the dawn of the returning King. Therefore, lift your heads, O remnant of God! Let not weariness overcome your witness. The same Christ who walked among lampstands still walks among His Church, trimming wicks, restoring light, and calling His people to burn bright until the end.

Hear the word of the Lord: "I am shaking the nations and exposing the hidden altars built in My name but not by My Spirit. The idols of greed, pride, and political idolatry shall crumble before My presence. You have turned My house of prayer into a stage for performance and politics. You have sought power more than purity and influence more than intimacy. Therefore, I am stripping away the illusions that blind you."

"I am raising a remnant who fear Me more than they fear rejection, who preach repentance without apology, and who love righteousness more than reputation. These shall carry My fire into dark places."

The Spirit of the Lord declares: the days of pretending are over. The Church can no longer blend with Babylon and call it relevance. The compromise of holiness for popularity has provoked the jealousy of God. The nations stand at a crossroads between mercy and judgment. America, once a beacon of spiritual light, now wrestles with rebellion at its roots. The same God who blessed her now calls her to repentance before the lampstand is removed.

Across the globe, kingdoms are trembling; governments are divided; moral order has collapsed. Yet through the shaking, God is calling His people to return—to rebuild not cathedrals, but character, not empires, but altars. Just as Paul confronted the idols of Athens, the modern Church must confront the idols of our age: nationalism that replaces kingdom identity, entertainment that replaces worship, and comfort that replaces conviction.

The Spirit weeps over pulpits that refuse to cry aloud and spare not. Too many shepherds have exchanged prophetic truth for political approval. But the voice of God still calls: "Who will stand in the gap and speak what I command? Woe to the leaders who twist My Word for gain, who justify sin for applause, and who feed themselves while My sheep scatter!" says the Lord. "I will raise shepherds after My heart who will feed My people with truth."

As in the days of Paul, the gospel must again confront every philosophy that exalts itself against the knowledge of Christ. This is not a time for timid sermons, but for truth that pierces through deception and awakens conscience. The nations cry for peace yet reject the Prince of Peace.They build walls of ideology but ignore the cornerstone of salvation. God's patience is mercy, but His delay is not approval—judgment is already at the door. Yet even in wrath, God remembers mercy. He calls to His bride, "Come out from among them and be separate. Touch no unclean thing, and I will receive you." This is the hour for holiness, humility, and healing to return.

For the Lord is purifying His bride. Every false prophet will fall, every counterfeit kingdom will crumble, and every hidden work of darkness will be exposed by the light of His truth. The Church that endures will emerge radiant and ready.

The final call of this generation is clear: Repent, restore, and return. The Judge stands at the door, but so does the Redeemer. Those who bow now will reign with Him when He appears in glory. Those who resist will be swept away by the storm they ignored.

And now the Spirit says: "Behold, I come quickly, and My reward is with Me. Let the Church awaken, let the nations tremble, and let every heart prepare the way of the Lord. For the trial of the Church is ending—but the reign of Christ is about to begin."

Lord, search for us, expose us, break us, and lead us into true repentance. For Your church has stood before men for applause, but now we stand before God for judgment. We come not with excuses, not with pride, but with trembling souls and humbled hearts.

There comes a moment when God silences the applause of men and replaces it with the trembling echo of eternity. When the lights of religion fade and the robes of men fall powerless to the ground, the soul must stand naked before the One whose eyes pierce the thoughts and motives of the heart. This is that moment— the chapter where the Church no longer hides in programs, titles, platforms, or stained-glass sanctuaries, but kneels in the dust like David in the cave, stripped of royal dreams and earthly assurances, learning that before God crowns, He crushes pride, exposes false motives, and humbles those He loves.

We have preached about the throne, but God begins in the cave. We have lifted palaces, spotlight pulpits, and political alliances, yet God shapes His servants in obscurity. David was not called from a palace but from a sheepfold; he learned obedience not in courts but in caves of exile, danger, and hidden warfare. And we, too, must confess we have admired crowns more than crosses and platforms more than purity. But God brings His people to lonely caves, where applause cannot follow and ambition cannot breathe, so that humility may rise and pride may die.

Jesus Christ, the greater David walked the path we avoid. Rejected, misunderstood, hunted, betrayed, and humiliated, not because He lacked power but because redemption is forged in surrender. He did not come with legions but with wounds; He did not rule by force but by sacrifice. If the perfect Son of God embraced a cave and a cross before glory, how dare we demand crowns without crucifixion? How dare we preach comfort without repentance, authority without obedience, platforms without brokenness?

Church, we have boasted in our buildings while neglecting the broken. We have pursued influence among kings but ignored the cries of the widow, orphan, immigrant, and wounded soul hungry for truth. We have praised men more than God, defended institutions more than righteousness, protected reputations more than victims, and feared losing members more than grieving the Holy Spirit. And now the Spirit of God stands in the doorway, calling us out—not for condemnation, but for cleansing.

The church is on trial not before media, not before culture, not before political critics, but before the Holy God of Heaven. This is not a courtroom of men where evidence can be spun and witnesses bought; this is the throne room where truth stands unbending, and every hidden idol, every secret sin, every unrepentant leader, every abusive shepherd, every manipulative prophet, every proud worshiper will be exposed by fire. Not to destroy, but to purify. Not to shame, but to sanctify.

Oh Church, we have loved influence more than intercession, platforms more than presence, applause more than altar tears. We have crowned charisma and strangled character. We have tolerated wolves because they preached well, sang beautifully, led powerfully, or filled seats. But God does not measure success by crowds; He measures surrender by obedience, humility, repentance, and truth. And today, heaven demands the Church to cry again—not the tears of emotional worship, but the tears of broken repentance.

Some of you reading feel like David pushed into caves by betrayal, hunted by jealousy, wounded by those who should have protected you. And the enemy whispers, "God has forgotten you." But hear this truth: the cave is not rejection is preparation. Exile is not abandonment is refinement. The silence is not judgment; it is divine shaping. God is not punishing you; He is making you unshakeable.

But others, if honest, have been Saul. We feared losing control more than losing Christ's presence. We fought to maintain position rather than posture. We resented the rising of others instead of celebrating God's calling on them. We spoke in God's name but obeyed reputation, ego, and power. And the Spirit now whispers: *Lay down your sword of pride before heaven lays you low.*

Yet mercy stands open. The same Christ who endured betrayal, humiliation, and the cross extends redemption not to the strong but to the surrendered. Salvation is not earned by years in pews or robes of ministry, or the praises of congregations received only by brokenness before the Lamb slain. Acts 4:12 declares salvation is in no other name, not presidents, pastors, bishops, prophets, denominations, nations, or constitutions, but Jesus Christ alone.

So, come. Lay down every title, every excuse, every whispered justification, every secret sin, every hidden bitterness, every political idol, every spirit of superiority, every self-righteous thought. For the trumpet of repentance is sounding. And like blind Bartimaeus who cried, "Jesus, Son of David, have mercy on me!", let us cry with desperation, not ritual, not eloquence, but groaning souls desperate for cleansing.

There is a trembling season when God rises from His holy throne and asks His people, *"Where is your fear of Me? Where is your awe? Where are your tears?"* We have wept over elections, over stock markets, over losing influence, but where are the tears for a grieving God? Where are the tears for the lost? Where is the trembling at the altar? The Church has shouted for national revival without first seeking personal repentance. But revival never begins in capitals; it begins in caves of humility, on the knees of the broken, under the weight of holy conviction.

The fire of God is returning, not the fire of hype, but the fire of holiness. A fire that consumes pride, exposes spiritual manipulation, and burns away the religious masks we have carefully crafted. We shouted "fire" in our worship, but feared the fire that refines the soul and purifies the heart. But the Spirit whispers: *"If I burned in the bush for Moses, if I burned on the altar in Elijah's day, if I fell at Pentecost — shall I not burn again?"* Yet only the surrendered will stand in that flame without being consumed.

There are altars God will overturn before He rebuilds His Church. Some pulpits will fall, platforms that will crumble, and names once praised that heaven would erase not because God delights in shame, but because God refuses to share His glory with flesh. The Church does not need celebrities; it needs servants. The kingdom does not advance through charisma, but through crucifixion. And the cross is not merely a message; it is a lifestyle that kills the ego, crushes pride, and resurrects only Christ.

Yet to the weary, to the wounded, to the one falsely accused, to the one betrayed by leaders, to the one cast aside for speaking truth, heaven sees you. Your tears have not fallen unnoticed. Your prayers have not been ignored. Like David in the caves of Adullam, you have been hidden, not abandoned. God hides His anointed before He reveals them. He wounds His warriors before He sends them. Do not forget you are being fashioned.

Repentance is not shameful; it is liberation. It is not condemnation; it is an invitation. It is not punishment, it is purification. The enemy tells you repentance means God is angry; the Spirit tells you repentance means God is nearby. For the Lord is close to the brokenhearted, and He saves those crushed in spirit. Fall to your knees, not because you are worthless, but because He is worthy. We regret it not because we are rejected, but because we are loved.

Let the American church hear that political allegiance cannot save us; only the blood of the Lamb can. No movement, flag, party, candidate, or nation can cleanse sin or save the soul. Many have shouted *"God bless America"* without first whispering, *"America, bless God."* Our hope is not in Congress, courts, or constitutions but in Christ crucified and risen. For kingdoms rise and fall, nations tremble and fade, but the government upon His shoulders shall never collapse.

Let the modern church hear that platforms cannot sustain what pride builds. A sermon can move a crowd, but only the Spirit can move a soul. We have mastered production but forgotten presence. We have perfected performance but neglected prayer. We have multiplied programs but starved the altars. Yet the Lord whispers, *"Return to Me, and I will return to you."* Not to your talent, not to your brand, not to your strategy, but to your heart.

Let every heart hear: holiness is still required. Grace is not permission to sin; grace is the power to be free from sin. Mercy is not an excuse to remain broken; mercy is the miracle that heals. Christ did not die to make us comfortable. He died to make us holy. And holiness is not cold religion; it is fiery love for a God who is worthy of all.

There is a shaking coming, not by politics, pandemics, or world systems, but by the hand of God. He is purifying His bride. He is separating the sincere from the superficial, the faithful from the fashionable, the worshipers from the performers. And those who remain will not be those with the largest stages, but those with the lowest knees.

So once again, we cry: "Jesus, Son of David, have mercy on us! Purify us! Break us! Restore us! Lead us to repentance that births revival, surrender that births strength, and brokenness that births glory!" For when the church falls at His feet, heaven stands in our defense. Let judgment begin not in the world, but in the house of God, and let redemption rise like the dawn.

There comes a moment when God silences the applause of men and replaces it with the trembling echo of eternity. When the lights of religion fade and the robes of men fall powerless to the ground, the soul must stand naked before the One whose eyes pierce the thoughts and motives of the heart. This is that moment, the chapter where the Church no longer hides in programs, titles, platforms, or stained-glass sanctuaries, but kneels in the dust like David in the cave, stripped of royal dreams and earthly assurances, learning that before God crowns, He crushes pride, exposes false motives, and humbles those He loves.

When God hides a man in a cave, it is not punishment; it is preparation. The palace polishes crowns, but caves polish souls. David did not learn humility on a throne; he learned it in the dust, in the darkness, in the secrecy of rejection and accusation. And so it is with the Church today, we have known lights, platforms, microphones, and visibility, yet we have forgotten the sacred school of silence.

We forgot how to tremble, how to weep, how to pray until heaven shakes and flesh dies. We became people who speak much but listen little, who perform ministry without being pierced by God's presence. But the Lord whispers again from the caves of purification: *Come out of self promotion and into surrender, come out of status and into sanctification, for what I raise in hiddenness no man can tear down.* Blessed is the believer who embraces obscurity if it means gaining the heart of Christ.

The modern church looks at influence and assumes favor; God looks at brokenness and sees obedience. David was hunted not because he did wrong, but because he was marked for a divine purpose. Likewise, Christ was hated not because He sinned, but because heaven's authority confronted earth's corruption.

Today, many believers misinterpret warfare as abandonment. They see rejection as failure, when often it is heaven's protection removing us from voices that would distort our calling and places that would dilute our anointing. If the modern believer understood the mercy of exile, they would praise God in the wilderness, not complain in it. For God sends His chosen away from applause so they may hear the only voice that matters, *His.*

And now, the Church stands in its own cave, stripped of moral power, stained by scandals, trembling under the weight of compromise. This generation has witnessed pulpits rot with pride, politics invade the sanctuary, and personalities replace the presence of God. We thought favor was respect from the world, but biblical favor is repentance before heaven. The Church must now bow low, not as a gesture, but as a confession: *Lord, we have admired image more than righteousness, popularity more than purity, crowds more than truth, applause more than obedience.* This is our Goliath, not a giant warrior, but a giant within: pride dressed as ministry.

David pretended madness before Achish in 1 Samuel 21:14, not because he lacked power, but because the appearance of weakness was safer than the spotlight of strength. Sometimes God allows His chosen to look foolish in the eyes of men so He may make them wise in the courts of heaven. Christ Himself looked defeated on the cross, yet hell trembled as redemption unfolded. The Church must stop fearing looking weak and start fearing looking self-sufficient. Our strength has never been in programs, institutions, or personalities; it has always been in Lamb, who chose suffering over spectacle. If the world laughs at a repentant Church, let it laugh for heaven crowns the humble, and the cross is still the only throne of authority.

We must confess our fascination with palaces. We envied kings and influencers, forgetting that God chooses shepherds and servants. We sought titles more than tears, positions more than purity, platforms more than prayer. And so, God stripped us, not to destroy us, but to heal us. The cave is God's mercy, a sacred crucible where corruption dies and calling is reborn. We do not come out of these caves polished by public approval but scarred with surrender. Only then can we carry authority without arrogance, truth without self-righteousness, and power without pride. The Church must embrace the cave again, for revival will not come through celebrity Christianity, but through crucified Christianity.

Jesus, the greater David, walked into rejection willingly, not hidden by circumstance but by divine assignment. He surrendered not only His throne, but His right to be understood. *He came unto His own, and His own received Him not.* If the Church truly followed Christ, we would stop demanding acceptance and begin embracing the holy misunderstanding that comes with obedience to heaven. The cross does not make us popular; it makes us holy. Christ was not crowned because He fit into culture, but because He broke its chains. Let the Church return to the cross where our agendas die, our flesh bows, and our love becomes pure enough to heal nations again.

There is a shaking upon the land, political, spiritual, moral, and the Lord is asking

His Church: *Will you trust Me when the nations tremble? Will you stand when leaders fall? Will you follow My voice over the noise of the world?* For we have idolized earthly kings and feared earthly laws more than we feared dishonoring God. But no president, no king, no judge, no institution holds the future Christ alone does. Earthly thrones crumble, heaven's throne reigns forever. It is time to repent not only of sin, but of misplaced trust. For salvation is not in laws, systems, or elections, salvation is in the name above every name, *Jesus Christ.*

Just as David fled without sword or armor, we must return to the simplicity of salvation naked before God, dependent on Him alone. Our strategies cannot save us. Our budgets cannot deliver us. Our influence cannot redeem us. Only the blood of Jesus calls us holy. Only the Spirit of Jesus makes us new. Only the Word of Jesus keeps us from deception. We must lay down every false covering pride, denominational superiority, cultural favoritism, political loyalty disguised as faithfulness, and cling to Christ alone. A Church stripped of idols is a Church clothed in glory.

Some reading this feel betrayed by leaders, by friends, by systems, by congregations who did not see you or protect you. Some feel falsely accused, misunderstood, silenced, pushed aside because you refuse to compromise truth. Hear the word of the Lord: *Your cave is not abandoned; it is an appointment.* God sees every tear. God remembers every wound. He will vindicate you in His time, but first He must purify your heart so that your victory does not poison you with bitterness. Healing comes not when people apologize, but when you surrender your pain at the feet of the Healer who understands wounds more than any human ever will.

This is the hour for intercessors to rise, for watchmen to weep, for pastors to repent before preaching, for churches to fall on their faces until the altars burn again with purity, not performance. God is not impressed with our productions. He is moved by broken spirits and contrite hearts. Revival will not come through schedules and branding; it will come through tears and trembling. God is not asking for a louder Church first; He is asking for a cleaner one. A humbled Bride becomes a holy Bride.

So now the trumpet sounds repent, O Church! Come out of pride and into purity, out of politics and into prayer, out of self-will and into surrender. Cry like Bartimaeus once cried, *"Jesus, Son of David, have mercy on me!"* For only mercy can save us, only grace can wash us, only Christ can restore us. Let every pastor cry out, every mother kneel, every father bow, every leader tremble before the King who judges righteously. This is not a chapter to read; it is a call to fall on your face before Holy God. Repent, return, and be restored, for the cave is not where you die, but where resurrection begins.

There comes a moment in every believer's journey where God strips away every illusion of strength so we may discover the only real strength is His. David did not become a king in the palace; he became a king in the place of loss, in the silence where every support system failed, every friend abandoned, and every earthly source of protection dissolved. The modern Church must walk through this same refining, for we have leaned too long on charisma instead of character, applause instead of anointing, and strategy instead of surrender. The refining fire is not cruelty; it is mercy preparing us for glory. A Church that has never been emptied cannot carry the weight of heaven.

In this hour, God is not merely exposing evil in governments or media; He is exposing it in pulpits, choirs, leadership boards, prayer circles, and private hearts. Ministries built on gifting without godliness are crumbling; platforms raised on personality rather than presence are collapsing. This shaking is not Satan's victory but God's mercy for a Bride polluted cannot be presented before the Bridegroom. Judgment begins in the house of God, not to destroy the house, but to cleanse it. We weep not because He is harsh, but because He loves us too much to leave us filthy.

The time has passed for churches addicted to applause, sermons built on inspiration without conviction, and congregations comfortable with sin so long as talent is present. It is not skill that heaven seeks; it is surrender. It is not noise that moves God; it is brokenness. A Church that entertains but does not repent has already fallen. A Church that fills seats but empties altars is already dead. God is calling His people back from spiritual performance into raw, trembling holiness where every song is a prayer, every sermon a warning, every gathering an encounter with the living God.

When David hid in the cave, God was silent to him — but not absent from him. Silence is not abandonment; silence is surgery. God sometimes removes His felt presence to purify our motives. He hides His face not to punish, but to teach us to seek Him not for miracles, not for blessings, not for influence, but because He alone is life. The true Church is being drawn back to the place where worship is not a performance but a pouring out; where prayer is not routine but desperation, where the presence of God is not optional but oxygen.

We have seen political leaders promise salvation, and religious leaders promise revival, but only Christ can redeem. The Church must repent for making idols of parties, presidents, pastors, prophets, movements, and platforms. When nations shake, our faith must not shake because our kingdom is not of this world. We do not serve political saviors; we serve a crucified King. Let every believer sever the invisible chains of nationalism disguised as Christianity, pride disguised as patriotism, and tradition disguised as truth. We belong to Jesus and Jesus alone.

Many have suffered betrayal, church wounds, leadership manipulation, character assassination disguised as discernment, and spiritual abuse hidden under religious language. Heaven has seen every tear. Hell has hoped those wounds would harden your heart, but God intends them to humble you, soften you, and anchor you in His compassion. Do not allow the failures of man to rob you of faith in God. Broken by the Church does not mean rejected by Christ; many saints were wounded by religion before they were healed by the Savior. If you bleed today, bleed at His feet for there, wounds become worship.

The Church must confront the sin of silence. Silence when truth should be spoken. Silence when injustice cries out. Silence when the vulnerable are harmed. Silence when racism hides in pews. Silence when sexual sin is excused. Silence when the pulpit protects abusers. Silence when pride masquerades as holiness. Heaven will not excuse what earth ignores. God does not overlook sin because a ministry is successful; He confronts sin so ministry can be sanctified. The comfort of silence has killed more souls than the violence of persecution ever could. This is the hour to speak not with anger, but with authority, not with pride, but with purity.

We must repent of preaching truth without love and preaching love without truth. One cuts without healing, the other comforts without conviction. Real gospel wounds and restores, tears down and builds up, exposes sin, and offers salvation. Christ did not come to make bad people good; He came to make dead people live. And the Church cannot revive the world until the Church itself is revived. Revival is not energy; revival is repentance. Revival is not loud worship; revival is purified hearts. Revival is not a service; it is surrender.

If you feel like the world is closing in, if you see wickedness advance and righteousness mocked, if you are grieved by deception spreading like a disease, remember this: darkness does not mean defeat; it means destiny. David's darkest season bears his calling. Christ's darkest hour birthed salvation. The Church's greatest shaking will be her greatest awakening. But awakening does not begin with prophecy; it begins with repentance. It begins not when we accuse the world of sin, but when we confess our own.

God is calling His people to fall to their knees, not in ritual, but in desperation. To weep for the state of our souls, not for the state of our comfort. To cry out, *"Lord, break me before You use me. Cleanse me before You send me. Humble me before You raise me."* Every move of God begins with someone who breaks before God. Not the proud, not the confident, not the polished, but the desperate. And God says to His Church now, *Return to desperation, for complacency is the coffin of revival.*

Let every preacher examine his pulpit. Let every prophet examine his motives. Let every singer examine her worship. Let every believer examine their heart. Revival is not measured by crowds but by confession. Not by lights but by tears. Not by reputation but by repentance. A church that refuses to confront sin cannot carry glory. A Christian who refuses to crucify flesh cannot carry anointing. Holiness is not legalism; holiness is liberation from the slavery of self.

This generation needs not softer sermons but surrendered hearts. Not motivational speeches, but prophetic warnings wrapped in compassion. Not celebrity pastors, but weeping shepherds. Not entertainment, but an encounter. Not polished religion, but purified worship. The time of casual Christianity has ended. The church that survives will not be the stylish church, but the sanctified one. The believer who endures will not be the gifted one, but the crucified one.

Perhaps you feel you have failed too deeply, wandered too far, sinned too greatly, doubted too long. Hear the mercy of God — the cave is where failures are forgiven, not final. David sinned, but he repented. Peter denied Christ, but he returned. The thief died in shame but woke up in paradise. Grace does not excuse sin, but grace rescues sinners. There is no condemnation for the one who cries, *"Lord, have mercy on me."* The only soul beyond redemption is the one who refuses repentance.

Let every barrier fall now: pride, offense, stubbornness, rebellion, bitterness, fear. The door of mercy is open, but it will not remain open forever. Christ is calling His Bride not to comfort, but to consecration; not to status, but to surrender. Fall on your face before the Holy One and say, *"Search me, O God, and know my heart. Purify me, cleanse me, remake me."* For only the broken can be remade, and only the humbled can be exalted.

And now the Church stands where David stood between what was and what will be, between rejection and resurrection, between cave and crown. The question is not whether Christ is ready. He is. The question is whether we will bow low enough to rise with Him. There is only one prayer left for a Church on trial: *Jesus, Son of David, have mercy on us. Break us, cleanse us, revive us, restore us. Let us be a Bride worthy of Your return.* For the King is coming, and the cry of repentance must rise before the trumpet of glory sounds.

The Lord is shaking the foundations of every church that has trusted in numbers over obedience. Congregations may be full, programs may be popular, but if holiness is absent, the house stands on sand. David's cave reminds us that God honors hidden faith, secret prayers, and obedience when no one is watching. Today, God calls His Church to return to the secret place, to weep in silence, to fast in humility, and to prepare for His glory. What is visible to man may be impressive, but what is hidden from men is precious to God.

Leaders who have climbed through manipulation or compromise will fall unless they humble themselves. God has no favorites of convenience. His anointing rests on surrendered hearts, not on smooth speeches or polished appearances. Every crown that is built on pride will crumble. Every platform built on compromise will collapse. The Church must repent for exalting human hands over the hand of God, for bowing to influence instead of obedience, and for serving the applause of men rather than the approval of Heaven.

The blood of Christ alone is the refuge of the betrayed, the falsely accused, the abandoned, and the imprisoned. As David fled from Saul with nothing but a sling and his faith, so many today feel stripped, hunted, or voiceless. Yet the cave is not a prison; it is a sanctuary. The wilderness is not rejection; it is preparation. God sees, God remembers, and God will act. Every tear will be accounted for. Every insult endured will become testimony. Every injustice suffered will become glory.

God's Church cannot afford the luxury of neutrality. Compromise in the name of unity is rebellion in the eyes of Heaven. The Spirit cries: *"Come out of conformity, put off pretense, speak truth, even when men hate you. Serve justice, even when*

461

leaders oppose you. Walk in holiness, even when the world applauds impurity."
We have traded courage for comfort and obedience for compromise. The Church is on trial, but mercy still waits for the humble. God's call is urgent: repent before revival is replaced by reckoning.

David's exile teaches us endurance. Christ's cross teaches us to surrender. The modern Church must learn both lessons. To endure trials without grumbling, to surrender pride without hesitation, to trust God when human wisdom fails, is the mark of a faithful remnant. Those who remain faithful in the caves of testing will one day walk into glory. Those who bow low in seasons of humiliation will one day wear crowns of honor. God's purposes are never thwarted by man, but often hidden in patience, silence, and tears.

We must repent of trusting in flesh in presidents, in politicians, in movements, in denominations, in doctrines, in human leaders rather than in God alone. David could not save himself. Jesus, Son of David, could save no one except through God's will. So, too, the Church must abandon reliance on human wisdom. Salvation, revival, and freedom come only from Christ, the King of kings. No lawmaker, no preacher, no monarch can stand in His place. Every heart must recognize dependence on the Almighty alone.

The Church has tolerated hidden evil gossip, manipulation, favoritism, greed, sexual sin, and pride. Some have endured it silently; some have perpetuated it unknowingly. God sees all. God judges all. God calls His people to repentance and to holiness. Nothing can remain hidden. The cave of humility is where the Church confesses, cleanses, and consecrates itself. Only when we confront hidden evil can we rise as a holy bride, prepared for the return of Christ.

We must not fear shame. David faced shame in his cave, yet he remained God's chosen. Jesus bore ultimate shame on the cross, yet He became the salvation of the world. The Church today must be willing to endure shame for righteousness, to be misunderstood for truth, and to be rejected for holiness. The world may mock us, but heaven sees us. The kingdom of God is never advanced by comfort; it is advanced by sacrifice.

Repentance is more than confession; it is a turning of the heart, a total surrender. We must turn from pride, anger, offense, compromise, fear, and self-will. We must turn from idols of politics, denomination, fame, wealth, and social approval.

We must turn entirely to Christ, who alone redeems and restores. The Church cannot walk partially and surrender and claim revival. Partial surrender births disappointment; full surrender births glory.

The Lord reminds us that even in exile, His presence is near. Even in caves, His hand guides. Even in humiliation, His purpose unfolds. David's journey from shepherd to king teaches the Church that trials are not detours; they are divine instruction. Suffering is not rejection; it is refinement. Persecution is not punishment; it is preparation. Those who endure with faith will witness God's glory, and those who remain humble will bear eternal honor.

The modern Church must weep for its own failures. We have preached truth selectively, loved partially, judged unfairly, and ignored cries for justice. God's Spirit is grieved by our neglect of righteousness and mercy. He calls us to weep, to pray, and to intercede for the nations and for His Bride. Tears are not a weakness; they are a strength when guided by God. A weeping Church is a praying Church, and a praying Church is the instrument of God's power on the earth.

We must repent of empty rituals, superficial worship, and hollow service. The Church has become accustomed to appearances over authenticity, activity over intimacy, noise over holiness. God desires substance, not show. He desires hearts that tremble, lives that surrender, and lips that speak truth with love. Only a Church willing to remove the façade can experience genuine revival and manifest the presence of Christ to a watching world.

The Holy Spirit calls for leaders to humble themselves first. Pastors, prophets, teachers, elders, and intercessors, examine your heart. Confess your failures, abandon ambition, embrace truth, and walk in integrity. The Church's credibility depends on the obedience of its leaders. Heaven does not honor titles; it honors character. Obedience before God precedes influence among men. Those who lead must first follow Christ completely.

The call of God is urgent: rise from comfort, step away from pride, and pursue holiness with urgency. There is no time to delay. The trumpet of judgment sounds, the hour of repentance is now, and the opportunity for revival is passing. The Church must return to the cave of humility, to the altar of confession, to the secret place of prayer, and to the feet of the Savior. Only there will strength, wisdom, and anointing be restored.

And so the final call resounds: *Jesus, Son of David, have mercy on us! Forgive our sins, redeem our failures, break our pride, purify our hearts, restore Your Church, revive Your people, and prepare us for Your coming!* This is not a suggestion; it is an urgent decree from heaven. The Bride stands at a crossroads: return to the Lord or face His discipline. The cave is mercy, the cross is redemption, and the King waits with open arms. Bow, confess, repent, and rise, for God is faithful to restore those who seek Him fully.

The Lord calls the Church to confront its deepest compromises. We have allowed pride to dictate decisions, fear to silence truth, and comfort to replace courage. David's cave reminds us that God trains His leaders not in palaces, but in places of humility, danger, and dependence. The Church must learn the same lesson: greatness is born from surrender, not status; influence is earned through obedience, not applause. Every ministry that resists purification will fall when the fire of God tests it.

Even when the Church feels abandoned, God is present. David was haunted, hunted, and humiliated, yet God never left him. Christ Himself endured betrayal, rejection, and the cross, yet He completed the work of salvation. We, too, must endure trials, persecution, and injustice without turning from God. Each struggle, each season of humiliation, is an opportunity to experience God's presence more deeply. What looks like failure in the world's eyes may be a divine appointment for preparation and refinement.

Repentance demands honesty. We must name our sins, confess our failures, and confront our complicity in hidden evil. The Church has tolerated corruption, covered abuse, and excused pride. God is not silent about these things; He is calling His people to holiness. This is not a gentle whisper; it is an urgent summons. Those who refuse to examine their hearts will be caught in the collapse of structures built on compromise. The cave teaches that salvation is found in surrender, not in survival by cunning or compromise.

The Church must recognize the danger of spiritual self-reliance. David could not save himself, and no preacher, politician, or institution can deliver the Bride of Christ without the Spirit. We have leaned on human wisdom, political agendas, and institutional security, but God's kingdom operates on obedience, faith, and the blood of Jesus. The Church must forsake its illusions of independence and bow fully before the Lord. Only then will revival come, only then will righteousness prevail, only then will the Bride be ready.

Jesus Christ, the Son of David, the Son of God, is our ultimate refuge. He endured betrayal, mockery, false accusations, and the shame of the cross to redeem mankind. Like David, He trusted God through every humiliation, but unlike David, He was perfect and without sin. The Church must remember this example — suffering is not a sign of God's absence; it is the path of sanctification. The cross is the template for leadership, ministry, and life: humility, obedience, and total surrender to God's will.

The Church must repent of following men rather than Christ. We have lifted pastors, politicians, presidents, and platforms above the Savior. We have sought guidance from voices that cannot save. Acts 4:12 reminds us that salvation is found in no one else: there is no other name given among men by which we must be saved. No matter how impressive a leader appears, no matter how persuasive their speech, no one can redeem a soul. Only Jesus Christ, the Son of David, is our hope, our deliverer, and our King.

Every believer must examine personal compromise. Pride, self-righteousness, stubbornness, and worldly ambition must be laid aside. David's exile teaches that God often shapes leaders through hardship, not through honor. Likewise, the Church is called to embrace seasons of difficulty as divine instruction, not punishment. Those who cling to comfort over obedience will be unprepared for revival. Those who embrace humility, surrender, and repentance will carry the authority of God to a broken world.

The Church must weep for its failures in truth and love. Preaching without conviction, ministering without compassion, and leading without integrity have corrupted our witness. God is grieved by compromise, and His Spirit calls us to brokenness. Tears are not a sign of weakness; they are a sign of spiritual sensitivity and strength. A Church that cries before God rises above human judgment and enters divine purpose. We must allow our pain, our shame, and our remorse to drive us into His presence.

God is calling for radical obedience. David left behind family, comfort, and security to follow God's calling. The Church today must leave behind reputations, ministries, traditions, and attachments that conflict with Christ's authority. Everything we trust outside of God is an idol, whether political, religious, or cultural. To be effective in the kingdom, we must surrender all.

Revival cannot coexist with divided loyalties. Holiness demands exclusivity: Christ must be first, last, and all in between.

Repentance also demands courage. The Church must confront hidden evil within its own ranks, injustice, favoritism, hypocrisy, and abuse. To ignore these is to condone them. David's courage in exile, Christ's courage on the cross, and the perseverance of the apostles show that obedience often requires facing opposition. The Church must rise with boldness, not arrogance; with love, not compromise; with conviction, not fear. True leadership is forged in the fires of challenge and accountability.

The Lord is shaking nations, systems, and churches, but the shaking is a mercy for the obedient. Those who repent will be purified; those who resist will fall. David's time in the cave demonstrates that preparation and patience precede coronation. Christ's path to the cross demonstrates that suffering precedes salvation. Likewise, the Church must embrace seasons of trial, humiliation, and hiddenness to be ready for God's next move. The world's judgment is temporary; God's approval is eternal.

The Church must repent for tolerating sin in its midst. From gossip to injustice, from greed to favoritism, hidden evil has infiltrated altars and pulpits. Heaven is calling for confession, not convenience. Leaders, elders, teachers, and congregants alike must admit failure, confront wrongdoing, and pursue righteousness. Without cleansing, the Bride cannot stand before the Bridegroom. The cave of humility is open — enter it with tears, with confession, and with total surrender.

Even when exiled, betrayed, or falsely accused, God's purpose endures. David's journey shows that persecution is often divine protection. Christ's path demonstrates that rejection is a gateway to salvation. Likewise, the Church must not despair when facing opposition. Our suffering is never wasted; our pain is never ignored. God sees, remembers, and will vindicate those who repent, remain faithful, and cling to Christ alone. The cave is where destiny is forged, even in the absence of human comfort.

We must embrace humility and dependence upon God. Every idol, whether political allegiance, church affiliation, or social status, must be removed from the heart.

David could not save himself, nor could we. Only God redeems, restores, and establishes. Christ alone is sufficient. The Church must forsake self-reliance and embrace total surrender. The cave, the cross, and the desert are not punishments; they are paths to power, authority, and victory under God's plan.

The time for repentance is now. The Church is on trial, and every heart will be examined. Bow before the Lord, confess hidden sin, release offense, abandon pride, and cry out: *"Jesus, Son of David, have mercy on us!"* Heaven waits not for our excuses, but for our surrender. Like David in exile, we must leave behind the things of the world, comfort, approval, and control, and embrace the cave of God's preparation. Only there will we rise in holiness, power, and authority to fulfill His divine purpose.

The Church must now reject complacency. David could not sit in comfort while Saul hunted him; Christ could not wait for acceptance while the world condemned Him. Likewise, the Bride of Christ cannot rest while compromise reigns, while pride dominates, while hidden evil persists. Repentance demands action, a turning from sin, a rising from apathy, and a running toward holiness. The cave of preparation requires us to shed every worldly attachment that hinders intimacy with God.

The Lord is calling the Church to see itself as it truly is a bride in need of cleansing. Every altar must be purified, every pulpit must be sanctified, every heart must be examined. No more pretense, no more hiding behind tradition, no more excuse for sin. David was prepared in the shadows; Christ was glorified through suffering. The Church will only be prepared for revival through humility, confession, and the total surrender of its will to God.

We must acknowledge the spiritual and political deceptions that have infiltrated our lives. Leaders, systems, and ideologies cannot replace obedience to God. David depended on the Lord in exile, Christ depended on the Father in obedience, and we, too, must recognize that no human authority holds ultimate power. The Church must repent of placing trust in flesh and return to faith in God alone. Only then will we experience freedom, protection, and divine guidance.

Repentance is not passive; it is a radical realignment with God's will. The Church must abandon pride, self-righteousness, and self-will. We must leave behind every worldly attachment — comfort, reputation, influence, and control. David abandoned his comforts; Christ surrendered everything. We, too, must surrender completely. Only in total surrender can the Bride experience resurrection power, holiness, and the authority to stand firm in the midst of spiritual and political storms.

The Church must weep for its failures. Every unconfessed sin, every compromise, every hidden evil tolerated grieves God's Spirit. Tears are not a weakness; they are a weapon in spiritual warfare. David wept in the cave; Christ wept over Jerusalem. Likewise, the Church must weep for loss, for the deceived, and for itself. This weeping is not despair; it is preparation for the joy of restoration, revival, and righteous authority.

The cave teaches patience and dependence. David could not force his coronation; Christ did not force the cross. Likewise, the Church must trust God's timing. Repentance and humility precede elevation. We must endure seasons of invisibility, rejection, and trial, knowing that God is faithful to fulfill His promises. Those who embrace the cave will emerge purified, strengthened, and equipped to fulfill their divine destiny.

God's mercy is abundant, yet urgent. The Church cannot delay confession and surrender. Every day spent in pride or compromise is a day lost from holiness. David was hunted, and Christ was rejected, but both fulfilled God's purpose because they obeyed. The Church must choose obedience now, before judgment comes in a more visible and devastating form. Repentance is the gateway to revival, and mercy will not wait indefinitely.

We must confront the idols within the Church. These are not only physical symbols but attitudes and allegiances: loyalty to leaders over Christ, preference for comfort over truth, allegiance to systems over the Spirit. David abandoned worldly idols; Christ rejected earthly power. Likewise, the Church must dismantle every idol that competes with God. Only then can holiness prevail, and only then can the Bride be ready for the King.

Repentance calls for courage. It demands facing the reality of hidden evil, sin, betrayal, and personal failure. The Church cannot hide from the truth any longer. David faced enemies and uncertainty; Christ faced the cross. We must face our failures, confess them fully, and turn to Jesus for mercy. Only through courage and honesty will the Church be restored, strengthened, and purified.

The Lord calls the Church to unity in holiness. True unity is not uniformity of opinion or allegiance; it is alignment with God's truth. David led a divided people through obedience and faith; Christ brought together sinners through love and truth. Likewise, the Church must reject division born of pride, politics, or personal preference. Repentance requires humility, and humility births unity that honors God.

The Church must pray with intensity. Not casual prayers, but desperate, Spirit-led cries for mercy, cleansing, and revival. David prayed in his cave; Christ prayed in Gethsemane. Only persistent, passionate, and contrite prayer aligns the Church with God's will. Prayer is the instrument that shifts heaven and earth, that tears down strongholds, and that opens the doors for redemption and restoration.

Repentance is a call to action, not mere confession. The Church must live out holiness, justice, and truth daily. David acted courageously despite fear; Christ acted obediently despite rejection. Likewise, the Church must act in obedience, confronting injustice, protecting the vulnerable, and proclaiming truth. Without action, repentance is incomplete, and revival cannot manifest.

The Lord calls for transparency. Hidden sin, secret agendas, and concealed corruption are incompatible with the Bride of Christ. David faced public trials; Christ endured public shame. Likewise, the Church must confront and expose evil within its ranks, not for shame but for sanctification. Only in truth can healing, unity, and revival flourish. Hidden evil has no place in God's plan for the Church.

The Church must cry out collectively: *"Jesus, Son of David, have mercy on us!"* Every leader, every member, every believer must join in confession and surrender. The voice of one is powerful; the voice of the united Bride is unstoppable. God's mercy is ready; His Spirit is present; revival is possible. But only for those willing to humble themselves, forsake pride, and embrace the cave of preparation.

The days we are living in echo ancient warnings, yet too many are deaf to the trumpet. Pride has lifted its head not only in political palaces but behind pulpits, in ministries, in church boards, and among those who once called themselves servants of the Highest. Like Nebuchadnezzar, many believed that the kingdoms they built, the platforms they grew, and the influence they commanded were the work of their hands and the result of their brilliance. They forgot the God who gave breath, who positioned them, who gave them favor, and who alone is worthy of glory.

When the Church begins to boast in itself rather than in Christ, judgment must begin at the house of God. For God will never share His glory with flesh, and He will never allow His name to be used to prop up egos, political idols, or cults of personality masquerading as ministry. Those who misuse His name for gain invite the same humbling Nebuchadnezzar endured, yet many today ignore the signs of God's discipline already shaking the foundations of religious institutions.

There is a shaking across pulpits because too many shepherds became celebrities, too many ministers became businessmen, and too many altars became stages for human applause rather than sacred places of repentance and worship. The Church is now on trial because God is reclaiming His bride, purifying His temple, and reminding His people that no empire, secular or spiritual, can stand when it is built on pride and self-exaltation.

We live in a time where spiritual leaders speak more about building influence than making disciples. Where sermons focus on self-promotion and branding rather than brokenness before God. Where emotional hype is mistaken for the Holy Spirit, and where crowds are mistaken as proof of God's approval. But God is exposing the hidden motives, the secret sins, and the corrupted ambition that has polluted sacred leadership.

Just as Nebuchadnezzar looked over Babylon and declared it the work of his own greatness, many today look at their ministries, their titles, their followers, and their wealth and whisper the same prideful words in their hearts. Yet Scripture warns us — when pride rises, a fall follows. When man glorifies himself, God must humble him. When leaders exalt themselves above obedience and holiness, divine judgment awaits.

The downfall of Nebuchadnezzar did not begin when he lost his throne; it began the moment he lost sight of who placed him there. Likewise, the downfall of many houses of faith today is not sudden; it has been quietly unfolding as faith leaders began trusting in connections, money, prestige, and influence more than the presence and counsel of God.

When a church forgets to bow before the King of Kings, God will bend it low again. When a ministry becomes a monument, God dismantles it. When a shepherd exploits the sheep, God removes the shepherd and scatters the flock for their protection. And when spiritual leaders treat God's people as stepping-stones to wealth or power, God Himself intervenes.

But even in judgment, God's mercy endures. Nebuchadnezzar's humiliation was not destruction; it was discipline intended for repentance. God does not discipline to destroy; He disciplines to restore. He humbles Himself to heal. He tears down pride so humility can rise again, and His sovereignty is recognized above human throne rooms.

Today, God is calling His church to remember that the throne belongs to Christ alone. Authority flows from heaven, not from human brilliance or political endorsements. Security comes from obedience, not charisma. And the true mark of anointed leadership is not influence but surrender.

True greatness in the Kingdom has never been measured by earthly acclaim. Daniel's greatness was not in Babylonian honors but in unwavering obedience. His strength was not political power but his posture in prayer. His victories were not won in courts or councils but in the secret place where he bowed before the God of heaven.

Daniel's integrity was tested in Babylon, not in Jerusalem. Likewise, God is watching how His people behave in a world hostile to truth, not merely how they act inside church walls. The exiled believers of Scripture did not compromise in foreign systems, yet many today compromise within the sanctuary.

Some ministers preached repentance, but now preach what brings applause. Churches once focused on holiness now emphasize comfort. Spiritual leaders, once committed to truth, now avoid offense to maintain influence. Yet the faithful remnant God is raising looks more like Daniel, unshaken, uncompromised, unbent by pressure.

A church that blends in with culture cannot transform it. A believer who fears rejection more than God cannot lead others to righteousness. Daniel stood firm in a wicked land because he feared God more than man. He refused to bow before idols even when it was convenient, expected, or lucrative. And because he stood, Heaven stood with him.

We need Daniels again. We need believers who do not sell truth for networks, partnerships, or donations. We need leaders who cannot be bought by political favor or silenced by public shame. We need saints who would rather lose everything than dishonor the God who gave everything. The call in this hour is not to blend in it is to stand apart. The church was never meant to be admired by the world but to confront it with truth, grace, holiness, and justice. A church more concerned with looking successful than being faithful has already fallen, even if the seats are full and the lights are bright.

The days of lukewarm faith are over. The days of comfortable Christianity are finished. We are in a season where only those rooted in truth will endure, for the winds of deception, corruption, and societal pressure are intensifying. But those grounded in Christ will not be moved. Many ask why judgment begins at the house of God, and the answer is simple: God purifies His own before He confronts the world. He corrects His family first because His name is on His Church. And before the nations tremble, His people must tremble before Him again.

The Church cannot call a sinful world to repentance while ignoring pride, greed, manipulation, abuse, compromise, and hidden sin within its own ranks. We cannot preach holiness while leaders secretly indulge in moral corruption. We cannot speak against idols while many in ministry worship influence, wealth, and applause. God is exposing what has been hidden, not to shame the Church but to save it. Exposure is mercy when it leads to repentance. But if repentance does not come, judgment follows. For the holy God of Daniel is the same God who judges every generation's rebellion.

God is searching for hearts. He is weighing motives. He is purifying pulpits. He is dismantling idols in His house. A bride polluted by worldliness cannot welcome the Bridegroom. A sleeping church cannot proclaim the return of the King. And a prideful church cannot experience revival. True revival does not come through marketing campaigns, worship concerts, or emotional highs. Revival is born when pride dies, when hearts break, when sin is confessed, when idols fall, and when repentance becomes more important than reputation. Revival begins where surrender begins.

The Spirit of God is calling the Church back to godly sorrow, the kind that bends the knee and breaks the heart. Not the shallow apology that seeks image protection but the deep repentance that seeks soul purification. Not tears for being exposed but tears for grieving God. The Church must cry again, not for attendance, not for political favor, not for cultural relevance, but for righteousness, holiness, and intimacy with Christ. We must cry for lost souls, not lost platforms. For the broken, not for brand success. For truth, not trend.

When the Church stands before God, He will not ask what we built but what we surrendered. He will not ask how many followed us, but how many we led to Him. He will not ask how well we were known but how faithfully we obeyed. Every crown will be cast down. Every accomplishment will fade. Every title will dissolve. Only what was done in obedience to Christ will endure. In the Kingdom, only surrendered hearts carry weight. There is a holy shaking occurring, and it is not to destroy but to restore. God is realigning His Church for purity, not popularity. For holiness, not hype. For power in the Spirit, not power in optics. For truth proclaimed boldly, not truth negotiated for convenience.

This purification is painful, but it is necessary. God is removing false shepherds who used His sheep. He is a silencing prophet who speaks dreams instead of Scripture. He is a humble leader who trusted charisma over consecration. And He is raising a humble remnant who bow low before the King of Glory. These humble ones will not be moved by trends or tempted by applause. They will serve without seeking fame. They will pray more than they perform. They will preach truth even when it pierces culture and challenges comfort. They will shepherd with tears and trembling, not ego and entitlement.

The coming move of God demands vessels who are emptied of pride, ambition, and self-glory. God will not pour new wine into proud skins. Revival cannot flow through hardened hearts. Renewed influence will not come to those seeking platforms, but to those who embrace purity and brokenness before Him. We must choose who we resemble, Nebuchadnezzar in pride or Daniel in humility. Saul in disobedience or David in repentance. Judas in ambition or Peter in restoration. The path of humility is narrow, but it leads to life. The path of pride is wide, but it ends in ruin.

Many have admired Daniel's promotion but overlooked his posture. Before honor came humiliation. Before elevation came surrender. Before influence came persecution. His faithfulness in private prepared his authority in public. Today, God is calling us to that same hidden obedience. Daniel prayed when no one was watching, fasted when no applause existed, and stood firm when threats arose. His devotion was not seasonal or situational; it was steadfast. And that steadfastness led not only to personal blessing but to national awakening.

Our nation needs Daniels again, men and women who rise early to seek God, who intercede for the nation, who weep for the lost, who speak truth to power without fear, and who refuse to bow before idols of culture, politics, or corrupted religion. The Nebuchadnezzars of this world — both in government and in pulpits must face God or fall. Their pride may be tolerated for a time, but Heaven always answers arrogance. And those who refuse humility will meet humiliation until they acknowledge the King of Heaven rules all.

The Church must no longer confuse earthly power with divine approval. Just because someone stands high before men does not mean they stand clean before God. The Lord does not look at position but posture, not success but surrender, not noise but holiness. There is a sobering truth many avoid: some who are celebrated on earth will be rejected in heaven because they served the crowd but never bowed to Christ. They performed ministry but lacked repentance. They preached God's name but lived for their own.

Christ warned that many will say, "Lord, Lord," only to hear, "I never knew you." Not because they never spoke His name, but because they never surrendered their hearts. They used Jesus' platform without living His lifestyle. And heaven will not be fooled by earthly applause. This chapter in history demands genuine faith. God is searching for worshippers in spirit and truth, not performers in public and pretenders in private. He is calling us back to our first love, not ministry success, not spiritual gifting, but Christ Himself.

The final cry of repentance is sounding across the earth, a cry for humility, holiness, and heart transformation. The King is returning, and He is coming for a pure bride. He will not settle for a mixture, compromise, or divided loyalty. His Church must be ready, cleansed, and aligned with heaven. We must fall before Him now, willingly, rather than fall like Nebuchadnezzar in forced humility. Blessed is the one who bows before God, humbles himself. Blessed is the leader who repents before exposure comes. Blessed is the church that returns to the altar before judgment falls.

Repentance is not a punishment; it is a gift. It is God inviting us back into alignment, back into intimacy, back into purity, back into power. It is how we return from the exile of the soul. It is how we regain spiritual vision. It is how we recover the fear of the Lord, which is the beginning of wisdom. Pride is a fast road to spiritual blindness. Humility opens the eyes again. When pride dies, discernment lives. When we decrease, Christ increases. When we surrender, the Spirit fills. And only then can the Church once again be a light to the nation rather than a mirror of the world.

The world does not need a church that imitates culture; it needs a church that reflects Christ. It needs holiness that convicts. Love that heals. Sacrifice that inspires. Truth spoken in power, not silence born of fear. A courageous witness, not a compromised presence. Let the Church rise again, but rise in repentance. Rise in humility. Rise in purity. Rise in intercession. Rise in truth. For God is not finished with His people; He is refining them for greater glory than before, but glory that belongs to Him alone.

We must not waste this divine reset. For when God humbles a people, it is because He intends to heal them. When He breaks pride, it is because He intends to restore honor. When He calls for repentance, it is because revival is near, but revival that flows from brokenness, not bravado.

Let every pastor, minister, church leader, and believer search their heart. Let every hidden motive be laid before God. Let every idol be torn down. Let every unconfessed sin be surrendered. For God is not seeking perfect vessels, but purified ones. If we cry out in repentance, He will heal. If we turn, He will restore. If we humble ourselves, He will lift us again, not for our glory, but for His Kingdom. And His glory will rest on those who bow low before Him now.

Heaven records every tear of repentance and rejects every excuse of pride. The one who kneels will stand strong; the one who stiffens their neck will be broken. Choose humility now, for the hour is late, and the Judge stands at the door. The cry of the Spirit is calling us to return — return to holiness, return to prayer, return to fasting, return to Scripture, return to communion with God, return to authentic fellowship, return to righteous leadership, return to first love devotion.

Let the Church rise again as a beacon of truth, not a system of performance. As a sanctuary of healing, not a platform of ego. As a place where the presence of God dwells, not a marketplace for religious transactions. Let the fire return to the altar, not merely lights to the stage. The Church on trial can still be the Church triumphant if it repents. For the God who humbled kings and restored them is the same God who humbles churches and revives them. And the God who disciplined Nebuchadnezzar restored his dignity when he lifted his eyes to heaven.

So, lift your eyes, Church. Lift them from pride. Lift them from fear. Lift them from politics. Lift them from human saviors. Lift them from worldly validation. Lift them to the hills from whence your help comes, for your help comes from the Lord, Maker of heaven and earth. Let the proud bow. Let the weary kneel. Let the broken rise. Let the deceived awaken. Let the prodigal return. Let the Church find its humility and its power again in Christ alone. For those who humble themselves under the mighty hand of God will be lifted in due time. And when God lifts you, no man can pull you down. When God restores you, shame cannot hold you. When God breathes on you, ministry becomes holy again. When God purifies you, the fire falls. And when God reigns in you, your life and ministry will bear eternal fruit.

The greatest revival in history is not coming through proud voices but repentant hearts. The greatest moves of God will not be televised but birthed in hidden altars, late-night prayers, and quiet rooms of surrender. The final cry of repentance will precede the final trumpet of Christ's return. So let every believer weep for sin, not defend it. Let every leader confess failure, not justify it. Let every church renounce idolatry, not hide it. Let every ministry seek God's face, not human applause. Only a repentant church can carry a holy fire.

Let the fire of repentance burn pride away. Let it cleanse the pulpit and purify the pew. Let it expose every counterfeit and empower every true servant. Let it prepare a bride without blemish for the soon-coming King. The Church that bows now will rise in glory later. The Church that repents now will rejoice when Christ appears. The Church that mourns sin now will celebrate eternal victory. For repentance is not the end, it is the gateway to restoration.

In this hour, God is not simply asking His Church to do better; He is commanding His Church to **return**. Return to holiness. Return to reverence. Return to the altar where tears stain the floor and hearts are rebuilt in repentance. Return to true discipleship, not digital influence. Return to shepherding souls, not managing audiences. Return to fasting, not feasting on entertainment. Return to trembling at His Word, not twisting it for applause.

For the Judge of all Creation stands at the door, not pacing in hesitation but positioned in righteousness. He is not coming as the gentle Lamb to be slain again — He is coming as the Lion of Judah, with fire in His eyes and justice in His hand. He is coming to separate wheat from tares, shepherds from wolves, servants from performers, worshipers from pretenders.

And yet even now His voice is not only thunder; it is still a whisper for those willing to hear. "Return to Me, and I will return to you." His judgment is not aimed at destroying but to awaken, not to crush but to cleanse, not to condemn but to redeem. The God who disciplines is the God who restores. The hand that corrects is the hand that gathers the broken back to His heart.

Many in the church fear the exposure of sin, but few fear the absence of God. That is the true danger, not humiliation before men but separation from the presence that gives life. A church can lose its building and still live, but if it loses the presence of God, it becomes a shell, a museum of former glory where Ichabod silently hangs over the door: *"The glory has departed."*

God is not seeking a polished church; He is seeking a purified one. He is not impressed by performance but moved by purity. He is not entertained by worship services; He is enthroned by worshippers in spirit and truth. He is not after religious professionals; He is calling for repentant sons and daughters.

Some have mistaken delay for approval. Some assumed, "Nothing has happened yet, therefore God must be pleased." But God's silence has been mercy — time to repent, space to turn, a window to humble our hearts. Yet windows do not stay open forever. Ships of compromise eventually hit storms of consequence. And mercy ignored becomes judgment embraced.

The Nebuchadnezzars of this age, political rulers, wealthy influencers, and spiritual celebrities are shaking. Thrones wobble. Platforms tremble. Institutions crack. And God whispers again: "Acknowledge Me as Lord, or I will humble you for the sake of those you mislead."

But the Daniels of this age are rising. Quiet. Holy. Uncompromised. Hidden but chosen. They do not bow to idols, nor dilute truth, nor mortgage eternity for earthly acceptance. Their authority is not earned online but in prayer rooms where eternity hears them before earth sees them.

And the Shadrach, Meshach, and Abednego, the faithful remnant, are standing tall in the furnace of cultural hostility. Others panic; they praise. Others bow; they believe. And the Son of God still walks with them in the flames. When the Church stands before God, titles will mean nothing, but tears will speak. Reputation will fade, but righteousness will endure. Success will dissolve, but surrender will shine. And only those who fell on their faces in repentance now will stand with boldness then.

For there is a day when every voice will cease except the voice of the King. Every knee will bow willingly or unwillingly. Every crown will fall except the crown upon His holy head. And every church will give an account not to critics, but to Christ Himself.

Oh, church, this is the moment to wake up. Not tomorrow, not when scandal comes, not when culture collapses, not when persecution increases **now**. The Spirit says, "Today if you hear His voice, harden not your heart." Pride resists this call. Religion excuses it. The ego argues against it. But the humble fall to their knees and whisper, "Lord, cleanse me first." A humbled church will become a healed church. A repenting church will become a revived church. A purified church will become a powerful church. And a surrendered church will become a shining city on a hill once again.

We are not losing influence; we are shedding illusions. We are not dying; we are being pruned. We are not collapsing; we are being cleansed. For God does His greatest work not when we appear strongest, but when we kneel lowest. Blessed is the church that bows now, for it will stand in glory later. Blessed is the leader who repents in private before rebuke reaches the public. Blessed is the believer who refuses compromise and chooses consecration.

Let every pastor examine their heart. Let every prophet weigh their words. Let every worship leader check their motives. Let every church member assess their devotion. The holiness God seeks is not loud but loyal, not flashy but faithful, not impressive but obedient. The days of shallow faith are ending. The era of showmanship is closing. The time of the remnant has arrived. And God is not looking for crowds. He is gathering soldiers of truth, worshippers of purity, disciples of sacrifice.

You do not need a platform to have purpose. You do not need applause to have anointing. Influence born in humility will outlast influence bought by hype. Quiet obedience shakes more kingdoms than loud self-promotion ever could. Success without surrender is spiritual suicide. Power without purity is a snare. Ministry without brokenness becomes manipulation. But surrender births authority. Brokenness births healing. Humility births revival.

There is no revival without repentance. There is no awakening without weeping. There is no restoration without surrender. Before God rebuilds, He tears down what pride erected. Before glory comes, idols must fall. Hear the word of the Lord: *"Return to Me, and I will restore you."* Not return to programs, return to prayer. Not return to branding, return to brokenness. Not return to crowds return to the cross.

For the Cross is where pride dies. The Cross is where the ego collapses. The Cross is where kings remove crowns and sinners find mercy. And only those who bow at Calvary now will reign with Christ later.

Let this chapter be etched into the spiritual walls of every church: *We were warned. We were invited. And we chose repentance.* If we do, heaven will write: *And God breathed on them again.* The final cry of repentance is not a cry of despair; it is a cry of awakening. It is the sound of chains breaking. It is the sound of idols crashing. It is the sound of prodigals running home. It is the sound of demons losing territory. It is the sound of glory returning.

May we be a people who humble ourselves before God humbles us publicly. May we be a generation that responds to His whisper before He sends thunder. May we be a Church that honors Christ more than culture, truth more than comfort, and holiness more than hype. And when we stand before God not as spectators but as His redeemed, may we stand not in shame but in gratitude. May we stand forgiven, purified, humbled, and restored. May we stand knowing that when pride tried to destroy us, repentance rebuilt us. May we stand proclaiming that Christ alone is worthy, forever and ever, Amen.

Finally, the Church must rise from repentance to restoration. David emerged from his exile as a king; Christ rose from the cross as Savior. Likewise, the Church will emerge from humility, trial, and confession into glory, power, and authority in Christ. The cave was preparation, the cross was redemption, and surrender is the path to resurrection. Today, God calls every believer to kneel, repent, and cry out: *"Jesus, Son of David, have mercy on me, redeem me, and restore Your Church to holiness and power!"* The final cry of repentance has sounded; the choice is ours: surrender or continue in hidden destruction.

Chapter 40: Epilogue: "The Nations Tremble, the Heavens Speak"

The Epilogue unfolds as a prophetic revelation from God addressing the spiritual, political, and moral collapse of the modern world. The Lord speaks directly to the nations, especially the nations of the world and the global Church, declaring that the chaos, wars, corruption, and division we see are not coincidences but signs of divine shaking.

God exposes the world's moral decay, warns the Church of its compromise, and reminds Israel of His unbroken covenant. The global crises are revealed to be labor pains before Christ's return. Yet amid the warnings, God offers mercy and hope to the repentant, calling His people to revival, holiness, and unwavering faith.

The Lord says, "I am not blind to what is happening in your nations. My eyes see the corruption that parades as leadership, the deception that dresses itself in righteousness, and the blood that cries from the ground of the innocent."

Nations of the world, you were once a nation that carried My name in your pledge and upon your currency. Yet now, you legislate rebellion, call sin freedom, and silence those who speak truth in love. You have replaced altars with agendas and prophets with politicians.

From your highest courts to your local councils, justice has become selective. My Word has been mocked, My laws debated as opinions. You exalt the wisdom of man above the fear of the Lord. But I say again, *the fear of the Lord is the beginning of wisdom.*

I gave you abundance so that you would bless nations, not boast in power. I gave you liberty so that you would proclaim My truth, not redefine it. But your liberty has become lawlessness, and your freedom is a banner for rebellion. Therefore, the shaking will not be avoided. Systems will collapse, idols will fall, and those who built their empires on deceit will see their foundations crumble. Yet in the ruins, a remnant will rise — purified, humbled, and hungry for righteousness.

To the Church leaders across the world: I am calling you back to your first love. You have mirrored the culture instead of transforming it. You sought to fit in when I called you to stand out. Return to your altar of tears, for revival is born from repentance. And to Israel, My covenant nation, the world watches your turmoil and war. Yet My covenant remains unbroken. Though nations gather against you, I, the Lord, will not forsake the seed of Abraham. What you see as chaos, I am using to fulfill prophecy.

The nations rage, the kings of the earth take counsel together, saying, "Let us break their bands asunder." But He who sits in the heavens laughs. For the time of the Gentiles is ending, and the restoration of My people Israel is near. There will be wars and rumors of wars. The land I promised will be contested. Yet every arrow, every missile, and every act of terror will remind the world that prophecy is alive, for I declared these things before they came to pass.

The nations surrounding Israel will tremble, for My Word will stand even when governments fall. I am setting the stage for the return of the Son of Man, when every eye shall see Him and every knee shall bow. Europe groans under moral decay; Asia burns with persecution against My children; Africa battles corruption and bloodshed; South America struggles with spiritual deception. Yet on every continent, I am awakening remnants who will not bow to Baal.

In the Middle East, blood cries out from the soil, but so do the prayers of My saints. I am revealing Myself even in the deserts, in visions, in dreams, and in the secret gatherings of believers who risk their lives to bear My name. I am not absent from the suffering; I am present in it. I am not silent amid injustice; I am speaking through it. What the world calls chaos is My divine confrontation — exposing lies, dismantling idols, and calling humanity repentance.

The alliances of nations, the wars for territory, the propaganda for control, all are part of the shaking that reveals what cannot be shaken: My kingdom. Governments will rise and fall, but My Word will endure forever. Even within My Church, I am dividing truth from tradition, faith from fame, and calling shepherds to repent for neglecting My sheep. Those who repent will find mercy; those who resist will be removed.

Many will say, "Where is God in all this?" But I tell you, I am in a storm, not as destruction but as purification. I am not the author of evil, but I am the Judge of it. What you see unfolding is not the end it is the beginning of awakening. I am raising voices from unexpected places — prophets from prisons, worshipers from war zones, intercessors from broken homes — to cry out for the nations and prepare the way of the Lord.

The world's crises are not random; they are redemptive. I am shaking the visible to reveal the invisible. I am overturning governments to reveal the true King. I am allowing famine and fire to remind the world of its dependence on Me. Let every pastor, politician, and prophet hear you cannot serve two masters. You cannot bless what I have cursed, nor curse what I have blessed. Choose this day whom you will serve: the approval of men or the authority of God.

The cries of the persecuted, the tears of the righteous, the groans of creation all reach My throne. And I am answering, not with mere comfort but with correction, not with delay but with divine disruption. The return of My Son is nearby. The stage is being set. The trumpet is being polished. The angels are preparing for the great gathering. The nations may not see it, but Heaven is already in motion.

My people, prepare your heart. The kingdoms of this world are becoming the kingdoms of your Lord and of His Christ. Every headline, every shaking, every war is a trumpet announcing that the King is coming. To those who stand firm: fear not. You were born for this hour. You are the Daniels, the Esthers, the Paul's, and the Deborahs of this generation. Shine in the darkness, for the darkness cannot overcome you.

The Church is on trial, but soon the Judge will rise from His seat. When He stands, every lie will fall silent, every false prophet will flee, and every faithful servant will hear the words, "Well done, good and faithful servant." And the Spirit concludes: "Behold, I make all things new. The kingdoms of man are fading, but My kingdom is forever. Let the nations tremble, let the Church awaken, and let every heart prepare for the Lord your God is coming in power and great glory."

Thus says the Lord of Hosts: *The nations are in turmoil, and the hearts of men fail them for fear of what is coming upon the earth. But I, the Lord, remain enthroned above the flood. My Word stands eternal, though kingdoms crumble beneath their own pride.* America, I once called you a beacon to the nations — a land that declared "In God We Trust." But now you trust in your own strength, your own systems, your own idols of politics and power. You raise leaders who speak My name but deny My truth. You have sown division and call it democracy.

Your cities burn with corruption, your courts twist justice. From the highest office to the pulpits of compromise, deception flows like polluted waters. You have exchanged holiness for entertainment and truth for tolerance. You legislate what I call abomination, then lift your hands in worship, as though I cannot see the blood on them — the blood of the innocent, the exploited, the voiceless. Have you forgotten that I am the God who hears the cry of the oppressed?

My prophets warned you, but you silenced them. My Spirit tugged at your hearts, but you quenched Him. You mocked those who stood for righteousness and applauded those who rebelled. Therefore, I will shake your foundations until idols fall and truth is the only thing that remains standing. The winds of shaking are not punishment for the righteous but purification for the remnant. For I am raising voices from the wilderness — voices that do not bow to political thrones or cultural applause but stand only for My kingdom.

To My Church in America, I say: you have mirrored the world when you were called to transform it. You have sought popularity more than purity, membership more than discipleship, and offerings more than obedience. Repent before the candlestick is removed. I walk among the lampstands again, trimming the wicks, removing the soot, and igniting fresh oil. I am raising a Church not dressed in glamour but clothed in glory — not known by its wealth but by its witnesses.

Look to Israel, My covenant nation surrounded, slandered, and under siege. Yet My promises stand firm. Though rockets fall and enemies gather, I, the Lord, am her keeper. I neither slumber nor sleep over Jerusalem. The nations gather around her borders and plot her ruin, but I have decreed her restoration. Every attack is a reminder that prophecy is alive, and every shaking draws the world closer to the revealing of the Son of Man.

From the land of Abraham to the nations far away, I am aligning events to fulfill what was written. The time of the Gentiles wanes, and the eyes of the world turn once more to Zion, where history began and where redemption shall be completed. The wars you see from Gaza to Ukraine, from Africa's deserts to Asia's seas — are not random. They are the labor pains of a groaning creation, awaiting the manifestation of the sons and daughters of God.

I am shaking every system: political, financial, religious, and cultural. The towers of pride are falling, the economies of greed are trembling, and the altars built on deception are collapsing beneath My judgment. Europe has lost its moral compass,

483

chasing shadows of humanism while rejecting the Light of the world. Asia rises in power yet wages war against My saints. Africa wrestles between revival and corruption, while Latin America groans under false religion and oppression.

But in every continent, I am raising remnants nameless, faceless, fearless. They will not be silenced by censorship or controlled by fear. They will cry out for righteousness until the nations tremble and the heavens open. I hear the prayers of the persecuted in underground churches, in refugee camps, in prison cells. I see the tears of the mothers who have lost children to war and violence. I hear the cries of those who call upon My name amid famine and fire.

The world asks, "Where is God?" I answer, *I am here — in the shaking, in the storms, in the silence before the trumpet sounds.* I am purifying the earth, exposing the false, and revealing the truth. Those who trust in idols, whether political parties, economic systems, or human leaders, will be confounded. For I am tearing down every throne that has exalted itself above My Word.

Many who claimed to speak for Me have spoken from ambition, not anointing. They prophesied prosperity while ignoring purity. But I will not share My glory with flesh. Every false voice will be silent, every hidden agenda revealed. Yet even in wrath, I remember mercy. My hand is stretched out still — not to destroy, but to deliver those who will humble themselves and turn from wickedness. For I take no pleasure in the death of the wicked but rejoice when the prodigal returns.

I am calling for repentance, not reform. For reform adjusts behavior, but repentance transforms the heart. This is the hour to rend your heart, not your garments, to return to Me with fasting, weeping, and intercession.

Conclusion

The Church is indeed on trial—not in the courts of men, but before the throne of God. The trials we see in the world today expose hidden evil, hypocrisy, and falsehood within the body of Christ. Yet even in judgment, God's mercy calls His people to repentance, restoration, and renewal.

This is not the time for silence or compromise but for boldness in truth and holiness. The Church is refined not by comfort but by fire. And through the refining fire, God reveals a remnant—a people committed to His Word, His Spirit, and His mission. Let us remember: the Church does not belong to man. It belongs to Christ, the Head, who gave His life for her. While evil may be uncovered, God's glory will shine brighter, and His purposes will prevail. May we each examine our hearts, return to the cross, and live as witnesses of truth in a world desperate for light.

Reflection / Study Guide Questions

1. In what ways have you seen "hidden evil" in the Church or in your own life that God has revealed?
2. How can believers respond to the uncovering of corruption and hypocrisy without losing faith in God's true Church?
3. What Scriptures remind you that God refines His people through trials and judgment?
4. What practical steps can you take to remain steadfast in God's Word when the Churchfaces pressure from the world?
5. How does this book challenge you to walk more boldly in your faith and to call others to truth?

Bibliography – The Church on Trial – God Rebukes Hidden Evils

Primary Source – The Holy Bible

- The Holy Bible, King James Version (KJV). Thomas Nelson, 1769.
- The Holy Bible, New International Version (NIV). Zondervan, 1978.
- The Holy Bible, English Standard Version (ESV). Crossway, 2001.

Scripture References

Old Testament

- Genesis 1:26–27; 3:1–7
- Exodus 20:1–17
- Deuteronomy 30:19–20
- 2 Chronicles 7:14
- Psalm 1:1–6; 34:18; 51:10; 139:23–24
- Proverbs 3:5–6; 4:23; 10:12
- Isaiah 5:20; 14; 29:13; 53:5; 59:1–2; 61:1–3; 65:5–7
- Jeremiah 6:16; 17:9; 31:33–34
- Ezekiel 22:30; 28:12–15; 36:26–27
- Joel 2:12–13
- Amos 5:24
- Micah 6:8
- Habakkuk 2:4
- Zechariah 7:9–10

New Testament

- Matthew 5–7; 16:18–19; 22:37–40; 23
- Mark 5:19; 12:30–31; 13:10–13
- Luke 5:16; 6:31; 12:2–3; 15:11–32; 19:8–9; 22:42
- John 3:16–18; 4:23–24; 8:32; 13:34–35; 14:27; 15:12–13; 17:21–23; 18:36
- Acts 2:42–47; 10:34–35; 16:16–18
- Romans 1:18–32; 5:8; 7:19; 8:1–2; 12:1–2, 9–10; 13:1
- 1 Corinthians 3:16–17; 6:19; 13:1–13
- 2 Corinthians 4:5–6; 5:17–19; 6:14; 11:13–15; 12:7–9
- Galatians 3:28; 5:16–25; 6:2
- Ephesians 4:3; 4:15; 5:11–14; 5:25–27
- Philippians 2:3–11; 4:8
- Colossians 2:8; 3:12–14
- 1 Thessalonians 4:3–7; 5:23
- 1 Timothy 4:1–2
- 2 Timothy 1:7; 3:1–7, 16–17
- Titus 2:11–14
- Hebrews 4:12; 10:22–24; 12:14
- James 1:22–27; 2:17; 3:15–17; 5:16
- 1 Peter 1:22; 4:8; 4:17
- 2 Peter 2:1–3
- 1 John 1:9; 2:3–6; 3:16–18; 4:1–3, 7–12, 18–21
- Jude 1:20–23
- Revelation 2–3; 3:15–16; 19:7–9; 20:11–15; 21:1–8; 22:12–17

Secondary Christian Authors & Resources

- Bonhoeffer, Dietrich. *The Cost of Discipleship.* SCM Press, 1937.
- Tozer, A. W. *The Pursuit of God.* Christian Publications, 1948.
- Lewis, C. S. *Mere Christianity.* HarperCollins, 1952.
- Ravenhill, Leonard. *Why Revival Tarries.* Bethany House, 1959.
- MacArthur, John. *The Gospel According to Jesus.* Thomas Nelson, 1988.
- Piper, John. *Desiring God: Meditations of a Christian Hedonist.* Multnomah, 1986.
- Keller, Timothy. *Every Good Endeavor: Connecting Your Work to God's Work.* Dutton, 2012.

- Sproul, R. C. *The Holiness of God.* Tyndale House, 1985.
- Warren, Rick. *The Purpose Driven Church.* Zondervan, 1995.
- Grudem, Wayne. *Systematic Theology: An Introduction to Biblical Doctrine.* Inter- Varsity Press, 1994.
- Blackaby, Henry & Blackaby, Richard. *Experiencing God: Knowing and Doing the Will of God.* B&H Books, 1990.
- Murray, Andrew. *Humility: The Beauty of Holiness.* Whitaker House, 1982.
- Wright, N.T. *Simply Christian: Why Christianity Makes Sense.* Harper One, 2006.

Recovery, Mental Health, and Trauma Resources

- Substance Abuse and Mental Health Services Administration (SAMHSA). *National Recovery Month.* SAMHSA, 1989–present.
- Alcoholics Anonymous World Services. *The Big Book: Alcoholics Anonymous.* 4th Edition, 2001.
- Narcotics Anonymous World Services. *Narcotics Anonymous Basic Text.* 6th Edition, 2018.
- American Psychiatric Association. *Diagnostic and Statistical Manual of Mental Disorders, 5th Edition (DSM-5).* APA, 2013.
- Herman, Judith Lewis. *Trauma and Recovery: The Aftermath of Violence— from Domestic Abuse to Political Terror.* Basic Books, 2015.
- van der Kolk, Bessel A. *The Body Keeps the Score: Brain, Mind, and Body in the Healing of Trauma.* Penguin Books, 2015.

Faith-Based Mental Health and Healing

- White, David W., & Ellis, James. *Christian Counseling and Mental Health: Integrating Faith and Psychology.* Baker Academic, 2020.
- Tan, Siang-Yang. *Counseling and Psychotherapy: A Christian Perspective.* 3rd Edition, Baker Academic, 2011.
- Johnson, Eric L., & Jones, Robert L. *Addiction and Grace: Love and Spirituality in the Healing of Addictions.* Zondervan, 2002.
- Koenig, Harold G. *Religion, Spirituality, and Mental Health: Evidence for an Association. International Review of Psychiatry,* 2015.
- Clinton, Tim & Hawkins, Ron. *The Quick-Reference Guide to Biblical Counseling.* Baker Books, 2009.

Trauma-Informed Church Practices

- Akin, Daniel L., & Alexander, Paul. *Trauma-Informed Ministry: How Churches Can Heal from Crisis and Pastoral Stress.* Baker Publishing, 2021.
- Guenette, Fiona. *Creating Safe Spaces: Trauma-Informed Care in Faith Communities.*
- Routledge, 2020.
- Felitti, Vincent J., & Anda, Robert F. *The Adverse Childhood Experiences (ACE) Study. American Journal of Preventive Medicine,* 1998.

White Christian Nationalism References

- Pew Research Center. *Religion and Politics in America: Trends in Christian Nationalism.*
- Washington, D.C.: Pew Research, 2021.
- Whitehead, Andrew L., & Perry, Matthew J. *Taking America Back for God: Christian Nationalism in the United States.* Oxford University Press, 2020.
- Marsden, George M. *Religion and American Culture.* Harcourt Brace, 1990.
- Lovett, Bobby, and Leith, John. *Faith and Politics in Contemporary America.* University of Chicago Press, 2018.
- Smith, Christian. *American Evangelicalism: Embattled and Thriving.* University of Chicago Press, 1998.

Additional Resources

- National Institute of Mental Health (NIMH). *Mental Health Information.* NIMH, 2023.
- World Health Organization (WHO). *Mental Health and Substance Use.* WHO, 2023.
- Barna Group. *The State of the Church 2023.* Barna, 2023.
- Christianity Today. *Global Revival and Church Renewal in the 21st Century.* Christianity Today Publications, 2022.

Invitation to Know Christ / Devotional Ending

Beloved, the greatest trial is not what happens to the Church in this world, but what happens to your soul in eternity. The Judge of all the earth is also the Savior who died for you. Though the Church may be on trial, Christ has already borne the greatest judgment on the cross so that you may be free.

If you do not know Him yet as Lord and Savior, this is your invitation. Jesus says: *"Come to Me, all you who are weary and burdened, and I will give you rest."* (Matthew 11:28)

Pray this simple prayer from your heart:

Lord Jesus, I acknowledge that I am a sinner in need of Your grace. I believe You died for my sins and rose again on the third day. Today, I repent and invite You into my heart as Lord and Savior. Wash me, fill me with Your Spirit, and make me a new creation. From this day forward, I choose to follow You. Amen

If you prayed this prayer, welcome to the family of God. Seek out a Bible-believing church, immerse yourself in God's Word, and live boldly for Christ.

As the Church stands on trial these last days, may your life testify to the power of the cross, the truth of Scripture, and the hope of eternal life.

About the Workbook Study Guide

The book *The Church on Trial – God Reveals Hidden Evil within the Church* is a prophetic call to awaken the Body of Christ. It reveals the hidden sin, compromise, and spiritual apathy that have quietly infiltrated the church, calling both leaders and members to personal and corporate examination. The Workbook Study Guide has been created to serve as a practical, interactive companion to the book, designed to equip believers, church leaders, small groups, and communities to respond faithfully to God's call for revival, holiness, and restoration.

Purpose of the Workbook Study Guide

The primary purpose of this Workbook Study Guide is to provide a structured, engaging pathway for readers to engage with the truths presented in the book. Through reflection questions, discussion prompts, practical action steps, prayers, and creative exercises, participants are encouraged to:

1. **Examine the Heart and Church Practices:** Identify areas of compromise, hidden sin, and spiritual lukewarmness within personal lives and the church.
2. **Respond in Faith and Obedience:** Move beyond awareness to actionable steps, including prayer, repentance, accountability, and advocacy for righteousness.
3. **Foster Spiritual Growth and Maturity:** Develop habits, disciplines, and leadership practices aligned with God's Word and the Spirit's guidance.
4. **Promote Community Healing and Unity:** Equip church groups and leaders to confront issues such as hypocrisy, pride, injustice, and spiritual deception while fostering transparency, reconciliation, and compassion.

Vision Behind the Workbook

The vision of this study guide is to empower the church to rise as a holy, fearless, and unified bride of Christ. Guided by the Holy Spirit, it seeks to ignite spiritual discernment, courage, and revival that transform individual believers, families, churches, and the broader community. The aim is to prepare the Body of Christ for God's revelation, His shaking of hidden evil, and the glorious return of Jesus Christ.

Alignment with the Book

Each chapter of the book addresses a specific area of hidden evil, spiritual compromise, or divine correction. The Workbook Study Guide mirrors this structure, providing tools to:

Reflect on the Scripture and messages in each chapter.
Discuss and apply for lessons within small groups or leadership teams. Implement practical steps for personal and communal spiritual growth. Engage in prayerful and Spirit-led action for revival and renewal.

Who This Workbook Is For

This guide is intentionally designed for:

- **Church Leaders:** Pastors, ministry leaders, and mentors seeking to lead with integrity, discernment, and spiritual authority.
- **Small Groups and Study Teams:** Encouraging open dialogue, accountability, and practical application of God's Word.
- **Church Members and Communities:** Anyone who desires to deepen intimacy with God, confront personal and communal sin, and participate in the church's purification and revival.

A Call to Spiritual Awakening

The Workbook Study Guide is not merely a companion to read; it is a tool for transformation. It challenges participants to:

- Confront sin honestly and transparently.
- Pursuing holiness and obedience with fervor.
- Engage in intentional prayer, worship, and service.
- Lead and influence others toward revival, unity, and righteousness.

As you journey through this Workbook Study Guide, allow the Holy Spirit to guide you. Let it stir conviction, inspire action, and produce lasting change within your heart, your church, and your community.

Let this guide be your companion as we heed the call of God: to rise, awaken, and prepare the Church for His glory.

A Call to Awakening

The church stands at a pivotal moment. *The Church on Trial – God Reveals Hidden Evil* exposes the hidden sins, compromise, and spiritual apathy that quietly erode the Body of Christ. This Workbook Study Guide is designed to help believers, leaders, and church communities engage these truths practically, prayerfully, and courageously.

Through reflection questions, group discussions, action steps, prayers, and creative exercises, this guide will:

1. Illuminate areas of personal and corporate compromise.
2. Encourage repentance, holiness, and transparency.
3. Equip the church to confront deception, injustice, and pride.
4. Inspire spiritual growth, unity, and readiness for revival.

This workbook is more than studying; it is a journey of transformation. As you move through each chapter, allow the Holy Spirit to convict, guide, and strengthen you. Embrace His call to awaken, purify, and prepare the church to stand holy, fearless, and radiant for Christ's return.

Let this guide lead you to renewal, restoration, and revival—personally, corporately, and in your community.

Introduction: A Holy Fire in God's Nostrils

This introduction sets the tone for the book, highlighting God's righteous anger toward hidden sin and compromise in the church. It calls believers to awaken, examine themselves, and prepare for revival and restoration.

Key Scripture
Hebrews 12:29 – For our God is a consuming fire.

Reflection Questions
1. What does it mean that God is a consuming fire?
2. How does hidden sin affect the life of the church?
3. In what ways can we prepare for revival personally and corporately?

Group Discussion Prompts
How can the church today reawaken to God's holiness?
What are some examples of compromise in modern congregations?

Action Step / Weekly Challenge
Commit to a daily time of self-examination in prayer this week, asking God to reveal any hidden compromises in your heart.

Prayer Focus
Lord, purify my heart and cleanse Your church. Let us walk in holiness and truth, prepared for Your revival fire.

Creative Response Option
Create a journal entry or poem reflecting on what it means for God to be a consuming fire.

Self-Assessment
☐ I am actively seeking God's holiness.
☐ I sometimes overlook compromises in my life.
I ☐ am prepared for revival and restoration.

Chapter 1: A Church That Lost Its First Love

Chapter Summary

This chapter examines how the church's neglect of intimacy with Christ leads to spiritual decline. It calls for rekindling devotion through prayer, worship, and love for God above all else. When passion for Christ fades, religion replaces relationship. The church of Ephesus was once burned with zeal but grew cold in devotion. Today's Church mirrors that same apathy—busy in service but empty of intimacy. This chapter calls believers to return to their "first love," reviving prayer, worship, and holiness before the Lord.

Key Scriptures

- Revelation 2:4–5 – "You have forsaken your first love… Repent and do the works you did at first."
- Revelation 2:4 – Nevertheless, I have somewhat against thee, because thou hast left thy first love.
- Matthew 22:37 – "Love the Lord your God with all your heart…"
- Jeremiah 2:2 – "I remember the devotion of your youth…"
- Psalm 51:12 – "Restore to me the joy of your salvation…"

Reflection Quotes

When love for God cools, ministry becomes mechanical.

Revival is not found in noise, but in returning to intimacy with Jesus.

Reflection Questions

1. In what ways can a church lose its 'first love' for Christ?
2. Have I noticed seasons in my own life where zeal for God grew cold? What caused it?
3. What daily habits could help me rekindle intimacy with Jesus?

Action Step / Weekly Challenge

Spend one hour daily this week in uninterrupted prayer and worship, not asking, but adoring. Ask God to reignite your love for Him.

Commit to spending at least 20 minutes each day in undistracted worship and prayer this week, asking God to renew your love for Him.

Challenge Verse

"Draw near to God and He will draw near to you." – James 4:8

Group Discussion Prompts
- What are some signs of a church or believer losing their spiritual passion?
- How does returning to prayer and worship restore first love?

Biblical Character Connection
The Church of Ephesus (Revelation 2) – Commended for works but rebuked for lost passion. Their example teaches that zeal without intimacy leads to burnout.

Key Quote / Takeaway Box
"A church without love is a lampstand without light."

Weekly Song Suggestion
"Heart of Worship" – Matt Redman

Creative Response Option
Write a love letter to Jesus expressing gratitude for His faithfulness and confessing where your affection has grown cold.

Self-Assessment
1. What competes most for your affection toward Christ?
2. How does lost intimacy affect your ministry or service?
3. When was the last time you truly wept in His presence?
4. What would it look like to rekindle that fire again?
5. Who around you needs to see revived love for Christ through you?
6. ☐ I feel closer to Christ than I did a year ago.
7. ☐ I sometimes let busyness crowd out my time with God.
8. ☐ I am actively cultivating intimacy with Jesus.

Devotional Prayer for Repentance and Renewal

"Lord, forgive me for replacing relationship with routine. Strip away spiritual apathy and restore the fire of my first love. Ignite my heart until passion for You consumes every distraction. Lord, reignite my passion for You. Strip away distractions and idols that have taken Your place in my heart. Restore to me the joy of my salvation. In Jesus' name, Amen."

Final Reflection

A loveless church may have crowds, but it lacks power. Revival begins when hearts fall in love with Jesus again.

Chapter Summary

This chapter explores how pretense and hidden sin weaken the church from within. Authenticity and transparency are crucial for spiritual health and growth. Hypocrisy corrupts the church internally. When believers pretend righteousness while concealing sin, integrity suffers. God desires truth in the innermost parts. Genuine faith fosters transparency, confession, and repentance that bring freedom and purity.

Key Scriptures

- Luke 12:1 – "Beware of the leaven of the Pharisees, which is hypocrisy."
- Psalm 51:6 – "You desire truth in the inward parts."
- Matthew 23:27 – "You are like whitewashed tombs…"
- Proverbs 28:13 – "He who conceals his sins will not prosper…"

Reflection Quotes

"God cannot bless who we pretend to be."

"Hypocrisy blinds others—but destroys the soul of the deceiver."

Reflection Questions

1. What are some examples of hypocrisy in the church today?
2. How can hidden sin spread like "leaven" in a congregation?
3. In what ways can I pursue greater authenticity before God and others?

Group Discussion Prompts

Why is transparency vital for true fellowship in the body of Christ?

How does hypocrisy damage the church's witness to the world?

Action Step / Weekly Challenge

Confess one hidden struggle to a trusted accountability partner or Spirit-filled believer this week. Allow light to expose darkness.

Challenge Verse

"If we walk in the light… the blood of Jesus cleanses us from all sin." – 1 John 1:7

Biblical Character Connection

Ananias and Sapphira (Acts 5) – Their pretense before God cost them their lives. They remind us that the Holy Spirit cannot dwell in deceit.

Key Quote / Takeaway Box

"What's hidden in darkness will one day be shouted from the rooftops."

Weekly Song Suggestion

"Refiner" – Maverick City Music

Creative Response Option

1. Create a mirror prayer journal—write the truth about your inner struggles beside a column of Scriptures declaring freedom.
2. Draw or journal an image of "leaven" spreading through dough and reflect on how quickly hidden sin multiplies.

Self-Assessment

1. In what areas are you tempted to appear more spiritual than you are?
2. What fears keep you from being transparent?
3. How can confession bring healing in your community?
4. What is the cost of remaining silent about hidden sin?
5. How will you choose authenticity this week?
6. ☐ I strive to live with integrity before God.
7. ☐ I sometimes struggle with keeping up appearances.
8. ☐ I am learning to walk in greater transparency

Devotional Prayer for Repentance and Renewal

"Lord, cleanse me from hypocrisy. Let truth dwell deep within me. Remove the masks I've worn before you and others. Make me honest, humble, and pure. Lord, remove every trace of hypocrisy in me. Teach me to walk in truth and sincerity before You and others." In Jesus' name, Amen."

Final Reflection

The church's power returns when its people stop pretending and start repenting.

Chapter Summary

This chapter warns against false leaders who exploit the vulnerable. It emphasizes discernment, Scripture-based oversight, and accountability in leadership. The enemy often disguises himself through deceptive leadership. False shepherds exploit the weak for gain, twisting Scripture to serve ego and greed. God calls His people to discernment and courage to confront manipulation and protect the flock.

Key Scriptures

Matthew 7:15 – "Beware of false prophets… inwardly they are ravenous wolves."
Ezekiel 34:2–4 – "Woe to the shepherds… You feed yourselves but not the flock."
Acts 20:29–30 – "Savage wolves will come in among you…"
1 John 4:1 – "Test the spirits…"

Reflection Quotes

"Not every preacher is a shepherd—some are salesmen in shepherd's robes."
"True shepherds bleed for the sheep; false ones feed on them."

Reflection Questions

- What qualities distinguish a true shepherd from a false one?
- How can discernment help us protect ourselves and others from spiritual deception?
- Have I ever encountered leadership that exploited rather than served? How did it affect me?

Group Discussion Prompts

1. Why does the church sometimes struggle to confront false leaders?
2. How can accountability structures help prevent abuse in ministry?

Action Step / Weekly Challenge

1. Pray daily for discernment and ask God to expose any false influences in your spiritual circle or ministry.
2. Pray for your pastors and leaders daily this week, asking God to keep them faithful, humble, and protected from deception.

Challenge Verse

"My sheep hear My voice, and I know them." – John 10:27

Biblical Character Connection
Paul (Acts 20:28-31) – Warned the early church against false teachers and modeled servant leadership grounded in humility and truth.

Key Quote / Takeaway Box
"Discernment protects what deception seeks to destroy."

Weekly Song Suggestion
"Spirit Lead Me" – Influence Music / Michael Ketterer

Creative Response Option
Draw a symbolic sketch of a shepherd's staff breaking chains—representing deliverance from manipulation. Write a prayer or song of intercession for the spiritual leaders in your life.

Self-Assessment
1. ☐ I test teachings against Scripture before accepting them.
2. ☐ I sometimes follow personalities without discerning the fruit of their lives.
3. ☐ I pray regularly for my leaders' integrity and faithfulness.
4. How can you identify a true shepherd versus a false one?
5. What warning signs of manipulation have you seen in ministry?
6. How does discernment grow in your life?
7. Have you been spiritually wounded by false leadership?
8. How can you protect others through truth and prayer?

Devotional Prayer for Repentance and Renewal
"Lord, open my eyes to deception. Guard my heart from manipulation and misuse of Your name. Raise righteous shepherds and heal those misled. Strengthen me to discern and stand for truth. Lord, give me discernment to recognize truth from error. Protect Your church from those who would exploit Your people. Amen."

Final Reflection
The wolves will always come—but a discerning Church will not be devoured.

Chapter 4: When Love Is Thrown to the Wolves: Michal, David, and the Judgment Against Power That Betrays the Faithful

Chapter Summary

This chapter explores the betrayal of loyalty, the weaponization of love, and the silencing of women across history and modern society. Through the story of Michal, Saul, and David, readers learn how power and pride can corrupt institutions—whether political, religious, or cultural. The chapter exposes spiritual abuse, political manipulation, and societal patterns that marginalize women while highlighting God's ultimate justice, vindication, and restoration. Readers are encouraged to recognize the ripple effects of corruption and to rise with prophetic understanding, courage, and discernment.

Key Themes & Scripture References

Key Themes:
Love vs. Power
Spiritual and political abuse
Silencing of women in faith and society Divine vindication and justice
Ripple effects of systemic corruption

Scriptures:
- 1 Samuel 18:20–28 – Michal's loyalty to David
- 1 Samuel 19:11–17 – Saul's jealousy and oppression
- 2 Samuel 6:16–23 – Michal's silencing and lost legacy
- Proverbs 31:8–9 – Speaking for those who cannot
- Psalm 34:18 – God sees the brokenhearted
- Isaiah 61:1–3 – God restores justice and vindicates

Reflection Questions
1. How does Michal's story reflect the struggles women face today in religious, cultural, or political systems?
2. In what ways can love be weaponized by authority figures, and how have you seen this in society?
3. Reflect on a time when someone's loyalty or devotion was taken for granted. How did it affect your heart or community?

4. How does God's vindication of Michal encourage you to trust Him in situations where you feel silenced or marginalized?

5. What lessons can be learned about standing firm in faith and integrity when confronted with abuse of power?

Group Discussion Questions

1. Compare Michal's experience with modern-day examples of women silenced in religious or political spaces. What similarities and differences do you observe?

2. How can churches, organizations, or communities prevent loyalty and love from being exploited?

3. Discuss the ripple effects of spiritual abuse in families and society. How can these be mitigated?

4. How can men and women work together to promote justice and restore voices that have been silenced?

5. What practical steps can your group take to identify and confront systemic corruption while honoring God's justice?

Action Steps / Weekly Challenge

- Identify one area in your life, church, or community where women's voices are overlooked or silenced. Take one intentional action to amplify, advocate, or support them this week.
- Pray for leaders—political, religious, or social—to be held accountable and guided by humility and justice.
- Record one instance of loyalty, integrity, or courage you witnessed in someone and reflect on how it impacted your life.

Biblical Character Connection

Michal: A woman whose love and loyalty were silenced by corrupt authority. She represents all women who experience oppression yet remain devoted to God and righteousness.

David: A God-chosen leader opposed by corrupt authority, representing the faithful who face jealousy and manipulation from those in power.

Key Takeaway Box

"God sees the silent, remembers the overlooked, and vindicates those whose loyalty has been exploited."

"No Longer Slaves" – Bethel Music
"Raise a Hallelujah" – Jonathan David & Melissa Helser
"Way Maker" – Sinach

Creative Response Option
- Write a letter from the perspective of Michal, expressing her thoughts, emotions, and prayer for justice.
- Draw or create a visual representation of "broken chains" or "vindicated loyalty" as a reminder of God's justice.

Self-Assessment Activity
- List areas in your life, church, or workplace where you feel silenced or marginalized.
- Rate your level of confidence in speaking truth in those spaces (1–10).
- Identify practical steps or spiritual disciplines to increase courage, clarity, and discernment in those areas.

Devotional / Prayer Section
Prayer:
Lord, You see every woman whose voice has been silenced, whose loyalty has been exploited, and whose heart has been wounded by pride and power. Restore honor to those who have remained faithful.

Vindicate the faithful, convict the oppressors, and release a wave of courage, clarity, and prophetic authority into Your daughters. Let Your justice roll like waters, and let Your glory be revealed in every faithful heart. Amen.

Chapter Summary

This chapter urgently confronts the risks of turning ministry into a business and exploiting faith for personal gain. True ministry demands service that stems from a genuine love for God and people, not a quest for monetary profit, fame, or influence. When the Gospel is treated as a commercial endeavor, the profound significance of the cross is undermined. Ministry must be rooted in purity and purpose, prioritizing service over sales. This chapter unequivocally warns against the exploitation of faith, asserting that true ministry should be driven by love, not by a craving for material rewards. It's time to reclaim the integrity of ministry and ensure it remains focused on what truly matters.

Key Scriptures

Matthew 21:12 13 – "You have made My Father's house a den of thieves."
1 Peter 5:2 3 – "Feed the flock of God… neither as being lords over God's heritage but being examples to the flock."
Acts 8:20 – "May your money perish with you…"
Matthew 6:24 – "No man can serve two masters… Ye cannot serve God and mammon." 2 Corinthians 2:17 – "For we are not as many, which corrupt the word of God: but as of sincerity, but as of God, in the sight of God speak we in Christ."

Reflection Quotes

"When ministry becomes a market, miracles become merchandise." "True ministers are not for hire—they are for service."

Reflection Questions

1. How has commercialization affected modern churches and ministries?
2. What's the difference between supporting ministry and exploiting the Gospel for profit?
3. How can I guard my heart from treating God's work as a transaction?
4. How can financial gain or recognition corrupt the ministry?
5. What does true servanthood in ministry look like?
6. How can the church balance fundraising with maintaining

spiritual integrity?

Group Discussion Prompts
- What does it mean to serve God with pure motives?
- How can believers keep ministry Christ-centered instead of money-centered?
- Share examples of ministries that may have been tainted by commercial interests.
- How can churches encourage transparency and integrity in finances and leadership?

Action Step / Weekly Challenge
- Examine your motives for serving. Fast from self-promotion and spend time interceding for purity in ministry.
- Give this week in a way that stretches your faith—not out of obligation but out of love for God.
- Identify one act of service this week where you serve without expectation of reward or recognition.

Challenge Verse
"Freely you have received; freely give." – Matthew 10:8

Biblical Character Connection
Simon the Sorcerer (Acts 8) – Tried to buy the Holy Spirit's power. His story reminds us that God's gifts cannot be purchased or sold.

Key Quote / Takeaway Box
"The Gospel cannot be priced—it was paid for by blood."

Weekly Song Suggestion
"Nothing Else" – Cody Carnes

Creative Response Option
Write a declaration of purity for your ministry, committing every talent and platform to glorify Christ alone.
Create a list contrasting "true ministry" vs. "false commerce" in the church today.
Write a reflection on how you can contribute to ministry with humility and integrity.

Self-Assessment

1. ☐ I give and serve out of love for God, not personal gain.
2. ☐ I sometimes struggle with wrong motives in giving or ministry.
3. ☐ I desire to see ministry remain pure and Christ-centered.
4. ☐ I recognize areas where pride or ambition might affect my service.
5. ☐ I seek to maintain integrity in all acts of ministry.
6. What motivates your service—profit, popularity, or purpose?
7. How has the commercialization of faith affected the modern Church?
8. What can you do to restore sincerity to your calling?
9. Where might you be tempted to compromise purity for gain?
10. How will you live as a servant, not a salesman?

Devotional Prayer for Repentance and Renewal

"Lord, purify my motives. Deliver me from greed and the desire for fame. Let every act of ministry be an offering of love, not a transaction. Teach me to serve as You served. Lord, purify my motives in giving and serving. Let me never exploit Your Gospel for selfish gain. Lord, purify my heart from motives of gain. Help me serve You and others with pure devotion. Amen."

Final Reflection

The Church must choose: to be a marketplace or a holy dwelling where God's glory abides.

Chapter Summary

This chapter uncovers manipulative and controlling spirits within ministry. It requires vigilance, spiritual authority, and the breaking of unhealthy power structures. It also reveals the presence of controlling, pride-driven, and manipulative spirits within church leadership and ministry. The Spirit of Jezebel seeks to dominate, intimidate, and influence personal gain or power, often undermining godly authority. Believers are called to discernment, prayer, and exercising spiritual authority to overcome such influences. This spirit seduces, manipulates, and controls, infiltrating leadership and worship to dominate and corrupt. The Jezebel spirit resists authority and seeks power through intimidation. The Church must reclaim spiritual authority, discernment, and deliverance through prayer and humility.

Key Scriptures

- Revelation 2:20 – "Notwithstanding I have a few things against thee, because thou sufferest that woman Jezebel… to seduce my servants to commit fornication."
- 1 Kings 21:25 – "No one so completely sold himself to do evil as Ahab, whom Jezebel, his wife, incited."
- Ephesians 6:12 – "We wrestle not against flesh and blood…"
- James 4:7 – "Submit yourselves to God. Resist the devil…"
- 1 Corinthians 16:13 – "Watch ye, stand fast in the faith, quit you like men, be strong."
- Ephesians 6:11 – "Put on the whole armor of God, that ye may be able to stand against the wiles of the devil."

Reflection Quotes

"The Jezebel spirit thrives where accountability dies." "It seeks to control what it cannot possess."

Reflection Questions

1. What are the signs of manipulative or controlling behavior in ministry?
2. How can unchecked pride lead to spiritual bondage within the church?
3. What steps can I take to guard against the influence of this spirit?

4. How can the Spirit of Jezebel manifest in church leadership or ministry today?
5. What practical steps can a believer take to resist manipulation or control?
6. How does exercising spiritual authority help maintain godly order?

Group Discussion Prompts

1. How can spiritual authority be exercised with humility instead of control?
2. Why is discernment important when dealing with manipulative influences?
3. Discuss ways to identify unhealthy power structures within the church.
4. Share examples of how prayer and accountability helped overcome manipulation

Action Step / Weekly Challenge

- Identify areas of control, fear, or manipulation in your relationships or ministry. Renounce them in prayer and choose humility and submission to God's authority
- Spend time in prayer asking God to reveal any unhealthy influences in your life or church and commit to confronting them with His truth.
- Spend time this week praying for discernment and boldness to confront manipulation lovingly and biblically.

Challenge Verse

"Not by might, nor by power, but by My Spirit." – Zechariah 4:6

Biblical Character Connection

Elijah (1 Kings 18–19) – Faced Jezebel's intimidation with divine courage and intercession. His perseverance models how to overcome spiritual warfare.

Key Quote / Takeaway Box

"The Jezebel spirit falls where the Spirit of Truth reigns."

Weekly Song Suggestion

"Break Every Chain" – Tasha Cobbs Leonard

Creative Response Option
- Create a "freedom decree" declaring your household, ministry, and heart free from controlling influences.
- Write a prayer declaration of freedom from manipulation and control.
- Write a short strategy plan for how your church or small group could guard against manipulative influences.

Self-Assessment
1. How does manipulation appear subtly in spiritual environments?
2. What emotions or fears does the Jezebel spirit exploit?
3. How can submission to God protect you from deception?
4. In what ways must your ministry or leadership be purified?
5. What does true spiritual authority look like in your life?
6. ☐ I walk in humility and submission to God.
7. ☐ I sometimes struggle with control or manipulation.
8. ☐ I am committed to fostering spiritual health and accountability.
9. ☐ I can recognize controlling or manipulative behavior.
10. ☐ I rely on God's authority and wisdom to confront spiritual deception.
11. ☐ I am committed to maintaining integrity and godly order in ministry.

Devotional Prayer for Repentance and Renewal
"Lord, expose and break every controlling spirit operating in or around me. I renounce fear, pride, and manipulation. Empower me with Your Spirit to walk in freedom, humility, and authority. In Jesus' name, Lord, expose and remove any Jezebel-like influence in my heart and in my church. Restore purity, humility, and holy authority. Lord, protect me and my church from controlling spirits. Grant discernment and courage to walk in Your truth. Amen."

Final Reflection: Where Jezebel rules, the altar is broken—but where Christ reigns, deliverance flows and truth triumphs.

Chapter Summary
This chapter highlights sins such as pride, greed, and oppression that grieve God deeply. It calls for repentance and consecration to avert judgment and seek restoration. Jesus warned that false teachers would arise, disguised as shepherds but inwardly destructive wolves. They twist God's Word, exploit others for gain, and lead people astray with half-truths. This chapter exposes their tactics and equips believers to test every teaching against Scripture. It also identifies sins that deeply grieve God, such as pride, greed, oppression, and neglect of justice. God's anger is revealed as a call to repentance, consecration, and holiness. Sin is not merely moral failure; it's a stench before a holy God. This chapter exposes the sins that deeply grieve His heart: pride, greed, and oppression. When the Church tolerates what God detests, His presence withdraws.
Yet, where there is confession and consecration, His mercy flows.

Key Scriptures
Isaiah 65:5 – "These are smoke in My nostrils, a fire that burns all day."
Proverbs 6:16-19 – "There are six things the Lord hates, including pride and deceit." Romans 12:9 – "Abhor what is evil; cling to what is good."
2 Chronicles 7:14 – "If My people who are called by My name will humble themselves..." Matthew 7:15 16 – "Beware of false prophets, which come to you in sheep's clothing, but inwardly they are ravening wolves."
2 Peter 2:1 3 – "There shall be false teachers among you... and many shall follow their pernicious ways."
Acts 20:29 30 – "Grievous wolves shall enter in among you, not sparing the flock."

Amos 5:21–24 – "I hate, I despise your feast days... But let judgment run down as waters."

Reflection Quotes
"God's holiness cannot coexist with hidden sin." "What the Church excuses, Heaven exposes."

Reflection Questions
What types of sin does Scripture say especially provoke God's anger?

Why do pride and greed spread so easily within the church? How can I practice consecration in daily life?

How can you discern between a true teacher and a false one?

What role does the Holy Spirit play in guarding your understanding of truth?

Have you ever encountered teaching that seemed appealing but conflicted with Scripture? How did you respond?

Which sins grieve God the most in the church today? How can I examine my own heart for these sins?

What steps can be taken to align with God's holiness?

Group Discussion Prompts

Why is repentance both personal and corporate?

What are examples of sins today that "burn in God's nostrils"?

Why do you think false teachers are often so convincing?

Share examples of how false doctrine has harmed people or communities. Why do sins like pride and oppression anger God?

How can the church create accountability to prevent sin?

Action Step / Weekly Challenge

Fast from all forms of entertainment or indulgence for three days. Use that time to pray for God to reveal and remove anything in your life that offends His Spirit. Fast from one area of personal indulgence this week and use the time to seek God in prayer. I commit to reading and meditating on Scripture daily this week. Compare every sermon, teaching, or advice you hear to God's Word. Identify one area of sin in your life or church to repent of this week.

Challenge Verse

"Create in me a clean heart, O God, and renew a right spirit within me." – Psalm 51:10

Biblical Character Connection

Achan (Joshua 7) – His secret sin brought defeat upon Israel. His story warns that private disobedience has public consequences.

Key Quote / Takeaway Box

"Revival cannot come where sin is still being justified."

Weekly Song Suggestion

Clean Hands" – Chris Tomlin

Creative Response Option

Write a personal confession list before God. Burn or tear it afterward as a symbolic act of surrender and cleansing.

Write a confession prayer or poem, laying your sins before God.

Draw or write about the image of a wolf in sheep's clothing.

Reflect on how appearances can be deceiving. Write a reflection on how God's holiness inspires

your daily choices.

Self-Assessment

1. What "small" sins have you tolerated in your life or ministry?
2. How does unrepentant sin affect the collective body of Christ?
3. What steps are you taking to live a consecrated life?
4. What does true repentance look like in your walk with God?
5. Are there injustices or oppressions you've ignored or justified?
6. ☐ I am aware of sins that deeply grieve God.
7. ☐ I sometimes excuse or justify sinful habits.
8. ☐ I am pursuing repentance and consecration.
9. ☐ Do I regularly test teachings against Scripture?
10. ☐ Am I grounded enough in God's Word to recognize falsehood?
11. ☐ How can I grow in discernment?
12. ☐ I recognize sins that grieve God.
13. ☐ I commit to confession and repentance.
14. ☐ I desire to walk in holiness.

Devotional Prayer for Repentance and Renewal

"Lord, let Your holiness burn away every trace of sin in me. I surrender pride, greed, and compromise. Purify me until I reflect Your righteousness. May my life release a fragrance pleasing to You. Lord, forgive me for sins that grieve Your heart. Cleanse me and set me apart for Your holiness. Lord, give me wisdom and discernment. Protect me from deception and help me to recognize truth by the light of Your Word. Lord, reveal and purify my heart from all sin that grieves You. In Jesus' name, Amen."

Final Reflection

Sin stinks in the nostrils of God, but repentance releases the aroma of grace.

Chapter Summary

This chapter challenges pastors and leaders who remain silent about sin. It emphasizes the need for courage in preaching truth. Silence allows compromise to flourish. Bold, Scripture-based preaching is essential for holiness. When preachers grow silent on sin, truth is replaced by comfort. This chapter exposes the cost of cowardice in the pulpit. God calls leaders to speak boldly, even when truth offends. A silent church cannot heal a sinful world.

Key Scriptures

Ezekiel 33:7–9 – "If you do not warn them… their blood I will require at your hand."
2 Timothy 4:2 – "Preach the word… correct, rebuke, and encourage."
Isaiah 58:1 – "Cry aloud, spare not, lift your voice like a trumpet."
Galatians 1:10 – "If I were still trying to please men, I would not be a servant of Christ." Ezekiel 33:8 – "When I say unto the wicked, O wicked man, thou shalt surely die; if thou dost not speak to warn the wicked… his blood, will I require at thine hand."
Ezekiel 3:17 – "I have made thee a watchman… if thou warn the wicked… their blood will I require at thine hand."
James 3:1 – "Be not many masters, knowing that we shall receive the greater condemnation."

Reflection Quotes

"A mute pulpit breeds a dying Church."
"Silence in the face of sin is consent to its spread."

Reflection Questions

1. Why do some leaders avoid addressing sin from the pulpit?
2. How does silence harm the spiritual health of the church?
3. What does it mean to preach with both truth and love?
4. Why is silence from leaders dangerous?
5. How does bold preaching influence spiritual health?
6. In what ways can I encourage accountability in leadership?

Group Discussion Prompts

- How can congregations support pastors in speaking truth boldly?

- Why does society pressure churches to remain silent?
- Discuss examples of where silence led to compromise.
- How can congregations encourage responsible accountability?

Action Step / Weekly Challenge

Speak truth this week in one area where you've been silent—whether in family, ministry, or workplace, using wisdom and love.

Pray for boldness for your pastor or leaders this week, that they will preach truth without fear. Pray for pastors and leaders to speak truth boldly and consistently this week.

Challenge Verse

"The righteous are bold as a lion." – Proverbs 28:1

Biblical Character Connection

John the Baptist – Spoke truth to power even when it cost him his life. His courage exposes today's need for fearless voices in ministry.

Key Quote / Takeaway Box

"If the Church won't cry out, the streets will."

Weekly Song Suggestion

"I Speak Jesus" – Charity Gayle

Creative Response Option

- Compose a short prophetic declaration to read aloud in prayer, proclaiming truth over your city or congregation.
- Write a sermon outline on a subject that may avoid, using Scripture as your foundation.
- Journal a message you would want to hear from a godly leader.

Self-Assessment

1. When have you remained silent out of fear of rejection?
2. What topics has the Church avoided that must be addressed?
3. How does silence harm both the preacher and the people?
4. What does it mean to speak truth in love?
5. How can you intercede for pastors under pressure to compromise?

6. ☐ I listen openly to sermons that challenge me.
7. ☐ I sometimes prefer messages that make me comfortable.
8. ☐ I pray for courage in those called to preach truth.
9. ☐ I value bold preaching.
10. ☐ I sometimes excuse silence or compromise.
11. ☐ I pray for courageous leadership.

Devotional Prayer for Repentance and Renewal

"Lord, forgive us for fearing man more than You. Fill every pulpit and believer with holy boldness to declare Your Word. Restore truth to our preaching and conviction to our hearts. Lord, raise voices of truth in this generation who will not compromise Your Word. Lord, raise leaders who honor You in word and deed, speaking truth without fear. Amen."

Final Reflection

The Church cannot heal the land with closed lips. Courageous truth restores holiness.

Chapter Summary

This chapter exposes the church's failure to care for the marginalized. True righteousness is measured by compassion, generosity, and advocacy for the needy. It also exposes the church's failure to care for the poor and marginalized. True righteousness is measured by compassion, generosity, and advocacy. God measures righteousness not by sermons but by compassion. When the poor, the widowed, and the oppressed are forgotten, the Church loses its credibility. This chapter confronts apathy toward the needy and calls believers to act as the hands and heart of Jesus.

Key Scriptures

Proverbs 19:17 – "Whoever is generous to the poor lends to the Lord."
Matthew 25:35-40 – "Whatever you did for the least of these, you did for Me."
Isaiah 58:10 – "If you spend yourselves on behalf of the hungry…"
James 2:15-17 – "Faith without works is dead."
Proverbs 14:31 – "He that oppresseth the poor reproacheth his Maker: but he that honoureth him hath mercy on the poor."
James 1:27 – "Pure religion… is to visit the fatherless and widows in their affliction."

Reflection Quotes

"A Church that ignores the poor has silenced the Gospel it preaches." "Compassion is the evidence of true conversion."

Reflection Questions:

1. How does neglecting the poor dishonor God?
2. In what ways can my church actively serve the marginalized?
3. How can generosity transform both the giver and receiver?
4. How does neglecting the poor affect God's judgment?
5. In what practical ways can I help the marginalized?
6. What barriers keep churches from serving the needy?

Group Discussion Prompts

- Why is caring for the poor central to true worship?
- Share examples of how churches have made a difference in

their communities.

- Share ministry ideas to serve the poor.
- Discuss why compassion is an essential measure of true faith.

Action Step / Weekly Challenge

1. Serve at a food pantry, donate clothing to the homeless, or help a struggling neighbor.
2. Let your love be visible this week.
3. Give time, food, or financial support to a ministry serving the poor this week.
4. Volunteer, donate, or pray for someone in need this week.

Challenge Verse

"Let your light so shine before men…" – Matthew 5:16

Biblical Character Connection

Tabitha (Dorcas) – Acts 9:36 – Known for good works and generosity. Her ministry of compassion caused revival in her community.

Key Quote / Takeaway Box

"Mercy is the language Heaven understands best."

Weekly Song Suggestion

"Hosanna" – Hillsong United ("Break my heart for what breaks Yours…")

Creative Response Option

Create a "mercy jar." Each day, put in a small offering or note of gratitude. At week's end, give it to someone in need or sow it into a local ministry. Create a "Compassion List" of practical ways you can bless the marginalized. Write a list of practical ways your church can help marginalized communities.

Self-Assessment

1. How often do you intentionally serve the poor or marginalized?
2. What biases prevent compassion in your community?
3. How can your church better reflect Christ's love to the needy?
4. What spiritual reward does generosity produce?
5. What is God asking you to give today—time, love, or resources?
6. ☐ I actively care for the needs of the poor.

7. ☐ I sometimes overlook those in need around me.
8. ☐ I desire to honor God by serving the least of these.
9. ☐ I care about the needs of the marginalized.
10. ☐ I sometimes overlook opportunities to serve.
11. ☐ I desire to live out true religion through compassion.

Devotional Prayer for Repentance and Renewal

"Lord, forgive us for walking past the wounded. Open our eyes to see You in the hungry, the homeless, and the forgotten. Make us a people of compassion who serve not for recognition but for love. Lord, break my heart for the things that break Yours. Help me see and serve the poor with compassion. Lord, open my eyes to see the needy and give me a heart to serve them. Amen."

Final Reflection

When the Church feeds the poor, Heaven takes notice—and revival draws near.

Chapter Summary

This chapter addresses the subtle ways pride enters leadership and worship. Humility is the foundation of authentic ministry and unity. Pride subtly infiltrates worship and leadership. Humility protects unity, promotes spiritual growth, and ensures God receives the glory. Pride is the silent killer of ministries. It turns worship into performance and service into self-promotion. God resists the proud but gives grace to the humble. This chapter calls for brokenness and humility that attract God's glory.

Key Scriptures

Proverbs 16:18 – "Pride goes before destruction..."

James 4:6 – "God resisteth the proud, but giveth grace unto the humble."

Isaiah 66:2 – "To this one I will look... who is humble and contrite." Luke 18:14 – "Whoever exalts himself will be humbled."

1 Peter 5:5 – "Clothe yourselves with humility toward one another."

Reflection Quotes

"When pride walks into the sanctuary, the Spirit walks out." "Humility is the posture that keeps Heaven's doors open."

Reflection Questions

1. How can pride subtly enter into ministry or worship?
2. What is the danger of seeking recognition in the church?
3. How can I intentionally practice humility in service?
4. How does pride manifest in worship or leadership?
5. How can humility be cultivated personally and corporately?
6. Why is humility foundational to spiritual health?

Group Discussion Prompts

- How has pride divided churches historically?
- What are biblical examples of humility in leadership?
- Share examples of how pride has caused conflict in ministry.
- How can humility protect the church from internal strife?

Action Step / Weekly Challenge

Intentionally serve in a hidden way this week—do something kind without recognition.

Let humility shape your actions. Serve someone this week in a hidden way without seeking recognition.

Perform one act of service this week with complete humility and no recognition.

Challenge Verse

"He must increase, but I must decrease." – John 3:30

Biblical Character Connection

Nebuchadnezzar (Daniel 4) – His pride brought him low until he acknowledged God's sovereignty. His story warns that no throne stands taller than God's.

Key Quote / Takeaway Box

"Worship without humility is noise without power."

Weekly Song Suggestion

"Here I Am to Worship" – Tim Hughes

Creative Response Option

1. Write a humility prayer or poem titled *"Less of Me, More of You."*
2. Write a list of ways to replace prideful attitudes with humble actions.
3. Write a reflection on areas of your life where humility needs to grow.

Self-Assessment

1. How does pride disguise itself in ministry or worship?
2. What areas of your heart crave recognition?
3. How do you respond when corrected or overlooked?
4. Why is humility necessary for revival?
5. How can you cultivate humility daily?
6. ☐ I check my motives before serving.
7. ☐ I sometimes seek recognition for my service.
8. ☐ I am growing in humility.
9. ☐ I practice humility in relationships and service.
10. ☐ I sometimes struggle with pride.

11. ☐ I value unity over personal recognition.

Devotional Prayer for Repentance and Renewal
"Lord, humble me before Your throne. Remove every trace of self-glory and ambition. Let my worship be pure and my heart lowly. May Your glory, not mine, fill the sanctuary. Lord, strip me of pride. Teach me to walk humbly and serve with grace. Lord, humble my heart and remove all pride from my life and church. Amen."

Final Reflection
A proud Church boasts of gifts; a humble Church bows before the Giver.

Chapter Summary

This chapter examines how superficial harmony can mask sin and moral compromise. Genuine unity requires truth, holiness, and accountability. Superficial unity hides sin and moral compromise. Genuine unity requires truth, holiness, and accountability. Compromise threatens revival and God's blessing. Not all unity is holy. When peace is bought at the price of truth, it becomes deception. This chapter exposes the counterfeit unity that tolerates sin for the sake of appearance. Genuine unity is rooted in holiness, not hypocrisy.

Key Scriptures

Amos 3:3 – "Can two walk together unless they are agreed?"
John 17:17, 21 – "Sanctify them by the truth… that they may be one."
2 Corinthians 6:14 – "Do not be unequally yoked."
Ephesians 4:3 – "Make every effort to keep the unity of the Spirit…"
Ephesians 4:15 – "Speaking the truth in love, may grow up into him in all things."

Reflection Quotes

"Unity without truth is a treaty with darkness."
"The Church must unite in holiness, not in compromise."

Reflection Questions

1. What is the difference between true unity and false unity?
2. How can compromise damage the testimony of the church?
3. In what areas must I stand firm without compromise?
4. How can compromise masquerade as unity?
5. Why is truth essential for lasting harmony?
6. How can I promote accountability in relationships and ministry?

Group Discussion Prompts

- Why do churches sometimes prioritize appearances over holiness?
- How does truth protect unity in the body of Christ?
- Discuss practical steps to maintain integrity without creating division.
- Share experiences where compromise caused spiritual decline.

Action Step / Weekly Challenge

1. Pray for wisdom to distinguish between godly collaboration and ungodly compromise.
2. Reevaluate any alliances or partnerships that dilute biblical truth.
3. Examine one area where you may be compromising truth for comfort and take a stand for righteousness.
4. Identify one area where truth needs to be spoken, even if uncomfortable.

Challenge Verse

"Stand firm in the faith, be courageous, be strong." – 1 Corinthians 16:13

Biblical Character Connection

Micaiah the Prophet (1 Kings 22) – Refused to agree with lying prophets for favor's sake. His boldness shows that real unity stands on truth alone.

Key Quote / Takeaway Box

"Compromise may build crowds, but it cannot build the Kingdom."

Weekly Song Suggestion

"Build Your Church" – Elevation Worship & Maverick City Music

Creative Response Option

1. Design a visual collage or poster contrasting "True Unity" vs. "False Unity" based onScripture.
2. Draw two paths: one of compromise, one of truth.
3. Reflect on where each path leads.
4. Create a visual or written representation of "unity built on truth versus compromise.

Self-Assessment

1. What compromises threaten the purity of today's Church?
2. How can unity exist without abandoning truth?
3. Have you ever stayed silent to avoid conflict?
4. What does it mean to pursue unity in the Spirit?
5. How can you model holy unity in your relationships and ministry?
6. ☐ I value truth even when it costs me.
7. ☐ I sometimes choose peace over righteousness.

8. ☐ I pursue unity rooted in holiness and Scripture.
9. ☐ I value truth over superficial peace.
10. ☐ I sometimes avoid confrontation to keep harmony.
11. ☐ I seek genuine unity in my life and church.

Devotional Prayer for Repentance and Renewal

"Lord, guard my heart from compromise. Help me to walk in unity, rooted in Your Word. Let truth and love work together in me and in Your Church. May we be one as You and the Father are one. Lord, help me seek unity that is rooted in Your truth and holiness, not in compromise. Lord, help me pursue unity rooted in truth and holiness. Amen."

Final Reflection

The unity that pleases Heaven is not built on comfort—it is built on the cross.

Chapter Summary

God disciplines His people first to cleanse and restore. Exposure of hidden sin is an act of mercy aimed at revival. It also reminds us of Christ's warning to the churches in Revelation. A church that abandons love and truth risks losing its witness and presence of God. Deception has found a seat in the sanctuary. Many pulpits echo words that sound holy but lack the Spirit of Truth. The enemy has camouflaged lies in religious language, and what once convicted now entertains. God is uncovering deception to restore discernment. This chapter reveals how Satan masquerades as light among leaders who have traded revelation for reputation.

Key Scriptures

2 Corinthians 11:13–15
1 John 4:1
Matthew 24:11 12
Acts 20:29–30
1 Peter 4:17 – "For the time is come that judgment must begin at the house of God."
Hebrews 12:6 – "For whom the Lord loveth he chasteneth."
Revelation 2:5 – "Repent and do the first works; or else I will come unto thee quickly, and will remove thy candlestick out of his place, except thou repent."

Reflection Quotes

"Deception thrives where discernment dies."
"Truth without the Spirit becomes tradition; Spirit without truth becomes deception."

Reflection Questions:

1. How does divine correction demonstrate God's love?
2. Why must exposure precede revival?
3. In what areas do I need God's correction?
4. What does it mean for a church to lose its lampstand?
5. How is the presence of God more valuable than programs or numbers?
6. What first work should I return to personally?

Group Discussion Prompts:

- Share personal experiences of correction leading to growth.

- Discuss how churches can respond to the exposure of hidden sin.
- How do we know when God's presence has departed from a church?
- What is the difference between outward success and spiritual fruitfulness?

Action Step / Weekly Challenge

1. Ask the Holy Spirit to expose any deceptive influence in your life, church, or leadership.
2. Fast one day this week, asking God to increase your discernment.
3. Ask God to reveal one hidden sin in your life and take steps toward repentance.
4. Spend intentional time in prayer and Scripture, returning to your "first love.

Challenge Verse

Ephesians 5:11 – *"Have nothing to do with the fruitless deeds of darkness, but rather expose them."*

Biblical Character Connection

Ananias and Sapphira (Acts 5) – They deceived the Holy Spirit for appearance's sake, teaching us that falsehood in the house of God brings divine judgment.

Key Quote / Takeaway

"When deception hides in the pulpit, deliverance must begin at the altar."

Worship Song Suggestion

"Refiner" – Maverick City Music

Creative Response

- Write a personal prayer asking God to cleanse your motives and remove any spiritual blindness that prevents truth from flourishing.
- Journal a testimony of how correction has strengthened your faith. Write down your testimony of when you first encountered God's love and passion.

Self-Assessment Questions

1. How does deception manifest subtly in modern ministries?
2. What does it mean to test every spirit?

3. How can discernment be strengthened through prayer?
4. Have I ever been swayed by charisma instead of character?
5. What guardrails can protect me from deception?
6. ☐ I welcome God's correction.
7. ☐ I sometimes resist exposure of sin.
8. ☐ I desire revival through holiness and obedience.
9. ☐ I recognize signs when my love for God grows cold.
10. ☐ I sometimes focus more on work than on relationships.
11. ☐ I am seeking to return to my first love.

Devotional Prayer

"Lord, remove every veil of deception from my eyes. Let Your truth be the mirror of my soul. Expose hidden motives, correct false doctrine, and purify my heart to walk in Your light. "Lord, cleanse me of hidden sin and prepare me for revival. Lord, do not let Your presence depart from me or my church. Restore my first love." Amen."

Chapter Summary

Leaders are tested and refined through trials. God uses challenges to restore, remove, or strengthen them. Leadership integrity ensures the church's spiritual health. It also reflects God's judgment through the image of divine scales, weighing motives and actions. It highlights holiness, integrity, and purity of heart. The modern church is filled with many voices—some sent by God, others self-appointed. Wolves wear robes of righteousness while devouring the vulnerable. This chapter reveals how false shepherds exploit the weak for personal gain, yet God is raising true watchmen to protect His flock.

Key Scriptures

Matthew 7:15–16
Ezekiel 34:2–5
John 10:11–13
Acts 20:28–30
1 Timothy 3:2-7 – Qualifications for overseers, emphasizing character and faith.
James 1:2-4 – Trials produce perseverance and maturity.
Daniel 5:27 – "Thou art weighed in the balances, and art found wanting."

Reflection Quotes

"A true shepherd bleeds for the sheep; a wolf feeds on them."
"The robe may hide the wolf, but it cannot silence the growl of greed."

Reflection Questions:

1. How do trials reveal leadership character?
2. What role does accountability play in leadership refinement?
3. How can the congregation support leaders during testing?
4. What does it mean to be "weighed in the balances"?
5. How does God judge motives as well as actions?
6. What areas of my life might be found "wanting"?

Group Discussion Prompts:

- Share examples of leaders who grew through trials.
- How can transparency and accountability prevent abuse of leadership?
- Why is holiness more than just outward appearance?
- How does God's justice differ from human judgment?

Action Step / Weekly Challenge

- Study John 10 and identify the traits of a true shepherd.
- Pray for discernment to recognize spiritual predators in leadership and community spaces.
- Write a note of encouragement to a leader, affirming their faithfulness.
- Draw or describe what "God's scales" might look like and reflect on what He values most.

Challenge Verse

Jeremiah 23:1 – *"Woe to the shepherds who destroy and scatter the sheep of My pasture!"*

Biblical Character Connection

The false prophets of Israel who misled the people, while Jeremiah cried the truth alone.

Key Quote / Takeaway

"Not every voice behind a pulpit speaks from the throne."

Worship Song Suggestion

"Shepherd" – Bethel Music

Creative Response

- Sketch or write an image of a healthy, protective shepherd and what spiritual safety looks like in God's flock.
- Pray for a church leader this week, asking God to refine and strengthen them.
- Ask God to reveal one hidden area of your heart where He desires repentance.

Self-Assessment Questions

1. How can I tell if a leader truly loves God's people?
2. What are the signs of spiritual abuse?
3. How can believers stay watchful without being judgmental?
4. Who in my life models true shepherding?
5. How can I protect others from manipulation?
6. ☐ I understand trials refining leaders.
7. ☐ I sometimes criticize without understanding challenges.
8. ☐ I desire to support godly leadership.
9. ☐ I invite God to search my motives.

10. ☐ I sometimes focus only on outward deeds.
11. ☐ I desire to walk in holiness and integrity.

Devotional Prayer
"Lord, make me wise as a serpent but harmless as a dove. Teach me to discern wolves in disguise and to follow the voice of my true Shepherd—Jesus. Keep me in the fold of truth and love. Lord, raise leaders of integrity and faithfulness for Your church. Lord, search for me and know me. Purify my motives and weigh me according to Your righteousness. Amen."

Chapter 14: Hidden Sin Brought to Light – Transparency and Confession

Chapter Summary
Secret sin destroys communities. Exposure enables confession, healing, and purification. God calls for transparency to maintain holiness and unity. It also teaches that God tests every believer's works by fire. Only what is built on Christ will endure. Holiness has become performance instead of purity. Many display spiritual power publicly but harbor hidden sin privately. This chapter confronts religious hypocrisy, the outward image of sanctity that hides inward rebellion. God is calling His people back to authenticity, where holiness is not a mask but a lifestyle.

Key Scriptures
John 8:32 – "And ye shall know the truth, and the truth shall make you free."
James 5:16 – "Confess your faults one to another, and pray one for another, that ye may be healed."
1 Corinthians 3:13 – "Every man's work shall be made manifest: for the day shall declare it, because it shall be revealed by fire."
Matthew 23:27–28
Isaiah 29:13
1 Peter 1:15–16
Hebrews 12:14

Reflection Quotes
"Holiness is not a stage performance; it's a surrendered posture." "God sees beyond robes and rituals—He weighs the heart."

Reflection Questions:
1. Why is transparency essential for spiritual health?
2. How can hidden sin harm the church body?
3. How do confession and accountability lead to freedom?
4. What kind of work will stand the test of fire?
5. How does fire purify rather than only destroy?
6. Am I building my life on Christ or on worldly pursuits?

Group Discussion Prompts:
- Discuss ways to create safe environments for confession.
- Share experiences of healing after exposing hidden sin.
- What is the difference between good works and God-approved works?
- How does fire reveal authenticity?

Action Step / Weekly Challenge
1. Examine your life in the light of Matthew 23.
2. Confess one area where your actions haven't matched your words and ask God for integrity in your walk.
3. Confess one hidden sin to a trusted believer and pray for accountability.
4. Examine your current commitments—are they rooted in Christ or in personal ambition? 5.

Challenge Verse
Psalm 51:10 – *"Create in me a clean heart, O God, and renew a right spirit within me."*

Biblical Character Connection
The Pharisees, who exalted religious image over true repentance.

Key Quote / Takeaway
"True holiness starts in the heart, not on the platform."

Worship Song Suggestion
- "Give Us Clean Hands" – Chris Tomlin
- Creative Response
- Write a brief poem or journal entry titled *"Unmasked."*
- Write a prayer of confession and thanksgiving for God's forgiveness.

List activities in your life under two columns: "Eternal Value" and "Temporary Value."

Self-Assessment Questions
1. What areas of my faith have become outward performance?
2. How does God define holiness versus human religion?
3. What keeps believers from living authentically?
4. Why does hypocrisy grieve the Holy Spirit?
5. What changes will I make this week to pursue real holiness?
6. ☐ I recognize the danger of hidden sin.
7. ☐ I seek accountability in my spiritual walk.
8. ☐ I desire freedom through transparency
9. ☐ I seek to build on Christ's foundation.
10. ☐ I sometimes pursue recognition more than eternal fruit.
11. ☐ I welcome God's refining fire in my life.

Devotional Prayer
"Father, strip me of pretense and pride. Let my life reflect inward holiness that glorifies You. May my words and actions align, and may purity of heart be my offering. Lord, give me courage to bring hidden sins into the light for Your healing. Lord, let my works be refined by Your fire, that they may glorify You and endure. Amen."

Chapter Summary

This chapter speaks to the church that once burned with passion but now sits in comfort. The Spirit of God is confronting spiritual complacency and calling believers to reignite their first love. A lukewarm heart offends God more than rebellion because it pretends devotion while living in apathy. It explores the tragedy of losing God's glory because of sin, neglect, and disobedience. The presence of God is not automatic; it requires reverence. Spiritual complacency and indifference grieve God. Zeal, obedience, and wholehearted devotion are required to remain pleasing to Him.

Key Scriptures

Revelation 3:15–16 – "I know thy works, that thou art neither cold nor hot: I would thou wert cold or hot... I will spew thee out of my mouth."
Samuel 4:21 – "And she named the child Ichabod, saying, The glory is departed from Israel."
Revelation 3:15–16
Romans 12:11
Timothy 1:6
Matthew 24:12

Reflection Quotes

"Lukewarm faith is the grave of revival."
"When passion dies, compromise reigns."

Reflection Questions:

1. How does lukewarm faith manifest today?
2. What steps can I take to rekindle zeal for God?
3. How do obedience and devotion protect from spiritual indifference?
4. How can the glory of God depart from a church or individual?
5. What signs reveal when God's presence is missing?
6. How can I invite His glory back into my life?

Group Discussion Prompts:

- Share personal experiences of rekindled passion for God.
- How can churches motivate members toward wholehearted devotion?
- What role does holiness play in maintaining God's presence?
- Why is His glory more vital than religious activity?

Action Step / Weekly Challenge
- Spend three consecutive days in prayer, asking God to rekindle your spiritual fire.
- Remove one distraction that hinders intimacy with Him.
- Take one intentional action this week to grow your personal zeal for God (prayer, study, worship).
- Set aside a time of personal or group repentance this week, seeking the return of His glory.

Challenge Verse
Revelation 3:19 – *"Be zealous therefore, and repent."*

Biblical Character Connection
The Church of Laodicea—wealthy but spiritually poor.

Key Quote / Takeaway
"God would rather a cold sinner than a comfortable saint."

Worship Song Suggestion
"Set a Fire" – Will Reagan & United Pursuit

Creative Response
- Write a personal revival declaration—what you are rededicating to God in this season.
- Journal a "revival plan" for personal spiritual growth.
- Create a short prayer or song inviting God's glory to dwell in your home.

Self-Assessment Questions
1. What does it mean to be lukewarm in faith?
2. How can spiritual comfort lead to moral decay?
3. What does true zeal look like?
4. Where have I lost my spiritual fire?
5. How can I sustain revival personally?

6. ☐ I am aware of areas of spiritual lukewarmness.
7. ☐ I commit to growing in zeal and obedience.
8. ☐ I seek wholehearted devotion in my life.
9. ☐ I value the presence of God above all.
10. ☐ I sometimes go through motions without His glory.
11. ☐ I seek His presence daily.

Devotional Prayer

"Lord, ignite my heart again. Burn away the ashes of apathy and light the flame of devotion within me. Let my life be a living fire for Your glory. Lord, ignite in me a passionate, devoted heart for You. Lord, do not let me live without Your presence. Restore Your glory in my life and church. Amen."

Chapter 16: The Deception of White Christian Nationalism — When Faith Becomes a Weapon Against God's Kingdom

Chapter Summary
In this chapter, we examine the rise of White Christian Nationalism, a movement that distorts the Gospel to promote racial supremacy, political dominance, and fear-based obedience. While it masquerades as Christianity, it opposes God's Kingdom by elevating nations and races above Christ, manipulating Scripture for human agendas, and fostering division within the Church. The chapter explores its historical roots, global influence, and the danger it poses to democracy, unity, and true Christian witness.

God's Word provides clear warnings about pride, hidden evil, and misuse of authority. True faith is measured by obedience, love, and service—not by political allegiance or cultural identity. Believers are called to discern deception, reject manipulation, and stand firmly in truth. The chapter concludes with a call to repentance, encouraging the Church to realign with God's Kingdom and demonstrate justice, mercy, and humility. The modern church celebrates blessings but avoids the burden of the cross. Many preach prosperity without persecution, grace without surrender. This chapter calls believers back to the altar where true discipleship begins—where self dies, and Christ reigns.

Key Scriptures
Luke 9:23–24
Galatians 2:20
1 Corinthians 1:18
Philippians 3:10

Reflection Quotes
"The cross is not decoration—it's the declaration of dying to self."
"A gospel without the cross is not the gospel at all."

Reflection Questions
1. What are the key characteristics of White Christian Nationalism, and why do they conflict with God's Kingdom?
2. How do fear and political ambition distort the practice of genuine faith?
3. In what ways has the Church historically been complicit in

promoting nationalism or racial supremacy?

4. How can Scripture guide believers in recognizing and resisting deception in faith movements?
5. Why is unity in the Church essential to counter the divisive tactics of Christian nationalism?
6. How does the pursuit of earthly power differ from true spiritual authority in God's Kingdom?
7. What steps can you personally take to align more fully with God's will and resist cultural or political idolatry?

Action Step / Weekly Challenge
1. Reflect on what it means to "take up your cross daily."
2. Identify one area where you need to surrender your will to God's.
3. Identify one area in your community or church where fear or cultural allegiance may be overshadowing Christ-centered love.
4. Pray for clarity and discernment.

Challenge Verse
Luke 14:27 – *"Whoever does not bear his cross and come after Me cannot be My disciple."*

Biblical Character Connection
Simon of Cyrene – the man who helped carry Jesus' cross, symbolizing every believer's shared call to bear Christ's burden.
Consider Daniel, who remained faithful to God despite pressures from political and cultural powers (Daniel 1–6). Reflect on how his courage applies to resisting deceptive movements today.

Key Quote / Takeaway
"The church that forgets the cross forgets Christ."
"True faith is measured by obedience to Christ, love for all people, and humility before God— not by allegiance to nations, races, or political power."

Worship Song Suggestion
"When I Survey the Wondrous Cross" – Chris Tomlin

"Build My Life" – Focus on surrendering all authority to God's Kingdom rather than earthly power.

Creative Response

Draw or journal your reflection of what the cross personally represents to you today. Write a letter (unsent) to a leader or community promoting fear-based or exclusionary ideologies,

explaining God's call to love, justice, and repentance.

Self-Assessment Questions

Why is the cross central to Christian life?

What happens when we remove suffering from discipleship? How can embracing the cross bring victory?

In what ways have I avoided my personal cross?

What does it mean to "die daily" to self?

Reflect and journal:

Am I prioritizing God's Kingdom over political or cultural loyalty?

Do I see any areas in my heart or church where fear or pride might be influencing decisions?

What action can I take this week to demonstrate God's love over fear?

Devotional Prayer

"Jesus, remind me of the power of the cross. May I never glory in anything but Your sacrifice. Teach me to carry my cross with humility and joy, knowing it leads to eternal life. Amen."

Chapter Summary

This chapter exposes the spirit of greed that has commercialized God's Word and calls the Church to return to purity and generosity. It also declares repentance as the doorway to revival. God's mercy is extended when His people humble themselves and turn back to Him. Counterfeit prophecy misleads and manipulates. True prophecy aligns with Scripture, promotes holiness, and glorifies God. Believers must discern, test, and submit to the Holy Spirit. The sacred altar has been turned into a marketplace. The Gospel—once freely given—is now sold for profit. Many have exchanged the anointing for applause, and ministry has become a brand rather than a calling.

Key Scriptures

Deuteronomy 18:20–22 – "The prophet who speaketh a word presumptuously… shall die."
1 John 4:1 – "Beloved, believe not every spirit, but try the spirits whether they are of God."
2 Chronicles 7:14 – "If my people, which are called by my name, shall humble themselves, and pray, and seek my face, and turn from their wicked ways; then will I hear from heaven, and will forgive their sin, and will heal their land."
Matthew 21:12 13
2 Peter 2:3
Acts 8:18–20
Micah 3:11

Reflection Quotes
"The Gospel is not for sale; it was paid for in blood."
"When the altar becomes a marketplace, the presence departs."

Reflection Questions:
- How can counterfeit prophecy be recognized?
- What is the role of Scripture in discerning prophetic words?
- How can the church guard against deception?
- Why is repentance more than just words?

- What does it mean to "turn from wicked ways"?
- How does humility prepare the way for revival?

Group Discussion Prompts:
1. Share experiences of discerning true vs. false prophecy.
2. Why is accountability essential in prophetic ministry?
3. Why does revival always begin with repentance?
4. How can repentance be modeled in a community of faith?

Action Step / Weekly Challenge
1. Evaluate your giving, service, and ministry motives.
2. Are they driven by gain or grace?
3. Commit to one act of generosity this week without expecting anything in return.
4. Evaluate a recent prophetic word you received—does it align with Scripture?
5. Confess one specific sin to God this week and commit to turning from it.

Challenge Verse
Matthew 6:24 – *"You cannot serve both God and money."*

Biblical Character Connection
Simon the Sorcerer (Acts 8) – who tried to purchase the Holy Spirit's power, exposing the danger of greed in ministry.

Key Quote / Takeaway
"Where money becomes the motive, ministry loses its meaning."

Worship Song Suggestion
"Nothing Else" – Cody Carnes

Creative Response Option:
List the characteristics of true prophecy versus false prophecy. Write a personal repentance prayer in your journal.
Design a symbolic "receipt" of surrender, list all the things you refuse to sell or trade for the sake of Christ.

Self-Assessment Questions

1. How has commercialization affected today's Church?
2. What does it mean to "freely give as you have freely received"?
3. How can I guard my heart from greed?
4. Have I ever placed value on recognition instead of righteousness?
5. How can generosity restore purity in ministry?
6. ☐ I test every word against Scripture.
7. ☐ I rely on the Holy Spirit for discernment.
8. ☐ I seek truth over emotional appeal.
9. ☐ I acknowledge areas where I need repentance.
10. ☐ I sometimes mistake emotions for true repentance.
11. ☐ I am actively turning back to God in daily life.

Devotional Prayer

"Lord, cleanse Your temple once more. Remove every motive tainted by greed or vanity. Let my ministry and my life reflect pure devotion to You alone. Lord, grant me discernment to recognize Your voice from deception. Lord, I humble myself before You. Heal my heart and my land through true repentance. Amen."

Chapter 18: Exposing the Sin of Racism and the Forgotten Voices in Scriptures

Chapter Summary

This chapter unmasks how racism, prejudice, and silence in the church corrupt the witness of Christ. God calls His people to embrace the full body of Christ in unity and truth. When leaders fall, entire generations lose direction. Yet behind every public collapse is a private compromise that went unaddressed. This chapter examines the tragic downfall of once-powerful voices who lost their anointing to pride, lust, or disobedience. It calls the Church to humility and accountability, for no one stands taller than when kneeling before God.

Key Scriptures

Proverbs 16:18
Corinthians 10:12
Samuel 12:7–9
Galatians 6:1
Galatians 3:28 – "There is neither Jew nor Greek, there is neither bond nor free, there is neither male nor female: for ye are all one in Christ Jesus."

Reflection Quotes

"The fall of one leader becomes the test of many followers." "Anointing does not exempt us from accountability."

Reflection Questions

How does racism contradict the gospel?

Why is silence in the face of injustice a sin?

How can I be a voice for forgotten and marginalized people?

Group Discussion Prompts

What practical steps can churches take to combat racism in their community?

How do the Scriptures uplift forgotten or silenced voices?

Action Step / Weekly Challenge

Reach out to a mentor or spiritual accountability partner. Share one area where you need coverage or correction.

Reach out to someone from a different cultural or ethnic background this week. Listen to their story.

Challenge Verse

James 4:10 – *"Humble yourselves before the Lord, and He will lift you."*

Biblical Character Connection

King David – Anointed but fallen, yet restored through repentance and brokenness.

Key Quote / Takeaway

When pride builds the platform, humility becomes the rescue plan."

Worship Song Suggestion

"Gracefully Broken" – Tasha Cobbs Leonard

Creative Response Option

Write or create a visual that represents what unity in Christ looks like to you.

Write a personal letter to God titled *"Before I Fall."* Confess areas of weakness and ask Him to keep you standing in grace.

Self-Assessment Questions

1. Why do spiritual leaders fall?

2. What warning signs can help prevent spiritual decline?
3. How can we restore fallen leaders with grace and truth?
4. What does humility look like in leadership?
5. How can I guard my anointing?
6. ☐ I recognize racism as sin.
7. ☐ I sometimes avoid hard conversations about justice.
8. ☐ I desire to walk in Christ-centered unity.

Devotional Prayer

"Lord, keep me humble, teachable, and true. Let me never mistake gifts for godliness. Guard me from pride and keep my heart anchored in repentance. Lord, break down walls of division and prejudice in my heart and in Your church. Amen."

Chapter Summary
Modern idolatry is not golden statues but human platforms, success, image, and comfort. Many worship ministries instead of the Master. This chapter calls the Church to tear down every idol— celebrity culture, materialism, and self-promotion—that competes with God's glory.

Key Scriptures
Exodus 20:3–5
Ezekiel 14:3–5
1 John 5:21
Colossians 3:5

Reflection Quotes
"Idols today wear suits and titles."
"Whatever steals your worship becomes your god."

Reflection Questions
1. How do you personally define political violence, and where have you seen it impact communities or churches?
2. What are the dangers of confusing nationalism with true Christian faith?
3. How can Christians discern between true and counterfeit churches?
4. Have you witnessed performative religion in your community? How did it affect others?
5. How does Isaiah 5:20 speak to your own beliefs or church environment?
6. In what ways are you tempted to prioritize political allegiance over obedience to God?
7. How can you actively resist supporting white supremacy or racial prejudice in your community?
8. What steps can you take to strengthen critical thinking in your spiritual life?
9. How does your understanding of God's Kingdom challenge the notion of a "Christian nation"?
10. How can you be part of a faithful remnant calling the church back

to righteousness?

Group Discussion Questions

1. Why do some Christians gravitate toward Christian nationalism, and what biblical warnings address this?
2. How can your church actively expose and resist counterfeit teachings or political collusion?
3. What is the difference between patriotism and Christian nationalism, and why does it matter?
4. How can the church maintain unity despite cultural, racial, or political divisions?
5. What role do prayers play in confronting political violence and counterfeit churches?
6. How do biblical prophets inspire the church to speak truth to power today?

Action Step / Weekly Challenge

- Identify one "idol" in your life—something that consumes more time or passion than God—and lay it down for a week of fasting or separation.
- Identify a political or cultural issue where faith and nationalism are being confused.
- Research it and compare it with Scripture. Journal your findings and pray for wisdom on how to respond faithfully.
- Attend a church service or gathering and evaluate whether the teaching reflects true Gospel values or performative religion.
- Record insights and discuss them in a small group.

Challenge Verse

Corinthians 10:14 – *"Therefore, my beloved, flee from idolatry."*

Biblical Character Connection

King Solomon – who began with wisdom but ended in compromise due to idolatry.

Daniel – In a hostile political environment, Daniel refused to compromise his faith. He prayed faithfully, upheld justice, and influenced leaders without joining their corrupt systems (Daniel 6). Like Daniel, believers today are called to stand against Christian nationalism and counterfeit churches while remaining faithful to God.

Key Quote / Takeaway

"You can't have revival where idols still reign."

"A nation is not Christian because of its leaders, laws, or flags. A nation becomes Christian when Christ reigns in the hearts of its people, embracing justice, mercy, and truth for all."

Worship Song Suggestion

"Clear the Stage" – Jimmy Needham

"Hosanna" by Hillsong United – Reminds believers that God's Kingdom transcends nations and earthly powers, emphasizing justice, mercy, and His reign over all people.

Creative Response

Draw or list the idols of today's church and write what true worship would look like without them. Draw or write a comparison of two "churches": one counterfeit that aligns with power, fear, or racism, and one faithful that reflects Christ's justice and love.

Use this as a visual reflection for personal meditation or group discussion.

Self-Assessment Questions Activity

1. What are the modern idols that distract believers?
2. How can self-promotion be a hidden form of idolatry?
3. What happens when the church exalts man above God?
4. How can we keep Christ central in ministry?
5. What does surrender look like practically?
6. Rate yourself on a scale of 1–5 (1 = Needs Growth, 5 = Strong):
7. I discern when political ideologies conflict with God's Word.
8. I resist aligning my faith with nationalism, racism, or power.
9. I actively pursue justice, mercy, and reconciliation in my community.
10. I can identify performative or counterfeit religious practices.
11. I practice critical thinking and evaluate teachings against Scripture.

Total your score and reflect prayerfully: Where is God calling you to grow?

Devotional Prayer

"Father, reveal and remove every idol in my heart and in Your Church. Be my only pursuit, my only passion, my only praise. Reign without rival in me. Amen."

Chapter Summary

This chapter reveals Satan's role as accuser and deceiver, seeking to prosecute God's people. Believers overcome through Christ's blood and faithful testimony. Throughout history, prophets have been rejected, silenced, and killed because their voices exposed corruption. Today, the same spirit persists—truth-tellers are labeled as divisive, while flatterers are celebrated. God is restoring prophetic voices who fear Him more than popularity. The Church must reopen her ears to the cry of correction.

Key Scriptures

Amos 3:7
Matthew 23:37
Jeremiah 7:25–27
Timothy 4:2–4
Revelation 12:10–11 – "The accuser of our brethren is cast down... And they overcame him by the blood of the Lamb, and by the word of their testimony."

Reflection Quotes

"A silenced prophet becomes a grieving God."
"When truth is unwelcome, deception becomes home."

Reflection Questions

1. How does Satan act as an accuser against believers?
2. What role does Christ's blood play in overcoming accusations?
3. How can my testimony silence the voice of the accuser?

Group Discussion Prompts

- Why is understanding spiritual warfare important for the church today?
- How can believers guard against deception and accusations?

Action Step / Weekly Challenge

Spend time listening in silence before God. Write what the Holy Spirit is warning or calling you to do in this season.
Speak aloud your testimony of salvation to someone this week as a declaration

of victory.

Challenge Verse
Jeremiah 1:9 – *"Behold, I have put My words in your mouth."*

Biblical Character Connection
Jeremiah – the weeping prophet who was rejected by his own people yet remained faithful to his call.

Key Quote / Takeaway
"The Church that silences the prophets will soon be silenced by judgment."

Worship Song Suggestion
"Speak to Me" – Kari Jobe

Creative Response Option
Write a short prophetic declaration to the Church calling for repentance and return to truth. Write your testimony on one page as a reminder of God's victory in your life.

Self-Assessment Questions
1. Why does the modern Church often reject prophetic correction?
2. How can we discern true prophetic voices from false ones?
3. What does it mean to carry a prophetic burden?
4. How can I support and honor God's prophets?
5. What happens when truth is ignored?
6. ☐ I understand the enemy's tactics of accusation.
7. ☐ I sometimes struggle with feelings of guilt or condemnation.
8. ☐ I rely on Christ's blood and my testimony to overcome.

Devotional Prayer
"Lord, give me ears to hear what the Spirit is saying. Raise voices that will cry aloud and spare not. Let truth thunder again in the pulpits of the earth. Lord, strengthen me to overcome the accusations of the enemy by Your blood and my testimony. Men."

Chapter Summary

The Church was meant to be a refuge for the broken, but many have found rejection instead of restoration. This chapter confronts spiritual coldness, where religious duty replaced compassion. God is calling His people to weep again for souls, to love the poor, the hurting, and the lost as Jesus did. False prophecy thrives when people seek comfort over truth. True prophecy aligns with Scripture and glorifies Christ, never self or deception.

Key Scriptures

Matthew 25:35–40
James 2:15–17
Luke 10:33–37
1 John 3:17–18
Jeremiah 23:16 – "Hearken not unto the words of the prophets that prophesy unto you: they make you vain: they speak a vision of their own heart, and not out of the mouth of the Lord."

Reflection Quotes

"A loveless church is a lifeless church."
"We are never more like Christ than when we show compassion."

Reflection Questions

What are the marks of counterfeit prophecy?
Why is discernment critical in today's church?
How can we measure prophecy against Scripture?

Group Discussion Prompts

How do false prophecies damage individuals and churches?

What role should accountability play in prophetic ministry?
Action Step / Weekly Challenge
Perform one act of compassion this week—feed someone hungry, call someone lonely, forgive someone undeserving.
Study one biblical prophet this week and compare their message with modern

prophetic voices.

Challenge Verse
Colossians 3:12 – *"Clothe yourselves with compassion, kindness, humility, gentleness and patience."*

Biblical Character Connection
The Good Samaritan – who demonstrated love beyond religion or race.

Key Quote / Takeaway
"If the Church stops caring, Christ stops being seen."

Worship Song Suggestion
"Give Me Your Eyes" – Brandon Heath

Creative Response
Create a "Compassion List" — names of people God is calling you to love or serve this month. Write down three questions you will ask when discerning whether a message is from God.

Self-Assessment Questions
1. Why is compassion central to Christian witness?
2. How can apathy creep into ministry?
3. What does mercy look like in modern times?
4. Who around me needs tangible love today?
5. How can the Church rebuild trust through compassion?
6. ☐ I test every word against Scripture.
7. ☐ I sometimes chase after words that please my emotions.
8. ☐ I desire to follow truth over comfort.

Devotional Prayer
"Lord, soften my heart again. Let me see through Your eyes, love with Your hands, and feel with Your heart. Restore compassion to Your Church until the world sees Jesus through us. Lord, give me discernment to recognize truth from deception in every prophetic word. Amen."

Chapter Summary

In an age of compromise, God is raising a remnant that fears nothing but sin and reveres no one but Him. The Holy and Fearless Church stands firm in truth despite persecution, political pressure, or cultural rejection. This chapter calls believers to live courageously in holiness, to proclaim righteousness without apology, and to stand unwavering in the power of the Holy Spirit. A holy church is fearless because it walks in truth and obedience. Fear of man is replaced with reverence for God, enabling bold witness in a hostile world.

Key Scriptures

Acts 4:30–31

2 Timothy 1:7

Ephesians 6:13 14

Joshua 1:9

Acts 4:29 – "And now, Lord, behold their threatening: and grant unto thy servants, that with all boldness they may speak thy word."

Reflection Quotes

"Courage is not the absence of fear—it is obedience in the face of it." "A holy church cannot be a silent one."

Reflection Questions

1. What does it mean to be both holy and fearless?
2. How does fear of man hinder the church's mission?
3. Where do I need greater boldness in my faith?

Group Discussion Prompts

- Why does holiness produce courage?
- How can the church stand fearless in times of opposition?

Action Step / Weekly Challenge

Ask God to reveal one area where fear or compromise silences your witness. Confront that fear this week through prayer, Scripture, and faith-driven action. Take one step of boldness this week, share your faith, pray publicly, or speak truth in love.

Challenge Verse

Psalm 27:1 – *"The Lord is my light and my salvation; whom shall I fear?"*

Biblical Character Connection

Daniel – who stood fearless in the face of lions because his conviction was stronger than his fear.

Key Quote / Takeaway

"A fearless church becomes a flame that darkness cannot extinguish."

Worship Song Suggestion

"Spirit Lead Me" – Influence Music & Michael Ketterer

Creative Response Option

Write a declaration titled *"My Holy Boldness"*—a personal statement of what you refuse to be silent about anymore.

Write a short declaration beginning with, "I will not fear…"

Self-Assessment Questions

What fears have hindered your obedience? How does holiness strengthen courage? What does it mean to be fearless yet humble? How can the Church model holy boldness today? Where do I need to take a stand in love and truth?

I walk in reverence for God more than fear of man.

I sometimes shrink back from bold witness.

I desire to live holy and fearless before God.

Devotional Prayer

"Lord, clothe me with courage from heaven. Let holiness be my armor and faith my weapon. Teach me to speak truth in love and to stand strong when the world bows to compromise. Lord, clothe me with holiness and boldness to stand unashamed in Your name. Amen."

Chapter Summary

Before every revival comes exposure. God reveals hidden sin not to destroy His people but to cleanse and ready them for renewal. This chapter teaches that exposure is mercy—it brings darkness to light so that healing can flow. The Church must humble itself before the shaking, for revival begins when repentance runs deep. God is preparing His church for the final exposure of sin and for revival. Repentance, purity, and prayer prepare us for His refining fire and awakening. He is God also prepares the church for revelation, purification, repentance, and spiritual renewal are essential to experience revival.

Key Scriptures

Peter 4:17 – "For the time is come that judgment must begin at the house of God."
Chronicles 7:14 – "If my people... shall humble themselves... then will I hear from heaven, and will forgive their sin, and will heal their land."
Joel 2:12–13 – "Return unto me with all your heart... for I am gracious and merciful."
Luke 8:17
Psalm 85:6

Reflection Quotes

"God exposes what He intends to heal."
"Before the fire of revival falls, the fire of refinement must come first."

Reflection Questions

Why does judgment begin in the house of God?
How is exposure an act of mercy?
What steps can I take to prepare for revival?
How can I prepare personally for spiritual exposure and revival?
Why is repentance crucial before revival occurs?
What role do prayer and fasting play in readiness?

Group Discussion Prompts

Why must exposure precede revival? How does prayer usher in awakening?
Share personal or church practices that foster revival.
How can we encourage accountability and humility in preparation for revival?

Action Step / Weekly Challenge

Spend three days in prayer asking God to expose anything in your life that grieves His Spirit. Journal what He reveals and surrenders it at His feet.

Join with others in a prayer meeting specifically focused on repentance and revival. Spend time each day this week in prayer and fasting, seeking God's guidance for spiritual renewal.

Challenge Verse

Psalm 139:23–24 – *"Search me, O God, and know my heart."*

Biblical Character Connection

King Hezekiah – who purified the temple and restored true worship, preparing the nation for revival.

Key Quote / Takeaway

"Exposure is not God's wrath—it's His mercy calling you to revival."

Worship Song Suggestion

"Refiner" – Maverick City Music

Creative Response Option

Compose a short revival prayer to pray daily this week.

Create a personal "revival readiness plan" highlighting spiritual disciplines.

Draw or list "walls" that need to fall before revival—both personal and corporate—and pray for their collapse.

Self-Assessment Questions

1. How does exposure precede revival?
2. Why is confession vital for renewal?
3. What areas of darkness still need God's light?
4. How can churches create safe places for repentance?
5. What signs indicate that revival is near?
6. ☐ I recognize that exposure is for my good.
7. ☐ I sometimes resist correction or discipline.
8. ☐ I long for God's revival fire.
9. ☐ I pursue holiness and repentance.
10. ☐ I commit to personal and corporate preparation for revival.
11. ☐ I prioritize God's work over personal comfort

Devotional Prayer

"Father, search and cleanse me. Expose what's hidden, purify what's impure, and ignite my heart for Your glory. Let revival begin in me. Lord, purify Your church and prepare us for the fire of revival. Lord, purify my heart and prepare me for Your Spirit to move mightily. Amen."

Chapter Summary

This chapter warns of manipulative and controlling spirits that undermine godly leadership. Spiritual discernment and authority are needed to guard the church. It also offers strategies to identify and overcome manipulative, controlling influences within ministry. Spiritual authority, discernment, and prayer are key tools. The spirit of Jezebel is alive in the modern church— manipulating, controlling, and deceiving leaders into submission to unholy influence. This chapter reveals how this spirit operates through charm, intimidation, and spiritual abuse. God calls His servants to discern, confront, and cast down every manipulative power that threatens His order and holiness.

Key Scriptures

Revelation 2:20–23
Kings 21:25
Ephesians 6:12
Kings 9:30–33
Revelation 2:20 – "Notwithstanding I have a few things against thee, because thou sufferest that woman Jezebel… to teach and to seduce my servants."
Revelation 2:20–23 – Warning against tolerating the Jezebel spirit.
Ephesians 6:12 – "For we wrestle not against flesh and blood, but against principalities…"

Reflection Quotes

"Jezebel doesn't always wear makeup—sometimes she wears ministry titles."
"The spirit of Jezebel fears true prophets who walk in obedience."

Reflection Questions

1. How does the Jezebel spirit operate in the modern church?
2. Why is discernment essential for leaders and members alike?
3. What safeguards can I put in place to avoid manipulation?
4. How can leaders detect manipulative influence in ministry?
5. What steps can a church take to remove unhealthy power structures?
6. How does discernment protect the body of Christ?

Group Discussion Prompts

- How do we balance grace with firm confrontation of ungodliness?
- What role does accountability play in overcoming controlling spirits?
- Discuss real-life examples of manipulation in church leadership.
- Share best practices for accountability and spiritual protection.

Action Step / Weekly Challenge
- Pray for discernment over your church and personal life.
- Ask the Holy Spirit to reveal any controlling influences you've tolerated and to give you wisdom to confront them in love.
- Pray for your pastors and leaders, asking God to shield them from manipulation.
- Pray for discernment and identify one area in ministry where spiritual manipulation could be addressed.

Challenge Verse
Ephesians 5:11 – *"Have nothing to do with the fruitless deeds of darkness, but rather expose them."*

Biblical Character Connection
Elijah – who stood fearlessly against Jezebel and the false prophets of Baal.

Key Quote / Takeaway
"When truth rises, manipulation falls."

Worship Song Suggestion
"Break Every Chain" – Tasha Cobbs Leonard

Creative Response
1. Write a prayer declaration breaking agreement with any spirit of control, fear, or intimidation that has hindered your calling.
2. Journal about a time you discerned manipulation and how God helped you overcome.
3. Write a plan for cultivating healthy leadership and accountability structures.

Self-Assessment Questions
1. How does the Jezebel spirit manifest in churches today?
2. What role does discernment play in leadership?

3. Why must spiritual authority always be rooted in humility?
4. How can leaders avoid manipulation in ministry?
5. What happens when Jezebel is confronted by the truth?
6. ☐ I pray for discernment in spiritual matters.
7. ☐ I sometimes overlook manipulative behavior.
8. ☐ I stand firm in truth against ungodly influence.
9. ☐ I can recognize unhealthy power dynamics.
10. ☐ I rely on God for discernment in leadership matters.
11. ☐ I support transparency and integrity in ministry.

Devotional Prayer

"Lord, expose every Jezebel spirit within and around me. Give me the courage of Elijah to stand firm and the humility of Jesus to respond in righteousness. Deliver Your Church from manipulation and restore spiritual purity. Lord, expose and remove every ungodly influence from my life and church. Lord, give me wisdom to confront control and manipulation in Your name. Amen."

Chapter Summary

This chapter calls believers to live open, honest lives before God and man, reflecting His truth without hypocrisy. God is calling His Church to walk in the light. Hidden sin, secret agendas, and concealed wounds are being brought to the surface—not for shame, but for freedom.

Transparency invites accountability, and accountability preserves holiness. Transparency protects holiness. God calls His people to live openly before Him and others, walking in truth, humility, and accountability. Living openly and accountable before God protects holiness and prepares the church for divine evaluation. Transparency fosters trust, unity, and spiritual growth.

Key Scriptures

1 John 1:7–9
James 5:16
Proverbs 28:13
Luke 8:17
Ephesians 5:13 – "But all things that are reproved are made manifest by the light: for whatsoever doth make manifest is light."

Reflection Quotes

"Transparency is not weakness—it's worship."
"The Church cannot heal what it refuses to reveal."

Reflection Questions

- Why is transparency vital to holiness?
- What keeps people hiding in secret?
- How can I practice accountability in my walk with God?
- 1 John 1:7 – "The blood of Jesus... cleanseth us from all sin."
- James 5:16 – "Confess your faults one to another and pray one for another."

Group Discussion Prompts

1. How does confession bring freedom?
2. Why is secrecy dangerous for leaders and members alike?

3. Why is transparency essential in the church?
4. How does accountability strengthen spiritual communities?
5. What practices can encourage openness and honesty?

Action Step / Weekly Challenge
Confess a struggle or weakness to a trusted spiritual mentor or prayer partner this week. Let light bring healing.
Share an area of struggle with a trusted accountability partner this week. Identify one area in your life to walk more transparently before God and others.

Challenge Verse
Psalm 32:5 – *"I acknowledged my sin to You, and You forgave the guilt of my sin."*

Biblical Character Connection
Nathan and David – the prophet who confronted the king, and the king who chose repentance over reputation.

Key Quote / Takeaway
"Transparency is the bridge between conviction and cleansing."

Worship Song Suggestion
"Clean Hands" – Chris Tomlin

Creative Response Option
Write a short prayer of confession, offering it as an act of transparency.
Journal a personal plan to foster accountability and transparency.
Write your personal "truth statement" about one area God has healed or is healing. Use it as a testimony of grace.

Self-Assessment Questions
Why is transparency vital for holiness?
What are the dangers of secrecy in leadership? How can confession lead to restoration?
What keeps believers from walking in the light?
How can churches foster a culture of honesty and accountability?
☐ I invite God's light into hidden areas.
☐ I sometimes keep secrets that hinder my walk.
☐ I value accountability and openness.

☐ I prioritize honesty and openness in relationships.
☐ I seek to maintain integrity in all interactions.
☐ I encourage others toward transparency in Christ.

Devotional Prayer

"Father, teach me to walk in the light as You are in the light. Let nothing remain hidden that hinders my relationship with You. Make Your Church transparent and truthful again. Lord, shine Your light into every hidden area of my life. Lord, help me live with integrity and openness for Your glory. Amen."

Chapter 26: Return to the Altar – The Spirit of Repentance and Revival Fire

Chapter Summary

This chapter is a divine call for the Church to return to the altar—the sacred place of sacrifice, surrender, and renewal. Revival doesn't start with shouting—it begins with weeping. The Spirit of repentance is the foundation from which true revival is born. This chapter reveals the power of contrition, brokenness, and humility before God. When the Church turns from sin, heaven turns toward her again. Revival fire falls where hearts are fully surrendered.

Revival begins where repentance causes knees to bend. The altar symbolizes the heart of worship and the meeting point between man and God. When the Church rebuilds the altar, the fire of the Spirit falls once more. Revival begins at the altar of God's presence. Returning to prayer and worship restores intimacy, faithfulness, and spiritual fire. Returning to God's presence restores closeness, faithfulness, and spiritual power. Repentance is vital for renewal and revival.

Key Scriptures

Joel 2:17 – "Let the priests, the ministers of the Lord, weep between the porch and the altar."

Joel 2:15–16 – "Blow the trumpet in Zion, sanctify a fast, call a solemn assembly."

Psalm 51:10 – "Create in me a clean heart, O God; and renew a right spirit within me." Joel 2:12–13

Romans 12:1

1 Kings 18:30–38

Hebrews 13:10

Psalm 51:11–13

Acts 3:19

2 Chronicles 7:14

Reflection Quotes

"There can be no revival without a return to the altar." "When hearts become the altar, heaven sends the fire."

Repentance is not punishment—it's permission to be restored." "The fire of revival falls only on altars soaked in tears."

Reflection Questions

1. What does "returning to the altar" mean personally?

2. How does prayer restore broken fellowship with God?
3. What sacrifices of time or pride might God be calling me to make?
4. How does returning to the altar foster personal and corporate revival?
5. What barriers prevent believers from repenting?
6. How can the church encourage a culture of returning to God?

Group Discussion Prompts

Why does revival always start at the altar of prayer? How can families and churches rebuild the altar today?

Share experiences of spiritual renewal through repentance.

How can churches help members return to wholehearted devotion?

Action Step / Weekly Challenge

- Set aside time each day this week to kneel before God—literally or spiritually—and rededicate your heart to Him.
- Dedicate 15 minutes each day this week to uninterrupted prayer at your "altar."
- Spend time at the altar (physically or spiritually) in prayer and repentance this week.
- Spend a day in fasting and repentance—personally or with your church group.
- Journal what God reveals and how He restores your hunger.

Challenge Verse

Hosea 6:1 – "Come, let us return to the Lord."

Acts 3:19 – "Repent, then, and turn to God, so that times of refreshing may come from the Lord."

Biblical Character Connection

Elijah – who rebuilt the broken altar before the fire of God descended. David – who was broken by sin but restored by grace

Key Quote / Takeaway

When the altar is restored, the presence returns." "Revival is not a service—it's a surrender."

Worship Song Suggestion

"Fire Fall Down" – Hillsong United

"Send Revival" – CeCe Winans

Creative Response

Draw or create your "altar map"—a visual symbol of areas in your life where God is calling for renewal and surrender.

Create a simple altar space in your home for prayer and devotion. Write a personal prayer of return and commitment to God.

Write a personal revival confession—a letter to God expressing repentance and renewed commitment.

Self-Assessment Questions

What does the altar symbolize in your life today?

How has modern Christianity drifted from the altar of repentance? What is God asking you to lay down before Him?

How can you rebuild intimacy through daily worship and prayer? How can the corporate Church rebuild the altar collectively?

What is the true evidence of repentance?

Why does revival die when repentance is ignored?

How can leaders cultivate a repentant culture in the Church? What personal changes can usher revival fire in your home? How do brokenness and boldness coexist in revival?

☐ I value time at God's altar.

☐ I sometimes neglect prayer and worship.

☐ I seek intimacy with God daily.

☐ I value returning to God in repentance.

☐ I recognize areas needing restoration in my life.

☐ I commit to personal and communal holiness.

Devotional Prayer

"Lord, I return to the altar today. Take my pride, my comfort, and my sin. Let Your fire purify me again. Restore passion, presence, and purity to Your people until Your glory fills the earth. Lord, draw me back to Your altar. Restore passion and intimacy in my worship. Lord, draw me near and restore my intimacy with You. Lord, break me to make me. Heal what sin has hardened and restore what pride has ruined. Let revival begin in me, and let Your fire purify Your Church once more. Amen."

Chapter 27: Holiness Unto the Lord – Pursuing Moral and Spiritual Purity

Chapter Summary
This chapter calls the people of God back to a lifestyle that reflects His nature, not the culture's compromise. Holiness is not perfection; it is separation unto God. The modern Church has dressed in grace but undressed in purity. To be holy is to be whole, walking daily in reverence, purity, and surrender before the watching world. Holiness is not optional; it is God's standard. This chapter calls for moral and spiritual purity as the foundation for revival. Holiness is the foundation for revival, unity, and readiness for Christ's return. Pursuing moral and spiritual purity is a daily commitment.

Key Scriptures
Peter 1:15-16 - "Be ye holy; for I am holy."
Hebrews 12:14"Follow peace with all men, and holiness, without which no man shall see the Lord."
Leviticus 20:7–8
Corinthians 7:1

Reflection Quotes
"Holiness is not about rules—it's about relationship."
"The closer you walk with God, the less you desire what defiles."

Reflection Questions
1. Why is holiness foundational to revival?
2. How is holiness both inward and outward?
3. In what areas is God calling me to greater purity?
4. What steps can I take daily to pursue holiness?
5. How does personal holiness impact church unity?
6. Why is holiness necessary for revival?

Group Discussion Prompts
- What is the difference between legalism and true holiness?
- How can we pursue holiness in a world of compromise?
- Discuss practical ways to pursue holiness individually and corporately.
- Share strategies for resisting temptation and sin.

Action Step / Weekly Challenge

Identify one area where you have allowed compromise.

Repent, and take one practical step this week to realign your lifestyle with the holiness of Christ. Choose one area this week to surrender fully to God in holiness. Identify one habit or area to improve in holiness this week and implement change.

Challenge Verse

Hebrews 12:14 – *"Without holiness no one will see the Lord."*

Biblical Character Connection

Joseph – who fled temptation and chose integrity over indulgence.

Key Quote / Takeaway

"Holiness is heaven's language—learn to speak it fluently."

Worship Song Suggestion

"Take Me Back" – Maverick City Music

Creative Response Option

Write a "Holiness Covenant" with God—three commitments to guard your purity, thoughts, and speech this week.

Write a declaration of holiness and place it somewhere visible. Create a checklist of spiritual disciplines that cultivate holiness.

Self-Assessment Questions

1. How does holiness protect intimacy with God?
2. Why is holiness often misunderstood in modern churches?
3. What are the practical fruits of a holy life?
4. How can we teach holiness without legalism?
5. What area in your life needs cleansing today?
6. ☐ I pursue holiness with intention.
7. ☐ I sometimes confuse rules with true holiness.
8. ☐ I long to be set apart for God.
9. ☐ I actively pursue moral and spiritual purity.
10. ☐ I resist compromise in thought, word, and deed.
11. ☐ I encourage others to live holy lives.

Devotional Prayer

"Father, cleanse me from within. Let Your holiness flow through my thoughts, words, and actions. Make me a vessel of honor, set apart for Your glory. Lord, set me apart for Your glory. Make me holy as You are holy. Lord, sanctify me wholly and guide me in Your ways. Amen."

Chapter Summary

This chapter confronts the creeping worldliness that has entered the sanctuary—materialism, pride, entertainment-driven worship, and moral compromise. It also calls for sincerity, devotion, and Spirit-led praise. Then the Church starts imitating the world, and she loses her influence.

God calls His Church to come out and be separate, to shine as light in darkness rather than blend in with it. True worship is centered on God, not performance or self. Authentic worship is central to revival and spiritual renewal. Worship must be sincere, God-centered, and marked by devotion rather than ritual.

Key Scriptures

Romans 12:2

1 John 2:15–17

James 4:4

2 Corinthians 6:17

John 4:23-24 – "The true worshippers shall worship the Father in spirit and in truth."

Psalm 95:6 – "O come, let us worship and bow down: let us kneel before the Lord our maker."

Reflection Quotes

"The world should see Christ in the Church, not the Church in the world."

"If the Church looks like the world, who will show the world what holiness looks like?"

Reflection Questions

1. What makes worship "true" or authentic?
2. How does worship shape my relationship with God?
3. Am I more focused on style or substance in worship?
4. How does authentic worship affect spiritual growth?
5. What elements distinguish true worship from empty ritual?
6. How can worship lead to personal and corporate revival?

Group Discussion Prompts

- Why do we often confuse entertainment with worship?

- How can we cultivate a culture of authentic worship in church?
- Share experiences of encountering God through true worship.
- How can your church cultivate authentic, heartfelt worship?

Action Step / Weekly Challenge

Do a "heart inventory." Where have worldly desires replaced godly focus: finances, fashion, social media, pride, pleasure?

Choose one for seven days.

Set aside time to worship God privately this week without music or distractions.

Participate in worship this week with a renewed heart, focusing on God alone.

Challenge Verse

1 John 2:17 – *"The world and its desires pass away, but whoever does the will of God lives forever."*

Biblical Character Connection

Lot, who settled near Sodom and paid the price for comfort over conviction.

Key Quote / Takeaway

"The Church that flirts with the world will eventually lose her purity."

Worship Song Suggestion

"Set a Fire" – Will Reagan & United Pursuit

Creative Response Option

Write a personal song, poem, or prayer of worship to God. Write a worship reflection or song of praise from your heart.

Create a "Separation Wall" in your journal: on one side, list worldly habits; on the other, godly virtues that replace them.

Self-Assessment Questions

1. How has worldliness disguised itself as relevance?
2. What does it mean to be "in the world but not of it"?
3. How can we restore purity in our worship and lifestyle?
4. What areas of compromise weaken the Church's witness?
5. What does true separation look like in daily living?
6. ☐ I worship God in spirit and truth.
7. ☐ I sometimes focus more on outward expression than

inward devotion.

8. ☐ I desire to restore true worship in my life.
9. ☐ I engage in worship sincerely.
10. ☐ I avoid empty rituals and habits.
11. ☐ I inspire others to authentic worship

Devotional Prayer

"Lord, remove the love of the world from my heart. Teach me to love what You love and reject what defiles. May Your Church be pure, radiant, and unshaken by worldly desires. Amen. Lord, cleanse my worship of pride or distraction. Receive my heart of devotion. Lord, help me worship You in spirit and in truth."

Chapter Summary
This chapter explores the dark days of King Ahab's reign, paralleling it with the current state of church and political leadership. It underscores the exploitation, manipulation, and corruption seen in some modern leaders, warning against the Jezebel spirit of greed and deception. While highlighting the consequences of unrepentant sin, it also points to God's mercy and the need for repentance (2 Chronicles 7:14). The chapter emphasizes the importance of prophetic voices, like Elijah's, in confronting sin and restoring justice, urging them to rise amid a world where truth is silenced. True prophets must listen for divine guidance before speaking, carrying a message of repentance rather than seeking approval.

Key Scriptures
Amos 3:7
Jeremiah 1:9–10
Ezekiel 33:7–9
Acts 2:17–18

Reflection Quotes
"True prophets don't predict trends—they reveal truth." "The prophetic mantle carries both fire and tears."

Reflection Questions
1. How does King Ahab's story mirror some of the leadership challenges in today's church and political world?
2. What are some examples of the Jezebel spirit in modern times, according to this chapter?
3. How do hidden abuses affect the Church's credibility and witness?
4. What does Scripture in *2 Chronicles 7:14* say about repentance and healing for leaders and the land?
5. Why is the role of Elijah-like voices critical in confronting modern corruption?
6. How can leaders ensure that repentance is genuine rather than superficial?
7. What lessons can the laity learn about discernment and

accountability from this chapter?

Discussion Prompts
- Share an example of a leader (political or church) who needed to repent.
- What were the consequences of their choices?
- Discuss how fear and manipulation allow corruption to flourish in institutions.
- Brainstorm practical ways the Church can support victims and confront abusive leaders.
- Reflect on times when you witnessed or experienced injustice. How can faith communities respond effectively?
- Debate: Can a leader truly be restored without leaving their position or making amends?

Action Step / Weekly Challenge
- Observe & Reflect: Identify one area in your church, community, or workplace where corruption, greed, or abuse is tolerated. Pray for God's guidance and discernment on how you can address it.
- Speak Truth in Love: Choose one situation where you can respectfully and biblically confront injustice or encourage a leader toward repentance.
- Repent & Restore: Ask God to reveal any ways you may have contributed to hidden evils—through silence, indifference, or compromise—and make amends where possible.
- Set aside one hour this week to intercede for your city, nation, and leaders. Ask God to raise voices of righteousness in this generation.

Challenge Verse
Jeremiah 1:9 – *"I have put My words in your mouth."*

Biblical Character Connection
- Jeremiah – the weeping prophet who spoke unpopular truth to a rebellious nation.
- **Elijah:** A prophet who boldly confronted King Ahab and the prophets of Baal, exposing sin and calling for repentance. He serves as a model for courage, obedience, and reliance on God's power in confronting wicked leadership.

Key Quote / Takeaway

"Before prophets speak to people, they must first listen to God."
The dark days in our church and political world are an invitation to awaken, confront sin, embrace obedience, and trust God to heal the land. The choice is ours, the time is now, and God's promise remains true: repentance brings restoration."

Worship Song Suggestion
- "Speak to Me" – Koryn Hawthorne
- **"Lord, I Need You" – Matt Maher**

Emphasizes humility, dependence on God, and seeking His face

Creative Response Option
1. Journaling Exercise: Write a letter to God reflecting on the areas of darkness you've witnessed in leadership. Include prayers for repentance, justice, and healing.
2. Art Exercise: Create a visual representation of "light breaking through darkness" in your church or community.
3. Write a "Prophetic Prayer" declaring God's will for your community or church, aligning it with Scripture.

Self-Assessment Questions
On a scale of 1–5, evaluate your awareness of corruption or hidden sin in your church, workplace, or community.
List three practical steps you can take this month to encourage accountability and justice. Identify one personal area where you need repentance or renewed commitment to integrity. What distinguishes true prophets from false ones?
Why is the prophetic voice necessary in this generation? How can prophets guard their purity and humility?
What happens when prophetic voices are silent?
How can the Church embrace and test the prophetic anointing biblically?

Devotional Prayer
"God, raise Your prophets again. Purify their hearts, sanctify their lips, and strengthen their voices. Let them cry aloud with truth, grace, and fire until the Church awakens. Amen."

Chapter 30: The Five P's Pillars of a Church on Trial - (Passion · Presence · Prestige · Powerbase · Process)

Chapter Summary:

This chapter discusses five foundational pillars that influence the Church's strength or collapse when tested by God's truth: Passion, Presence, Prestige, Powerbase, and Process. Each pillar represents an area where God reveals hidden motives and addresses evils within His people and leaders. Passion without purity becomes performance; Presence without repentance is deceptive; Prestige and power without humility turn into idols; and Process without the Holy Spirit leads to religion without revelation. God calls His Church to rebuild these pillars on righteousness, compassion, and truth so that His presence can reside among a pure people. The Church must become a haven for those struggling with trauma, addiction, and mental health challenges. This chapter highlights the Church's vital role in offering healing, hope, and support for those in crisis.

Key Scriptures:

Passion: Revelation 2:4 – *"Nevertheless I have somewhat against thee, because thou hast left thy first love."*

Presence: Psalm 51:11 – *"Cast me not away from thy presence; and take not thy Holy Spirit from me."*

Prestige: Matthew 23:12 – *"Whoever exalts himself will be humbled, and whoever humbles himself will be exalted."*

Powerbase: Zechariah 4:6 – *"Not by might, nor by power, but by my Spirit, saith the Lord of hosts."*

Process: Isaiah 1:16 17 – *"Wash you, make you clean; put away the evil of your doings… learn to do well; seek judgment, relieve the oppressed."*

Rebuke of Hidden Evil: Luke 12:2 – *"For there is nothing covered, that shall not be revealed; neither hid, that shall not be known."*

Psalm 34:18 – "The Lord is nigh unto them that are of a broken heart; and saveth such as be of a contrite spirit."

Psalm 34:18 – "The Lord is nigh unto them that are of a broken heart."

Matthew 11:28 – "Come unto me, all ye that labor and are heavy laden, and I will give you rest."

Reflection Quotes:

"God is not impressed by our pillars of reputation — He examines the foundation of our hearts." "Passion without holiness becomes performance; presence without purity becomes pretense." "When prestige overshadows purpose, the Church becomes a monument instead of a movement."

"True power is not found in politics or influence, but in submission to the Spirit of God." "The process of God refines what pride tries to conceal."

Reflection Questions

1. How can the church respond to those carrying deep wounds?
2. Why is it important to integrate faith with mental and emotional healing?
3. How can I personally support someone on their healing journey?
4. How can the church address mental health and trauma better?
5. What is the role of faith alongside professional help?
6. How can believers foster safe spaces for healing?

Group Discussion Prompts

- Why do churches often overlook mental health issues?
- How can compassion transform the way we minister to the hurting?
- Discuss ways your church can respond to trauma and mental health needs.
- Share testimonies of hope and healing.

Action Step / Weekly Challenge:

1. Reflect and Repent: Examine each of the five pillars in your own life and church.
2. Where has passion dimmed?
3. Where is God's presence missing?
4. Has prestige or influence replaced humility?
5. Has power been misused?
6. Has the process of faith turned into an empty ritual?
7. Write a prayer of repentance for any pillar that has been compromised.
8. Ask God to rebuild your foundation with integrity and spiritual discernment.
9. Reach out to someone struggling emotionally and offer a listening ear.
10. Offer encouragement or practical support to someone struggling with mental health or trauma.

Challenge Verse:
Psalm 139:23–24 – *"Search me, O God, and know my heart: try me, and know my thoughts: and see if there be any wicked way in me, and lead me in the way everlasting."*

Biblical Character Connection:
King David: His passion for God turned to repentance after sin exposed hidden evil (Psalm 51). Saul (Paul): Once driven by prestige and power, he was transformed into a vessel of grace through divine process (Acts 9).
Moses: A man of presence who learned that true power came not from Egypt's palace, but from God's presence in the wilderness (Exodus 3).

Key Quote / Takeaway:
"God is rebuilding His Church not on the pillars of popularity, but on the foundation of purity."

Worship Song Suggestion:
"Refiner" – Maverick City Music
"Clean Hands" – Chris Tomlin
"Build My Life" – Pat Barrett

Creative Response Option
1. Create a written or visual reflection expressing hope and healing in Christ.
2. Create a resource list or ministry plan to support mental health in your community.
3. Create a **visual diagram or drawing** of the Five P's Pillars, labeling which ones in your life or ministry are strong, weak, or in need of rebuilding.
4. Write a **personal psalm or poem** asking God to restore His presence and passion within you.
5. Record a **spoken word declaration** of how you will guard against prestige and power that corrupts purity.

Self-Assessment Questions:
1. Which of the five pillars (Passion, Presence, Prestige, Powerbase, Process) has God recently tested in my life?
2. Do I serve from genuine love for God or for the prestige and

praise of others?

3. How do I invite God's presence daily into my ministry, family, and decision-making?
4. Have I trusted in human systems or the Spirit's leading when facing opposition?
5. What does the "process" of purification look like in my walk with God right now?
6. ☐ I acknowledge the reality of trauma and mental health struggles.
7. ☐ I sometimes feel unsure how to help others in pain.
8. ☐ I want to be a safe place of compassion for others.
9. ☐ I am aware of mental health and trauma needs.
10. ☐ I offer compassion and support.
11. ☐ I commit to integrating faith and care for holistic healing.

Final Reflection

The Church on trial must return to its foundation. The Five P's are not just principles; they are divine tests. God is purifying His Bride so that passion burns with truth, presence rests in holiness, prestige bows to humility, power submits to the Spirit, and process reflects justice.

When these pillars stand firm, the Church will rise again as the dwelling place of God's glory, unshaken by corruption and steadfast in love. In Jesus' name, Amen.

Chapter Summary

Every healthy church stands on five divine pillars: Purity, Prayer, Power, Purpose, and Presence. These pillars served as spiritual foundations for a victorious Church in the last days. Weakening any pillar invites corruption, but when they all remain strong, the Church becomes a powerful force in a fallen world. Disunity is one of the enemy's most effective weapons against the body of Christ. When pride, jealousy, or competition disrupts collaboration, the anointing through unity is hindered. This chapter highlights how Satan exploits these fractures to weaken the Church's effectiveness. God calls His people back to genuine partnership, humility, and spiritual oneness. Disunity delays revival and hinders healing. However, through repentance and submission to the Holy Spirit, unity can be restored, allowing the Church to move forward as one body for the glory of God.

Key Scriptures

Matthew 21:13

Acts 1:8

1 Peter 2:9

Ephesians 4:11-13

Psalm 133:1 – "Behold, how good and how pleasant it is for brethren to dwell together in unity!"

John 17:21 – "That they all may be one; as thou, Father, art in me, and I in thee…"

1 Corinthians 1:10 – "I appeal to you… that there be no divisions among you, but that you be perfectly united in mind and thought."

Ephesians 4:3 – "Make every effort to keep the unity of the Spirit through the bond of peace." Philippians 2:3-4 – "Do nothing out of selfish ambition or vain conceit. Rather, in humility value others above yourselves."

Reflection Quotes

1. "Purity guards power."
2. "Prayer fuels presence."
3. "Purpose without purity leads to destruction."
4. "Unity is not uniformity—it is harmony birthed in humility."
5. "The Church cannot conquer the world while divided within."
6. "Broken collaboration is a sign of broken communion with Christ."
7. "Satan doesn't need to destroy a Church that destroys itself

through division."

Reflection Questions
- What are some signs that collaboration has broken down in your ministry or church community?
- How has pride, offense, or mistrust hindered your ability to work with others for the Kingdom?
- What personal steps can you take to be a peacemaker or restorer of unity where division exists?
- How does unity invite God's presence and blessing according to Psalm 133?
- Reflect on a time when collaboration brought greater fruit than working alone—what changed?

Group Discussion Prompts
1. Discuss how the early Church maintained unity despite persecution and diversity (see Acts 2:42-47).
2. What role does forgiveness play in restoring collaboration among believers?
3. How can leadership teams cultivate unity without silencing accountability or truth?
4. What does a "spirit of collaboration" look like in your local church or ministry today?

Action Step / Weekly Challenge
1. Evaluate your life and church through the five pillars.
2. Identify which one needs strengthening and develop a practical growth plan this week.
3. Identify one relationship, ministry, or partnership where unity has been strained.
4. Reach out this week to initiate reconciliation, prayer, or dialogue.
5. Let humility lead the way.
6. Seek restoration not for appearance's sake, but to honor Christ's prayer for unity among His followers.

Challenge Verse
Ephesians 3:20 – *"Now unto Him who can do immeasurably more…"*
Romans 12:18 – *"If it is possible, as far as it depends on you, live at peace*

with everyone."

Biblical Character Connection
The Early Church – whose devotion to prayer, unity, and purity birthed a global movement. Paul and Barnabas (Acts 15:36–41) – Once strong ministry partners, their disagreement caused separation. Yet God used both men mightily afterward, proving that reconciliation and maturity in Christ can still bring fruit beyond conflict. Their story reminds us that broken collaboration can be redeemed when both hearts remain surrendered to God's will.

Key Quote / Takeaway
A Church built on purity and prayer cannot collapse under persecution."
"Unity releases power, but division drains purpose. God's glory dwells where His people walk together as one."

Worship Song Suggestion
"Build Your Church" – Elevation Worship & Maverick City Music
"Make Us One" by Jesus Culture
(Theme: Asking the Holy Spirit to unite hearts, heal division, and restore harmony within the body of Christ.)

Creative Response Option
1. Create a "Unity Covenant" board or personal journal page.
2. Write down the names of people or ministries you want to reconcile with or pray for unity over. Decorate it with Scriptures, prayers, and declarations of restoration.
3. Keep it as a reminder that God blesses peacemakers.
4. Draw a five-pillar diagram representing the foundation of your faith.
5. Label each pillar with Scripture and a personal commitment.

Self-Assessment Questions
1. Which of the five pillars is most vital for today's Church?
2. How can prayer protect the Church's purity?
3. What happens when the Church loses her purpose?
4. How do power and presence sustain ministry?
5. Which pillar will you strengthen first—and how?
6. Do I celebrate others' gifts or feel threatened by them?

7. Have I allowed offense to block collaboration in ministry?
8. Do I pray regularly for unity in my church and leadership?
9. Am I willing to humble myself first to repair relationships?
10. Do I seek the Spirit's direction before making divisive decisions?

Devotional Prayer

"Lord, restore Your five pillars in us—Purity to cleanse, Prayer to connect, Power to impact, Purpose to guide, and Presence to sustain. Build Your Church that the gates of hell shall not prevail against it. Lord Jesus, Forgive us for every moment we've allowed pride, jealousy, or misunderstanding to divide what You intended to unite. Heal the fractures in your body. Restore true collaboration rooted in humility, love, and obedience. Help me to be a peace vessel, not strife, a bridge builder, not a wall builder. May Your Spirit unite us for the work of Your Kingdom so that the world may believe You sent us. Amen.

Final Reflections

The Church stands on trial when its members refuse to walk in unity. God is not impressed by outward performance but by inward alignment with His heart. Collaboration is sacred—it is how the Kingdom advances. When the Church chooses humility over ego, reconciliation over rivalry, and love over competition, heaven rejoices, and revival begins. Unity is not optional—it is the call of every true disciple.

Chapter Summary

This chapter addresses the reality that all actions, words, and intentions—within the Church and the broader world—will face God's judgment. The time for divine reckoning has arrived, as hidden sins and spiritual hypocrisy cannot remain concealed. God is urging His Church to return to purity and responsibility, emphasizing that leadership without accountability breeds corruption. While He is merciful, He also demands truth. This reckoning is meant for refinement, calling for repentance before judgment befalls the world. God's justice is impartial, focusing first on those in spiritual authority. When leaders and congregations stray from righteousness, God disciplines them for restoration. The lesson remains constant from Eli's household to today's churches: God holds His people accountable for the light they've received..

Key Scriptures

Romans 14:12 – "So then, each of us will give an account of ourselves to God."
1 Peter 4:17 – "For it is time for judgment to begin with God's household…"
Ecclesiastes 12:14 – "For God will bring every deed into judgment, including every hidden thing."
Luke 12:2–3 – "There is nothing concealed that will not be disclosed, or hidden that will not be made known."
2 Corinthians 5:10 – "For we must all appear before the judgment seat of Christ…"
Luke 12:47–48
1 Samuel 2:29–30
Acts 5:1–11

Reflection Quotes

"Accountability is not punishment—it's proof of God's love."
"Every hidden deed will one day be weighed on God's scale of truth." "Accountability before man is good; accountability before God is eternal." "The fear of the Lord restores what the comfort of sin has stolen." "Judgment begins not in the world's courts but in God's house." "Exposure is not punishment—it is purification."

Reflection Questions

    1. What does it mean for judgment to "begin in the house of God"?

2. How have you experienced God's correction in your personal life or ministry?
3. What areas of accountability are lacking in the modern Church?
4. Why do you think God allows hidden sin to be exposed publicly?
5. What changes must you make today to walk in greater integrity and transparency?

Group Discussion Prompts
1. Discuss how accountability strengthens spiritual communities.
2. What systems of godly oversight should churches adopt to protect against moral failure?
3. Why is confession and repentance essential before revival can come?
4. How can believers practice accountability with one another in love?

Action Step / Weekly Challenge
Examine your leadership, relationships, and commitments this week.

- Ask: *Am I managing what God has entrusted me with faithfully?*
- Journal areas where repentance or accountability is needed.
- Take one area of your life or ministry and invite a trusted spiritual mentor or peer to hold you accountable.
- Confess struggles, seek prayer, and set boundaries that lead to spiritual growth and holiness.

Challenge Verse
Luke 12:48 – *"To whom much is given, much will be required."*
Hebrews 4:13 – *"Nothing in all creation is hidden from God's sight; everything is uncovered and laid bare before the eyes of Him to whom we must give account."*

Biblical Character Connection
Eli – the priest who failed to correct his sons and suffered the consequences of neglecting accountability.
King David (2 Samuel 12) – Though a man after God's heart, David faced the reckoning of his hidden sin when confronted by Nathan the prophet. His story teaches that exposure is an act of mercy that leads to restoration, not rejection.

Key Quote / Takeaway

"The Church cannot hold the world accountable until she first submits to God's judgment herself." "Accountability is the bridge between conviction and transformation."

Worship Song Suggestion
"Refiner" – Maverick City Music
"Refiner" by Maverick City Music
(Theme: Asking God to cleanse and purify the heart, even when it costs comfort.)

Creative Response Option
Write a personal "Accountability Covenant" listing areas where you will seek godly correction and support. Include Scriptures that anchor your commitment to holiness.
Create an "Accountability Covenant" with God and one trusted believer—detailing spiritual goals, prayer habits, and moral commitments.

Self-Assessment Questions
1. What does divine accountability look like in leadership?
2. How does ignoring sin within the Church invite judgment?
3. Why does God begin judgment with His people?
4. How can transparency protect against moral failure?
5. What will your record show when you stand before God?
6. Do I invite correction or resist it?
7. Is there anything I've hidden from spiritual mentors or God?
8. Do I live daily as though I will give an account to Christ?
9. Have I been honest in my words, finances, and relationships?

Devotional Prayer
"Righteous Judge, search my heart and expose what is hidden. Teach me to walk uprightly before You and those I serve. Let Your refining fire purify my motives, so that I may stand blameless in Your sight. Examine my heart and reveal what is unpleasing to You. Cleanse me from hidden faults and restore my integrity. May Your discipline produce holiness in me and in Your Church. Help me to walk in truth, accountability, and humility until the day of Christ Jesus. Amen.

Final Reflections
God's reckoning is not cruelty—it is mercy in motion. He exposes only what

we refuse to surrender. The Church's credibility in the world depends on its accountability before heaven. When purity is restored, power returns.

Chapter Summary
This chapter emphasizes the Church's duty to confront the often-overlooked issues of mental health, trauma, and emotional wounds. Many who suffer are silenced by stigma and shallow theology. God calls His Church to care for not just souls but minds, creating safe spaces for the broken. Healing requires honesty, compassion, and Spirit-led care to restore faith and emotional wholeness. It recognizes that many in the body of Christ bear unseen wounds. God is both Judge and Healer, inviting His people into wholeness. The Church must shift from judgment to compassion, where truth, empathy, and faith unite in Christ's love, especially in addressing mental health, trauma, and addiction.

Key Scriptures
Psalm 34:18 – "The Lord is close to the brokenhearted and saves those who are crushed in spirit."
3 John 1:2 – "I pray that you may enjoy good health and that all may go well with you, even as your soul is getting along well."
Isaiah 61:1-3 – "He has sent me to bind up the brokenhearted…"
Matthew 11:28-30– "Come to me, all you who are weary and burdened, and I will give you rest."
Romans 12:15 – "Rejoice with those who rejoice; mourn with those who mourn."

Reflection Quotes
1. "Healing flows where honesty begins."
2. "God cannot heal what the Church refuses to acknowledge."
3. "Spiritual strength and emotional health were never meant to be enemies."
4. "The Church must become a hospital again, not a courtroom."
5. "Ignoring mental suffering is ignoring the cries of Christ in His people."
6. "Healing begins where judgment ends."

Reflection Questions:
1. How can the church address mental health and trauma better?
2. What is the role of faith alongside professional help?

3. How can believers foster safe spaces for healing?
4. How has the Church historically failed in addressing mental health?
5. What does it mean for God to "bind up the brokenhearted"?
6. How can faith communities become trauma-informed and compassionate?
7. Why is emotional healing vital to spiritual revival?
8. What steps can you personally take to support those struggling with mental illness or grief?

Group Discussion Prompts:
Discuss ways your church can respond to trauma and mental health needs. Share testimonies of hope and healing.
Share examples of how the Church can partner with mental health professionals.
Discuss the balance between prayer, counseling, and community support.
How can we change the narrative around mental illness within faith spaces?
What role does vulnerability play in communal healing?

Action Step / Weekly Challenge
1. Take one intentional step toward inner healing and seek counseling.
2. Confess pain in prayer or talk with a trusted believer.
3. Allow God's Spirit to mend your hidden places.
4. Offer encouragement or practical support to someone struggling with mental health or trauma. Reach out to someone who may be struggling silently.
5. Listen without judgment.
6. Offer prayer and help connect them to practical or professional support if needed.

Challenge Verse
Psalm 34:18 – *"The Lord is close to the brokenhearted and saves those who are crushed in spirit."*
Galatians 6:2 – "Carry each other's burdens, and in this way you will fulfill the law of Christ."

Biblical Character Connection
Hannah – who prayed through her pain and was healed through surrender.
Elijah (1 Kings 19:1–8) – After a great victory, Elijah fell into despair and suicidal thoughts. Yet God met him not with condemnation but care—providing rest,

food, and a renewed mission. His story reminds us that spiritual giants also need emotional healing.

Key Quote / Takeaway
"True revival begins when the Church becomes a hospital for the wounded."
"You can't heal what you hide—bring your wounds to the Healer."

Worship Song Suggestion
"Broken Vessels (Amazing Grace)" – Hillsong Worship
"Come to the Altar" by Elevation Worship
(Theme: Inviting those who are broken and weary to receive Christ's healing and grace.)
Seether - Broken ft. Amy Lee

Creative Response Option:
Create a resource list or ministry plan to support mental health in your community. Create a "Healing Letter" to God expressing your pain and asking Him to transform it into purpose.
Create a "Healing Wall" journal section. Write prayers, Scriptures, or art that represent your healing journey. Add names of people you're interceding for who need emotional or mental healing.

Self-Assessment Questions
1. How does trauma affect spiritual growth and faith?
2. Why is it vital for the Church to address mental and emotional wounds?
3. What does healthy vulnerability look like among believers?
4. How can leaders balance truth and compassion in ministry?
5. Where is God calling you to extend grace and healing to others?
6. Do I feel safe being honest about my struggles?
7. Have I offered empathy to someone in pain, or avoided them?
8. Do I understand that healing can be both spiritual and psychological?
9. Am I willing to be vulnerable before God and others?
10. ☐ I am aware of mental health and trauma needs.
11. ☐ I offer compassion and support.
12. ☐ I commit to integrating faith and care for holistic healing.

Devotional Prayer

"Heavenly Healer, touch the places in me that still ache. Restore my joy, renew my mind, and give me peace beyond understanding. Let my healing become a testimony of Your mercy and grace. Lord, bring healing and restoration to those in pain and guide me to help them. Loving Father, Heal the wounds that words can't express. Restore my mind, my peace, and my faith. Teach me to see through the eyes of compassion and to carry the burdens of the broken. May Your Church become a refuge for those in pain, reflecting Your heart of mercy. Amen."

Final Reflections

The Church on trial must be the Church that heals. When compassion replaces criticism and empathy replaces ignorance, Christ's heart is revealed. Healing is holiness in motion—and the world is waiting to see it through us.

Chapter Summary

This chapter envisions the end-time Church as the radiant Bride of Christ, purified and adorned in righteousness. Through trials and persecution, God prepares His people for a divine wedding, requiring them to let go of worldly compromise and hidden sin. The Bride must be holy and faithful, with garments washed in Christ's blood. The Church's radiance comes not from worldly success but from divine sanctification. Every trial refines believers, removing hypocrisy and pride. Purity is essential for the Bride; it is her wedding garment. The vision is for the Church to be presented to Christ as spotless and pure, emphasizing sanctification, unity, and spiritual readiness. Maturity as a mark of readiness. Presents the church as the spotless bride of Christ.

Emphasizes sanctification, unity, and spiritual maturity as marks of readiness.

Key Scriptures

Ephesians 5:25–27 – "…that He might present her to Himself a glorious church, not having spot, or wrinkle, or any such thing…"

Revelation 19:7–8 – "For the wedding of the Lamb has come, and His bride has made herself ready."

2 Corinthians 11:2-3 – "…I promised you to one husband, to Christ, so that I might present you as a pure virgin to Him."

Malachi 3:3 – "He will sit as a refiner and purifier of silver."

1 John 3:3 – "Everyone who has this hope in Him purifies himself, just as He is pure."

2 Corinthians 7:1 – "Cleanse yourselves from all filthiness of the flesh and spirit, perfecting holiness in the fear of God."

Reflection Quotes

"The Church's beauty is found in her obedience." "Holiness is the wedding dress of the Bride of Christ." "Purity is not perfection—it is full surrender."

"The Bride's beauty is her obedience."

"The Church cannot wear the world's garments and expect heaven's invitation."

"Every trial is a tailor's stitch preparing the Bride's final gown."

Reflection Questions

1. What does it mean to be the Bride of Christ in today's world?
2. How do trials and correction prepare us for Christ's return?

3. What "spots or wrinkles" is God calling the modern Church to remove?
4. How can believers pursue holiness without becoming self-righteous?
5. What does readiness for Christ's return look like in daily life?
6. What does it mean to be the bride of Christ?
7. How does sanctification prepare us for His return?
8. What "spots or wrinkles" is God cleansing from my life?
9. How can the church pursue spiritual maturity collectively?
10. What personal steps contribute to sanctification?
11. How does holiness prepare the church for Christ's return?
12. How can the church pursue spiritual maturity collectively?
13. What personal steps contribute to sanctification?

Group Discussion Prompts

1. Discuss what spiritual purity means in a culture of compromise.
2. How can the Church collectively "make herself ready"?
3. What does Christ's love for the Church teach us about divine commitment?
4. How do we maintain hope and purity in the last days?
5. How do holiness and unity prepare the church for Christ?
6. Why does Christ use the image of a bride for His church?
7. Share strategies for fostering unity and maturity in your church.
8. Discuss the challenges to be living as a spotless bride.
9. Share strategies for fostering unity and maturity in your church.

Action Step / Weekly Challenge

1. Take time to examine your life for "spots" or "wrinkles" that hinder your readiness.
2. Confess, repent, and recommit yourself to spiritual purity.
3. Dedicate a time of fasting and repentance this week.
4. Ask the Holy Spirit to reveal areas needing cleansing.
5. Choose one habit, relationship, or mindset to surrender fully to God.
6. Commit to a fast or act of consecration this week as preparation for Christ.
7. Commit to one practice this week that promotes holiness and unity.

Challenge Verse

Ephesians 5:27 – *"That He might present her to Himself a glorious church, not having spot or wrinkle."*
Revelation 22:17 – "The Spirit and the bride say, 'Come!' And let the one who hears say, 'Come!'
Commit to one practice this week that promotes holiness and unity.

Biblical Character Connection
Esther – purified and prepared. Before entering the king's presence, Esther underwent months of purification and preparation. Likewise, the Bride of Christ is being prepared through sanctification for her royal union with the King of Kings.

Key Quote / Takeaway
"Purity prepares the Bride; compromise delays the wedding."
"The purified Church is not perfect but perfected in love."

Worship Song Suggestion
"Ready for You" – Maverick City Music
"Even So Come" by Passion
(Theme: Anticipation and readiness for the return of Christ, the Bridegroom.)

Creative Response Option
1. Design a symbolic "wedding garment" page in your workbook. Write Scriptures and promises representing your spiritual preparation for Christ's return. Reflect on what holiness means to you personally.
2. Design a "Spiritual Wedding Garment" list—attributes and virtues you want God to clothe you with (faith, patience, humility, purity).
3. Write a letter to Christ as His bride, expressing readiness and devotion. Write a vision statement for your church as a spotless bride.
4. Write a vision statement for your church as a spotless bride.

Self-Assessment Questions
1. What does spiritual purity mean for the modern Church?
2. How do trials prepare the Bride for Christ?
3. Why is obedience more beautiful than outward success?
4. How can believers keep their garments white daily?
5. What will readiness look like when the Bridegroom comes?

6. Am I living as though Christ could return at any moment?
7. What areas of my life still need purification?
8. Do I long for the Bridegroom, or just His blessings?
9. Have I allowed trials to refine me or harden me?
10. ☐ I see myself as part of Christ's bride.
11. ☐ I sometimes feel unprepared for His return.
12. ☐ I seek to live sanctified and ready.
13. ☐ I seek personal sanctification.
14. ☐ I contribute to unity and growth in the church.
15. ☐ I am preparing for Christ's return in holiness.
16. ☐ I seek personal sanctification.
17. ☐ I contribute to unity and growth in the church.
18. ☐ I am preparing for Christ's return in holiness.

Devotional Prayer

Holy Bridegroom,

Prepare me to be a vessel of Your glory. Wash me clean and clothe me in righteousness. Help me love purity more than pleasure, and holiness more than comfort. May Your Church rise spotless and radiant, ready for Your coming. Lord Jesus, make me ready for Your return. Wash me in Your Word and clothe me in righteousness. May Your Bride be pure, unified, and radiant in love until You come again. Lord, sanctify me and Your church to be ready for Your return. Lord, prepare me as Your bride, holy and ready for Your coming. Lord, sanctify me and Your church to be ready for Your return. **Amen.**

Final Reflections

The story ends not in shame, but in glory. The Church that endured rebuke will be the same Bride that reigns beside the Lamb. Every trial, every exposure, every tear was part of the preparation. The Bridegroom is coming—let the Bride make herself ready.

Chapter 35: When the Church Becomes the Crime Scene — God's Verdict on Hidden Evil and the Call to Repentance

Chapter Summary

This chapter serves as a divine wake-up call to the modern Church. It exposes the hidden sins, hypocrisy, and deception that have crept into pulpits and pews alike, reminding us that *judgment begins at the house of God* (1 Peter 4:17). It calls out leaders who have traded truth for applause and congregations that have become comfortable with compromise. The chapter also serves as a divine courtroom scene. The Church is both the witness and the accused. God reveals hidden injustices, spiritual abuse, and corruption that have wounded His people. The verdict is clear— repentance or removal. Yet mercy still pleads: if the Church confesses her sins, healing and revival will follow. God's justice is redemptive, not vindictive. Yet amid the rebuke, the voice of God offers mercy. He invites repentance, restoration, and revival. The abused, the rejected, and the silenced will rise again as vessels of His power. The Church that endures this refining fire will emerge radiant—pure, holy, and filled with the fear of the Lord. This is not the end of the Church; it is her purification before the coming of Christ, the Bridegroom who is soon to return.

Key Scriptures

1 Peter 4:17 – "For the time is come that judgment must begin at the house of God."
Joel 2:12-13 – "Return to Me with all your heart, with fasting, weeping, and mourning… for He is gracious and merciful."
Matthew 7:21-23 – "Not everyone who says to Me, 'Lord, Lord,' will enter the Kingdom of Heaven."
Revelation 3:19 – "Those whom I love I rebuke and discipline. So be earnest and repent." Romans 8:19 – "The creation waits in eager expectation for the children of God to be revealed." Revelation 22:17 – "The Spirit and the Bride say, 'Come.'"
1 Peter 4:17
Jeremiah 7:30–34
Isaiah 1:16–18
Revelation 2:4–5

Reflection Quotes

"God's exposure is not to destroy, but to deliver."

"The greatest crime in the Church is the silence that covers sin."

Reflection Questions

1. In what ways has the modern Church become distracted or compromised by comfort, fame, or performance?
2. How can leaders and members alike embrace public humility and private repentance?
3. What does it mean for judgment to begin at the house of God, and how should that truth shape our worship and service?
4. How can the Church restore its credibility to those who have been wounded, silenced, or betrayed within it?
5. Are there areas in your own life where you have tolerated spiritual apathy, pride, or fear of man? What step of repentance will you take this week?
6. How can you personally become a voice of healing, truth, and integrity in your local church or ministry?
7. What might revival look like in your city if the Church collectively returned to holiness, humility, and prayer?

Action Step / Weekly Challenge

1. Spend this week in a *spiritual audit*.
2. Ask the Holy Spirit to search your heart and expose any area where compromise, offense, or pride may be hindering your walk.
3. Then, take one specific step of obedience—apologize, forgive, confess, or serve someone in humility.
4. Write down what God reveals and how you respond.
5. Fast and pray for your church, community, or nation.
6. Ask God to expose hidden evil and bring truth, justice, and restoration.

Challenge Verse:
Psalm 139:23–24 — "Search me, O God, and know my heart… and lead me in the way everlasting."
Isaiah 1:18 – *"Though your sins are like scarlet, they shall be as white as snow."*

Biblical Character Connection: King David
Nathan the prophet – who courageously confronted King David's hidden sin.

King David, though anointed by God, fell into sin and deception. Yet when the prophet Nathan confronted him, David's response was not denial but repentance (Psalm 51). His humility restored his fellowship with God and preserved his calling. Like David, the modern Church must not cover sin—but confess it and be cleansed, for *a broken and contrite heart God will not despise.*

Key Quote / Takeaway Box
1. *"Exposure is God's mercy in motion."*
2. "Public sin demands public humility. The Church will only be healed when its leaders stop hiding behind titles and start kneeling in truth."
3. Write your reflection on what this means personally:

_____

_____

Worship Song Suggestion
"Refiner" by Maverick City Music
"Lord, I Need You" – Matt Maher
"I want to be tried by fire, purified / You take whatever You desire Lord, here's my life." Let this song become your personal altar of surrender. Play it as you pray for cleansing and revival in your own heart and in the Church.

Creative Response Option
Create a symbolic *"altar of repentance"* at home or in your church group.

1. Write on slips of paper the areas God has revealed that need surrender, personal or corporate, and place them before a cross, praying over each one.
2. Then, burn or bury them as a sign that the old is gone and the new has come.
3. Write a "Repentance Decree" declaring God's verdict over your heart and church truth, cleansing, and restoration.

Self-Assessment: Heart Check
Rate yourself from 1 (Needs Change) to 5 (Spiritually Healthy) in each area, and write one improvement step beside each:

Spiritual Area   1 2 3 4 5   Action Step

Integrity in daily life	☐ ☐ ☐ ☐ ☐	_____
Prayer & devotion consistency	☐ ☐ ☐ ☐ ☐	_____
Willingness to forgive	☐ ☐ ☐ ☐ ☐	_____
Boldness in truth-telling	☐ ☐ ☐ ☐ ☐	_____
Humility & teachability	☐ ☐ ☐ ☐ ☐	_____
Compassion for the wounded	☐ ☐ ☐ ☐ ☐	_____
Obedience to God's call	☐ ☐ ☐ ☐ ☐	_____

1. Why does God expose sin rather than overlook it?
2. How does exposure lead to mercy and revival?
3. What are the modern "crimes" committed within the Church?
4. How can believers respond to exposure without defensiveness?
5. What does a repentant Church look like in today's world?

Devotional Prayer of Repentance and Renewal

Heavenly Father,

We come before You as Your Church, broken but willing, wounded but yearning to be whole. Forgive us for our silence when we should have spoken, for our comfort when You called us to courage. Expose every hidden sin, every false motive, every mask we've worn in Your name.

Wash Your Church in the blood of Jesus. Purify Your leaders and awaken Your people. Let judgment turn to mercy and rebuke to revival. Revive our first love, restore our witness, and renew our passion for holiness. Righteous Judge, we repent for every hidden sin, every injustice covered by silence. Cleanse Your house, purify our leaders, and renew Your Bride. Let Your verdict lead to victory and revival.

Make us a Church of power and purity, a Bride without spot or wrinkle, ready for Your return. In

Jesus' name, Amen.

Final Reflection: "The Church on trial will soon become the Church triumphant."

Take a few moments in silence. Ask the Lord:

"What do You want to cleanse in me so You can cleanse through me?"
Write your answer below:

_____

_____

Chapter Summary

This chapter declares victory! The purified, tested, and refined Church shines with glory, remaining faithful despite persecution and corruption. This is the Church Christ will return for— radiant in love and unity. Heaven rejoices as the earth witnesses the restoration of this unstoppable Bride. The vision concludes with a fully prepared Church, emphasizing readiness through prayer, obedience, and active mission.

Key Scriptures

Matthew 24:12-14

Romans 8:18–21

Philippians 3:20–21

Revelation 19:7-9– "Let us be glad and rejoice and give honour to him: for the marriage of the Lamb has come, and his wife hath made herself ready."

Revelation 19:7–8 – "The marriage of the Lamb is come, and his wife hath made herself ready."

Matthew 24:44 – "Be ye also ready: for in such an hour as ye think not the Son of man cometh."

Reflection Quotes

"The end-time Church will not hide in fear but rise in glory." "The Bride is not escaping darkness—she's illuminating it."

Reflection Questions

1. What does a "glorious church" look like?
2. How do prayer and obedience prepare us for Christ's return?
3. What role does mission play in readiness?
4. How can the church remain vigilant and prepared for Christ's return?
5. What practices promote spiritual readiness individually and corporately?
6. How does obedience ensure glory for God?
7. How can the church remain vigilant and prepared for Christ's return?
8. What practices promote spiritual readiness individually and corporately?

9. How does obedience ensure glory for God?

Group Discussion Prompts
- Why is the church called to both holiness and mission?
- How does hope in Christ's return shape daily living?
- Discuss ways your church can maintain readiness and holiness.
- Share methods to inspire members to active participation in God's mission.

Action Step / Weekly Challenge
- Live every day as if Christ will return tonight.
- Share the Gospel, love deeply, forgive quickly, and serve humbly.
- Share the gospel with one person this week as preparation for His return.
- Create a personal and church plan for readiness in devotion, service, and holiness

Challenge Verse
Revelation 22:12 – *"Behold, I am coming soon; My reward is with Me."*

Biblical Character Connection
The Wise Virgins (Matthew 25) – who kept their lamps burning until the Bridegroom came.

Key Quote / Takeaway
"A glorious Church is not perfect—but perfectly surrendered."

Worship Song Suggestion
"Even So Come" – Chris Tomlin

Creative Response Option
Create a vision board or journal entry of what a glorious church looks like. Design a visual or written plan for a fully prepared, radiant church.

Create a "Readiness Manifesto"—a declaration of how you will live in light of Christ's soon return.

Self-Assessment Questions
1. What defines a glorious Church?
2. How can believers prepare for the return of Christ?

3. Why does endurance matter in the last days?
4. How does unity reflect the glory of Christ?
5. What personal commitment will you make before His return?
6. ☐ I live with the expectation of Christ's return.
7. ☐ I sometimes lose focus on eternal readiness.
8. ☐ I want to be part of a radiant, unified, holy church.
9. ☐ I am spiritually vigilant and ready.
10. ☐ I actively participate in God's mission.
11. ☐ I seek personal and corporate holiness for Christ's return.

Devotional Prayer

"Come, Lord Jesus! Prepare Your Bride to be spotless, faithful, and full of oil. Let our lamps burn with love and our hearts overflow with Your glory. Until You come, keep us steadfast and ready. Lord, make us a glorious church, ready and waiting for You with joy. Lord, help me and my church to be ready for Your glorious return. Amen."

Chapter 37: The Kingdom of Heaven at War – When the Gates of Hell Rise Against the Righteous

Chapter Summary:
This chapter reveals the ongoing spiritual battle between the Kingdom of Heaven and the gates of Hell, highlighting how fear, corruption, political upheaval, and injustice are used to silence the righteous. It exposes hidden evil within church leadership and societal structures while emphasizing that Christ's victory on the cross equips believers to stand firm. The chapter calls the Church to courage, truth, compassion, and justice, showing that God's Kingdom will prevail despite opposition. It encourages readers to embrace their role in this spiritual battle, resist compromise, and align their lives with God's purpose.

Key Scriptures:
1. Matthew 16:18 – *"The gates of hell shall not prevail against it."*
2. Ephesians 6:12 – *"We wrestle not against flesh and blood... against spiritual wickedness in high places."*
3. Revelation 11:15 – *"The kingdoms of this world have become the kingdoms of our Lord and of His Christ."*
4. 2 Timothy 1:7 – *"God has not given us a spirit of fear, but of power, love, and a sound mind."*
5. Colossians 2:15 – *"Having spoiled principalities and powers, He made a show of them openly, triumphing over them."*
6. Amos 5:21 – *"I hate, I despise your feasts, and I take no delight in your solemn assemblies."*
7. John 14:27 – *"Peace I leave with you; My peace I give unto you."*

Reflection Quotes:
- "Fear silences the voice of the righteous, but faith amplifies the voice of Heaven."
- "The gates of Hell may roar, but the cross has already won the victory."
- "Corruption cannot withstand the fire of a repentant, obedient heart."
- "The remnant rises not for recognition, but for the glory of God."

Action Step / Weekly Challenge:
1. Challenge: Identify one area in your life, church, or community

where compromise, fear, or injustice has silenced truth.
2. Take one practical action this week to confront it in alignment with God's Word—through prayer, advocacy, or speaking truth with love.
3. Keep a journal of how God strengthens you in this battle.

Challenge Verse:

Joshua 1:9 – *"Have I not commanded you? Be strong and courageous. Do not be frightened, and do not be dismayed, for the Lord your God is with you wherever you go."*

Biblical Character Connection:

Daniel: Stood firm in Babylon despite fear, political pressure, and cultural compromise. Esther: Risked her life to save her people, showing courage in the face of systemic injustice.

Jesus: Faced corruption, political manipulation, and betrayal but remained obedient to God's mission.

Key Quote / Takeaway:

"The Kingdom of Heaven advances not by human compromise but by obedience, courage, and love. Even when the world resists, God's purposes prevail."

Worship Song Suggestion:

"Oceans (Where Feet May Fail)" – Hillsong UNITED
"Way Maker" – Sinach / Leeland
"Reckless Love" – Cory Asbury

Creative Response:

Write a personal letter to God confessing areas of fear, compromise, or silence in your life. Draw or create a visual representation of the "battlefield" in your heart, community, or church, labeling areas where Heaven is advancing and where gates of Hell resist.

Compose a short worship song, poem, or spoken-word piece declaring God's victory over hidden evil.

Self-Assessment Questions:

1. Where in my life or community have I allowed fear to silence truth?
2. Have I witnessed or participated in any form of compromise or

corruption that contradicts God's Word?

3. How do I actively stand for justice, mercy, and truth, even when it's unpopular or risky?
4. Who are the people I can support or pray for this week who are facing inhumane situations or systemic injustice?
5. In what ways do I rely on God's power instead of my own to confront spiritual battles?

Devotional Prayer for Those Facing Inhumane Situations and Their Families:
Heavenly Father,

You are recognized as the Defender of the vulnerable and the Champion of justice. We express our concern for those who endure oppression, violence, corruption, and injustice. We request that you provide these individuals with your protection and grant them the courage to uphold the truth. Strengthen their families and offer comfort in times when fear and suffering may seem insurmountable. May Your Kingdom be evident in their lives, revealing the tactics of malevolence, and allow Your love to shine amidst chaos. Equip Your Church to serve as a refuge, a voice for those who are silenced, and an instrument of Your mercy. Let the victory of the cross be evident in every challenge they confront. You observe every instance of injustice, every corrupt system, and every weary individual striving for righteousness within a context of compromise.

Fortify those who encounter oppression, persecution, and manipulation. Restore their passion where it may have diminished; may Your presence provide both comfort and conviction.

Uncover the insidious evil that affects Your people and rejuvenate the integrity of Your Church. Healing families fractured by injustice and uplifting those who bear the burdens of corruption.

May Your Spirit impart light, courage, and purification, ensuring that Your Kingdom remains steadfast in truth. We request healing for the brokenhearted and ask to be utilized as instruments of comfort. We seek healing and restoration for those in distress and express our willingness to assist them in the name of Jesus, Amen.

Final Reflection:
The Kingdom of Heaven is not passive. Every believer is called to participate in

the spiritual battle through obedience, courage, and love. Reflect on your personal role in confronting injustice, corruption, and fear in your world. Consider how God is asking you to stand firm, speak truth, and act with mercy. Remember, even in the midst of opposition, Lamb has already triumphed.

Chapter 38– The Modern Athens: God's Final Rebuke and the Unveiling of Hidden Idols

Chapter Summary

This chapter draws the lessons from the prophetic revelation of Chapter 36 into practical application for the Church and believers. It emphasizes the responsibility of God's people to respond to His rebuke through holiness, repentance, discernment, and intercession. The chapter challenges the Church to examine its priorities, realign with God's Word, and prepare spiritually and morally for Christ's return. It also addresses leadership accountability, faithful witness, and the spiritual influence of the Church in a world that continues to embrace deception and idolatry.

The central message: *God's rebuke is both a warning and a call to action; His people must respond with faith, obedience, and courage.*

Key Scriptures

- James 4:7–10 (KJV) – "Submit yourselves therefore to God. Resist the devil, and he will flee from you. Draw nigh to God, and he will draw nigh to you. Cleanse your hands, ye sinners; and purify your hearts, ye double-minded."
- Romans 12:1–2 (KJV) – "Present your bodies a living sacrifice, holy, acceptable unto God, which is your reasonable service. And be not conformed to this world: but be ye transformed by the renewing of your mind."
- Ephesians 5:11 (KJV) – "And have no fellowship with the unfruitful works of darkness, but rather reprove them."
- 1 Peter 4:17–18 (KJV) – "For the time is come that judgment must begin at the house of God: and if it first begins at us, what shall the end be of them that obey not the gospel of God?"
- Micah 6:8 (KJV) – "He hath shewed thee, O man, what is good; and what doth the Lord require of thee, but to do justly, and to love mercy, and to walk humbly with thy God?"

Reflection Quote

"God's rebuke is not the end of hope — it is the beginning of revival for those who obey and the awakening of those who hear."

Reflection Questions
- Considering God's rebuke, what areas of compromise do you recognize in your own life or ministry?
- How can the Church act as a moral compass and prophetic witness in a culture that embraces deception and idolatry?
- What steps can you take to ensure your personal devotion aligns with God's Word and not the approval of men?
- How can believers balance intercession with action in addressing systemic corruption or injustice?
- Which biblical principles in this chapter challenge you the most, and how will you respond to them this week?

Action Step
- Choose one specific area of personal or ministry life that requires realignment with God's
- Word. Write it down and commit to a 7-day plan of action:
- Prayer and fasting
- Scripture study
- Accountability check-in with a mentor or pastor
- Acts of obedience and witness in your community

Biblical Character Connection
Nehemiah, when confronted with the broken walls of Jerusalem and the compromise of the people, led with prayer, fasting, and strategic action. He exemplifies leadership that responds to God's rebuke with courage, vision, and unwavering obedience.

Key Takeaway
"Obedience is the proof of hearing God. Repentance is the gateway to revival. The Church that responds faithfully becomes the light that no darkness can overcome."

Worship Song Suggestion
"Refiner's Fire" – Brian Doerksen
A song of surrender, purification, and alignment with God's holiness.

Creative Response
Write a prophetic letter or personal pledge to God, stating how you and your

church will respond to His rebuke. Include tangible commitments for spiritual growth, ministry accountability, and moral courage.

Self-Assessment Activity
Evaluate your spiritual posture (1–10):
1 = passive / distracted | 10 = actively obedient and vigilant
☐ I pray daily for personal holiness and for the Church's alignment with God's Word.
☐ I discern worldly influence from spiritual truth in leadership and media.
☐ I actively participate in intercession for my nation and global issues.
☐ I pursue accountability in my personal, family, and ministry life.
☐ I intentionally teach and model God's truth in my sphere of influence.

Reflect: Which two areas need your immediate attention, and what practical step will you take this week?

Chapter 39: *When the Church Stands Before God — The Final Cry of Repentance*

Chapter Summary

This chapter calls the Church and individual believers to confront hidden evil, compromise, and reliance on human authority instead of God. Using David's story in 1 Samuel 21:14 and the ultimate example of Jesus Christ, the chapter emphasizes that God often shapes leaders in caves, exile, and seasons of trial. Believers are reminded that salvation is found in Jesus Christ alone, and the Church must be purified from pride, hidden sin, and compromise before fulfilling God's divine purpose. The chapter is a clarion call to repentance, surrender, and restoration. God exposes hidden evils in the Church, calling leaders and members to repentance. Pride, false prophecy, political compromise, and self-exaltation are being judged. The faithful remnants, like Daniel, Esther, and Paul, will rise. Revival comes through holiness, obedience, and surrender. The Bride is called to return to her first love before Christ returns.

Full Narrative / Reflection Content

The story of Nebuchadnezzar reminds us that being in control and doing what we want without listening to God and those who placed us in power will bring ruin. Pride brings downfall, but God gives second chances to those who humble themselves. No human power is permanent. God alone rules over nations, countries, kingdoms, palaces, presidents, spiritual leaders, and those in authority who desire to be authoritarian or corrupt in churches, governments, and institutions.

Nebuchadnezzar learned that true greatness begins with humility, listening to reason, and submitting to God. Wealth and power cannot replace obedience, and the poor and needy reveal whether leadership is just. You do not have to blend in to make an impact; rather, stand firm in your faith with God as Daniel and his friends did, never compromising. They, like David, obeyed God in exile and were rewarded.

Success without surrender leads to ruin. Influence does not come from titles, empires, or leadership achievements—it comes from knowing God alone reigns. He raises and removes kings, political and church leaders who misuse their power to get rich over those they serve. God can lead any man or woman to repentance, and real strength begins when you give up control, honor, and seek God first instead of relying on your own strength.

Prayer:

Heavenly Father, we come before you because of your greatness, recognizing that we, too, have fallen short of your glory. Like Nebuchadnezzar, we have built our kingdom, chased after power, and taken credit for not only what You could have made possible. We confess our pride, self-reliance, and our failure to see Your hands in every blessing. Forgive us for the times we have forgotten that You alone are the ruler of all things. We acknowledge that in our pride, we often ignored Your warnings and signs, choosing our own decisions rather than Your wisdom and guidance. We have chased after success, riches, greed, and power, ignoring the consequences, forgetting that true greatness comes from being surrounded by You. We have built our lives around things and wealth that will fade, not realizing that only what is done in Your name will endure. We remember the faithful of Daniel, Shadrach, Meshach, and Abednego who stood firm in the face of pressure and refused to bow to false idols, politicians, and corrupt church leaders. Help us to have that same unwavering faith even when the world around us demands compromise. Lord, we ask for Your mercy, just as You extended grace to Nebuchadnezzar, allowing him to return to You after his time of brokenness. We ask for Your grace to return to You and restore us. In Jesus' Name, Amen.

God Will Not Let His Bride Be Defiled

The Lord is jealous for His Bride. He is not passive, silent, or indifferent to spiritual abuse, manipulation, hidden sin, or counterfeit prophecy. He sees every tear shed by the one who sat in the sanctuary, feeling unseen and unheard. He hears the silent cries of those broken by leaders who cared more about image than souls.

God saw when prophetic words were twisted to shame instead of edifying. He noticed that when church politics silenced the humble and elevated the prideful. He recorded every moment when titles sat higher than truth. Now He stands to judge: *"For the Lord is the judge; He puts down one and sets up another."* He is dethroning those who crowned themselves and raising those who bowed low. Not the famous, the faithful. Not loyal. Not the polished, the pure.

The Veil Is Tearing Again

God is ripping the curtains off private hypocrisy. He is exposing secret pride disguised as spiritual authority, diluted doctrine, voices claiming revelation without consecration, leaders weaponizing Scripture for control, worship teams performing for applause, not presence, prophets speaking in the name of nationalism, pastors who shout holiness but whisper repentance to themselves, and church members who gossip in pews but mute conviction in prayer.

If you built a ministry on charisma instead of character, this shaking exposes it. If you built relationships on loyalty to man instead of loyalty to God, this shaking reveals it. God is tearing down the counterfeit version of His Church.

The Spirit of the Pharisee Has Returned
They wear robes of righteousness but walk with hearts of self-exaltation. They prophesy judgment on others yet refuse to repent themselves. They call division "discernment" and control "covering." They say "God told me" as if the Holy Ghost is a personal servant for their ambitions.

But Jesus is walking through His temple again — not with applause, but with a whip. He is overturning tables of ministry corruption. He is cleansing altars polluted by ego. He is calling out spiritual brokers who sell influence for loyalty. And He is saying to this generation:

"My house shall be called a house of prayer — not performance, politics, or personalities.

When God Cuts the Mic Off
There will be ministers whose influence evaporates overnight. There will be prophets who wake up and hear nothing. There will be churches once packed that slowly empty. There will be spiritual influencers whose audience vanishes like mist.

Not because they were attacked — but because God removed the oil they misused. Some will try to force it—manufacture glory, simulate power, copy others—but without God's breath, it will sound hollow.

Spiritual theatrics cannot replace spiritual truth. Hype cannot replace holiness. Clapping hands cannot cover unrepentant hearts.

The Church Must Not Repeat Its Mistake
Some churches today look more like Babylon than Zion, more like Egypt than the Upper Room, more like political rallies than prayer gatherings, more like celebrity platforms than sanctuaries of repentance.

God is knocking, not dismissing. Heaven is calling the Bride back to purity: return to first Love, return to purity, return to reverence, return to humility, return to truth, return to prayer, return to the fear of the Lord.

Humility Is Heaven's Currency

God measures ministry by surrender. He searches not for talented voices but for broken vessels. Not those who command platforms, but those who command private altars. Not those who demand honor, but those who lay crowns at His feet.

The proud carry microphones. The humble carry crosses. And it is the cross, not charisma, that breaks chains.

The Bridegroom Speaks

"My Bride, return to Me. Come out from the noise and kneel at My feet again. You have chased platforms, come back to My presence. You have pursued influence, pursue My heart. I did not call you to be admired, to need a popular church; it needs a purified one. The nations do not need a relevant church; they need a repentant one. I am not coming for a celebrated Bride; I am coming for a consecrated Bride."

False Prophecy and Holiness

God is removing false tongues and silencing words that elevate self over Him. He calls for fasting that breaks pride, repentance that restores purity, and obedience that releases His fire. Political compromise and worldly agendas are exposed. The faithful will rise; the rebellious will fall.

The Final Cry

This is the last cry before the Bridegroom returns. It is a call to repentance, unity, humility, and holiness. Revival comes through consecration, obedience, and surrender. Those who respond will participate in God's glory. The remnant is being prepared; Heaven is moving; the earth is shaking. The time is now.

Key Scriptures

1 Samuel 21:14 – David in the cave, God's preparation in humility
Acts 4:12 – Salvation is found in Jesus alone Psalm 34:18 – God is near the brokenhearted
2 Chronicles 7:14 – Call to repentance and humility for revival James 4:10 – Humble yourselves before the Lord
Matthew 5:6 – Blessed are those who hunger and thirst for righteousness

Daniel 4:30–37
Proverbs 16:18
1 Samuel 15:23
Acts 12:21–23
Matthew 21:12 13
Revelation 2:4–5, 19:7
Matthew 7:21–23, 25:1–13
Psalm 51:17
Joel 2:12–14
Hebrews 12:26–29
Ephesians 5:27

Reflection Quotes
- "God does not shape kings in palaces, but in caves, in shadows, and in silence."
- "Salvation comes through surrender, not status; through humility, not human approval."
- "The cross shows us that rejection, shame, and suffering are the paths to redemption."
- "True greatness begins when you give up control and honor and seek God first."
- "Pride wears religious robes and calls itself leadership; humility carries the cross."
- "Revival begins not with shouting, but with surrender."

Reflection Questions
1. Where in your life are you relying on human leaders, political structures, or worldly systems instead of God?
2. What hidden sins, compromises, or attitudes do you need to confront and confess?
3. How do your current trials or "caves" reflect God's preparation for spiritual growth?
4. How can the Church collectively address hidden evil and restore holiness?
5. What idols (political, cultural, personal) must you renounce to experience freedom and revival?
6. How does pride manifest in the leadership or members of the Church today?

7. What steps can I take personally to humble myself and seek God's first place in my life?
8. How does the story of Nebuchadnezzar relate to the spiritual accountability of church leaders?
9. Who are the modern-day Daniels and Esthers in your life or community?
10. How can the Church respond to false prophecy and division without creating further conflict?

Group Discussion Prompts
- Discuss why God prepares leaders in caves or periods of trial rather than in positions of power. How does this principle apply to the Church today?
- How can the Church confront hidden evil without fear or compromise?
- Share personal experiences of seasons of trial where God shaped your faith or character.
- Reflect on Acts 4:12 — why is it crucial that salvation and revival cannot come from human leaders or institutions?
- What practical steps can your local congregation take to embody true repentance and humility?
- Discuss how political ideologies can infiltrate spiritual spaces.
- Share examples of how humility and obedience have brought restoration in church or personal life.
- Evaluate ways your local congregation can protect itself from false teaching.

Action Step / Weekly Challenge
- Spend 10–15 minutes daily in quiet reflection and prayer, seeking God's guidance in
- areas of hidden sin or compromise.
- Confess one area of pride, compromise, or hidden sin and commit to forsaking it.
- Pray for the Church, leaders, and nations for repentance, revival, and holiness.
- Perform one humble act of service or sacrifice without recognition this week.
- Commit to 24–48 hours of prayer and fasting focused on humility, purity, and intercession for your church leaders.
- Journal observations about areas where pride or compromise exists in your environment and how God might be calling for change.

Challenge Verse
"Humble yourselves before the Lord, and He will lift you." – James 4:10

Biblical Character Connection

1. David: Prepared in caves, hunted and humiliated, yet faithful and obedient. His life demonstrates perseverance, humility, and reliance on God.
2. Jesus Christ: The perfect Shepherd, misunderstood, rejected, and crucified, offering salvation to all who repent and surrender.
3. Daniel's faithfulness in exile
4. Esther's courage and fasting
5. Shadrach, Meshach, and Abednego's refusal to bow to false authority
6. Paul's unwavering obedience amid persecution

Key Quote / Takeaway

"The Church is purified not by human approval but by surrender, confession, and obedience to God alone." "The Church will breathe again when it bends again. Revival begins not with shouting, but with surrender."

Worship Song Suggestion
"Break Every Chain" – Jesus Culture
"Way Maker" – Sinach
"Refiner's Fire" – Brian Doerksen

Creative Response Option
1. Journaling Exercise: Write a letter to Jesus describing areas of your life and the Church that need repentance, surrender, or cleansing. Seal it as a symbolic act of surrender.
2. Prayer Mapping: Map out people, systems, or areas you are praying for and commit to interceding daily.
3. Accountability Partner: Pair with another believer to confess hidden sins and pray for one another's spiritual growth over a month.
4. Where in my life have I unknowingly followed personalities instead of God?

5. Am I willing to confront hidden pride or sin in my church or community?
6. What steps will I take this week to realign with God's purpose for my life?

Self-Assessment Questions
- On a scale of 1–10, how surrendered are you to God in areas of pride, self-reliance, and compromise?
- Identify three practical steps to move closer to full surrender and holiness.
- Are there idols (political, cultural, religious) in your life that compete with Christ's authority?
- How committed are you to confronting hidden sin in yourself and your community?

Final Reflection

The Church stands at a crossroads: return to God in true repentance or continue in hidden compromise. Like David in exile and Christ on the cross, the path to restoration, power, and holiness is through surrender, humility, and obedience. Today, God calls every believer to kneel, confess, and cry out:

This chapter calls the Church to urgent, heart-level surrender. God is exposing what is hidden, purifying what is contaminated, and preparing a remnant for His glory. Humility, obedience, and repentance are the only paths to restoration before Christ's return.

"Jesus, Son of David, have mercy on me. Redeem me and restore Your Church to holiness and power."

The cave is mercy, the cross is redemption, and the King waits with open arms. Respond now and step into revival.

Chapter 40: Epilogue: The Nations Tremble, the Heavens Speak

Chapter Summary

This chapter calls believers to stand firm, discern the times, and prepare their hearts for the soon- coming King. The central message: *The Church is on trial, the world is trembling, but God's sovereignty still reigns.* The Epilogue unfolds as a prophetic revelation from God addressing the spiritual, political, and moral collapse of the modern world. The Lord speaks directly to the nations, especially the nation of the world, and the global Church, declaring that the chaos, wars, corruption, and division we see are not coincidences but signs of divine shaking.

God exposes America's moral decay, warns the Church of its compromise, and reminds Israel of His unbroken covenant. The global crises are revealed to be labor pains before Christ's return. Yet amid the warnings, God offers mercy and hope to the repentant, calling His people to revival, holiness, and unwavering faith.

Key Scriptures

- Haggai 2:6–7 (KJV) – "For thus saith the Lord of hosts; Yet once, it is a little while, and I will shake the heavens, and the earth... and I will shake all nations, and the desire of all nations shall come."
- 2 Chronicles 7:14 (KJV) – "If my people, which are called by my name, shall humble themselves, and pray, and seek my face, and turn from their wicked ways; then will I hear from heaven, and will forgive their sin, and will heal their land."
- Isaiah 60:1–2 (KJV) – "Arise, shine; for thy light is come, and the glory of the Lord is risen upon thee... but the Lord shall arise upon thee."
- Matthew 24:6–8 (KJV) – "And ye shall hear of wars and rumours of wars... all these are the beginning of sorrows."
- Revelation 11:15 (KJV) – "The kingdoms of this world are become the kingdoms of our Lord, and of his Christ; and he shall reign for ever and ever."

Reflection Quote

"The shaking is not destruction — it is divine purification. God is removing what can be shaken, so that what cannot be shaken may remain."

Reflection Questions

What are some ways you see God "shaking" the nations and systems around the world today?

How has the Church mirrored the world instead of transforming it, and what does true repentance look like in this generation?

Why is it important to discern the difference between human reform and divine repentance?

In what ways can believers prepare their hearts and homes for the return of Christ amidst political and global turmoil?

What personal idols, distractions, or loyalties must you surrender to stand pure before God in these last days?

Action Step

Spend this week in personal prayer and fasting for your nation, your leaders, and the Church. Write down one specific area of compromise in your life or ministry that the Holy Spirit is calling you to surrender. Then, take one actionable step of obedience to realign yourself with God's truth.

Biblical Character Connection

Noah — In a time of global corruption, Noah stood as a righteous man who heard God's warning, obeyed His voice, and built an ark before judgment came. Like Noah, we are called to stand firm, prepare, and warn others while there is still time.

Key Takeaway

"The nations may tremble, but the faithful will stand. God's judgment reveals His justice; His shaking reveals His sovereignty."

Worship Song Suggestion

"Even So Come" – Passion (feat. Chris Tomlin)

A song of expectation, declaring, *"Like a bride waiting for her groom, we'll be a Church ready for You."*

Creative Response

Write a short prophetic prayer, poem, or letter to your nation — interceding for repentance, healing, and revival. Title it *"Let the Nations Tremble, Let the Church Awaken."*

Self-Assessment Activity

Rate your current spiritual posture (1–10):

1 = spiritually numb | 10 = fully awakened and ready for Christ's return

☐ I am daily seeking God through prayer and repentance.

☐ I am discerning the times through Scripture, not fear.

☐ I am interceding for my community and nation.

☐ I am detaching from worldly distractions.

☐ I am helping others prepare for Christ's coming.

Reflect: Which area needs the most attention this week?